Entrepreneur® MAGAZINE'S
ULTIMATE
SMALL
BUSINESS
MARKETING GUIDE

1500 Great Marketing Tricks That Will Drive Your Business Through the Roof

JAMES STEPHENSON

Ep
Entrepreneur®
Press

Managing editor: Jere Calmes
Cover design: Beth Hansen-Winter
Composition and production: Eliot House Productions

This publication is designed to provide accurate and authoritative information in regard to the subject matter covered. It is sold with the understanding that the publisher is not engaged in rendering legal, accounting, or other professional services. If legal advice or other expert assistance is required, the services of a competent professional person should be sought.

Library of Congress Cataloging-in-Publication Data

Stephenson, James, 1966-
  Entrepreneur magazine's ultimate small business marketing guide: over 1500 great marketing tricks that will drive your business through the roof! / James Stephenson.
      p. cm.
  Includes index.
    ISBN 1-932156-10-0
  1. Marketing—Handbooks, manuals, etc. 2. Small business—Management—Handbooks, manuals, etc. 3. Success in business—Handbooks, manuals, etc. I. Entrepreneur (Irvine, Calif.) II. Title.
    HF5415.S764 2003
    658.8—dc22

                                                        2003049405

Printed in Canada

09 08 07 06 05 04 03   10 9 8 7 6 5 4 3 2 1

CONTENTS

RESEARCH, PLANNING, AND COMPETITION

Marketing Tips for Your Business

EMPLOYEE

Marketing Tips for Your Business

CUSTOMER SERVICE

Marketing Tips for Your Business

HOME OFFICE
Marketing Tips for Your Business

ADVERTISING, DIRECT MARKETING, AND TELEMARKETING
Marketing Tips for Your Business

PUBLIC RELATIONS
Marketing Tips for Your Business

NETWORKING AND REFERRAL
Marketing Tips for Your Business

PROSPECTING
Marketing Tips for Your Business

PRESENTATION

Marketing Tips for Your Business

CLOSING

Marketing Tips for Your Business

CREATIVE SELLING
Marketing Tips for Your Business

RETAILING
Marketing Tips for Your Business

SERVICE PROVIDER
Marketing Tips for Your Business

TRADE SHOW AND SEMINAR
Marketing Tips for Your Business

ACKNOWLEDGMENTS

I would like to thank all of those who throughout the years have bestowed their marketing and sales knowledge upon me. A book such as this that covers so many marketing disciplines could not have been written without their assistance—thank you. Additionally a big thanks goes to Jere Calmes, Editorial Director at Entrepreneur Press, and his team of highly skilled professionals. I appreciate all of their input, encouragement, and continued support. And I would like to thank my biggest supporter in business and in life—my wife, Pamela, who has patiently listened to all of my ideas, the good and the sometimes off-center, for nearly 20 years.

Dedication

To My Great Grandmother Pearl Woodworth (1898–1994)
A fireball of contagious enthusiasm and generous giving who
inspired many to follow their entrepreneurial
ambitions and life dreams.

INTRODUCTION

Marketing, without question, is the single largest challenge facing small-business owners today. And to make matters worse, marketing success is always temporary. The minute you stop stoking the promotional boiler, the marketing train begins to stall. I wish there were a quick-fix solution that I could share with you or a magical marketing wand that you could wave to achieve instantaneous and permanent marketing success—but none exists.

However, for small-business owners who are prepared to roll up their sleeves and get to work to build and maintain a solid marketing foundation, I can offer you more than 1,500 great marketing tricks, tips, and ideas to help you achieve long-term marketing and business success.

Entrepreneur Magazine's Ultimate Small Business Marketing Guide has been specifically developed to help the millions of small-business owners across North America unlock the mysteries that surround marketing. This book will help you secure the big marketing opportunities and success you want and deserve. Each marketing trick, tip, and idea is presented in jargon-free terminology. This book is packed with information that is easy to understand and readily applied in a matter of minutes regardless of your marketing experience or skills. Successful marketing is a matter of dedication, hard work, research, planning, and a clear vision of what you want to achieve. The more than 1,500 marketing

ideas and strategies presented in this book are time tested and proven to work. In fact, these are the same marketing strategies and ideas that top business and sales professionals use daily to win new business, devour the competition, and secure customers for life.

GETTING STARTED

My objective when creating a small-business marketing guide was to feature and explain hundreds of great marketing tricks and ideas representing a wide cross section of marketing and sales activities from public relations to direct marketing to retailing—marketing ideas the pros use. Some of these ideas and tricks will be familiar to you, many will be new. The data and information featured for each marketing trick, tip, or idea is brief and is meant to give a short synopsis of the underlying marketing concept and principle. In other words, the theme of this book is not to give a definitive and lengthy explanation of each marketing idea and activity featured, but rather a collection of great marketing ideas that can be used as a catalyst to get you thinking about ways these ideas and tricks can be applied and implemented with your own small business for success. I have had the pleasure and have been in the enviable position of working with top small-business owners and marketers for many years. The information featured in this book has been compiled from my own business and sales experience as well as from numerous conversations with a multitude of small-business owners and sales professionals.

HOW TO USE THIS BOOK

This book should not be taking a restful nap on a dusty shelf. On the contrary, this is a workbook. Use this book daily and keep it with you for those times when you have a few moments to spare and you are looking for great ways to increase revenues and profits. Invest in a highlighter pen and mark the information that is the most beneficial for your business. Let's face it though, no one has time to identify, test, and implement more than 1,500 marketing ideas; it's simply not feasible or cost effective. Therefore, you must take a bit of time to really dig in and locate a few marketing ideas that you believe will work for you—then put them to work. Use the book incrementally and set a target of testing or implementing perhaps one new marketing trick every week or month until you have built a powerful marketing arsenal.

WHAT YOU WILL DISCOVER INSIDE

All the marketing ideas in this book are indexed by marketing activities such as retailing, selling, advertising, networking, and so forth. However, do not read only select chapters, read the entire book. You will find sales ideas in the retailing chapter, networking ideas in the research chapter, and online marketing tricks in the advertising chapter. My point is this: As much as I tried to index and group information into specific chapters, it is not possible, simply due to the fact that successful marketing is a mixture of many marketing disciplines. The following is a bit of what you will discover inside:

- *Research and planning.* You will find great tricks that will assist you to research your markets, identify your customers, and plan for future business and marketing success.
- *Competition.* Learn the tricks the pros use to devour the competition whole before they even know what hit them.
- *Employees.* Inside are numerous tricks that will help you to increase employee productivity,

enhance creativity, and become a strong leader and motivator.

- *Customer service.* Without customers, there is no business; with that in mind, extra attention was paid to present some really outstanding customer service ideas that will not only help you to serve your customers better, but secure their loyalty for a lifetime.
- *Home office.* Small-business owners and professionals working from a homebased location will find the ideas featured in the home office chapter to be particularly helpful and insightful.
- *Technology and communications.* Though not categorized in a separate chapter, you will discover throughout the book lots of great cutting-edge ideas for the use of technology in marketing as well as fantastic communications tricks that will help you convey your marketing message with perfect clarity.
- *Advertising and direct marketing.* Managing and making the best use of your precious marketing capital means your advertising, direct-marketing, and telemarketing efforts must be perfectly aimed at your target audience.
- *Public relations.* Discover tricks that will help you grab the attention of the press, secure free and valuable media attention, and develop a public-relations strategy that will produce results year in and year out. PR is not just for the big boys anymore.
- *Networking and prospecting.* Inside you will find powerful ways to network your present contacts for more business. You will also learn how to source new contacts for networking and prospecting purposes. If you don't know what the headcount rule is, you soon will.
- *Presentations and closing.* Closing is the natural progression of the sales presentation and in these chapters you will discover how this is accomplished and much, much more. And did I mention that you will learn the negotiation tricks that top sales pros use to ensure they never leave money on the table?
- *Creative selling.* Often the best and most profitable selling strategies are the simplest ones,

and that is what the creative selling chapter will reveal: easy, straightforward, and truly profitable creative selling strategies.

- *Retailing*. A chapter packed to the rafters with knockout retail marketing tricks that will set your cash register on fire.
- *Service providers*. A bonus chapter for service providers packed with great marketing ideas.
- *Web site and online marketing*. Simple tricks that will help you optimize your Web site for the flood of new traffic your site will get after you implement a few of the clever tricks and tips in this chapter.
- *Trade shows and seminars*. In this section you will find ideas to help you tap into the multibillion dollar marketing machines that are trade show and seminar marketing. You will find super-helpful planning checklists that will ensure your next exhibition event is a raging success.

CHECKLISTS

Throughout this guide you will find numerous helpful checklists that can be utilized as they are featured. Alternately, you can customize each checklist and create one that is relevant to your business, industry, products, services, or marketing objectives. Likewise, you will find many examples, such as a sample press release, to help explain the marketing trick that is being featured. You can also use these examples or samples as a template and from there customize to suit your business and objectives.

ICON SYSTEM

As you read through the *Ultimate Small Business Marketing Guide* you will notice a series of icons accompanying each great marketing tip and trick featured. These icons represent additional condensed information such as the approximate cost to implement the idea, whether the marketing trick is a do-it-yourself project or if you should call in a professional to help out. And, an icon that will let you know at a glance if there are legal issues that must be considered in terms of the marketing idea or activity. Additionally, you will find numerous handy online and publication resources. The purpose of the icon

system is to give you, the reader, additional need-to-know information at a glance. Information that can assist in helping you decide on marketing ideas, tricks, and strategies that might be right to be put into action for your small business.

$ Cost to Implement

All of the great marketing tips, tricks, and ideas featured in this book include an approximate financial investment needed to implement the marketing idea or activity. This is generalized information and should only be used as a yardstick to determine the approximate costs associated with the specific marketing trick, idea, or activity. Occasionally the dollar sign icon will be followed by a plus sign (+); this simply means that the cost to implement the idea greatly varies, but will be greater then the lowest cost indicated. Always keep in mind that successful entrepreneurs carefully research and plan every aspect of marketing, including what each new marketing idea will cost to activate.

$ Less than $1,000

$$ $1,000–$10,000

$$$ $10,000–$25,000

$$$$ Greater than $25,000

⚒ Do-It-Yourself

By their very nature, entrepreneurs are resourceful hands-on types of individuals accustomed to rolling up their sleeves and getting to work, building or providing innovative solutions. When you see the hammer-and-nails icon featured in the book, this means that the marketing trick or idea featured is one that you can tackle yourself without having to call in the professionals. You might still have to conduct a little research and be prepared to learn by trial and error, but most readers will already be accustomed to doing that. Occasionally you will see that the do-it-yourself and a call-in-the-professionals icons are featured together. This simply means that the marketing trick or idea might be a do-it-yourself project for the more experienced marketers, or that calling in the professionals should also be considered. But fear not, the vast majority of marketing tricks and ideas featured in this book are included because they can be successfully implemented or carried out by any small-business owners regardless of marketing experience.

Call in the Professionals

When you see the telephone icon featured in the book alongside a marketing trick you might just want to stop and call in the professionals for help and guidance. Sometimes all the best intentions, hard work, and effort cannot replace experience and special education in terms of accomplishing certain marketing tasks and activities. And, with that said, I have tried to take the guesswork out of what should be considered a do-it-yourself marketing activity and one that would be best left to the professionals to tackle. As mentioned previously, occasionally you will see the do-it-yourself and the call-in-the-professionals icons featured together on the same marketing idea. Every small-business owner's marketing experience and specialty will vary—while one person may find a particular marketing activity easy to carry out, another may want to seek assistance from an outside professional.

Legal Issues

The scale-of-justice symbol indicates that there might be one or a combination of permits, licenses, liability insurance, certificates, or training required to employ the marketing trick, idea, or strategy that is featured. Remember that it the responsibility of all small-business owners to carefully research any marketing activity prior to implementing or testing the effectiveness of the idea for their businesses. You must make sure that what you are doing is legal within the community in which you conduct business.

Web Resource

Located throughout this book you will find numerous handy Web resources that are indicated by a mouse icon. The purpose of the Web resources is not to promote or endorse any one company, product, service, individual, Web site, or organization, but to give you an additional research tool in terms of learning more about a particular marketing trick or idea featured. For instance, you might be interested in finding a source for printable advertising specialties such as pens, calendars, coffee mugs, and memo pads, and you may be able to find a source for these items online. In a nutshell, the numerous Web resources throughout this book are fantastic research tools that enable you to quickly explore and compile further data and information about a particular marketing idea, activity, or strategy that you would like to learn more about.

Book Resources

Located at the end of each chapter is a suggested additional reading list, the purpose of which is not to promote or endorse any one author, book title, or publisher. The book resources are there to give you a research tool in terms of finding additional information and advice about specific marketing activities and strategies. Likewise, the suggested reading list is not meant to inspire you to run out and spend hundreds of dollars on new books, though investments made into products that can assist you to become a better business operator and marketer are without question wise business and personal investments. However, once again do not feel compelled to purchase these titles, if you come across one that interests you, start your search at the local library and take it for a marketing test drive first, so to speak.

◆ ◆ ◆

Entrepreneur Magazine's Ultimate Small Business Marketing Guide is the most authoritative and comprehensive marketing book available. This book gives you the ability to identify numerous great marketing ideas that will work for your small business. Harness the power of this book and put it to work for you starting today.

RESEARCH, PLANNING, AND COMPETITION
Marketing Tips for Your Business

Research serves to make building stones
out of stumbling blocks.

—Arthur D. Little

THE MARKETING MUSTS

$+

To excel in education there are learning musts, to excel in sports there are training musts, and to excel in business there are marketing musts. I don't want to overly simplify the marketing process, but the following are what I consider to be the marketing musts. Some of these tips, ideas, and tricks are repeated throughout this book, but that is because their significance to successful marketing cannot be overlooked or underestimated.

First Impressions Are Vital to Business Success

First impressions are lasting impressions and, therefore, you must make a conscious effort to always project the most professional business image possible. First impressions go well beyond personal contact with prospects and customers—making a great first impression must carry through all of your business and marketing activities. These areas include the visual appearance or presentation of your store or office, company transportation, signage, printed marketing materials, product displays and packaging, service delivery, and all forms of advertising.

Always Build Win-Win Business Relationships

It should come as no surprise that in order to be successful in business it is smart to build win-win situations in terms of all your business relationships. You cannot expect customers, employees, business alliances, and suppliers to be loyal to your brand, treat you with respect, and believe in your business unless you strive to build situations and relationships in which they all stand to win as much as, if not more than, you do.

Develop a Clearly Defined, Unique Selling Proposition

One, if not the biggest, marketing must is to have a clearly defined, unique selling proposition. This is nothing more than a fancy way of asking the vital question, "Why will people choose to do business with you, or purchase your product or service instead of doing business with a competitor and buying their product or service?" In other words, what one feature or combination of features is going to separate your business from competitors? Will it be better service, a longer warranty, better selection, longer business hours, more-flexible payment options, or a combination of all these and more? You should be able to sum up your unique selling proposition in one clearly defined sentence that makes customers say, "I understand why I should buy from you."

Know Who Your Customers Are and What They Need

An obvious, but much overlooked and underestimated, marketing must is to know who your customers are and what their needs are at all times. The reason I say overlooked and underestimated is because it becomes much too easy to assume you know who your customers are and what they need, especially if you have been in business for a while, complacency kicks off its shoes, and sits for a spell. Customers change, their needs change, and the marketplace and competition constantly changes. Consequently, the task of knowing who your customers are and what they truly need is an ongoing, ever-evolving process that requires your constant attention if you plan on staying one step ahead of the competition and want to make a profit.

Make It Easy for People to Do Business with You

Making it easy for people to do business with you is a marketing must that transcends all industries and marketplaces worldwide. You must always remain cognizant of the fact that few if any customers will work hard just for the privilege of giving you their hard-earned money. The shoe is on the other foot—you must work hard to earn your customers' business and make it as easy as possible for them to do business with you. Making it easy for people to do business with you means that you have to be accessible. Your staff should be knowledgeable about the products and

services you sell, and you must be able to provide customers with what they want and need when they want and need it.

Make Customer Service One of Your Top Priorities

How important is customer service? Even if you ignore the simple fact that without customers you have no business and concentrate only on the proven fact that it is ten times easier to sell to an existing customer than to try to find a new one. It is safe to say that customer service is very important to every business and definitely qualifies as a marketing must. Tear apart your current customer service program and policies and carefully analyze everything that you are doing now: What can be improved and what will have the biggest beneficial impact right away? The sad truth about customer service is that if you are not prepared to go the extra mile for your customers, a competitor gladly will.

Talk Is Cheap, Prove It to Them

Proof is one of the small-business owner's most tangible and marketable assets, making it an absolute marketing must. With proof will come credibility and trust, all of which will go a long way to build your business. Don't just tell prospects and customers how great your products and services are—show them, educate them, and prove to them beyond any doubt that your marketing claims are built on results, not something that you just pulled from thin air. Use customer testimonials, statistics, and most of all be prepared to overcome objections with believable and credible explanations if you want to earn your customers' business and loyalty for life.

Always Sell the Benefits

Your advertising, your sales presentations, your printed marketing materials, your product packaging, your trade show exhibit, your signage—every time that any person comes into contact with any marketing message from your business you must always be selling the *benefits* associated with your product or service and not the *features*. A treadmill may have 30 features, but the salable benefit is the fact that if you buy and use the treadmill you will become more physically fit. This can be translated into selling terms such as you will lose weight, you will become more healthy, you will enjoy increased self-confidence, and you might even live longer. Clearly demonstrate to prospects how your product or service will benefit them and you will sell more. This is a marketing must that should be practiced by all small-business owners.

Make Branding the Cornerstone of Your Marketing Activities

Brands sell, they don't have to be sold. That should be more than enough argument to convince all small-business owners that they should be making an effort to make branding the cornerstone of all their marketing activities. Develop a unified corporate image and marketing message and consistently project and deliver both in all your business and marketing activities. If brand management becomes a regular business activity, then brand management becomes habitual and not an afterthought.

Constant Contact, Follow-Up, and Follow-Through with All Customers

Constant contact, follow-up, and follow-through with customers should be the mantra of every small-business owner, and without question a wise marketing must to employ. Talk is cheap, and customers are never won for the long term by what you say, but instead by what you do. Keep in close contact with customers so you know what they need. Follow up with customers after the sale to make sure they are 100 percent happy with their purchase. Follow through on every promise you make. Best of all, this is very easily accomplished by building and maintaining a customer database system that enables you to update customer files, plug in their individual needs, and track their purchasing history and overall satisfaction with your business, employees, and what you are selling them.

Reduce Buying Risk to Increase Profits

What is the biggest obstacle to overcome to ensure that prospects buy and that customers buy more and

more often? Risk. You must develop ways to reduce the risk associated with buying your goods or services, especially if you are a new start-up business, introducing a product or service, or have plans for rapid growth and increased market share. You can reduce risk by offering trial product or service periods, no-hassle money-back guarantees, installment and other creative payment plans, and by using customer testimonials that show prospects that other people have bought before them and have benefited because of it. Reducing buying risk is a marketing must for small-business owners that have yet to establish brand name awareness and brand trust in their trading areas.

Always Grab Their Attention

Every marketing activity you engage in must be designed in such a way that it grabs the attention of your target audience. Your print advertisements and headlines must leap off the page screaming, "Look at me!" Your signage must grab so much attention that people will turn so quickly to see it they run the risk of getting whiplash. Your radio and television advertisements must make people turn up the volume at the mere mention of your business name, product, or service. And your window displays must nearly cause auto accidents as passing motorists slam on the brakes to check them out. If you want to stand out in today's extremely competitive business environment then everything you do to market your business must be aimed at grabbing the attention of your target audience. A small-business owner cannot waste money on marketing activities aimed at building awareness solely through repeated exposure—if you do, you will go broke long before this is ever accomplished. Instead every marketing activity you engage in has to put money back in your pocket so you can continue to grow your business. And this can only be accomplished by grabbing your target audience's attention and pulling them into your store, office, Web site, trade show booth, or sales presentation to find out more and to buy what you are selling.

Always Ask for the Sale

Marketing, advertising, and promotional activities are completely worthless regardless of how clever they are or how much money you spent to develop them or even if they are perfectly aimed at your target audience unless one simple thing is done: ask for the sale. Remember, as much as it helps to be a great salesperson, an advertising copywriting whiz, or a public relations specialist, the average small-business owner will win more times than not by following one simple rule: always ask for the sale. In your advertising, ask people to buy. In your store, ask people to buy. In your signage, ask people to buy. In your promotional materials, ask people to buy. The last eight words that you ever say to a prospect or current customer should be, "How would you like to pay for that?"

Master the Art of Negotiation

Becoming a master in the art of negotiation provides two benefits. First, it will enable you to never leave money on the table in terms of negotiating with a customer over a sale. And second, when you know how to negotiate, you will buy products and services for resale or use in your business for less and, more importantly, on better terms. Learning to negotiate forces you to question the other person's motivations or responses rather than simply accepting them without explanation. Simply learning to master the art of negotiation will increase the average small-business owner's bottom-line profits by 5 percent or more annually, based on nothing more than selling your goods and services for 2.5 percent more and paying suppliers 2.5 percent less. And when you look at it in these basic terms, you see how 2.5 percent would seldom be the basis of a deal breaker with customers or suppliers.

Go Out of Your Way to Get Involved

Also an important marketing must is to get involved with the community that supports your business. Go out of your way to help local charities and community events. Join associations and clubs that concentrate on programs and policies that are designed to improve the local community for the better of all residents. Besides the fact that it is every small-business owner's responsibility to help support the local community, going out of your way to get involved will open many new doors in terms of networking, prospecting, and increased selling opportunities.

Never Stop Investing in Yourself

The final marketing must is to never stop investing in ways to make yourself a better businessperson and marketer. Buy and read marketing books, magazines, reports, and industry publications. Attend marketing seminars, workshops, and training courses. Invest in equipment and technology that will help to improve your marketing efficiency—things such as computers and software, multifunction telephone systems, and office equipment that will increase productivity and profitability.

WHY SPEND TIME RESEARCHING?
$ ✎

A marketing plan is only as strong as the research foundation that it is built on; a lack of research makes the plan just words on pages and nothing more. A marketing plan is a strategy, a road map compiled from information about how and when you will reach certain objectives and goals. The research that goes into the planning process is what makes all of the planning, goals, and objectives feasible and attainable. By researching the various components of business—customers, products, services, competition, marketplace trends, customer service, the industry as a whole, and technology—you gain the insights you need to construct the marketing plan. It has often been said that failing to plan in business is planning to fail. However, without research, a plan is purely fiction, assumptions based on what you think or, more so, what you hope might happen. Without research you do not know if you are paying too much for an advertisement, or if that advertisement even reaches your target audience. But then again you wouldn't know who the target audience is because there was no research conducted to identify the target audience. It's funny, we might spend a day researching various kinds of DVD players before we buy one—the manufacturer, the warranty, the features, the price, and the reputation. All this work spent researching an item that costs perhaps $250. And even worse, it's an item that has no direct impact on our income or livelihood.

But how much time did you spend on research before you committed to that $500 a month Yellow Pages ad, or that $2,000 golf tournament sponsorship, or the $5,000 you spent to have a new four-page color brochure designed and printed? At some point we are all guilty of not committing to and conducting the proper research to maximize our marketing plans. This includes neglecting to conduct the proper research to maximize that plan and not putting forth the effort to ensure the best results, business success, and profitablitity. However, knowing this is the first step to committing to a new marketing plan, or revamping the marketing plan.

Simply put, research gives you answers so you dont have to make assumptions. Here are a few examples of what research could reveal:

- Whether shoppers are prepared to pay $200 for your custom-manufactured picnic tables before you invest $100,000 in the manufacturing facility.
- If the local marketplace can support a fifth weekly newspaper before you get the presses rolling.
- Whether expanded store hours will make your business more profitable before you hire ten new employees to meet staffing requirements.
- If your product will sell overseas before you set up international distribution channels.

DEFINING PRIMARY DATA
$+ ✎

Primary data is the data and information that you generate through various methods of research or that you collect from your customers, suppliers, employees, subcontractors, prospects, and business alliances. The ways you can collect or generate primary data for research and marketing planning purposes is nearly unlimited. Some forms, such as formal surveys, cost money to develop, conduct, tabulate, and analyze while other methods, such as listening to what your customers are telling you, are absolutely free for the taking. Here are a few ways that you can collect or generate primary data:

- Talk to customers, employees, suppliers, and business alliances.

- Conduct formal or informal surveys and polls and question people to learn more about your customers, market, products, and services.
- Host brainstorming sessions or focus groups.
- Analyze your customer and prospect database to learn more about your customers' buying habits and your prospects' needs.
- Conduct product or service sampling exercises and demonstrations.
- Install a suggestion box in your store, office, or Web site and encourage employees and customers to make suggestions, comments, or complaints.
- Make general observations about your store, customers, products, services, and marketplace and record these observations.
- Observe the competition and compare.

These are only a few ways to collect and record primary data about your business, products, services, customers, and marketplace. There are many more, some of which are featured later in this chapter. Business owners are surrounded by primary data; the key to success is not to be oblivious to this information. Make a conscious effort to collect and compile this data so that it can be analyzed and acted upon accordingly for the benefit of your business and bottom-line profits.

DEFINING SECONDARY DATA
$+ ✎

As the name suggests, secondary data comes from outside or secondary sources—such as government agencies, nonprofit organizations, business associations, and privately and publicly held corporations—that have generated, collected and compiled the data. Like primary data, this information can be used to learn more about your business, customers, competition, industry—basically any aspect of business or marketing that you want to understand better for the benefit of your business or position in the marketplace. Obtaining secondary data for research and planning purposes is very easy; it's everywhere, and, much like primary data, the vast majority of secondary data is free for the taking. Listed below are some sources where you can obtain valuable secondary data that can be used for research and planning purposes, some of which are explained in greater detail later in this chapter.

- Local, state, and federal government agencies
- Library and Web sites
- Business, industry, and trade associations
- Media companies, publishers, radio and television stations
- Schools
- Nonprofit associations
- Books, newspapers, magazines, trade papers, newsletters, and reports
- Suppliers, competitors, and business alliances

However, before you consider the source, you must first identify your research and marketing objectives. What do you want to fix? What do you want to learn? What type of data are you seeking? In other words, what do you want to accomplish with the use of secondary research data? For instance if it is trademark related, then the logical place to search for this type of data is the Trademark and Patent Office. Perhaps you are looking for scientific data to back product claims. Trade journals and scientific associations would be the place to seek this type of data. The following are categories of various types of data that are available from secondary sources. Keep in mind only some types, as the list is almost unlimited.

- Patent, copyright, and trademark data
- Manufactured products specifications
- Demographic statistics
- Psychographic data reports
- Public opinion polls
- Transportation data
- Media surveys and polls
- Legal data
- Business statistics
- International statistics
- Pricing data
- Arts and entertainment information
- Political statistics and data
- Crime statistics
- Weather statistics
- Military statistics
- Personal finance and monetary markets data

I could quite literally fill this entire book with the various types of data, statistics, and information available from secondary sources and who these secondary sources are, but that is not the point nor would it be practical. The point is that there is an unlimited about of secondary data and information that is available for small-business owners to tap for research and marketing planning purposes. In fact, at the time of writing this book, it is estimated that the amount of information that is available to the populations is doubling every three years. Given this astounding rate, once again the objective is not to know what type of secondary data and information is available, but what type of data will meet your specific research and planning needs.

DEFINING QUANTITATIVE AND QUALITATIVE DATA
$ ✎

Quantitative Data

Quantitative data is expressed in numbers, quantities, and percentages. The vast majority of data analyzed and used by small-business owners to create marketing plans and marketing strategies is quantitative data. The reason for this is straightforward: Because quantitative data is expressed numerically, it is very tangible and measurable. Therefore quantitative data is easy to understand and transfer into charts, lists, and graphs, and apply to planning. Examples of quantitative data include the following:

- Results of a questionnaire that asks yes or no questions. The results can be tabulated easily in numbers; either a fixed quantity such as 53 said yes, while 47 said no, or in percentage terms such as 53 percent said yes and 47 percent said no.
- Comment cards that ask customers to rank your service on a scale of 1 to 5. Once again, the results are turned into numbers such as 15 people out of 30 who ranked our service gave us a 5 out of 5. This could then be translated into a further result in percentage terms such as 50 percent of our customers are 100 percent satisfied with the level of service we provide.
- Another example of quantitative data would be a survey conducted by you as the primary

source or by a secondary source that revealed 55 percent of woman under the age of 25 plan on having two children before they reach 35 years old.

Quantitative data is valuable to small-business owners because it enables them to look at and understand the marketplace in broad terms at a glance.

Qualitative Data

Qualitative data is not expressed in tangible numbers, but rather in answers and statements. It is what people say about your business, products, services, prices, quality, or just about anything else that cannot be grouped or placed into numerical terms and results. Examples of qualitative data include:

- surveys, questionnaires, or polls where people freely answer questions in their own words, not by giving multiple choice, ranking, or yes or no responses;
- open discussion groups, such as forums and focus groups, that generally consist of your target audience and who are encouraged to speak openly or comment about how they feel about or perceive a product, service, price, value, or quality; and
- informal discussions held with customers, suppliers, or employees wherein their personal comments about questions you ask are recorded, such as, "I think the price of the widget is more than most people can afford or would be willing to pay."

Qualitative data is valuable to small-business owners because it can reveal more precise details about what your customers think of specific things relevant to your business.

THE GEOGRAPHICS, DEMOGRAPHICS, AND PSYCHOGRAPICS DATA TRAIL
$+ ✎ 🐷

Identifying your customers and prospects, in other words your target audience, is a process that should be broken into three distinct groups: geographics, demographics, and psychographics. In marketing this is commonly referred to as market segmentation and it enables you to know who your customers are,

where they come from, and what common characteristics they share. It is the combination of these three market segments that will help you to identify and group your customers and to create a target customer profile.

Geographics

Geographics is segmenting your customers geographically, such as by country, state, city, neighborhood, and right down to the street. This information is really the beginning of the process of trying to segment and identify your target customers. Where do your customers come from, or where are your customers located? While your goods or services may sell well in Toronto, that certainly doesn't mean you will automatically enjoy the same market acceptance and success in Tampa. There are five basic questions that have to be considered and identified in terms of geographics:

1. Where are your target customers geographically located?
2. Is the target audience in the geographic area large enough to be profitable?
3. What is required to access that geographic area?
4. What means of promotion is available to tap the target market in that geographical area?
5. Will the target audience respond to the promotional activities?

Even on a basic level, geographical segmentation is extremely valuable information. For example, the owner of a retail shoe store that is located in the center of the city can access his customer database to find out in which part of the city the majority of his customers live. Knowing this information will enable the shoe-store owner to then target marketing and advertising efforts in the area (e.g., north, south, east, or west) of the city that the majority of current customers live.

Demographics

Demographics is segmenting your customers by sex, age, race, religion, education, income, profession, and so forth. Demographics can be further expanded to include information such as the type of car that your customers drive and how many people reside in their houses. In a nutshell, demographics are statistical facts about the population. It is the second step in determining who your target customers are. Start by compiling a list of what you know to get the demographics ball rolling:

- Are the majority of your customers or your target audience male or female?
- Into what age range would the majority of your target audience fall?
- Is the majority of your target audience married, single, or divorced?

These are just a few of the demographic profiling questions that need to be answered. If you are already in business, then you can start by surveying your current customers and prospects for answers. If you are looking for demographics information to help target potential customers, then start with local government agencies, schools, and business associations to find this secondary demographics data.

Psychographics

Psychographics is segmenting your customers by their common characteristics such as lifestyle, values, behavior, and opinions. Psychographics is used as a continuation of geographic and demographic data. Or simply put, once you know where your target market is (geographics) and who your target market is (demographics) then you can begin to find out what they think and care about (psychographics) in terms of your business and what you sell or provide. Start by asking a few basic questions:

- What do my customers have in common? Perhaps many belong to one particular local association, group, or church.
- What do my customers care about most: price, quality, fast service, value, or wide selection?
- What do my customers read or watch on television? What activities do they participate in on weekends?

You can make basic assumptions in terms of psychographical profiling of your target market, providing they are logical assumptions. For instance, it is a safe assumption that the target market for $200,000 sports cars are not young families that reside in the-suburbs.

WEB RESOURCES

- www.srds.com SRDS (Standard Rate and Data Service): Media Solutions, print and online lifestyle and demographic publication sourcebooks.
- www.demographics.com: *American Demographics* magazine.

CUSTOMER DATABASE RESEARCH
$+ ✎ ☏

One of the best sources of primary research data available to small-business owners, professionals, and salespeople is their own customer database. Information extracted from a well-maintained and planned database can reveal the average age of your customers, whether the majority are male or female, where they live, who buys the most often, and what the average sales value of their purchases are, just to mention a few. However, this is a catch-22 situation, because in order to use your customer database to generate and compile valuable primary data that can be used for market research and planning purposes you must first have a customer database.

This begs the question that if a customer database is such a powerful research and marketing tool, then why doesn't every single small-business owner invest in the equipment, technologies, and training required to build and maintain their own in-house customer relationship management database? The answer is there is no reason, especially when you consider that the price of computer equipment and database software has fallen dramatically over the past decade while the usability and custom features that can be personalized to meet individual marketing objectives have increased dramatically. However, don't fret if you are not plugged into your customers by way of a database; it is never to late to get the data train rolling and benefit from what you learn about your customers. Customer relationship management technologies are revolutionizing the way that small business competes for and captures market share and customer loyalty. Though the type of information that you choose to capture and record about your customers will change depending on your business and your marketing needs, the following are a few suggestions:

- Name of individual (consumer)
- Name of company, including contact people and titles
- Type of company and related information such as product/service description, number of employees, etc.
- Address, including mailing address if different from the physical location
- Telephone number, fax number, e-mail address(es), Web site
- Job description/job title
- Demographic information including age, sex, education, etc.
- Buying history including date of first purchase, date of all subsequent purchases, type of purchases, units sold, average units each sale, average value each sale, sale value to date
- How a person became a customer, for instance networking, cold call, advertising, trade show, sales visit, etc.
- Customer ranking
- Special requests, complaints, payment history
- What specific benefits and features are needed and/or wanted

WEB RESOURCES

- www.oracle.com: Oracle/Netledger Small Business Suite
- www.maximizer.com: Customer and contact management software.
- www.salesforce.com: Customer relationship management solutions.

INFORMAL SURVEYS AND DISCUSSIONS RESEARCH

$+ ✎

Another method to generate and collect primary data for research and planning is to informally survey or discuss particular business- or marketing-related topics with people that can assist in delivering or divulging the type of information you want to meet your specific objective. These people would include the following:

- Current and past customers
- Suppliers, subcontractors, and business alliances
- Community leaders and those who influence the decisions of others
- Employees, consultants, and trainers
- Current and past prospects

The informal survey or discussion sessions could happen over a coffee break, at the point of purchase, during a business or social function, or just about any other place or time. Even something as routine as asking a customer if she enjoyed her steak dinner is a way of collecting primary data. Of course it is the customer's response and your reaction to the response that will dictate how this data is used in your business.

FORMAL SURVEY RESEARCH

$+ ✎

Formal survey research consists of polls, questionnaires, or surveys, or whatever you want to call them. Sometimes you have to develop and conduct a formal survey to get the response you need for important business and marketing decisions. So, with that said, the following are a few surveying methods to consider.

Mail Surveys

Mail surveys are a popular way to find out what customers and prospects think. They can be developed and conducted in two ways. The first is to create a survey and mail it to current and past customers and prospects on your in-house mailing list. You can also rent mailing lists that are compiled from people who meet your target audience. The second method is to have your survey published in a newspaper, magazine, newsletter, or trade journal that is read by your target audience and ask readers of these publications to complete the survey and mail it in or drop it off at your store or office. In both cases you will likely have to provide some sort of incentive to motivate people to take the time to complete and mail in or drop off your survey. The incentive or special gift could be that by doing so their names will be automatically entered into a contest, or you can send them back a discount coupon, gift certificate, or a free gift or product. Most of the formal surveying methods mentioned here will cost in the range of $5 to $50 a person when direct costs and indirect costs are combined, something important to keep in mind when budgeting.

Ballot and Comment Surveys

As mentioned above, holding a contest in association with your survey is a great way to motivate people to participate in the survey. You can develop contest entry ballots and comment cards that ask specific questions regarding what you would like to learn about your customers, products, or services. These ballot survey cards can then be dropped into the ballot box as a way for customers and prospects to enter your contest. Ballot surveys can be distributed in your store, at malls, trade shows, seminars in the form of tent or table cards, and through the mail.

Telephone Surveys

Calling your customers or target audience at home or at the office is also a survey method, but one that requires skill and a thick skin to do well. In fact, this is a surveying method that should be left to the professionals who have the people, skills, equipment, and expertise to ensure good results. However, if you do tackle telephone surveying yourself, make sure to call general consumers in the early evenings and business consumers during the day. Evening calls are best placed between the hours of 6 P.M. and 8 P.M., and daytime office calls on Tuesdays, Wednesdays, or Thursdays between 10 A.M. and noon or 2 P.M. and 4 P.M.

Online Surveys

An easy, fast, and frugal way to conduct customer and prospect surveying is to do it on the Internet. This can be accomplished through your own Web site if you have one. Alternately, there are literally hundreds of survey services that for a fee will develop a survey for you and place it in Web sites on the Internet that are frequented by your target audience. Online survey are a great option for small-business owners who are on tight budgets and need results quickly. In the online marketing chapter of this book you will find more detailed information about developing and conducting online polls, surveys, and questionnaires.

In-Person Surveys

In-person surveys are another way that you can find out what your customers and target audience think about your products and services. These in-person surveys can be conducted right at your business location, at malls on weekends with permission, or at trade shows and seminars. The benefits of personally surveying customers and prospects is that it enables you to ask questions of a more qualitative nature, as respondents will often answer these kinds of questions verbally but not take the time to answer them if they have to write their answers down. As with any survey method you choose, make sure that you carefully develop your questions prior to conducting the survey and don't let respondents catch you off guard and take you down paths that you have not planned for nor need information about.

Product and Service Sampling

Product and service sampling is obviously one of the best ways to conduct market research and for some businesses, such as food manufacturers, it is an absolute must. The downside of sampling is that it is very easy for the results to be skewed—when consumers receive something for free, even if the something is a small sample, they view it as a gift and their responses or comments about the product or service may be affected by their feelings of gratitude. When was the last time you told someone that you hated a gift they gave you? However, if you can get past this stumbling block, then firsthand testing of a new product or service by the end users is one of the best marketing research methods.

A Few Survey Question Tips

- Start by identifying exactly what you want to learn from your customers' or prospects' responses. In other words what is the marketing objective of the survey?
- Ask closed questions such as those that require a yes or no response, or multiple choice if you want quantitative results. Alternately, ask

open-ended questions that require respondents to write down how they feel or what they think if you want qualitative results. Of course you can combine both methods to meet specific survey objectives.

- Make sure that your wording in the questions is not biased toward the answer that you would like to receive. You would be amazed at how easily this can happen mainly because of your own expectations and perceptions. However, the surveying exercise should always be focused on real results, free of bias, leading, or manipulative questioning techniques.

- Pretest your survey prior to wide release to make sure that your questions are easily and clearly understood and that you have not inadvertently placed questions out of the desired sequence order. Pretesting also ensures that the survey can be completed in a reasonable amount of time so respondents do not terminate early.

- Choose wording carefully so that it is easy to read and understand; skip technical jargon, slang words, and abbreviations.

- Questions should be very easy to answer; never make a respondent have to work or think hard to answer because they won't. Many people view surveys as fun, so if possible try to stick with easy multiple choice, straight yes or no, and "on a scale of" questions. The easier and more fun you make it for participants to complete, the more likely they will fully complete it honestly and accurately.

Web Resources

- www.oneminutepoll.com: One Minute Poll, customizable survey and poll software.
- www.websurveyor.com: Web Surveyor, customizable survey and poll software.

CUSTOMER SERVICE INQUIRIES AND COMPLAINTS RESEARCH

$ ⚒

Customer service inquiries and complaints are perhaps one of the best sources of primary data that

you can collect, record, and analyze simply because it comes directly from the source that can make or break your business. Call it the standing-in-front-of-you-and-knocking-you-over-the-head type of important research that every business owner has to be totally aware of. Get started by recording all customer inquiries and complaints you receive and use the information you collect to find weak areas within your business, products, services, staff, or customer-service policies—basically repetitious problems that need to be corrected. Or, use the information to identify requests from customers about specific products or services that they would like and need; in doing so you can potentially expand your product or service line and fill this need. By recording and analyzing customer inquiries and complaint information you will generally see patterns start to develop and you will be able to react and plan accordingly. Even the smallest business can benefit by recording all customer comments, inquiries, and complaints, by writing them in a daily journal, or by using your computer and customer-management software. Additionally, by recording complaints, you'll be able to measure the performance of your supplier's products and services as well. Once again, if you find that patterns start to develop with a particular supplier, you'll be armed with the information you need to confront that supplier and look for mutually beneficial ways to fix the deficiencies or find a new supply source. Reacting to the same problem over and over and over accomplishes nothing, but costs a lot in terms of time, money, and potentially lost customers. By logging complaints, you can identify those that are repeated and fix them so they do not continue. Hence, not only is it important to listen to what your customers are saying, but even more so to act on what is revealed through these inquiries and complaints.

HARNESS THE POWER OF THE WEB FOR RESEARCH

$ ⚒

Just one short decade ago, finding a foreign distribution source for your widget, or even something as simple as learning about out-of-state laws and regulations pertaining to business expansion was an extremely time-consuming and often frustrating task. Countless hours could be spent on the telephone, writing letters, or purchasing expensive books and directories just to get the business information you needed. Fortunately all of that has changed thanks to the advent of the Internet. Facts, information, leads, and just about anything you ever wanted to know or needed to know about business, domestically or internationally, is now just a painless mouse click away. If you're not hooked up to the Internet already, then do it. Get Internet savvy and take advantage of the Internet for business research and planning purposes. Educate yourself about how the Internet can help you grow your business and keep it on track for years to come. Use the Internet to keep on top of your competition, discover new business and selling opportunities, and even showcase your products and services to a worldwide audience of buying consumers. All of this and more can be done using the Internet, but only if you make a conscious decision that the Internet is going to play an important role in how you research, plan, and take action in and for your business. Bill Gates once referred to the Internet as the "Information Superlibrary," a very accurate observation, wouldn't you agree?

GET SCHOOLS ON BOARD TO HELP WITH RESEARCH

$ 📞

Would you like to conduct focus groups, market research surveys, and new-product testing forums, but unfortunately it's not in the financial budget? If so, perhaps you should look to local schools as a possible solution. Many schools offer small-business owners the opportunity to work together in joint partnerships with business and marketing students to assist in things such as market research, new product forums, marketing plans, and marketing polls and surveys. Get started by creating a proposal outlining the details of the marketing activity you would like to conduct or research. Once your

proposal is ready to go, simply set appointments with school administrators, teachers, and professors of local learning institutions and pitch your proposal. As a rule of thumb the vast majority of teachers and schools see these types of partnerships between students and community small business as very positive, win-win situations. Students need real-life experience that classroom training cannot provide, but that working hands on with local entrepreneurs can. If your proposal is well planned and can provide students with beneficial learning opportunities, in all likelihood you will have few problems forming these research and marketing partnerships with schools and thus find a cost-effective solution for conducting various types of marketing research and planning activities.

HOMEMADE FOCUS GROUPS

$+ 🔨

One of the best ways to research the viability of a new product is to conduct a focus group to see if the people in the group like the product and its features, benefits, competitive advantage, durability, reliability, performance, and price point. The only problem is that conducting focus groups can be very costly for budding entrepreneurs with limited financial means or access to research capital. Consequently as an inexpensive research solution, consider creating your own homemade and hand-picked group of people to form a focus group to test, suggest, and report on your product. Selecting the members of the group is not rocket science, just choose people that are within your intended primary target audience for the product. For instance, if you have designed a new toy and want to test it and research the product, then strike a deal with a local daycare and let the kids run the toy through a vigorous workout while you watch from the sidelines and take notes. Big corporations often spend thousands, sometimes millions, of dollars forming focus groups to give feedback on new products; you can get results as useful as the pros do simply by being creative and frugal in the way you form your own focus groups.

Some Helpful Focus Group Tips

- Ideally the focus group should comprise six to eight participants to ensure accurate results. The members in the group should be representative of your target audience for the product or service.

- Create a general outline of the topics, points, and ideas that you would like the focus group to consider, but remain open to the process and allow for deviations from the outline if warranted and useful.

- Everyone in the group should be made aware of the fact that their input, ideas, suggestions, and complaints are important and will be heard. After all that is the whole idea behind the process. Likewise each person in the group should have the opportunity to voice their individual opinions. If you feel the individual opinions could sway, influence, or alter group opinions, then let each individual describe his or her experiences or thoughts about the product or service in private. Once this has been completed, have them discuss and debate the merits and faults openly as a group.

- Provided you get the okay from everyone in the group, you may want to consider taping the discussions to ensure that no information is overlooked or left unrecorded.

LOOK-OUT-THE-WINDOW RESEARCH

$+ ✎

One research method that should never be overlooked or underestimated by small-business owners is the good old look-out-the-window method of collecting primary data for marketing and business planning purposes. What's going on in your trading area and community? Is the market growing, has it matured, or is it declining? What is the competition doing? Are they expanding, remaining static, or going out of business? And what is the overall state of the local economy? Is it heated and energized or are people lined up at the unemployment office looking for work? Even something as simple as counting passing motorist and pedestrian traffic at peak and nonpeak hours can help you compile information in terms of selecting a retail location. Look-out-the-window research is more than looking out your window in the literal sense. It is keeping your finger on the pulse of the community at all times to keep in step with trends and gain knowledge and have access to information that can effect your business and the decisions you make in planning for the future.

CUSTOMER DEMOGRAPHICS QUESTIONNAIRE

$+ ✎

The more you know about your customers, the better informed you will be about who they are and what they like. More importantly, you can create a customer profile that will enable you to clone your best customers. There is a sample customer demographics questionnaire on page 14 that you can use as a guideline to create one that will work for your particular business. Distribute the questionnaire directly to your customers in person, or by mail, fax, or e-mail. Stress that they do not have to include information that will identify them personally and that the information will be held in the strictest of confidence and used only internally so you can understand and better serve your customers' needs. Additionally, you may want to include a small incentive such as a discount coupon or gift as a method to motivate people to complete the questionnaire.

WEB RESOURCES

- 🕭 www.demographics.com: *American Demographics* magazine.

- 🕭 www.srds.com: SRDS (Standard Rate and Data Service) media solutions, print and online lifestyle and demographic publication sourcebooks.

Sample Customer Demographics Questionnaire

Please tell us a little more about yourself.

The following is a simple questionnaire that (your business name here) has developed so we can better serve our customers. Your answers will be kept in the strictest confidence and not shared with anyone outside of our organization.

Sex
- ❏ Male
- ❏ Female

Age
- ❏ Under 17
- ❏ 18–25
- ❏ 26–35
- ❏ 36–45
- ❏ 46–55
- ❏ 56–65
- ❏ 66+

Marital Status
- ❏ Married
- ❏ Divorced
- ❏ Widowed
- ❏ Single

Family Members
Total number of family members living at home
- ❏ 1
- ❏ 2
- ❏ 3
- ❏ 4
- ❏ 5
- ❏ 6+

Education
Please check the highest completed level
- ❏ High School
- ❏ Trade/Technical School
- ❏ College/University
- ❏ Other _____

Occupation
Are you employed ❏ full time, ❏ part time, or ❏ seasonally?
- ❏ Laborer
- ❏ Skilled Labor/Trade
- ❏ Office/Clerical
- ❏ Management
- ❏ Executive
- ❏ Self-Employed
- ❏ Retired

Personal Income
- ❏ $0–$9,999
- ❏ $10,000–$19,999
- ❏ $20,000–$29,999
- ❏ $30,000–$39,999
- ❏ $40,000–$49,000
- ❏ $50,000–$59,000
- ❏ $60,000–$69,000
- ❏ $70,000+

Household Income
- ❏ $0–$24,999
- ❏ $25,000–$49,999
- ❏ $50,000–$74,999
- ❏ $75,000–$99,999
- ❏ $100,000+

Residence
Do you currently ❏ own or ❏ rent?

How long have you been at your current residence?
- ❏ 1–5 years
- ❏ 6–10 years
- ❏ 11+ years

Which type of housing?
- ❏ Apartment
- ❏ Townhouse/Co-op
- ❏ House
- ❏ Vacation Home
- ❏ Other _____

Hobbies/Interests
Please list three hobbies or special interests that you have.

_____

_____

_____

Language
Please list any languages you are fluent in other than English.

_____ Spoken ❏ Written ❏

_____ Spoken ❏ Written ❏

_____ Spoken ❏ Written ❏

_____ Spoken ❏ Written ❏

_____ Spoken ❏ Written ❏

Thank you for your cooperation; we appreciate it.

TARGET CUSTOMER PROFILE

$ ✎

Once you have compiled and analyzed all of your research data, you should have a very good idea of who your target customers are and the special characteristics that make them your target audience. At this point you should create a simple profile of your target customer, so you can use the profile as a handy reference tool when planning advertising and marketing activities. However, keep in mind that you will want to update your customer profile every year.

Target Customer Profile Worksheet (Consumer)

Sex
❏ Male   ❏ Female

Age Range
❏ Under 17   ❏ 46–55
❏ 18–25   ❏ 56–65
❏ 26–35   ❏ 65+
❏ 36–45   ❏ Specific _____

Where do my customers live? _____

_____

_____

Education Level
❏ High School   ❏ University
❏ College   ❏ Trade/Technical

Additional comments _____

_____

_____

Income

Personal Income Range $ _____

Family Income Range $ _____

Occupation (list)

_____

_____

_____

_____

Hobbies and Interests (list)

_____

_____

_____

_____

Common Characteristics or Lifestyle (e.g., go to church)

_____

_____

_____

_____

What is (are) the biggest benefit(s) my customers get from buying my products/services?

_____

_____

_____

_____

General Questions
(add/subtract questions depending on relevancy)

Do my customers own homes?   ❏ Yes   ❏ No

Do my customers own cars?   ❏ Yes   ❏ No

Do my customers travel often?   ❏ Yes   ❏ No

WHY PLAN?

$ ✎

Get in the habit of creating a plan for every marketing activity or method that you decide to test or implement, even if you already have an overall marketing plan for the current year in place. Why? Writing down what you want to do and what you want to achieve by doing it forces you to research and gather information, which in turn will enable you to make educated decisions based on factual information as opposed to assumptions. Furthermore, having what you want to do and how you will achieve it on paper enables you to use the plan as a yardstick to measure the success of the marketing undertaking and the success of how it was implemented. Your marketing plan may indicate that you want to run print advertisements in November to promote Christmas specials. But has this section of the overall plan been broken down into what size advertisement, budget, featured section of the newspaper, and more? Probably not. That's why creating a mini plan for every marketing action you decide to take is wise. Besides, no plan should be set in stone. You may find during your current year that you have to switch gears for some reason, thus creating another reason to get in the habit of planning all marketing decisions.

THE NUTS AND BOLTS OF A MARKETING PLAN

$+ ✎ ☏

Many small-business owners take a "fly by the seat of their pants" approach to business and market planning and, in spite of this practice, some are still very successful. Yet some are not and go broke as a direct result of lack of planning. Admittedly I can chalk up a few marketing experiences gone awry because of my lack of planning—most entrepreneurs can. We learn from our own mistakes and the mistakes of others. Consequently, it only strengthens the argument that you should have some sort of business plan and marketing plan in place that will work as a compass to assist in leading you through the murky waters of today's highly competitive small-business environment. The small-business marketing plan does not have to be a sophisticated and highly detailed hefty volume like those the multinational corporations need to satisfy nervous bankers and investors. In fact, even just a few detailed and well-documented pages that cover the basics are often sufficient. Keep in mind, however, the objective of the marketing plan is to create a map that details what you currently know and how this information can be used to increase market share, attract new customers, fend off competition, and generate more revenues and profits. With that said, the following are the basic components required for creating a small-business marketing plan.

Section 1. Overview

The overview should be brief—a few paragraphs that summarize the overall plan. The overview should include your business purpose (mission statement) such as, "We strive to lead the industry by providing our customers with incredible service, value, and convenience." Also in the overview should be a short description of the product(s) or service(s) that you sell and a strategic goal such as, "Through the expansion of our vendor plus program, ABC Hot Tubs will increase market share to 33 percent and revenues will top $5,000,000 annualized within two years."

Section 2. Company Analysis

Don't be intimidated by the phrase "company analysis"—it simply means the stuff that you already know about your own business, such as your strengths, weaknesses, and market share. The company analysis will include the following information:

- Key managers and strategic employees within the organization.
- A brief history of the company, when it was formed, and growth or decline in recent years.
- Key joint-venture or cross-promotional partners, which could include suppliers, business alliances, and competitors.
- The trading area that you currently operate in or serve.
- Company strengths such as highly trained service personnel.
- Company weaknesses such as lack of capital that could be used to fuel growth.

- Obstacles or challenges that stand in the way of reaching key marketing goals and objectives.

Think of your company analysis as the stuff your company currently does great, stuff that could be done better, and opportunities that could be capitalized upon within the marketplace. Likewise, think of the company analysis in relation to the marketing plan as where the company is currently situated, and where your company will be situated should you meet the objectives as set out in the marketing plan.

Section 3. Market Analysis

The market analysis is the information about the marketplace your business operates in currently, or the marketplace that you want to enter. The key concept to keep in mind about a market analysis is that much that is going on in the marketplace is out of your immediate control. All you can do is identify challenges and opportunities and guide your business accordingly. But without this information and subsequent planning, you face a full barrage of unknowns and uncontrollables. Conducting and recording a market analysis means that you reduce your exposure to risk while increasing your chances of capitalizing on opportunity. Market analysis should detail information in three areas: market size, market segmentation, and marketing environment.

MARKET SIZE

- What is the current market size and how big is the potential market?
- How many other companies are currently competing for this market?
- Is the market growing, static, or declining?

The market size should be detailed in broad terms and statistics. This information will be based on and supported by your own primary research data, as well as any secondary research data that you have used as a yardstick to determine the current and future market situation.

MARKET SEGMENTATION

As mentioned earlier in this chapter, market segmentation is breaking your target audience into groups for easy identification and targeting. These three market segments you should include in your marketing plan are:

1. *Geographics.* Include where your target audience is geographically. This information can expand into multiple geographic markets; however, if more than one marketplace is included then also be sure to include the number of potential customers in each geographic market.
2. *Demographics.* Include the basic demographic facts of your target audience in your marketing plan. These facts include sex, age range, education, profession, and income.
3. *Psychographics.* List the common characteristics, behaviors, and lifestyle similarities that your target customers share, things such as they go to church, they prefer to drive sports cars, and live in high-rise apartments.

MARKETING ENVIRONMENT

The marketing environments are current conditions or emerging trends that can affect the way you do business and market your products or services. These marketing environment issues can be positive, negative, or both and include issues such as the following:

- *Economic.* Economic trends and influences can range from increasing or decreasing employment rates or interest rates to impending changes in income tax structure that could leave consumers with less discretionary income.
- *Social/Cultural.* Fewer people going to church, more people working longer hours, and just about any other social or cultural change that you can think about may affect your marketing plans.
- *Political/Legal.* Political and legal trends and issues can run the gamut from an election year, to new regulations that will alter the way your business operates, to public interests groups that may not have your business in their best interests.
- *Technology.* Are emerging technologies changing or likely to change the way you do business, distribution, promotion, or pricing? If so, include any emerging technological trends that can influence your marketing plans.

- *Environmental.* Some environmental issues that could effect your plans, such as weather, are obviously hard to account for, while others such as energy costs and raw materials supplies, can easily be included if they are relevant.
- *Infrastructure.* Road construction, transit construction, and buildings being renovated and/or constructed that are in your immediate trading or market area can all affect your revenues and marketing plans. Therefore, they must be identified number one, and number two workable solutions and must be included in the plan.

Keep in mind that you do not have to include all or any marketing environment trends. Only those that can or will potentially influence or affect your business and marketing plans.

Section 4. Customer/Prospect Analysis

Imagine how easy it would be to win at business and in marketing if you knew exactly what your customers and prospects wanted all of the time? That is the next component of the marketing plan to concentrate on: a customer/prospect analysis. This section of the marketing plan should be able to answer the following types of questions about your customers and prospects:

- What decision process do they use when buying?
- What are the critical benefits that they look for?
- How are choices made between competitors?
- How sensitive are price, quality, service, and value issues?
- To what promotional or marketing activities are they attracted?

You have two options in terms of selling to consumers. The first is to know exactly what your target audience wants and needs and then give them exactly that. And the second option is to change consumer perceptions or buying habits so they will buy what you are selling. The vast majority of small-business owners will find their first choice to be the path of least resistance and expense, which is to know exactly what your customers and prospects want and need and then deliver it to them on a silver platter. Therefore, figure it out and get it in writing and into your marketing plan.

Section 5. Competitor Analysis

Much like death and taxes, small-business owners can rely on the fact that there will always be competition in the marketplace, and often this competition will want your market share, meaning your customers. Of course, the shoe is also on the other foot and there is a very good chance that you also want your competitors' main asset, their customers. Competition can be measured and analyzed in many ways, but perhaps one of the most proven and accurate forms to conduct a SWOT analysis on each competitor that competes for the same target market as you. SWOT is an acronym for Strengths, Weaknesses, Opportunities, and Threats. Later in this chapter you will find a complete explanation about how to conduct a SWOT analysis; it would be a wise decision to conduct, competitor analysis for each competitor you face and include this information in your marketing plan. Likewise, when creating your marketing strategies, try to think about how your competitors will react to these marketing strategies. Remember Newton's third law, "for every action, there is an equal and opposite reaction." Therefore, you have to be cognizant of the fact that your competitors will react or to counteract your marketing efforts. The trick is to know beforehand what action they will take so you can stay two steps ahead, even when they think you are one step behind.

Section 6. Marketing Objectives

The next component to include in your marketing plan is your goals and objectives. State your marketing goals in numerical terms that are easily measured, such as the company goal is to increase revenues by 15 percent to $505,000 or the company goal is to decrease customer complaints by 25 percent. Your objectives should be statements that support your goals and give details as to how you will reach these goals, such as "We will increase revenues by hiring four new territory sales representatives," and "We will decrease customer complaints by increasing our sales representatives' understanding about our products so they can better educate our prospects and customers."

Section 7. Marketing Strategy

The marketing strategy component consists of two parts. Part one is your marketing strategy—your philosophy about how you can best reach your target audience and deliver the goods and services they need in the manner that they would like these products or services to be delivered. This component includes choosing quality over price and filling a well-defined niche in the marketplace. Part two is how your strategy relates to the four marketing P's: product, price, place (distribution), and promotion. Marketing strategies will be based on several things including:

- market conditions.
- target audience.
- current customers.
- how you want to brand your business.
- the position you want to fill in your target audience's minds.

Brands and branding are discussed later in this chapter, but in short once you have chosen how and what you will brand, then the key to success is consistency. Therefore, your marketing strategy must be consistent with the brand that you want to establish and project. Think of "position" as your competitive advantage. You must have at least one aspect of your business that is unique and can become the cornerstone for all marketing and promotional activities. Once again, link brands in a unified and consistent manner. The following are a few aspects that should be discussed in the marketing plan in terms of product, price, place, and promotion.

PRODUCT

- Benefits the consumer receives from buying and using
- Scope and range of the product line
- Packaging both in the literal sense and in bundling
- Branding (how this relates to your marketing strategy such as "we won't be undersold" or "quality is our mantra")
- Quality, warranty, and features

PRICE

- Standard or list pricing

- Price specials and discounts, including to vendors, agents, and wholesalers and for bulk purchases
- Payment terms and financing and leasing options
- Payment methods (credit card, electronic check, etc.)

DISTRIBUTION (PLACE)

- Where and how the product will be placed for consumer access
- The type of distribution channel (direct, vendors, agents, wholesaler, etc.)
- The management of multiple distribution channels, if required
- Transportation and warehousing

PROMOTION

- Advertising, including frequency and media
- Sales promotions
- Direct marketing
- Personal/contact selling
- Sponsorships and public relations
- Internet
- Event marketing including trade shows and seminars
- Promotional materials including catalogs, brochures, signs, and ad specialties

Section 8. Budgets and Projections

The next step is to determine a marketing budget identified to correspond with the marketing and promotional activities identified in the plan, including a media budget, commissions forecasts, and special events budget. The obvious question is "how much should my marketing budget be?" There can be only one answer to that question: "How much will it cost to reach your marketing goals and objectives?" I wish I could give you a more accurate estimate, but every small-business owner will have different marketing objectives, different activities planned to meet them, and be on different timetables to reach them. However, you can create an estimate based on previous years and use a break-even analysis based on project expenses versus the projected increase as identified in the plan. If you want to increase revenues from $100,000 to $150,000, then you could apply the same percentage toward your marketing budget—if it was $10,000, then increase it by 50 percent to $15,000.

The same can hold true for financial projections based on marketing activities. You can base your projections starting with what you know: last year's sales and profits. And increase these numbers based on the goals that you set for each marketing activity or segment of your business as well as the overall marketing goal. However, the danger in doing so is that if you did not reach previous goals and forecasts, then you do not have a clear picture of the effectiveness of previous marketing plans and activities. Therefore monies may have been directed into the wrong areas for the wrong purposes. A ground-up approach to building marketing budgets is always the preferred method.

Section 9. Action Plan Timetable

The final component of your marketing plan should be an action plan timetable, which is a calendar outlining when each new marketing activity will be implemented throughout the calendar year. Or, when each existing marketing activity will be improved or implemented throughout the year. Your action plan should also include times when you will measure success or accuracy to date, I would suggest every three months, or quarterly.

STICK TO THE PLAN
$+ ✎

The key to marketing success is once you have developed and written your marketing plan, stick with the plan closely and give your plan time to materialize. Far too many small-business owners expect immediate results from marketing. When the results are not immediate, their first line of defense is to start to fiddle with their marketing plans—not little changes but a complete 180-degree turn about. Unfortunately, this does not give the original plan a chance to find its legs and work in the marketplace. There is no question that it is okay to fiddle with a marketing plan—in fact you

should never stop tweaking it to ensure maximum performance—but you have to stay true to the core ideas and not stray too far from these researched strategies. The worst part of drifting from the marketing plan is the fact that much money can be wasted—printed materials that change, other advertising that will no longer be suitable to use in the new marketing direction, and all the time that was wasted researching and drafting the marketing plan and perhaps creating a new one. The moral of the story is to take your time and carefully research and create a marketing plan that identifies your core marketing objectives and how they will be implemented and carried out correctly and with patience the first time around.

WEB RESOURCE

⊘ www.entrepreneur.com: Online business and marketing resource center for small-business owners and professionals.

IT'S ALL IN THE NAME
$ ✎

Skip the hip and latest fads in terms of naming your new business enterprise. Instead stick with the time-tested and proven formula of keeping it simple and making a good and memorable first impression on consumers. In a flash your business name should instantly tell people what you do and what's in it for customers (the benefit). It should be memorable and easy to spell and pronounce. ABC Pool Cleaning, granted, is not a very original business name. But it does tell people what you do (clean pools), what's in it for them (not having to slave all day cleaning their own pool), it's memorable (we all learned our ABCs), and it's very easy to spell (once again. we all learned our ABCs). More than anything else your business does or sells, it is your business name that will promote your business and get used the most, in print and verbally. The importance of having the right business name cannot be understated. Avoid names tied into your specific geographic area in case you want to expand the business nationally or internationally down the road. Seattle Pool Cleaning just wouldn't have the same recognition and impact in

Miami or in Dallas as it would in Seattle. Yet, National Pool Cleaning would be a name that would be universally adaptable regardless of geographic operating location.

CREATE A MARKETING CALENDAR

Throughout this book you will find hundreds of great marketing ideas, many of which I am sure would help your business grow if they were implemented. But let's face reality, small-business owners are busy people. In fact most work in excess of 60 hours a week to begin with so it begs to question, how will you ever find the time to implement any of these great marketing ideas into your business? One way is to create a marketing calendar, and in doing so you can prioritize the importance of each change you want to make in your current marketing activities. Or prioritize each new marketing idea you want to implement into your marketing routine. Developing a marketing calendar is actually quite simple to do, even if you already have a marketing plan in place. Get started by making two lists; the first should be comprise the new marketing ideas you would like to test or implement. The second list should comprise current marketing activities that you feel could be improved upon or done better. Each list should be prioritized with the most important things at the top. Once you have created the lists, simply place each item into your yearly business planner on the dates you feel each new or improved marketing task should be started or implemented in your marketing and action plan.

JOIN THE BETTER BUSINESS BUREAU

Before they spend their hard-earned money, most consumers want to know they are doing business with a credible and honest firm. One of the best and most affordable ways for you as a business owner to drive home the fact that your business is both credible and honest is by becoming a member of your local branch of the Better Business Bureau.

Membership in the BBB is especially important if you're in the business of providing consumers with services. As a service provider, one of your main sales and marketing tools is your business reputation and how you treat customers. Being a member of the BBB will help form an instant impression of credibility and good reputation. Once your business is registered with the BBB, be sure to promote the fact by including the BBB member logo in all advertisements and sales materials you use. Furthermore, most BBB branches publish an annual *Better Business Pages* or similar publication that lists member businesses and what they do. Advertising in these BBB publications is inexpensive and you'll quickly discover that many people, especially those have had bad past experiences purchasing a product or service, will only deal with businesses that belong to the Better Business Bureau.

WEB RESOURCE

 www.bbb.org: Better Business Bureau.

GET THE LATEST SCORES AT SCORE

For more than 30 years SCORE, The Service Corps of Retired Executives, has been assisting small-business owners with free advice and guidance on tough business issues and marketing. The SCORE team is comprised of seasoned professionals (most of whom are retired) who represent a wide range of business experience and backgrounds, from bank executives to CEOs of major international corporations. In addition to joining up for one or more of the many workshops SCORE hosts monthly, you can educate yourself though SCORE publications. Member coaches can even help you directly with a one-on-one coaching session to answer specific business questions and problems. SCORE is not limited to business management and operations information and help. The members are also well versed in all sales and marketing methods, and SCORE has many publications and training programs aimed directly at ways to increase revenues and profits by utilizing various marketing techniques and methods. By tapping into the SCORE network, you will be tapping into a wealth of free business knowledge and experience.

WEB RESOURCE

✍ www.score.org: Service Corps of Retired Executives.

TAP INTO THE SBA
$ ✍

Since 1953 the United States Small Business Administration (SBA) has been a one-stop source of information, products, and services for new and existing small-business owners. Through the SBA, you can apply for business start-up funds, secure loan guarantees, or apply for venture capital to expand an existing business operation. Additionally, SBA products and services include a vast online research database, management and marketing advice, business-specific training workshops, specialized reports and manuals, and access to international export markets worldwide. Every year the SBA assists more than one million small-business owners to start a new business, manage an existing business, or expand a business. There is no one source of business and market research information, products, and services available larger than the SBA. So make sure you tap the SBA and take advantage of the incredible range of research and marketing tools they provide.

WEB RESOURCES

✍ www.sba.gov: United States Small Business Administration.

✍ www.cbsc.org: The Canadian Business Service Center, the Canadian equivalent to the SBA.

JOIN ASSOCIATIONS
$$+ ✍

Many business owners are hesitant to join industry and business associations for two reasons: the cost to join and the time commitment required to participate in association events. Both can be valid objections providing you have taken the time to fully research and understand the association and decided that membership has little or no value to

your particular situation and business. Create a list and check it against what the association offers members in terms of exposure and services. At the top of your list should be the question "Can I recoup membership cost and get paid for the time I spend at association functions and events?" Almost 100 percent of the time the answer to this question will be yes. The key is to mine the value of membership, which can include member discounts on products and services, networking opportunities, creating new business alliances, advertising opportunities, and education opportunities through seminar and workshop series. Remember business and industry associations must provide value and benefits to their members in order to secure and retain them. Most associations provide great opportunities, but the rest is up to you. Profiting through membership requires a plan and participation to realize the value and benefits of membership to the fullest extent. The checklist on page 23 represents a few opportunities that can be created or exploited in terms of joining business and industry associations. Use this checklist for two reasons. One, identify areas in business that are your current weaknesses and that could be improved with help and advice from other small-business owners. And two, use the checklist as a yardstick to measure each association that you are considering joining. The associations that meet your needs will be a higher priority than those that do not.

WEB RESOURCES

✍ www.marketingsource.com/associations: Online directory listing more than 35,000 business associations.

✍ www.uschamber.com: The United States Chamber of Commerce.

✍ www.chamber.ca: The Canadian Chamber of Commerce.

GREAT BRANDS ARE CONSISTENT
$+ ✍

One characteristic that all great brands share is they are consistent in what they look and feel like, as well as what they do. Bayer aspirin has changed little

Business and Trade Association Checklist

❑ Does the association offer member discounts on products and services that I commonly purchase and use in my business? Examples would include reduced credit card merchant rates, courier fees, and office products and supplies.

❑ Are there advertising opportunities within the association's publications and Web site?

❑ Does the association host events that would be suitable for networking purposes?

❑ Does the association have resources that I can tap into that would be helpful? These resources would include a print and electronic library or industry-related information, rentals of meeting space and displays for trade shows and such, and experts on staff to answer questions.

❑ Does this association provide educational opportunities such as workshops, training classes, and seminar series?

❑ Does this association have a strong voice in regional and federal levels of government, and does this voice influence policy makers?

❑ Does this association have a strong voice within the industry and is it respected within the industry?

❑ Do the current members match my target audience and are there opportunities to market my products or services directly to association members?

❑ Does the association provide members with valuable and up-to-date industry research, news, and forming trends?

over the decades and still does the same thing today that it did 50 years ago: gets rid of headaches. Everything you do to promote and manage your brand needs to be consistent, including design, look, feel, tone, voice, benefit, and message. The reason brands must be consistent is they take a long time to build, maintain, and evolve, and this is what builds consumer awareness of the brand. In other words, it makes consumers think of your particular business, service, or product when they have a specific need to be filled that is relevant to what you do or sell. Even brand king Coca-Cola got caught in the consistency trap when they tried to change the recipe for the soft drink after more than 100 years of it being the same. Consumers revolted and Coke was forced to issue two recipes of their cola, New Coke and Classic Coke. The consistent Classic Coke that looked and tasted the same won out hands down over New Coke.

Tricks for Building a Great Brand through Consistency

- Develop and maintain a central marketing or selling message that is consistent throughout all your advertising, promotional, and marketing activities. Your central marketing message should also be your unique selling proposition, which is your main argument or reason people should buy your product or service rather than a competitor's product or service.

- Create a central image and use this image consistently throughout your business, advertising, and marketing activities. Your unified corporate image should include a memorable and easily identifiable logo, color scheme, font type, size, and style. Your unified corporate image should be used in all printed materials, in your logo, in your store or office, on signage, company uniforms, and in all advertising.

- Develop and maintain a consistent pricing model or system. Don't be known for low prices today and high prices tomorrow. Pick a pricing model and stick with it for the long run. In other words, brand your pricing philosophy, be it low, high, or in the middle.

- Clearly define your position in the marketplace. For instance, your community may have ten residential house-cleaning services, but perhaps yours is the only residential-cleaning service committed to consistently using environmentally friendly organic cleaning supplies instead of chemical-based cleaning supplies.

- Maintain consistent operating procedures for your business including store or office hours, customer service policies, employee policies, and all other aspects involved with the day-to-day operations of the business.

GREAT BRANDS TAKE TIME TO EVOLVE

$+ ✎

While a great brand might be developed and introduced overnight, it cannot become known as a great brand until it has been tested, proven, and accepted by consumers. This can take years, even decades to accomplish. Consequently, you must be committed to developing and maintaining a brand for the long term. This is the point where many entrepreneurs and marketers become unglued in terms of their commitment to their own research. Research takes extremely careful planning. You must first decide that you want to create a great brand, and then determine if there is even merit in the brand you are considering attempting to turn into a great brand. Think of it as building a 5,000-square-foot log house, but instead of using 24-inch diameter logs, you are using toothpicks. Now you see the point, faced with such a commitment of both time and financial resources, it becomes easy to lose sight of what you set out to accomplish. Therefore before you decide to take one element out of your business—be it a product, service, logo, competitive advantage, or whatever—be careful because it may be that specific thing is what you want to build a great brand out of or around. Be aware of the fact that brands take time and commitment to evolve into great and instantly identifiable brands.

OK, so you own and operate a small business and as important as taking the time to "evolve" a brand is, that doesn't change the fact that in all likelihood you need the benefits that branding can bring to your business today as well as down the road. You can speed up the process simply by getting your brand "out there" and consistently promoting it over and over. Repetitious exposure is one of the key ingredients for building a great brand image and awareness.

Tricks for Speeding Up the Brand Evolution Process

- Become a publicity hound by creating clever ways to develop news, stories, and ideas that revolve around your brand and using these ideas seek as much publicity and media coverage as you can. Once you have devised newsworthy stories, ideas, and events, contact media outlets by way of press releases, media advisories, and pitch letters to make your case for media coverage and exposure.

- You can also speed up the time it takes to establish your brand image and awareness by investing heavily in targeted advertising where it will benefit your business the most. Short-term financial pain for long-term beneficial brand gain. Yes, the additional expenditure on extra or increased exposure through paid advertising can be costly. However, if you take the time to clearly identify your target audience and create an advertising campaign that is aimed directly at them, you can greatly reduce wasted advertising efforts and dramatically improve advertising and branding results.

- Be your brand's biggest fan and network your way to brand success. Join business associations, get involved in your local community, pitch in and help out a worthwhile charity—all of these are great ways to speed up the branding process. Providing you are your brand's biggest cheerleader and not timid in terms of letting everyone you come into contact with know about your brand. In other words, network your way to brand success.

- Become known as an expert and speed up the branding process as a result of continual exposure to your target market. Write articles and stories about your area of expertise and tag your "brand" to the end of each feature, such as "This article was written by security expert John Doe, qwner of John's Alarms and Home Security." Getting published is one of the best ways to brand your expertise. You can write for newspapers, print and electronic newsletters, magazines, trade papers, Web sites and get featured on talk radio and television programs; all are ways to increase your brand's exposure to your target audience and speed up the brand evolution process.

- You can also speed up the branding process by ensuring that all employees and business alliances are reading from the same page in terms of the image (brand) that you want your business to project. There is strength in numbers, and by using and believing in a consistent and unified brand message everyone that your business team speaks to will be exposed to your brand in a consistent fashion.

GREAT BRANDS REQUIRE HANDS-ON MANAGEMENT

$+ ✎

Think of a great brand as a finely manicured lawn free of weeds and thatch; let the lawn go untended for just one season and you risk having to devote years of hard work to get the lawn back into its finely manicured state. Great brands are no different than the manicured lawn—they require constant hands-on management to ensure the brand continues to deliver the benefits that are associated with it to consumers. And more importantly, to continually be on consumers' lips, minds, and in their consciousness on a daily basis, or at least through visual identification. Though the largest fast-food chain in the world and known worldwide, McDonald's still continues to spend more money on advertising and promotional marketing activities yearly than the total annual GDP of many countries. Why? To remain a brand that is known, trusted, and utilized by consumers from around the world. You can never stop managing and maintaining the brand name that you build, period. Therefore, if your objective is to build a brand name, which is synonymous with your product, business, or what the brand does, then be prepared to manage that brand in the short and long term.

Tricks for Successfully Managing Your Brand

- Make your brand one of your highest business and marketing priorities and never lose sight of the fact that brands sell without having to be sold.
- Have a clear definition of what your brand is so there will be no "gray zone" in terms of the image and message you want to send or project. You can't successfully manage something that changes focus daily, weekly, monthly, or yearly.
- Be prepared to spend money to manage your brand through paid advertising and by maintaining your business image, including areas such as your store, office, signs, transportation, work force, operations, and packaging. Your brand is the total sum of the parts or ingredients that go into creating it. Therefore, all the parts must be managed and maintained in order for the brand to remain powerful and effective.
- Protect your brand through the use of trademarks, registration, and copyrights. An important aspect of brand management is brand ownership. You want to own your brand so no one else can profit from the work you have put into building and maintaining your brand, and, alternately, so no one can misuse your brand and do damage to the brand image.
- Make branding the cornerstone of all of your marking activities. If brand management becomes a regular business activity, then brand management becomes habitual and not secondary, or an afterthought.

GREAT BRANDS PROVIDE MORE ADVANTAGES

$+ ✎

Great brands provide more advantages than disadvantages, yet a great brand can have faults, and most do. But to be considered a great brand, it must have more advantages than disadvantages. What is in it for consumers? If there are no benefits to the product or service, it will never become a great brand, simply because there is no reason for people to buy it. This may seem elementary, but many companies have launched a product or service aiming to turn them into a great brand name only to discover that the benefits of what they offered were short term, easily matched, or exceeded by a competitor's brand. Some found the spin-off disadvantages of taking ownership and using the product or service eventually outweighed the benefits. Though initially cheap to buy (beneficial advantage), most people who purchased a Yugo car soon discovered that the cars were prone to mechanical breakdowns. And because Yugo had poor distribution channels in North America, parts were expensive and hard to come by, and service personnel to fix the cars were even harder to find. These factors eventually led the manufacturer to retreat from the North America, automotive retailing market, leaving behind junkyards full of prematurely broken-down Yugo cars. Over the longer term, the disadvantages of maintaining this particular car far outweighed the benefit of the low initial purchase price, ultimately killing the Yugo brand in North America. The moral of the story: For a product or service to be considered a great brand it must provide consumers more advantages than disadvantages.

Tricks You Can Use to Ensure Your Brand Provides More Advantages

- Make quality of product or delivery and execution of service the number-one priority. In other words, give consumers good value for their hard-earned purchasing dollars.
- One of the easiest ways to provide more advantages is to put your money where your marketing mouth is by backing up your claim of superior advantages with ironclad guarantees. Longer product warranties, superior workmanship warranties, and customer satisfaction guarantees are a good starting point.
- Know exactly what your customers want and need, then go out of your way to ensure that you not only meet these expectations, but you exceed them. Exceeding perceived value is one of the best ways to ensure your brand provides more advantages.
- Take steps to ensure that the word-of-mouth advertising your brand is receiving is positive and not negative. It is true that unhappy customers will tell ten times as many people about

their experience, than happy customers will. Knowing this fact enables you to take steps to ensure that all your customers are happy with the benefits your brand provides. Do this by staying in constant contact with customers—conduct follow-up satisfaction surveys, and call customers who have complained even after the resolution to ensure that they are 100 percent happy with the brand, the way the complaint was handled, and the way the problem was resolved.

- Strive to always be looking for ways to improve your brand and the advantages it provides while never straying far from the core brand beliefs or what makes it a great brand. Change is inevitable, but change must be managed properly. You can develop new ways to provide more advantages, but the changes must enhance or be compatible with your core brand.

GREAT BRANDS ARE NEVER FADS
$+ ✎

Another characteristic that great brands share is they are never fads; in fact, they resist and transcend fads. Good old Coke has been around for generations and bucked many fads in its industry to remain at the top and to be enjoyed by a broad demographic; 5 to 95 years old, all sorts of people buy and use the product. This is a very important aspect in terms of building and developing your own brand for the simple reason that new products and ideas often are nothing more than fads, which is fine if your objective is quick market saturation and vanishing with the loot. However, if you want to be around for the long haul, then your brand must not be a fad. For instance, the pet rock, as weird, wonderful, and highly successful as it was back in the '70s was not a brand; it was a fad that appealed to a limited audience for a limited amount of time.

Tricks You Can Use to Ensure Your Brand Will Have Timeless Appeal

- The first trick to ensuring timeless brand appeal is simply to build a brand around a product or service that will always be in demand or an improved version will always be in demand. We all require food, shelter, clothing, transportation, information and education, and security (be it financial, family, or safety). While many of these things will change over time in their appearance, makeup, style, delivery, and obviously cost, at the core they are things that will always be in demand, people from every walk of life will need them.

- The second trick to timeless brand appeal is to understand the difference between a fad and trends in the marketplace. You must know this if you want to ensure that your brand remains trendy but is not a flash-in-the-pan fad. The automobile is a good example of an item that can be branded yet still remain timeless while being trendy by adding new features and altering appearance and style. The amphibious car of the '60s is a good example of taking an item that had already been branded (car) but the change or altered state was merely a fad, something that is neat today but has limited appeal to the mass market for any kind of sustained marketability.

- Another way to ensure your brand enjoys timeless success is to appeal to a wide and varied demographic audience. As mentioned above, 5 or 95, Coke has mass appeal regardless of age.

GREAT BRANDS REINVENT THE WAY WE THINK $+ ⚒

What truly defines a great brand is the effect the brand has on the way consumers act or think; a great brand reinvents the way we think about a business, product, service, person, or even entire industries. Look what Subway did for the simple sandwich, Michael Jordan for the once grossly underrated sport of basketball, and Starbucks for the cup of Joe. All of these great brands have one thing in common: They reinvented the way people think about the product and, more importantly, how people act toward them. More sandwiches are sold now because of Subway, even if they are not always Subway sandwiches being purchased. The

NBA has skyrocketed in popularity, both in game attendance and in merchandise sales, because a single person made us stand back and look differently at the game, which in turn increases the popularity of basketball outside of the NBA. And Starbucks turned a $.50 cup of coffee into a $5 taste experience and entertainment activity that has created an entirely new gourmet coffee industry modeled on their success. Yet before, Subway, Michael Jordan, and Starbucks went to work on reinventing the way we think about these things, for the most part the average consumer thought of sandwiches, basketball, and coffee in generic terms.

Tricks for Reinventing the Way People Think About Your Brand

- The first trick to reinvent the way people think about your business, industry, or brand is through first impressions. Be professional to a fault, including how you present you business, your image, your products or services, and your staff. It has often been said that a first impression is a lasting impression. If you want to change or heighten the way people think about your brand, then go the extra mile to present a great first impression wherever and whenever people come into contact with your brand.

- Your approach to customer service and customer service policies is another way to reinvent the way people think about your brand, usually through changing their expectations. While customers may expect a tough time in terms of getting a complaint or problem solved, instead make it easy for this to happen, and in doing so, you will drastically change the way they think about your brand.

- Reverse the way you think about branding and look at it from the customer's perspective. What is the first thing you want people to think about your business? Build a list, and through the process of elimination and prioritization narrow your list down to a few key points. Make these key points the main thrust of your marketing and branding activities.

- Perhaps the best way to change the way people think about your brand is to operate your business at a level that is higher than industry standards. This is especially true where stereotypes may come into play.
- And finally, reinvent the way people think about your brand by offering that one thing they cannot get from anyone else, at least not within your geographical trading area. In other words, find a niche in the marketplace and cater to those people need that particular product or service. Doing so will enable you to build from one point with a stable customer base already in place, thus changing the way these people think about your particular brand.

SUBSCRIBE TO TRADE PUBLICATIONS
$$ ✎

Trade publications can provide a wealth of great business and marketing ideas and keep you informed about the latest trends, regulations, and news within your industry. Therefore, subscribing to trade publications is a great way to hone marketing skills and keep abreast of what competitors are doing and subsequently not doing. There are literally thousands of trade publications covering every industry imaginable. In addition to subscribing to publications within your own industry, it is wise to regularly read publications from other industries to search for unique promotional, sales, marketing, and advertising ideas you can put to work for your particular business, products, or services. In terms of marketing, being a trailblazer and the first to go into uncharted waters is not always the best policy. Usually following time-tested and proven marketing techniques is a much safer and better approach that will have the best chance of producing the desired results, especially for small businesses with a limited marketing budget. Look for success marketing stories in trade publications and use them as a template to create similar programs for your business and watch your sales and market share increase with each great new marketing idea you implement.

WEB RESOURCE

✍ www.tradepub.com: Online directory listing hundreds of trade publications indexed by industry.

CREATE A POWERFUL MISSION STATEMENT
$ ✎

What Is a Mission Statement?

A mission statement is a group of words strung together to form sentences and/or phrases that clearly state who you are, what you do, what you stand for, and why you do it. These words should not be taken lightly, as your mission statement should be an honest reflection of your core values and what you hold to be important. Remember your mission is your purpose at the time you create the statement.

Who Needs a Mission Statement?

Any people, businesses, or organizations that want to publicly or privately state their purposes for being or what they stand for need a mission statement. It also makes a heck of a handy tool for reminding us what our purpose is when we forget, get sidetracked, or suffer from a temporary loss of focus.

BUSINESSES

Businesses large and small should take the time to identify and create mission statements. Once again, it will state in a consistent manner who you are, what you do, what you stand for, and why you do it. Basically, why you are in business and for whom you are in business.

ORGANIZATIONS

Often organizations will create mission statements so they can state their purpose. For instance, The Red Cross mission statement reads, "Provide relief to victims of disaster and help people prevent, prepare, and respond to emergency." Without question a very clear statement of what they do and for whom they do it.

PERSONAL

Another form of mission statement is a personal mission statement that once again clearly states who you are, what you do, why you do it, and for whom you do it. Even if who you do it for is yourself. A sales professional or business professional might create a mission statement that reads something along the lines of, "My purpose in business is to provide my customers with unsurpassed value, quality, and service, and always conduct business in an ethical and fair manner." And a personal mission statement does not have to be limited to business or career; students, homemakers, seniors, kids, anyone who wants to create a mission statement that will help his or her define their purpose can do so. Think of it as a compass that can help guide you through the fog.

Who Is the Mission Statement For?

The audience that a mission statement is designed for and aimed at will vary depending on the objective that one sets and for whose benefit one created the mission statement. The mission statement can be meant for an internal audience, an external audience, a personal audience, or for a combination of these.

INTERNAL AUDIENCE

A mission statement can be created for an internal audience only, such as management and employees. Often the purpose of an internal mission statement is to motivate people within the organization by helping them understand the larger vision of the company, or what they can expect from the company should they live up to their end of the bargain—their end being hard work, honesty, loyalty, and creativity.

EXTERNAL AUDIENCE

A mission statement can be created for external audiences including any one or all of the following: customers, suppliers, investors, vendors, and business alliances. Of course, in terms of the external audience, usually the mission statement is created for the customer, because without them, your marketing efforts are totally useless and wasted.

PERSONAL AUDIENCE

You can create a mission statement that is specifically written for you and for no one else. The biggest benefit for having your own personal mission statement is that it can be used as a source of inspiration and motivation for when things are going well and not so well. Many top businesspeople create personal mission statements that they print on cards, laminate, and keep with them at all times so they can occasionally escape the moment and reflect on what they truly stand for.

MULTIPLE AUDIENCES

And, of course, a mission statement can be created to address all three audiences, either as one mission statement or as a larger one with various components that address each audience.

How Do You Create a Mission Statement?

There are no hard and fast rules in terms of creating a mission statement. Ask 100 experts how to write a mission statement and chances are you will get 100 answers. However, most agree that the following are key points to consider when developing a mission statement.

- As a general rule most mission statements are brief, two or three sentences long and less than 40 words. Keep your mission statement brief especially if you want people to read it and be able to remember it.
- A mission statement is not an advertisement, business plan, or promotional message activity, but it should be used as a component of these and other marketing activities.
- Don't rush when creating your mission statement, take your time and edit it accordingly.
- Look at other mission statements to get ideas about how they were crafted. Check to see if the company or organization is living up to its purpose. Never copy someone else's mission statement, but instead review many to get a feel for what the authors are trying to say and who they are trying to appeal to.
- The best mission statements are simple, real, and honest. Never create a mission statement that you do not believe in, people will be quick to spot the difference between what you say in your mission statement and what you actually do in hands-on, practical terms.

- Your mission statement should be flexible; don't be afraid to alter it to meet your customers' changing needs or your new purpose.
- Skip "puffery" such as how great you are and what a great job you do and instead stick with what your audience will receive as a result of your mission statement, the benefits to them through quality, value, and uncompromising service.

Here are the mission statements of a few well-known companies; to find more simply log on to Google or Yahoo! and type in "mission statement." The search will render thousands of matches.

AVIS RENT-A-CAR

"To ensure a stress-free rental experience by providing safe, dependable vehicles and special services designed to win customer loyalty."

BLOCKBUSTER VIDEO

"To help people transform ordinary nights into Blockbuster nights by being their complete source for movies and games."

THE CHICAGO BULLS

"The Chicago Bulls organization is a sports entertainment company dedicated to winning NBA championships, growing new basketball fans, and providing superior entertainment, value and service."

DELL COMPUTERS

"Dell's mission is to be the most successful Computer Company in the world at delivering the best customer experience in markets we serve. In doing so, Dell will meet customer expectations of, highest quality, leading technology, competitive pricing, individual and company accountability, best-in-class service and support, flexible customization capability, superior corporate citizenship, and financial stability."

YOUR COMPETITIVE ADVANTAGE SHOULD BE BENEFICIAL

$+ ✎

Your competitive advantage is what sets your business apart from your competitors. Think of it

as the reason people will buy your products or services instead of your competition's. Because of the importance your competitive advantage plays in positioning your business, products, or services in the marketplace, the competitive advantage you create should be used as the anchor for all your sales and marketing activities and should be thought of as your number-one marketing tool. Likewise, the message you develop around your competitive advantage should be consistently used in all marketing media. Your competitive advantage is what people will get out of buying your product or service, or even what they will get out of doing business with you. Customers subconsciously think of this as the "what's in it for me" factor. If there is no benefit, then why do business with you? Why not do business with the competition that provides something beneficial. The benefit you provide will be directly related to the service you provide or product you sell, but you have to identify what benefit your customers will receive. Will they save money? Make money? Feel better? Will your product or service solve a problem they have? To truly beat the competition, you must have or create an advantage that your competition does not have, and that advantage must benefit your customers.

YOUR COMPETITIVE ADVANTAGE SHOULD BE EXCLUSIVE

$+ ✎

A competitive advantage must be exclusive, not necessarily exclusive in the sense that no other business or person sells it or provides the service in the way you do. Creating a competitive advantage that is exclusive is a task that many small-business owners struggle with on a regular basis; they often associate "exclusive" products and services with large corporations that have unlimited access to manufacturers, advertising campaigns, and research and development budgets so they can make or buy their way into "exclusivity." However, creating a super-effective and beneficial competitive advantage that is exclusive to your business does not have to be difficult or costly to achieve. In fact, it could be something as simple as a residential cleaning service using organic cleaning products as opposed to chemical cleaning products, which is the industry standard. Thus, in this example (that would cost a mere few hundred dollars to implement) the advantage is the fact that the residential cleaning service is environmentally friendly, an exclusive competitive advantage that is guaranteed to appeal to a certain segment of environmentally conscious consumers. As this example illustrates, an exclusive competitive advantage does not have to reinvent your business, the way you do business, or the industry you operate in, it just has to be something that you do or sell that is different and not available from competitors in your area.

YOUR COMPETITIVE ADVANTAGE SHOULD BE SIMPLISTIC
$ ⚒

Your competitive advantage should be very easy to remember, simplistic in nature, and, more importantly, one that people can easily identify with your business. For example, a roofing installation company's competitive advantage might be that they "guarantee a leak-free roofing installation." Or a dry cleaner's competitive advantage might be "dress shirts cleaned in 30 minutes or they're free." In both examples these competitive advantages are extremely simplistic and easy to remember. Yet they are beneficial to the customer and while perhaps not exclusive entirely within their respective industries, definitely exclusive to each of their businesses, especially if their respective competitive advantages become the anchor of all their marketing activities. Many businesspeople create competitive advantages that are far too hard to remember, to explain, or for the average consumer to understand how they will directly benefit from buying. Basically if you cannot explain your competitive advantage in one sentence, or in less than ten seconds in such a way that people say "Yeah I get it, now let me buy it," then chances are your competitive advantage will never be truly beneficial to your business. It must be simplistic enough for people to remember it, identify your business with it, or understand how they will benefit from it.

THE SWOT ANALYSIS
$+ ⚒

SWOT—Strengths, Weaknesses, Opportunities, and Threats—is commonly used in business as a method of analyzing your ability to compete against other businesses that sell products or services similar to yours in the same marketplace and to the same target audience. Additionally, conducting a SWOT analysis can help you identify your position within the marketplace—how consumers view your business and products or services in direct relationship to your competition and their products or services. The true purpose of this book is to boil down business mumbo jumbo into easily digestible information bites that make sense and that can be readily applied by small-business owners and managers. So, I have taken the "scratch your head factor" out of trying to make heads or tails of a SWOT analysis and broken it down into five simple steps.

Step 1. Definition

The first step is to simply understand what strengths, weaknesses, opportunities, and threats are and how they relate to your particular business.

STRENGTHS

Strengths are resources your business has that can be used as an advantage in business, or a specialty that your business excels at that can be effectively used to reach your business and marketing objectives. For instance, a company strength might be that you have the most highly trained service technicians in your geographical trading area.

WEAKNESSES

Weakness is a critical factor that diminishes a company's competitiveness, a limitation that stands between you and your business and marketing objectives. An example of a weakness may be that your business lacks sufficient venture capital that could be used to stimulate growth.

OPPORTUNITIES

An opportunity is best characterized as a positive situation upon which you can capitalize. A true opportunity can potentially improve your company's position in the marketplace and profitability. For instance, the recent deregulation of automated teller machines in Canada created opportunities for entrepreneurs to own banking machines and offer cash withdrawal and deposit services to consumers for a fee.

THREATS

A threat is best characterized as a negative situation that can potentially damage your position in the marketplace and profitability. For instance, the ATM example above represents a threat to the Canadian banking industry that once held a monopoly on the ownership and operation of ATMs. This threat came in the form of deregulation of the industry by the government to open the industry to enable private ATM ownership. The banks no longer control a monopoly and now face stiff competition from the private business sector.

Step 2. Internal Analysis

The second step is to analyze the strengths and weaknesses within your business. This is best accomplished by using a blackboard, whiteboard, or large sheet of paper and later transferring the information to your computer to create and print the analysis.

INTERNAL STRENGTHS

Take a moment to consider what your company's strengths are and write these down. I always try to develop the list to include five strengths, but list only what I believe to be major strengths that are highly marketable. To develop your strengths list, ask yourself questions:

- What are your current competitive advantages in the marketplace?
- In what does your business specialize?
- What is the biggest benefit that people receive from buying your products or services?

The questions that you ask and your answers will be directly related to your business and what you sell. When you develop your questions and subsequently answer them, try to view the questions from your customer's perspective. Doing so may help you to identify a new strength, or

alternately reveal a weakness that you thought of as a strength.

INTERNAL WEAKNESSES

Next, take a moment to consider what internal weaknesses your business has. Remember, weaknesses can come in any and all forms—poorly trained or motivated employees, cash flow problems, lack of credibility, or narrow product selection are just a few. Once again, write these down and try to include at least five major weak points that may diminish your ability to effectively compete in the marketplace. The questions you develop should be relative to your business and what you do or sell. Questions should revolve around important topics and issues:

- What are the causes of the current complaints we receive?
- What could we be doing better?
- What are we currently doing that is hurting our business?

Step 3. External Analysis

The third step is to analyze the external opportunities and threats that face your business. Once again, use a blackboard, whiteboard, or large sheet of paper and later transfer the information to your computer to create and print the analysis.

EXTERNAL OPPORTUNITIES

Take a moment to consider what external opportunities may be currently available or coming available that could be capitalized upon for the benefit your business. Here are some examples of external opportunities:

- Changes in technologies that would enable you to increase productivity or market share.
- Changing trends in consumer buying habits that would favor your product or service.
- Changing demographics in your trading area that would favor your particular business.
- Forthcoming changes in government rules and regulations on a local, state, or federal level that would have a positive impact on your business.

External opportunities can come in almost any form; for instance, the closing of one of your main competitors is an opportunity. Dig deep and try to identify at least five current or forthcoming external opportunities that could potentially benefit your business and prioritize them from the greatest opportunity to the least beneficial opportunity.

EXTERNAL THREATS

Next, take a moment to consider what external threats your business might be facing currently or could face in the future and write them down. Here are some examples of external threats:

- Is there new or increased competition in the marketplace?
- Is your industry in the maturing or declining phase?
- Are there changes coming in government regulations or changing technologies that could have a negative impact on your business?

Step 4. Data Analysis

The fourth step is to carefully analyze and prioritize the data for each section. Start with strengths and list them from your greatest to your smallest. Repeat this for each of the internal and external categories. Often you will see patterns start to form, such as competitor strength built upon one of your internal weaknesses and so forth.

Step 5. SWOT Action Plan

Once you have analyzed and prioritized all of your data, you will be able to create an action plan covering the following.

MAXIMIZE STRENGTHS

Knowing what your greatest internal strengths are will allow you to build upon these and maximize their positive impact on your business. For instance, if your great strength is your highly trained work force, then this should become your main competitive advantage and the cornerstone or anchor message for all marketing activities.

MINIMIZE WEAKNESSES

Knowing what your internal weaknesses are forces you to resolve them or work out ways to minimize

their impact on your business. Often a SWOT analysis will work as an important "wake-up call to the facts" that no longer allows you to simply hope problems will go away.

CAPITALIZE ON OPPORTUNITIES

Identifying external opportunities enables you to properly plan for the future. It also allows you to take immediate action and capitalize on opportunities that can have a positive impact on your business almost instantly.

ELIMINATE THREATS

Now that you have identified external threats and how these can potentially affect your business and profitability, you can create a course of action that will reduce or entirely eliminate these threats. Or you may choose to simply find a way to avoid the threats if it is possible to do so without the potential to damage your business.

IF YOU CAN'T BEAT 'EM, JOIN 'EM
$ ⚒

Are you sick and tired of butting heads with your competition? Perhaps you don't have the deep pockets necessary to outlast the competition in a prolonged price war. If so, then maybe it's time to embrace the old saying, "If you can't beat 'em, join 'em." Send your competition a letter, give them a call, or set up an appointment to meet in person and let them know that you're available to handle their overflow work during their busy times of the year. This simple marketing tactic is especially useful for the business owners working from home on their own, as most often your operating and fixed overheads will be far less than your larger competitors. This, provides you with the ability to slightly discount products and services to secure business and still enable the competition that you are subcontracting for to add a markup and make a profit on the products or services you provide to their customers. Working for the competition is definitely not the best strategy to use for building a successful business over the long term. However, in the short term it can be a source of new business revenues and every business needs cash flow in order to survive. Consequently, depending on your current business situation, it might be well worth careful consideration as to whether you should be working for and with the competition.

EMBRACE CHANGE
$$ ✎

Never be afraid to embrace change; in fact seek out new ways of doing old things and be ready to create new opportunities or at least keep an open mind to new opportunities as they come along. As the old saying goes "in this world nothing can be said to be certain, except death and taxes." And this could not be more true—think back to how you use to live, how you operated your business, and what you felt was your priority 20 years ago. Chances are most things, if not everything in your life has changed. Nothing remains the same forever—business changes, customers change, the way we conduct business changes, products change, and the value of money changes. But what does not change is that smart entrepreneurs realize, understand, and embrace the fact that change is inevitable, and, therefore, they must stay open to new ideas and ways of doing things, especially things that can affect their business. Case in point, in the early 1990s I had the opportunity to secure the exclusive Canadian distribution rights to a manufacturer's flooring product that was catching on in Europe, but had yet to be tested in North America. I passed on this opportunity because I felt the product it was designed to replace was too well ingrained in our society and too popular to ever be replaced. Basically, I was trying to resist change because I was complacent in the way things were at that moment. The product that I declined to secure the Canadian distribution rights for was floating laminate flooring, which had been designed to be a less-expensive alternative for real hardwood flooring, but still retain the same good looks and practical durability. What do you think, was resisting change in this example a mistake? My wife sure does think so every time she visits the bank, especially when you consider that more floating laminate flooring products are now sold and installed

than any other type of replacement flooring products. The moral of the story: keep an open mind and learn to embrace change, it's all part of being a successful entrepreneur.

CAPITALIZE ON COMPETITORS' DISTRIBUTION CHANNELS
$$+ ✎ ☎

Is a 10 percent slice of the pie better then no pie at all? This is a question that some small-business owners must ask themselves, especially new start-ups and under-capitalized business ventures. Building a market or securing market share for a new product can be a difficult, time-consuming, and very expensive process. Often the lure of enormous potential profits (on paper) overshadows fact and reality, which often is that many small businesses that manufacture or distribute a limited product line are really only a single cog in a much larger machine. For that reason, carefully consider the true attributes of your product to identify if you might be better off blending your goods or single product in with a larger competitor and utilizing their proven marketing programs and established distribution channels to move your product to consumers. In terms of financial remuneration, you could devise a royalty or license agreement or work on a percentage of sales on goods sold; there are many options. In some situations, such as where a business is really only a product, it makes more sense to let competitors with well-defined market share and distribution channels take over your product. This way, you retain a royalty without the risk of ever-present financial disaster looming over you like a dark cloud ready to let lose at any moment.

COMMISSION A STUDY
$$+ ✎ ☎

Outsmart the competition by having a study or report commissioned with results that will reflect that your business, product, or service is superior to your competitors' business, product, or service. Ideally, you want the study to conclude that your product or service is superior in reducing something such as cholesterol, improving something such as a good night's sleep, outlasting something such as the life of a battery, and so forth. Basically, you want conclusive evidence that can back up a promotional or marketing claim that you feel will have the biggest and most positive impact on your business in terms of generating new leads and closing more sales. This claim could then become the backbone or anchor of all your marketing activities—your biggest competitive advantage much like Wal-Mart's "we sell for less." Government, large corporations, unions, and organizations of all sorts have beneficially used studies and reports to back up countless claims and statements. Obviously you want the study to be independent, but you also want the results to be favorable. Therefore, be creative in how and whom you choose to conduct the study. This could be by forming a consumer or business focus group, by way of a scientific laboratory, or through an existing organization be it large or small, known or unknown. Of course, the better the testing organization or group is that will be compiling information and conducting research to make conclusive results for the study, the greater impact and benefits it will have for your business.

PROFIT FROM COMPETITORS' CLOSE OUTS
$$+ ✎

Your competitors' loss may very well be your gain if you are prepared to profit by taking steps to secure their real business capital. Most business owners will pawn off their inventory, fixtures, and equipment for pennies on the dollar when closing out. Yet few think about selling off the most valuable stuff, business telephone numbers and customer lists. When competition in your area goes out of business try to buy their telephone number and have the phone number forwarded to your location. Buy their customer mailing list and mail out a notice to their past customers letting them know you are there to serve them better and for a long time to come. Swoop in and make a quick offer to nab the stuff that will generate revenues and profits instead of the stuff that doesn't, such as store fixtures, equipment, and out-dated inventory.

Additionally, look at any business close out in your area as a potential target to mine what's left of that business's value. The customer list of a bankrupt jewelry store would be a wise purchase for a retailer of luxury cars. The customer list of a lawn maintenance service would be of great value to a pest control company. The trick is to know who is going out of business, look for pieces of their operation that can be purchased for next to nothing, and mine it for all it is worth before the competition does.

SUBSCRIBE TO COMPETITORS' MAILINGS
$ ✎

Get to know your competition better by subscribing to any and all information offerings they make to their prospects and customers. This can include print and electronic newsletters, catalog mailings, free seminar series, and any other types of information your competitors provides to their clients and customers as a promotional tactic. Of course, if you or your business is well known to the competition, then make sure to ask an employee, family member, or friend to subscribe and have the information sent to their home address or computer via e-mail. Subscribing to your competitors' mailings is one of the best and least expensive ways to keep abreast of what your competition is up to in the marketplace. Additionally you will want to occasionally order a product or service and carefully analyze how they handle distribution, customer service, and other key operational aspects of their business. Doing so will help you better understand your competitors' strengths and weaknesses and how your business can effectively compete against their products and services. Remember knowledge is power, so let your competitors empower you with as much knowledge about their business as they are willing to give you, especially if they don't even realize they're doing it.

START A MARKETING IDEA FOLDER
$ ✎

How many times have you seen a commercial on television, read an article in the newspaper, or heard an advertisement on the radio that makes you say, "hey, now that's a great marketing idea"? Then "poof," a day later the great idea vanishes without a trace because you didn't write it down or cut it out and save it? If you are like most small business owners this scenario is a weekly occurrence, but it doesn't have to be. Instead profit from other people's great advertising and marketing ideas by creating a marketing idea folder or box. Every time you see, hear, or read a great marketing or advertising idea, write it down in detail or cut it out and put it in your folder or box. Set aside a few moments each week to mine your box for ideas that can benefit your business, or perhaps provide a helpful solution to a current marketing dilemma. Encourage staff and friends to collect great marketing ideas from various sources they come into contact with, too, and file them for future review and use in your marketing program and business.

HIRE A CLIPPING SERVICE
$$ 🐎

Keeping up to date on important industry news, trends in the marketplace, and your competition is a daunting task, not to mention extremely time consuming. If you're like most businesspeople, you know the benefits of staying informed, but you simply do not have the time available that is required to scour countless publications and Web sites to gather this information on a regular basis. And for that reason, hiring a news clipping service to do it for you is such a great idea. A news clipping service employs skilled researchers to monitor news publications, trade journals, and Web sites for topics and specific information as requested by its clients. Clipping services can provide this to you for a fraction of the cost that it would take you or an employee to get the same results, especially when you factor in search time and publication subscription costs. Clipping services work in volume and in all likelihood the information they send you will also be sent to additional clients seeking information on the same topic. Most clipping services will customize service packages based on clients' needs and budgets. This can range from how you receive information—mail, fax, or e-mail—to the geographic area or type of publications the information is gathered from.

WEB RESOURCE
🐎 www.google.com: To find a clipping service that might be right for your needs, go to the search engine Google or the directory Yahoo! and search for "Clipping Service Directory."

YELLOW PAGES RESEARCH
$+ 🔨

Smart entrepreneurs never overlook the good old Yellow Pages telephone directory as a fast, cheap, and very effective way to conduct market research in terms of the competition. In the Yellow Pages you will find a nearly unlimited amount of information about your competitors. Open to any page and carefully study your competition's advertisements and you will discover information about their businesses, products, and services, including things such as the following:

- What they do and sell, including their specialty or what they believe to be their competitive advantage and unique selling proposition.
- Their hours of operation, how many stores or office locations they have and where those stores or offices are located.
- Complete contact information, including mailing address; telephone, toll-free, and fax numbers; e-mail address, and Web site URLs.
- Product and workmanship warranty information and customer satisfaction guarantees.
- How long they have been in business and the main geographic area they service, as well as their main target audience.
- The payment options they accept, such as credit cards, checks, debit cards, financing and leasing plans, and in-house installment plans.
- Special discounts they provide, such as senior discounts, association discounts, and trade-in discounts.
- Special incentives to motivate people to call or to buy, such as free delivery, free installation or setup, free parking, free estimates, free consultations, and radio-dispatched personnel or service trucks.

- Special requirements and documentation in terms of insurance, licenses, and trained and certified personnel.
- Affiliations they may have with professional or business associations.

Get smart and put the Yellow Pages to work for you when you want to learn as much as you can about your competition.

LOOK BEYOND TRADITIONAL MARKETS
$$+ ✎

Never allow restrictive financial budgets and large competitors stop you from getting your product into the marketplace. Instead get creative and look beyond what might be viewed as traditional markets for your product and develop distribution channels through nontraditional sales venues. For instance, if you manufacture swimsuits but do not have the brand name recognition or financial resources needed to get your product into major retailing chains, then consider tanning salons, fitness clubs, and day spas as potential retail outlets for selling your swimsuits. Or, if you manufacture specialty sauces but can't afford the shelf or slot fees to get your products into supermarkets, then consider pubs, restaurants, cookware retailers, and gift shops as potential retail outlets. The objective is not to let restrictive budgets or larger competition dictate where and how your products will be sold. The objective is to create new selling opportunities by discovering or inventing new venues to sell through. Never let someone else dictate your dream and how you go about realizing that dream.

SEND IN THE MYSTERY SHOPPERS
$$ ✎ ☎

Spy on competitors and measure your own business's level of customer service by employing mystery shoppers to conduct random shopping excursions to your competitor's businesses and your own. Professional mystery shoppers will get the best results as they are specifically trained to identify customer service strengths and weaknesses in competitors' operations as well as in your own. You'll find

these professional mystery-shopping services generally charge in the range of $25 to $35 an hour, or some will contract for services in an all-inclusive package price basis. However, if your budget is too tight to afford these services, then you might want to consider enlisting a friend or family member to mystery shop for you. Just make sure to carefully develop a plan first to identify the exact information you would like to gather about your business and employees as well as your competitors' businesses, employees, products, or services. Major corporations routinely use mystery shoppers to spy on their competitors and their own businesses, and so should you; the information that can be revealed can be invaluable in terms of identifying competitor strengths and your own business weaknesses. Here are a few key points that mystery shoppers always look for.

Greeting

All mystery shoppers will tell you that one of the first things they look for is a warm and friendly greeting from staff when they enter a store. By not warmly greeting customers as they enter, you may as well be telling them that they are a bothersome interruption and to take their business elsewhere. A smile and a warm "welcome to our store" alone will prompt 50 percent of new customers to return at a later date without having to do anything else to win them over.

Attention to Detail

Is the store clean, are the aisles well laid out, is merchandise neatly displayed, and does the store have an overall pleasant shopping atmosphere? Attention to even the smallest details can mean the difference between business success and failure; so take the time to carefully analyze your store from a customer's point of view and not your own.

Sincerity

Does the staff take an honest and sincere interest in helping customers find what they need and in answering questions, no matter how trivial they may seem? Your staff has to be interested in the customer and not in the radio or a co-worker or the clock that is ticking ever closer to the end of their shifts. For mystery shoppers, this is an area of great concern—if your staff does not take a sincere interest in your customers, then don't be surprised when your customers no longer take a sincere interest in your business and shop elsewhere.

Appreciation

And finally, does staff thank your customers for coming to the store before they leave and welcome them to please come back soon even if they did not purchase? Well, if they are not, then most mystery shoppers will tell you that you are missing out on the potential for a lot of future business. Often it is the last words spoken to a customer that are remembered the most and the clearest. Therefore it only stands to reason that if they are asked to please come back again they in all likelihood they will.

WEB RESOURCES

- www.shoppercomments.com: Mystery shopping services.

- www.mysteryshop.org: Mystery Shopping Providers Association, a searchable database of companies and individuals that provide mystery-shopping services, indexed geographically.

BE MORE CONVENIENT THAN YOUR COMPETITION
$$ ⚒

Price, service, and quality are three important factors in determining why people will choose to deal with one business instead of another, but also in the mix is the equally important aspect of convenience. People want to do business with companies that make it easy for them. Analyze your competition to identify what special conveniences they provide their customers. Do they stay open longer hours? Do they offer more flexible payment options, such as credit cards, checks, and consumer financing plans? Do they provide free parking and free delivery and setup of products? If so, are these customer conveniences making their business busier and more successful than yours? If the answer is

yes, then chances are the conveniences your competition is providing their customers will definitely be a contributing factor in their success. In a nutshell, to compete for and secure customer loyalty in today's fast-paced and extremely competitive business environment you must be willing to do business when and how potential customers want to do business. Do not focus on what is convenient for you, but for them, your prospects and customers. This means your business must be accessible to keep your current customers loyal, and you must be prepared to put customer convenience ahead of what you might find as operational convenience in order to lure customers from the competition. The customer conveniences checklist on page 39 as well as the payment options checklist will help you identify which ways that you can make it more convenient for customers to do business with you and more convenient ways that they can pay for products and services they purchase.

WEB RESOURCES

- www.visa.com: Visa credit card financial services.

- www.mastercard.com: MasterCard credit card financial services.

- www.discovercard.com: Discover credit card financial services.

- www.amercianexpress.com: American Express credit card financial services.

- www.internet-e-checks.com: Software enables you to accept electronic checks by mail, fax, telephone, and e-mail.

GET THE LOWDOWN ON COMPETITORS FROM YOUR SUPPLIERS
$+ ⚒

It's not uncommon for competing businesses to purchase products and services from the same suppliers. In fact, about 50 percent of competing businesses share one or more common suppliers. For that reason, it only makes logical sense to quietly ask your suppliers' sales reps what your competitors are up to, how they're doing businesswise, and, more importantly, what they will be doing soon.

Customer Conveniences Checklist

❑ Free product delivery

❑ Free and paid product assembly and setup options

❑ Free and paid product installation options

❑ Free consultations and estimates

❑ A toll-free telephone number

❑ Sales of handy items such as stamps, transit passes, and calling cards

❑ 24-hour emergency telephone service line

❑ Provide shopping carts or baskets

❑ Provide a carry-out-to-the-car service

❑ Provide umbrellas for rainy days that can be returned later

❑ Product ordering by telephone, fax, e-mail, or Web site services

❑ Free inside courtesy telephone for local calls

❑ 100 percent handicap accessible and compatible store

❑ Offering free coffee in the winter and water in the summer

❑ Free while-you-wait gift-wrapping service regardless of the season

❑ Good parking and close to public transit

❑ Extended business hours, especially during holidays and sales in-store promotional events

❑ Accepting various payment options such as credit cards, debit cards, financing, and checks

❑ Providing a gift registry and management service

❑ Gift certificates and gift baskets available with free delivery

❑ Rain checks provided on out of stock items, along with a special discount

❑ No-hassle product return and refund policies

❑ Follow-up service on all large purchases

❑ Courtesy seating benches inside and outside the store

❑ Exterior bicycle rack

❑ Automatically fill out and submit all warranty cards for customers free of charge

❑ Offer an automatic product replenishment system so high-volume buyers do not run out

❑ Prompt service and knowledgeable staff

❑ Free and helpful information booklets and tip sheets about the products you sell

❑ Stock a wide selection of products that customers want and need

❑ Free seminars to inform customers about new products or how to use specific products

❑ Valet parking

❑ Coat-, bag-, hat-check service

Payment Options Checklist

❑ Visa credit card

❑ MasterCard credit card

❑ American Express credit card

❑ Discover credit card

❑ Diners Club credit card

❑ In-house credit card

❑ Business checks

❑ Personal checks

❑ Electronic checks

❑ Debit cards

❑ On-site ATM

❑ Money orders

❑ Foreign currency

❑ Gift certificates

❑ Travelers' checks

❑ In-house revolving credit account

❑ In-house creative 90-day same-as-cash financing

❑ In-house 30-day bill-me-later programs

❑ Consumer and business financing options in association with lending institutions

❑ Consumer and business leasing options in association with leasing companies

❑ Barter and exchange programs and points

Don't be shy about asking, because it's human nature for people to talk and share information; besides in all likelihood your competitors are getting information about your business in the exact same fashion. Of course, pumping suppliers and sales reps for information about your competitors requires tact and you must have a pretty good working relationship established with them first before you start prying for "confidential" information. Perhaps you can even be a little tricky about how you get answers about your competition by asking questions like, "So who orders the most of this particular product?" Or, "Am I the only business in the area that buys this product from you?" The responses to your questions will enable you to ask more questions and dig a little deeper with each one until you have the information that you want and need about competitors.

HAPPILY ACCEPT THE COMPETITIONS' COUPONS
$$+ ⚒

Mom-and-pop operations can battle back against large corporations that frequently distribute coupons by gladly accepting all competitors' coupons. Post a sign in the window and by the cash register letting your customers know that you will accept and honor a competitor's coupon for the same product. This simple marketing trick will not likely secure you new business, but it can go a long way to making sure your customers stay loyal to your business and continue to support it. There is a cost associated with accepting competitors' coupons, but this can easily be offset by retaining customers for the long term and by customers' purchasing impulse noncoupon products when redeeming competitors' coupons. Additionally, you may want to advertise that you will match or beat any competitor's price on the same products. As risky as this may sound, few people will actually go back and forth between two businesses and force a price war. What it does do, however, is make the customer feel comfortable with the knowledge that they are receiving the lowest price, regardless of if they really are.

IDENTIFYING DIRECT COMPETITION
$ ⚒

Direct competitors are businesses that sell the same or similar products, provide the same services, target the same demographic market, and operate in the same geographic area as your business. Direct competitors are your biggest competition because they want to sell to, and build customer loyalty with, the exact same people you want. Direct competitors want your customers and therefore your business. As obvious as this statement may seem, many business owners, sales professionals, and managers fail to properly identify their direct competition. Because it's a fact that there will be direct competition in the marketplace, why bother to identify who they are and what makes them successful or not? Because they want your business and the savvy operators have or soon will have a plan in place to make sure they get your business. But don't let them. Instead develop a competition plan that identifies all four types of your competition (direct, indirect, phantom, and future), how they operate, how they currently have an effect on your business, and, most importantly, what steps you can take to secure your customers and steal their customers. Implement the strategies you outline in the plan and keep the plan updated. Your plan will give you your best chance of staying one step ahead of competitors who are out to steal your investment and livelihood.

IDENTIFYING INDIRECT COMPETITION
$ ⚒

Indirect competition is becoming more and more of a concern for small business simply because in most cases, your indirect competition will be large corporations operating super-sized box stores carrying a wide range of products including ones similar to or the same as your core product line. For instance, an indirect competitor for a clothing retailer is Wal-Mart, as they both stock and sell clothing. Service providers fair somewhat better in terms of indirect competition because by nature most companies that provide services tend to specialize, such as plumbers. But once again, in larger centers, even service providers face indirect competition from superstores that also offer installation services on products they sell. Indirect competition can even come in the form of a fair or carnival that rolls into town once a year and draws paying customers away from other businesses within the community that compete for consumer entertainment and restaurant dollars. Identifying who your indirect competition is will enable you to create strategies and action plans to ensure that you can do battle and survive.

WATCH OUT FOR PHANTOM COMPETITION
$ ✎

Phantom competition can range from self-help books to consumers who choose simply not to buy for whatever reason, to unusual weather patterns, to media influences that sway or change consumer opinion. For instance, a story about tainted beef at a local food market can be phantom competition for the local steak house restaurant. Though these two businesses have little in common, the steak house can be affected if the media is running stories about tainted beef from the market making people ill. Customers might think twice about going out for a steak dinner. Cold, rainy weather in the summer months is phantom competition for the ice cream stand and boat rental dealer as we assume summer to be warm and dry, and when it is not, many summer activities are curtailed. Likewise, a self-help book about installing a patio deck might cost the local deck installer a job should a homeowner decide to buy the book and tackle the job of installing the deck without professional assistance. Phantom competition is the hardest to predict and control simply because you never know where, why, when, how, and who it may be and what effect this will have on your business and, subsequently, revenues and profits.

PREDICTING FUTURE COMPETITION
$ ✎

Future competitors are the businesses that will open in the future and compete in your marketplace. Or, they are the businesses that will expand their offerings to include products and services that you currently sell, and compete in your marketplace. Future competition is easier to predict then most think. All that is required is a commonsense approach to figuring out who or what form the future competition will come in. For instance, if you own and operate the busiest video rental store in town, then it is a safe bet that you will soon have new competition, or existing competition in the marketplace will expand their operation under current or new ownership. This is a safe assumption simply due to the fact that when people see a successful business and the opportunity to make money, then they copy that model with the anticipation of taking away customers from number one in the marketplace and making money in the process. Also if you operate a business in a geographic area that is undergoing a large population expansion, it is a safe assumption that new competitors will soon move in to help serve the increased population base of consumers. Or, if you're one of the first to open a "trend" business, such as video rentaes were a decade ago, then expect to see competition soon until the marketplace reaches saturation or critical mass and becomes stagnant or begins to decline. Gather as much economic and demographic information about the geographic area that you operate in. Collect as much information as you can about your industry and the products and services you sell. Analyze this information, and more often than not common trends will start to appear, enabling you to use this information to predict who, when, and how many future competitors you may have.

MAKE AN INCENTIVE YOUR COMPETITIVE ADVANTAGE
$$ ✎

Develop an exclusive incentive as a method to separate your product or service from the competitors' and as a way to motivate prospects to buy. However, before you do, remember that the incentive you offer must represent real value to prospects in order for it to effectively motivate them to buy and for it to be useful to you as a competitive advantage tool. Additionally, the incentive you create must fit in with your offering; for instance, a realtor who offered free certified home inspections with every property sold would be offering her customers a truly valuable and beneficial incentive to purchase a property using her service. This is because most homes sold today are on a conditional basis subject to a property inspection report, something that can cost a potential homebuyer hundreds of dollars but save thousands of dollars down the road if the inspection reveals major structural or mechanical problems with the property and buildings. Therefore, by including an inspection as an incentive, the realtor is providing a very valuable and beneficial service that would have cost money and been required regardless. Here are a few other points to keep in mind in terms of offering an incentive to customers as your competitive advantage.

The Incentive Must Represent Value

You should always attach a dollar value to the incentive so it will have bigger impact and represent true value. If you're offering a one-hour free consulation as an incentive, for example, then put a dollar figure on that hour to increase the perceived value, "Call me now for a free one-hour personal consultation, a $250 value absolutely free to the next ten people who call!"

There Must Be Minimum Requirements

Always try to place a minimum purchase requirement in order to qualify for the incentive or a "buy before date" to take advantage of the incentive. Online retailer Amazon has mastered this simple trick to increase the value of the average transaction, "Buy $39 worth of books and receive free shipping." The incentive is very valuable and directly related to their offer, which is books. But at the same time few books cost $39, most are generally in the $15 to $25 price range. Which means that in order to take advantage of the incentive (free shipping) people who might have purchased one book are now purchasing two or three books to qualify for the free shipping.

Only Quality Incentives Work

Your incentive must represent real value and be beneficial in order for it to work effectively. Cheap premiums or products of visibly poor quality will only hurt, not help. I learned this the hard way when I offered a free patio furniture set as an incentive to motivate prospects to buy custom-designed and constructed sun decks. But the furniture was flimsy plastic and was so cheesy that the people who went ahead and hired my firm to install a sun deck didn't want it. I couldn't even give the stuff away; sadly I was way off base, not much of an incentive to buy.

BUILD COALITIONS WITH COMPETITORS
$$+ ✎ 📞 ⚖

Strategic alliances, relationship marketing, or joint ventures, the business world is abuzz with such terminology as we enter into a truly global marketplace the likes of which we've never seen before, with fierce competition around every corner. Perhaps one of the best ways to grow your small business is by joining forces with competitors that operate outside of your geographic trading area to build strong business coalitions—a strength-in-numbers approach to business in the 21st century wherein companies that share similar goals and objectives can band together to share risks and the potential rewards. In doing so you may find that as a group you will be able to negotiate lower supply costs based on increased purchasing power. And as a larger coalition you may also find that you are able to bid on and secure goods and services supply contracts that would normally be too large for your business to handle alone but can be shared among the larger business coalition that you have established with your competitors. Additionally, by building and being involved in the coalition, you will be able, as a group, to mutually identify and overcome marketing and business challenges facing the industry through collective brainstorming and planning.

WEB RESOURCE

⚲ www.entrepreneur.com: Online business and marketing resource center for small-business owners and professionals.

WHEN TO BE REALISTIC
$ ✎

Often it is best to avoid the temptation of going after a large corporation's market share, no matter how appealing the revenue and profit picture may appear to be on paper. Much thought has to be given to what the corporation has and you do not. This will most likely include venture and working capital; pre-established and proven distribution channels; in-house legal, accounting, marketing, and sales professionals; and an extensive network of business alliances. Remember, as a small business you have advantages that larger corporations do not have and cannot create. First, you can implement marketing strategies to take advantage of new market trends and opportunities within a matter of days, not months or years like the big corporations. Second, you can usually provide customers with individualized service based on each one's specific needs; that is something a large corporation can only dream. Get big by finding your own niche and competitive advantage within the marketplace, and as revenues and profits start to increase and build, look at ways that you can take nibbles of the big guy's market based on tight geographic and demographic conditions. Then, over time and through continuous nibbling, quietly amass their market share while they are not looking, instead of diving in and trying to take it from the start.

MORE WAYS TO BEAT THE COMPETITION
$$+ ✎

Listed below are more great ways that you can employ to beat the competition hands down.

Performance

Beat the competition by making your product longer lasting and more dependable, or your service more reliable. Consumers are willing to pay more for a Porsche car because they want the performance the car is renowned worldwide to provide. People will pay a premium to ship packages with FedEx because they know it will arrive the next day, guaranteed.

Selection

Outdo the competition by offering customers a wider selection of products or more services than the competition provides. Home Depot thrives partly because they offer the do-it-yourself homeowner more product and service selections than any other hardware or building products retailer in the industry. Obviously not every small-business owner can offer more selection than the big-box retailers, but if you specialize and cater to a small niche market, you can.

Price

Beat the competition by offering lower prices, or alternately find ways to save customers money. Wal-Mart sells for less, one call to GEICO can save you money on your car insurance. Beating the competition on price does not always mean selling for less, you can increase the value of your products or services to justify a higher price.

Guarantees

Offer guarantees and warranties that are the best in the industry and leave your competition in the dust because of your incredible warranty program. Midas guarantees installed brake pads and mufflers for as long as you own your car.

Great Service

Go out of your way to provide incredible customer service to distinguish yourself from competitors. Domino's will deliver your pizza in 30 minutes or less, or it's free. Create your competitive advantage around a service aspect, and go the extra mile to deliver incredible service to all your customers.

Specialization

Do one thing better than your competition and make it your competitive advantage. Starbucks doesn't serve coffee, they serve a taste experience and command a premium for it. In fact, they have reinvented the way people drink and think about coffee.

THE ULTIMATE COMPETITION WORKSHEET
$+ ✎

Copy the following worksheet and use it to rate all your competitors, and of course your own business (honestly). Once you have completed this worksheet you can use this information to help you identify your own and your competitors' strengths and weaknesses. Use this information to improve your weaknesses or to build upon your strengths.

Complete only the items that are relevant to your specific business or industry. You may also discover a few items that you want to add to the worksheet.

Competition Worksheet

Competitor Company Name: _____

Years in Business: _____

Estimated Annual Sales: $ _____

Number of Employees: _____

Estimated Market Share: _____ percent

Market Share
- ❏ Increasing
- ❏ Decreasing

Industry
- ❏ New
- ❏ Growing
- ❏ Saturated
- ❏ Declining

Reputation	Poor	Fair	Good	Great
Company reputation	❏	❏	❏	❏
Product(s) reputation	❏	❏	❏	❏
Service(s) reputation	❏	❏	❏	❏
Customer service reputation	❏	❏	❏	❏
Pricing reputation	❏	❏	❏	❏

Product(s)	Poor	Fair	Good	Great
Benefits	❏	❏	❏	❏
Positioning	❏	❏	❏	❏
Quality	❏	❏	❏	❏
Value	❏	❏	❏	❏
Reliability	❏	❏	❏	❏
Performance	❏	❏	❏	❏
Ability to meet market trends	❏	❏	❏	❏
Ability to meet market needs	❏	❏	❏	❏
Availability	❏	❏	❏	❏
Packaging	❏	❏	❏	❏
Labeling	❏	❏	❏	❏
Private label/exclusive	❏	❏	❏	❏
Warranties	❏	❏	❏	❏

Competition Worksheet, continued

Service(s)	Poor	Fair	Good	Great
Benefits	❑	❑	❑	❑
Positioning	❑	❑	❑	❑
Quality	❑	❑	❑	❑
Value	❑	❑	❑	❑
Reliability	❑	❑	❑	❑
Performance	❑	❑	❑	❑
Ability to meet market trends	❑	❑	❑	❑
Ability to meet market needs	❑	❑	❑	❑
Availability	❑	❑	❑	❑
Exclusive/proprietary	❑	❑	❑	❑
Warranties	❑	❑	❑	❑
Workmanship warranties	❑	❑	❑	❑

Business Location	Poor	Fair	Good	Great
Interior cleanliness/repair	❑	❑	❑	❑
Exterior cleanliness/repair	❑	❑	❑	❑
Exterior signage	❑	❑	❑	❑
Interior signage	❑	❑	❑	❑
Interior lighting	❑	❑	❑	❑
Exterior lighting	❑	❑	❑	❑
Customer/staff security	❑	❑	❑	❑
In-store displays	❑	❑	❑	❑
Window displays	❑	❑	❑	❑
Parking	❑	❑	❑	❑
Transit accessibility	❑	❑	❑	❑
Pedestrian accessibility	❑	❑	❑	❑
Street visibility	❑	❑	❑	❑
Conveniences (washrooms, carts, etc.)	❑	❑	❑	❑
Business Hours	❑	❑	❑	❑
Store Fixtures	❑	❑	❑	❑
Atmosphere	❑	❑	❑	❑
Computerized	❑	❑	❑	❑
Payment options (credit or debit cards, etc.)	❑	❑	❑	❑

Marketing Activities	Poor	Fair	Good	Great
Advertising	❑	❑	❑	❑
Yellow pages	❑	❑	❑	❑
Radio	❑	❑	❑	❑
Television	❑	❑	❑	❑
Direct mail	❑	❑	❑	❑

Competition Worksheet, continued

Marketing Activities, continued	Poor	Fair	Good	Great
Trade shows	❑	❑	❑	❑
Seminars	❑	❑	❑	❑
Publicity	❑	❑	❑	❑
Contests	❑	❑	❑	❑
Newsletters	❑	❑	❑	❑
Networking	❑	❑	❑	❑
Seasonal events	❑	❑	❑	❑
Telemarketing	❑	❑	❑	❑
Event sponsorships	❑	❑	❑	❑
Cross marketing/promotional	❑	❑	❑	❑
Customer clubs/loyalty programs	❑	❑	❑	❑

Operations	Poor	Fair	Good	Great
Customer policies	❑	❑	❑	❑
Reliable	❑	❑	❑	❑
Consistent message	❑	❑	❑	❑
Leadership	❑	❑	❑	❑
Proactive thinking/planning	❑	❑	❑	❑
Customer service	❑	❑	❑	❑
Communications	❑	❑	❑	❑
Technologically advanced	❑	❑	❑	❑
Community involvement	❑	❑	❑	❑
Charity involvement	❑	❑	❑	❑
Corporate citizenship	❑	❑	❑	❑
Business associations	❑	❑	❑	❑
Better business report	❑	❑	❑	❑
Vendor(s) support	❑	❑	❑	❑
Manufacturing capabilities	❑	❑	❑	❑
Research/development	❑	❑	❑	❑
Distribution channels	❑	❑	❑	❑
Equipment	❑	❑	❑	❑
Transportation	❑	❑	❑	❑

Employees	Poor	Fair	Good	Great
Loyal	❑	❑	❑	❑
Training	❑	❑	❑	❑
Remuneration	❑	❑	❑	❑
Benefits	❑	❑	❑	❑
Work conditions	❑	❑	❑	❑

Competition Worksheet, *continued*

Employees, continued	Poor	Fair	Good	Great
Education	❑	❑	❑	❑
Specialized	❑	❑	❑	❑
Subcontractors	❑	❑	❑	❑
Professional appearance	❑	❑	❑	❑
Energized/motivated	❑	❑	❑	❑

Financial	Poor	Fair	Good	Great
Overall financial stability	❑	❑	❑	❑
Accept credit cards	❑	❑	❑	❑
Accept paper/e-checks	❑	❑	❑	❑
Offer financing options	❑	❑	❑	❑
Pay suppliers on time	❑	❑	❑	❑
Pay employees on time	❑	❑	❑	❑
Pay fixed costs on time	❑	❑	❑	❑

Web Site	Poor	Fair	Good	Great
Regularly updated	❑	❑	❑	❑
Relevant content	❑	❑	❑	❑
Efficient shopping model	❑	❑	❑	❑
Customer service support	❑	❑	❑	❑
Visitor interactive (community)	❑	❑	❑	❑
Fast/efficient	❑	❑	❑	❑
Relevant to audience	❑	❑	❑	❑
Links	❑	❑	❑	❑
Navigation	❑	❑	❑	❑
Useful user tools	❑	❑	❑	❑
Keyword search	❑	❑	❑	❑
Opt-in/e-zine/e-newsletter	❑	❑	❑	❑
Online advertising	❑	❑	❑	❑

Follow-Up Questions

What do you think this company's biggest competitive advantage is and why?

_____

_____

What do you think this company's greatest strength is and why?

_____

_____

Competition Worksheet, continued

What do you think this company's greatest weakness is and why?

_____

_____

What opportunities do you see in terms of competing against this company or in terms of filling a niche that they do not, or for piggy-backing on their positioning? Why?

_____

_____

What is the greatest threat that this company poses to your business and why?

_____

_____

What is the greatest threat that your business poses on this company and why?

_____

_____

What is your greatest advantage in terms of competing against this company?

_____

_____

What does this company do well that you should also be doing?

_____

_____

Now that you know this company better, what products or services can you provide to their customers to lure them onto your team? What marketing activities can you implement to reach this company's core target audience?

_____

_____

📖 SUGGESTED ADDITIONAL READING

Abraham, Jay. *Getting Everything You Can out of All You've Got: 21 Ways You Can Out-Think, Out-Perform and Out-Earn the Competition.* New York: St. Martin's Press, 2000.

Andersen, Alan, and William A. Smith. *Marketing Research That Won't Break the Bank: A Practical Guide to Getting the Information You Need.* New York: Jossey-Bass, 2002.

Bangs, David H. *The Marketing Planning Guide: Creating a Plan to Successfully Market Your Business, Products and Services.* Chicago: Dearborn Trade Publishing, 2002.

Collins, Jim. *Good to Great: Why Some Companies Make the Leap . . . And Others Don't.* New York: HarperCollins, 2000.

Jensen, Bill. *Simplicity: The New Competitive Advantage in a World of More, Better, Faster.* Cambridge, MA: Perseus Publishing, 2001.

Krueger, Richard A., and Mary Anne Casey. *Focus Groups.* Thousand Oaks, CA: SAGE Publications, 2000.

MacKay, Harvey. *Swim with the Sharks without Being Eaten Alive: Out Sell, Out Manage, Out Motivate and Out Negotiate Your Competition.* New York: Random House, 1996.

Porter, Michael E. *Competitive Strategy: Techniques for Analyzing Industries and Competitors.* New York: Free Press, 1998.

Ries, Al, and Laura Ries. *The 22 Immutable Laws of Branding.* New York: HarperCollins Publishing, 2002.

Sclein, Alan M., J. J. Newby, and Peter Weber. *Find It Online: The Complete Guide to Online Research.* Tempe, AZ: Facts On Demand Press, 2002.

Stucker, Cathy. *Mystery Shopper's Manual.* Sugar Land, TX: Special Interests Publishing, 2002.

Travis, Daryl, Richard Branson. *Emotional Branding: How Successful Brands Gain the Irrational Edge.* Roseville, CA: Prima Publishing, 2000.

Trout, Jack, Al Ries. *Positioning: The Battle for Your Mind.* New York: McGraw-Hill, 2000.

Trout, Jack. *Differentiate or Die: Survival in Our Era of Killer Competition.* New York: John Wiley & Sons, 2000.

Underhill, Paco. *Why We Buy: The Science of Shopping.* New York: Simon & Schuster. 1999.

KEY

COST TO IMPLEMENT	$
DO-IT-YOURSELF	
CALL IN THE PROFESSIONALS	
LEGAL ISSUES	
BOOK RESOURCES	
ONLINE	

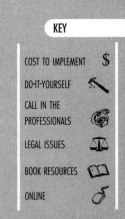

EMPLOYEE
Marketing Tips for Your Business

If we hire people worse than ourselves we become a company of dwarves. If we hire people better than ourselves, we become a company of giants.

—David Ogilvy

WHAT EMPLOYEES NEED
$

Every employee needs certain things to be productive in the workplace. If these needs are not met, then it can have a very negative effect on that employee's ability to carry out his or her duties in a productive manner, and therefore negatively affect any marketing abilities. The following are the basic things every employee needs.

To Feel Challenged

All employees at every level from the warehouse to the boardroom need to feel challenged; without it work is boring, repetitive, and workers will soon become lax, unmotivated, and uninvolved. People want and need to win, solve problems, find solutions, and be tested and challenged on a regular basis. Nothing motivates people quite like meeting a challenge head on and beating it hands down, especially when an audience of peers has witnessed the victory.

To Contribute

All employees want to know that their suggestions, ideas, and input are valuable and that through their work they are making a positive contribution to the team and to the success of the business. At the end of the day an employee must be able to stand back and tell someone, "Hey, I did that."

To Have Freedom

All employees need a certain degree of freedom within their jobs to express themselves. Freedom to be creative, to be productive, to implement and test their own ideas and theories, and to make mistakes and learn from those mistakes.

To Be Part of a Community

All employees need to feel as though they are part of your business community—that within the work environment they can forge new friendships and mentoring relationships, that the competitive spirit is alive and well defined within the workplace. Most important, all employees from the stockroom to the boardroom must have the ability to earn the mutual respect of the others.

To Develop Themselves

All employees need and want to be able to better themselves both personally and professionally. Smart business owners and managers realize this and put tools in place that workers can utilize to achieve personal and professional development success. These tools include specialized training, career promotion potential, learning new and valuable professional and social skills, and of course financial rewards based on individual performance and exceeding expectations.

THE BENEFITS OF TEAM BUILDING
$+ ⚒

It has often been said that teamwork and productivity go hand in hand, one cannot exist without the other. And in terms of marketing success and profitability, this is a true and sound premise; it takes a team composed of individuals that are committed to the common goals and objectives of the business to make it work. Therefore, wise business owners and managers have long known that investing in and maintaining team-building training and activities is indeed a wise investment to make, one that will repay the investment many times over. But one also has to keep in mind that it takes a commitment of time, money, effort, and energy to build and maintain a strong team. You cannot start today, expect results tomorrow, and give up when these results do not materialize. Alternately, once you have assembled your business dream team, you still must continually strive to maintain it and make it better. However, with that said, the benefits of team-building training and activities can be terrific, as the following will illustrate.

Support

Through team-building activities, employees and managers learn to support and understand each other's roles, responsibilities, and priorities within the business. Because of this in-depth understanding

and knowledge they acquire, when problems do arise, as undoubtedly they will, each member of the team will have the ability and knowledge needed to pitch in and help resolve challenges. Think of it this way: If the defensemen know what role the goalie plays in the game and what is expected of this role, then it becomes very easy for them to help the goalie when an opponent attempts to score.

Common Objectives

Problems and challenges faced by an individual team member are more easily overcome using the collective expertise of the entire team as opposed to that of one individual person. And the objectives of the entire team become the focus as each individual member understands and can identify with their own personal contributions—contributions that will get the entire team one step closer to its objectives.

Collective Effort

By the very nature of team-building activities, the lines of communications remain open, thus encouraging collective brainstorming in terms of creative thinking, problem solving, and seeking ways to meet challenges and exceed expectations. It is the old saying that two heads are better than one.

Increased Productivity

Because no one member of the team wants to let down the other members, everyone will place a high priority on productive work habits that conform with or stay in cadence with the rest of the team members. The true benefit of this is that the top producer will set the yardstick and every team member's abilities will improve as they strive to reach the benchmark set.

WEB RESOURCE
⚓ www.teambuilding.com: Teambuilding Adventures, corporate and team-building programs.

INSTALL AN EMPLOYEE MARKETING IDEA BOX
$ ⚒

Start tapping employees for potentially great marketing ideas by installing a marketing idea box in a common area of your business such as the lunch room or reception area. Encourage all staff, regardless of title or duty, to submit at least one new marketing idea per week, in fact insist they do and check up to make sure that are filling the box as requested. The ideas they submit could be original and unique to your particular business, product, or service. Or they could be sales and marketing ideas they have seen, read, or heard elsewhere that are linked to competitors, or noncompetitors' businesses. Set aside time each week to review and consider the ideas that are submitted. To motivate employees to work hard and think creatively about the marketing ideas they submit, offer incentives such as money, time-off, or a gift of appreciation to employees who suggest marketing ideas that are tested or implemented in your marketing program. Additionally, don't be afraid to ask employees to submit ideas and thoughts about what they think may be good or bad about your current marketing strategies and activities. Never penalize them if you happen not to agree with their expressed opinions.

THE MAGICAL MONEY INCENTIVE
$$ ✎

Assuming that you take all the necessary steps to ensure that employees know how to profitably sell your product or service, the next logical step is to give them incentives based on performance as a motivation to sell more. No one can dispute the fact that every business could dramatically increase sales and revenues if every member of the team were highly effective marketers. Therefore, instead of just paying employees a salary that trades time for a wage, develop an incentive plan that includes money as a reward for delivering results. Money has always been one of the best incentives to increase employee effectiveness and productivity. Offering a financial incentive can be accomplished in many ways, but for showroom or field salespeople it should be a commission based on results or a combination of a base salary and commission based on productivity results. For nonselling employees (if there is such a thing) consider giving cash rewards for marketing ideas, generating referrals, or for providing great customer service. The

objective is to create an overall peak marketing environment that includes all employees and from which all employees can benefit financially by delivering individual and team results.

WEB RESOURCE

✆ www.ctm-incentives.com: A full-service company specializing in the design, implementation, and operation of motivation and performance improvement programs.

MOTIVATE BY RECOGNITION
$$ ✎

Marketing and business leaders such as McDonald's and Wal-Mart have long used recognition incentives to motivate and reward employees who go above and beyond the call of duty. An "employee of the month" plaque or photograph by the entrance, or an employee of the year who wins an all-inclusive trip to a tropical destination. There are many ways to recognize employees for performing great work and exceeding expectations. The key to success is to develop a recognition system that all employees want to be part of—something they want to win and makes them feel important because they have won. Perhaps the best way to find out what type of recognition incentive would work best for your business is simply to ask employees what they would like, collect these ideas, and put it to a democratic vote. Additionally a handwritten note from you placed inside weekly pay envelopes thanking employees who have done an excellent job is a great way to recognize their performances and make them feel as though they're part of the team and contributing to the success of the business. This might seem like a small thing, but I guarantee that they will proudly show off the thank-you note to co-workers, family, and friends, simply because we all need to feel as though we are positive contributors.

WEB RESOURCE

✆ www.serviceawards.com: Online retention solutions to help recognize, reward, and retain employees.

MOTIVATE BY PILING ON THE RESPONSIBILITIES
$ 🔨

The key to the kingdom has often been described as one of the best methods of turning a mediocre employee into a highly productive team leader who can motivate others to also be more productive. Who would have thought that a simple one-dollar key that opens the front door would be such an effective motivational tool? But it is. Everyone wants to feel important; it's human nature. Handing out responsibilities to employees is a great way to motivate them to do more and a better job. In a sense, when you delegate responsibilities that typically fall outside of an employee's normal duties, you are telling that person that you trust him and that he is a valued member of your business team. Beyond responsibilities, promotions and titles—even without additional financial remuneration—also work well as incentives to motivate employees to do a better job. The theory is that with a promotion or a title comes the feelings of self-worth and self-confidence; this theory works extremely well in practical terms. Put people in charge of other people, give them challenging tasks, or make them personally responsible and accountable for something within the business and watch their on-the-job productivity soar.

WEB RESOURCES

✍ www.motivationusa.com: Employee motivation products, programs, and awards.

WITH AGE COMES EXPERIENCE
$ 🔨

The demographic trend in North America is toward an aging population base, so not only will you as a business owner or manager have to carefully consider hiring older workers, in some cases you might have no choice as the competition heats up for the limited supply of younger workers in or soon to be entering the workforce. However, don't despair—with age often comes wisdom and experience. Tapping into this "gray power" can benefit a business immensely in terms of hands-on sales and marketing know-how, which can be especially beneficial to small and new businesses. Never underestimate an older person's value to your organization when it comes time to hire new employees to fill key positions. Not only are older people generally more loyal, less concerned with wages, and more reliable, but you can also tap into their knowledge and experience of sales and marketing for new ideas to help your business grow. Not to mention many of these people who have 30, 40, and even 50 years of experience also have extensive customer and business contact lists that can be tapped and turned into money in the cash register.

CHANGE CAN ONLY TRICKLE DOWN
$ 🔨

As a business owner or manager you face a constant challenge—to make your employees more productive in their jobs and, therefore, increase the productivity of the entire business to capture more revenues and profits. However, many of these same business owners and managers fail to understand that change can only start at the top and be implemented at the top. You can't expect employees to take the initiative to be more productive in sales, marketing, customer service, or whatever their duties may entail unless you are prepared to do the same. A "lead by example" method as opposed to a "do what I say and not as I do" method. Saying you want increased productivity or performance is not good enough. You have to be able to clearly demonstrate to employees how this can be achieved, and often by your own actions, especially in small-business operations with few employees. Change can only trickle down, never up. If you want change, then you must take the initiative and make it happen, because blaming employees who are only following your lead simply makes no sense and will accomplish nothing but creating more headaches.

BUILD A MARKETING LIBRARY FOR EMPLOYEES
$+ 🔨

Give employees access to tools and information that will enable them to become expert marketers, which, in turn, will help to increase revenues and profits for your business. One of the best ways to do this is to create an educational marketing library that includes books, software, journals, and audiocassettes covering a wide range of marketing disciplines and topics, such as sales, customer service, creative promotions, and innovative thinking. Set a monthly budget for purchasing these materials and encourage all staff regardless of job duty to participate by reading or listening to the materials. In fact, make it mandatory that they take this material home and study it on their own time. Let all employees know that it is for the benefit of the business and their careers to become marketing superstars and create an incentive system based on increased individual performance to reward their efforts. Building an employee marketing library is a very low-cost, highly effective way to train and continually upgrade employees' marketing skills. However, if your budget is tight, don't despair; just turn to your local library as a source to secure these marketing information products. Select a topic each month, such as sales in February, customer service in March, and stock up, return the titles the following month and select a new topic—very simple and cost effective.

Web Resources

- www.amazon.com: Amazon, online bookseller.
- www.bn.com: Barnes & Noble, online bookseller.
- www.smallbizbooks.com: Online retailer of business and marketing books, guides, and software.

GIVE THEM ALL BUSINESS CARDS
$$ ✎

Give all employees business cards, regardless of their job positions or the duties they perform within the organization. We all want to feel important; it's human nature. And we all want to feel as though we are contributing in a positive way as a productive member of the team that is collectively reaching for and meeting set objectives and goals. Therefore, giving employees their own business cards is a great way to reinforce this basic human need and illustrate to them how important they are to the overall success of the business. Don't be shy in creating titles to be displayed on the cards either. A shipping employee could become the warehouse supervisor and a secretary could become the office manager or executive assistant and salespeople could become product or service consultants. The bigger- and better-sounding the titles printed on the cards are, the more likely those employees will be to distribute their business cards outside of the working environment to generate referrals. With that said, also make sure to demonstrate to employees how they can use their business cards effectively for networking purposes and give rewards to all employees who bring in new business.

BRAINSTORMING ROUNDTABLES
$

You never know from where the next great marketing idea may come. That is why getting all staff together for monthly brainstorming roundtables is such a good idea. All employees should participate regardless of job duty because often a fresh perspective will reveal new ideas or a fresh approach to an old marketing idea or activity that you are currently using. Often the most productive brainstorming roundtables are the ones that take place away from the store or office and away from daily business distractions and interruptions. Hold the roundtable in a park before work if weather permits, or at a restaurant after work. Also make sure to prepare an agenda prior to the meeting with a number of points that you would like to discuss listed. But don't be rigid with the agenda, allow employees to talk freely about marketing ideas they have. In fact, encourage all employees to bring at least three new marketing ideas to each roundtable. And be sure to hear them out because every idea is one more than you currently have and once again you never know from where the next great marketing idea that could potentially increase revenues and profits may come. Here are a few more basic ideas to incorporate into your brainstorming sessions.

Brainstorming Tips

- Appoint a moderator, be it you or an employee, to ensure you stay on topic and stay within the time you have allowed for the meeting.

- Have a basic outline for the ideas that you would like to cover, but keep the meeting open and encourage all ideas.
- Select one person (preferably someone with good penmanship) to record the ideas and the key points that are discussed as a result of each idea.
- Avoid the formality of hand raising or taking turns to talk; instead encourage people to let loose so great ideas do not get lost waiting for a turn.

"MANAGE" TO MINIMIZE WASTED TIME
$+ ✎

What is the best use of your time right now? This is a question that many business managers and owners must ask themselves, because invariably the answer will be to increase business revenues and profits. Therefore any wasted time directly reduces the amount of time you have to concentrate on marketing activities aimed at increasing revenues and profits. Here are a few tricks you can use to minimize wasted time in the workplace, allowing you to focus more time on marketing and growing your business.

- Computerize your business and introduce new technologies to make your business more efficient; ensure that all staff is computer literate and knows how to use the system.
- Avoid taking unimportant telephone calls and attending unimportant meetings. Also, make it a policy to never meet with anyone who does not have a prearranged appointment unless it is a customer who has a complaint or a suggestion about how they can spend more money at your business—then drop everything to meet with them at once.
- Set policies and work procedures for all employees to learn and follow. This will go a long way to reduce duplication of work, eliminate questions about what they are supposed to be doing, and provide a clear picture of each employee's duties and responsibilities. Through repetition, people get better and faster at doing tasks, and this can increase productivity enormously.

Openly communicate with employees and clearly state directions, instructions, and expectations.

- Get in the habit of using a daily, weekly, and monthly planner to plan your business activities as a way to prioritize and save time. Make sure that you work from one schedule or planner and not multiple planners.
- Match employees' skills and talents to the job you want accomplished. When time is tight, training employees to do new tasks is wasted time.
- Create an agenda before all meetings and adhere to it, but build 10 percent into the agenda for free time to allow for impulse ideas and creativity as they arise.
- Set priorities and deadlines for all projects and make sure that staff are aware of these and have confirmed they can meet them. Hold them personally accountable if they do not.
- Master the art of delegating small jobs, tasks, and routine work to others. And finally learn to say no, no matter how hard this may seem to be.

BRING IN PROFESSIONAL TRAINERS
$$+ ☎

Whenever you are in doubt don't risk or bet the farm, instead bring in the professionals. Every small-business owner or manager can't be an expert in every area or discipline of business, it's impossible. So rather than jeopardize one aspect of the business by passing on your weaknesses to employees, take steps to identify those weaknesses and bring in professionals to conduct the training for you so you do not pass your weaknesses on to employees. If sales are your weakness bring in a sales trainer; if it's customer service, then bring in a customer service trainer. Or, if computers and technology are your weakness, then bring in a computer consultant to computerize your business and bring you and your staff up to speed on how to operate and benefit from the system. Each segment of your business can only be as good as you are at it. Yes, there is always room for improvement, but you have to identify the weak spots, and then call in the professionals to rectify the problem. Remember it's the sum of the parts that create the whole, and each part must be sound in order to create a solid foundation for the structure to built upon. Have just one defective part and the entire structure can come crumbling down like a cheap house of cards.

WEB RESOURCE

✍ www.trainingregistry.com: National online directory listing professional business, management, and employee training consultants and training courses and products indexed geographically and by topic.

CREATE AN EMPLOYEE MARKETING HANDBOOK
$$ ✎

Promote consistency by creating a marketing handbook for your business that every employee can use and refer to for answers about what is expected in terms of customer service, sales, and marketing. Stress the fact that without paying customers, there is no business, thus the importance for every employee to understand the role marketing plays in your business—it's their job. Also outline the history of your business in the marketing handbook, including information about where the business has come from and where it is heading in the near and long-term future. Give employees as much knowledge about your marketing plan and ideas as possible. By doing so they will know what is expected from them and how they can help add to the overall success of the business by becoming better individual marketers within the team and in line with your marketing goals and objectives. Update the marketing handbook annually when you draft and update your marketing and action plans. Include relevant data such as sales and marketing goals that have been met and goals that were not met in the previous years. Employees who know and understand your overall approach to marketing will become more productive and more consistent in terms of meeting your marketing expectations and objectives.

ASK FOR CUSTOMER REFERENCES
$ ✎

There is a great deal of truth to the old adage that a business is only as good as its employees. Poor customer service will alienate customers, and salespeople who prefer to talk when they should be listening can drive business to the competition faster than a speeding bullet. Unfortunately, discovering that you have hired the wrong person for the right job generally comes after the damage to your business has been caused. There is a way that you can fight back and help ensure that you hire the right people for the job, or at least get as close as possible the first time around. Instead of solely relying on a resume and character references, go directly to the source and ask job candidates to furnish customer references. That's right, people they have sold to and serviced accounts for in their past employment positions. No one is better qualified to give you the honest lowdown on a person's commitment to customer service and selling than the actual customer has had dealings with the applicant. However, don't ask up front; instead ask for customer references during the interview. Those employment candidates who truly provide great customer service and deal in an open and honest fashion with all clients will have no problem furnishing a few customer reference names on the spot. Those who cannot might be suspect and best sent packing so they can pull the wool over some other manager's eyes, just as long as it is not yours.

MASTER THE ART OF DELEGATION
$ ✎

Business owner or business manager, a key component for reaching your marketing goals will be to learn to master the art of delegation. This applies to internal staff as well as external suppliers, vendors, alliances, and contractors. It is impossible to clone yourself and far too many small-business owners and managers feel as though they must wear many hats and complete many tasks in order for anything to ever get completed. First, understand that the world's leading and most productive and creative businesspeople learned mostly through trial and error that the best way to clone themselves was to train others to work and think as they do and then delegate work, tasks, and responsibilities to those people. Second, these same top businesspeople learned that you must let go of trying to control everything that happens, and put faith and trust in other people's abilities to do the job. But there are a few golden rules for delegating tasks and responsibilities; they are training, supplying, and supporting. Never delegate a task to anyone who has not received the proper training for the task, or clear and concise instructions. If you do, you are only setting up that person for failure and yourself for disappointment, ultimately leading to wasted time and money by having to duplicate and repair efforts. Supply the tools needed to get the job done right the first time, on time and on budget. And if you do not have these tools, then let whomever you are delegating to know where these tools can be found, and make sure they know how to use them. Asking an employee to dig a hole only works if you give his a shovel. And finally, support efforts of the person you have asked to do something; never undermine his capabilities with negative criticism and praise him when he has successfully completed the task assigned.

LEARN FROM CO-WORKERS
$ ✎

Let your best-performing employees train new employees—in fact insist they do—and offer a little incentive or bonus to get them motivated about conducting new-employee training sessions. Many business owners and managers make the mistake of training new employees when this job is often best left to other employees who have mastered specific responsibilities within the business. New employees often feel intimidated when they are being trained by either the owner of the business or senior management and concentrate on trying to impress the trainer instead of learning the finer details of the position that they have been hired to fill. And in some cases it gets worse because new employees are so worried

about doing something wrong that they become totally gripped by panic and fear and their performance suffers dramatically because of this constant feeling that they are on the verge of making a colossal error. However, when new people are trained by other employees who are on their level and who they will be working with daily, they have a tendency to be more relaxed and open to the training process and experience. Besides if you have employees who are top performers, why wouldn't you want them to train others to become top performing clones of themselves? Obviously you would want them to train new employees and pass on their productive work habits. In doing so, they free up more of your time so you can concentrate on finding or creating new ways to grow your business, revenues, and profits.

GET UNIFORMED
$$+ ✎

Visually separate your employees from your customers by ensuring that you get the team into uniforms that are appropriate for your business and target audience. Employee uniforms can dramatically raise the perceived professionalism of your business and even increase revenues and profits as a result of this increased professionalism. Top retailers, restauranteurs, and corporations have long understood the benefits of having employees decked out in sharp, matching uniforms emblazoned with the business name and corporate logo, and so should you. Uniforms needn't be expensive; you can start with smart, casual golf-type shirts silk-screened or embroidered with the business name, which can be purchased for as little as $20 each. Often you'll find employees very receptive to the idea of matching uniforms and even willing to pay for them out of their own pockets because it means not having to purchase more expensive clothing for work and not having to waste time trying to decide what to wear to work. Additionally, you will find that customers like employee uniforms because it identifies the employee making it easier to get assistance.

⚒ www.uniforms.com: National online directory listing manufacturers and distributors of workplace and professional uniforms, indexed geographically.

MAKE SOME NOISE
$ ⚒

Installing a noisemaker in the office such as a brass bell, trumpet, or siren can go a long way to building team spirit for all staff, as well as a friendly competitive selling environment among sales staff. Once you have installed the noisemaker, insist that all employees ring it every time they make a sale, save a sale, provide great customer service, receive a referral, collect a testimonial, or just about any other business-building occasion that warrants special recognition. Not only is this a great way to recognize their individual accomplishments, but it is also a great wake-up call for other salespeople to get hustling and sell more, and for all employees in general to get motivated and improve their own on-the-job performance. I installed a brass bell on the wall in our office and found it to be a great motivator. In fact, the salespeople got in the habit of purposely waiting until the end of the day or the following morning when they knew everyone would be present in the office before they would ring the bell so they could get some extra mileage and let everyone know they made a sale.

MANAGE BY OBJECTIVES
$ ⚒

A common trait that great managers have is that they have learned to manage employees by the objectives they wish to reach. What this means is that all employees must know what is expected from them, what the result of their work or contributions should be, and what objectives the company seeks from them. These objectives must be clearly stated, clearly defined, and mutually understood to maximize productivity and positive results. The overall "objectives plan" with each employee should include individual goal setting, creating and implementing action plans and time tables for reaching these objectives, regular review of the plan and progress to date, and evaluation and feedback upon each completed segment of the plan. Boiled down, everything in life has an objective. You run a marathon to reach the end; your objective then is to finish the marathon. Managing employees is no different; you hire a person for a specific task and expect that person to meet or exceed your expectations in terms of reaching the objectives you set. Therefore, you must understand that you are managing by objectives and when you do, you will increase productivity and efficiency because of this understanding.

LET YOUR CUSTOMERS EDUCATE YOUR EMPLOYEES
$$ ⚒

Sending out a shipment of blue widgets instead of red widgets, or missing a shipping deadline by ten minutes may not seem like the end of the world to your employees, but what about to your customers? Chances are an error on your end will have a much greater impact on your customers than your employees and this is definitely a situation that you want to turn on its ear. One of the best ways to do this is to get employees working as a team. To help them truly understand the impact their actions have on your customers, ask your customers to attend employee meetings and explain their business to all of your employees in greater detail. By doing so, your employees will have a better understanding of how your clients' businesses work and how something as seemingly harmless as one missed item on an order can cause a chain reaction of devastating events for your customers, resulting in them losing revenues, profits, and perhaps even a customers. These types of interactive miniworkshops between your customers and employees can go a long way to boost employee morale, motivation, customer service, and productivity—all of which of course will help to build a solid business foundation that is capable of supporting future growth.

IDENTIFYING SALES PERSONNEL
$ ✎

Identify the type of salesperson you need to fill the objective before you choose a candidate for the job. There are three main types of sales personnel and knowing the personality type of the applicant is important for creating a good match with the duties that need to be filled.

Handlers

Order handlers are sales personnel who come in direct contact with customers but do nothing more than receive payment for goods and services or a voucher for goods and services. An example of the order handler is the person who collects ticket stubs at the movie theater. These people must be pleasant, knowledgeable about your business, and thick-skinned as they are often the front-line people who will be faced with the most customer questions and complaints.

Takers

Order takers, on the other hand, serve similar roles as order handlers with one major difference: these sales personnel are in the position to make suggestions to the customer that can result in higher sales averages. Therefore they must have an intimate knowledge of all the products and services you sell in order to have the ability to make these suggestions. Suggestions that ultimately benefit the customer and represent value to your customers.

Makers

Order makers are the salespeople who are supplied with leads or generate their own sales leads and hit the street or telephone with one purpose in mind: find new prospects and sell your goods and services to them often. By the very nature of the job, order makers must be outgoing, motivated, and have personal goals.

A FAMILY AFFAIR
$$ ✎

You can increase employee productivity and reduce on-the-job stress by helping all employees better balance their home lives with their work lives. It is a proven fact that employees who are having a difficult time trying to balance both are far less productive than employees who have learned to balance both the family and work aspects of their lives. Therefore, go out of your way to create or assist with small things that can make a big and beneficial difference in your employees' lives. Give employees the ability to create flexible work schedules, either in terms of setting their own hours or by working with other employees to create work schedules so they can meet outside family commitments. Look for ways some employees might telecommute even if it is only one day a week. Offer prescreened daycare and babysitting referral lists; if you can and the demand is great enough, have a daycare center at the office or at least an after-school daycare service available so employees will concentrate on their work and not on the welfare of their kids. Pets now also play a major role in people's family lives, so if health regulations allow, space permits, and the majority rules in favor, you might even let employees bring dogs to work.

GREAT LEADERSHIP TIPS THAT EVERY BUSINESS OWNER AND MANAGER NEEDS TO KNOW
$+ ✎

Successful businesses are comprised of three main fundamentals: customers, employees, and the leadership of the organization. Remove any one and the business cannot function and, therefore, cannot be successful. Throughout this book I share tips and ideas about how to secure paying and repeat customers, as well as tips and ideas on the subject of motivating employees to be more creative and productive. However, the following are tips that business owners and managers can make use of to become more effective leaders.

People Are Your Most Valuable Resource

People are the only resource that a business has that can and should, with proper training and supervision, appreciate in value; everything else will eventually depreciate and require capital expenditures to repair or replace. You can utilize the latest and best technology, have an incredibly high-profile location, use only the best equipment for the job, but all of this will be for nothing if you do not have dedicated employees who care about the business in the same manner as you. Therefore it stands to reason that you should treat all employees as the valuable business resource and assets they are now, will continue to be, or will eventually become.

Personally Accountable

Demand that all employees be personally accountable for their own decisions and actions and how these decisions and actions affect the business, customers, projects, other employees, and their own performance. Insist on commitments in terms of when projects will be completed, how they will be completed, and what can be expected of the finished product.

Develop Mutual Expectations

Clearly state to each employee what is expected of him or her and, in turn, what they can expect to receive in return for meeting these expectations or, subsequently, not meeting expectations. Mismatched management-to-employee expectations are one of the main reasons for repetition, interruption, and low productivity in the workplace.

Be Likable

Be a likable boss and employees will go out of their way to do the best job they can for you. It is human nature for people to want to go that extra mile to help a friend or someone they like, especially a boss they look up to, respect, and consider a great mentor. The more likable you are, the harder your employees will work to impress you. Also take a personal interest in the people who work for you and with you. Chances are you will be spending as much time with these people as you do your own family,

therefore get to know them and what makes them tick.

Keep Emotions in Check

Always avoid showing anger or criticizing employees in front of other employees or worse, customers. Instead opt to hold closed-door meetings to resolve problems and find solutions. Scared employees are the least productive because they spend all of their time worrying about being yelled at, instead of focusing on their jobs. Besides it is bad for team spirit and moral.

Take Concerns Seriously

Take every employee concern or complaint seriously, regardless of how small or trivial it may seem to you. Chances are what you may find trivial won't be thought of in the same way by the person who raised it, or they would not have brought it to your attention in the first place.

Lead by Example

Lead by example, be what you want your employees to be, do what you want your employees to do, say what you want your employees to say, and act as you want your employees to act. "Do as I say, not as I do" is dead. Instead make sure that you set a positive example that all employees will want to follow. Be a positive role model and never forget that employees look to the boss and all levels of management for clues about how they are suppose to behave in the workplace, interact with other employees, and more importantly, how they are supposed to treat customers.

Never Settle for Second Best

Never settle for hiring anyone you feel would be less than ideal for the position you want to fill. You have to match a person's special skills, experiences, interests, and motivation with the needs of your business. An employee can grow within an organization and eventually reach new levels that qualify him or her for advanced positions, but a new employee brought in with hopes for growth into the advanced position seldom, if ever, works out.

Hard Decisions

Never think things will get better over time in terms of problem employees or low producers, because they never do. Problems cannot fix themselves, they require intervention from a person who can make decisions, identify challenges, and find solutions—in other words a leader. Meet these challenges head on and take the required action immediately. Also be direct and to the point when asking people what you want them to do, how you want it done, and when you want it completed. You have to design the map and set the parameters before any meaningful or beneficial discussion in terms of the project or task can take place.

Create an Orientation Program

Develop and implement an orientation training program for new employees so they will learn who all of the other team members are, where things are located, and who to ask for assistance as the need arises. This will help to eliminate duplication of tasks and needless interruptions at the last moment.

Keep Employees in the Loop

When you are considering a change in the way things are done within the organization, make sure to discuss this with the people that the changes will impact. You must get employees involved in the process if you want them to truly understand the reasons for it and the beneficial results that can be achieved because of it. Also consider setting aside time to work with each staff member to develop or update the standard operating procedures for his or her position. In doing so, you will eliminate duplication of tasks between departments and repetitious questions from employees seeking clarification. Additionally, these types of exercises often lead to discovering new and more efficient ways to carry out tasks.

Provide the Best Training

Employees are only as good as the training they receive to accomplish specific tasks. Never expect peak performance unless you have or are willing to have that employee trained to handle a specific task

or project. Feeling let down by an employee you thought could handle the job even though she or he was not qualified to do so is simply irresponsible management. Additionally strive to provide adequate training and task instruction the first time around. Having to redo, re-explain, or repair things done incorrectly costs money, wastes time, and can become the basis of resentment from both an employee and management perspective.

One-on-One Meetings

Meet with all staff members on a one-on-one basis at least every four months to address any concerns they may have in terms of the workplace, other employees, their performance, or their jobs before the concerns become problems. This will also help you better understand each individual employee's motivation and drive in the workplace, and how he or she interacts with the rest of your business team. Likewise, end important employee meetings by writing down a follow-up date in your calendar. When the date arrives, make sure to follow up with the employee. Not only does this demonstrate to the employee that you take an interest in their well-being, but also that you care about every issue, whether positive or negative.

LEARN TO CHALLENGE EMPLOYEES TO DO BETTER

$+ ✎

The main focus of learning to challenge employees to do a better job is to first avoid constantly telling them what to do, when to do it, and how to do it. Instead give employees the leeway required to let them think their way through a problem or challenge and create solutions for themselves. Handholding does not create great employees; it only works to make mediocre business owners and managers great babysitters. Additionally, when employees ask for help, try to lead them though a solution-finding process rather than outright fixing the problem for them. Ask questions that will challenge them to find solutions through research or through trial and error. Likewise, echo back their questions with your own "What if you tried this" questions. This will force employees to think about solutions on their own and cut down on the number of times they seek assistance. The goal is to create ways that challenge employees to think independently and learn how to do things for themselves. Reward and recognize those who meet and exceed expectations through independent creativity and productivity.

SIMPLE TIPS THAT CAN INCREASE EMPLOYEE PRODUCTIVITY
$+ ⚒

Increased employee productivity is one of the fastest and least-expensive ways to grow a business and make it profitable. And with that said, the following are a few simple tips that can be used to increase employee productivity.

- People want to feel important and that they are involved with and part of the total business process. Therefore give them an important job, task, or project to complete on their own or with other employees. Raising self-confidence levels in all employees will go a long way to building loyal and highly productive employees who are goal oriented.

- Start each workday with a quick five-minute employee pep rally. Let them all know what a great job they are doing and how each one is helping the business to reach objectives and goals.

- Develop a remuneration system that enables employees to earn what they are truly worth and not what you think they are worth. Many employees will surprise you by their level of personal ambition, especially if the reward comes in the form of money.

- A few weeks before an employee leaves on a vacation or for a extended period of time away from the office or workplace, make sure to mutually identify and develop a list of things to do before leaving and a list of things to do immediately upon return. This will ensure maximum productivity and minimum before-and-after vacation excitement distraction.

- Avoid a centralized employee memo or bulletin system and instead send memos only to specific employees you want the message to reach. Centralized memo systems or stations tend to get congested with employees making repeated trips back to read the latest memos even if they are not directly involved or affected by the memo. This, in turn, wastes an incredible amount of time, resulting in lost productivity.

- Give employees all the tools necessary to ensure they succeed. Anything less than a 100 percent effort on your behalf, and you will be setting employees up to fail and dramatically decreasing their on-the-job productivity.

- Reveal to employees exactly why they are doing something; they will work harder to achieve the desired result if they can recognize and feel good about their role in the satisfactory completion of the product.

- Write key business and marketing ideas down on paper and circulate this paper throughout the office to get valuable employee feedback and thoughts. Not only can this assist in the planning and decision-making process, but you'll also make employees feel as though their input and thoughts are important and valued by the organization.

- Clearly explain, and if need be demonstrate, how staff will benefit from doing their jobs well. When people understand how they will personally benefit from their work, they are more motivated to do a good job the first time, and exceed expectations so the personal benefits to them become even greater.

- Schedule development and goal-setting meeting with all employees on a semiannual basis. The meetings should be conducted on a one-on-one basis and be focused on how to help each individual employee reach his or her true potential through mutually identified performance enhancement techniques that can be practiced and implemented; as well as setting attainable personal goals that can be reviewed at the next scheduled development meeting.

- Never offer employees help or assistance unless they ask for it. Premature intervention only displays your lack of trust in an employee's ability to perform appointed tasks. Instead let them know that you are there to help, all they have to do is ask. This will enable employees the opportunity to solve problems independently and seek out help only when they are truly stumped.
- Encourage all employees to develop their own personal action plan and agree on how it should be implemented and what the key objectives and goals to be reached should be. Likewise set review dates to assess performance and alter the action plan as required.
- Never set up employees for failure just to make a point, especially in front of other employees. One of the best ways to increase employee productivity is to team low producers with top producers, not to sit back and tell yourself "I knew it" when the employee fails at the task you assigned.
- And finally, strive to get 95 percent performance out of each employee and forget about the last five because trying to squeeze out the last five will take twice as long as it took to get the first 95 percent, making the exercise counterproductive.

LEARN TO SAY THANK YOU
$+ ⚒

Get in the habit of sending thank-you notes to employees to recognize a job well done. Feeling appreciated is one of the most basic human needs, and knowing that we are appreciated is one of the greatest catalysts for craving more by working harder to earn the appreciation of others. Here are a few more ways to say thank you for a job well done and, in doing so, motivate employees to want to work even harder.

- Motivate employees to reach new levels of personal achievement in their jobs through the use of encouraging feedback and words of positive encouragement.
- Share the credit you receive from customers or senior management with all the employees who

helped make it happen. In fact, take a backseat and push employees into the limelight and lead the rest in applause.
- Always be polite and treat others the way in which you like to be treated. Don't tell, ask and remember to say please and thank you. No one likes to be taken for granted and feel as though he or she is not appreciated, or worse, feel as though someone is taking advantage of him or her.
- Create a database listing birthdays, wedding anniversaries, and other special occasions for all employees. Even a simple birthday card and a few words of congratulations can go a long way to making an employee feel special, important, and like a valued member of the business team.

EMBRACE AN OPEN-DOOR POLICY
$+ ⚒

The most successful small-business owners and managers are the ones who have embraced an open-door policy in terms of how they interact with employees. Empower all employees, regardless of job title or duty, to speak their opinions and forward ideas and suggestions in terms of the business, marketing, operations, other employees, and management without fear of ridicule from management or other employees. You may have a marketing star in your midst and never know it because employees are afraid to speak up or out of turn for fear of being ignored or, worse, reprimanded for it. Likewise, develop an ironclad one-day response policy wherein you guarantee to respond to all employee inquiries, problems, or suggestions within one day of being asked. Nothing motivates employees more to do a better job than knowing that what they have to say is important and not falling on deaf ears. And don't be afraid to ask employees what you can do and what they think you should be doing differently. Over time, even the most productive and proactive people managers can become complacent in their jobs and lose the edge that made them great leaders. However, this can easily be fixed and often it is the front-line employees you manage daily who can pinpoint the necessary changes for you.

ENCOURAGE EMPLOYEES TO BE CREATIVE

$+

Encourage employees to come up with new ideas and create new ways of doing things, and recognize and reward them for a job well done when they do. Even if the suggestions and ideas do not pan out, make sure you still encourage them to keep trying. If you do not, they may simply stop trying to be creative and productive in their jobs because they are not receiving the support and encouragement they need and require as a catalyst for motivation. Therefore get employees personally invested in projects by involving them in the creative and planning processes right from the beginning. Not only will this motivate them to do a better job, but it will also make them understand what the desired result is and how it will be achieved. This will give them a road map that will eliminate the need for too many unnecessary questions as the project progresses. Also try to limit the amount of control you exercise over employees. Understand that everyone needs space to make right and wrong decisions, as this becomes the basis for improving one's own performance and measuring one's own success and effectiveness. The more time you spend trying to control others, the less time you'll have to encourage others to achieve more by being creative thinkers.

ENLIST STUDENT TRAINERS

$$

Training employees how to use and get the most out of the latest computer hardware and software technologies can be very expensive, especially when you consider that computer training consultants are now charging an average of $100 a hour. This kind of fees, regardless of value received, leaves many small-business owners with restrictive training budgets out in the cold and unable to take full advantage of being up to speed using and working with cutting-edge computer technologies. However, as a way to get employees trained in understanding and using the latest computer technologies, consider hiring students from local technology and business schools to come in and train your staff. In some cases these schools already have student trainer programs in place and all that is required is a quick call to the administration office to inquire. If not, post help-wanted ads in the school newspapers and on school bulletin boards listing the details of exactly what type of trainer you are seeking. Hiring student trainers has numerous benefits. First, you'll save a substantial amount of money, as student wages even for computer trainers are a fraction of what professional training and computer consultants charge. Second, you will be helping out local students by providing much-needed employment opportunities and income. And ultimately, by harnessing the full power of current technologies, you may be able to increase revenues and profits for your business.

INCREASE PRODUCTIVITY BY REDUCING INTERRUPTIONS

$+

One of the best ways to increase productivity at the office or store is to reduce the amount of interruptions to the daily routine. Even the most basic interruptions can reduce productivity in the workplace for all employees. Featured below are a few ideas of how you can increase productivity by reducing interruptions.

- Insist that all employees and managers be on time for work shifts and meetings. People who arrive late gain the attention of those around them, thus reducing the effectiveness and productivity of the entire team, not just the latecomer.
- Ask employees and managers to take careful notes at meetings so they do not have to ask unnecessary questions later and reduce productivity.
- Don't allow your own train of thought to be interrupted while you are working on tasks and projects. Instead take a brief moment to write down your thought or idea and come back to it afterward, once you have completed your project in the works.
- Ask employees to write down questions prior to a staff meeting. Let them know that at the beginning of the meeting there will be a

scheduled question-and-answer period, thus eliminating interruptions with questions during the meeting.

- Let employees know that your open-door policy is an invitation for real and important issues that benefit the business and not just a quick, irrelevant chat session. If this still does not work, try keeping your door closed and post a schedule of availability times on the outside of it.
- Expect employees and managers to give you 100 percent of their undivided attention during meetings and give them the same in return. Once again this will reduce redundant questions and duplicating explanations at later dates.
- Get in the habit of carrying a "questions page" and list questions that you have to ask employees and managers as you think of them. Do this throughout the day and make your question-asking rounds at the end of the day so you can save time and not interrupt employees as they work.
- Distribute meeting agendas and ask all managers and employees to come prepared. At the end of the meeting, recap all ideas, information, and discussions to limit the number of questions later.
- Give all employees and managers the tools they need to do their work efficiently so they do not need to waste time borrowing from others. As an example, having one central three-hole punch for everyone to use may seem like a frugal, good idea. Take a moment to calculate the true cost in terms of wasted time for each time an employee has to get up and take time away from what he is doing just to find the paper punch and punch a piece of paper. By the end of the year, a $5 three-hole punch could end up saving you thousands in interrupted productivity.

GREAT QUESTIONS FOR EMPLOYEE INTERVIEWS

$ ⚒

The following is a list of great interview questions you can ask potential employees to ensure that

you will be hiring the best candidate for the position you want to fill. Not all the questions will be applicable to every situation, therefore, use this list to create your own customized list of questions to ask potential employees during a specific interview. The questions are broken into two categories: Section A includes general interview questions and Section B includes more sales-specific interview questions.

Section A: General Employee Interview Questions

- How did you hear about this job opening, and why did you apply for this position?
- Briefly summarize your employment history and education.
- Tell me about yourself.
- What are your short-term and long-term career goals?
- What motivates you to want to work harder? And what holds you back from wanting to work harder?
- Why are you leaving your current/past position?
- Do you prefer working alone or as a member of a team?
- How would you define success, and is success important to you?
- How well do you work under pressure? Please give a brief example.
- What are your greatest strength and weakness?
- In terms of your career or employment history, what has been your greatest accomplishment to date—what are you the most proud of?
- How would you describe the company you are working for or used to work for?
- What do you or did you like best about your current/past job?
- What supervisory experience have you had? Please elaborate.
- What do you do to motivate others?
- What specific aspects of your work experience have prepared you for this position and why?
- Which of your work skills do you feel needs improvement and why?
- What is the most important thing you look for in a career and in a company?

- What do you like and dislike about your current job?
- What specialized training have you received that qualifies you for this position and when did you complete it?
- How do you feel about customer service?
- What do you think is the most important aspect of customer service?
- How would you handle an irate customer, either in person or on the telephone? Do you have an example you can share?
- Do you think that it is the employee's or the company's responsibility to provide great service?
- Please give me one example of great customer service that you have personally provided without being asked to do so?
- How would you describe yourself as a person, and what is your strongest personality trait?
- What things give you the greatest job satisfaction?
- What do you find the most frustrating in your current/past position and how do/did you cope with it?
- Do you prefer to work under close supervision or independently? Why?
- Do you hold yourself personally accountable for the decisions you make at work, or do you think the company is accountable for your decisions?
- What was your most difficult work-related decision to make in the past year and why?
- What is your definition of success at work?
- What examples do you think you set that other employees would want to follow and why?
- Do you feel comfortable leading a team or do you prefer to follow?
- Do you work more efficiently alone or in a group/team atmosphere?
- What is your experience with public speaking? What was the topic, why did you speak, when was it, and how many people were in attendance?
- How would you rank your telephone skills— fair, good, or excellent? Why?
- Have you ever created a report for your current/past company? What was the topic? Were your recommendations implemented?
- What is the most creative marketing idea you have suggested to your current/past employer? Was it implemented, and if so, what were the results?
- Do/did you feel pressure/stress in your current/past job? If so, what is/was the source of the pressure? How do you deal with it?

Section B: Sales-Specific Employee Interview Questions

- What do you like/dislike about sales or selling in general?
- What do you like/dislike about the products/ services you are currently selling?
- Do you generate/prospect for your sales leads or are they supplied?
- In what specific sales-training courses, workshops, or seminar series have you participated? What was the most valuable point you took away from them?
- Who is your favorite sales speaker/trainer? What sales books and programs do you read and/or participate in and why?
- Which part of the sales cycle are you the most comfortable with and why? Which part of the sales cycle are you the least comfortable with and why?
- What do you know about our products/services? What would you describe as the biggest benefit people will receive from owning/using them?
- Have you ever been responsible for your own sales territory? If so, what were the main sales-building activities you used to prospect, secure new customers, and service new and existing accounts?
- What do you know about our specific competition and the competition in our industry?
- How would you describe your negotiation skills? Give an example where you persuaded a client to buy using value and service as opposed to a price concession?

- How much time do you typically spend daily prospecting, presenting, following up, and on administration?
- Given what you know about our products/services, what three qualifying questions do you think you would have to ask a prospect in terms of determining its need and ability to buy?
- In your current position, how do you qualify prospects and what questions do you ask?
- What is your favorite closing technique or method? Why?
- How many times do you think you should ask a prospect for a sale?
- Give me one example of how you overcame a 'no' and eventually closed the sale?
- Do you ever contact a prospect that did not buy? If so, for what reason?
- What is your typical closing-to-presentation ratio?
- What is the ratio of time you spend with prospects in person as opposed to on the telephone?
- How would your customers describe your selling abilities and your commitment to their account/purchase?
- What do you like/dislike about group presentations or one-on-one presentations?
- Are you comfortable speaking publicly? How large was the last group you spoke to? What was the topic?
- Would you sell to a prospect that wanted to buy but you knew they did not need what you were selling?
- Describe a sale you made that has gone bad and why? What did you do or not do to win the customer or sale back?
- You have exactly one minute to pitch me on why I should hire you for this sales position, starting now.

📖 Suggested Additional Reading

Blanchard, Kenneth H. and Sheldon Bowles. *Gung Ho! Turn on the People in Any Organization.* New York: William Morrow & Company, 1997.

Blanchard, Kenneth H. and Spencer Johnson. *The One Minute Manager.* Berkeley, CA: Berkeley Publishing Group, 1983.

Coffman, Curt and Gabriel Gonzalez-Molina. *Follow the Path: How the World's Greatest Organizations Drive Growth by Unleashing Human Potential.* New York: Warner Books, 2002.

Coffman, Curt and Marcus Buckingham First. *Break All the Rules: What the World's Greatest Managers Do Differently.* New York: Simon & Schuster, 1999.

Gleeson, Kerry. *The Personal Efficiency Program: How to Get Organized to Do More Work in Less Time.* New York: John Wiley & Sons, 2000.

Hiam, Alexander. *Making Horses Drink: How to Lead & Succeed in Business.* Irvine, CA: Entrepreneur Press, 2002.

Nelson, Bob. *1001 Ways to Energize Employees.* New York: Workman Publishing Company, 1997.

———. *1001 Ways to Reward Employees.* New York: Workman Publishing Company, 1994.

Smart, Bradford D. *Topgrading: How Leading Companies Win by Hiring, Coaching and Keeping the Best People.* Upper Saddle River, NJ: Prentice Hall Press, 1999.

Von Oech, Roger. *A Whack on the Side of the Head: How You Can Be More Creative.* New York: Warner Books, 1998.

KEY	
COST TO IMPLEMENT	$
DO-IT-YOURSELF	
CALL IN THE PROFESSIONALS	
LEGAL ISSUES	
BOOK RESOURCES	
ONLINE	

CUSTOMER SERVICE
Marketing Tips for Your Business

Problems and complaints are only
opportunities in work clothes.

—HENRY KAISER

WHY IS CUSTOMER SERVICE SO IMPORTANT?
$

Let's face it, without customers, you have no business. If you do not provide and practice incredible customer service, your current customers will unquestionably find a business that does. A recent survey conducted by the U.S. Small Business Administration (SBA) revealed that more than 60 percent of respondents stated that the number one reason customers stopped doing business with a particular business and opted to go to the competition was poor customer service. That is more than all of the other reasons, such as moving, death, or changing priorities, combined. This survey clearly illustrates the importance of providing great customer service—and when you think about it providing great customer service is much easier than continually trying to find and satisfy new customers. Featured below is what the SBA survey discovered about why

customers stop supporting one particular business. The customer

- dies or becomes physically immobile: 1 percent.
- moves out of the geographic trading area: 4 percent.
- goes to competitors because of lower prices: 15 percent.
- stops shopping because of dissatisfaction with what they buy: 15 percent.
- stops shopping because of poor service from employees or the business: 65 percent.

NEVER FAIL TO TELL CUSTOMERS HOW IT IS
$

In times of crisis, never fail to tell customers exactly how it is when it comes to specific problems or challenges that involve their accounts or purchases. Don't pass the buck to others, create long-winded excuses, dodge calls, or point blaming fingers. None of these are solutions; they only work to magnify the problem and ultimately cost more time, effort, and money to sort out and overcome. There are four major benefits for telling customers exactly how it is when dealing with complaints or challenges.

Maintain Integrity

By telling customers exactly how it is, you maintain personal and business integrity. More importantly, you maintain the trust and credibility relationship you have worked hard to build with your existing customer base. Lose credibility and you will lose business.

Open the Lines of Communication

By telling customers exactly how it is, you open the lines of communication and thus shift the focus of the discussion from the problem to a collective effort to find a mutually agreeable solution. It is much easier to overcome challenges when both sides are working for ways to find a solution.

Save Time

By telling customers exactly how it is, you create far less work and save enormous amounts of time. Being proactive and forthright from the start will save the time and effort needed to be reactive and searching for solutions—often after it is too late and the damage to the customer relationship is already beyond repair.

Retain the Customer

Best of all by telling it like it is, you keep your customer. Likewise, customers that have encountered problems that were dealt with professionally and in a timely manner often become your best source for referrals and word-of-mouth advertising.

SAVVY DEBT COLLECTION
$ ⚒

The first rule to getting paid in full and on time is to take your billing procedures seriously. As obvious as this statement may seem to be, it's not. If you're late sending out invoices or lax in any way about the way you collect payments or the billing or the debt collection process, then how can you expect your customers to be any different in their attitude and the actions they take in paying you? Additionally, avoid issuing legal threats unless you are prepared to follow through and proceed with legal action to collect your money. If you are not prepared, then instead calmly ask customers how they intend on making good on the bill. Often it is easier to come up with collective solutions that will work for both sides. Be polite but firm and get right to the point. Never make small talk or make light of the issue, once again you send customers the wrong message. The bill collection objective should always be to get paid in full. The intention also should be to keep the customer if you are confident that the unpaid debt was an isolated situation that is likely not to be repeated. Here are more points to consider when collecting debts.

Talk to the Right Person

Make sure you are talking to the right person. It will do you little good to vent about an unpaid bill if the person you're talking to doesn't have the ability to pay the bill or make decisions in regards to payment.

Look for Other Payment Options

Find out if they have access to other means to pay the debt—credit card, bank loan, or a loan from a friend or family member. You're not a bank, so don't let them use you or your business as their own personal bank. As a last resort, accept any item that has value and that can be resold to recoup losses, if for no other reason than the principle of the matter.

Demand Explanations

Make them explain why the bill or debt is not paid in full and on time as agreed upon. Doing this makes most people very uncomfortable and strangely enough many will pay up instead of being under the spotlight of having to go into too many details.

No Excuses

Close the conversation by telling them that this is a serious matter that must be resolved immediately and without excuse. Make them commit to how they will pay the bill before you end the conversation, whether it's over the phone or in person.

CLEAR ALL CHALLENGES BY THE END OF THE DAY
$ 🔨

Do yourself a favor and get in the habit of always trying to clear all customer complaints or challenges by the end of each working day. This is especially important advice for small-business owners and managers with few if any support staff available. Seldom are customer complaints more than a simple miscommunication, something small that has been misinterpreted or not fully understood somewhere along the line between the two parties. However, even the smallest of complaints has a way of quickly manifesting into full-blown problems unless it is dealt with in a timely and decisive fashion. Don't let yourself get caught in the procrastination trap of "I'll look after it tomorrow." Instead make a conscious effort to clear all customer challenges by the end of each business day and carry over only those problems that require input from an unavailable source. If you are unable to clear up the problem that day, then let your customer know why and when the problem will be corrected, give a firm call-back time, and assurance that this concern is priority number one. Ultimately, clearing all challenges by the end of each day will save time, headaches, and money. Most important, you'll earn the respect of your customers and make them your best and most loyal repeat customers for life.

THE ONE-MINUTE TRAINER
$$ 🔨

Turn all staff into expert one-minute trainers; but before you do, make sure that everyone working for you knows your products and services inside out and upside down. This marketing and customer-service strategy works wonders mainly because of the high standard of customer service it sets. Every business can benefit from implementing strategies geared at improved customer-service levels. For instance, if you sell bicycles then all staff members should be able to give every customer who purchases a bike from your store a quick rundown on how to properly maintain the bike so it will provide years of trouble-free riding enjoyment. Likewise if you operate a mini-golf center, then take just a quick moment to give all customers a few tips that might improve their games. This may seem elementary, but think of it this way—when a person buys a product or service from your business, they have certain expectations about how it will perform, how it will fill their needs, or how they will benefit from taking ownership. And if you can give your customers a quick training session that will increase the benefits, their performance, and ultimately their enjoyment of the product or service, then in all likelihood your product or service will exceed their expectations. This will lead to happy customers who are more likely to refer your business to others and be repeat customers themselves. The theory is sound and basic: Empower customers with the knowledge and skills to get the most benefits out of your product or service and you will secure a customer for life.

COMMIT TO A CALL-BACK TIME
$ 🔨

Value your customer's time as much as you value your own time. Prove this to your customers by committing to a firm call-back time for all customer complaints that cannot be immediately remedied within a few minutes during the initial call. To a customer (which we all are) with a problem there is no thing worse then being placed on hold for extended periods of time or being promised that someone will call right back only to wait hours or sometimes days before you hear a peep. Make a pledge to abolish slow and frustrating call-back periods by implementing and committing to a firm call-back time for all customer complaints. Tell customers when you will be calling them back with information or a solution to their complaint, problem, or concern. Let them know that you value and respect their time and you will not waste it. Even if you have not found the solution by the time you have promised to call them back, at least your customer will be happy in the knowledge that you are trying, which is reconfirmed by sticking to your commitment to the promised call-back time.

PRECUSTOMER CONTACT
$$ ✎

Get smart by getting busy to develop a precustomer contact employee-training program before you place new employees or subcontractors on the front lines and in contact with your most valuable business asset, your customers. Your precustomer-contact plan should include training and information sessions about the following topics:

- Provide geographic and demographic information about your primary and secondary target audience. Additionally, train staff about why your customers shop at or buy from your business, your competitive advantage in the marketplace, and how customers benefit from buying.
- Training should include explanations that enable employees to have an in-depth knowledge and understanding of all company policies, procedures, and rules, and why these policies and procedures are in place.
- In-depth knowledge of your products and services including statistics, manufacturer's information, warranty information, and, of course, the biggest benefit a customer receives by taking ownership of your product or service.
- Why your customer base is the single most important asset to the business, and what marketing activities you have in place to reach your target audience.

The more employees and subcontractors understand about who your customers are, why they choose to deal with your business and not with your competitors, and how customers benefit as a result of doing business with you, the better equipped your employees will be to serve your customers and understand their importance to the business.

ASK EMPLOYEES HOW TO IMPROVE CUSTOMER SERVICE
$ ✎

Often the best way to improve the level of customer service within your organization is to go directly to the frontline people who provide it—your employees. Ask your employees what they think the current customer service problems are and how these problems can be solved. Also ask what the positive aspects are of current customer service policies and procedures; and how these positive aspects can be expanded into other areas of the business and used as a successful platform upon which to build. Often frontline employees will identify consistencies in terms of repeated customer-service complaints, but not report them to management because they feel powerless to fix the problem—not to mention that management also has a tendency to pass the problems back to employees in the form of reprimands without providing workable solutions so the problem is not continually repeated. You can fix that by letting your employees tell you what they need to provide better customer service or what they think the company should do to provide better customer service. You may be pleasantly surprised by the insightful suggestions employees put forward.

REMEMBER IMPORTANT DATES
$$ ✎

Do you know when your best customer's birthdays are? How long has your biggest client has been in business? This is important information that you need to find out about all of your best customers so you can send a card, small gift, or place a quick call to congratulate them on their special occasion. This is powerful marketing and customer service. Your customers will be impressed that number one, you remember a date that is important to them, and number two you acknowledged it in some way that made them feel special, important, and not just another dollar sign to your business. The easiest way to develop a system of capturing important and valuable customer information is to create a small questionnaire and ask each new customer to complete it. Ask for information about your clients, their business, and their families. Additionally, make sure to send the questionnaire to current customers and ask that they complete and return it. Ideally you will want to record this information electronically on your PC and use software that will automatically remind you of these dates. This is an easy system to develop and the payoff is the fact that you are building very strong ties with your customers; they really become part of your business team.

WEB RESOURCE

⚲ www.maximizer.com: Sales-and-client management software.

CULTIVATING CUSTOMERS
$$+ ⚒

Small-business owners—or, for that matter, any businesses or corporations—are not in the business of selling products or services. They are all in the business of finding and keeping customers who want to trade their hard-earned cash for products and services that are distributed through small and big businesses alike. For that reason, being in business is about knowing your customers as well as, if not better than, what you are selling. Let's face it, at the end of the day, if you have customers who are loyal to you, believe in you, and want to give you their money, you will sell whatever they need and want to buy. In essence that is what business is all about, catering to the wants and needs of people (customers) who want to spend money. So it makes sense that to truly know and understand customers, you have to take a few steps to identify them, know what they are buying, know how often they buy, and figure out ways to sell them more of what they want and need. Below are a few steps that you can take to track your customers, rank your customers, identify your most profitable customers, sell your customers more, and build lifetime selling relationships with your customers. It is a five-step process to set up and maintain on a regular basis.

Step 1. Build a Customer Database

The first step is to set up some form of customer database so you can compile and store information about who your customers are, what they are buying, how often they buy, and additional information such as mailing address, telephone number, and e-mail address. Every small-business owner must take the time and invest the money required to build a customer database. It is an essential business and marketing tool that is required to survive in today's hypercompetitive business environment.

Step 2. Rank Your Customers

Next, based on the information you capture in your database, develop a simple customer ranking system so you can identify who your best customers are and any similarities they might share. Assign each customer a rank—A, B, C, or D or use numbers such as one as great, two as good, three as fair, and four as poor. Rank each customer on factors such as buying frequency, types of products or services they buy and the profitability associated with these purchases, special requests, complaints, and if they pay on time or are notoriously slow payers.

Step 3. Concentrate on Your Most Profitable Customers

Ranking your customers will enable you to pinpoint who your best and most profitable customers are. Knowing this, you will be able to direct more of your marketing efforts at your core target group to increase sales values, introduce new products, and ask for referrals.

Additionally, through customer ranking and analysis, you will generally discover that 20 percent of customers are responsible for 80 percent of sales and profits; this is called the 80/20 rule and is a widely accepted measure of customer loyalty principles. Focus the majority of your marketing efforts and activities on 20 percent of your best and most profitable customers. As I have mentioned many times throughout this book, it is ten times easier and less expensive to sell more and more frequently to existing customers than it is to find new customers. Ultimately the goal is to turn every existing customer and new customer into a lifetime customer. But start with your core of best customers who give you the largest profits with the least amount of trouble.

Step 4. Look for Ways to Increase Buying Frequency

Now that you know who your best customers are, look for ways to sell them more products or services more frequently. This can be accomplished in many ways, including introducing a product- or service-of-the-month club, gift registry service, automatic replenishment service, reminder or alert service, or whatever you feel is relevant to your business, customers, and what you sell. Regardless, the key to success is to know who your best customers are and then create ways that will entice them to buy more and more often.

Step 5. Cement Relationships with Customers for Life

The final step in cultivating great customers is to go out of your way to secure customers for life. Do this by catering to each customer's individual needs and paying close attention to the small details of each of your best customer accounts. Additionally, institute customer-loyalty programs, rewards, and appreciation gifts; work with customers to keep prices low and value and service high. Doing so will go a long way to cement lifelong business relationships with your best customers and also ensure that your business remains strong and profitable.

MAKE IT EASY FOR CUSTOMERS TO COMPLAIN
$$+ ✎

Far worse than a complaining customer is the customer who chooses not to complain and instead decides never to return to your business. With so much at stake, make it as easy as possible for customers to complain if they are unhappy with the product they have purchased or with the service they have received. In fact, go one step further and encourage customers to complain by creating a toll-free complaint telephone hotline as well as a complaint hotline e-mail address. Both of these should be included in print materials such as brochures and survey forms as well as on package labeling, in-store signage, sales invoices, and warranty cards. When customers complain, you have the ability to fix the problem and, in doing so, have the potential to keep that customer and secure their future business—maybe even for life. However, quite the opposite is true when unhappy customers do not complain; often you will lose their repeat business to the competition and never be the wiser of it, just poorer because of it. So making it as easy as possible for customers to complain and backing that up with a customer-first attitude focused on finding solutions to all concerns regardless of scope just make good business sense.

CREATE INFORMATION BOOKLETS
$$ ✎

Create an information booklet about your company, products, and services, and give the company information booklet to every customer. Information in the booklet should include a brief but exciting company history, key staff profiles including name, title, and direct telephone number. The booklet should also include information and details about your main product lines and services that you provide, their benefits, why they are the best available in the marketplace, and why your company is an industry leader. Likewise identify your competitive advantage in the booklet and use them in all of your marketing efforts; your competitive advantage is your most powerful tool; it is why people should do business with you. Company information or profile booklets such as these are great marketing and customer-service tools. It gives your customers insight into your business and it gives them confidence in your ability to quickly solve problems as they have key contact information to go directly to decision-makers should the need ever arise. Update the booklet annually and send it to all customers. You can even use the booklets to introduce a special offer or to add a response survey asking how you can better serve your customers.

A CURE FOR MISMATCHED EXPECTATIONS
$ ✎

The vast majority of customer-service complaints arise from mismatched expectations, generally caused by a breakdown in communications, or in the way a product or service was described or marketed, causing misunderstandings. The cost to business resulting from mismatched expectations is enormous, especially when you factor in the potential for lost customers and the amount of time to find solutions and fix these problems. Therefore, it makes a lot of sense to reduce the chances for mismatched expectations between what you are selling and what customers expect they are buying by developing a predelivery customer expectation form. The form should review the details of the sale and ask specific questions about what the customer expects the product or service to do for them or for their business. The number of small miscommunications and wrong details that such a simple, yet effective, form will uncover will amaze you. But with that said, you will also be armed with the information you need to avert potential disaster down the road after the product has been delivered or the service has been provided. Also select one employee to carry out the task of speaking to the customer and completing the customer expectation form or survey; be sure it is not the salesperson who wrote the order as the same mismatched customer expectations would likely be overlooked a second time.

SEND OUT REMINDER NOTES
$$ ✎

For years veterinarians have used reminder notes about annual vaccinations due as a subtle but powerful marketing tool and customer service. I'm sure that all veterinarians care about the well-being of your beloved family pet, but they are also businesspeople that understand that you must keep in contact with your customers. What better way to do that than providing a valuable reminder service. Sending out reminder notes can benefit any business, not just veterinarians. A pizza shop could send out monthly reminder notes, "Hey you haven't ordered pizza in a while, here's a dollar-off coupon to let you know that we're thinking about you and your empty stomach." Or, an auto mechanic could send out semi-annual car-service reminders to all customers, one in the spring for the presummer tune-up and inspection and one in the fall for the prewinter tune-up and

inspection. Really just about every business can come up with a reason to send customers a reminder that they are still in business and care about their customers. Use friendly terms, don't make it all marketing—demonstrate through appropriate words that you really are thinking about them and that you have their best interests in mind. This is a low-cost marketing trick that is guaranteed to boost revenues and profits, while also providing a valuable customer service.

PROVIDE A 100 PERCENT CUSTOMER SATISFACTION GUARANTEE
$$ ✎

Due to manufacturer's restrictions, you may not be able to provide 100 percent product guarantees, but you can provide all customers with a 100 percent customer satisfaction guarantee. Create a written document that boldly states you provide a 100 percent customer satisfaction guarantee and include this document with all customer purchases. This is not to say that you want to unconditionally guarantee every product or service you sell. But do state that your business strives for 100 percent customer satisfaction and will go above and beyond the call of duty to ensure that every customer is treated with respect, and should any problems arise they will be solved in a fair and honest manner. Customers want assurances that once they have paid for a product or service, they will not be hung out to dry should a problem arise down the road. When you think about it, that's not a very big demand to meet, no more of a guarantee than we all would like to have every time we part with our hard-earned money. So take the time to create a 100 percent customer satisfaction guarantee and back it up by making 100 percent of the people who buy from you satisfied. High customer-satisfaction ratings are the easiest and least expensive way to secure repeat business and grow revenues and profits.

CUSTOMER COMMENT CARDS
$$ ✎

Creating customer comment cards is another great way to gauge how your customers feel about the level of service they receive from your business and about their satisfaction with the products and services that you sell. Developing your own customer comment cards is very easy to do—simply ask questions on the card that you feel are relevant to your business and that would help you understand and assess your level of customer service. The cards can be given to customers to complete at the cash register, or alternately they can be prestamped and addressed on one side and customers can complete them at their convenience and mail them back to you at a later date. Below is an example of what the card could look like. Ultimately, you will likely want to customize your own customer comment card that will be relevant to your business. However, you can use this one as a template for designing your own right on your desktop personal computer.

WEB RESOURCE

☞ www.mycommentcard.com: Custom comment cards.

Sample Customer Comment Card

How did we do today? Customer comments welcomed.

(Your Business Name Here)

To help serve you better, we kindly ask that you rate our store, products, and service.

Poor	Good	Great	
❑	❑	❑	The cleanliness of our store
❑	❑	❑	Helpful, friendly, and knowledgeable staff
❑	❑	❑	Price
❑	❑	❑	Value
❑	❑	❑	Selection
❑	❑	❑	Overall satisfaction

Additional Comments: _____

_____

Customer Information

Name: _____

Street address: _____

City: _____ State: _____ Zip code: _____

Telephone number: _____

E-mail address: _____

I am a new customer. Yes _____ No _____

* May we send you our monthly (newsletter, special offer, e-newsletter)? Yes _____ No _____

We appreciate your business and comments!

TRICKS TO CALM IRATE CUSTOMERS
$ ✎

Make friends and allies from angry customers by trying a few of the following tricks when you receive customer complaint calls. Remember the old adage that an unhappy customer will tell ten people is true, so it is in your best interests to follow these tricks to ensure that every customer remains a happy customer.

Don't Interrupt

Let people get what's on their minds off first. Interruptions only further infuriate a person who is already angry, frustrated, and upset. By interrupting you are, in effect, telling customers that you do not care about them or their problem with your business.

Empathize

Once customers are through venting, empathize with them and show them that you're on their side by telling them that you understand their situation. Tell them your name so they are dealing with a person and not a company and continually use their name so they feel valued and important.

Confirm

Ask the customer to restate the chain of events that lead to the call and ask them to include details such as other people in the company they might have spoken to or who were involved, product or service problems, and resulting problems caused by the deficiency.

Don't Lay Blame

Never admit to any fault or lay blame on a person who is not involved in the conversation. Instead first make sure that there have been no miscommunications on either side, and then seek solutions by asking the customers how they would like the problem resolved. This will instantly show them that they're valued customers.

Fix What You Can

Fix what you can in the first call. For the problems that cannot be fixed during the first call or contact, make promises about when the customer will be called back and restate the solution that both sides feel will correct the situation.

ADD CUSTOMER SAFETY TO CUSTOMER SERVICE
$$+ ✎ ⚖

Recently I purchased a new bicycle and was very surprised to learn that the retailer holds a monthly bicycle safety course for all customers who purchased bicycles within the current calendar month. In fact this retailer didn't stop there; any person who wanted to attend was invited to do so and the course was publicized through in-store and direct-mail promotions. This is a great customer-service and marketing idea that many retailers could benefit from. Not only does it illustrate to the customer that the business has their best interests in mind by ensuring that they are informed about how to use the product safely, but also it provides an opportunity for the retailer to sell new products and build a loyal customer base. Which, in the case of this particular bicycle retailer, was achieved because when the safety seminar was over many people purchased products that were suggested as "safety-related and needed," including helmets, tire pumps, elbow pads, tool kits, first-aid packs, and many more. Basically this was a very well-planned and savvy marketing exercise disguised as a safety course. However, the retailer accomplished this in a very subtle manner and did provide excellent and valuable safety tips for all in attendance. See if your business can benefit by developing monthly courses to keep your customers safe, it should be a very worthwhile exercise.

LOG ALL COMPLAINTS
$ ✎

Get customer-service savvy by getting in the habit of recording all customer complaints you receive. Use the information you collect to find weak areas within your business, products, services, staff, or customer-service policies—basically repetitious problems that need to be corrected. Once you have identified your weaknesses in these areas, you will be able to look for solutions and ways to fix the problems. By recording and analyzing this customer-complaint information you will generally see patterns start to develop, and therefore you will be able to react accordingly. Even the smallest business can benefit by recording all customer complaints and writing them in a daily journal notepad or entering them on your PC using customer-management software. Additionally, by recording complaints, you'll be able to measure the performance of your suppliers' products and services as well. Once again, if you find that patterns start to develop with a particular supplier, you'll be armed with the information you need to confront that supplier and look for a mutually beneficial way to fix the deficiencies—or find a new supply source. Reacting to the same problem over and over and over accomplishes nothing, but costs a lot in terms of time, money, and potentially lost customers.

FOLLOW UP AFTER THE RESOLUTION

$ ✎

A customer-service complaint that appears to be resolved on the surface is not always so. For that reason, it is wise to implement a program of following up with customers who have complained and had their complaint "resolved." A few days after the problem has been fixed, call the customer to find out if they are truly satisfied with the way the problem was handled and resolved by yourself or employees. Develop a script for the follow-up calls with a checklist of questions you should ask during the conversation with the customer: Are you satisfied with the way we responded to your complaint? Are you happy with the way the problem was resolved? Would you purchase from our business in the future? Would you refer our business to other people? These are just a few questions you should be asking customers after there has been a complaint and a resolution. Develop more specific questions that are tailored to your business. But keep in mind that it is important to find out if a customer is truly satisfied with the solution. The old saying that an unhappy customer will tell ten times more people about their bad experience with a business, product, or service than a happy customer will about their good experience is very true.

SURVEYS CAN SHOW WHAT CUSTOMERS REALLY THINK

$$ ✎

Conduct formal surveys that are much more in-depth than customer comments cards to find out what your customers really think about your business, products, services, and customer service. Customer surveys have long been one of the best methods to identify weak areas within a business so you can develop a plan to find and implement corrective solutions. There are a number of ways you can conduct these surveys—by a forum, by telephone, online via your Web site, or create a survey form and distribute it to existing customers with self-addressed and stamped return envelopes. Budget will likely determine which is the best surveying method for your business, but don't get too caught up in the financial realities of conducting surveys; what you can learn from your customers about your business could prove to be much more valuable than the few hundred dollars it costs to conduct a simple customer-service survey. Once you have identified a surveying method that works and gets results, continue to use it quarterly to ensure that your business keeps up with ever-changing customer needs and wants.

PROMOTE RELIABILITY

$ ✎

Every business should promote reliability, but it is especially important for service-oriented businesses. If you say you'll be there at 12, then be there at 11:55. Many service providers rely on selling intangibles; your track record of happy clients is often your main marketing tool and in some cases your only marketing tool that carries any weight. Make a pledge of reliability to all customers and stick to it like glue. No one wants to be left waiting, and worse no one wants work that they have bought and paid for to not live up to promises of reliability. One of the most memorable and successful advertising campaigns of all time is built on the topic of reliability, "Like a good neighbor, State Farm is there." As a general rule when there is an insurance claim, something bad has happened. State Farm has brilliantly recognized this fact and is in effect telling people, "Purchase insurance with us and should an unfortunate event occur, you can count on us to be right there to assist you in any way we can." People want to know that when they buy a product or service, the company that sells it to them is reliable and will be there for them as promised. You can never go wrong by promoting and being reliable.

ALWAYS FIX THE CUSTOMER FIRST
$ 🔨

Every small business can benefit by adopting an "always fix the customer first" approach to customer complaints and challenges. What this means is make your customer happy, quickly, and without hesitation, and once this has been accomplished, turn your attention to the source of the problem. "I'll get back to you," or "That is a manufacturer's problem," just doesn't work in today's highly competitive business environment. These are dinosaur excuses used to skirt customer-service problems. Think of it this way, if you have an angry customer on the telephone line or standing in front of you, you have the ability to rectify that situation. Things that might be at the source of the problem can wait. In all likelihood you cannot do anything about the source at that moment; the cause of the problem will in all likelihood be out of your immediate control. However, what is in your immediate control is to make your customer happy. Remember the person who pays your bills, office rent, employee wages, and generates your income is the person who deserves your immediate and undivided attention. Not a product, a manufacturer, a supplier, or an employee. As long as you have happy customers who are buying and therefore paying the bills, you have a business. Fix the customers first to keep their business, then turn your attention to the source of the problem.

STRIVE TO FORM CUSTOMER PARTNERSHIPS
$ 🔨

Let your customers know that you think of them as a valuable business partner, and that without their support, you would have no business. Stress the partnership aspect, as it requires their continued support in order for you to be able to continue to provide them with goods and services that they need and want. No longer can businesses, regardless of size and reputation, afford to treat customers as numbers or blips on a bar graph; there is way too much competition and way too many choices for consumers to put up with anything less than being treated as a valuable business partner. Treat your customers as friends and with respect, and in turn you will develop buying relationships and mutually beneficial partnerships with your customers that can last a lifetime and even span to new generations within the same families. Marketers are learning that they must return to the roots of business and provide spectacular customer service that was the norm decades ago, and that means forming powerful relationships with all customers. Even large and multinational and multilocation corporations have adopted this new idea in marketing, which is really a centuries-old practice with new life being breathed into it to meet today's fast-paced business atmosphere. Therefore, get smart and strive to form a lifelong relationship with every customer to ensure new or continued business success.

CREATE A CUSTOMER-FIRST
TEAM ENVIRONMENT
$ 🔨

Be diligent about building and maintaining a business team that feels the same way you do about customers and customer satisfaction, including employees, strategic alliances, and suppliers. Use education as your main tool in your quest for customer-service excellence by ensuring that staff and management get and stay trained in the best and latest customer-service techniques. Also make sure that suppliers and subcontractors are trained in the same manner, as they will reflect on your business if they provide poor service to your customers. People rank the one who took their money in exchange for goods and services in terms of customer service and overall satisfaction. Remember that your customer will view installers, delivery personnel, and others involved in the transaction as part of your business team even if you have little if any control over them. So it is very important that every member of your business team is reading from the same manual to provide excellent customer service in the way you think it should be provided. Reward your team for meeting and exceeding customer expectations. No successful business can be built on and by one person; it takes a team with a common and collective goal that is reading from the same script.

GO THE EXTRA MILE
$$ ✎

Develop a strategy that requires you and your staff to go the extra mile for all customers, especially for your best and most loyal customers. Recognize that customers are not all the same; they're people who want and need different things. Each person must be viewed as an individual and not merely as cash in the register or a number in a database. Be flexible and willing to bend the rules once in a while when your customers need you to, even if it's an inconvenience to you and your business. Ask customers what they truly want and develop solutions to meet each individual's need. Let them know that customer satisfaction is really your primary concern and let them know that you will strive to go that extra mile when called upon to do so. Adopt an "all you have to do is ask and I will deliver" attitude. Going the extra mile for customers has many benefits for your business:

- Price no longer will be a determining factor in buying decisions; service and how you deliver upon your promises or on customers' special requests will be the determining factor.
- When you treat people specially you no longer have to work as hard to persuade them to purchase more products and purchase more often. When was the last time that you stopped shopping at a particular business because you received exceptional treatment?
- Everyone knows someone else, be it family, friends, or co-workers. Going that extra mile will give you access to your customer's circle of potential prospects. A warm prospect is ten

times easier to sell to than a cold prospect. Not to mention the fact that securing a referral costs a mere fraction of what it costs to market to and find a new customer.

CAREFULLY EVALUATE POLICIES
$ ✎ ⚖

Are your customer-service policies and procedures designed with your customers and their best interests in mind, or with your business in mind? Many small-business owners create customer-service policies based on and for their own convenience and what is easiest for them, when in fact these same policies should always be focused on what is best for the customer. Is a "No shirt, no shoes, no service" sign really necessary? When was the last time you saw a stampede of shoppers without shoes or shirts? Not often, if ever I'll bet. Do the sales of discounted goods have to be final? Probably not, as the vast majority of people are honest and do not purchase goods with the intention of returning them at a later date. And, should you tell customers a month after their warranty has expired that there is nothing you can do for them? Only if you want to send that customer's future business to your competition at lightning speed. The point is that all business owners and managers should carefully examine their business policies and how these policies relate to and affect their customers. Policies and procedures should be designed with the customer's best interests in mind, not yours, because over time bad policies make for bad businesses that will eventually lose business and go broke.

EMPOWER EMPLOYEES TO MAKE DECISIONS
$$ ✎

For a customer with a legitimate complaint, nothing is more frustrating than not being able to get a straight answer or speak to someone who can make a decision to rectify the problem or create a suitable solution. While it is probably not possible to allow all employees to make decisions about customer complaints, you should train a core group of employees and empower them with the ability to make decisions and react immediately to customer complaints. During all business hours there must be at least one employee on duty and readily available who has the power to make decisions and solve customer-service problems that are outside your normal customer-service policies. This is especially important for small- to mid-size businesses that do not have a dedicated customer-service manager or department. Value your customers' time, don't ask them to wait or tell them that someone will call them back. Instead train employees to deal with customer-service challenges and give them the tools and power they need to solve these problems in a quick and efficient manner. Customers are every company's greatest assets—you wouldn't mistreat a thousand-dollar bill for fears of destroying it and making it valueless. So why would you risk losing one customer who can represent a lifetime value that far exceeds a thousand dollars just because they couldn't get a firm answer and decisive action to resolve a problem?

KEEP THE LINES OF COMMUNICATION OPEN
$ ✎

A customer who jumps ship and starts doing business with the competition is not necessarily lost; there is always the opportunity to win him or her back in the future. That's why it is important to always keep the lines of communications open with all customers even if they are no longer customers. Sometimes the grass looks greener on the other side, and it's not until we are on the other side that we realize the pasture we just left wasn't so bad. In fact, it might be better than the situation we currently find ourselves in. This is common, especially in business. Clients get lured away from one business to another only to discover that the new business does not live up to its claims, making the transition a bust. People do not like to admit that they made a mistake—especially small-business owners. By keeping the lines of communication open with past clients, you are in effect leaving the door open should they wish to come back on board and do business with your team once again. Drop the lost-but-not-forgotten customer an occasional letter or telephone call reconfirming the

benefits of doing business with your company; keep it light, personal, and professional, but always let past customers know that you would welcome the opportunity to win back their business now or in the future. Keep the lines of communication open and you just might find that you win back some business.

PROFIT FROM PROVIDING CUSTOMER SERVICE
$$ ✎

Provide all customers with a very comprehensive and free customer-service plan. But also make sure to develop extended customer-service plans for those customers who are prepared to pay extra for the peace of mind and security that these extended service plans provide. There are two benefits for doing so: first, consumers want options and by creating a few levels of customer-service plans, you empower them to make decisions based on what they feel is best for their particular situation. Second, providing customer service is a cost to business that comes directly off the bottom line. And while smart business owners build the cost of providing after-sales customer service into the original purchase price, that will only work some of the time. In many cases customers who have purchased a product or service begin to think that because they have done so, your business should be forever in their debt and at their beck and call. That is fine, but their must be a value placed on services that exceeds what can be interpreted as normal customer-service levels, and customers who want these services must be prepared to pay for these services. Extended customer-service plans can and should go well beyond just a basic extended warranty to include extended technical support by phone, extended technical support in person, extended training periods, extended upgrades or guaranteed future value trade-ins, and so on. Create various levels of customer-service plans and empower your customers to choose what works best for them.

WEB RESOURCE

✎ www.entrepreneur.com: Online business resource center.

CATCH LATE CUSTOMERS
$$ ⚒

We have all raced through traffic at breakneck speeds trying to get to a business before they close only to finally arrive five minutes late and be greeted by a locked door and all employees gone for the day. Though no fault of the business, we stomp our feet in anger, throw our arms in the air, and angrily march back to our cars vowing never to return again. This situation is played out thousands of times every day across the country. Even if you do post and maintain regular business hours, there will always be customers who arrive minutes after you close; unfortunately many of these same people will never come back to your business because the door was locked. To combat this problem, create a rotating employee schedule that keeps one employee a day behind for an extra half-hour after you close. This person can greet customers arrived late outside and explain in a pleasant way that you are closed and offer the customer an incentive to come back the next day. The incentive could be a coupon, a printed discount card, or even a T-shirt or ball cap imprinted with your business name and logo. This is not to say that the employee should open up for the customer, but just be there to soothe the beast so that person will remain a customer and not take the business and money to the competition the following day. Or, if you really want to impress customers, then make it a standard policy to remain open for one-half hour after posted hours.

SUPPORT YOUR VENDORS
$$+ ⚒

Often due to lack of interaction with the end users, it is easy for manufacturers and suppliers to lose sight of the value of providing vendors with customer service solutions that they can in turn pass on to their customers, which are of course also your customers. Provide 100 percent vendor support by sending out field reps to train your vendors and the vendor's employees in the finer points of your products and how they truly work to ensure maximum customer benefits and enjoyment. Staff a toll-free customer-service hotline that is available to both vendors and their customers. Develop a Web page that vendors and end users both can have access to so they can ask questions, and get answers in relation to the products your manufacturers' supply. The easier you make it for your vendors to handle customer inquiries and complaints about your products, the more motivated they will become to sell your products instead of a competitor's product.

Here are a few areas of training that you should provide to your vendors:

- In-depth product knowledge.
- In-depth warranty information, including the small print and your guarantees in terms of repair, replacement, or refunds.
- What separates your products from competitors' products—the advantages, features, benefits to the user, durability, reputation, and reliability.
- What the most common questions are that the end user will ask and how they can answer these questions in an easy, fast, and helpful way.
- What the major objections are and how these objections can be turned into advantages and positive selling points.

CALCULATE THE TRUE COST OF A LOST CUSTOMER
$ ⚒

Help your employees understand the importance of providing great customer service by calculating the true dollar cost of just one lost customer. Use that figure to clearly illustrate what is at stake in terms of the success of the business and their income. To calculate the lifetime value of a customer, multiply your average sales value by the average number of times a customer buys from your business. Then multiply that figure by 15 years, which is widely accepted as the span of a lifetime customer. For instance, say your average sale is $50 and the buying frequency of your average customer is once a week. Then the yearly value of one customer would be $2,600 ($50 x 52 weeks). And the lifetime value of that same average customer would be $39,000 ($2,600 x 15 years). The result of calculating the true cost of each lost customer has a much greater impact than just saying "we lost another customer today." The dollars lost can be put into tangible terms such as in the above example—$39,000 would pay three part-time employee wages for an entire year. And using this example, if you lost ten customers a month for just one year, you would in effect be losing in excess of $4.5 million worth of lifetime customer sales value!

THROW CUSTOMER APPRECIATION PARTIES
$$ ⚒

There is no better way to thank customers than occasionally throwing a party in their honor. Get in the habit of hosting an annual customer-appreciation party and invite your best customers, current prospects you would like to close, and even customers who have taken their business elsewhere. Social activities such as customer-appreciation parties are a great marketing and customer-service tool for reinforcing existing business relationships and showing new prospects and past clients how much you care about and appreciate all customers. Additionally, having new prospects mingle with current and past customers is a good way to build credibility and confidence by demonstrating your honest and open approach to your business, as if to say, "We have nothing to hide, feel free to talk to all of our customers." Customer-appreciation parties can be held at local restaurants or banquets facilities. Or, if your financial budget is tight, you can even host the party right at your business location or for fun at an outdoor location such as a local park or a beach if weather permits. Make the annual event as fun as possible and you'll soon discover that customers start to look forward to it, thus creating an even stronger bond with clients.

GIVE BIG-IMPACT GIFTS
$+ ⚒

Forget about flowers or a box of chocolates when gifting your best clients. Instead get creative and give them a customer-appreciation gift that they will actually like, use, and more important, appreciate. Get to really know your clients, ask them questions about their hobby, likes, dislikes, and special interests, and use this information to select or create gifts that will have real impact. Additionally, don't stop with just your clients; find out what their family members' hobbies are as well, and occasionally give them a gift that their entire family or a specific family member would appreciate. Gifts need not be expensive; often the best gifts that have the most positive impact on clients are ones that have special meaning to them or that demonstrate that some real thought went into finding it or making it. Also keep in mind that the best gifts are nonperishable, meaning that they do not go bad or get thrown in the trash in a week. That way every time your client sees or uses the gift you gave they will think about you and your business.

GIFTS THAT DO GOOD
$+ ⚒

Are you searching for that perfect gift for that special client, but just can't seem to find the right one? If so, consider making a donation to a charity in your client's name and send your client a nice greeting card with the details of the charitable donation you made on her behalf. Of course if possible try to find out which charities your clients favor prior to making a donation on their behalf. This is a very high-impact gift as it makes two statements. First, you care enough about your clients to find out what charities or special causes are close to them. Second, you demonstrate to your clients that there are more important issues and realities in life than just business and material possessions. Both of these statements can go a long way to earn your client's respect and gratitude. Years back I mentioned to a supplier that my grandmother had recently passed away due to cancer. The following Christmas I received a card from that supplier with a note inside that they had made a donation to the cancer society on my behalf. Needless to say I was appreciative and have not forgotten about that kind gesture to this day. So when in doubt about what to gift special clients don't forget the possibility of making a charitable donation on their behalf.

🔨 www.charitywatch.com: Directory listing hundreds of charity organizations indexed by type and cause.

POWERFUL BIRTHDAY DISCOUNTS

$$ 🔨

Celebrate your customers' birthdays in grand fashion by passing along a special discount on purchases they make on their birthdays. Promote your special birthday discount in your newsletter, on your Web site, in customer loyalty programs, and with in-store signage posted by the cash register. Try to make your birthday discount 15 percent, as a 10 percent birthday discount is far too common and does not have the same big value impact that a 15 percent discount has. Besides, it is not the discounted business that you want to secure, it is the regular business at full price that is your real goal; the birthday discount is just a way to say "thank you for your business." Once word is out about your special offer you'll soon discover a whole new crop of customers coming in to make purchases and claim their birthday discounts. Of course the objective is to lure customers in with the discount and then wow them with great products and service to turn them into loyal buying customers 365 days a year and not just on their birthdays. This can be accomplished by providing incredible service and selection. This simple and effective marketing trick can also be extended to include other special occasions or milestones such as graduations and anniversaries.

WORK WITH CLIENTS TO HOLD THE LINE ON PRICE INCREASES

$ 🔨

As an alternative to customer gift giving, another great way to show your best clients that you appreciate their business is to not raise prices on goods or services they frequently purchase from you—this is a gift that they will really appreciate. Work with your clients to find mutually suitable solutions to abolish price increases. Not only will this marketing trick show clients that you have their best interests in mind, but it can also help turn good customers into lifetime customers and even motivate them to buy more and more often; not to mention the spin-off referral business that can result from this type of strong customer management and relationship practice. These "price-holding solutions" could include having clients cover the cost of delivery or transportation of products instead of you paying for shipping or having clients supply part-time employee labor to help produce products or supply services. When faced with the potential for increased prices you'll find that most clients will be more than happy to work with you to find mutually beneficial ways that they can use their existing resources as a way to hold prices in check.

MAKE IT A FAMILY AFFAIR

$ 🔨

When it comes time to thank your best customers for their business and continued support don't forget to include their family members. Inviting customers to dinner, or sending them concert or game tickets is a great way to say thank you. But have you taken the time to find out if your gift will cause more bad than good, and therefore diminish the effectiveness of what is supposed to be a big thank you? Think about things, such as will your customer have to find a babysitter to look after the kids and be forced to spend more money to take advantage of your gift than the value of the actual gift you are giving them? Or, is your gift something that the entire family can benefit from? These are just a few questions you must get answers to so that when you gift that special client it will have the biggest and most positive impact and not be view negatively. Ask customers about their families, find out what they enjoy doing as a family, and tailor each gift to each individual client's family and specific interests. Let's face it, the purpose of the appreciation gift is to say "thank you" and to keep that customer loyal to your business for life. So the few extra moments that you spend to find out what your best customers truly enjoy doing in family time is a wise investment of your time that can go a long way to ensure that your customers remain yours and not the competition's customers.

FOCUS ON CUSTOMERS TO STAY MOTIVATED
$$ ✎

Keep yourself and your employees motivated to provide incredible customer service by creating "customer walls of fame" in your store or office areas. The customer walls of fame should include photographs of your customers, letters of appreciation and testimonials that your business has received from them, news articles written about them, and print advertisements clipped from newspapers and magazines showing what products and services that they sell if they are business clients. The customer walls of fame can be located behind the cash register, in lunchrooms, along hallways, and even in reception areas and waiting rooms. Of course, if the customer walls of fame are located in areas visible to customers, then frame the materials that you display and have explanation signs professionally made to go with the material. Keeping the focus on customers is a great way to stay motivated. By displaying your customers in a highly visible location in your business, you and your staff will be constantly reminded of your customers and how important they are to the business.

STAYING FRESH IN YOUR CUSTOMER'S MEMORY
$+ ✎

One downside of giving appreciation gifts to your best customers is that if the gift is perishable, such as a box of chocolates, or a consumable such as a imprinted pen, the lasting advertising or memorable value is somewhat depreciated. Here is a list of a few gifts that customers will use and that will keep you in their thoughts.

Subscriptions

Find out what newspapers or magazines your customers like and get them a monthly subscription for it as an appreciation gift. Every time they receive the magazine or newspaper they will think of you and your business.

Imprinted Items

Key chains, pens, note pads, calendars, coffee mugs, travel mug, clocks, mouse pads, basically anything that they will use on a day-in, day-out basis and that keeps your name in front of them. Of course your business name, logo, and message must be boldly emblazoned on these items so that they will create the desired impact on your customer's memory.

Education

Find out what interests your customers, both business interests and personal hobbies. Tickets to an ongoing seminar or workshop series make a great gift, as well as enrolling a customer into training classes of their choice such as photography, music, or sports. As the old adage goes, the gift of education is one that lasts and is remembered for a lifetime.

Referrals

If your customers are business owners and professionals then make an effort to send them three referrals each month. Make a real presentation of it by printing the referral information on your best letterhead or an awards-type certificate. What better gift is there than helping someone build their business, practice, or career? This one will definitely make sure that you are remembered.

WEB RESOURCE

⌘ www.promomart.com: Billed as the world's largest online source for promotional and advertising specialty products.

THE QUIET MASSES
$ ✎

Here is a simple yet truthful customer service and marketing premise that can potentially make you rich or alternately bankrupt your business if you choose to ignore it: for every one customer who speaks out and says it, there are many more customers who are thinking it. That customer who just complained that his steak was rare and not medium rare as ordered, might just be the person that saves your business from financial ruin if you're prepared to listen to what he has to say and react accordingly. It's no mystery that some people are comfortable with complaining about a product or service they do not like, but be aware that there are many more people who are not comfortable with speaking up. This is for many reasons—they feel intimidated, don't like confrontations, or they just expect that complaining will get them nowhere so they simply decide never to come back instead of speaking up. So in fact the customer who complained about the way his steak was cooked might just be speaking up for and representing the quiet masses who choose to say nothing. Believing in this premise is your first line of defense and will enable you to take every customer complaint seriously.

CUSTOMER SERVICE IDEAS CHECKLIST
$+ ✎

Listed below is a collection of great customer service ideas; some have been featured in this chapter, while others have not. Customize this checklist by adding in your own customer service ideas and deleting those that do not apply to your business to create your own checklist that is specifically suited and relevant to your business. Use it—copy it and distribute it among management and staff to ensure that they never stop giving your valued customers the best service possible.

Customer Service Ideas Checklist

❑ Provide your customers with customer service satisfaction guarantees and written warranties that are better than your competitors' guarantees.

❑ Create a customer service mission statement that clearly defines your customer service objectives. Tie these objectives in with all your marketing activities so customers know exactly what to expect from your busines. Then go the extra mile to far exceed their expectations.

❑ Always search for and find ways to fix the customer first, and the problem second.

❑ Create service and business policies that have your customer's best interests in mind and not policies that are simply convenient for your business. Chances are if it is convenient for you, it won't be for your customer and they will find another business that is more convenient to do business with and that will happily accept their money.

❑ Strive to clear and resolve all customer complaints and challenges by the end of each working day. Small complaints have a way of quickly manifesting into gigantic problems when ignored or put off. When it comes to your customers, never procrastinate.

❑ Never point fingers: all frontline staff should take ownership of problems and provide solutions or immediately put the customer in contact with those who can provide solutions.

❑ Empower employees to make customer service decisions. Don't make your customers spend the rest of their lives trying to track down and speak to someone with decision-making powers. Eventually they will give up and run into the waiting arms of your competition.

❑ Log and analyze all customer complaints so repetitive problems can be identified and corrected, saving time and money.

❑ Develop a "three rings or faster" telephone answering policy.

❑ Train and support frontline staff to deliver the best customer service by developing a customer service guideline and expectations handbook.

❑ Create a valuable customer loyalty program to reward your best customers and implement VIC (Very Important Customer) discount cards.

❑ Offer free workshops, training classes, and seminars to make sure that your customers know how to get the most out of what they have purchased from you.

❑ Create a new customer kit that includes discount coupons on goods and services you provide, an information booklet about your business, and contact information for key managers and employees. Freely distribute this kit to all new customers and update it on a regular basis.

Customer Service Ideas Checklist, continued

❏ Keep your store spotlessly clean, your displays in top condition, and your store designed with your target customer in mind.

❏ Use mystery-shopping services to make sure that your employees are providing optimal customer service.

❏ Never pass your own weaknesses on to your employees: if customer service is not your strength then bring in professionals to train staff on the finer details of providing great customer service.

❏ Make customers look forward to doing business with you by never failing to amaze them with incredible customer service delivered with a smile.

❏ Become an expert source of information about your business and industry. Encourage customers and prospects to tap into your knowledge by asking questions and making special requests.

❏ Train your suppliers, vendors, resellers, and subcontractors great customer service techniques that are the same that your business practices so that your customers will receive a consistent level of service regardless if it comes from one of your employees or one of your vendors.

❏ Continually survey your customers asking them to rate your service levels, give feedback, and make suggestions about ways your business can serve them better.

❏ Create a precustomer contact training program that every employee must successfully complete and pass with flying colors before they can come in contact with any customer.

❏ Calculate the lifetime value of one single lost customer so that your staff can identify and understand the importance that each and every customer represents to your business. An actual dollar figure makes it tangible and often scary, thus having real impact from that point forward as to how staff treats all customers.

❏ Examine your business from the customer's point of view. Identify problems that impede great service and performance, such as wider aisles, faster delivery, larger portions, etc.

❏ Strive to ensure that all the goods and services you sell exceed your customer's expectations. Referrals will skyrocket!

❏ Make sure that customers can easily connect with the departments and people they want. Never leave them dangling helplessly on hold, instead commit to a call back time.

❏ Always keep an open mind and learn from what your customers are telling you when they complain or challenge a policy.

❏ Go out of your way to welcome newcomers to the community and to your business.

❏ Identify and develop ways to turn customer service activities and contact with customers into revenue and profit centers.

❏ Think in terms of customer safety in addition to customer satisfaction. When customers are directly engaged with your business or with a product or service you sell, one of your top priorities must be their safety and security.

❏ Create a system to route some of your customer service functions through your Web site to increase visitor volume and promote online shopping.

❏ Educate your customers via a book, special report, or newsletter about your business, staff, what you do, and why you do it so they will have a better understanding about your business, how it operates, and what they can expect from you. This can dramatically reduce repetitive customer service inquiries.

❏ Regularly send out reminder notes letting your customers know that you are thinking about them. Include an incentive or reason for them to come and see you with the note. Always develop ways to stay in front of your customers so that you stay on their minds.

❏ Always strive to project a professional and reputable business image.

❏ Make it as easy and convenient as possible for people to do business with you and pay you.

❏ Strive to out-benefit your competition in terms of providing great customer service.

❏ Utilize all currently available technology to stay in contact with your customers.

Customer Service Ideas Checklist, continued

❏ Keep the lines of communications open with past clients and never stop trying to lure them back as customers.

❏ Treat each and every customer with respect and in the way that you expect to be treated.

❏ Carefully study the industry-leading businesses to see how they provide and maintain excellent customer service; copy and implement their strategies for the benefit of your customers and your business.

❏ Build and maintain a Customer Relationship Management database.

❏ Train all staff how to deal with irate customers so that they do not take it personally and foolishly get combative and aggravate the problem so that you lose customers.

❏ Make it easy for customers to complain; in fact encourage them to. Far too many times customers won't complain and instead just never return or stop buying and head to competitors. Install toll-free complaint telephone lines, let them know to where they can write, have a complaint page in your Web site, and most importantly follow up, resolve, apologize, and build customer loyalty.

❏ Use incentives, recognition, and rewards to motivate employees to provide and practice exceptional customer service.

❏ Make all staff one-minute trainers and show your customers how they will receive the biggest benefits from owning and using your products and services. Often the difference between customers not being satisfied with a purchase and being 110 percent satisfied is about 60 seconds of extra training or instruction about how to use, maintain, or enjoy a product or service.

❏ Are your customers really happy with the way a problem was resolved or fixed? If you are unsure, then get in the habit of following up after the resolution. Remember it is your responsibility to ensure 100 percent satisfaction, not your customers'.

❏ Go the extra mile for all customers, but especially your best customers who buy the most and always pay in full and on time.

❏ Always promote reliability and a consistent customer service message, and become known as the industry leader. And continually update and improve your customer service policies to reflect changing trends in customers' wants and needs.

❏ Double check and reconfirm all the details; miscommunications and mismatched expectations are responsible for 90 percent of all customer complaints and problems.

❏ Strive to clear all customer complaints and problems by the end of each working day.

❏ Never fail to tell customers exactly how it is. Honesty is one of your most powerful customer service tools and the easiest one to master.

❏ Regularly send your best customers appropriate gifts to show them how much you appreciate their business and continued support.

❏ Never stop asking customers for glowing testimonials and for new business referral opportunities. Your customers benefit from doing business with you, why shouldn't their friends, family, and business associates?

❏ Give back to the community that supports your business by supporting charitable causes, sponsoring community events, and by always being a good corporate citizen.

❏ Extend your customer service benefits and interests to include and involve your customers' families. And, host an annual customer appreciation party and invite your customers and prospects.

❏ Make customer service your number-one competitive advantage, because it is the easiest and least expensive advantage to create and maintain.

❏ And finally, smile, have fun, enjoy your job, and acknowledge every customer who comes into your store or office by way of eye contact and a smile when you are busy.

📖 SUGGESTED ADDITIONAL READING

Anderson, Kristin and Ron Zemke. *Delivering Knock Your Socks Off Service*. New York: AMACOM, 1998.

Barlow, Janelle. *A Complaint is a Gift: Using Customer Feedback as a Strategic Tool*. San Francisco: Berrett-Koehler, 1999.

Blanchard, Ken and Sheldon Bowles. *Raving Fans: A Revolutionary Approach to Customer Service*. New York: William Morrow & Company, 1993.

Carlow, Peggy and Vasudha Kathleen Deming. *The Big Book of Customer Service Training Games*. New York: McGraw-Hill, 1998.

Dyche, Jill. *The CRM Handbook: A Business Guide to Customer Relationship Management*. Boston, MA: Addison-Wesley Publishing, 2001.

Fox, Jeffrey J. *How to Become a Rainmaker: The Rules for Getting and Keeping Customers and Clients*. New York: Hyperion Books, 2000.

Johnson, Michael D. and Anders Gustafsson. *Improving Customer Satisfaction, Loyalty, and Profits: An Integrated Measurement and Management System*. San Francisco: Jossey-Bass, 2000.

Leland, Karen and Keith Bailey. *Customer Service for Dummies*. New York: John Wiley & Sons, 2001.

Morgan, Rebecca L. *Calming Upset Customers*. Englewood Cliffs, NJ: Crisp Publications, 1996.

Sher, David and Martin Sher. *How to Collect Debts: And Still Keep Your Customers*. New York: AMACOM, 1999.

KEY

COST TO IMPLEMENT $

DO-IT-YOURSELF

CALL IN THE
PROFESSIONALS

LEGAL ISSUES

BOOK RESOURCES

ONLINE

HOME OFFICE
Marketing Tips for Your Business

*Thought, not money is the real business capital, and if you
know what you are doing is right, then you are bound
to accomplish it in due season.*

—Harvey S. Firestone

INVEST IN YOU
$$ ⚒

Great entrepreneurs never stop investing in ways
to become better businesspeople and marketers.
They know that every dollar they invest into edu-
cational activities and items that are geared to
make them better in business and more productive
and innovative will pay back tenfold or greater.
Strange, but most of us don't think twice about
spending money on golf lessons so that we can
become better golfers, or on dance lessons so we
can become better dancers. But how many small-
business owners use that same logic in terms of
investing in things that will make them better busi-
nesspeople? Unfortunately the vast majority do
not. Invest in training courses to become a better
manager or public speaker, buy books that will
help you improve your marketing skills, attend
seminars that are geared toward making you a bet-
ter salesperson. Invest in and learn to use technologies
that will make your business more competitive and
profitable in today's highly competitive business
environment. Never stop investing in your most
powerful, effective, and best business and market-
ing tool—you!

- Read business, marketing, and sales books reg-
  ularly.
- Subscribe to monthly business and marketing
  magazines and journals.
- Attend business and marketing training and
  information seminars.
- Join business and industry associations to keep
  up with the latest trends.
- Attend industry trade shows.
- Invest in specialty training such as learning a
  new language if it will help you to enter into
  new markets.
- Take courses that will help you to use current
  or new technologies in your business to be
  more productive and efficient.

- Network with other successful small-business owners, salespeople, and professionals.

WEB RESOURCE

✆ www.smallbizbooks.com: Online retailer of business and marketing specific books and guides.

MEET ALL REQUIREMENTS
$$+ ✎ 🐾 ⚖

Develop a policy that clearly states that you and your business will meet and strive to exceed all requirements in terms of starting and operating a business from home. Many people falsely believe that because a business is operated from a homebased location it means they do not need to secure licenses, permits, or insurance, or that these things can wait because the business is not really official. Avoid that mindset like the plague. Register for a business license, secure required insurance and permits, and open bank accounts in the business name. In a nutshell operate your homebased business as though it were a business operating from an office or other fixed location because that is what it is and should be; a legitimate business entity. Besides, the more documentation you have to present to prospects that clearly demonstrates that your business operates above board and is covered in case of mishap, the more credibility and trust you will build with your prospects. Business documents are wonderful sales tools; get them copied and let all potential customers know that you are committed to your business and their best interests for the long run. Keep in mind that there is no "across the board" set of standard rules and regulations in terms of operating a business from a home. It is the responsibility of every home-based business owner to become acquainted with and conform to the rules and regulations governing homebased business ventures as set forth by local governments. However, with that said listed below are the basics that must be considered.

- Liability, fire, and theft insurance
- Zoning and building use codes
- Fire and health regulations
- Certificates of training

- Licenses, permits, and tax conformity
- Exterior signage ordinances

WEB RESOURCE

✆ www.nolo.com: Nolo is the one-stop source for online law information and forms pertaining to small business.

TAKE IT SERIOUSLY
$ ✎

You cannot be an effective marketer unless you truly believe in your business and the goods and services that you provide to your clients. Far too many homebased business owners fail to take their business seriously because of the misconceived notion that a "real business" needs a "real" location to operate from such as a street storefront or commercial office space. However, this notion could not be farther from the truth. According to the National Association of Home Based Businesses more than 50 million people in the United States work from home on a full- or part-time basis. And, not surprisingly, of that number close to 30 million are self-employed, owning and operating a homebased business venture. In fact, homebased business ventures create more jobs annually in the United States than any other business or industry sector. Your homebased business is not merely a hobby and should not be treated as such, even if you operate the business part time. Take your business seriously and in return you will reap all the benefits and financial rewards and security that business ownership can provide to the serious business owner.

WEB RESOURCE

✆ www.entrepreneur.com: Online business and marketing resource center for small business owners and professionals.

PROJECT A PROFESSIONAL IMAGE
$$ 🐾

The majority of homebased business owners do not have the advantage of elaborate offices or elegant storefronts to wow prospects and impress customers.

Instead they must rely on imagination, creativity, and paying attention to even the smallest detail when creating and maintaining a professional image for their homebased business. Consequently, it is wise to budget extra to have business cards, stationery, and sales materials such as catalogs and brochures printed on high-quality paper that is rich in texture and heavy to the touch. Additionally have your corporate identity logo professionally designed so that it truly identifies with your business and make sure to consistently incorporate your logo into all printed communications. Attire is also an important aspect of creating and maintaining a professional image; therefore consider having smart, casual golf shirts and sweaters embroidered with your business name and logo. The more you strive to create a professional business image, the more likely your prospects will see your business as credible and overlook the fact that it is operated from a homebased location. The best corporate identity images are used in a consistent fashion throughout the business; this includes color scheme, marketing message, and logos.

Professional Business Image Checklist

❑ Professionally designed logo that clearly identifies and brands your business

❑ Unified marketing message that is used throughout your business, the cornerstone of all marketing activities

❑ Consistent business image that carries through all business and marketing activities

❑ Consistent company color scheme

❑ Sharp uniforms and attire emblazoned with the company name, logo, and marketing message

❑ Rich and bold professionally printed business stationery

❑ Professionally designed signage for trade shows, seminars, and vehicles

❑ Professionally designed and printed presentations, catalogs, and promotional materials

❑ High-quality imprinted advertising premiums and specialties embossed with the business name, logo, and marketing message

❑ High-quality color business cards

TAKE ADVANTAGE OF REDUCED OPERATING COST

$ ⚒

High rent, support and administration staff, water coolers, a fleet of company cars, a raft of expensive employee benefits, and bloated expense and entertainment accounts—these things are just a few reasons you should have no problem in undercutting your larger competition with the price that you sell your goods or services at. Take full advantage of the fact that you operate your business from home on a shoestring budget and use your low overhead costs to lure customers away from the competition by offering lower prices. Not lower value or quality only the price you charge for the same or better quality and value. And moreso, let them know that you can offer the same great service, products, and value cheaper than the competition because you maintain a tight budget and keep costs in check by running your business from a homebased location. However, as a cautionary note, make sure to agree to payment terms in advance and in writing prior to carrying out any work for clients. Some business owners, managers, and even consumers are under the misconceived notion that homebased business owners can wait for payment or will take substantially reduced payments for goods and services because the business is operated from a nontraditional business location. That is why it is vital to agree to payment terms with clients in advance and in writing so that should a problem arise after delivery you will have the necessary documents to ensure that you can secure payment by legal means if required.

GO OUT OF YOUR WAY TO GET INVOLVED
$ 🔨

By its very nature operating a homebased business can often mean hours of isolation or even days spent cut off from the outside world. It is critical that you get out of the house and get involved in your community in some capacity; preferably one that provides for networking and lead generation opportunities. For many people who work from home, especially those new to it, isolation starts to become habitual, and can eventually lead to a decrease in motivation and focus. Leading businesspeople know and understand the importance of networking and mingling with others who are like-minded and who share similar interests. You feed off the other people's energy, thus fueling your own desire and need to succeed. There is no greater motivator than other people's success stories to get you wound up and charging forward. Not even money can have the same effect, because money is always the same and constant; business and marketing success stories and energized conversation can change with each new person with whom you come in contact. Here are a few suggestions for ways that you can get involved in the community.

- Join local business associations such as the chamber of commerce.
- Select a local charity and pitch in to help out with administration, charity drives, and organizing special functions and events.
- Join or start a networking club in your area.
- Get involved in amateur sports as a player or coach.
- Get involved in local politics or even take a run for a seat in office.
- Become active in your church or children's school.

WEB RESOURCE

🖱 www.marketingsource.com/associations: Online directory listing more than 35,000 business associations.

MAKE INVESTMENTS IN DISGUISE
$$+ 🔨

The smartest small-business owners are the ones who know where and when to economize and where and when to spend extra loot in terms of marketing their businesses. They know that spending more money on a telephone system with far more business functions is a wise expenditure, and that spending less on a disposable pen imprinted with your name is also a smart and frugal business move. They know that spending money on items for their business that can be used over and over again like professional artwork for advertising is a very wise investment, while spending money on items or services that can only be used once or on a very limited basis is a poor and ultimately costly decision. Top entrepreneurs know that in order to compete in today's extremely competitive business environment every purchase they make must be a investment in disguise that will have the biggest and longest beneficial impact on their business and their marketing program as possible. Learn to get 150 percent, not 50 percent, value out of every dollar that you spend on marketing.

HANDLING PRESSURE
$ 🔨

Every business owner faces various forms of pressure daily—irate clients, damaged inventory shipments, or cost overruns on major projects. However, these common business pressures can especially take a toll on homebased business owners simply due to the fact that the entire problem usually rests on one person's shoulders, yours. Unfortunately the worst part of being under pressure is that it can cause you to make poor marketing and business decisions, which can ultimately slow the growth of your business or even worse cause you to go out of business. Listed below are a few methods that you can employ to handle pressure and remain levelheaded in the process.

Evaluation

Create a written outline of what form the pressure is taking—customer complaint, supplier, family, financial, or other form. In doing so you can better understand the nature of the problem and have a tool that you can use to evaluate and find solutions. You only worry about what you don't understand and therefore cannot fix. If you know what is causing the pressure then you can take the required action to reduce it or eliminate it entirely.

Flexibility

Be flexible and always seek a compromise solution to the cause or source of the pressure. With a supplier, be flexible to their needs and look for mutually identifiable payment solutions. With a client, create a mutually beneficial payment plan so that you will get paid, keep the customer, and reduce or eliminate the cause of the pressure.

Action

Once you have identified the source of the pressure take immediate and affirmative action to reduce or eliminate it entirely. Left unchecked, pressure will only become worse, never better; and it will continue to grow and could even manifest into a major situation that may even cause health problems as a result.

Advice

Look to those people around you who you trust and ask them for advice when the pressure gets to be too much. Simply talking to someone else is often enough inspiration and opportunity to vent to get thinking clearly again, get beyond a problem, and relieve pressure.

Separation

Know when to separate your business life from your personal and family life. Make sure that you have pursuits outside of the business and that you plan and take time away from the business to engage in these pursuits. You must clearly define what your priorities are in terms of the business, your family, your friends, and yourself.

OUT-BENEFIT THE COMPETITION
$$+ ✎

One of the biggest secrets to homebased business success lies within your ability to match or exceed the benefits that your larger competition provides their customers. Many homebased business owners tend to use their small size as an excuse for such things as why they don't offer 24-hour service, extended warranties programs, or flexible payment and financing options. But don't use these excuses or create any others; instead match your competitors by going toe-to-toe with them, and if possible strive to exceed them, providing a wide range of useful and valuable customer benefits and conveniences. Look at the small size of your business as a benefit or advantage, not a disadvantage. Your smaller size is an advantage that empowers you to move quickly and be flexible meeting specific customer needs and deadlines on an individual basis and not a one-size-fits-all approach to marketing or service. Offer everything the competition does and then dig a little deeper to discover what prospects truly want and need. Use this information to create a benefits package that is tailored to each individual client. Most mid- to large-sized corporations can't come close to matching that type of personalized customer service; their chain of command and need to generate mountains of paper for justification doesn't allow for this type of service to ever be financially recouped. Remember, don't back down or make excuses; give prospects every reason to do business with you, then blow them away with results that far exceed their expectations.

DESIGN YOUR WORK SPACE FOR SUCCESS
$$$ ✎ ☏

Carefully plan and design your home office work space to ensure maximum performance and professionalism. Ideally, you'll want a separate room or office with a door that closes, to keep business in and family members out, at least during prime business and revenue generating hours of the day. Likewise, keep what makes you money whether it be the telephone or computer the closest and get rid of the stuff that doesn't make you money. Basically eliminate clutter and streamline your office to allow you to work productively and efficiently at all tasks and projects. Also if your office does not have it's own separate outside entrance, yet you routinely have customers and business alliances visit you, then consider installing a separate entrance into your office space. A good quality entrance door can be installed in most cases for less than $500. And often the job of cutting a hole in the outside wall to install the door is a lot less painful and complicated than it might seem to be at first glance—a comfortable weekend project, making it a worthwhile expense by providing clients access to your office without having to walk through your home. Remember nothing screams unprofessionalism louder then a vacuum cleaner as background music when you are engaged in a telephone conversation with a very important client or prospect.

WEB RESOURCE

✍ www.officebydesign.com: Online retailer of office furniture and a custom design studio and office design tips.

DEVELOP A ROUTINE
$ ✍

Temptations are many when you work from home, yet personal motivators are few. Avoid getting caught in the procrastination trap that many new work-from-home business owners find themselves bogged down in. Instead be diligent and develop a daily routine right from the get-go. Your plan should include short- and long-term business and marketing goals, as well as segment business objectives and action plans to reach these objectives. Additionally, at the end of each business day complete a "to do list" to tackle the following day, and don't forget to reward yourself for regularly meeting goals and objectives. I have more than a decade of experience in working from a homebased location so I can tell you firsthand that it can be difficult to get and stay motivated when you do not have others pushing you to do so. This is why it is so important to develop your own system of goals and rewards as a method of motivation. Not to mention the fact that by setting goals and objectives you will have a standard that can be used as a yardstick to measure performance and success. Procrastination and television have destroyed hundreds if not thousands of promising homebased business ventures, so make sure to develop and stick to a work schedule and routine so that you

don't become a homebased business casualty as a result of procrastination.

TRICKS FOR WRITING GREAT BUSINESS COMMUNICATIONS
$ ✍

Business communications that are well written, to the point, and that state a clear and concise message stand a far better chance of securing the desired results or meeting your specific objectives than communications that are not. Utilizing the following great tricks will go a long way to increasing the effectiveness of your written business communications.

- If time allows write a first draft and let it sit for at least a day or two before you go back to review the draft and make changes. Often you will find key messages or points within the first draft that you want to expand upon or delete.

- Even if your mood is not positive, your words and the tone of your message must be, so it stands to reason that if you are in a bad mood it will be reflected in your written communications and the reader will pick up on this instantly. You have two options. One, wait until your mood is more positive before you write the communication. Two, write the communication in draft form and wait a day or two before you go back to it and make revisions.

- Get to the point quickly and state your message clearly. The "what's in it for your reader" should be boldly stated within the first few lines of the first paragraph and repeated again in the body of the communication as well as in the postscript. The reader must know why they will benefit if you expect to hold their interest long enough to read what you have to say.

- Skip the technical jargon, and stick to plain English when writing business communications. You do not want to use words and terms that your reader might not understand; it will only serve to make them feel stupid. Most experts agree that you should try to communicate with other adults both verbally and in writing at about an eighth-grade level.

- Never write or send a communication when you are angry with the reader or others. Hold off a few days and you will usually begin to see the situation in a new or different light. Do not burn your bridges might be a dated cliché, but it is time-tested and advice to practice.

MORE TRICKS FOR WRITING GREAT BUSINESS COMMUNICATIONS
$ ✎

Listed below are a few more great tricks for writing effective and results-oriented business communications.

- Communicate in a writing style and tone that suits who you are and avoid trying to appear or sound like someone else, it will only complicate the task; you will work twice as hard and accomplish half as much by trying to be someone or something that you are not. And worse, this will be reflected in your written communications and easily picked up by readers, especially those who know you.
- Write in short paragraphs using a subheading for each new section. This will ensure that the "skimmers" get the message and stay engaged and interested in your message. Thanks solely to life's hectic pace most people now skim written communications as opposed to reading them word for word. Bold subheadings at the beginning of every paragraph will pull attention to the key messages and benefits that you are trying to relay.
- Write from the reader's point of view and try to anticipate what questions, concerns, and objections the reader might have and answer these throughout your communication. I cannot state the importance of this enough: if you can leave readers satisfied with your primary message then in all likelihood they will respond positively and take the action you want them to take—call, drop in, e-mail, fax, buy, or whatever the desired action might be.
- Make sure that you clearly indicate in your written communications what action you want the reader to take: call me, visit my Web site, or drop by the office for a demonstration. People are not mind readers, nor do they have a crystal ball, you have to let readers know what you want them to do next. This message should be repeated at least two to three times in the body of your communication and again in a postscript.
- Include a postscript in all written communications that restates the main theme of your message and the big benefit the reader will receive by taking action and responding to your communication.

USE TECHNOLOGY TO LEVEL THE PLAYING FIELD
$$$ ✎

Just because you operate a small business from home doesn't mean that you should not streamline your operation by effectively using technology. Take advantage of current technologies to level the playing field with your larger competition and gain wider access to a larger base of potential customers. Create a Web site and use it for marketing and communication purposes. Install an integrated telephone system with features such as voice mail, call forwarding, and fax on demand options. Use wireless devices like cell phones, Palm Pilots, and beepers to stay in contact with clients and prospects at all times. Use laptop computers for presentations, and have your own virtual presentation created and placed on CD-ROM to use as a powerful sales and marketing tool for your small business. And, most important, never stop learning about new technologies, how they work, and how they can be integrated into your business to make your homebased business operation seem taller, larger, and wider just like the competition. Never think that you should wait to invest into technologies because of the myth that as soon as you do, it will be obsolete. Few things ever become obsolete, they only improve over time. Below is a checklist of basic technology tools that can help you succeed in business.

- ❑ Personal computer, software, and printer
- ❑ Modem and Internet connection
- ❑ Business Web site and e-mail

❏ Prospect, sales, and customer management software such as Maximizer

❏ Telephone with features, such as facsimile capabilities, on hold, voice mail, and multiple extensions

❏ Cellular telephone and pager

❏ Digital camera, still and video formats

❏ Portable or notebook computer and computerized palm-held recording and scheduling devices

❏ CD-ROM and DVD rewriters

❏ All-in-one scanner, photocopier, and printer

❏ Microcassette voice recorder

GO FOR THE BIG OPPORTUNITIES
$$ ✎

Don't let the fact that you operate your business from home stop you from going after the big-selling business growth opportunities. You might operate a small homebased business, but your thinking and goals for the future do not have to be small-minded. Adopt a can-do attitude and go after and land the big sales opportunities that can provide a springboard to bigger and better things in the future. Make a conscious effort to land new jobs or sales that were larger than the previous, thus creating a snowball effect that gets larger and larger as it steams down the hill. The more you can demonstrate to your prospects your ability to handle larger jobs or orders, the more confidence they will have in your ability to perform, and the snowball will continue to roll and grow larger with each new or larger account you land. Almost all big businesses started small, but the ones that grew were headed by leaders who were not afraid to chase the big opportunities because they knew that securing these opportunities were the best bet to get them where they wanted to be in the shortest amount of time.

GET CREATIVE WITH APPOINTMENTS AND MEETINGS
$+ ✎

As a general rule, clients, prospects, and sales representatives will feel extremely uncomfortable traipsing through your home for a meeting unless they know you really well. And even then, key meetings and presentations should always be conducted outside of the home office at a suitable location. Here are a few suggestions for conducting appointments and meeting outside of the home office.

- Many business associations such as the Chamber of Commerce rent meeting and boardroom facilities to members who need meeting or presentation space for short periods of time, even by the hour. Check with your local business association to inquire if they provide members this service; if so it may be well worthwhile joining.

- Strike a deal with a key business alliance or supplier so that you can use their office space and meeting facilities when you need to conduct meetings and presentations. Most will be happy to accommodate you, providing that there is something in it for them, such as increased sales, new partnerships, or whatever you can think up.

- Check to see if any restaurants in your local area would be suitable meeting places. Many have small banquet and meeting rooms that can be rented by the hour very inexpensively.

- And finally, take clients to unusual places for meetings; maybe a park, or a boat ride, or even a drive through the country. I used to use my sailboat as a place to conduct meetings and appointments with clients and prospects. Everyone loved it and thought it was a great change of pace and scenery.

REPLACE YOUR COMMUTING TIME WITH PROSPECTING TIME
$ ✎

One of the biggest advantages of working from home is the amount of new time that will be created by not having to spend countless hours every day, week, month, and year commuting to and from an out-of-the-home office. Get the most out of this newfound time by specifically setting it aside for the sole purpose of aggressively prospecting for new business. Imagine what you can accomplish in terms of generating new business if you spend just one hour a day prospecting instead of being stuck in traffic? To really ramp up the effectiveness of this simple yet effective marketing trick, don't reduce the amount of time that you currently devote to prospecting. Instead double your prospecting efforts by adding this newfound time to it, and watch your sales and revenues skyrocket because of the additional prospecting effort. Securing just one new client a week as a result of this technique will multiply into in excess of 50 new clients a year, not even including referral business and additional sources of word-of-mouth advertising that can be gained as a spin-off result. One major key to business success is to always keep your "prospecting pipeline" full and current.

BUILD A TOP-NOTCH TEAM
$$ 🐾

Almost all homebased business owners have one problem in common or a challenge that they face on a daily basis: there is not a support system in place to assist in growing the business and help out in the day-to-day operations of the business. Mid- to large-sized corporations have the benefit of having in-house, or on-hand support staff that most small-business owners cannot afford to pay in the form of employee wages or service retainers. These support people can include public relations people, sales/marketing specialists, bookkeepers and accountants, lawyers, and financial analysts just to mention a few. This is why it is important that you take the time now while your business is small to build a top-notch support team for the eventuality of needing this support team in the future when your business grows. Once again, one common trait of successful businesspeople is that they are proactive and look to the future, rather than react to an event or situation as it may arise. Look to your local community and find out who can help your business grow. Set appointments with these people and let them know what your future business plans are, and the fact that in all likelihood you will be calling on their professional advice, or service in the very near future. The added bonus of conducting such an exercise is

that this will get your name out there regarding what you do and therefore will greatly increase the odds of being referred from the people that you come into contact with during meetings.

THE ART OF MAKING DECISIONS
$ ⚒

One of the most difficult aspects of working from home and being self-employed is having to make all of the decisions in terms of the business. And if that is not difficult enough for some you must also factor in that the decisions you make will often affect your personal and family life as well, further pressuring you to make the right decision. However, making decisions is one of the most important aspects of being self-employed and all business owners must learn to master the art of decision making. Therefore here are a few ideas that you can use to help you master the art of making wise and profitable business decisions.

Don't Have Regrets

Realize that every decision you make will not be a good one; in fact some will be terrible. But fear not as this is called learning by trial and error. Of course the trick is to learn from good and bad decisions equally, and clone only the goods ones and try never to repeat the bad ones. Additionally, never regret bad decisions because all businesspeople have made them, you must be able to learn from it, and move on. If not you'll spend countless hours thinking about what went wrong instead of devising a plan to make it right.

Set a Financial Limit

Set a limit in terms of making money decisions. For instance, any purchasing decisions that require you to spend more than $1,000 must be held off for at least 24 hours. Call this a cooling off or thinking period. Whatever you want to call it in the end it will assist you in making a wise and carefully thought out purchasing decision, instead of a spur of the moment, impulse, or emotional purchasing decision that can do your business and bank account much harm.

Don't Procrastinate

Once you have made a decision to do something don't procrastinate, implement your decision right away. If not, the decision can't be called a final decision, you're still locked in the deciding mode. Talk is cheap, decisions require actions to be called decisions, otherwise they are still talk.

Take Calculated Risks

Never be afraid of making a risky decision as long as you have done your homework and you feel good about the decision. By nature, entrepreneurs are calculated risk takers and that is what separates them from the working masses who fear risk so much that it controls them and instead of them controlling it. Every single successful business is built on a foundation of calculated risks.

Consider the Consequences

Always research major decisions including the opposite reactions that these decisions will have. Remember Newton's third law, "For every action there is an equal and opposite reaction." Just make sure that the equal and opposite reaction to your decision is manageable, meaning carefully consider all of the consequences your decision will have.

Seek Advice

When in doubt seek advice from business colleagues, family, and friends; second opinions are good but never base your decisions on anything but your own final decision. If you do then you'll point fingers at those who made the suggestion if things go bad. Taking responsibility for one's decisions and actions and a willingness to be held personally accountable is another common trait shared by most entrepreneurs.

TARGET YOURSELF
$ ✎

When identifying who your customers will be for your homebased business make sure not to overlook potential prospects like you—people working from a home office and people operating a business from home. You'll find that in most cases other homebased

business owners and workers will be far more open to cold calls and proposals simply due to the fact they share a common bond with you, which of course is working from home. People who work or operate a business from home can understand, relate to, and appreciate the challenges that other homebased business operators face as they struggle daily to build their business and take on larger competitors. Targeting prospects who are like minded can be a powerful icebreaker and a proven way to get a foot in the door. Go online to source and buy mailing lists that specifically include homebased business owners and join homebased business associations such as SOHO (Small Office Home Office). Many homebased business associations like SOHO operate only in the cyber world so you'll be able to network and prospect with other small-business owners right online from home via e-mail and discussion boards.

WEB RESOURCES

⚓ www.soho.org: Small Office Home Office America

⚓ www.soho.ca: Small Office Home Office Canada

PLACE A HIGH PRIORITY ON EVENT MARKETING
$$$ ✎

Exhibiting at tradeshows or industry events or speaking at seminars can all be great ways for homebased business owners to get the word out about their business and help build and maintain a recognizable brand image. Web site, print advertising, direct mail, and other methods of marketing and advertising are great, but like the old saying goes "it's always nice to put a face with the name." Not to mention that event marketing can pay off large generating a mountain of qualified leads in a very short period of time and go a long way to assist in making new and valuable business contacts. I know businesspeople who operate from home and market by no other means than exhibition events and seminars. Some of these same businesses generate revenues in excess of six figures monthly, leaving no doubt as to the validity of placing a high priority on event marketing. Even if you discover that event marketing is out of the financial reach of your business, still be sure to attend trade shows and seminars that are related to your industry and target audience for networking purposes. Get out of the office and network with other businesspeople who can help you grow your business.

WEB RESOURCE

  www.tradeshows.com: Online directory listing trade show and exhibition events indexed by geographical location.

TAKE ADVANTAGE OF ALL AVAILABLE RESOURCES
$ ⚒

Be like the neighbor who has nothing but needs everything and learn to master the art of taking advantage of all available resources that are around you. This is especially important information for homebased business owners operating on very tight financial budgets. Take inventory of what you currently have and write it down in one column. Then create a second column comprising things that you need in order to increase sales and revenues. Once you have created the list set about identifying those who can help supply things on your list. If a PowerPoint projection system would assist in presentations then find out which one of your business alliances or suppliers has one that you can borrow. Or maybe additional warehousing space is needed but not in the budget; call friends to see who has an empty garage or basement that they're willing to let you use. Writer and director Robert Rodriguez describes in his book *Rebel Without A Crew* how he followed this system of listing resources he had and resources he needed to make his film *El Mariachi*. By doing so he was able to get what resources he needed from friends, family, and his entire town to make his first feature film on a budget of less than $10,000. *El Mariachi* went on to eventually gross millions of dollars and was responsible for launching his career. Needless to say a valuable lesson can be learned from his experience in taking advantage of the resources that are around you. People want to help other people succeed; it's human nature. However, don't forget to thank the people who helped you get to the top once you reach the top.

LIMIT THE NUMBER OF HATS YOU WEAR
$$+ ⚒

It is difficult for most business owners not to take a hands-on approach and try to do as much as possible and tackle as many tasks as possible in terms of operating their businesses. However, you have to look beyond today to determine what is in the best interests of the business and yourself over the long run. Farm out duties and chores that you know you are not well equipped to handle and that would be better handled by an expert in that specific field or area of business. Yes there is a cost in doing so; there are no free lunches in this world. But the cost of trying to do something that you know little if anything about could wind up being substantially higher through lost sales or through not getting the desired results that you want and need. As an example, don't stuff and mail envelopes if your specialty is prospecting and sales. Hire out envelope-stuffing to someone, and in most cases you'll find that by sticking to your specialty, you'll generate far more revenues and profits than what you'll spend in farming out some of the more mundane and unproductive tasks associated with operating your business. Likewise if copy writing is not something that comes naturally to you then hire a professional to create advertising and catalog copy for you.

CREATE POLICIES JUST LIKE THE BIG COMPANIES
$$ ⚒ 🐾

Even if your business only employs one person, namely you, still make sure to create policies just like the big companies. What are your service guarantees or product warranties? What is your product return and money back policy? What is your policy in terms of dealing with negative publicity in the unfortunate event that you suddenly are steamrolled with some? What are your employment and termination policies in case you find yourself hastily hiring employees to help meet a sudden demand in new business? These are just a few policies to consider; there are many more. But what is important is that you preidentify and develop policies that will help your business grow and prosper if not today then tomorrow. Not having policies in place can have potentially devastating effects depending on the circumstances and the time, money, and resources that it will take to address them as they arise. In business it is always better to be proactive and plan for the unforeseen and for the future, rather then reactive as needs or challenges arise. You should be able to answer every challenge or inquiry with a definitive answer, one that represents the policy of your business.

BECOME A SHAMELESS SELF-PROMOTER
$ ⚒

The greatest and generally the most underutilized marketing tool that you have to promote your home-based business is you. Become a shameless promoter of the goods or services that you sell by creating unique promotions, seeking publicity, and building a network of other people who believe strongly enough in your business that they too will become supporters and shamelessly help spread the word for you via word-of-mouth advertising. Never stop asking everyone who you come into contact with for new business. This simple trick works because the worst you'll ever hear is "no," which is usually a "yes" once you dig a little deeper to expose and understand your prospect's true needs and the obstacle that stands between you and a yes. Success never happens by accident or a lucky break, success is always a result of planning, hard work, and tireless promotion. Marketing success is always temporary; it's like a steam engine going uphill and the moment you slow down with stoking the promotional boiler, the engine begins to sputter, and the moment you stop promoting entirely, even if only briefly, the engine stalls and begins to roll backward.

BUILD THROUGH BARTER CLUBS
$$ ⚒

Business barter clubs can be valuable sources of new contacts and business opportunities, especially for small-business and homebased business owners with limited marketing budgets and limited time for prospecting and networking. Business barter clubs have been around for decades, but have really taken off in popularity with small-business owners in the past few years. For those not familiar with the business barter club concept, they are simply clubs that enable members (business owners) to freely trade goods and service among each other for goods and services they may need for business or even personally. Usually no money changes hands with these transactions, just a trade of goods and services. However, these business relationships often extend beyond the club and alliances are formed between members to create or seek new business opportunities that will be mutually beneficial. Additionally, not all members accept full "barter-or-swap" payments for products and services, some work on a part-barter, part-cash payment basis.

WEB RESOURCES

- www.barter-bay.com: Local, national, and international online barter club.
- www.barternews.com: *Barter News* is an online magazine dedicated to the world of business barter clubs, organizations, and industry information.

GOALS NEED TO BE ON PAPER
$ ⚒

Many believe that if you can think it, then you can do it; I happen to agree with this simple premise. However, if you can think it, that also means that you can forget it. The following are reasons you should write down your goals.

- It gives you something to use as a yardstick to measure progress and success. Otherwise, you will never know if you are getting close or are on track with reaching your goals.
- It helps to better organize and implement action plans to realize your goals. Goals are great, but you have to have a plan in place that will clearly indicate how you will reach your goals and when.

- It increases your effectiveness by being able to focus on results that serve only to get you closer to your goals. Additionally you will save time by knowing where you want to get to and how you will get there.
- It reduces stress, worry, and frustration. Think about it, if you do not know where you are going, how you will get there, and why you are doing it, then this can be very stressful. What's it all for? Goals clearly answer that question.
- It builds self-confidence and vision for the future.
- It reduces internal conflicts in making decisions that will affect your short- and long-term future. You can weigh the decision against your goals to see how they correspond, or if the decision will get you one step closer or one step farther away from your goals. If your goal is to make an extra $10,000 this year then the decision to make one extra prospecting call each day becomes an easy one.
- It helps you to stay on track and motivates you to reach for something you want and gives you the ability to focus your creativity, ingenuity, and hard work on reaching them.
- It increases your enthusiasm for what you are doing, especially as you begin to move toward what you seek. Once you see proof that setting goals and working to realize them is working for you then you will work harder and smarter to reach your goals, and have a lot more fun doing it.
- It gives you the ability to control your future and the discipline to see it through.

BENEFIT BY BEING FLEXIBLE
$$ ✎

One of the most powerful marketing tools that homebased business owners enjoy, that businesses that operate from a fixed location do not, is flexibility. You have the flexibility to meet customer's individual specific needs and benefit because of it. The mass marketing model of squeezing everyone through a funnel and into the same box that was developed in the '70s and continued into the '80s and '90s is drawing to a close for all but big-box retailers. In the new millennium customers want to be viewed and treated as individuals. Which in turn means that in order to provide this service and meet the demand, you must be flexible. Once again, this is an area where homebased business owners have a competitive advantage over much of their larger and more "structure-restricted" competition. Make a pledge to your customers that you will structure your operation and how you deliver goods and services to them around what they deem to be the most important and beneficial to their individual and specific needs. And best of all, in doing so not only will you impress clients and prospects, but also you will be able to charge a premium, or at the least easily justify your prices, because of your individual and unique customer care policy.

GREAT TIPS TO INCREASE YOUR PRODUCTIVITY IN THE HOME OFFICE
$+ ✎

Increased personal productivity can help you achieve profitability by accomplishing more in less time, and with that said here are some great tips that you can employ to increase your productivity in the home office.

Invest in the Right Tools

The first rule of increasing productivity in the home office is to have the right tools to do the job. Therefore make an investment in office and business equipment and supplies that will enable you to be 100 percent effective and productive. Having to remove your client files from the kitchen table every time a family member wants to eat is not making the best use of your time. Likewise, running down to your local printing center and using their fax machine to send and receive a fax is also not a very effective time management strategy. Invest in the tools that you need in order to be more productive and therefore profitable. Don't fret if your budget is tight; office and business equipment can be leased or rented. Or, good quality equipment can usually be purchased at auction and liquidation sales for a fraction of the cost new.

Take Some Time Off

To increase productivity get in the habit of scheduling personal time for yourself, time away from your business and office. This is very important because "small business burn out" is caused largely due to the fact that as a small-business operator you are one person who does the work of many people and puts in long hours to stay on top of it all. However, the downside of trying to stay on top of it all can be small business burn out which is one of the fastest ways to become ineffective and less productive; therefore time away from the office is rewarded with increased productivity in the office. Additionally make it a personal goal to stay fit and healthy. If you do not feel good physically or mentally it is very difficult to be 100 percent effective and productive. Eat right, get lots of sleep, and start and maintain a regular physical exercise program; even a mere 20 minutes a day will suffice.

Work from One Calendar

Create a single calendar to work from, not multiple sets for individual tasks or jobs. Your single calendar should also incorporate your family schedule as well as your own personal time off so that each do not inadvertently overlap when scheduling. Also try to create a to-do list each evening for the next day's activities and start your new to-do list for the following day in the morning and build it throughout the day on one single sheet of paper or electronic organizer, allowing enough expansion room as your list grows. Working from a single well-reviewed scheduling calendar and daily to-do list as opposed to multiple calendars and lists is perhaps one of the best ways to increase productivity and reduce duplication of tasks.

Get Appointment Savvy

Carefully plan your appointments out of the office and for other business-related matters so that you can minimize such things as needlessly waiting in rush hour traffic or standing in long bank and post office lines around lunch time. Also be sure to plan out-of-office client meetings in blocks of time such as an entire morning, afternoon, or the entire day to reduce the amount of time wasted driving back and forth to your office only to have to leave a half hour later for the next appointment. Likewise confirm appointments twice, a few days prior to the appointment and again before you leave the office for the appointment. A telephone call takes but a moment, but hours can be wasted fighting traffic only to arrive and find out that the person you were scheduled to meet with is not available for whatever reason.

Supply and Delivery Tips

Install a whiteboard or blackboard on the office wall and keep an ongoing list of supplies that are running low so you can purchase these supplies once a week or month to ensure that you never run out. Dashing down to the office supply store in the middle of the day to pick up a printer cartridge so you can get a proposal finished can end up taking an hour or more if traffic is snarled. Do it a few times a month and over the course of a year you will lose a week's worth of productivity. Also try to have deliveries to your home office arranged to be dropped off on the same day so you are not tied down and left waiting on multiple days out of the week. And get in the habit of logging all ordering information in a spiral notebook including contact names, dates, and times so that if a problem arises on delivery day it will only take a few moments to sort out and not days' worth of telephone tag and waiting on hold.

Simple E-mail Tips to Increase Productivity

Use e-mail autoreponders as a way to reduce the amount of time you spend responding to low-priority e-mails. But always try to respond to all e-mails you receive within 24 hours, as this will go a long way to help build a sense of credibility and reliability with your clients and suppliers alike. Also set up various e-mail accounts as a way to determine importance and priority of incoming messages. Such as customer service@yourmail, newcustomerinquirery@yourmail, order@yourmail, and so on. Keep all e-mails in your in-basket until you have had the opportunity to read, respond to, or delete them. And, set a block of time aside each day to deal with e-mail communications all at once instead of multiple times that can distract from other work. Additionally, be sure to print the most important e-mails and keep a paper record in your client files.

Establish a Primary Workstation

Establish a primary workstation in your home office for working on client projects and other key "money-making" projects and a secondary workstation for lesser things such as mail sorting, filing, and general administrative work. Separate workstations will help you to stay organized and focused on the areas of your business that make you money, while still keeping other required business activities organized but secondary in priority. Also be sure to invest in a good paper-filing system so you can spend more time working on a client's file and less time looking for a client's file. Perhaps creating a system using color-coded files to indicate the projects of the highest priority, such as red for "must do now" down to blue for the least important tasks to be completed. Likewise purge your paper file and electronic files of outdated or irrelevant information on a monthly basis. Amazingly enough, 80 percent of what we store or file for business will never be read or needed again.

Ergonomically Correct

Ensure that your office and work space are ergonomically designed for maximum productivity. Ergonomics and medical experts agree that this can increase productivity and quality of work by as much as 20 percent per annum. Invest in books that will explain the finer points or ergonomics considerations such as chair and seating position, eyes and lighting, upper body position, and monitor and keyboard position. Proper ergonomic office design and layout will create a healthful and productive work environment.

Telephone Efficiency

To increase productivity and save time, plan your telephone calls before you make them, know what you want to ask and what you want to accomplish. This will greatly reduce the amount of time you spend on the phone and the amount of calls you

make back to the party to get additional information you didn't get the first time around. Also create a system for making telephone calls wherein you set aside blocks of time each day for specific calls such as follow-up, prospecting, and administrative-related calls. Bouncing back and forth with no focus can really chew up time and make you unproductive and not very effective. Likewise when you leave a voice-mail message, give the person you are calling a specific time range and day they can call you back when you will be in the office such as "I'll be in the office Tuesday morning between nine and eleven. Can you please call me then?" This will greatly reduce the amount of time you spend engaged in telephone tag. Additionally, turn on the answering machine when you are buried in a project with a specific deadline, but make your message as professional and promotional as possible. Get back to callers within the same day if possible and never longer than 24 hours.

Learn to Delegate and Say No

If you have employees, willing family members, or suppliers who are able to help out in terms of your workload then don't be afraid to ask for help. Or better, learn to delegate as many of the mundane or low-priority business and administrative tasks as you can or that others are happily willing to handle for you. Also learn to say no; no matter how hard saying no is. Nothing will kill productivity as fast as taking on too much work and spreading yourself too thin, or saying yes to work-related projects that you know nothing about and therefore cannot effectively complete for a profit. Saying yes too often is one of the biggest challenges faced by small-business owners, and one of the most difficult to overcome and correct. Likewise be sure to invest in a $1 "do not disturb" sign for your office door or make a pact with family members that if your door is closed you are working and do not wish to be disturbed. Even the most basic interruptions to a work routine can cause mayhem in a daily schedule and drastically reduce productivity.

Get Organized

Set aside specific times of the week that you open all mail, pay all bills, and complete all administrative paperwork. This simple trick can save a huge amount of time when factored over a yearlong period. And of course this extra time can be put to good use on other more important money-making initiatives such as prospecting and client follow-up. Also try to set aside an open time slot each day, perhaps 20 minutes in the middle of the day so that you can deal with unexpected or last minute crises that arise or special client requests. Prescheduling this extra small block of time will reduce stress and enable you to be productive; if nothing arises then use this time on things that will benefit you the most, such as prospecting and follow-up. And finally, banish all personal items such as the basketball, brochures on your forthcoming trip to Jamaica, or last week's newspaper from your workspace. More often than not access to personal items will only work against you as a temptation that quickly gets picked up and studied, thus turning into a full-on, time-wasting distraction. Always strive to keep your office and work space clean and clutter free.

WEB RESOURCE

- www.maximizer.com: Sales and client management software.

- www.autoresponders.com: Online directory listing various autoresponder programs and services.

- www.mailloop.com: E-mail and e-business automation and autorepsond software.

- www.ergonomics.org: Online ergonomics information, articles, and links.

📖 SUGGESTED ADDITIONAL READING

Barrett, Niall. *The Custom Home Office: Building a Complete Workspace*. Newtown, CT: Taunton Press, 2002.

Carter, David. *American Corporate Identity*. New York: Hearst Books International, 2003.

Edwards, Paul, Sarah Edwards, and Peter Economy. *Home-Based Business for Dummies*. New York: John Wiley & Sons, 2000.

Gleeson, Kerry. *The Personal Efficiency Program: How to Get Organized to Do More Work in Less Time*. New York: John Wiley & Sons, 2000.

Hayden, C. J. *Get Clients Now: A 28-Day Marketing Program for Professionals and Consultants*. New York: AMACOM, 1999.

Miller, Steve. *How To Get The Most Out of Trade Shows*. New York: McGraw-Hill, 2000.

Silber, Lee T. *Self-Promotion for the Creative Person: Get the Word Out About Who You Are and What You Do*. New York: Crown Publishing, 2001.

Smith, Douglas K. *Make Success Measurable: A Mindbook-Workbook for Setting Goals and Taking Action*. New York: John Wiley & Sons, 1999.

Steingold, Fred S. *Legal Guide for Starting & Running a Small Business*. Berkeley, CA: Nolo Press, 2001.

Von Oech, Roger. *A Whack on The Side of The Head: How You Can Be More Creative*. New York: Warner Books, 1998.

ADVERTISING, DIRECT MARKETING, AND TELEMARKETING
Marketing Tips for Your Business

A headline should single out your prospect like a bellhop
paging a man in a crowded hotel lobby.

—CLAUDE HOPKINS

WHY ADVERTISE?

$ 🔨

The following was created by the Michigan Directory Company to promote their publication Home Town Directories. This humorous yet very accurate message clearly demonstrates the importance of advertising. A man wakes up in the morning after sleeping on an advertised bed, in advertised pajamas. He will bathe in an advertised tub, wash with advertised soap, shave with advertised shaving cream, eat a breakfast of advertised juice, cereal, and toast that was toasted in an advertised toaster. He will put on advertised clothes, glance at his advertised wristwatch, and then ride to his office in his advertised car. At the office he will sit at his advertised desk, in his advertised chair, and write with his advertised pen. Yet this man hesitates to advertise, saying that advertising doesn't pay. Finally when his business fails, he will advertise it for sale. Still not convinced of the power of advertising? Then consider the old newspaper story. The first time people look at an advertisement, they don't see it. The second time they look at an ad, they don't notice it. The third time, they become conscious of the ad's existence. The fourth time, they vaguely remember seeing the ad somewhere before. The tenth time, they think someday I am going to buy that. The 20th time they see the ad, they finally get in their cars and head down to the store to buy what was in the ad. Through constant exposure advertising builds awareness and influences consumer buying habits, period.

TAKE A DESKTOP PUBLISHING COURSE

$$ 📞

Taking a basic desktop publishing course will certainly not make you a professional graphic designer, but it will enable you to design simple, yet extremely useful printed promotional materials for your business. Beginner desktop publishing courses are available in just about every community across the nation, either through community colleges or private institutions and tutors. Generally these courses are held nights and weekends and span only a couple of weeks and cost only a few hundred dollars—money that can be easily and quickly recouped by designing your own printed promotional materials instead of paying the printer to do it for you. Likewise, desktop publishing software is widely available and the competition in the marketplace has driven the price of these programs to a level that makes them very affordable for every budget level. Adobe and Corel desktop publishing programs are regarded as the best and most user-friendly in the industry. If you're not yet convinced, consider these additional reasons listed below and I am sure that you will agree that taking a basic desktop publishing course makes good business sense.

Save Money

Artwork and layout is very costly; in fact most commercial printers charge in the range of $60 to $80 an hour for graphic design services to create marketing materials like brochures, newsletters, and other printed items commonly used for small-business promotion. But taking a desktop publishing course can put that money back in your pocket and to better use on other marketing efforts. Yes your time is also valuable and has to be factored in, but instead of spending the evening in front of the television, why not put that time to better use creating powerful marketing materials for your business? You can if you have the basic skills and knowledge to do so.

Experiment

Imagine that one day you can design, print, and test a two-for-one coupon offer, the next day a tips sheet, the following day a customer appreciation gift voucher, the sky is the limit. Having the equipment and skills needed to produce your own promotional materials gives you the ability to experiment with various print marketing tools until you find the right mix without having to break the bank getting these materials printed professionally every time you want to experiment with a new marketing message or printed medium.

Professionalism

Imagine being able to print the name of your customer right on gift certificates and other promotional materials, all with the simple click of a mouse? You can if you have the skills and equipment to do so. Personalize every correspondence with your best customers: homemade thank-you notes, greeting cards, and more that have been individually created with the customer in mind instead of a broad, generic, unappealing message. Now that is powerful marketing and customer appreciation.

Timely

Get your message out the same day, sometimes within the same hour if you choose. No working with the printer's schedule and making numerous trips back and forth to proofread and sign off on artwork. Have a hot idea for a special offer? Get it in front of your customers in a flash, or change an existing offer or message in the matter of minutes. Having the ability to design and print your own marketing materials can save you time and more importantly enables you to react quickly to changing offers or a promotional message.

Freedom

For me one of the best aspects about being my own boss is the freedom. Freedom to make decisions, freedom to devise and implement a plan, and freedom to write my own paycheck based on my abilities rather than a time clock. Therefore having the freedom to design my own basic promotional materials fits in with my plan. I don't like to wait, I want to have the ability to react right away to a good idea, and I want to be able to test my ideas without having to spend a small fortune in layout and artwork charges to do it. Experimenting and having the freedom to do it is great, but make sure you have someone else proofread your homegrown print materials.

WEB RESOURCES

⚲ www.corel.com: Corel, a leading software development company with numerous desktop publishing products for a wide variety of user applications.

⚲ www.adobe.com: Adobe, a leading software development company with numerous desktop publishing products for a wide variety of user applications.

WASTED ADVERTISING

$ ⚒

Advertising will not put money in your business bank account; it is the follow-up to advertising that will. Yes advertising can make the telephone ring, motivate people to come to your store, and drive them online and to your Web site, but all of that will be for nothing unless you are prepared to sell your advertising. Being prepared to sell your advertising means many things such as: Is your sales force trained and armed with the tools they need to turn those advertising inquires into profitable sales? Have you created a system to capture every advertising inquiry and turn it into a prospect database so that you can forge long-term customer relationships? Is your store stocked with a wide selection of inventory, clean, and geared up with customer conveniences and service solutions ready to go and to handle the onslaught of new business your advertising might generate? Have you completely debugged your Web site and is it ready for optimum performance to turn visitors into paying customers? And are all employees trained and armed with the information and tools they need to overcome prospect concerns and objections? These are only a few things to consider prior to running that first advertisement, or continuing with an established advertising campaign. The objective is to maximize every single dollar you spend on advertising by being 100 percent prepared to sell and to turn every prospect into a lifetime customer. If not, you can advertise till the cows come home and it will not put money in the bank and it will be of no value and serve no purpose.

MEDIA QUESTIONNAIRE

$+ ⚒

Knowing what your customers and target audience like to read, watch, and listen to is important information to have so you can create an advertising campaigned that is directly aimed at reaching them. But how do you find out this sort of information? There are a few ways, but perhaps the easiest is to create a simple media question and ask your current customers to kindly complete the questionnaire; also ask people who fit your target audience who are not currently customers, but who you would like to become customers. Asking existing customers to complete the questionnaire is pretty straightforward. You can give it to them in person, fax it to them, mail it to them, or take advantage of your opt-in list and e-mail it to them. In terms of your target audience who are not currently customers, you will have to be a little more innovative about how you get the questionnaire to them and how you motivate them to complete it. This could be accomplished in a number of ways including setting up a survey booth in a mall or other high traffic area and giving away a small gift to people who will take the time to complete the questionnaire; block geographic areas in a city or community and mail or hand deliver the questionnaire to homes along with a prestamped response envelope and a discount coupon that is redeemable toward the purchase of products or services. A sample media questionnaire that you can use as a guideline to create one suitable for your business and advertising objectives is on pages 110–112.

TURN ALL BUSINESS MAILINGS INTO SALES TOOLS

$ ⚒

You're paying for the postage anyway, so you may as well get as much marketing mileage as you can out of all your monthly business mailings. Print an extra paragraph on each sales invoice you send out to customers stating a incredible monthly offer, or add a brief marketing message headline on the outside of your envelope. These are soft-sell techniques that reinforce your company's business and statement of purpose in a positive way. Think of how many hands an envelope or invoice can pass through before the person who pays the bills receives it, and multiply that by the number of mailings you send out in any

Sample Media Questionnaire

(Your business name here)

We kindly ask that you take a moment to complete the following media questionnaire. Your responses will be used to help us serve our customers' needs better. Thank you.

Newspapers

Please list any newspapers that you typically read along with your favorite section.

	Subscription	Favorite Section
1. _____	Yes ❑ No ❑	_____
2. _____	Yes ❑ No ❑	_____
3. _____	Yes ❑ No ❑	_____

Magazines

Please list any magazines that you typically read.

	Subscription
1. _____	Yes ❑ No ❑
2. _____	Yes ❑ No ❑
3. _____	Yes ❑ No ❑

Special Interest Publications

Please list any special interest publications such as trade journals, newsletters, or reports that you frequently read.

	Subscription
1. _____	Yes ❑ No ❑
2. _____	Yes ❑ No ❑
3. _____	Yes ❑ No ❑

Radio

Please list any radio stations that you typically listen to and any specific programs that you try not to miss.

	Program
1. _____	_____
2. _____	_____
3. _____	_____

Where do you typically listen to the radio?

❑ Home

❑ Car

❑ Office

❑ All

Sample Media Questionnaire, continued

What time of the day would you typically be listening to the radio?

❏ 6:00 A.M.–9:00 A.M.　　　　　　　　　❏ 3:00 P.M.–6:00 P.M.

❏ 9:00 A.M.–12:00 Noon　　　　　　　　❏ 6:00 P.M.–9:00 P.M.

❏ 12:00 Noon–3:00 P.M.　　　　　　　　 ❏ After 9:00 P.M.

Television

Please list any television stations that you typically watch and any specific programs that you try not to miss.

　　　　　　　　　　　　　　　　　　　　　　　　Program

1. _____　　　_____

2. _____　　　_____

3. _____　　　_____

What time of day do you typically watch television?

❏ 6:00 A.M.–9:00 A.M.　　　　　　　　　❏ 3:00 P.M.–6:00 P.M.

❏ 9:00 A.M.–12:00 Noon　　　　　　　　❏ 6:00 P.M.–9:00 P.M.

❏ 12:00 Noon–3:00 P.M.　　　　　　　　 ❏ After 9:00 P.M.

Which news program do you watch and at what time?

Program: _____

❏ Morning　　　　　　　　　　　　　　❏ Diner Hour

❏ Noon　　　　　　　　　　　　　　　　❏ Late Night

Internet

Are you currently connected to the Internet?

❏ Yes　　　　　　　　　　　　　　　　　❏ No

What search engine do you use to find information, products, and services online?

❏ AOL　　　　　　　　　　　　　　　　❏ MSN

❏ Google　　　　　　　　　　　　　　　❏ AltaVista

❏ Yahoo!　　　　　　　　　　　　　　　❏ Other _____

Do you receive or subscribe to any online or electronic publications? If so please list.

_____

_____

_____

_____

_____

_____

Sample Media Questionnaire, *continued*

What is the most common type of Web site you visit?

❏ General News

❏ Financial News

❏ Sports

❏ Shopping

❏ Entertainment

❏ Travel

❏ Other _____

General Questions

What type of advertising has the most influence on your buying decisions/habits?

❏ Newspaper

❏ Magazine

❏ Radio

❏ Television

❏ Internet

❏ Other _____

Have you ever purchased anything through mail order?

❏ Yes

❏ No

Do you belong to any shopping clubs such as a music club, book club, etc.? Please specify.

1. _____

2. _____

3. _____

Do you receive any product catalogs? If so, which ones?

1. _____

2. _____

3. _____

Do you clip coupons and special offers out of newspapers and magazines?

❏ Always

❏ Sometimes

❏ Rarely

❏ Never

What do you do with the advertisements you receive in the mail?

❏ Read and save

❏ Read and trash

❏ Straight to the trash without reading

❏ Other _____

Thank you for your cooperation, we appreciate it.

given month. You'll quickly discover that you can send a marketing message for free that can reach an additional 100 people or more every month by doing nothing more than paying your bills or sending out account statements and general business correspondents. Additionally, for any special offers or information that are more than a sentence or paragraph long don't be afraid to include a company promotional brochure in with all your mailings. Remember it's the sum of the parts that creates the whole for a successful marketing program, so no worthwhile effort can be discounted as trivial.

TRICKS FOR CREATING GREAT ADVERTISING COPY

In writing good advertising copy the headline is king. Later in this chapter you will discover some great tricks for writing attention grabbing headlines that pull your target audience into your marketing message. Great advertising or marketing copy is needed for more than just print advertisements. You need clever and convincing copy for brochures, fliers, catalogs, and every other medium that communicates your marketing message with your customers and prospects. Like all advertising, great copy should do four things: grab attention, build interest, create desire, and force the reader to take action. This is commonly referred to in advertising as AIDA, an acronym for attention, interest, desire, and action. Below you will find a few tricks for creating great advertising and marketing copy.

A Single Clear Message

Great advertising copy starts by presenting a singular straightforward message that is simplistic and above all clear. Keep your copy short, to the point, and everything you say should support your headline or your focal point message. If the main thrust of your message is price, then your copy should reflect this by supporting your focal message. Likewise, if your main marketing thrust is customer service then your copy should support your main message. This is referred to as your unique selling proposition (USP), which is your statement about why people

should buy what you are selling instead or what the competition is selling. Your USP or competitive advantage should underscore all your marketing activities including creating copy.

Appeal to Your Audience

Emotional triggers—things that all humans feel and need—are very powerful advertising copy tools. Things such as the need for friendship, the need for security, the need to achieve, the need for education, or the need to lead are emotional triggers. These are only a few and there are many more emotional triggers that can be appealed to. The objective is to relate an emotional trigger or need to what you are selling. For instance, a home alarm company can appeal to the need for physical or property security in their advertisements while a financial consultant would appeal to people's need for financial security in their advertisements. Likewise, a university would try to appeal to the need to achieve and learn in their advertisements. Figure out what emotional trigger is best suited for your goods or services and then build a unique selling message around the need.

Develop a Consistent Theme and Style

Develop a central theme and personality and consistently use your theme or personality in all of your advertising and marketing copy. Consistency is one of the key, if not the most important, requirements for building brand name recognition and awareness. Changing the way your ads look and read and the way your supporting marketing materials look and read will only confuse your target audience and customers. Develop a central theme and stick to it throughout all your advertising and marketing activities.

Credibility Counts

A key aspect for creating great copy is to back up your claims with facts and proof, as you always want your ads and copy to come off as credible and believable. If you say you are number one at providing customer service then tell people how you got there; if you state your quality is unsurpassed then back this up with facts that reveal why. And if you say that people benefit from doing business with you then clearly spell out the benefits they receive. As a whole we are a society of doubting Thomases. The more that you strive to eliminate doubt and fear, the more people will be open to receiving your marketing message. If you fail to back up your advertising claims with credible proof and evidence then the power and effectiveness of your marketing message is greatly if not entirely diminished, it's just that simple. Refer to the advertising believability checklist in this chapter for more great ideas about how you can make your advertising and copy more credible and believable.

Supply Ample Motivation

In your advertising and supporting marketing material motivate your customers and target audience to take action. You can accomplish this by adding a deadline to your main offer to create a sense of urgency. Or by boosting the appeal of your offer with tactics such as extended warranty offers, free delivery, or some other form of freebie—a price discount or increased value techniques such as two-for-ones and upgraded features at no additional cost.

Keep Your "Drivers" in Mind

When creating ad and marketing copy always keep what drives your customers and target audience to buy in mind and in your headlines and copy. Do they shop or buy based on convenience, image, price, value, quality, or service? These are called consumer drivers and are culled from psychographics market segmenting and customer profiling. Your copy must single out and talk directly to your target audience in the same way that they would think and act. That is what great copy does; it makes your target audience feel as though you are talking to them directly as an individual while reaching the masses.

Project a Professional Image

As mentioned above, invest in basic computer equipment and software that will enable you to create great-looking marketing tools such as presentations, catalogs, fliers, brochures, and advertisements. Likewise, invest in the time necessary to learn how to use this software so that your marketing materials will look professional and highly polished. Professional image is one of the many elements that go into creating great copy.

Pricing Sensitivities

Unless you have some really big news to reveal in terms of price then underplay its involvement in your copy. The problem is that pricing issues can become very complex thus destroying the first rule of creating great copy, which is to keep it simple. Secondly, consumers are not wowed by 10 percent off or even 25 percent off, it has become too commonplace; we expect sales to be spectacular events of 50 percent off or more. Consequently, offering 10 percent is no motivation nor is it likely to get your ad noticed.

Always Ask for the Sale

Regardless of the medium, all great copy asks for the sale, always. Never assume that your reader will know what to do next, tell them what to do and tell them to buy. Come to the store, drop by the showroom, visit the Web site, call and order now—your wording will be in direct relationship to what you want readers to do. Your call to action and asking for the sale should be visible in your copy and repeated throughout two or more times. When space will allow and you can keep your copy and the presentation looking professional also include additional information that will motivate prospects to take action, such as store and office hours, location, and types of payments accepted. Also use words and phrases that are designed to grab attention and persuade people to buy, such as free, clearance, and quality. At the end of this chapter you will find the 200 most persuasive words to use in advertising and marketing copy.

DEVELOP A UNIQUE HOOK
$+ ✎ ☎

What can you do so that your advertisements grab attention, are memorable, and separate your business and advertising messages from the thousands of other advertising messages out there? One solution is to develop a interesting and unique hook that can be used in all forms of advertising that you may participate in—radio, print, television, and Internet. The next question would be what kind of unique hook could you create? Much of that will greatly depend on the type of business you operate, your industry, and the products and services you sell. But perhaps the easiest way to get thinking about ways to create unique advertising hooks is to conduct a brainstorming session with your employees, suppliers, or even friends and family members so that collectively you can toss around some ideas that could eventually lead to a unique hook being created. As a catalyst to getting you thinking about what type of advertising hook would be right for your business, I have given a few ideas below. However, keep in mind that the success of the hook you create will depend on factors such as repetitious use of the hook, consistency using the hook, using advertising media aimed at your target market, and, of course, budget considerations.

Mascots and Characters

A common advertising hook is to develop a mascot or character, like Charlie the Tuna for Starkist or Ronald McDonald for McDonald's. The character or mascot you create can be living or a drawing or cartoon character. Once again, the key is to develop a character that is relevant to your business and what you do as well as a central marketing message or slogan that your mascot or character can consistently use in all forms of advertising. The owner of a flooring center close to my home has developed a character referred to as the "King of Floors," which is the owner dressed in a medieval king's costume; he uses this character throughout all of his advertising. Additionally he also uses a mascot, which is a dog he refers to as "Sir Scruffy." As kooky and goofy as this may seem to be, it works well for his particular business; in fact you cannot escape his ads, they are on local television, radio, and just about every type of print publication in the area. His store is busy and much of this success can be directly contributed to his advertising campaign with a unique hook and of course the fact that he is consistent in the ads and repetitious in their delivery.

Themes

You can also develop a central theme into a unique advertising hook and once again use this theme hook throughout your entire advertising campaign. Themes could range from sporting themes to space themes to jungle themes to old west themes; it really is endless when you consider how many various themes can be created and turned into a hook. However, as a caution make sure that you do not base your entire theme-advertising campaign on a fad, such as a hot movie at the box office or popular television show or personality—once these fads are over you will have to re-create your entire advertising hook and lose the forward momentum you have built to date. You can tie popular fads in with your advertisements, but make sure they enhance your central and consistent hook and are secondary to the main theme.

Music and Jingles

Can't get that silly little radio jingle out of your head? Well it must be doing what it was designed to do then—hook you! Radio jingles work well to make your business memorable to a radio listening audience. In fact, great jingles can transcend time; many of us still remember advertising jingles we heard 10, 20, and even 30 years ago. And even more important we remember exactly what the jingle was advertising. Memorable jingles, background music, and music soundtracks are another fantastic way to create a unique advertising hook; it won't do you much good for print ads but for radio and television it is one of the best unique hooks to create.

Spokesperson

And finally another great way to create a unique hook for your advertising campaigns is to enlist the services of a spokesperson. The spokesperson does not necessarily have to be famous or a household name, just a recognizable figure in the geographic area in which you do business and in which you will be running your advertising campaign. For instance, a handyman with a locally produced and aired television show or newspaper column would make a good advertising spokesperson for a hardware store, customer home builder, or renovation contractor.

Likewise a local athlete, amateur or professional, would make a good advertising spokesperson for a fitness center, athletic shoe store, or sporting goods store.

HOW-TO HEADLINES
$ ⚒

If you subscribe to the "Pareto Principle," better known as the 80/20 rule, then you already know and believe that 80 percent of the time you spend creating an advertisement should be spent on crafting an attention-grabbing headline while the remaining 20 percent should be dedicated to the balance of the advertisement and marketing message. It's a fact that you only have a passing second to grab a reader's attention. That's why a bold, powerful headline that pulls a reader's attention and interest into your article, advertisement, press release, or any other type of printed promotional material is so vital in terms of marketing effectiveness. One of the best headlines to use is a "How-To," which can deliver a powerful, beneficial, and clear message in few words. For instance, a realtor might use "How to buy a home with no money down." Or, a publisher of business opportunity information might use "How to earn $1,000 a week from home!" The best aspects of the how-to headline are that they deliver the message efficiently, have dream appeal, or solve a problem, and there is no guessing what the content of the message or advertisement is about from the reader's perspective. Of note though, the fact remains that a headline in a "how-to" format must still speak to your target audience, or the largest segment of your target audience in order for the headline to work as you wish it to. In both examples above, the "how-to" headlines speak directly to the intended target audience—people with restrictive budgets who want to buy a home and people who desire to work at home. Above all the headline must motivate the reader to take a sincere interest in your message and dive in to find out more.

MAKE A PROMISE IN YOUR HEADLINE
$ ⚒

Make a promise in your headline to stand out in the sea of advertisements and grab the attention of readers, "If it's not in stock you get it for free!" or "We will not be undersold!" The promise you make will be reflective of your business, your marketing objective, and the message you want to send or perhaps the action or response you want the reader to take. The best headline promises to make are ones that specifically solve a customer's problem or meet a need. For that reason before you make a promise you have to identify exactly what your customers need or in a broader sense what your target audience's needs and wants are, then deliver this solution to them in the form of a bold advertising "promise" headline. Another example of a promise headline would be a headline printed on the front cover of this book that states "great marketing tricks that will drive your business through the roof!" A promise that has mass appeal to any person in business seeking marketing solutions and advice to help him solve a problem or meet a need, which in both cases is sure to find more customers and increase revenues and profits. By making a bold promise you pull the reader into your article or advertisement; they want to believe in your promise because it appeals to them, once again by fixing a problem they may have or filling a need.

PRESENT A TESTIMONIAL IN YOUR HEADLINE
$ ⚒

Testimonial headlines work best when they are accompanied by a photograph or illustration. A picture of a smiling baby wearing nothing but a diaper and holding an umbrella in the pouring rain, along with a equally bold headline that reads "I've never been so dry" is an example of a testimonial headline, one that a diaper manufacturer might use in an advertisement to illustrate how good their diapers work to keep a baby dry and comfortable. Some advertising experts feel the person in the picture or photograph should be a known personality to grab attention and really pull readers to the advertisement. In theory this is true but in practical terms not every small-business owner can afford to shuck out big bucks for an instantly recognizable spokesperson. For that reason, in the absence of such a personality, the objective should then be to match the image and headline testimony to your target audience. As with the example above you can see that using a well-known personality would have no beneficial impact on the ad, as it is meant to appeal to parents with a tot in diapers. And I know of few tots who remain tots long enough to gain such celebrity notoriety. The true power of a testimonial headline is that it directly relates to your target audience; they read it and see the accompanying picture or photograph and think that the person featured and their situation is the same as their own situation or need. And that this "testimonial" person is no different from me and if it works for them then why not me? Remember that no one wants to be the first to sail into uncharted waters, especially when it comes to putting out hard-earned cash to buy an unknown or unproven product or service. We all want the security of knowing that someone has gone first and benefited because of their purchase. That's what a testimonial is designed to accomplish—it lets people know that they are not sailing into uncharted waters alone and that there is safety in numbers.

MAKE YOUR HEADLINE LOOK LIKE NEWS
$ ✎

Formatting headlines to look and read like news headlines is also a popular and time-tested way to grab the attention of readers and spike their interest. For example, a fruits and vegetables stand carrying a new line of organically grown foods might create a headline for their advertisement along the lines of "Metro Vegetables saves the planet!" The concept of disguising an advertising headline as a news angle is not new; it's been used successfully by copywriters for decades. What makes the news headline so effective is the fact that readers are bombarded with advertisements every time they pick up a publication. Consequently, many people have become immune or numbed to advertisements and skip right past them to the news instead. So by disguising an advertisement as news you will often at least get readers' attention and pull them into the text of the marketing message you want them to read and act upon. Remember it is no secret that the vast majority of people read newspapers and magazines for news and information, generally not

advertisements. Therefore, if you can make your advertisement look and read newsy then readers will be more apt to be drawn into your advertisement because of the news appeal created by a news headline.

ASK A QUESTION IN YOUR HEADLINE
$ ✎

Headlines that speak directly to your target audience in the form of asking a question are another popular way to grab a reader's attention and get your message read. For instance, if you operate a fitness or health club, a target question headline in a print advertisement overtop of a photograph of a happy and stress-free person running on a treadmill might ask, "Does gain really require pain?" With a bold sub-headline under the photograph answering, "No!" Follow this with the marketing message you want to get out to your target audience, be it a special, operating hours, or other information pertaining to your fitness business. Or, in this example perhaps the message or body of the ad would read, "Stop in for a free fitness consultation and we'll show you the fastest way to a pain-free, great new you." Any person with an interest in becoming more fit would pay close attention to this headline example, as it is designed to appeal to them on a conscious level. And in all likelihood this immediate interest will pull them into the entire message giving your advertisement and main marketing message or pitch their undivided attention. Asking a question is a good way to grab a reader's attention and draw her into your article or advertisement, but first make sure you know what question would appeal to the largest segment of your target audience. Think of this question from your target audience's perspective—what are they thinking about and for what questions do they really need answers and information?

TAP SUPPLIERS FOR ADVERTISING ASSISTANCE
$ ✎

Even small-business owners have some leverage in terms of getting your products and service suppliers to assist in footing part of the costs associated with advertising and marketing. What is this leverage you may ask? Your account, of course! Look to your suppliers for assistance in the form of high-gloss brochures, product samples, and even splitting print and electronic advertising costs. Explain that even though you may be a small business now, soon your business will grow large and the companies that support and assist in this expansion will eventually reap large returns via product and service supply orders. Many corporations have advertising assistance programs in place to help out the smaller businesses that they regularly supply products or services to; generally these programs are called advertising cooperatives, marketing cooperatives, and the like. Often all that is required is to ask for help, or to demonstrate by way of a written proposal how both parties will benefit and ultimately realize a return on investment. A section of your overall marketing plan should include an advertising strategy and action plan, which outlines in detail the methods of advertising you will employ, as well as a general timeline of when they will be implemented. Use this as a tool to help identify which suppliers may be able to assist with various segments of your program. Remember the worst answer you will ever receive is a no, and usually that just means you have to be more persuasive in showing suppliers the upside to cooperative advertising. The following are a few advertising and marketing activities that you should look to your suppliers to provide assistance for.

What You Should Tap Your Suppliers For

- Interior/exterior and special event signage
- Product packaging and design assistance
- Product labels and price tags
- In-store product displays and point-of-purchase displays
- Product catalogs and promotional fliers, brochures, and business cards
- Advertising specialties such as pens, notepads, hats, and totes
- Printed gift certificates and coupons
- Co-op print display and classified ads
- Co-op radio spots and television commercials
- Co-op Internet advertising including e-newsletter and e-zine advertisements

- Spokesperson special in-store appearances and other endorsements
- In-store and event marketing posters, banners, table tents, and signage
- Product samples for presentations, demonstrations, and gift and prize giveaways
- Contest assistance and prize donations

WEB RESOURCE

⌔ www.nationalregisterpub.com: National Register Publishing produces an annual co-op advertising program source directory.

GREAT MAGAZINE ADVERTISING TRICKS
$$ ✎

Next to radio, magazine advertising offers small-business owners one of the best opportunities to reach a very select target audience in a relativity cost efficient manner. And unlike newspapers, which are usually here today and in the recycling bin tomorrow, magazines have a tendency to be around for a while, on a desk, in the waiting room, in the lunchroom, or on the coffee table. Because of this magazines are almost always read by numerous people, and generally more than once even by the same person.

Target Audience

You can never say enough about effectively utilizing advertising methods and media to reach your customers and target audience; after all these are the people who are currently buying your goods or services and the people who are likely to buy your goods and services. And with that said magazines are one of the best advertising media to reach your target audience. This is simply because magazines have a tendency to cater to one specific portion of the population based on geographic, demographic, and psychographic profiling, or a combination of market segmenting. The first place to find out more about a magazine's particular target audience is through the publisher's media kit or fact sheet. In the kit you will find information about who reads their magazine, how many subscribers there are, what their average income is, what they like to do as a hobby, their education and income level, and the list goes on and on.

Magazine publishers go to great lengths to research and compile this information about their readership base because this is the information that sells advertising space. Not features or articles, not the editorials, not the glossy photographs, and certainly not the joke of the month—just facts and figures about their readers, what they like to buy, and how they can best be reached. Therefore, prior to jumping in and signing up for years' worth of full-page magazine ads, carefully research the publication's readership to determine if these people meet your target audience requirements.

Frequency

Frequency refers to the number of times that your target audience is exposed to your magazine advertisement or how many times you advertise in the same magazine, which should be a minimum of three times but preferably six to twelve times concurrently. Perhaps the only thing that should stop small-business owners from testing magazine advertising as a way to reach their target market is budget. If your budget won't allow you to commit to a longer-term ad run—once again at least three months for a monthly publication or four to six weeks for a weekly magazine publication—then you will likely be better off investing your advertising dollars in alternate forms of advertising media.

Ad Size Position

Simply put, the full-page players get the preference. However, there is much debate about which is best, full-page ad, half-page ad, third, or quarter and so forth. All sizes have their pros and cons; full-page ads are costly but get great exposure, while quarter-page ads are much cheaper but are often shoved near the back of the magazine. If full-page ads are not in the budget, try two different tactics to increase the exposure for your ad. The first is to negotiate for a second ad the same size as the first to run in the same magazine and in the same issue. Sometimes the discount can be substantial, in the range of 40 percent. The benefit of this tactic is that it increases the odds of your ad being noticed by readers if the same ad is in two locations within the magazine. This is especially

useful for an advertiser who is new to the magazine and needs to get noticed by readers. The second tactic is to try to negotiate a specific position within the magazine, preferably a location beside a regular column or feature. This is a good idea simply due to the fact that readers will be exposed to your ad for a longer period of time as they read the feature or column.

Plan Ahead

Unlike newspaper or even radio, magazine advertising requires planning well in advance of the publication date. But I say this with a qualifier—have an advertisement ready to go at all times and keep a list of cut-off ad commitment dates close by for magazines that you would like to advertise in. On the day of the cut-off date, call a sales rep or the publisher and ask about availability of ad space. Often you can negotiate as much as a 50 percent discount for last-minute ad insertions. But I stress you have to have everything ready to go in a package that can be couriered or e-mailed to the publisher as soon as you hang up the telephone.

Call in the Professionals

Due to the cost of magazine advertising, it is best to have a professional design your ad. The first place to start looking for a pro is through the magazine sales representative. Most magazine publishers have in-house design and copy editors to craft some pretty elaborate and clever ads for clients. And the small publishers that do not offer this service certainly will be able to refer you to a trusted local source.

Ask for a Feature

Another tactic, which is a favorite of mine, is to call magazines that you would like to advertise in and ask that they mail or e-mail you their editorial calendar. An editorial calendar is a schedule of forthcoming events and special features defined by when they will be taking place throughout the year. The value of having this information is threefold. Number one, let's say that you sell camping equipment and an outdoors and recreation magazine is running a special issue in the spring about camping supplies and products. Obviously because you sell camping supplies this would be an issue that you would want to run an advertisement in. Number two, try to negotiate a trade off with the publisher in that you advertise in their magazine in exchange for them running a feature or story about your business. Don't be fooled by the simplicity of this trick, trades such as these are negotiated all the time especially in small publications that quite simply need ad revenue to stay alive. Number three, knowing what special issues and features are forthcoming will enable you to create and send press releases to specific magazines that will be covering topics relevant to your business or what you sell.

Don't Stop with Just the Ad

Most magazine publishers offer advertisers additional methods or ways to reach their subscribers. These additional methods can include the following:

- Card deck programs, which are postcard-size direct response advertisements mailed to subscribers three to four times annually.
- Bingo cards in which readers circle or check off a box asking for more information from a particular advertiser about their featured product or service. (Readers mail the cards back, postage prepaid.)
- Loose insert and flier programs.
- Special issues or added publications that enhance the core publication.
- Advertising opportunities on the publisher's Web site and in the publisher's e-newsletters and e-zines if available.
- Reprints of full-page ads that can be used as marketing brochures, self-mailers, table cards and tents, and envelope stuffers.
- Many magazine publishers sponsor trade shows and seminars that are directly related to their magazine topic and target audience. There are opportunities for advertisers to sponsor the events or participate with exhibits and display booths.
- Some magazine publishers, especially the national and international ones, offer regional or city issues, which are a spin-off of their larger

national coverage magazines; advertising space in these often costs a mere fraction of what it would in the national issues.

Don't Expect Immediate Results

Magazine ads are not like direct mail or classified advertisements in your community—you are not likely to see immediate results from the ad. It takes continuous and consistent exposure to your target audience before results will begin to surface. Be patient and do not be too quick to pull the plug if your telephone doesn't start ringing the day after publication and distribution. Stick to your advertising plan and in time results will begin to surface.

WEB RESOURCES

- www.apsmagazine.com: Online magazine directory indexed by publication topic.
- www.newsdirectory.com: Online magazine and newspaper directory featuring worldwide listings and indexed by geographical region and publication topic.

STOCK UP ON REPRINTS
$$ ✎

Whenever you run a key or important full-page and full-color advertisement in a magazine or specialty publication make sure to order a lot of reprints of the advertisement from the publisher. Reprints are very inexpensive and can be used for a wide variety of activities in your marketing efforts.

- Include a reprint in all of your mailings, invoices, sales letters, newsletters, letters to the editor, and just about any other type of mail or business correspondence that you send out. Reprints are like a full color brochure, but available at a fraction of the cost of designing and printing a brochure.
- Include a reprint in your media kit along with your press release, company history and bio sheets, and product information sheets. Remember a photograph is worth a thousand words so in effect when media personnel see your advertisement they can quickly establish

what your business sells. Besides a full-page glossy ad tells them that you are a serious player in business and your industry.

- Include a reprint of your color magazine advertisement in your sales presentations. This is a very impressive sales tool and prospects and clients like knowing that they are doing business with a winner.
- Frame a color magazine advertisement reprint and hang it in your reception area for prospects and clients to see.
- And finally, have the reprints made into table tent cards and handouts for seminars, workshops, and trade show events.

Once again, the idea at work here is that if you have created and paid for a great-looking advertisement, why let it stop producing results for you just because the publication is no longer current? Instead stock up on reprints and get the most promotional mileage you can from attractive advertisements.

GREAT TRICKS FOR YELLOW PAGES ADVERTISING
$$+ 🔨

Remember that people do not read the Yellow Pages for the entertainment value, they read it because they are searching for information, generally because they want to buy something or need a service. However, not every business needs to spend hundreds if not thousands of dollars every month for a full-page display advertisement in the Yellow Pages when a simple two-line ad will be sufficient. But other types of businesses should— for instance, service providers that rely heavily on the Yellow Pages advertising to secure new customers. In fact for many service providers, it is their main source of marketing to generate new business. But before all of you plumbers put a second mortgage on your house to rent the biggest and boldest Yellow Pages advertisement money will buy, consider the following tricks that can give your Yellow Pages advertisement more impact for less money.

Skip the Covers

Never purchase an inside front or inside/outside back cover advertisement, because just about the time you do, a promotional advertising company will swing through town and give away thousands of plastic "phone book protection covers" to local residents. And guess what? Those protective plastic covers are always covered in display advertisements from local businesses. Once the covers are on the telephone book your very expensive, one-time, high-profile advertisement will be forever out of sight and out of mind.

Forget Renaming

Don't worry about renaming your business to "AAA something," as businesses that purchase full-page advertisements now get placed at the front of the section. However, it doesn't hurt to add an 'A' in front of your name to get priority placement in the line or nondisplay advertisements. Don't change your business name; just add an 'A' in front of it for Yellow Pages advertising purposes. For instance "Peachtree Heating" would become "A Peachtree Heating."

List It All

Yellow Pages display advertising is one of the rare exceptions where you should list everything you do, sell, how people can pay for it, and how they can get to your business. If you sell, install, and service five kinds of lawnmowers, then list all five in the ad. If you take credit cards, provide financing options, and accept checks then state it. If your service trucks are radio dispatched then tell it in the ad. Other critical information to include is contact information. List all your telephone numbers, toll-free numbers, fax numbers, your Web site URL, e-mail address, street address including multiple locations if applicable, and a map if your business is hard to find. Here are a few additional things that you should try to list in your Yellow Pages advertisement.

- How long you have been in business, especially if it is a long time or a long time owned by the same person or family.

- Special free offers or no-charge services and information that you may have in place such as estimates, reports, catalogs, seminars, or personal consultations.
- Your main competitive advantage: "We sell for less" or "We're the only 24-hour emergency roof repair service" or whatever your competitive advantage may be. Think of it as the reason a person will call from your ad and not the competitors.
- List special information such as liability insurance coverage, bonding, special certificates or permits, and professional association memberships.

The Big Benefit

Make your most important customer benefit the largest and boldest headline in your ad. If that's 24-hour service then scream it out followed by your telephone number. When people shop out of the Yellow Pages it's often because of need, not because of want. They call a roofing company in the middle of the night because the roof is leaking and they NEED to get it fixed right away. This is why your most important customer benefit should be the biggest and the boldest in the ad and not your business name. Likewise to secure more calls also offer another big benefit for free, such as free consultations by phone, in person, or via your Web site.

Track

If you advertise in more than one directory (the Yellow Pages is just one of many, and some of the others are even yellow!) be sure to track from where your calls are coming. The areas with the highest response rate get the biggest ads the following year; low response areas get a smaller advertisement. And this goes for testing ads also—the most popular ad that gets the highest response should also get duplicated into other Yellow Pages-type directories.

Don't Check Us Out

And finally, never tell people verbally or in any other advertising medium be it print, radio, television, or the Internet to check out your Yellow Pages advertisement for further details. By doing so all you accomplish is sending prospects right to your competition that also advertises in the Yellow Pages.

ALWAYS ERR ON THE SIDE OF POLITICAL CORRECTNESS
$ ⚒

When creating ads, sales materials, presentations, or just about any other type of promotional material for your business that includes a message, make sure to carefully examine what you are saying so that you do not inadvertently offend some people. Skip stereotypes like the pennywise Scotsman cartoon used to depict a big sale. Instead of gender specific terms like he or she, opt to use generic terms like people or person unless the product is specifically met and designed to be used by one gender. Additionally, avoid all references to religious and political views and opinions. Creating good copy is more difficult to accomplish than most people think it is; you have to take into account diverse perceptions, feelings, and values. It's best to always adopt the policy that if you think something might offend just one person, then don't bother using it at all. Find a word, phrase, picture, or illustration that you know won't.

GETTING NEWSLETTER SAVVY
$$+ ⚒ 🏺

For many small-business owners and professionals, regularly publishing and distributing a promotional newsletter could easily replace many other forms of advertising while still generating beneficial results. Or, alternately the newsletter could be used to enhance and complement your other advertising and marketing activities. A newsletter is a great way to keep your business name and the products or services you sell in front of prospects and clients alike in a consistent manner. Not only are newsletters highly effective in terms of their marketing power but they are also extremely cost effective, especially if you take the time to learn how to put together and publish the newsletter yourself. Newsletters should provide valuable information that is aimed directly at your target audience. They should be brief, yet long enough that the reader forms a favorable opinion about what they have learned from reading it. For instance, if you operate a property maintenance service, you could include a section in your newsletter every month that describes a new type of property maintenance service and the benefits of the service. Existing customers reading this will feel compelled to give you a call if they find the service would be beneficial to them. This is a powerful tool because it enables you to build on the existing credibility and trust that you have established with customers. However, with all that said newsletters still require time and energy to put together and to make it look professional, not to mention the fact that you must consistently come up with new ideas for content.

The Benefits of a Newsletter

The following are a few of the benefits that your business can receive by publishing and distributing a scheduled newsletter.

- Build awareness and brand your business
- Become known as an expert in your industry and field
- Introduce new or improved products or services
- Announce important company news
- Promote sales, contests, and events
- Build credibility and trust
- Stay in contact with prospects and customers
- Have a relatively inexpensive marketing and advertising tool that has no competitors' ads
- Showcase customer testimonials and industry and association awards

Electronic or Print, Which Is the Best Option?

Another consideration will be if your newsletter should be designed and distributed for print format or in electronic format. Both have their pros and cons. While the printing and distribution costs are near negligible with electronic newsletters, unfortunately in our ever-increasing jammed e-mail inbox pushing delete is very easy. Print newsletters stand a better chance of being read more thoroughly, but this comes at the higher cost to print and distribute them. Ultimately you will have to size up your target audience, marketing objectives, and budget needs to determine which newsletter format will be best for your business.

Who Should Design, Produce, and Distribute Your Newsletter?

A few more considerations will include the following:

- Who will create and maintain the newsletter?
- From where will the budget to produce the newsletter come?
- What kind of computer equipment and software will be needed to produce the newsletter?
- Will you print and distribute the newsletter or hire it out?

You can design, produce, and distribute the newsletter in-house or you can hire a service to do it for you. Once again, much of this decision will depend on your budget, marketing objectives, how often you plan to publish and to how many people you plan to send the newsletter. If you plan a relatively small production and distribution run of say less than 1,000 newsletters, then you will most definitely want to design, produce, and distribute the newsletter in-house. To hire a service for such a small run would likely prove to be far too cost prohibitive. For larger distribution numbers or more complicated newsletters you will likely want to get some help from a professional at least to design and produce the newsletter. If you do tackle the job yourself, most software packages such as Microsoft Office and Corel have newsletter templates in their word processing programs that can be used for design and guideline purposes.

Who Should Get Your Newsletter?

Ideally you want to get your newsletter into the hands of people who will buy your product or service, or into the hands of those people who can influence the buying habits and decisions of other people. Much of this will depend on your budget and how you distribute your newsletter, in print or electronically, but with that said the following are a few of the people that you should consider getting your newsletter out to.

- Current and past customers and clients
- Current and past prospects

- Suppliers, vendors, and subcontractors
- Editors, journalists, producers, and reporters
- Business alliances
- Employees and their families
- Influential leaders in your community, business associations, and industry

In addition to the above-mentioned people, you may also want to distribute your newsletter to places were it could be read by many people, thus increasing your exposure to a broader audience. The places where you distribute your newsletter could include restaurants, waiting rooms, public libraries, schools, and community centers. Basically anywhere in the community where people have a tendency to gather and read what is in close proximity to them while they wait for appointments, eat lunch, or have a quiet coffee break.

How Should You Distribute Your Newsletter?

Distributing your newsletter can be accomplished a few ways, including the following:

MAIL

Mail is the first option and the preferred way to distribute printed newsletters. However, keep in mind that if your mailing list is large, you will want to use a postage meter and possibly a lower class mail delivery system to reduce postage costs. Also make sure to include your newsletter in your regular outgoing business mail—account statements, sales letters, catalogs, and presentations.

HANDOUT

The second method to distribute printed newsletters is by hand. Give them personally to your customers and prospects and include them in packaging or with sales or product presentations. Additionally, keep a few on hand so that you can distribute them at trade shows, workshop sessions, and seminars.

FAX

The third and least preferred method for distributing a printed newsletter is by fax. However, if you can afford to avoid this method then do. The low distribution costs that faxing offers is more than negatively offset by the reduced print quality coming out on the recipient's end. Remember, image and presentation are an important aspect of the marketing mix.

E-MAIL

E-mailing your electronic newsletter is the final option in terms of distribution. And while this is certainly the least expensive way to distribute your newsletter, it does require the setup and constant maintenance of a database and opt-in subscriber list. Otherwise if you simply e-mail it to names that you collect randomly you will be sending "spam," which is unwanted e-mail correspondence and is illegal. Therefore, you will want to build an in-house opt-in list of names and e-mail addresses for the people that you want to send your e-newsletter to. Featured in the next section are a few clever ways that you can build an opt-in subscriber list to receive your e-newsletter.

Getting People to Subscribe to Your Electronic Newsletter

As powerful a marketing tool as electronic newsletters can be, they are of little value if you have no one to send them to. For that reason here are a few ideas that you can employ to build your opt-in subscribers mailing list for your electronic newsletter.

- Offer people free and valuable information if they subscribe to your e-newsletter. The information could be in the form of an e-book or e-report, but should be relative to your business, what you sell, and your target market. For instance, if you operate an antiques auction then create a valuable antiques pricing guide and give it away as a free gift to everyone who subscribes to your antiques auction newsletter.
- Provide a free sample of your e-newsletter on your Web site. You will generally find by doing so visitors will read it and benefit from the information and therefore be motivated to subscribe so that they will be able to further benefit from the information you provide via your e-newsletter.

- Offer a discount on all the products and services you sell to people who subscribe to your e-newsletter. Be bold and tell your visitors that if they subscribe they will receive 5, 10, or 15 percent off the first time they purchase a product or service from your business.

- Create a members-only section in your Web site and offer free and exclusive access to this section to people who subscribe to your e-newsletter. Increase the perceived value of your members-only section by including information, discounts, and other special offers that only members have access to.

- Host a subscription contest wherein everyone who subscribes is automatically entered in a drawing or contest to win fabulous prizes. Use deadlines to motivate people to subscribe or hold a new drawing every month so that you can continually add new names to your subscription opt-in list.

- Give away something that you would normally charge for. This is a great way to motivate people to subscribe. Your freebie could be delivery, more products for the same price, or an extended warranty providing they sign up to receive your e-newsletter.

- Place a dollar figure on the value of your e-newsletter and then motivate people to join by offering it for free for a limited time or to a limited number of people. "The next ten people to sign up will receive our monthly e-incredible tip sheet, a $200 value, absolutely free!"

A Few Ideas for Newsletter Content

First and foremost, a newsletter's main purpose must be for marketing and promotional reasons, with communications second. Like any good advertisement, you want your newsletter to be the vehicle that motivates your customers and prospects to call you, stop by the office or store, or to visit your Web site and buy. But you also must maintain a balance by making your newsletter more than just four pages of aggressive advertisements. In short you have to give your target market some information that they would find interesting and beneficial and pepper this information with promotional messages and advertisements for your products and services. So here are a few ideas for the type of content that you could include in your newsletter.

- Interview your customers and include their stories in your newsletter, especially customers who have benefited from doing business with you. Include their photos and, if they are in business, give them a plug that describes their products and services and how they can be contacted.

- Feature news concerning your industry, joint ventures, mergers, impending government legislation, statistics, and special events. Include stories on local, national, and international news concerning your industry.

- Talk about company milestones such as years in business, number of customers served, complaint-free or employee injury-free days on the job and so forth.

- Include some fun stuff, such as trivia, crosswords, word puzzles, and quizzes and reward readers with small prizes for the first person to correctly answer skill-testing questions.

- Also spotlight a new product and service each month and perhaps offer a special discount to entice customers to try them. You can extend this to include new products and services that you will soon be introducing as well.

- Have some question-and-answer interviews with experts in the industry, real and valuable information that will benefit your readers.

- Include tips of the month, how-to articles, and case studies on competitor services that do not stack up against yours. And you could also include community and charity news, events, and volunteer opportunities.

WEB RESOURCE

- www.howtowriteanewsletter.com: Newsletter toolkit software.

- www.muse2muse.com: Muse 2 Muse Productions, professional design service and content providers for print and electronic newsletters and magazines.

MORE BANG FOR YOUR CLASSIFIED ADVERTISING BUCK

$+ ✎

Low-cost classified advertisements can be a great alternative to high-priced display advertising, especially for small businesses with restrictive ad budgets or for any business that wants to test the effectiveness of a particular advertisement, product, or service before committing to a long-term display advertising program. Not only are classified ads easy to create, change, and post, but they also generally have a higher response rate than display ads because people seek these ads out by section of interest and are usually motivated or in the mood to buy. Additionally, more and more publishers are realizing the important role that classified ads play in the small-business marketing mix and therefore are starting to create a wider variety of classified sections or headings for these small-business people to advertise their goods and services in. New classified advertisement sections are springing up all over the country and include Internet services, computer services, and many more. And even more encouraging is the fact that many popular publications, both in print and online that did not have classified advertising sections now do, giving small-business owners even more low-cost and highly effective advertising opportunities to get out in front of their target audience. However, there are a few tricks to consider in terms of getting the most bang and the highest response from classified advertisements, some of which include the following.

Grab Attention

Write an attention-grabbing headline that jumps off the page and pay the few extra dollars to have it in bold, or flagged with a graphic icon or thick, bold border. Just about every newspaper or publication that offers classified advertising now has numerous options available to highlight business or important ads, so be sure to ask what is available and at what cost prior to submitting your ad. Likewise, many newspapers and magazines also allow you to include a small photograph; if there is an additional cost it can be worth it. Not only will the photograph grab attention but a picture really is worth a thousand words in describing or explaining your product or service.

Placement

Give some thought to the type of publication and the classified heading or section under which your advertisement will appear. Pick publications that are read by your target audience, and choose a section that your target audience is most likely to be searching through. For example, if you sell furniture then place your classified ad under the household furniture section. But give readers a reason to call your ad with the help of a creative message such as "Why buy used furniture when (your business name here) sells new high-quality furniture for no money down?! Call now."

Aggressively Sell

One of the best aspects about classified advertising is that you can aggressively sell because readers expect aggressive selling techniques in the classifieds—that's what classified advertising is all about. Write short powerful copy that sells, create urgency by stating a deadline or limiting the number available, appeal to a basic human emotion like need, love, family, or friendship, and most important list the main benefit that a person will receive by taking ownership of what you are selling.

Repetition

Like any advertising strategy, once you find an advertisement and publication that is pulling the desired response and sales, repeat it over and over. Repetition is one of the main ingredients of successful advertising. However, at some point the effectiveness of your ad will start to dwindle through repeated exposure to your target audience; once people see it too much the ad will no longer be effective. So make sure that you track the response to the ad and if a pattern begins to develop wherein the ad is pulling less response then it is time to replace it with a new ad.

Test

Classified advertisements are relatively inexpensive so continually look for ways to improve the responses you pull and the sales you generate by testing new ads in various publications that are read by your target audience. Test your headline, your main message, your products, and your special offers on a regular basis.

WEB RESOURCES

- www.newslink.org: Online newspaper directory serving the Untied States, Canada, Mexico, and South America, indexed geographically and by type of newspaper.

- www.newsdirectory.com: Online magazine and newspaper directory featuring worldwide listings and indexed by geographical region and publication topic.

NEGOTIATE FOR A FREE FLAG AD
$

Newspaper display advertisements can be very expensive and, worse, they often get lost in a sea of other advertisements all fighting to attract readers who have to a certain degree become numb to them. Increase the odds of getting your display advertisement seen and read by insisting that the newspaper sales representative give you a free "flag ad" in the classified section of the newspaper. A flag advertisement is simply a small two- or three-line ad found in the classifieds section that directs readers to a larger display advertisement in a different area but in the same publication, "See our advertisement in the automotive section for details," for example. Get in the habit of requesting a free flag ad when you purchase display ads; in fact ask for two and never settle for less than one. Additionally get creative in the way you write the flag ad and what heading you place it under in the classifieds. For instance a video rental store might run a "rent one, get one free" display advertisement in the entertainment section and flag that with an ad in the classifieds under employment that reads, "Movie critic wanted, see our large advertisement in today's entertainment section for details." Always request a free flag ad and get creative with the way you use it to direct attention to your more expensive, main display advertisement.

GET CREATIVE WITH POSTCARDS
$$

Custom-designed postcards emblazoned with your company name, logo, and promotional message are a terrific way to keep in touch with customers and new prospects alike. You can have a postcard specifically designed and printed in bulk for less than $.10 each, making them less expensive than sending an ordinary run-of-the-mill sales letter. Use the postcards to promote a new product or service, or just to let customers know that you are thinking of them. Postcards also beat out business cards for networking purposes. You can say more on them, use bigger and bolder headlines for greater impact, and due to their size you're sure to be remembered as the person with the postcard as opposed to one of the masses with just an ordinary business card. Furthermore, you can have the front of the postcard printed with whatever picture or graphic you like that best describes and promotes your business. Leave the back blank so that you can personalize each one you send to customers. Either handwritten or by running them through a desktop printer to add your promotional message. Postcards are a very inexpensive and effective marketing tool and every small-business owner or sales professional could benefit from the many promotional uses.

WEB RESOURCE

- www.postcardprinting.com: Custom postcard design and printing.

BUY FROM REPS WHO HAVE DONE THEIR HOMEWORK
$

Purchase print advertising based on your marketing plan, budget, and the publication's ability to reach your target audience. It's no good to advertise to people who do not want or cannot afford your product or service. While this may seem like elementary advice, it's not. Far too many businesspeople get sidetracked into buying print advertisements from sales reps who have learned and know how to effectively push the hot buttons. They speak of frequency discounts, huge circulation, critical placement, and ways to trick readers into noticing your ad. But do these advertising sales reps really know your business, who your customers are, and what your customers want and need? Most often the answer is no and that's not to say that all print advertising sales representatives are not intelligent qualified salespeople, just that the industry has been built on numbers and sizzle that leaves little benefit for the small-business owner. Make print advertising sales reps do their homework if they expect to earn your business. Never buy from the ones who push price discounts or amazing results based on examples that are far removed from your core business or target market. And especially never buy advertising on an impulse because it seemed like a good idea or a good deal at the time.

PAY LESS FOR PRINT ADVERTISEMENTS
$+ ⚒

Obviously another way to make more profits in business is to spend less money on print advertisements. But the real trick is to still reach the same audience, secure the same amount of qualified responses, and sell the same amount of products and services as a result of the lower-cost advertisements. How can a lower-cost advertisement accomplish this? Listed below are a few tricks that you can employ to drive down the cost of print advertisements, keeping the quality, quantity, and effectiveness of the ads intact.

Volume Discounts

The first way is simply by negotiating a volume discount with a publisher, once you have identified and tested a publication that is getting the desired response in terms of your advertisements. Most small-business owners do not realize that volume discounts can cut advertising costs by as much as 75 percent over the long term. Additionally, your advertisement does not even have to appear in the same publication, providing the publisher publishes more than one magazine, newspaper, trade journal, or whatever their print medium might be on a regular basis. You can negotiate split publication runs or ads that can run concurrent in a single publication. But of course there is a catch—you must be willing and have the financial resources to commit to the publisher on a long-term basis. This generally means a 12-month commitment in terms of a monthly publication, a six-month commitment for a weekly publication and a one-month commitment for a daily publication such as a newspaper. The longer you are prepared to commit running an advertisement, the more substantial your volume discount will become.

Standby Discounts

The second way to reduce the cost of print advertising is to always have a list of preferred publications that you like to advertise in, as well as a current advertisement ready to go. By doing so that you can take advantage of any standby discounts the publisher might offer on a last-minute basis. Publishers have space that must get filled within their publications and the closer to the publishing date, the cheaper unfilled ad space becomes.

Rate Protection

Seldom if ever do advertising rates go down in cost. For that reason make sure to negotiate a price protection guarantee for print advertisements that you will be running over the long term in the same publication. Aim for a two-year price freeze in terms of the advertising rate and never settle for anything less than a twelve-month rate protection guarantee from the publisher.

Soft Periods

Every publication has soft periods when their ad sales are the lowest during the year and therefore more times than not, publishers and sales reps are prepared to make deals to secure advertisers and generate revenue during these slow periods. Soft periods will vary from publication to publication depending on their target audience and the industry they service. However, as a word of caution be careful when buying advertising in soft periods because there is a reason it is soft, which is almost always less audience interest in the publication's information during that particular time of the year.

Position Guarantee

Seldom do you get to select where your advertisement will appear in the publication unless you pay a premium for this service, usually referred to as a position guarantee. However, as a way to get preferred location or a position guarantee, commit to an advertisement in exchange for getting the position you want. You won't be saving any costs because you were going to advertise anyway, but you will get a better position within the publication and therefore have the potential to generate better results.

Distress Negotiations

Again if you have identified publications that you want to advertise in you can always make an offer, generally about 20 to 30 percent of going advertising rates, call it your distress card. Let publishers know how much you are willing to pay for what size ad and that you have your ad ready on a moment's notice and leave the rest up to them. During soft periods and special promotional times, chances are you will get a few desperate calls from publishers agreeable to your terms.

WEB RESOURCES

- www.newslink.org: Online newspaper directory serving the Untied States, Canada, Mexico, and South America, indexed geographically and by type of newspaper.

- www.newsdirectory.com: Online magazine and newspaper directory featuring worldwide listings and indexed by geographical region and publication topic.

- www.srds.com: SRDS Media Solutions, publishers of print and online advertising rate card sourcebooks.

ADVERTISING BELIEVABILITY
$ ✎

Below is a checklist that you can use as a reference to make sure that the basic advertisements you create are believable. You can also use this checklist as a reference when you are creating marketing and promotional literature, such as sales brochures, letters, fliers, presentations, and more. Once again the purpose is to ensure that what you

Advertising Believability Checklist

❏ Are the claims you make believable and backed up with facts, either statistical or testimonials? Never place yourself in the position of having your claims debunked, because there are people—potential customers and your competition—who will check your claims for accuracy.

❏ Are your claims realistic and will people be able to identify with them? Suspension of disbelief is best left for the movies, not advertisements. Even if your claims are factual you may have to tone them down a bit if they seem too unrealistic.

❏ Is the tone and content of your message exciting? While facts and technical jargon might be accurate, at the same time they can also be boring and uninteresting.

❏ Does your copy come across as honest and sincere? No one wants to feel as though they are being lied to and this is easy to pick up on.

❏ Does your advertisement or copy focus mainly on the benefit(s) of your product or service and not the features? Great advertisements and marketing literature give people a reason and motivation to buy, by clearly stating what benefits they will receive by using the product or service. If you're not giving people a reason to buy, then don't be surprised when they don't.

❏ Have you let your first draft sit untouched for at least a few days? Creating great advertisements, sales letters, and marketing brochures takes time and as a general rule if you take breaks in between when you come back to it you will almost always spot ways to improve it or add in things that you forgot.

❏ Are you asking readers to take action and buy? When creating advertisements or marketing materials always be asking readers to take action and buy and give them the means to do so and a reason to do so. Write to sell always.

Advertising Believability Checklist, *continued*

❑ Are you using language and terms that are appropriate for and that will be understood by your target audience? Skip the technical jargon and always write in plain English that is easy to read, understand, and relate to.

❑ Have you created a knockout headline that will leap out and grab a reader's attention? Follow the 80/20 rule and spend 80 percent of your time creating a great attention grabber and remaining 20 percent of your time writing the balance of the copy.

❑ Are you clearly stating your message and what you want readers to do? Once you have a reader's attention, the next job is to create interest in your offering. If you don't create interest, readers will simply tune out and move on.

❑ Are you using powerful words that hit home with the majority of readers? These words include free, benefit, proven, fact, amazing, and more. Later in this chapter is a list of the 200 most powerful words to use in advertising—read them and use them and watch your responses and sales skyrocket.

❑ Have you created a sense of buying urgency? Motivate people to buy because they fear losing out. Use deadlines, limited product numbers, free gifts for early responses, and more.

❑ Have you had at least two other people proofread your copy for grammar and spelling errors as well as omissions that should be included and/or things that should be deleted? Printing can be costly and being stuck with 1,000 brochures with a simple spelling error smarts.

❑ Have you appealed to a basic human emotion, be it love, friendship, greed, or any other? Every piece of advertisement or marketing literature should be written in such a way that it appeals to at least one basic human emotion or need.

❑ Have you positioned what you are selling? You must be convincing in terms of where your product or service fits into the marketplace: high quality-low price, superior quality—high price, etc.

❑ Have you singled out your target audience and written in such a way that you are speaking to an individual and not the masses? Your copy should make people say to themselves, "That's how I feel" or, "That's what I need." Additionally make it personal by using "you," "You can lose weight" or, "You can buy this car with no money down."

❑ Have you included some sort of postscript that reconfirms and restates your message and your big benefit to buyers? Be it a sales letter, an advertisement, or a marketing brochure, think of the postscript as a way to summarize your message and why people will benefit from buying your goods or doing business with you.

❑ Have you reduced doubt and fear by clearly stating a guarantee or warranty? One of the best ways to motivate people to buy is to reduce or eliminate the risk of doing so. Offer a free trial period, delayed billing, a 100 percent money-back guarantee, or the longest and strongest warranty in the industry. Nothing is more believable than offering to refund people's money if they are not happy with their purchases.

---

are saying comes across as believable, honest, and sincere.

GET BEHIND COMMUNITY SPORTS
$$+ ✎

Sponsoring community amateur sports teams can really pay off, especially if you get behind a team that has a winning season and as a result gets a lot of media attention and coverage. You can "buy in" at various levels of team sponsorship as many leagues or teams provide various sponsorship packages based on your budget and their sponsorship needs.

Sometimes this means your sponsorship will cover only partial requirements like uniforms, and from there can go right through to include a complete sponsorship package that includes uniforms, transportation, equipment, printed promotional materials, and more. My construction and renovation company sponsored a junior hockey team some years ago. While it was not inexpensive, the first year led directly to more than $30,000 worth of new business from parents of a few of the players who hired my firm to do renovation projects on their homes. The profits generated from this work sufficiently covered the cost of the sponsorship and I feel that this is work I would not have secured if my company were not a team supporter. At the end of the day if you can afford to get involved with sponsorship at any level with amateur community sports teams then do it because it helps to build a good corporate image and shows that you support the community that supports your business. But don't forget that it is not enough just to have your business name emblazoned across the backs of the team jerseys, you also have to get out to the games and cheer your team on, which I think is the most gratifying aspect of sponsoring a local sports team. Here are a few easy ways that you can maximize the marketing impact and value of community sports sponsorships.

- If possible try to have the team named after your business, which can usually be arranged with full sponsorships. Check with league officials. The team uniforms should boldly display your business name as the sponsor.

- Have a banner made promoting your team and business and fly the banner at games. Also consider setting up product or service displays and demonstrations at games, especially during tournaments.

- Attend games and network by handing out business cards, product coupons, and your monthly newsletter.

- If you sell products then arrange to have a door or seat prize drawn at every home game. Make sure the announcer names your business at least twice during the drawing and subsequent awarding of the prize.

- Have team pictures taken and display the team pictures in your office, store, and newsletter. Let your customers and prospects know that your business is a proud sponsor of community sports.

- Pay to have game rosters and schedules printed for distribution. Make sure that your business name, logo, and marketing message are boldly printed across the top of the first page and subsequent pages. Printed promotional opportunities can also extend into areas such as ticket stubs and player cards.

- Create team and individual player awards that include trophies and award certificates. Be sure

your business name and sponsorship is engraved or printed on these items. Likewise consider sponsoring a season-end celebration event inviting players, parents, fans, media, and coaches.

- Inquire about advertising opportunities at the playing field or in the arena. These opportunities can include signs, banners, and displays in the bleachers, around the field, or on the scoreboard.

- Give away tickets for special tournaments to your best customers as a appreciation gift or to your hottest prospects as a way to spend a little more "selling time" with them under the guise of an afternoon at the ballpark.

- Look for ways to turn sponsorship into media or publicity events. Send out press releases about the team, write a weekly community sports column for the local newspaper, or get the scores out to radio disc jockeys to read on the air— along with your business name of course.

AUTO WRAPS
$$$+ 🐾

In recent years a new advertising and signage method called Auto Wraps has really taken off in popularity and has expanded right across the country and into just about every community. In a nutshell, Auto Wraps pays everyday people to have their cars signed with advertisements. But these aren't your run-of-the-mill normal car signs. The host car, van, SUV, or truck is completely wrapped in a business, service, or product advertisement—roof, trunk, hood, and even over windows using special see-through vinyl Mylar. Auto Wraps has programs available starting at about $300 a month based on a 12-month commitment and advertisers can choose the state, city, or community they wish to advertise in. Based on figures supplied by Auto Wraps they claim that this method of advertising costs a mere fraction of what print displays ads, radio or television spots, or direct marketing mailings cost, based on the number of people who are exposed to the ad (Auto Wrap) over an extended period of time. For any business owners seeking a creative way to advertise, this may be one of the best and certainly worth further investigation.

WEB RESOURCE

⚲ www.autowraps.com: Auto wrap advertising agency.

INITIATE A DOOR HANGER PROGRAM
$$ ⚒

The biggest advantage that door hangers have over traditional mailbox inserts like single-sheet fliers and folding brochures is that door hangers always get noticed. People cannot open the front door of their homes without seeing them and more important without touching them because like the name suggests the flier is shaped so that it will fit over and hang from the doorknob. I used to hire cash-starved college students to deliver door hangers for my home renovation business and the results were always fantastic, averaging a greater than 5 percent response rate. Door hangers can also be used as a very clever public relations tool. For instance, say your company is getting ready to build an addition onto a home. Two weeks prior to beginning the construction work you hang door hangers on the neighboring houses with a message stating the renovation schedule and a telephone number that people can call should they have any questions or concerns. Now that is good public relations and customer service. When it comes time for renovation work at their own homes who do you think these people will be sure to call for a quotation? Door hangers are cheap, they get noticed, and they don't get lost in a mailbox full of junk mail, making them a great marketing tool for small-business owners to use and include in their marketing mix and activities.

WEB RESOURCE

⚲ www.printusa.com/quotes/door-hangers.html: Free online quotes for printed door hangers.

SITE SIGNS ... THE $10 MARKETING WONDER
$$ ⚒

If your business sells products or services in and for the home, I strongly suggest that you initiate a site sign or lawn sign advertising program. Site signs come in all shapes and sizes, but the most popular are simple plastic sleeves emblazoned with your business name, logo, and promotional message that fit over top of a preformed wire stand that pushes easily into the ground. When purchased in bulk, site signs are very inexpensive—less than $5 each—and they can be reused over and over again. What makes site signs such a powerful marketing tool is the fact that they are like a referral beacon that attracts the attention of people living in and passing through the neighborhood and encourage people to think "Hey, if Henry is using that company to reroof his house they must be pretty good. I think I'll give them a call." Site signs are especially effective when combined with distributing door hangers in the same area. This creates a double whammy that is difficult for neighbors to miss: Driving past they see the site sign advertising your business on their neighbor's lawn and when they get home your advertising message really gels when they find a door hanger promoting your service hanging from the front doorknob. A great advertising combination that gets fantastic results. Give site sign advertising a try; you'll be amazed by the number of good quality inquiry calls that just one sign can generate.

WEB RESOURCE

⚲ www.politicallawnsigns.com: Manufacturers and distributors of lawn signs.

TRY INFLATABLE ADVERTISING
$$+ 🐵 ⚖

Twenty-foot gorillas, blimps, and cartoon characters get noticed by passing traffic, especially when these large inflatables are sitting on your business rooftop with a "sale in progress" sign boldly emblazoned across them. There are two methods to secure an advertising inflatable to promote your business or next sales or promotional event. You can purchase one, or alternately advertising inflatables can be rented on an as-needed basis. The cost to purchase advertising inflatables greatly varies depending on size and style, but start at about a $1,000 and can go as high as five figures. Secondhand inflatables sell for about 50 percent of the original cost, but this too depends on size, style, and overall condition. Rental rates start in the range of approximately $200 a week and go up from there, but do include delivery and setup. Besides being a great attention grabber, if you use an inflatable often to promote a sale or event, your business will become known for it and therefore memorable. And becoming known through advertising, regardless of the medium you choose, should always be one of the key objectives of any advertising technique. However, before you purchase or rent an advertising inflatable, make sure to check into local regulations, as some cities and communities have restrictions in terms of using inflatable advertising devices due to safety concerns.

WEB RESOURCE

⌚ www.uniqueinflatables.com: Manufacturers and distributors of custom-designed and constructed advertising inflatables.

TURN CUSTOMERS INTO MODELS
$+ ⚒

Save money and greatly increase the chances of word-of-mouth advertising by using your employees and customers as models in your advertisements and printed marketing and promotional materials. When asked, you'll likely find that most employees and customers will be more than happy to act as models in your advertisements—and for free, simply because it is a fun and a unique experience. Real customers and employees make great advertising models because their smiles are genuine, lending a special confidence and easygoing feeling that paid performers cannot mimic. For proof of this look no farther than Wal-Mart, which has used employee and customer models in their advertising campaigns for years, and very successfully I might add. Additionally, by using real customers to promote your products and services in advertisements, you can include an endorsement or testimonial about how satisfied these particular customers are with their purchases. This lends an incredible amount of credibility to your message because it is a firsthand experience about how your product or service was a solution or fixed a problem they had or benefited

them in another but equally positive fashion. At the end of the day there is no doubt that your "customer and employee models" will excitedly spread the word about their modeling assignment, and your business, to their friends and family members for months to come, giving you much-welcomed free word-of-mouth advertising.

TAKE ADVANTAGE OF FREE COMMUNITY NOTICE BOARDS
$ ⚒

Entrepreneurs on a tight advertising budget should regard community notice boards as a free and very valuable source for advertising your products and services. Design a business flier complete with a description of your product or service, what it will do for people (benefits), how they can contact you, and most importantly a call for action. Or simply put why they should contact you right away to take advantage of your product or service offer immediately. Photocopy the fliers for pennies each at your local copy center and always stock a supply of the fliers and thumbtacks in your car so you can make a weekly run posting the fliers on every community notice board in your area. These boards are typically found in buildings and areas of your local community:

- Supermarkets
- Convenience stores
- Public libraries
- Community colleges, universities, and high schools
- Coin laundries and dry cleaners
- Automotive service stations
- Community centers
- Fitness centers
- Public markets
- Sports complexes
- Churches and club or association buildings

Once your advertising fliers are printed, community notice board advertising is free, so why not put it to work for your business? Be sure to use a telephone tear-away system on the bottom of the fliers so interested parties can take the number and call once at home or the office.

DRIVE-BY BROADCASTING
$$ ⟍ ⚖

Promote your business on the radio 24 hours a day year round for virtually free by using low-powered FM broadcasting transmitters. The Federal Communications Commission allows low-powered FM transmitters to be used without the purchase of a broadcasting license. There are regulations like a maximum broadcasting range and noninterference with licensed broadcasters. But, these regulations are easily conformed to and minimal. Typically a sign is used to promote the broadcast, asking people driving past to stop and tune into a frequency on their FM dial and listen to a prerecorded message, which usually plays on a continuous loop. At one time these prerecorded messages were of poor quality, but with the advent of digital technology it is now possible to record the messages digitally on a CD-ROM for playback. This type of advertising promotion is excellent for real estate agents to use for promoting house listings, car dealers to promote service specials or car listings, and for retailers and service providers of all sorts to promote products and services. FM broadcasting transmitters are reasonably priced in the range of $500 and can often be rented on a trial basis for business owners wanting to test the waters prior to making a commitment to purchase.

WEB RESOURCE

⌲ www.fmtransmitters.com: Distributors of low-powered FM transmitters and accessories.

MAKE IT MULTIUSE
$$+ ⟍

It goes without saying that small businesses generally have small advertising budgets and therefore small-business owners must try to develop ways to get the most bang for their buck out of any print advertising and marketing. For instance, never have artwork created for use in only one advertisement. Instead make sure that the artwork is suitable for a wide variety of promotional uses throughout your entire marketing campaign and that it fits in with every marketing tool you use to promote your business,

product, or service. One single piece of artwork should be able to be used on your Web site, in all printed promotional literature, signs, trade show exhibits, in-store point of purchase (POP) displays and in sale presentations materials such as brochures and product catalogs. Additionally make sure that once the artwork is created that you own it, never assume just because you have paid to have the artwork created that it means you own it. Get it in writing from the artist because you don't want to have to pay a royalty for the artwork or photograph each time you use it in your marketing. Promotional or advertising artwork is only one example of items that should be created with multiple uses in mind, there are many more. The goal is to create or develop marketing tools that can be utilized throughout your entire marketing program, thus maximizing the value of every dollar you spend on sales, marketing, and advertising materials.

FLOAT ON BY
$$$ ⟍ ☏

For small-business owners seeking a unique and fun way to promote their businesses look no farther than designing and building a parade float. Parade floats are very memorable as they glide gracefully down the street emblazoned with your business name and logo as hundreds if not thousands of people line the sidewalks cheering. They also promote your business as civic minded and community oriented, which is worth its weight in gold for building goodwill in the community. Community parade and event floats need not be expensive to design and build; a few thousand dollars will go a long way. And best of all, if properly stored these same floats can last virtually forever with little maintenance outside of an annual freshening up and a little updating now and then. Get extra mileage out of your "advertising" parade float by having bold and colorful signs made up and attached to the float proudly advertising your business, products, or services. In another gesture of community-building spirit, consider enlisting local school kids to ride on top and wave to onlookers as you travel down the parade route. And don't forget to use the pictures you snap of your float on parade day in some of your printed marketing materials and on your Web site.

WEB RESOURCE

☞ www.astroparade.com: Full-service parade float designer and builder or do-it-yourself parade float plans and hardware.

GET NOTICED WITH STICKERS
$$

Having promotional stickers designed and printed with your business name and logo is another low-cost, yet highly effective way to advertise your business and products. The stickers can be in the form of bumper stickers to give to customers who will put them on their cars providing you with loads of free advertising as they drive around town. Or, the stickers can be in the form of window decals and promotional stickers used to jazz up packaging, POP displays, mailings, and even sales presentations. Additionally, if you wholesale products into stores for retail purposes, make sure to have stickers made that announce that fact for your vendors to display at the cash register and in their windows, "Julie's Homemade Soaps Sold Here," as an example. Credit card companies have long used stickers and decals for years to promote their credit card services and to indicate which businesses accept them as a method of payment, therefore you'll be in good company by also using stickers as an effective advertising tool.

BENEFIT FROM BENCH ADVERTISING
$$+

Sometimes the best way to advertise your business comes from advertising opportunities that you consciously identify and create. In every community across the country there are many unique ways to advertise a business in a cost-effective yet highly productive manner. One such way is to look for areas within your community, inside or outside, where seating benches could be installed to give people a chance to sit down and take in the scenery or just give their feet a rest. Once you have identified these excellent,

highly visible locations try to strike a deal with the property owners or managers to install seating benches. You can purchase premade benches or have them designed and constructed locally. Both ways will work as long as the backs of the benches are solid so you can install a sign on them that promotes your business. Bench advertising is not new; in fact it's been around since the '30s. However, you don't have to wait to be approached by an advertising company wanting to rent you this type of ad space, you can get proactive and go out and create it for a mere fraction of what you would spend in rental fees over the long term. Consider if each bench cost $500 to purchase, install, and sign, and were on site for five years each. That breaks down to a mere $8.30 a month for each bench providing you don't have to pay a location charge, which you shouldn't as long as you push the convenience and public service message to the property owner where the bench is to be located. All installations are good as long as they are highly visible, there is a need for this type of bench, and the area is relatively free of vandalism.

WEB RESOURCE

☞ www.victorstanley.com: Manufacturers and distributors of park benches.

OUTDOOR BICYCLE RACK ADVERTISING
$$$ ✎ 🐾 ⚖

Like seating benches, bicycle lock-up racks can also be installed outside in high-traffic areas of the community and provide excellent advertising opportunities. Once again the goal is to seek out suitable locations to have the lock-up racks installed. These could include in front of supermarkets, movie theaters, public institutions, sports complexes, and retailers, just to name a few. The benefit to the location is that they will be able to provide a service to their valued customers or visitors at no cost. The benefit to you is that you can have advertising signs made that can be installed on the top of the racks and used to promote your business, products, or services. Truly a win-win situation for all concerned. Like benches, bicycle lock-up racks can be purchased premade or you can hire a local firm to design, construct, and install them for you. Costs will vary greatly as to the design and how many bikes they can hold. However, good quality bicycle lock-up racks can easily be purchased for less than $500 each, once again providing a very low-cost, long-term advertising opportunity for your business.

WEB RESOURCE

⚸ www.bikeparking.com: Manufacturers and distributors of bicycle lock-up racks.

ADVERTISE YOUR BUSINESS IN VACANT STOREFRONTS
$$ 🔨

Take a drive or walk through your local community and count how many vacant storefronts and ground floor offices are available for sale or lease. If your community is like most there will be quite a few, and best of all, most will be in high-traffic areas that are highly visible to passing motorists and pedestrians alike. Write down contact numbers from the for sale or lease signs and get in contact with the owners or managers of these premises to inquire about the possibility of installing temporary window displays or signs advertising your business until the location is tenanted. The window displays and advertisements you create will reflect your business and products or services that you sell. Setting up temporary window displays in vacant stores is a wonderful low-cost way to display your products and services, and benefits the landlord by making their empty store or office location more attractive thus viable from a potential tenant's prospective. In some situations you will have to pay a monthly rate to secure the storefront window. Only you can determine what amount is fair. Based on what financial or awareness building benefits you believe will be realized by this unique and effective advertising method that is a winner for small-business owners.

COURTESY TELEPHONES CREATE ADVERTISING OPPORTUNITIES
$$$ 🔨 ☏

Courtesy telephones are located in high-traffic areas and available for public use at no cost to make local calls. There are two advertising opportunities associated with courtesy telephones. The first is visual: Advertisements can be created and displayed on the booth that surrounds the telephone. The second opportunity is audio: prerecorded messages that users of the telephone must listen to before being able to place their calls. Securing a high-traffic location to install courtesy telephones should not prove difficult, simply due to the fact that the benefit to the business where the courtesy phone is installed will be increased foot traffic from people coming into the building to use the phone, thus leading to increased purchases within the store. This type of creative advertising is very inexpensive over the long range, but an initial investment of approximately a $1,000 will be needed to purchase the commercial phone, have it installed and to create your advertisements. Beyond the initial investment the only monthly cost will be for a commercial telephone line and occasionally a service call to keep the phone in good working order. Additionally, to offset the cost, you could always sell some advertising space on the booth or audio messages that broadcast alternately with your message. Having your own courtesy phones out in the community may just be the unique advertising opportunity that you have been searching for and certainly warrants further investigation.

WEB RESOURCE

⚸ www.payphoneproducts.com: Distributors of commercial telephone equipment.

GIVE AWAY BOOKS AND MAGAZINES
$$ 🔨

Here is a clever way to advertise your business relatively cheaply and that can have a really positive impact over the long term. Purchase books and magazines that are relevant to your business, such as books about pets if you're in the pet business, or books and magazines about recreation and camping if you're in the outdoor outfitters business. Next affix stickers inside the front cover of the books. The stickers should be an endorsement of your business and promote it by stating what you do, what you sell, contact information, and the biggest benefit people receive from buying your products or services. Once the stickers are stuck inside, donate the books to local libraries. Not all libraries allow this, but with shrinking financial budgets to purchase new books, many will overlook the "soft ads" and gladly accept the donation. Assuming the book is on loan from the library only 250 days a year and remains in the inventory for five years then your $10 "book ad" could potentially be seen by more than 1,000 people making it a highly effective yet low-cost advertisement. Another method is to have plastic covers made, those similar to the protection sleeves that go over telephone directories. The covers should be printed with your business name, logo, and message, basically your advertisement. Once this is completed then make arrangements with local professionals such as lawyers, doctors, and accountants to stock their waiting rooms with current magazines. Of course, the magazines you stock for free are the ones with your plastic cover advertisement over the cover. Change the magazines monthly and when you do simply switch the cover over to the new magazine and presto, you're ready to advertise for another month. Both of these unique advertising methods are cheap and can be highly effective since in both cases you are marketing to a captive audience.

ADVERTISE WITHIN OTHER BUSINESSES
$+ 🔨

Advertising within an existing business can take many forms, an elaborate sign in a sports complex or even something as simple as a promotional flier on a bulletin board in the local supermarket. These can be paid advertisements, cooperative advertisements, or on a cross-promotional basis. I even recently heard about a clever entrepreneur in New York City who was striking deals with barbershop and hair salon owners to install small advertising placecards on the tops of their mirrors in their shops. The concept was that the advertisement on the mirror would have the undivided attention of the person getting the haircut for at least 20 minutes. It seems like a fair assumption given that the people receiving the haircuts are looking at the mirror for almost the entire time they

are in the chair. Another idea is having your ads installed on the backs of stall doors in washrooms. Now that really is what I would call gaining a person's undivided attention. Warm up your noodle and get thinking about creative ways that you can develop unique advertising opportunities for your business, products, or services within existing businesses and institutions that are in your community.

CREATE ROLLING BILLBOARDS
$$

Just about every business owner has at least one vehicle, so why not sign it and turn your car into a rolling billboard that advertises your business? Even if your business vehicle doubles as your personal vehicle you can always invest in a set of simple magnetic door signs that can be removed and easily stored in the trunk when the vehicle is being used for personal reasons. Additionally ask employees to sign their cars for business advertising reasons, and even offer a small incentive for doing so, say $50 dollars a month. Props can also be used in combination with signs to better describe your business and make a more memorable impression on people who see them. Examples of props could include a plumber replacing the door handles on their service vans with faucets. Or, a pizza shop replacing ordinary hubcaps on all their delivery vehicles with hubcaps that exactly resemble a pizza. Be sure to park your rolling billboard in highly visible and high-traffic locations when you're not using it, even if this means feeding parking meters. Listed below are a few ways to maximize the marketing value of vehicle signs.

- The look of your vehicle signs should be consistent with your overall business image include style, color, tone, logo, and unified marketing message.
- Ask employees to sign their vehicles and offer them an incentive for doing so, even if the signs they install are magnetic and only used during business hours.
- Park all signed vehicles in highly visible locations when they are not being used. Always think about maximizing the marketing value of these rolling billboards.

- Budget extra and make sure that your signs are professionally designed and installed. With today's high-tech computer sign design and printing, even very elaborate signs can be inexpensively designed and printed making for a very worthwhile marketing expenditure.
- Always include a call to action in the marketing message such as call now, visit our showroom, stop me for a free estimate, or log on to our Web site followed by the appropriate contact information such as street address, telephone numbers, and Web site URL.

A PICTURE IS WORTH A THOUSAND WORDS
$$ ⚒ ☎

Using photographs in your advertising and marketing materials can serve you well as it lends credability and makes your message tangible with nothing more than a passing glance. For instance, an advertisement describing a great new weight-loss method would have little impact without a photograph of an actual person who has benefited from this weight-loss product or program. But the same message with a before-and-after photograph of an actual person that clearly shows dramatic weight loss would have much more impact. It would be directed at the target audience who would be able to identify with the before photograph, "Hey that person used to look like I do now." And, they would think, "If they can do it, so can I." Recently I saw a very effective full-page advertisement sponsored by a local auto mall. It was a simple ad showing the interior of a car and dangling from the rearview mirror were about 20 air fresheners. Underneath, the message simply stated, isn't it time for a new car? An extremely effective advertisement that speaks volumes directly to the target audience, with few words. Photographs, especially those showing people or pets have the unique ability to showcase the best qualities of your product or service without saying a word and appeal to readers or viewers on an emotional level.

A Few More Great Ideas for Photographs in Advertisements
- If you operate a service-related business, use a photograph of yourself in all of your advertising efforts including print ads, business cards, and printed marketing materials. After all you are the business and your picture can help to brand your service.
- Go online to find royalty-free or very inexpensive royalty-paid photography images that can be used in advertisements as opposed to paying the high cost to have photography images produced. There are numerous Web sites that offer stock photography services, two are listed below.
- Humanize your print ad with the use of a photograph. If you are asking prospects to call now then include a photograph of an operator standing by complete with a headset and a caption that reads, "Jennie is waiting for your call," or something similar.

WEB RESOURCE

☞ www.indexstock.com: Thousands of royalty-free and royalty-paid stock photography images available for download.

☞ www.1stopstock.com: One million royalty-free and royalty-paid stock photography images available for download.

STRIKE A DEAL WITH LOCAL RESTAURANTS
$$ ⚒

Strike a deal with a local busy restaurant to supply them with free paper placemats in exchange for exclusive advertising of your business on the placemats. The placemats need not be printed in color. Eleven-by-seventeen color paper printed with black ink and in bulk will cost in the range of three cents each. This is truly a win-win situation. The restaurant receives free placemats, saving them money and getting you much-needed advertising exposure for your business. If the restaurant serves 200 customers a day, this will give you exclusive exposure to six thousand people a month for less than $200. Additionally, make sure to change your advertisement monthly to keep it fresh and keep people interested, perhaps announce a new special or news relating to your business, or incorporate some fun stuff like trivia and word games into the designs. One of the biggest benefits to this type of advertising is the fact that when people go to sit down in restaurants, there generally is a time lapse between ordering a meal and getting the meal. And more than likely your advertising placemat will get the diners' undivided attention at some point during this time. No competition and undivided attention equals a highly effective advertising opportunity for what it would cost to run one small print ad in your local paper.

BILLBOARD BASICS
$$$$ 🔨 🐾 ⚖️

Outdoor billboards can be a highly effective means of advertising your business, but be aware that billboard advertising requires a long-term commitment to get the most out of it. Simply renting one won't work unless it is in the highest-traffic and most-visible area available, which would be extremely difficult to secure if you're only willing to rent one, a catch-22 situation. Generally you must rent at least six to ten grouped in fairly close proximity of each other for there to be real benefits in terms of using billboard advertisements to build awareness of your business or brand. Also keep in mind that to raise the effectiveness of your advertisement you must use a picture(s) that depicts the biggest benefit that people will receive by purchasing your product, the "what's in it for me" factor. Limit the number of words on the billboard; most outdoor-advertising experts agree that six or seven words is the maximum amount. Drivers don't have time to concentrate on your billboard and the road at the same time. You have only a passing glance to grab their attention and for the message to be absorbed therefore your message and image must be potent, quick to absorb, and easily remembered. Keep in mind that no matter how hard the advertising company works to maintain their billboards there will always be a few mishaps that can slip through the cracks. So don't be afraid to take a drive around and make sure your billboard advertisement has not fallen victim to graffiti, that your ad has stayed affixed and is in good repair, has not become hidden behind obstructions such as brush, that the lighting works, and the overall visibility is generally good and what you expected.

Of course if all you can afford is to rent one billboard then use it for direct and immediate benefit rather than long-term recognition advertising—perhaps for your retail store "two miles ahead," or to promote an annual sale or event.

WEB RESOURCE

🔨 www.oaaa.org: Outdoor Advertising Association of America.

🔨 www.indooradvertising.org: Indoor Billboard Advertising Association.

🔨 www.emc-outofhome.com: Electronic Marketing Company, outdoor media buying service in the United States and Canada.

GIVE HUMAN BILLBOARDS A TRY
$$+ 🔨

Done right, wacky promotions can really pay off and perhaps one of the best wacky promotions is to hire a human billboard to promote a sale or event for your business. The best examples of human billboards are sports team mascots—who doesn't know what the mascot is of their favorite sports team? That is the principle behind this type of advertising technique, it's memorable and it's a real attention grabber. Look under "special event promotions" in your local Yellow Pages and you'll probably find a few companies that provide this type of service. Generally the cost is based on the number of people you want to promote the event and the type of props you want them to use, ranging from gorilla suits to chicken suits. So the next time you have a sale or special event, hire a human billboard and equip them with a sign promoting the event. You'll be amazed by the amount of attention and interest this generates as the human billboard marches outside of your location dressed as a chicken or gorilla handing out promotional coupons and fliers.

TRICKS FOR TRACKING ADVERTISEMENTS
$+ 🔨

When you are developing and testing various advertisements in various advertising media make sure that you create and implement a tracking system so that you will be able to identify which ads and which medium pulls the best responses and results. Knowing this information is important so that you can allocate your advertising dollars to where it will have the most beneficial impact in terms of reaching your target audience. Of course, certain forms of advertising such as outdoor billboards are designed to build brand awareness over a longer period of time through repetitive exposure, and therefore tracking these types of long-term ads can be difficult. However, with that said there is still much value to tracking your ads and listed below are a few methods that you can employ to accomplish this.

Special Codes

One way to track your advertisements is to use special codes. In order for the customer to take advantage of an offer they must use a special code that was printed in the advertisement or mentioned on television or radio, or use a coupon in person. Special codes can also be extended to electronic advertising media such as the Internet by simply having customers' type the special code into a submission box on your Web page to take advantage of your special offer. Of course, the idea is that each code is different for each advertisement and offer made so that you will know which ad and advertising medium had the greatest response.

Multiple Telephone Numbers

Feature different telephone numbers in different advertisements and make note of which telephone number received the most calls and generated the most sales. The most cost-effective way to do this is to hire a call center to answer the phones, record the information, then forward the caller directly to your place of business or to your voice-mail box. Remember if your advertisements span the nation then you must adjust your call center hours to receive both east and west coast calls.

Special Extensions

Another way to track your advertisements is to use different telephone extension numbers in each advertisement. You can purchase or rent telephone equipment that has this capability and inquiries can be made to your telephone service provider to find out about cost and availability. Once again, by using different extension numbers in the ads, you will be able to record and identify which ads and which advertising media pull the highest amount of responses.

Cloned URLs

Offline advertising that requires your prospects to go online to take advantage of your offer or to seek additional information from your Web site can also be successfully tracked so you can identify which ads are generating the best responses. Start by duplicating your home page and use different URL extensions for each separate advertisement your are running. Monitoring software such as ROIbot can tell you which home page extension received the most hits. Or, alternately you can run a different e-mail address or extension e-mail address in each ad and track the success using this method.

Gifts

Giving away different types of gifts or incentives is also a great way to track advertisements. In one ad you state "mention this ad and receive a free embossed tote bag." In another ad you state "mention this ad and receive a free one-year subscription to our recipe of the month club," and so on. You will quickly know which ads are working the best based on the gifts or incentives that are being sent.

Ask for a Person

One of the simplest ways to track advertising performance is to ask respondents to ask for a person by name. Even if there are only two people working in the office you can use different names in your various ads and ask readers and viewers to call in and ask for a specific person by name and then simply pass the telephone back and forth. Again by doing so you'll be able to track which ads are getting the greatest response.

Ask Customers How They Heard About You

And perhaps the best way to track the effectiveness of your advertising and marketing activities providing that your staff talks to each person who calls is to simply ask prospects and customers how they heard about your business. Create a simple form like the one shown below, listing all the marketing methods you are currently using to promote, advertise, and market your shop such as print ads, radio or television ads, direct marketing, coupons, referral, drive-by, and any other types of marketing you use. Print numerous copies of the form and keep them beside telephones so that they can be completed quickly and conveniently by employees. You will find that the vast majority of prospects and customers that you ask will not mind telling you how they heard about your business, in fact most will likely be impressed that you care enough to ask. Also make sure that all staff gets told the theory behind the new practice and they fully understand the importance of asking customers how they heard about your business so that the forms are completed accurately. Tabulate the results monthly and use the results to increase the marketing activities that work and drop marketing activities that are not working and therefore not cost efficient.

How Did Your Hear About Us? Form

How Did Your Hear About Us?

Advertising

❑ Newspaper
❑ Magazine
❑ Yellow Pages
❑ Trade publication
❑ Business directory
❑ Newsletter
❑ Internet/Web site
❑ Billboard

Referral

❑ Business alliance
❑ Supplier/vendor
❑ Customer
❑ Networking
❑ Business club
❑ School/institution

Direct Marketing

❑ Insert
❑ Mail drop
❑ Telemarketing
❑ Sales letter
❑ Response card
❑ Entry form
❑ Catalog
❑ Door hanger

Publicity

❑ Print article
❑ Radio
❑ Television
❑ Community event
❑ Charity event
❑ Internet article

Promotional Activity

❑ Sales visit
❑ Trade show
❑ Seminar
❑ Sponsorship
❑ Newcomer program
❑ Contest
❑ Cross promotion
❑ Gift certificate/coupon

Location

❑ Drive past/walk past
❑ Service vehicle
❑ Lawn sign
❑ Job in progress
❑ Store signs
❑ Window display

Additional comments: _____

_____

_____

Completed by (staff): _____   Date: _____/_____/_____

GET BEHIND A LOCAL CHARITY EVENT
$$+ ✎

There is great wisdom in the old saying "charity begins at home," and this should especially ring true to small-business owners. Support the community that supports your business by picking a worthwhile local charity or charitable event and help out any way you can, financially or with other resources that you may have at your disposal. Contributing to a charity within your community creates goodwill that over the long run will benefit your business from the contacts that you make. One of the best ways to support a charity is to create your own charitable event that can be hosted annually and include other members of the business community, a 10K run for cancer, bathtub races to raise money for community programs, or an annual food drive to collect nonperishable foods for those less fortunate, the charitable options are unlimited. Advertise the fact that you support one or more local charities and watch customer loyalty and repeat business grow because of it. Even small businesses on tight financial budgets can get involved by donating products or services to a charity or charitable event, or by providing assistance organizing the event, providing transportation, or even a location to host the event. Whichever charity avenue you choose, just make sure that you support the community that supports you and your business.

CREATIVE WAYS TO DISTRIBUTE FLIERS FOR FREE
$ ✎

Standard 8½" x 11" black-and-white advertising fliers can easily be designed on your desktop PC and copied in bulk for as little a two cents each at the local copy center, which makes them a great marketing tool for the financially strapped business operator. Here are a few creative ways that you can distribute fliers for free and get them into the hands of the buying public. Make sure you get permission first from the management of the various venues.

- Canvas busy parking lots throughout the community and tuck fliers underneath windshield wipers on parked cars. Saturday afternoons are the best as that is when parking lots are generally full.
- Stand outside of special event buildings like sports complexes, convention centers, movie theaters, and community centers and hand out fliers to people going in and coming out.
- Visit local businesses and institutions and ask if you can leave the fliers for their patrons. This works well, especially if you get some "please take one" plastic brochure boxes made up to leave at the location stocked with your advertising fliers. Be sure to return weekly to fill them with more fliers.
- Leave your advertising fliers in public transit areas like buses and subway cars for riders to read and take home, as well as in bus stations, train stations, airports, and bus shelters.

WEB RESOURCES

✺ www.corel.com: Corel is a leading software development company with numerous desktop publishing products for a wide variety of user applications.

✺ www.adobe.com: Adobe is a leading software development company with numerous desktop publishing products for a wide variety of user applications.

TARGET HOTEL AND MOTEL GUESTS
$$ ✎

Are hotel and motel guests potential customers for your products or services? If so, then design a basic promotional flier or information brochure about your business and products or services and strike deals with local hotel and motel operators to leave this promotional information at the front desk for their guests to take. Or better, right in the guest rooms if you can arrange it with the owner. An obvious match for this type of creative advertising is a pizza shop that offers free delivery right to the room, but there are many more good matches that could target hotel and motel guests, it just requires some creativity. For example, if you operate a wash-and-fold service or dry-cleaning service, offer guests one-hour service and free pickup and delivery. Or, a one-hour photo shop could offer free pick up of rolls of film and free delivery of the developed pictures back to the room an hour later—of course armed with a few new rolls of film at the same time. Also offer to sponsor "do not disturb" doorknob signs by giving them free to hotels and motels in your area, but with your business name, logo, and message also printed on them. Just about any business can seek out ways to profit from guests staying at local hotels and motels; it just takes a little bit of creative thinking.

OUTDOOR MOBILE MEDIA
$$$+ 🐶

Entrepreneurs who are searching for a unique way to advertise their businesses should consider the outdoor mobile media advantage. Recently a number of new media companies such as Outdoor Mobile Media have sprung up. For a fee, they will create a large billboard-style advertisement of your business, products, or services and attach the advertisement to one of their trucks, thus creating a mobile billboard. There are two basic styles of advertisement; the first is a paper-based advertisement like traditional billboards meaning that the ad is printed on sign paper or vinyl. And the second is an electronic advertisement meaning that your ad is shown on large stadium style video screens that are attached to these trucks. Of course, the advantage to the second method is that you can create an entire video or commercial production that can be continuously played on a loop. However, it goes without saying that creating and promoting this style of rolling electronic ad will cost you plenty, in fact the starting point is about $100,000. But fortunately for entrepreneurs with more modest budgets, you can still participate with far less by opting for the first style. The benefits to this type of unique and creative advertising method include the following:

- You have the ability to target specific audiences based on geography.
- You can rent one mobile billboard or many with no long-term contracts to worry about.
- You can use these rolling billboards to promote specific events such as sales, grand openings, trade shows, or seminars.

- The ads and the way they are delivered are very unique, thus ensuring great visibility and the ability to grab attention and generate interest.
- The advertisements and trucks use special backlighting so they can be used 24 hours a day, not limiting the marketing reach or potential.

WEB RESOURCE

🖱 www.outdoormobilemedia.com: Outdoor Mobile Media, truck-based mobile outdoor billboard systems.

WHY IS PRODUCT PACKAGING SO IMPORTANT?
$$$+ 🐶

Mediocre packaging can kill a great product, while incredible packaging will sell a mediocre product. You have to think of your product packaging as the silent salesperson; it doesn't talk, but it speaks volumes about what your product is, why customers should buy it, and the main benefit they will receive by taking ownership. What would you tell a prospect face to face to persuade him to buy your product? Your answer should be on your packaging. Great packaging is like a great advertisement—it grabs attention, builds interest, creates desire, and motivates people to action to buy it. The importance of product packaging cannot and should not be overlooked. In fact, if you could afford to hire just one professional in terms of everything having to do with your business, the professional that you would want to hire is a packaging expert. Someone who can design and create a package that will get the desired results: sales and plenty of them. To locate a professional package design firm simply submit "product package design" to any search engine and hundreds of matches will appear. Below are also two good online sites.

WEB RESOURCES

🖱 www.associatedbag.com: Stock and custom packaging products.

🖱 www.ajaxdesign.com: Product and packaging designers.

CREATE A STORY ON YOUR PACKAGING
$ ✎

Who can resist a great story? Not many, and for that reason it is wise to use your product packaging to tell customers interesting and unusual stories about the product they are purchasing or about your business, store location, or even your employees, past and present. The stories could be fictional works that revolve around characters who interact with your product, like a continuous soap opera but in print and on the inside or outside of your packaging label. Or the stories could be nonfiction pieces like interesting history about the product, how it is manufactured, where it came from, and so on. People like to hear a story, fact or fiction, and if you can get their attention and hold it then you can motivate them to buy more and more often by changing the story or continuing the story. For proof once again look no farther than popular television soap operas or popular book series. Likewise, if you can add educational benefit to the story then do so or even include customer testimonials. Creating stories on product packaging and labels is also a great way to separate your products from the competition, an interesting and clever competitive advantage.

ONE SUPPORTS THE OTHER
$ ✎

It should come as no surprise to you that the best-planned marketing campaigns are ones in which each advertising medium that is used to promote products or services supports other forms of marketing activities or advertising in the overall campaign. For instance, your infomercial should boldly promote your Web site URL, your radio spots should mention special events such as trade shows and seminars that you are participating in or hosting. And your special events like workshops should push your direct-mail and catalog program. Think of yourself in any one day: you watch television, you read the newspaper, you listen to the car radio on the way to work, you surf the Internet, and so forth. The idea behind this simple advertising trick is to direct a reader, listener, or viewer—in other words your target audience—in all the directions and places your advertising is, and you use all of your various advertising media to accomplish this. In doing so, you will increase the value of all advertising and promotional activities.

TRY ONLINE SPONSORSHIPS
$$ ✎

You already know the importance of targeting your audience in your advertising. Why not consider sponsoring online publications and forums whose readers or participants largely include your target audience? Many e-zines and electronic newsletter publishers already have a sponsorship program in place. And while you'll pay a few dollars more to be a sponsor over a standard advertisement, the extra cost can be well worth it. Not only does sponsorship give you the preferred location, which is generally on the header or near the top on the first page, but there is also a lot of credibility that goes along with being viewed as a sponsor rather than an advertiser. Likewise, many online forums like discussion boards and chatrooms also have sponsorship opportunities available. For those online forums that do not have sponsorship opportunities, approach the host and suggest you sponsor. Once again, the key to successful sponsorship advertising is to have a clear understanding of who your primary target audience is and what activities they participate in online, as well as what publications they read online or receive through electronic subscription. Use search engines such as Google to find directories listing discussion groups and e-zines that fit your target audience.

WEB RESOURCE
⚓ www.google.com: Possibly the most comprehensive search engine.

EFFECTIVE RADIO COMMERCIALS AND MORE GREAT TRICKS
$$$+ ✎ ☏

Radio has long been one of the favorite advertising media for small-business owners simply because of its ability to reach a very broad audience cheaply. And radio has the ability to speak to your target audience on a more intimate basis, usually one-on-one as listeners will be in their cars, offices, or at homes. The key to successful radio advertising is repetition, which in radio lingo is referred to as frequency or the number of times the audience is exposed to your broadcasted message. When you start to get sick of hearing the ad then leave it on the air for another few months to ensure that it is seared into the minds of your target audience. If you choose to use radio to advertise your business then you must commit to the program at least three months. In fact, radio-advertising contracts are commonly sold in 13-week blocks, which is three months or a quarter of a 52-week year. Radio ads do not have the ability to create a need for a product or service, unlike a live demonstration. That is why repetition is so important—through repeated exposure, your message will be on the prospect's mind when a need for a particular product or service arises. Another consideration is placement. Ideally, you will want to have the same time slot day in, day out. Most small-business owners find the morning or afternoon drive slots are the best. These are between six to ten in the morning and three to seven in the afternoon. Of course, ideal time slots will greatly depend on what you are selling and who your target audience is. You should be consistent in your message and always stay focused on a central theme or topic. Like a jingle, people get used to radio ads that consistently carry a theme, like the video store that counts down the top five movie rentals weekly. Or the restaurant the reads the daily special.

A Few More Great Radio Advertising Tricks

- Keep your radio ads free of information about your company that is unlikely to be remembered, such as telephone numbers and a physical address. Instead repeat your business name at least three times throughout the message and use a "landmark" such as located beside the courthouse if you must describe your physical location. If you have to use a telephone number try to get one that spells something related to your business. For example a roofing company might use 555-ROOF (7663) or a pet foods store, 555-PETS (7387).

- Skip all company puffery unless there is real reason to include it. Stick to the stuff that sells—what benefits people receive from buying your products or services—and crystal clear, simple messages free of technical jargon and detailed explanations that build brand name awareness for your business.

- Radio is like any other advertising medium; you are buying an audience and never a station—important information to keep in mind when it comes time to select the station, time slot, and price. Match the image of your business to the image of the station: If you operate a golf course then advertise on adult contemporary and easy listening stations. If you operate a retail fashion business aimed at young women then advertise on pop, hip-hop, and rock stations. On the surface this advice may seem obvious but don't be fooled. It has often been said that the most convincing and persuasive sales professionals in the world are the ones selling radio advertising.

- Ask your advertising rep what type of remote broadcast programs and promotions they have in place and carefully consider if such a promotion is right for your business. Live and on-location broadcasting can draw huge numbers of shoppers to the remote location. Grand openings, storewide sales, celebrity appearances and signings, trade show exhibits can all be enhanced with on-location broadcasting.

- Use your radio ads to support other advertising and marketing activities that you have on the go, such as, "Drop by our booth at the auto show," "Visit our Web site today," "Stop by the office for a coffee on us," "See our full page ad in this Friday's newspaper," and so forth. Every advertising and marketing activity you participate in should support, complement, and enhance the rest of your advertising and marketing activities.

- Before you hire a production company and voice-over expert to make a radio commercial check with local stations. Most will include the cost of producing the radio spot providing you sign up for a minimum 13-week contract.

Likewise try to negotiate to get one of their more popular disc jockeys, program hosts, or on-air personalities to record the ad or read it live.

- Opt for 30-second spots over 15-second spots, which almost always do not allow enough time to create a lasting and memorable message. Sixty second-spots are generally too long, not to mention you will try to fill all the space with about 200 words and start to lose the effectiveness of the message. Thirty seconds will enable you to get across about 50 to 75 words comfortably along with a simple jingle or memorable background music or hook without coming off as too fast, slow, or confusing.

- When writing copy for your radio ad think visually. Remember that you have to paint an exact visual portrait of what your product looks like, how it works, and how people will benefit, all without the aid of sight. Listeners must be able to paint a visual picture in their heads of what you are describing.

- Use your radio ads to generate leads with terms such as free estimates or information and free trial periods. As a rule of thumb radio ads do not sell. They grab attention, build awareness, and position your brand, business, product, or service within the market, but seldom sell. That job is left up to you when customers and prospects make contact.

- Radio audiences are extremely loyal to particular stations, on-air personalities, and on-air programs. Therefore, once you have identified your target audience, the station and programs they listen to, stick with that station, time slot, and program like glue. You want these listeners to have and feel the same loyalty to your brand and through repeated exposure to your marketing message this will begin to happen.

WEB RESOURCE

⌐ www.radio-locator.com: Online directory linked to more than 10,000 radio stations indexed by format and geographic location in the United States and Canada.

CONSIDER PUBLIC BROADCASTING
$$$+ ✎ ☎

Not long ago the Federal Communications Commission made it much easier for corporations and small businesses alike to advertise on public radio and television, mainly due to the reduced amount of funding that public broadcasting is receiving from the federal government. For this reason, great advertising opportunities have been created under the flag of sponsorship programs that small-business owners can take advantage of to reach the estimated 150 million people who tune in to public broadcasting on a monthly basis. According to a study conducted by the Public Broadcasting System (PBS), the majority of PBS viewers feel that companies that fund PBS through sponsorship programs have a commitment to quality and excellence. Viewers also believe that sponsorship underwriters (sponsors) are leaders within their industry, and that everything else being equal they would purchase products and services from a company that supports PBS over a company that does not support PBS. Given the results of the study, I would say that it is safe to assume that by becoming a PBS sponsor you have a certain amount of instant credibility built in, at least with PBS viewers. Visit the PBS Web page to find out more about their sponsorship programs.

WEB RESOURCE

⌐ www.pbs.org: Public Broadcasting System. Follow the "Sponsorship" link on the home page to the "Corporate Sponsorship" page.

CREATE A JINGLE
$$ ✎ ☎

Can't get that silly little radio jingle out of your head? Well it must be doing what it was designed to do then. Radio jingles work well in terms of making your business memorable to a radio listening audience. In fact, great jingles can transcend time; many of us still remember advertising jingles we heard 10, 20, and even 30 years ago. And even more important we remember exactly what the jingle was advertising. One of the great things about radio jingles is that they do not have to be terribly expensive to have written, produced, and recorded. Actually, you can get a highly effective and memorable jingle made for next to nothing by enlisting the help of music students and amateur musicians right in your own community. All that is required is a little bit of research to track down and approach the right person or people to take the project on and run with it. Once you have your jingle you can buy air time on radio stations that reach your target audience; you can also use the jingle in your shop, at trade shows, for on-hold telephone messages, and just about anywhere else that you think it will do your business good. However, on a more serious note, regardless of who writes, records, and produces your advertising jingle, make sure that it is clearly understood in writing that you own the copyright to the jingle and are free to use it as you wish. This is very important because you don't want a hit jingle on your hands only to find out that it will cost you cash every time you want to use your own jingle in a radio advertisement or elsewhere to promote your business.

INTERNET RADIO
$$ ⚒

Internet radio stations are popping up all over the Web as the popularity of listening to online radio continues to increase daily, especially for people working in offices who keep their computers tuned in to Web casts from around the country. Best of all advertising on these stations costs a fraction of what it costs to advertise on traditional radio stations. And, there are still other advertising opportunities available beyond standard radio spots. These additional advertising opportunities include things such as specific program sponsorships and even being featured as a guest on a call in, live, or taped talk show. However, don't try to record your own advertisement, hire a professional to make sure that you get the sound you want. This can be accomplished very inexpensively. I hired a local radio DJ once to record an audio commercial for $200 and for that he even improved the script by adding in a few great promotional ideas that I overlooked.

WEB RESOURCES

⚓ www.radiotower.com: Internet radio directory listing more than 1,300 Web casts indexed by format and region.

⚓ www.virtualtuner.com: Online directory of more than 10,000 Internet radio and television stations broadcasting from more than 100 countries in 75 languages directly to your computer.

GREAT ADVERTISING TRICKS FOR THE TUBE
$$$$ 🍪

The face of television has changed dramatically over the past decade with the introduction of more specialty cable channels. How broadcast signals are delivered to homes across the nation has changed, too. The one-time hold that the big three network broadcasters had on the viewing public is not nearly as tight as it once was. And this increased competition on the airways has created many advertising opportunities for small-business owners to have their own television commercial produced and aired right alongside of some of the biggest corporate names out there. However, like any advertising medium, television must be carefully considered and the pros and cons weighed before jumping in with both feet. Television might be more accessible and in some cases less expensive than it once was to air commercials on a tight repetitive schedule, but that still doesn't mean that it is cheap. Television still ranks as the most costly advertising medium, but with good reason; television has the highest participation numbers of any medium including radio, the Internet, and even newspapers. In fact, on average North Americans now spend more than 30 hours a week glued to the tube. Only slightly less time than the average amount of time people spend working at a full time job. Needless to say the reach of television and its influence on consumer buying habits is almost unlimited.

A Few More Great Advertising Tricks for the Tube

- Demonstrate, demonstrate, demonstrate, that's the power of a visual medium like television. It allows you to fully demonstrate the benefits of your products, adding few words if you choose. Don't tell viewers what your product will do, show them.

- Keep your brand on screen at all times by making sure that your sign or a banner with your business name or logo can be seen throughout the entire commercial. Also use other brand building visuals like uniforms emblazoned with your business name and logo.

- Avoid tying your commercial in with a current fad. Stay fresh but fad free simply because production costs can be steep and you want to get the most mileage that you can out of all well planned and produced commercials without having to shoot a new one weekly or monthly.

- Ask your suppliers and the manufacturers of the products that you sell if they have any "pre-produced" television ads that can be broadcasted in your local area with the addition of your business name, message, and call to action tagged on or overlaid onto the commercial. The majority of these types of television commercials will fall under the manufacturers or suppliers cooperative advertising programs, and generally will require you to pay for a portion of the associated costs to air the commercial locally. The reduced airtime cost and saving that comes from not having to have a television commercial produced are great and very attractive especially to small-business owners. The downside is that these commercials usually do very little to brand your business name in your market, which by all accounts is one of the key objectives of any good television advertising campaign. So only you will be able to decide if there is value for your business and brand in cooperative television advertising programs with one or more of your suppliers.

- Always appeal to the emotional triggers of the viewers. These emotional triggers are numerous and include such things as the need for security—both physical and financia—the need to achieve and lead, the need to learn, the need for friendship and love, and so forth. Appealing to consumers on an emotional level is the cornerstone

of all modern advertising practices, simply because has been proven beyond any reasonable doubt to work.

- Avoid having a "talking head" commercial produced, which is simply 30 seconds of you, an actor, or spokesperson talking nonstop about your business and products. Talking head commercials come off looking cheap, unprofessional, and just plain boring.

- Like a print headline, you have only a moment to grab your viewer's attention and pull them fully "connected" into your commercial marketing message and story. Therefore, you must kick off or launch your commercial in a powerful way that reaches out of the television and grabs hold of the viewers as they watch. Get to the point quickly, tell them what you have, how they will benefit, and what they need to do next.

- Another way to get on the tube and advertising your business without the high costs associated with producing a television commercial is to sponsor a news ticker, entertainment feature, or traffic or weather update where your business name and logo are shown on a small portion of the screen and often read by the on-air personality, host, or anchor person. These are generally referred to as a billboard and for small-business owners with tight advertising budgets this may be well worth careful investigation as it will allow you to get your foot into the television ad door and your business name on the screen.

WEB RESOURCE

⟆ www.virtualtuner.com: Online directory of more than 10,000 Internet radio and television stations broadcasting from more than 100 countries in 75 languages directly to your computer.

PRODUCE A TELEVISION COMMERCIAL ON THE CHEAP

$$+ ✎ 📞

The capital costs to have a television commercial professionally produced can range from thousands right up to millions of dollars leaving financially strapped small-business owners out in the cold in terms of having a television commercial produced— or does it? Many small-business owners are turning to media training schools and wanna-be producers and directors to have their television commercial produced for a fraction of what it traditionally costs. Often the results can be indistinguishable from a commercial that costs $10,000 to make. Look in the Yellow Pages, call some schools, and find out who the up-and-comers are who want to gain experience and need finished filmed projects to advance their own careers. Contact these filmmakers and strike a deal to get your commercial made on the cheap. Also many people who are in the film production business, even at a start-up level, have a vast amount of resources that you can draw upon to help get your commercial made. They know film editors, writers, makeup people, sound editors, cinematographers, and more. Once you narrow your list, look at examples of their work to get an idea of their abilities and ask for creative ideas that they might have about your project to decide who you should choose to produce and direct your budget television commercial.

WEB RESOURCE

🖰 www.cheap-tv-spots.com: Full-service television commercial production services including scripts, directing, formatting, filming, editing, music, and narration with packages starting at $499 for the budget-minded small-business advertiser.

WHY USE DIRECT MARKETING?
$$+ 🔧

Simply put, when direct marketing works you know it; you don't have to wait months, years, and decades to find out. Unlike many individual methods of marketing and advertising, direct marketing is almost immediately measurable. You can tally your success and failure very easily making the efforts valuable from a research and marketing perspective. Additionally, regardless of the method you use— mail, telephone, e-mail, or fax—direct marketing is one of the best ways to directly reach your individual

customer, meaning that you can take advantage of your in-house customer database and market to them directly on a personal one-on-one basis. People like this personal approach because it singles them out, makes them feel special and important and not merely one person lost in the masses. Though direct marketing is the most expensive form of marketing based on the cost to reach each individual prospect or customer, it can also have the most immediate and profitable response in terms of selling new products or services, or up-selling additional features or selling more products and services.

What Sells Best

What sells best using direct marketing? Just about every type of product or service can be sold by using one or more direct marketing methods. However, the products and services that sell best share a few of the same characteristics.

- Unique, interesting, and not available locally
- Easy and inexpensive to pack and ship with an extended shelf life
- Something that serves a purpose with mass appeal or fills a highly specific niche
- Large markup and profit potential
- Something that unlocks a mystery or formula
- A consumable, meaning the consumer has to order more

WEB RESOURCE

🖰 www.the-dma.org: The Direct Marketing Association.

IDENTIFYING THE MOST COMMON MAILING LISTS
$+ 🔧 ☎

The lifeblood of any direct marketing enterprises or campaign rests on the operator's abilities to rent the best and most appropriate contact and mailing lists that directly relate to their target audience and to what they are selling to this audience. For that reason, before you expand your business to include or extend a direct marketing program, or before you venture into mail-order sales, listed below are the most common types of contact or mailing lists that you can rent or compile yourself to reach your target audience.

In-House List

In-house contact lists are the lists that you create. They are generally compiled of names of your customers, current prospects, and even people who did not buy from you in the past. In-house lists are without question the best mailing lists available simply because the majority of people on the list have purchased from you in the past or are currently purchasing products or services from you. Additionally, multiply the value of in-house mailing lists by trading your in-house mailing lists with other direct marketers' lists that offer similar, but noncompeting products as you. For instance, if you sell fishing lures by mail, a good match for in-house list trades would be a business that sells mail-order camping products and specialized outdoor and recreational clothing and equipment. However, before you do make sure that you have not promised your customers and prospects that their information would not be shared with others, and that the list you are trading for is also clear of the same promise by the list owner.

Opt-In List

Opt-in lists are e-mail address lists of people who have given a specific business, organization, or individual permission to send them information via e-mail. And more importantly, they have given the holder of the list permission to share this information with "friends," which is a nice way of saying that the lists will be rented, sold, and traded without the subscriber really understanding what the term "friends" means. Opt-in lists are best suited for electronic direct marketers who wish to steer respondents to a Web site for future details or to an e-mail address to be sent further information or instructions. Many cyber marketers rely almost exclusively on opt-in lists to generate new business because of the ease of contact and the low cost to reach each individual on the list. However, be aware that a good many opt-in lists are really spam lists that are composed of e-mail addresses without the holders' permission. There are

unscrupulous characters who send spider robots into cyberspace to retrieve e-mail addresses from every available source including classified ads, discussion boards, chat rooms, and more. And, once they have these e-mail addresses they compile them in a list and rent them as permission opt-in lists. Spamming is illegal, so do your homework prior to renting an opt-in list so that you can be sure the people on the list really do want to receive information and offers that are of interest to them.

Subscription List

Subscription mailing lists are composed of individuals and businesses that subscribe to a publication, both in print or electronic format. These subscriber publications can include magazines, newsletters, trade journals, industry reports, newspapers, and e-zines. Basically the name of the business or individual on a subscription list has a specific interest in a specific topic, whether it be for business or personal reasons.

Assembled List

Assembled lists are most commonly associated with business mailing lists, which are usually categorized by industry or profession such as plastics manufacturers, lawyers, engineers, or chiropractors. These lists are compiled from various published information sources such as telephone and business directories or industry association and trade lists. While assembled lists provide a great opportunity for business-to-business direct marketers to reach specific target industries and buyers within companies, they are not very valuable to direct marketers of consumer goods. Keep in mind that when you rent assembled mailing lists the only prequalification of the names on the list is that the businesses or individuals on the list belong to a specific industry or professional.

Response List

Response lists are compiled from names of people who have purchased via mail order or a direct mail or marketing offer in the past. Once again, response lists are broken into many groups representing various special interests, such as people who own recreational vehicles. For mail order purposes a good response list is second only to a good in-house list in terms of the potential pull and high response rate. The downside of response lists is that they can be very expensive to rent, even twice as much as other types of lists because the quality is generally very good, but the higher initial cost to rent the list is often justified by the total sales that result from the offer.

Card Holder List

The only common denominator of names featured on credit card lists is that the individuals included hold a credit card. But with that said, credit card holder lists are good for mail order and direct marketers simply by virtue of being a credit card holder these people have the ability to pay by credit card, which for many direct marketers is a bonus and a big obstacle out of the way. If you are marketing directly to business owners and managers, skip credit card holder lists as they will not generally work. These lists are best suited to reach a broad individual consumer audience and rely on an emotional element or impulse decisions in terms of motivating them to a buying decision.

Attendee List

Attendee lists are compiled of names of people who have attended a specific event—everything from seminars, trade shows, sports events, concerts, workshops, right to timeshare pitch sessions. Once again, attendee lists are available in various configurations based on geography, special interests, and even demographics depending on the event that the names of people in attendance were compiled from. Attendee lists are generally accepted as a good alternative to a response list or an in-house list, and because the lists are categorized they are useful marketing tools for both consumer and business-to-business direct marketing and mail purposes.

Web Resources

⚲ www.infousa.com: Billed as the world's largest supplier of mailing lists indexed by consumer, business, industry, hobby, geographic, and demographic.

⚲ www.paml.net: List of Publicly Accessible Mailing Lists, information about 6,900 public mailing lists.

⚲ www.messageboardblaster.com: Software that automatically submits your message to more than 1,300 online message boards and Usenet newsgroups.

MORE ABOUT MAILING LISTS

As mentioned above, securing quality mailing lists is the lifeblood for successful direct marketing. Mailing lists are generally rented; seldom will you find anyone who wants to sell a list. Sometimes you can get free mailing lists, especially those for electronic mailing, but publicly accessible e-mail or opt-in lists come with a word of caution: They are not well maintained, include many dead links, and most include spam addresses. For the serious direct marketer, there really are only three reliable sources for mailing lists. The first is to build your own list. Compiling addresses from directories, your current customers, holding a drawing or contest and retrieving the information from the entry ballots, or information from warranty cards and checks. The second option is to rent mailing lists directly from the list owner as many marketers and business owners who have spent considerable time, money, and energy to build lists often rent these lists out as a method to recoup some of the expenditures and generate profits. The third option is to rent lists from mailing list brokers, who are businesspeople and mailing list services that represent numerous mailing lists; they may manage them or own them outright. But generally list brokers simply represent numerous lists for owners and receive a commission based on the number of rentals the list generates. As is the case with any marketing or advertising activity, the number-one objective is to target the right audience. In terms of direct marketing this means securing lists that are composed mainly of names of people who fit your target market. There are different ways of narrowing the field of suitable lists. The first is obvious: Simply ask who is on the list, what they buy, how they buy, and how often. Much of this type of information will be available in the form of a media kit or data card, which are available from the list owner or broker. The media kit or data card should give the following types of information and statistics, all of which can be used to determine if the mailing list in question meets your needs.

Cost

Mailing list costs shown on the data card always reflect the cost for 1,000 names. Costs can range from $10, right up to $250 for highly specialized lists, such as lists that target specific professions and industries. However, never base your decision to rent a list on cost; base it on the value of the list in relationship to your particular needs. Saving $250 now on the rental of a less than perfectly targeted list could cost you thousands in lost profits by not generating the desired results.

Size and Minimum Order

The total number of names or size of the list will also be shown on the data card as well as the minimum number of names that can be pulled from the list and rented. Most list owners and brokers require that a minimum of 5,000 names be rented from each list. Generally in the case of small lists that are highly specialized, you will find that you must rent the entire list, no splitting or segmenting.

Profile

On the data card you will also find a profile or brief list description that will outline details such as the source of the list, history of the list, average value of orders, and hotline information (which means people on the list who have purchased in recent months). And more important a description of the type of product they purchased or publication they subscribed to, that led them to be included on that particular list. Knowing this information helps you to understand the people on the list better and to determine if they fit your target market, for instance, if you sell crossbows and accessories and the names on the list are people who subscribe to a hunting or outdoor recreational magazine.

Restrictions

On the data card you will also find information pertaining to restrictions. All list owners and brokers reserve the right to review and approve or subsequently decline your mailing based on their own restriction criteria. Check this part of the data card carefully to find out if your mailing would be restricted; if so, don't waste your time and move on. However, be aware that few mailings ever get declined, and those that do are generally declined for competitive or moral reasons.

Selections

The selections area of the data card is important because it will tell you if the list can be segmented and to what degree. The reason this is important is because only a certain portion of the list may appeal to you and meet your target audience while the rest does not. This is a very common occurrence especially for lists that are business related and for marketers who want to target specific businesses or industries or even job titles or managers within an industry. Selections information will generally be shown in a percentage indicating the amount or portion of the list that can be selected and the additional cost associated with doing so.

Web Resources

- www.infousa.com: Billed as the world's largest supplier of mailing lists indexed by consumer, business, industry, hobby, geographic, and demographic.

- www.paml.net: List of Publicly Accessible Mailing Lists, information about 6,900 public mailing lists.

- www.messageboardblaster.com: Software that automatically submits your message to more than 1,300 online message boards and Usenet newsgroups.

PLAN AND REVIEW TO CUT PRINTING COSTS
$

Another way to increase profitability in direct-mail marketing is to decrease the cost to reach each prospect or customer, and one method of decreasing costs is to reduce printing expenses. One of the best ways to reduce printing costs is to get exactly what you want printed the first time around. While on the surface this may seem like very obvious advice, knowing exactly what you want printed is often overlooked in the excitement and rush to get marketing. Many new direct marketers quickly realize the value of proofreading work and creating a complete sample mailer after they have picked up their completed printing runs. Spelling errors, poor phrasing, missed components, and last-minute changes are commonplace. And worst of all, in most cases you'll be on the hook for these errors financially because printers do not assume responsibility for errors from proofs that you have signed off on prior to the run being printed. In addition to proofreading every word and page yourself, always have a second person review the proofs for errors prior to signing off. Likewise, make sure to create a storyboard of your complete mailing package in draft form first. Creating a complete A-to-Z storyboard of your mailing package enables you to carefully review all the components of the package before you go to press with it to make sure that you have not left out critical information or included information that is not relevant to the offer.

STICK WITH STANDARD SIZES AND NEGOTIATE
$ ✎

Whenever possible try to use printing industry standard sizes and weights for paper, envelopes, catalogs, and all components of your direct-mailing package. Straying from printing industry standard sizes or having lots specially die cut and printed can be very costly. In fact, they can easily double and in some cases triple the cost for each thousand mailed. Additionally, ask your printer what sizes, weights, and colors work best for them and what they have in stock; this can be especially useful when it comes time to negotiating a discount on paper inventories they want to reduce. And on that note, asking your printer for a discount just makes good business sense and should be practiced with every run you have printed. Also use incentive to your advantage when negotiating printing costs. These incentives can

include the promises of future print work and offering customer referrals. Printers are like any other business and want to secure long-term loyal customers. You will never get a discount or negotiate a better price unless you ask. Remember it's the squeaky wheel that gets oiled.

NEVER DATE KEY MATERIAL
$ ✎

Here is a little trick that I learned the hard way a few years back: Unless absolutely necessary try never to date key components of your direct mail package like catalogs, brochures, response cards, and order forms, especially when colorful photographs and graphics are used in the package to create a theme. The two biggest benefits of not dating these printed materials is the fact that you can reuse the same inserts for future offers and mailings, and you will not be bound to meet specific mailing or offer dates. As an alternative to printing offer expiry dates or deadlines on key components of your mailer consider using colorful attention grabbing stickers that can be stuck on individually, hand printed on small runs, or run through a desktop laser printer and affixed for larger mailing runs. There is no question that dating offers is the backbone marketing strategy of direct mail and is often required to create a sense of buying urgency to motivate people to take action and respond. However, try to use stickers, small individually dated deadline inserts or response cards, and bold printing on cover letters to indicate when a special offer ends instead of dating key printed materials that otherwise could be used over and over in new campaigns.

DOWNGRADE TO SAVE MONEY
$ ✎

As a rule of thumb the vast majority of people who receive your mail offer will not care particularly what type of card stock or weight of paper your offer is printed on or in what type of envelope the information and offer arrived. In fact most people won't even pay any attention to it at all. So in a bid to increase profitability by reducing overall printing costs, especially in the testing and experimenting phases of your direct-mail campaign, examine all components of your mailing package carefully to see if there are ways to reduce costs by using lower grade paper or by reducing paper weight. At the end of the day always use what works best for the job at hand and that is relevant to what you are selling—meaning don't go cheap if you're selling high-end merchandise or luxury items. But be cognizant of the fact that the vast majority of people will not examine or scrutinize your choice of paper nearly as closely as they will your offer. The decision to buy or not will never be based on the paper you use, but what is said on the paper and what you are offering for sale.

NEVER STOP EXPERIMENTING
$$+ ✎

The great direct marketers of the world all have one thing in common: They never stop experimenting to find new ways to improve on their current direct marketing campaigns no matter how successful and profitable their current campaigns are. These same top direct marketers also strongly believe that a direct-marketing campaign or any one part of the campaign can never be perfect. There is and will always be room for improvement, ways to boost responses, ways to sell more, ways to sell more frequently, and ways to secure better mailing and contact lists and create better offers and marketing messages. In short, direct marketing is an ever-evolving process that requires continual experimentation and hands-on management to constantly generate better results. And to find more cost effective ways to market and continue to serve ever-changing customers with better products and services that are tailored to their individual wants and needs. There is no such thing as status quo in direct marketing. Successful campaigns are not an everlasting goal, they are a mere plateau to bigger and more profitable peaks in the future, providing you are prepared to experiment and change when change is required.

TEST, TEST, AND RETEST
$$+ ✎

One of the keys to a successful direct-mail campaign lies in your ability to know which offer and mail package will get the best response and what is the best use of your money that will secure the maximum return on investment. There is only one way to know for sure and that is to test everything in terms of constructing your direct-mail package and campaign before you spend thousands of dollars and spend countless hours developing and implementing the entire program. There is an old and wise saying about direct-mail marketing, which goes something like this: The first time you see a mailer it is a test. The second time means the first test was positive, the third time means the second test was profitable, and the fourth time means the third time reconfirmed the second mailer and it works. Don't laugh, even the biggest names in direct-mail marketing such as Time Life and Publishers Clearing House still routinely and regularly test variations of their core mailers that have drawn millions of responses and generated billions of dollars in sales revenue over the decades. I have sold everything from $15 videocassettes to $5,000 business-in-a-box programs through direct mail. And it never fails to amaze me that regardless of how much you think you know about how people will respond to your package and to your offer, the results of the test or tests will be vastly different from what you expected. Thus the importance of never making assumptions and testing your package becomes very apparent. So the next question would be how much should you test? How much you test will be directly related to your offer and your marketing objective, not to mention your budget. However, as a general rule you will want to test at least 1,000 mailers (names) if you are using untested mailing lists and are trying a new promotional offer. Therefore, if your list is 20,000 names, test about 5 percent of the list with a variation of your package and offer. The results should give you a sufficient idea about the success of the test packages and offers. Which would lead us to the second question, "what needs to be tested?" Once again, that will depend on your marketing objectives—do you want to sell, generate leads, or qualify? But regardless of your objectives, here are the four basics elements of your package that should be tested.

The List

The list is by far the most important item to test simply because unless it is your in-house list or a list that you have used previously, you have no idea about its quality. Of course the list broker will go to great lengths to ensure you that the quality is great, but then every list they rent is a great list.

The Product

If the product is new to you then I strongly suggest that you test variations of the offer, especially for higher-priced goods. You may believe that the product may require two, three, or even four mailings to qualify, build interest, and close when in reality it might be able to be sold directly, with one shot. Or the opposite could hold true and your prospect may need to be exposed to your product through a number of mailings before you can establish believability, trust, and reduce buying risk and fear.

The Price

Price is another must-test aspect of your package. Price and value are very subjective and this is compounded if you are the creator of the information or product that you are selling via direct mail. From a creator's perspective you may overvalue or undervalue your product, but surprisingly it is almost always undervalued. The reason is that you know what you are selling, in fact you probably know it so well that your perceived value of the product will begin to diminish over time. Think of it this way: If you knew how to send an e-mail and did it 500 times a day, what would you charge someone to show them how to send an e-mail? Likely you would do it for free because it is so easy to you. But what is the value of this knowledge to the person you teach to send an e-mail? The answer could be very high depending on how much they benefit by being able to send e-mails. So that is the point you never know—what someone is prepared to pay for your product, especially if it is an exclusive product that they cannot get anywhere else and that greatly benefits them.

The Response Booster

The final thing you should test is your response booster, which is the special offer, premium, or incentive that you use in your package to motivate prospects to respond and to create a sense of urgency to respond or buy. Response boosters range from free delivery to the next ten callers, to a two-for-one product offer if you respond before a certain deadline, to a free one-hour online consultation, or just about anything else that will increase your response rate. The response booster can have a dramatic effect on the overall success or failure of your package, and therefore a couple of variations should be tested to increase the odds of using what will work best. Later in this chapter you will find 50 great tricks for boosting responses.

Additional Test Considerations

Beyond testing the four basic elements of your direct-mail package and offer, here are a few other additional considerations to keep in mind in terms of testing.

- Every new product or offer should be tested. You can make some assumptions once you're up and running, but in the infancy stage, test all aspects of a new product and offer before you launch the entire direct-mail campaign.
- Always track your tests and keep detailed records of the responses or orders you receive; after all, testing is researching and unless you can store and instantly recall huge amounts of information, your tests will be worthless.
- Before testing, set a target that you believe will be considered successful and give yourself a little room for variation on responses. For instance, if a response rate of 5 percent is your goal for rolling out the entire program then move forward at 6 percent.
- Don't abandon testing if things are not going as expected or even horribly. After all, that is what testing is meant to reveal, problems that could be a lot more costly if you didn't take the time to test and find out.
- Even if your budget is tight don't try to fudge it and roll out your entire package. Blowing $500 on a test is money wisely invested, while wasting $2,500 on a full-scale direct-mail assault that gets zero responses is a waste of money and foolish.

CAPITALIZE WITH CARD DECKS

$$+

Direct response card decks or postcard advertising decks are another avenue for the direct marketer to get products and offers out to the buying public. And with more than 1,000 suppliers and mailing card deck services out there, the choices for reaching your specific target market are nearly unlimited. The vast majority of card deck advertising opportunities are provided by magazine and report publishers that mail their ad decks to their subscribers, generally three times a year though some offer the service more or less frequently. The typical card deck will include anywhere from 10 to 100 cards, which are mailed to prospects wrapped in plastic and generally are approximately 3½" x 5⅜" in size. Consequently, there is not a lot of space for copy, product descriptions, and photographs so clever copy skills and a bold attention grabbing headline are a must. Some offer different sizes and styles such as folding cards, but for the most part the majority are standard sizes and printed in black and white or limited colors. The key to success with card deck advertising lies within your ability to reach your target market. So great importance must be paid to whom and where the card decks are being mailed. A good source of information about market segmentation by lifestyle, geographics, demographics, and psychographics is the *Standard Rate and Data Sourcebook*, a link to their Web site is included below. However, be aware that this publication is very costly so you might want to check with the library first to see if it is available there or with a few of your suppliers to see if they have a copy on hand that you can borrow. Costs to get involved in card deck mailing programs vary greatly from a low of $15 for each thousand mailed to a high of $75 for each thousand mailed plus the cost of return postage, layout, and design of the ad. Response rates also greatly vary, though advertisements that offer money back guarantees, free trial periods, and special incentives or offers receive a much higher response rate, which can go as high as 5 percent or more based on the total mail out. However, shoot for between a .5 and 1 percent response rate in terms of conducting a break-even

analysis to be on the safe side prior to making an advertising commitment.

A Few More Card Deck Advertising Tips

- Concentrate your copy on selling the offer or incentive to respond and not on the product that you are trying to sell. Copy space is limited on cards, not to mention the competition from other cards in the deck. Therefore the objective is to get readers to respond so that you can increase your selling opportunities. The best way to accomplish this is with a powerful incentive or offer to motivate readers to respond.

- The card deck program that you are participating in must reach your primary target audience and not secondary markets; if it does not do not bother to waste your time and money on the effort. When in doubt ask the publisher or mailer for a media kit or list characteristics breakdown and information so that you will have a better idea about who their target audience is and if they match your target audience.

- Make it clear on the card that you want people to respond. Give brief step-by-step instructions: "To receive your free gift and our valuable information, check this box and drop it in the mail; it's just that easy." Remember that all good marketing regardless of medium tells the target audience what to do next.

- Never ask people to work and spend money in order to respond, always use postage-paid business reply cards. Likewise, do not just rely on prospects sending your card back. Instead include other ways that prospects can contact you and make sure these are printed on the card, including a toll-free telephone number, e-mail address, and Web site.

- Keep in mind that in all likelihood there are another 30 to 100 cards in the deck, all of which are fighting to grab the attention of the reader. So with that in mind, create a powerful headline that grabs attention and compels readers to read on and find out more about your special offer.

- If you are running display or classified ads in a particular magazine already call to find out if they have a card deck program in place. If they do, it may be well worth getting involved for the simple reason that readers will already have been exposed to your ads a few times in print. This can add credibility and build awareness.

WEB RESOURCE

- www.srds.com: SRDS (Standard Rate and Data Service) Media Solutions, print and online lifestyle and demographic publication source-books.

GUARANTEED TIPS TO BOOST YOUR MAIL RESPONSES
$+ ⚒

One of the keys to a successful direct-mail campaign is to ensure that you are receiving a high response rate to your mailing package and the offers included in it, otherwise the effort is for nothing. You can never have enough tricks up your sleeve in terms of boosting direct-mail response rates. In fact, you should always be testing new and unique ways to get more responses and better quality responses. With that in mind, here are a few time-tested and proven ways that you can use to boost your direct-mail response rates.

Set Your Objective

Focus on one specific objective or reason for this mailing. Your objective could be to sell, collect leads, to give away free product samples, or to qualify your prospects for a second or follow-up mailing. Of course, if your mailing is multisegment or conducted in phases, each mailing will have a different objective than the previous, but still must be cohesive and meet the overall objective of the marketing campaign. Likewise, never weaken your offer by trying to get the reader or prospect to take advantage of anything more than you want them to, your key objective for that particular mailing. Once again, multiple offers that meander away from your key objective will confuse and in some cases irritate readers. Stick to the plan and get them to do what you want them to do.

Create Deadlines

Another great method of securing a higher response rate is to always include a deadline that your target audience or recipients of your mailed materials must meet if they wish to take advantage of your main offer, response offer, or other special offers that you have made in the package. Deadlines, be it a firm order date, financial incentive, or limited product availability create a sense of buying or response urgency. Miss the order or response deadline and you miss a fantastic opportunity to buy and benefit from what you have purchased.

Simplicity Counts

It cannot be overstated that if you want a high response rate to your mail-outs you must make it as simple, convenient and easy for readers to respond to your offer as possible. Include toll-free calling options, Web site URLs for further details, self-addressed and stamped return envelopes and response cards, and access to a 24-hour toll-free order or information hotline. The response instructions should be bold, clearly stated, and simple. The more ways you give readers to respond the higher your response rate will be; it's just that simple.

Include a Postscript

Dramatically increase response rates by always including a bold P.S. (postscript) on your opening letter, reply card, and order form that restates all the following key information:

- The main benefit of your offer—what your product or service will do for your target audience.
- Your key marketing or sales message—the most important thing that you want your target audience to know about your product or service.
- Specific and clearly stated deadline information to create response or buying motivation and urgency.
- Toll-free hotline number or alternate contact method.
- Why the reader should take action and respond immediately—a special offer, limited quantity, financial incentive or gift, etc.

Try Keeper and Bonus Gifts

Offer readers a special and exclusive no obligation "keeper" gift just for responding. The keeper gift must represent enough value to the reader that it is worth their effort to respond. Additionally, clever direct marketers have figured out that if you make your keeper gift relevant to your main offering then there is a higher response and purchase rate. For instance if you're selling a book of cooking recipes, then great and relevant keeper gifts just for responding would include cookie cutters, a free subscription to your recipe of the month club, a chef's knife, and other small gifts that are relevant to the main product or offer. Likewise offer a special bonus gift or information to people if they respond before a specific date. This is another great way to increase responses and create a sense of urgency. Once again, keep in mind that your special gift offer should be relevant to your main offering to have real impact.

Guarantee Your Main Offer

Make a strong guarantee to reduce the prospect's fear of buying or to replying to your offer. The guarantee should be bold and repeated two or three times throughout your mailing package and again on your reply form, order form, or response card. Your stated guarantee has to be strong enough that it greatly reduces or completely eliminates the prospect's fear of buying or in the least responding to your offer. Of course the strongest guarantee to make is an unconditional guarantee with no strings attached.

Identify Your Niche

Before you write your main offer, compile a list of what makes your product or service different from competitors' products and services. Find what your niche is in the marketplace and build your offering around the benefits of your niche. Every offer needs to have a competitive advantage; without one why would people buy from you and not the competition or even at all? Your competitive advantage could be a lower price, exclusive products available nowhere else, fast delivery and setup, or perhaps special features that will greatly benefit the user.

Reduce Buying Risk

If possible avoid asking for money up front. Instead offer a "bill me" option, credit card payments, and installment plan options in place of up-front payments. It is a proven fact that the easier you make it for people to buy from a financial standpoint, the higher the percentage of people who will respond positively and take action and buy. Once again by not asking for money up front you will reduce the risk to the prospect of buying or responding to your offer because they will feel as though they have nothing to lose. Reducing financial risk to the buyer is a surefire way of generating more leads and securing more sales.

Ask for Referrals

Make sure to include a second order or response form in your package with specific instructions that they are to share and pass the second order or response form to a friend or family member. And really ramp up the effectiveness of this simple trick by offering a discount or special incentive if the person they share the second form with buys or responses to the offer. The recipients of your mailer may not be interested in your products or services, but they may know someone who would be. Therefore, it is wise to always develop creative ways to ask readers for referrals.

Facts and Figures

Use precise figures when giving statistical numbers. For instance, "increase your profits by 253 percent" has much greater and positive psychological impact than "increase your profits by more than 200 percent," or worse "increase your profits by two times." Facts and figures should always be used in your message and package, but don't round them off or minimize their value in any other fashion, instead make them look big, bold, and beneficial to the reader. Also be as specific in your claims as possible and back them up with factual and proven data and testimonials. Stating, "You need to buy our booklet because 50 percent of new businesses fail" is not nearly as powerful as, "A recent survey conducted by the United States Small Business

Administration discovered that 50 percent of new business enterprises fail. Buy our book and we guarantee that you will succeed in business."

Flag Key Information with Subheadlines

Use powerful and bold subheadlines throughout the various components of your mailing package so that "skimmers" will still understand the key sales message, main benefit, and the call for action when they are skimming through your package. Additionally, bold subheadlines have the ability to pull nonskimmer readers further into your letter when they glance at something of interest, and that is a key point of great copy; it must get the reader involved with the message.

Edit, Edit, Edit

Edit hard, as less is more. Generally from the first draft of your mailing package to the final draft, half will be edited out. Likewise don't feel a need to overcrowd pages—white, or blank, spaces make readers feel comfortable while crowded pages make them feel stressed and confused. Also avoid overuse of capitalized words, bold-faced words, headings and phrases, and exclamation marks. Use them only in areas where they will have the greatest impact on readers and motivate them take action. If you use too many capital words, bold phrases, and exclamation marks, readers will feel as though your letter is screaming at them. Many people find this offensive and will simply trash your offering instead of responding.

Invite Participation

One of the best ways to increase mailer response rates is to get the reader involved in the response process by using participation devices such as stamps and stickers that they have to move from one place to another. Check boxes also work well, but if you use any participation method that requires readers to write make sure that you include a inexpensive pen imprinted with your business and message in the package. Also consider combining skill testing questions and quizzes that can be redeemed for a prize or gift when responding to the main offer.

Consistency

Strive to keep the tone of your message and writing style throughout your entire mailing package consistent. Don't make readers have to work in order to understand what you are saying, how you are saying it, and what they will really get. The more they have to work, the higher the chances go of your mailer ending up in the trash. Fun participation is good and increases responses, but requiring people to think and work hard never succeeds and is guaranteed to draw a dismal response.

Power Words and Phrases

Freely use power words and phrases that make people feel good, important and want to take action. Free, save, profit, and rich are just a few excellent choices. In this chapter you will find the 200 most powerful words to use in advertising and writing for action. Using these words is guaranteed to boost response rates. Also be sure to break your copy into easily digestible sections or paragraphs. Once again overloading the reader with too much information or repetitive information at once will cause confusion and lack of interest.

Personalize

Whenever possible, try to use the recipients' first and last names throughout your package, as though the offer is exclusive to them to no one else is receiving your highly beneficial and secretive information. This makes people feel important and more likely to respond or act on your offer. If you cannot use their names throughout then always emphasize the word you, and not words like we, them, or us. You must create ways to engage each prospect as an individual. You might be marketing to thousands at one time, but you will always be reaching them one at a time.

Create Mystery

Create mystery by using a window or peek-a-boo style envelope so that people can catch a glimpse of a teaser offer or special incentive pasted inside the package. This compels people to want to open the package rather than toss it in the garbage without opening it. And in doing so you increase the potential to secure more responses simply due to the fact that more people come into contact with your offer. There is great power in mystery; so be creative in the way you use it to generate direct marketing sales and leads.

Make It Credible

Improve your response rate by building credibility and trust by way of true statements such as "1,000 customers can't be wrong," or "We belong to such-and-such business or industry association or the BBB." Always look for ways to include trust and credibility statements in your sales pitch. Additionally name-dropping will go a long way to help establish credibility. If your product is manufactured or used by a well-known name, then pepper that name throughout your mailing package. Being perceived as aligned with major and trusted names in business is extremely powerful marketing.

Benefits Are King

Always push the benefits and answer the "what's in it for me?" question throughout your mailer. Nothing will make readers respond better than knowing what great things (benefits) they are going to get because of it. Likewise be sure to repeat your major benefit and strongest argument for readers to respond immediately on your order form. Often people will set aside the order form or even complete it with the intention of mailing it or calling later. What happens is they forget why they completed the order form because there is no specific information on the order form. Or, they lose interest and therefore trash the order form because the BIG BENEFIT is not there to remind them why they must respond.

GREAT TRICKS TO SECURE BETTER QUALITY MAIL RESPONSES
$+ ✎

Direct marketing can be a game of give and take, while you may want to secure better quality responses to your offer, chances are it will come at the cost of securing fewer overall responses to your offer. Only you can determine what is more important for your particular situation. And with that said here are a few tricks that you can use to help increase the quality of

the responses you receive from your direct marketing campaigns.

Get a Financial Commitment

Ask people to pay for your catalog, book, report, or any other type of information about your offering up front, and agree to credit the cost back to them in full if they buy your product or service. This simple trick works extremely well to ensure that your responses are much better qualified; few people will part with money to learn or discover more about your product or service unless they are truly interested in what you have to offer. However, do be sure to clearly state that the money they pay up front for your catalog, etc. will be completely applied toward any purchases they make.

Let Them Pay to Contact You

Another way to increase the quality of your responses is not to supply toll-free telephone calling options and skip the stamped self-addressed return envelopes. Once again, if someone is truly interested in your offer they will be willing to pay for the call or for a stamp themselves. This simple trick is very effective at reducing the number of unqualified responses you receive.

Make Them Prequalify for Your Offer

If you want to really prequalify prospects who respond to your offer then let them know in your offer that they themselves will have to qualify in order to buy your product or service. Do this by running the prospects through a series of meetings with salespeople in person or on the telephone, or by including a questionnaire that they must first complete and send back before you will release further information about your offer. Many business and investment opportunities companies skillfully use this clever trick to both increase the quality of the respondents and to also motivate prospects to buy by creating fear that they might not be qualified to buy.

Be Picky about Who You Target

Perhaps the easiest way to ensure that you receive the most and best qualified responses to your mailings and other direct-marketing efforts is to be extremely picky about who you send your package to or call in the first place. Use your own in-house mailing list or rent lists that are highly specialized in terms of the target audience you want to reach.

THE LOW-DOWN ON CATALOGS

$$+

Product catalogs have long been a powerful marketing tool utilized by direct marketers, corporations, and small-business owners worldwide and for decades. In fact, some estimates place the Sears (including all incarnations of the company) catalog as the third most published and distributed source of print bound information, right behind the Bible and Chairman Mao's Little Red Book. Even with the advent of the Internet, which allows for lightning quick distribution of information, catalogs continue to flourish. Mainly because savvy marketers not only rely on print catalogs, but electronic catalogs distributed through the Web as well. However, like any marketing method or activity, there are a few questions to answer prior to launching your own product catalog.

Niche Purpose

The one great aspect of catalogs is that they allow you to fill a very specific niche in the marketplace if that is your objective. You can organize your catalog and feature products for a very specific target or niche market such as specialty replacement parts, used or collectable items, specialized software, or price. I say niche purpose simply because that is the market that catalog marketing appeals to—people who cannot find a specific product in their own area, or people who like the convenience that catalog shopping provides. Catalog shoppers are seldom impulse buyers unless there is a very compelling reason or offer on the table for them to be. Therefore, if you are hawking products through your catalog that consumers or business buyers can easily get elsewhere, you might have a rough trail to blaze. It works for Sears and others, but that is because of a very wide selection and loyalty to the brand that was established when shopping locally was neither

convenient nor available. Consequently, unless you have a core group of customers to sell to, or you have a product that people cannot get elsewhere, catalog marketing likely is not your best bet.

Distribution

Once again, product catalogs can be in print or electronic format, or both; much will depend on the purpose, products, and budget. The benefits to distributing an e-catalog are obvious—it's cheap, fast, and the results or orders can be almost immediate. However, on the downside people are being deluged with so much e-mail these days that pushing the delete button is very easy. Regardless of the format of the catalog there is also the question of who will receive it, current customers and prospects or new prospects, and how will you reach these people? In-house mailing list, rented mailing lists, or general mail-outs through the postal service? Of course, other distribution questions will be order taking, order fulfillment, and customer service beyond the sale, just to mention a few.

Design and Management

Another consideration will be who will design the catalog and manage the program? Will it be in-house or hired out to a professional, and what will your budget be? Catalogs can be produced very inexpensively if you want to strictly put out a budget version. Years ago we were able to produce a decent-looking black-and-white basic catalog for our mail-order venture for less than $1,000 for each 1,000 mailed including postage. But the catalog was designed, produced, and managed in-house and was certainly not one that would have been suitable for luxury items or top end products. So back to my point—depending on what you are selling and how many you want to produce, catalogs can be very expensive for small-business owners to get rolling and therefore require a lot of research, planning, and budgeting prior to making a commitment.

A Few More Great Catalog Tips

- Always include an order form with your catalog. In fact try to include two: one a loose insert and the second a tear-away or cut-out order form. Additionally, give prospects numerous ways to order beyond mail such as a toll-free number and a Web site. Also make it easy for people to pay for their purchases by accepting check, money order, credit cards, bill me options, cod's, e-checks, and installment plans.

- Feature your bestselling and most profitable products near the front of the catalog. The first few pages are almost always read or at least glanced at by customers and prospects while the middle and back generally receive less fanfare, especially from new prospects. Likewise a strong seller should be placed on the front and back covers along with a beneficial and powerful attention-grabbing headline.

- When you send out your catalog include a letter with a last minute or special offer, even if the offer you are making means selling at below cost. One critical aspect of direct-marketing mail order is to get the prospects to make that first purchase. Once they have and once they have discovered how easy the process was and how credible your company is, they are much more likely to continue to buy from you. So view the initial loss as a business cost that can be recouped over lifetime selling to the customer.

- Always push the benefits of your products, list the features in the copy, but make the benefits or what the product will do for the buyer leap off the page and speak directly to them.

- Use lots of photos in your catalog to help sell, explain, and describe. Ideally, if the photographs or illustrations can depict the main benefit of the product being featured, the better. A picture really is worth a thousand words.

Web Resources

- www.cataloguecreator.com: Custom software that enables you to design your own print and electronic product catalogs.

- www.catalogprinter.biz: Custom catalog design and printing service with free online quotes.

CONSIDER CABLE SHOPPING CHANNELS
$$+ ☎ 🐭

Providing you have the right product, gigantic sales opportunities can be realized by selling your goods through cable shopping channels. For more than a decade, three shopping broadcasters have dominated the shop from home airways: The Home Shopping Network and QVC (Quality Value Convenience) in the United States and The Shopping Channel in Canada. How big are these companies and the shop-from-home market? Very big, in fact huge. In 2000, the Home Shopping Network alone generated sales in excess of $1.8 billion and reached an estimated 143 million consumer households worldwide. However, before you ring them up and ask how you can get your goods featured on their networks, here are a few facts about products that sell well in these electronic retail forums. They all share similar characteristics.

- The products must demonstrate extremely well.
- The products must make life easier.
- The products must solve or fix a problem.
- The products must appeal to a broad audience.
- The products must have unique features and ownership benefits.
- The products must be timely.
- The products must not be readily available through traditional community distribution and retail channels.

In addition to selling opportunities through broadcast programs, they also provide selling opportunities via their Web sites and in some case printed catalogs distributed to customers and prospects. Listed below are the three major cable shopping channels in the United States and Canada; each has vendor information available on its Web site.

Web Resources

- www.hsn.com: Home Shopping Network (HSN)
- www.qvc.com: Quality, Value, and Convenience (QVC)
- www.tsc.ca: The Shopping Channel (TSC, Canada)

GETTING PAST THE TELEMARKETING STIGMA

$ ✎

Many small-business owners flat out refuse to use telemarketing as a promotional and marketing tool for their business simply because of the bad publicity generated by a few unscrupulous rogue telemarketing outfits that have cheated seniors, businesses, and consumers of all sorts in recent years. However, you shouldn't let a few rotten apples deter you from taking advantage of and profiting from a highly effective marketing medium. In fact, when it comes right down to it, there is not a single businessperson that does not telemarket daily in the form of client calls, follow-up calls, calls to set presentations, or calls to invite prospects to business events and so forth. Like it or not, and admit it or not, all these are examples of using the telephone for marketing purposes, or otherwise known as telemarketing. The telephone should not be ignored, as every business owner and manager can benefit and profit from learning to use this powerful marketing medium as a tool to increase business revenues and profits.

Keep in mind that as of October 1, 2003 the creation of the "Do Not Call Registry" limits telemarketing efforts to people that are not on the "Do Not Call" list. Calling consumers that register to be on the list can result in sizeable fines. See the Web Resources for more information about this matter.

Web Resources

✍ www.donotcall.gov: National Do Not Call Registry.

✍ www.telemarketing.donotcall.gov: Downloadable Do Not Call list for telemarketers.

FORGET COLD CALLS AND CONCENTRATE ON WARM CALLS

$ ✎

Unquestionably cold calling is one of the most difficult telemarketing techniques to master, and if you're like most, the thought of making cold calls can send shivers up your spine. But what if there was an easy way to turn cold telemarketing into warm telemarketing, would you benefit from this? Now that I have your undivided attention here is how you can turn cold calling into warm calling. Forget name lists, picking names at random from telephone directories, automatic software dialers, and subscription lists. Instead concentrate on targeting your telemarketing efforts on people who share similar interests as you, or your business, and use this as the all-important icebreaker. Have you ever noticed that two people riding motorcycles and passing each other from opposite directions will wave to each other, but not to people driving cars? Or, two people walking their dogs on opposite sides of the street will wave to each other, but not to other pedestrians? Why? Simply because they share common interests and that creates an instant bond. Therefore if you operate a homebased business, concentrate your telemarketing efforts on other homebased business owners. Or, if you belong to your local PTA, then secure lists of other PTA associations and call their members. Sharing a common interest with the person you are calling enables you to immediately break the ice by referring to that common interest in your introduction.

USE TELEMARKETING TO REINFORCE

$$ ✎

Use telemarketing to reinforce other marketing activities that you might have on the go such as direct mail, seminars, trade shows, print advertisements, mobile sales force, and radio and television advertising campaigns. The reinforcement telemarketing strategy should be two-part. Make calls prior to the launch of the marketing activity informing prospects about the nature or reason for the marketing activity, be it a special offer, an invitation to a trade show that you will be exhibiting at, or the introduction of a new product or service. The purpose of the precall is to alert prospects about this forthcoming activity and build excitement. This call should be made about three days before the marketing activity begins. The second, follow-up call should be made three days after the marketing activity has taken place. The focus of this call should be to close prospects, set further appointments, answer questions, or all of the above. Reinforcement telemarketing is a hands-on approach that makes prospects feel as though you care about their welfare and interests.

Additionally one of the biggest benefits to this technique is that print, radio, or mail cannot replace the effectiveness of personal selling simply because a prospect cannot ask an advertisement, piece of paper, or television spot for additional information or clarification of information. Used effectively this simple telemarketing technique can double the response you get to your marketing activity.

SMALL DETAILS EQUAL BIG IMPACT IN TELEMARKETING

$$ ✎ ☎ ⚖

Like anything we do in life, always paying attention to the small details can have the biggest impact on what you are trying to accomplish. For that reason, here are a few small details to consider in terms of ensuring big impact on the telephone.

- Clearly define the objective of your call before you make the call. Your objective could be to sell, set an appointment to present or demonstrate, notify a potential prospect about a forthcoming event, introduce a new product or service, pass along a special offer or incentive, or just about any other valid reason that will benefit the person you are calling and motivate a close. Know why you're calling and what action you want the prospect or your customer to do as a result of the call.

- Avoid technical terms. Speak in plain English that your customers and prospects will understand and appreciate. Never talk down to them or use terminology that they will not understand; all this accomplishes is to make prospects feel uneasy and, worse, stupid because they have no clue about what you are talking. What you really want to accomplish is for the person on the other end of the line to feel special and important.

- Always be polite and use phrases and words such as please, thank you, may I, and you're very welcome. And, engage in conversation in such a way that it requires your prospect's involvement right away. Few people will sit back and listen to another ramble on without quickly becoming irritated and tuning them out, especially when it is a telemarketer or salesperson.

- Get comfortable before you start making calls, especially if you plan to make numerous calls and be on the telephone for more than hour at one time. Getting comfortable should include having a glass of water in front of you; sitting in a comfortable chair; and having all your notes, presentations, and fact sheets ready to call upon and support your claims as required. Basically, you want to be armed and ready for maximum productivity while on the telephone.

- Clearly state the purpose of your call and get right to the point. Respect your prospect's or customer's time and never take it for granted or waste it. And finally, always use your customer's or prospect's first name throughout the conversation. As noted author and motivational speaker Dale Carnegie said numerous times, "There is no sweeter sound to a person's ears then the sound of his own name."

TRICKS TO SELL BY VOICE

$ ✎

Voice is perhaps the most important and powerful tool the telemarketer has at her immediate disposal, in terms of an instrument used to build excitement and motivate others to buy. Voice can sell, voice can explain, voice can calm, and voice can make messages sound exciting and desirable, therefore try out these tricks that professional telemarketers use to sell by voice.

- Unlike personal contact, you do not have the benefit of showing or demonstrating product samples because prospects obviously cannot see or touch them. Hence, you must rely on telling people what it is you want them to see. This is best accomplished by using very colorful descriptive adjectives and phrases to help prospects visualize your product and even the benefits of taking ownership. Sit down with a pen and notepad, close your eyes, and visualize your products; write down a description of what you see in your mind and build from there adding key phrases until you are happy with the verbal description of your products.

- Develop an interesting-sounding voice by practicing your speech and playing it back on tape.

Too low and monotone and you'll come off as boring and may not be heard by everyone you speak to on the phone. Too high or loud and you'll come off as irritating and pushy and alienate prospects right from the start.

- Pace your speech or pitch so that it comes off as natural and unscripted; talk too fast and you run the risk of people missing what you say or coming across as pushy. Likewise, talk too slow and you'll come off as boring and people will lose interest in what you have to say. Try to speak at a comfortable pace; most speech specialists agree that 150 to 180 words a minute is a comfortable pace for the speaker and the listener.

- Highlight key elements of your sales pitch by changing the tone of your voice and your emotion at the exact moment of presenting these key features and benefits. Once you have verbally punctuated your main point, be silent for a moment to wait for the prospect to respond. Listen for telltale signs of involvement in the conversation and interest in your offer. These signs include excitement in their tone, a line of questioning about your main point, and responding or making statements of agreement or relaying how your point would benefit them.

- Always restate the main benefits of your product or service and how they will meet or exceed your prospect's needs and benefit him or solve a problem before you disengage from the conversation.

TELEMARKETING MISTAKES TO AVOID
$ ⚒

The following are a number of telemarketing mistakes that you should avoid at all costs.

Wrong Purpose

If the purpose of the telephone call is to sell, then the product or service you are selling must be saleable over the telephone. If a demonstration is required, or if a demonstration greatly increases the likelihood of a sale then don't try to sell the product or service over the phone. The true purpose of the call would then be to qualify and send out a field representative to present or demonstrate the product or service, or alternately you could ask the prospect to attend a demonstration seminar or go to a dealer showroom in their particular geographic area.

Wrong Audience

The wrong audience could be an untested contact list or any audience that is not warm to your offer. The wrong audience is a very common mistake, especially for business- and salespeople who want to develop a telemarketing program, but rather than research, plan, and test, they instead dive right in and start with the phone book at *A* and quickly become discouraged with the poor results. To increase the chances of telemarketing success you have to first determine the audience that is likely to respond favorably to your offer more times than not.

Wrong Person

Simply put, talking to people who cannot make a buying decision, people who cannot afford to buy what you are selling, and people who have no interest in what you are selling are all the wrong people to be talking to. Once again, a very common error that many novice telemarketers make because they believe and are relieved that they have someone on the other end of the telephone line who is interested in what they have to say and sell. Unfortunately, often this person they are engaged in conversation with cannot make the decision to buy or does not have the ability to buy, they just want someone to talk with.

Wrong Reason

Beyond identifying yourself and your company right from the get go, you have to give the prospect a reason to want to talk to you on the phone. Simply asking their permission is a waste of time. You have to tell them what the benefit to them will be for taking the time to get involved and participate in the call and conversation. People have to know that the 10, 20, or 30 minutes they spend with you on the telephone can potentially have a positive and beneficial impact on their lives.

Not Listening

While scripts are required to break the ice and deliver a consistent and clear message, they also must be flexible. You cannot do all of the talking and expect that the answers you will receive will be the canned answers that you are anticipating. You have to listen to what prospects are telling you and be able to act accordingly.

Not Selling

The final mistake is not attempting to sell, or giving up after asking for the sale only once. Telemarketing should be about selling, and when your prospect buys, then get busy up-selling to increase the effectiveness of the call and sales value. And when that is accomplished, ask prospects for referrals, names of other people they know who would also benefit from what you have to offer. In person or on the telephone always practice your ABCs, which means always be closing.

VISIT YOUR BEST 20 PERCENT, TELEMARKET THE REST
$$ ⚒

It's true that if small-business owners took the time to identify their best customers in relation to their total revenues and profits that in the majority of situations you would find that 80 percent of your sales revenue and profits will be provided by 20 percent of your total customer base. While the remaining 20 percent of revenues and profits will be generated by the remaining 80 percent of your customer base. This is a widely accept notion and for that reason make sure to make the best use of your time and develop a system to identify who your best customers are. Once you have identified the 20 percent who are responsible for 80 percent of your business revenue, then visit those people in person and on a regular basis. The other 80 percent of your customers who are responsible for the other 20 percent of business revenues can be contacted via telemarketing. Not only will this simple system save time, but it also enables you to stay in close personal contact with your best customers while not leaving the other 80 percent who can over time become better customers out in the cold. This is one of the powerful benefits of adopting a telemarketing program. Telemarketing can enable you to make wise decisions about where your time is best spent in person while still staying in contact with all customers and prospects via the telephone.

DIRECT MARKETING MARKET PLACE®
$$ ⚒

The National Register Publishing Company publishes an annual direct marketing directory called Direct Marketing Market Place. This directory is packed with thousands of sources of information and resources that will benefit both the direct-marketer selling products and services to businesses and consumers as well as suppliers of direct marketing services and products such as printers, copywriters, and photographers. In total, this book contains more than 16,000 listings in 19 categories and is often referred to as "The networking source of the direct-marketing industry," making this directory an invaluable information source for any business owner or manager who is currently utilizing direct marketing activities or is considering adding direct marketing into their marketing mix. At $339 the book is fairly priced considering the vast amount of information that is included and the opportunities that can be realized and formed with other like-minded businesspeople listed in it. However, if your financial budget is tight, make sure to check the library first as the bigger ones might have the book on the shelf. And of course, if you have no luck tracking down a copy at your local library you can always partner with a few businesses to buy the directory together and split the cost.

WEB RESOURCE
⚓ www.dirmktgplace.com: National Register Publishing, Direct Marketing Market Place.

THE 200 MOST PERSUASIVE WORDS TO USE IN ADVERTISING
$ ⚒

The following 200 words are considered to be the most persuasive words that you can use in advertising and direct-marketing copy, as well as in radio and television commercials and on the telephone. Of course the number-one persuader is the word FREE. However, you cannot only use the word free so use these words alone or group them together into powerful and persuasive phrases that are guaranteed to attract the response that you want and desire from your advertising and marketing efforts. They have been selected because they are considered to be "appeal triggers." Meaning that each will appeal to basic human needs that we all share, such as the need for security, the need for relationships, the need to achieve, the need to lead, and so forth.

The 200 Persuasive Words for Marketing

A

Absolutely	Advice	Amazing
Announcing	Anticipation	Appeal
Appreciative	Approved	Attention
Attractive	Authentic	

B

Bargain	Beautiful	Believe
Benefit	Best	Big
Blowout	Brand name	Bright
Budget	Buy	

C

Call	Care	Challenge
Choose	Cost	Clearance
Compare	Complete	Confidential
Convenient		

D

Delicious	Delivered	Dependable
Deserve	Development	Direct
Discount	Discover	Drastically

E

Easy	Endorsed	Event
Excellent	Exciting	Exclusive
Expert	Extra	Extravaganza

F

Fabulous	Fact	Family
Famous	Fantastic	Fascinating
Fast	Feel	Fortune
Free	Fresh	Full

G

Gain	Genuine	Get
Gift	Gigantic	Give
Go	Great	Guarantee

H

Have	Health	Hello
Help	Helpful	Highest
Honest	Huge	Hurry

I

Incredible	Important	Improve
Informative	Interesting	Introducing
Invited		

K

Knowledge	Keep

L

Largest	Latest	Learn
Lifetime	Limited	Look
Low	Love	

M

Magic	Miracle	Modern
More	Most	

N

Need	New	News
Now		

O

Offer	Official	Open
Opportunity	Outstanding	

P

Personalized	Please	Popular

The 200 Persuasive Words for Marketing, continued

Powerful	Practical	Price	Start	Startling	Strong
Present	Professional	Profitable	Sturdy	Successful	Suddenly
Promise	Protect	Proud	Superior	Surprise	Support
Proven					
			T		
Q			Take	Team	Terrific
Qualified	Quality	Quick	Tested	Thank you	Time
			Today	Tremendous	Trust
R			Try		
Rare	Ready	Real			
Reassurance	Recommended	Redeemable	**U**		
Reduced	Referred	Refundable	Ultimate	Unconditional	Understand
Relax	Reliable	Remarkable	Unique	Unlimited	Useful
Responsible	Reputation	Results			
Reward	Revolutionary	Rich	**V**		
Right	Rush		Valuable	Vast	
			W		
S			Want	Wanted	Warranty
Satisfaction	Save	Safety	Wealth	Welcome	Win
Secret	Secure	Security	Wise	Wonderful	
Selected	Selection	Self-confidence	**Y**		
Sensational	Service	Simple	Yes	You	Youthful
Smart	Smile	Special			

PLACES TO ADVERTISE IDEA CHECKLIST

$+

Here are some great ideas about places that you can advertise your business. Some of these ideas are featured in the advertising chapters while others are not.

Cost range. Each advertising idea also includes the general cost associated with the particular advertising activity. They are grouped according to average cost, however, be aware that this is a yardstick cost estimate and make sure that you thoroughly investigate the costs of advertising before committing to purchase.

$	$0–$100
$$	$100–$1,000
$$$	$1,000–$10,000
$$$$	$10,000+

Business type. Each advertising idea also includes the type of business that it is best suited for. Once again this should only be used as a general guideline.

RT   Retailer
SP   Service Provider (including professionals and consultants)
DM   Direct Marketer
WS   Web Site Online Business
MF   Manufacturer
DW   Distributor/Wholesaler
AL   All Types of Businesses

Places to Advertise Idea Checklist

	Cost	Type	Advertising Idea
❏	$$	RT SP WS DM	Newspaper Display Ads
❏	$	AL	Newspaper Classified Ads
❏	$	RT SP WS	School Newspapers
❏	$$$	RT WS DM	Magazines
❏	$$	AL	Trade Publications and Journals
❏	$$	AL	Special Interest Publications
❏	$$	AL	In-House Newsletters
❏	$$	AL	Corporate, Institutions, Community Newsletters
❏	$$	MF DS	Business Directories
❏	$$	RT SP WS	Consumer Directories
❏	$$$	RT SP DW	Telephone Yellow Pages
❏	$	AL	Telephone White Pages
❏	$$	AL	Web Pages/Internet
❏	$	AL	Banner Advertisements
❏	$	AL	E-zine Publications
❏	$	AL	E-newsletters
❏	$	AL	Reciprocal Web Site Links
❏	$$	AL	Search Engine Keyword Queries
❏	$	AL	E-mail Signatures
❏	$	AL	Internet Directories
❏	$	RT SP WS DM	Web Malls
❏	$$$	RT SP DM	Radio Spot Advertising
❏	$$$	RT SP MF	Radio Program Sponsorship
❏	$$$$	RT SP DM WS	Television Commercial Advertising
❏	$$$$	RT SP WS MF	Television Program Sponsorship
❏	$$	RT SP	Drive-by FM Broadcasting (talking signs)
❏	$$	RT SP DM	Supplier Cooperative Advertising Programs
❏	$$$	AL	Direct-Mail Promotions / Catalogs
❏	$$$	RT SP WS MF	Interior/Exterior Billboards
❏	$$$	RT SP WS MF	Interior/Exterior Transit Advertising
❏	$	RT SP WS DM	Community Bulletin Boards (fliers)
❏	$$	SP	Door Hanger Drops
❏	$$	RT SP	Flier Distribution and Handouts
❏	$$	RT SP	Restaurant Placemats

Places to Advertise Idea Checklist, continued

	Cost	Type	Advertising Idea
❏	$	RT DM	Packaging Insertion Programs
❏	$$	RT SP WS DM	Coupon Books and Coupon Distribution Programs
❏	$$	AL	Event Sponsorship
❏	$$	RT SP WS	Team Sponsorship
❏	$$	RT	Window Displays
❏	$$	RT MF DW	Point-of-Purchase Displays
❏	$$	RT MF DW	Counter Displays
❏	$$	RT SP WS	Interior/Exterior Bench Advertising
❏	$$	RT SP WS	Exterior Bicycle Lock-Up Stands
❏	$$	RT	Cross-Promotion Inserts and Handouts (store)
❏	$$	AL	Postcards
❏	$$	AL	Christmas Cards and Calendars
❏	$$	SP MF	Lawn/Job Signs
❏	$$	RT SP DM	Fax Blasts
❏	$	AL	E-mail Opt-in Blasts
❏	$$$$	DM MF	Infomercials
❏	$$$	DM MF	Cable Shopping Channels
❏	$	SP	Guest Appearances/Radio TV
❏	$$	AL	Telemarketing
❏	$$	RT SP DM	Mailbox Drops
❏	$$$	RT SP WS MF	Arial Banners and Blimps
❏	$$$	RT	Inflatable Advertising
❏	$$	RT	Sidewalk Signs
❏	$$	RT SP WS MF	Human Billboards
❏	$$	RT SP WS MF	Mascots
❏	$	AL	Inserts in Outgoing Mail
❏	$$	RT SP	Take One Brochure Boxes
❏	$$	AL	Seminar and Public Speaking Engagements
❏	$$	MF DW DM	Product Packaging
❏	$$	RT MF DW	Shopping Bags and Boxes
❏	$$	RT	Store Signs
❏	$$	AL	Car Signs
❏	$$	AL	Magnetic Vehicle Signs
❏	$$	RT SP	Theatre Programs

Places to Advertise Idea Checklist, continued

	Cost	Type	Advertising Idea
❑	$$$	RT SP WS MF	Theater Screen Shots
❑	$$	SP	Event Programs
❑	$$	RT SP	Newcomer Programs
❑	$	AL	Business Card Networking
❑	$	AL	Free Booklets and Reports
❑	$$	RT MF DW DM	Product Demonstrations
❑	$$	SP	Service Demonstrations
❑	$$	RT MF DW DM	Free Product Samples
❑	$$	RT SP	Sports Complex Signs/Sponsorship
❑	$$	AL	Imprinted Novelties
❑	$$	RT SP WS	Bumper Stickers
❑	$$	MF	Window Stickers
❑	$$	RT SP WS MF	Imprinted Hats and T-shirts
❑	$$$	RT DM	Card Decks
❑	$	AL	Press Releases and Publicity
❑	$$	RT SP	Cash Register Receipts
❑	$$	RT	Portable and Flashing Signs
❑	$$	RT SP WS	Score Sheets (golf/bowling)
❑	$$	RT SP WS	Telephone Booths
❑	$$$	RT SP WS MF	Parade Floats
❑	$$	RT SP MF	Community Events
❑	$$	RT SP WS MF	Golf Tournaments and Charity Events
❑	$$	RT SP	Hotel/Motel—Take One Brochures
❑	$$	RT	Elevator Advertising (interior)
❑	$$	RT SP WS DM	Community Directory Boards
❑	$$	RT SP	Community Business Maps and Street Maps
❑	$$	RT	Promotional Buttons, Badges, and Stickers
❑	$$	RT SP WS	Hoarding Advertising (construction site safety fence)
❑	$$	AL	CD-ROM Business Card
❑	$$$	AL	Digital Video Presentations
❑	$$	MF	Public Tours of Your Operation
❑	$	AL	Telephone On-Hold Advertising Messages
❑	$	AL	Word of Mouth and Referral Programs

📖 SUGGESTED ADDITIONAL READING

Bly, Robert W. *Business to Business Direct Marketing: Proven Direct Response Methods to Generate More Leads and Sales*. New York: McGraw-Hill, 1998.

————. *The Copywriter's Handbook: A Step-by-Step Guide to Writing Copy that Sells*. New York: Henry Holt Publishing, 1990.

Catal, Joe. *Telesales Tips From the Trenches: Secrets of a Street Smart Salesman*. Omaha, NE: Business By Phone Books, 2002.

Cliff, Stafford. *50 Trade Secrets of Great Design: Packaging*. Gloucester, MA: Rockport Publishers, 2002.

Corbett, Michael. *The 33 Ruthless Rules of Local Advertising*. New York: Pinnacle Books, 1999.

Fowler, David. *Newspaper Ads that Make Sales Jump: A How To Guide*. New York: Marketing Clarity, 1998.

Hatch, Denny and Don Jackson. *2,239 Tested Secrets for Direct Marketing Success: The Pros Tell You Their Proven Secrets*. New York: McGraw-Hill, 1999.

Kobliski, Kathy J. *Advertising Without an Agency: A Comprehensive Guide to Radio, Television, Print, Direct Mail, and Outdoor Advertising for Small Business*. Central Point, OR: Oasis Press, 2001.

Krause, Jim. *Layout Index: Brochure, Web Design, Poster, Flyer, Advertising, Page Layout, Newsletter, Stationery, Index*. Cincinnati, OH: North Light Books, 2001

Levinson, Jay Conrad, Orvel Ray Wilson, and Mark S. A. Smith. *Guerrilla Teleselling: New Unconventional Weapons and Tactics to Sell When You Can't Be There in Person*. New York: John Wiley & Sons, 1998.

Maher, Barry. *Getting the Most From Your Yellow Pages Advertising: Maximum Profits at Minimum Costs*. Newport, RI: Aegis Publishing Group, 1997.

Ogilvy, David. *Ogilvy on Advertising*. New York: Vintage Books, 1987.

Schmid, Jack. *Creating a Profitable Catalog: Everything You Need to Know to Create a Catalog That Sells*. New York: McGraw-Hill, 2000.

Schulberg, Pete and Bob Schulberg. *Radio Advertising: The Authoritative Handbook*. New York: McGraw-Hill, 1996.

Scissors, Jack and Roger B. Baron. *Advertising Media Planning*. New York: McGraw-Hill, 2002.

Sugarman, Joseph. *Television Secrets for Marketing Success: How to Sell Your products on Infomercials, Home Shopping Channels and Spot TV Commercials from the Entrepreneur*. Las Vegas, NV: Delstar Publishing, 1998.

Sullivan, Luke. *Hey Whipple Squeeze This: A Guide to Creating Great Ads*. New York: John Wiley & Sons, 1998.

Usborne, Nick. *Net Words: Creating High-Impact Online Copy*. New York: McGraw-Hill, 2001.

Zeff, Robin Lee and Brad Aronson. *Advertising on the Internet*. New York: John Wiley & Sons, 1999.

PUBLIC RELATIONS
Marketing Tips for Your Business

What kills a skunk is the publicity it gives itself.

—Abraham Lincoln

USE PR TO LEVEL THE COMPETITIVE PLAYING FIELD

$ 🔨

One of the most overlooked benefits of developing and implementing a public relations campaign is the fact that a great public relations campaign enables a small business to level the playing field and compete against larger and, more often than not, better-financed competitors for customers. This is because public relations costs little if anything outside of time to create and implement. Yes it is true that certain advertisements in publications such as the Yellow Pages can be in front of your target audience longer than, say, a free newspaper article about your business, product, or service. But the newspaper article can be just the tip of the publicity iceberg if you learn to master and apply the art of seeking and securing free publicity for your business. Of course, whether or not media outlets pick up your "news" is completely up to you and your ability to make your "news" irresistible to the media. A well-received and publicized

press release can have the same pull or awareness benefit that an advertisement costing five figures has, but with the advantage that the press release costs little if anything to produce. Every business owner and marketer alike needs to plan and implement an ongoing public relations campaign as an active component of an overall marketing plan and strategy. Few forms of advertising or other marketing activities can match the effectiveness and credibility of the media; our daily lives revolve around media and the news. We read the newspaper, watch television, surf the net, and listen to the radio and do so because we want to be entertained, be informed, and learn. Great media exposure can have the same impact on readers, watchers, or listeners as ads that can cost thousands of dollars.

THE "OTHER" PUBLIC RELATIONS

$ 🔨

Public relations is more than just clever ways to secure free media attention and exposure for your business, products, or services though that is primarily the focus of this chapter. This book is not intended to include in-depth explanations about the structure and all practical applications of public relations. However, with that said I think that every small-business owner should be aware of the "other" public relations and how it can be used to help your business communications and position within the industry and your community.

Media

Media is the obvious component of public relations and is the one that the vast majority of small-business owners are aware of because it is the most publicized use of public relations. It is through print and broadcast media exposure that you gain access to a broad audience that is exposed in these media to your marketing message or general information about a business issue, event, or a product or service. And once again, that is the main focus of this chapter, how to use proven methods and clever tricks to secure free (or at least very cheap) media exposure for your business.

Community

The second component that falls under the umbrella of public relations is the interaction between your business and the community that your business operates in. Community-related public relations activities include joining business and nonbusiness associations, volunteering to pitch in with various community activities and events, and often throwing your small-business weight behind one or more local charities. Any time you are out in public within your community you are in effect a goodwill ambassador of your business. These goodwill activities are referred to as being a good corporate and personal citizen and a common characteristic that every successful small-business owner shares.

Government

Public relations is also building open lines of communication between your business and elected and appointed public officials including politicians, city and community planners, and police and fire personnel. The goal is twofold: One, to help local governments

understand what effects their decisions and actions have on your business and two, for you to understand what challenges local officials face in terms of the community as a whole and issues related to decision and policy making. Once again, being heard and listening to local officials is accomplished by being an active member of your community and taking a leadership role when necessary.

Industry and Alliances

Another role of public relations is the communications between your business and the industry you operate in as well as the alliances you form to help guide your business to success. These alliances include suppliers, your bank, accountant, and subcontractors. Industry and alliance PR is accomplished by attending events, hosting events, attending trade shows, and creating special meeting opportunities to discuss the challenges that face your business, industry, products, or service as well as through other means of contact and interaction, such as print and electronic newsletters, journals, and reports.

Internal

The final role that the "other" public relations play is an internal one, the communications between management and ownership of the business and employees. This PR is accomplished through the use of one-on-one meetings, group meetings, memos, internal newsletters, reports, and special events that are all designed to keep the lines of communication and information freely flowing between all parties.

WEB RESOURCE

⌁ www.prsa.org: The Public Relations Society of America

KEY PUBLIC RELATIONS CONSIDERATIONS
$+ ⚒

Before you spring into action you will first have to decide what your public relations goals and objectives are and how you will meet them. The logical starting point is to get out a pen and notepad and write down the following eight questions. Your answers to each will help define your public relations objectives that are best suited to your business and what you want to achieve as a direct result of public relations.

1. What marketing objectives do you want public relations to help you reach?

Your marketing objectives could be anything from wanting to increase sales, introduce a new product or service, generate sales leads, or perhaps separate your product or service from competitors. Or, of course your objective could be a combination of any or all of these. A well planned and executed public relations plan can help you achieve or build on each of these marketing objectives. However, that is the first rule of publicity: What do you want to achieve as a result of the publicity that you are seeking? Listed below is a basic checklist of common publicity objectives.

COMMON PUBLICITY OBJECTIVES

❑ Increase company, product, or service awareness.

❑ Promote a sale, contest, or special event.

❑ Promote a community or charity event.

❑ Drive traffic to a Web site, toll-free information line, or catalog.

❑ Become known as an expert information source within a specific industry or field.

❑ Introduce a new or greatly revamped product or service.

❑ Generate sales leads.

❑ Change public perceptions and consumer buying/spending habits.

❑ Share or announce information that benefits the local community, such as business expansion or new employees.

❑ Expand market share or create a competitive advantage.

❑ Seek the public's help to solve an internal problem, such as naming a new product.

❑ If your company is publicly traded, then release information according to SEC disclosure regulations or release information aimed at increasing stock values.

2. What is the message you want to send out?

The message you want to get out to the news-hungry public will likely change with each news release you send or every time you seek media exposure through another channel such as telephone calls or pitch letters. But at the end of the day each time you seek publicity there must be a key message that you want to get across. One message might be specific information about your products or services, while the next might be more focused on the community your business operates in and is supported by.

3. What audience do you want to reach?

Prior to launching a public relations program or a segment of the program, you have to identify who you want your message to reach—known as your target audience. Once again, your target audience might change with every new release or advisory you send out to the media, but at the core to effectively reach an audience you must first identify who that audience is. Identifying the target audience can be accomplished in a simple and basic way, which is to break it down into three categories and ask yourself questions relevant to these categories: Demographic—what is the age, sex, education, and income level of the audience you want to reach? Geographic—where is your target audience located geographically? Benefits—who will benefit the most from coming into contact with your news by way of media exposure?

4. What media do you want to target?

The importance of knowing which audience you want to reach is partly because you can use that information to identify which media reaches your target audience. For instance, if your target audience is business managers then you will want to target your publicity efforts at media outlets that cater to this particular group. Likewise if your target audience is high school students then you would want to target your PR efforts toward school publications and other forms of media that regularly cater to this demographic.

5. What action do you want people to take as a result of media coverage?

Regardless if your target audience has seen, read, or heard your message you have to know two things in advance: One, what action do you want them to take, and two, what tools will you give them to take the desired action? Do you want them to call you, stop by your store, attend a special event or meeting, or visit your Web site? Depending on the physical action you want your target audience to take you must put tools in place for them to be able to follow through. For instance, if your PR message is that you want people to come out and support a community cleanup that your business is sponsoring then you must include the details such as time, place, things they should bring, contact people, and registration information in your release.

6. What is your timeline for implementing your public relations plan, or a particular segment of the plan?

Sending out a press release or pitch letter in June to inform the media about an "ice castle sculpture contest" you are hosting to raise money for charity in January will garner little if any reaction or attention from the media. It is simply too far in advance to motivate them to take action in the present. You must identify your timeline in advance for each segment of your PR program and what you want to accomplish. Likewise, your own schedule will have to also be considered. If you are a one-person business then planning a media event or release during your busiest time of the year will likely be counterproductive.

7. What is your PR program budget and from where will the money come?

Though securing publicity is often referred to as free advertising, there is still a cost associated with creating, maintaining, and growing a PR program. You have to set a budget and know where the money will come from to support the program. Like many forms of advertising it is difficult to track the success of publicity, so once you have committed to the program, follow through and do not let early disappointments dissuade you from further PR endeavors.

8. Who in your organization will manage your public relations program?

Assuming that you will manage your public relations program in-house then you must decide who will be responsible for creating, managing, and growing the program as well as what tools and training you will be able to provide this PR manager to be effective and productive. These issues must be considered even if you plan to only occasionally put public relations to work for your business. Think of it this way: If you started with a penny and doubled it each day and set a target for 30 days at which point you would stop doubling the sum, then by the 10th day you would have $5.12, by the 20th day that would grow to $5,242, and by the 30th day an astounding $5,368,708. My point is this: there is no sense starting something unless you are prepared to see it through to the end. As this example clearly illustrates, the payoff is always in the follow-through, not in the implementation. Therefore, if you are going to develop and implement a PR program then you must put everything and everyone in place so that you can follow through to where the program will start to pay dividends.

YOUR PR PROGRAM OPTIONS
$+ ✎ ☎

Do-It-Yourself Option

The first option and most likely candidate for the vast majority of small-business owners will be to create and maintain your own ongoing public relations program and key campaigns. The following are a few points to consider in terms of creating and maintaining your own public relations campaigns and program.

- Determine your public relations objectives as outlined above and put together a basic outline of what you want to accomplish, the audience you want to target, how you will target this audience, and when you plan to launch the campaign.
- Conduct basic research to determine your target audience.
- Identify the media that reaches your target audience and contact them to find out who key

contact people are and how they can be reached. Use that information to build a contact media list, which will be comp0sed of media outlets and media personnel to whom you elect to send your "news."

- Practice writing press releases, fact sheets, media advisories, and pitch letters until you are comfortable with your ability to do so competently.
- Get creative and start listing ideas about how you can turn your promotional or marketing message into newsworthy information for mass media consumption.
- Create an outline of your plan and news idea including press releases, media kits, and so forth.
- Release your newsworthy information to the media and follow up with media personnel as required.

Intern Option

The second option is to hire an intern or student from a local college or university to help create and implement your public relations program and each campaign as the need arises. Ideally, the student or intern will be a public relations, marketing, or advertising major with a ton of creative ideas that she can bring to the table. To get started, contact local schools and inquire about work placements or internship programs that they have in place. If no suitable matches are found then think about creating your own program in association with a school. Or, alternately, advertise in the school paper or on bulletin boards outlining the details of your needs. Many students and professors understand the importance or real-world experience in terms of education and therefore are open to these types of joint business/student arrangement. Generally, you will not have to pay students involved in these types of programs, but you will be required to cover out-of-pocket expenses associated with the their work.

Freelance Option

The third option is to hire a freelance public relations consultant or a marketing/advertising consultant with a strong public relations background. Often freelancers break away from larger firms seeking to build their own agency and you will generally find that their fees are about 60 percent of what a full-service public relations agency will charge. To find freelance PR consultants contact your local chamber of commerce for referrals and also do a telephone book search.

Agency Option

The final option is to hire an agency that specializes in creating, maintaining, and growing public relations programs based on each client's individual needs and budget. However, the downside of hiring a PR firm is that most will not take on small jobs or one-time jobs. They prefer to sign longer-term contracts with monthly payment guarantees and extra billing for services provided beyond the basic agreement. If you are going to hire a professional PR firm be prepared to shell out $2,000 a month and that is only to get going. However, with that said the cost could easily be recouped many times over because when you hire a professional you gain access to their knowledge and contact base—that is what you pay them for, exposure and ins with the right people who can get you what you want.

WEB RESOURCE

⚲ www.prfirms.org: Council of Public Relations Firms, free online directory listing public relations firms nationwide.

BECOME A JUNIOR REPORTER
$ ⚒

It's a little-known fact that more than 50 percent of news is generated by non-news sources. What this means is that half of the news we read in publications or on the Web, hear on radio, or see on television was submitted or initiated by people who are not reporters, journalists, producers, editors, or media personnel in general. Who are these people who are creating the other 50 percent of the news we read, watch, and hear? They are professional publicists, business owners, politicians, salespeople, marketers, community leaders, and basically anyone else who has learned that becoming a "Junior Reporter" is one of the best ways to get their message out to a news-hungry public. Every single day journalists, editors, reporters, and producers have the daunting task of filling the news pipeline; it's a job that never ends because people have come to expect news and accept news as part of our everyday lives. However, this has created a problem for media workers. There simply are not enough people working in the media or hours in the day for those who do work in the media to research, write, film, or record enough news events and stories. Knowing this fact is what creates an opportunity for you to benefit by becoming a "Junior Reporter," developing news stories and angles that relate to your business, product, or service and submitting these news stories to media outlets. Everyday people just like you are benefiting by having their message (news) displayed in the media just by simply understanding how to become "Junior Reporters" and help media outlets serve their customers by assisting in the news gathering process.

PRESS RELEASE BASICS

$ 🔨

A press or news release can be considered the main tool that is used to secure media attention and exposure, and fortunately one that is very easy for every small-business owner to create regardless of experience. The following information will give you the basics in terms of format, style, and design of what is required to create a press release. See the sample on page 180.

Format

The format of a press release is pretty basic and the following overview will give you a guideline that can be used when preparing your press release.

- *Paper.* If you have company letterhead then you can use it to print your press release. If not just use standard 20 pound, 8½-by-11-inch white office paper. There is no need to use fancy, colored, or extra heavy paper stock to print your press release. In fact you're best just to stick with standard office paper. The same applies to

mailing envelopes if you plan to mail out your press release, pitch letter, or media advisories; just use a standard white office envelope with no window.

- *Font.* Standard 12-point fonts such as Times New Roman or Arial are fine. Stay clear of using fancy fonts or too much italics or bold face. Additionally, always use black ink on white. The only color should be in your business name or logo if you are printing the release on company letterhead.

- *Spacing.* Double-spacing makes the release easy to read at a glance. Use 1-inch to 1.5-inch margins all around.

- *Length.* Generally press releases are between one and three pages long. As a rule of thumb, expect to fit about 200 to 250 words on each page so it won't appear overcrowded and hard to read. Lots of white or blank space on the page is perfectly okay.

- *Templates.* Most of the popular word processing software programs such as Microsoft Office and Corel Word Perfect have press release templates that you can customize to suit your particular needs. Or, you can easily create your own press release template using Notepad, Word, or a similar word processing program. Also, use exclamation marks and other punctuation sparingly.

- *Proofread.* Always proofread your press release for grammar and spelling errors prior to sending it out. Do not solely rely on your word processor's spellcheck feature.

Contact Information

Contact information should be repeated a few times throughout your press release. First on the top of the press release; if you print it on company letterhead then chances are you will already have your full contact information included. If not, you can print your business name and address at the top of the page, followed by a contact name and the direct telephone number and e-mail address of the contact person. The contact information should be repeated at the bottom of the press release on the last page.

Release Information

Near the top on the left-hand side of your press release indicate a release date for the information or news. If the news can be released any time simply print in all upper case letters and underscored "FOR IMMEDIATE RELEASE." Alternately, if you have a specific date you would like the news or information to be released on, then the once again write that specific date in all upper case letters and underscored such as "TO BE RELEASED SEPTEMBER 1, 2002." However have a good reason for wanting to release the news or information on a specific date. When you narrow the date the information can be used or released on you greatly reduce the odds of securing media exposure because you are telling media personnel to work around your timetable and not what is convenient or works for them.

Headline

The headline is one of the more important aspects of the press release if not the most important. This is because your headline is what will grab the attention of the reader and separate your press release from the numerous other press releases that media personnel will typically come in contact with during any given week of the year. Your headline should be bold, larger-sized type, and printed directly across the top of the press release. Your headline could be in the form of a question, a statement that reveals part of the news, or a statistical fact. Use whatever you feel is relevant to your main message and that will grab the attention of the readers and draw them into the body of the release. Under the headline should be a subheadline that reveals just a little more information about your main marketing message or it can answer a question that your headline has asked. The subheadline should be used to generate additional interest from the readers' perspective.

Dateline and Lead Paragraph

Start your first paragraph with a dateline followed by your lead in to the news or story that you want to release. Make this powerful, interesting, and unique, as

this is as far as many readers will get before they begin to lose interest in what may seem like just another advertising message and not real news or information that would benefit their readers, viewers, or listeners.

Text Information

Follow the lead paragraph with the text information of the body of the press release. This should be a few paragraphs in length and tell the rest of your story, basically answer the who, what, why, when, where, and how information. Think of this as the area that you state your compelling case or argument about why this information should be made available to the public.

Boilerplate Information

The boilerplate information is a single paragraph that gives some brief information and details about your company or organization, how long you've been in business, current ownership, number of employees, and whatever else you feel is relevant or will help to support your news idea or story. After the boilerplate paragraph use three pound signs (# # #), triple x (x x x), or simply print "END" to indicate that the press release is done. You can also repeat your contact information on the bottom of the last page in your press release.

MORE GREAT PRESS RELEASE TRICKS

Due to the fact that a press or news release is such a valuable marketing tool for small-business owners to have in their arsenal of marketing weapons, the following are a few more great press release tips that are guaranteed to help you secure much-needed media exposure.

- Be creative and write about an event, news, information, or a story that is unique and that does not happen every day. Editors, producers, reporters, and journalists receive tons of press releases and you have to make sure that yours stands out in the crowd if you want to grab their attention and secure valuable exposure. What

Sample Press Release

Complete contact information here, including:
Business name, full address, and Web site URL

FOR IMMEDIATE RELEASE   CONTACT: John Doe

                                                                  555-5555

FINALLY A MARKETING TOOL THAT IS GUARANTEED TO HELP EVERY SMALL-BUSINESS OWNER TO SUCCEED

A Hot New Small-Business Book Packed With 1,500 Great

Marketing Tricks That Will Drive Your Business Through the Roof!

Irvine, CA, September 1, 2003—Finally, marketing information that was specifically developed for the millions of small-business owners in North America who want and deserve big marketing results from their small marketing budgets.

Entrepreneur's Ultimate Small Business Marketing Guide (Entrepreneur Press, 2003) is now available at bookstores nationwide and is the most authoritative and comprehensive small-business marketing book available. In fact, this book is a virtual marketing idea warehouse packed to the rafters with 1,500 great marketing tricks that are proven and guaranteed to boost small-business sales revenues, profits, customer loyalty, and drive your business through the roof. Discover the marketing tricks and secrets that top business and sales professionals use daily to devour competitors, close more sales, win new customers, and keep them coming back for life.

Author James Stephenson invests his 15 years of small-business marketing and sales experience into this book, and advises "that no marketing stone is left unturned" in this hefty volume. You will discover public relations, sales, retailing, direct marketing, advertising, networking, customer service, online marketing tricks, and many more. All presented in jargon-free terminology, easy to understand, and readily applied in the matter of minutes and for minimal cost.

Entrepreneur Magazine now in its third successful decade of providing small-business owners with the vital business and information know-how that they need to start and grow their businesses, is committed to helping small-business owners succeed through timely and expert information in book, magazine, and electronic formats.

#

If you would like more information about this book, a review copy, or to schedule an interview with the author, call John Doe at 555-5555.

you decide is news does not have to necessarily be groundbreaking stuff, just look for a new way to get the info across or put a new twist on an old story.

- Try to be objective about the information that you include in the press release and look at it from the perspective of the media's target audience. How will knowing this information benefit them? People will only read, watch, or listen to information that will help them in some way or that interests them. Additionally, think in terms of mass appeal—the more people who would be interested in knowing the information that is included in your press release then the higher the odds go of securing media exposure.

- Include additional supporting information or documents with your press release if you feel that it is relevant to your news or story idea and will help to get the desired response or action. Support documents can include a tip or fact sheet in bullet format that lists the highlights of your news, photographs, or illustrations that will help to paint a complete picture. Or a report or similar booklet information if you plan on making these available should your story get picked up by one or more media outlets.

- Make sure that you target the right media and the right media personnel. Spend a little time to research the media's target audience before you send them a press release or media advisory. You will attract little attention if the information you want to release does not benefit the media's audience. Likewise, if you are unsure what department or person should be receiving your press release for review and consideration, then call first and ask the receptionist. Try to get a full name and title of the person who should receive the press release and address the release directly to that person. These departments within one organization could range from real estate to lifestyles to business to book reviews, so it is important that you know specifically who you are writing the information for and who it must be sent to when complete.

- You have to think about two separate but equal calls to action. The first is the media—go out of your way in your press release to let them know what you would like them to do next, call us, visit our Web site, or stop by our booth at the trade show. Likewise, you have to be creative in the way that you motivate the media to take the action you want them to take. The motivation could be in the form of an exclusive story option or perhaps dangling a carrot in the form of other great ideas, stories, and features that you will share in terms of future news partnerships. The second call for action is aimed at the audience who will read, view, or listen to your message. What do you want them to do next? Once again, tell the reader what you want them to do—call us, visit our Web site, enter our contest, show up at the charity event to help volunteer, or whatever is required. It doesn't matter; just make sure to tell your intended audience what you want them to do next.

DISTRIBUTE YOUR PRESS RELEASE ELECTRONICALLY

$+ ☏

The Internet has transformed the way publicists and the media send and receive press releases and news information and you can take full advantage of this by distributing your press release electronically on the Net. Some editors and journalist still like to receive press releases the old-fashioned way, by mail or fax. But they are quickly finding themselves in the minority as more and more join the technology revolution and prefer to receive and review press releases via e-mail. Most media directories in print or online will include e-mail contact information for key media people and companies. The listings in these directories that indicate no e-mail address are the ones who prefer to receive press releases the old-fashioned way. So in a nutshell that is a simple way to know if it's okay to send a press release via e-mail or by mail. Of course, you could always contact the person you want to send it to and make sure an e-mailed press release is acceptable, but be forewarned, that process is very time consuming. Make it easy on yourself, and if a media person or company openly releases their e-mail address into the public domain then don't be afraid to use it. Besides sending press releases via e-mail is not only simple; it's also very inexpensive and fast.

WEB RESOURCE

✆ www.internetnewsbureau.com: Internet News Bureau, subscription-based online press release distribution.

⚲ www.xpresspress.com: Express Press, subscription-based online press release distribution.

⚲ www.prweb.com: PR Web, free online press release distribution.

⚲ www.onlinepressreleases.com: Online Press Releases, software that enables you to build a press release media database and distribute press releases via e-mail.

RESEARCHING PRESS RELEASES
$ ⚒

The best approach for creating a press release is to pay a professional copywriter with press release experience to write an attention grabbing "newsy" one for you. However, not all small-business owners can afford this type of costly luxury. So before you sit down and struggle to put your thoughts into words and onto paper make sure to research press releases first to get a feel and understanding of the style, tone, format, voice, and structure that is commonly used in the creation of press releases. The easiest way to accomplish this is to simply read lots of other press releases, especially releases that have been picked up and covered by the media. Think of it this way: Would you sit down and write a book without having read at least a few first? Not likely. So why would you attempt to write a press release without having read a few first? There are numerous Web sites where you can go and read current and archived press releases, but one of the best is PR Web, as not only can you browse and read through thousands of press releases for free, but they are also conveniently indexed by business industry. You don't want to reinvent the wheel, you just want to write an effective release that gets picked up, so use what's available and modify it to meet your own PR objectives.

WEB RESOURCE

⚲ www.prweb.com: PR Web, an online database containing thousands of press release postings in more than 60 industries.

CREATE YOUR OWN MEDIA KIT
$ ⚒

A media kit is generally in the form of a decorative folder with an interior pocket that holds various loose information sheets (8½" x 11") inside. The information sheets are intended to give the reader insights into your business, what you sell or what you do, who is involved, and other information that is considered newsworthy or relevant to your business, industry, products, or services. The media folder can be basic, but the outside should be visibly imprinted with your business name, logo, and contact information. These types of heavy paper presentation folders can be purchased at most office supply stores and, in bulk, cost about $.50 apiece. Additionally, there is generally a cutout on the outside so that you can insert a business card into it; this is a good alternative for small-business owners on a tight budget who cannot afford the expense of having media kit folders printed with their corporate name and logo.

Here are the basic elements that most media kits include. Of course, there are no rules set in stone; you can add or delete items as required to meet your own specific needs and marketing, business, public relations, and communications goals and objectives.

Summary Sheet

A summary sheet is much like a table of contents; it allows the reader at a glance to quickly decipher what is in the media kit and what may be of particular interest to them. Additionally, the summary sheet should include the name, address, and other contact information of the person that the media kit is intended for (journalist, editor, CEO, etc.) as well as the contact information of the author, public relations officer, or contact person within your organization. It is always a good idea to print your summary sheet on company letterhead.

Press Release

Included in the media kit should be a current and up-to-date press release. Additionally, have more than one press release ready to go at any one time; the theme or angle of each should be different so you can appeal to a broader audience of both the public and media personnel.

Review Sheet(s)

Generally a review sheet is a one-page sheet that lists the compelling reasons that a reader should give you media coverage. One paragraph can be devoted to describing the product or service. A second paragraph can be devoted to the benefits that using the product or service will deliver. And a third paragraph can be used to describe how the product or service can be used to solve a problem and any competitive advantages associated with the product or service.

Company Fact Sheet

A company fact sheet can be included the media kit. It briefly describes the history of your company and the vision for the future. You can also use this sheet to describe any awards your company has won and to point readers to a company Web site if you have one. If you are going to include a fact sheet in your media kit then make sure you print your company mission statement on this sheet. Your mission statement should instantly provide the readers with a clear understanding of what your company does, why you do it, and what people get out of doing business with your firm. Also you can use a highlighter pen to draw attention to key information on the company fact sheet and other information sheets in the kit, but don't go overboard with this. Also include more specific facts on the sheet about the industry your business operates in; try to make this exciting, interesting, and intriguing.

Bio Sheet

A bio sheet is simply a list of the key employees and managers within your organization, their titles, their education, their specialties, their awards, and how each person featured can be contacted directly. Often it is also best to list personal information about these key people and their families and even a hobby or interesting point about this person as this can appeal to readers on an emotional level. For instance, John Smith is a devoted family man and

weekend sailor who when not working can often be found circumnavigating Catalina Island with his three kids and wife, Helen. He has been with ABC Company for 15 years as the head of research and development and holds an MBA from Harvard.

Testimonials

You can include with your media kit testimonials that you have received from clients. However, make sure that if you add testimonials they include information about the person who wrote the testimonial—their company and title, how they can be contacted, what solutions your products or services provided them, and how they benefited as a result. Know that if you include testimonials that there is a better than average chance that the reader (media personnel) will contact this person to back up or support your and their claims. Be sure that is OK with the person providing the testimonial.

Visuals

Visuals can include everything from relevant photographs, condensed charts, maps, and graphs to specialized illustrations and step-by-step product instructions. Remember, that a picture really is worth a thousand words, so if you can include or incorporate a picture that leaves no doubt as to what your product or service is and how people benefit by using it, then make sure to include one.

Clippings

You might also want to include past press or media clippings that have featured your business, products, or services. Limit the number to one or two, don't go overboard and turn your press kit into a scrapbook of photocopied press clippings, especially dated ones that span decades and are now completely irrelevant.

PITCH LETTERS

$ ⚒

As the name suggests, pitch letters are exactly that: a letter that you write on company letterhead or standard white office paper that pitches your news idea, story, or the reasons your story or news should be featured in print or on air. Pitch letters are generally brief and to the point. Many public relations people like to use pitch letters to create mystery and motivate the media to call or set an appointment to find out more. This is a great idea providing you have some big news or an excellent idea for a story, feature, or interview that would be welcomed. Think of the pitch letter this way: you want to convince the editor, journalist, or producer that your story idea is a good one, and motivate her to give you a call. Additionally, you can also send accompanying support documents with a pitch letter, fact sheet, media advisory, photographs, or even product samples—basically anything that you feel will help to support your news story or reason for being interviewed. I always like to think of a pitch letter as being less formal than a press release. A good press release should be completely self-explanatory and in effect the media outlet should be able to print or air the news without further contact with the author of the release. (This is easier said than done of course.) A pitch letter is a tool to open the door and the lines of communication between the media and the people who want to use the media as a vehicle to get their message out to a broad audience.

MEDIA ADVISORY
$

A media advisory is a bit different than other forms of contacting the media discussed in this chapter. Media advisories or alerts are prepared and sent to the media outlining an event that will be taking place, as opposed to only pitching a story or photo opportunity idea that you think should take place or that would make a good feature in print or on air. In other words, a media advisory or alert is very much like an invitation that spells out the details of the event that you think should be covered by the print or broadcast media. The details in the media alert or advisory should include:

- *What.* What the event is all about—a special promotion, a charity event, or a publicity stunt.
- *Where.* Where the event will be taking place—at your store, office, or another location. You

should always include directions in the media advisory or attach a map for difficult-to-find locations.

- *When.* When the event will be taking place, including the date and time. Additionally, if the event will be broken into various segments such as a ribbon cutting at ten, celebrity appearance at 11, and so forth, then make sure to include a schedule or itinerary with the advisory.
- *Who.* Who will be attending the event. Once again this could include politicians, celebrities, company executives, contest winners, or children who will be getting their pictures taken with Santa. Basically, tell for whom the event is being staged.
- *Why.* Why will cover two aspects in the advisory. First, why the event is taking place—to raise money for charity, to conduct a contest, or to present award. The reason will be directly related to the event. And second and more important, why you think the media should attend. The reason could be a great opportunity for a human-interest story, a photo opportunity, or general information that benefits their audience and the community.
- *How.* And finally include how the media can find out further information about the event. This could include by telephone, directing them to your Web site e-mail, a press conference prior to the event, or more than likely a combination of all of these contact methods.

Media advisories can be mailed, faxed, e-mailed, or hand delivered to the media you want to target and can be printed on company letterhead or standard office paper. Additionally, make sure to send out your advisory at least a week prior to the event. There is no reason you cannot follow up with members of the media to check on whether or not they will be attending.

FACT SHEETS
$

Fact sheets are different than a company fact sheet that you would include in your media or press kit. As mentioned previously, company fact sheets include details or highlights about your company, employees, products, or services, wherein a general fact sheet should list information in bullet form about your news story, idea, or reasons for being interviewed. The fact sheet should be printed on company letterhead or standard white office paper and include your business name, a contact person, and a telephone number or e-mail address. Generally a fact sheet will accompany an introduction letter, press release, or pitch letter, and is not usually sent as a stand-alone item. But once again there are no hard and fast rules that cover every situation so if you feel you can get the main message of your news idea across suitably in bullet form on a fact sheet then go for it. The purpose of the fact sheet is to give the reader a quick overview of the details of your proposal or story in an easy and fast-to-read format that highlights the major points and your most compelling reasons why you think they should get involved.

MORE CLEVER WAYS TO INTRODUCE YOURSELF TO THE MEDIA
$ ⚒

In addition to creating and sending out a press release, media advisory, pitch letter, or a complete media kit here are more clever ways that you can contact media outlets and personnel with the objective of securing some free exposure in ink or on air.

Introduction Telephone Call

Another way to introduce yourself and news ideas and stories is to simply call the members of the media you want to target. However, if you do, make sure that you call the appropriate department, such as the business editor for business-related news, the lifestyles editor for news stories related to people or events in the community, and so forth. Once you have the right person on the other end of the line, introduce yourself, your business, and ask if they have a quick moment to discuss a story idea that you think would be of interest to them. Or would they prefer that you send the material by mail, fax, or e-mail. Some public relations experts will tell you that you should not call media personnel until after you have

sent an introduction letter, press release, or the like. While there is some merit in this advice, especially in terms of contacting larger or national media outlets, there is certainly no reason you cannot call regional or community media outlets and introduce yourself and pitch your story right over the telephone. I have called members of the media out of the blue to pitch stories and my ideas were always welcomed.

Introduction Letter

As mentioned above you can also introduce yourself to members of the media by crafting a general introduction letter on company letterhead and, as the name suggests, introduce yourself, your business, and what products you sell or services you provide. Introduction letters do not have to include a news story or pitch; they can in fact give the reader a brief explanation of your expertise in a particular field or industry. If you do take this route, though, do make sure that you ask the reader to store the letter for future reference. It is also wise to follow up with additional introduction letters twice a year. Or, alternately, you can pitch a story or news idea right in the introduction letter and cover the usual bases: who, why, what, where, when, and how. Once again there are no hard and fast rules in terms of contacting members of the media, as long as you do not waste their time and show a sincere interest in helping them out to make their news and story gathering and reporting job easier.

Introduction Visit

And finally another great way to meet members of the media is to get out of your shop or office, make a trip to their office, and personally introduce yourself. This is an especially useful tactic if you also take along a complete media kit and leave it with the media company after you have introduced yourself. You can go armed with a few story ideas or just let them know that you are available to supply them with information in your field of expertise when they may need it. Always keep in mind that the media is in the business of supplying news, stories, and information to the public. That is their business and the more sources they have to call on to get news and useful information that is suited to their target audience the easier their job becomes.

EXPERT POSTCARDS
$$ ⚒ 🏵

Creating "expert postcards" is a very clever way for media-savvy business owners and professionals to become known as an expert in their field or industry by members of the local and even national media. As the name suggests, expert postcards are a king-sized version of a business card that states all of your qualifications, training, special permits, and anything else that can be used to substantiate your expert claim or build credibility in the minds of media personnel. The expert postcards should be professionally printed in high gloss color like a regular postcard and you may even want to include your photograph or a photograph relevant to your business, industry, product, or service on the front and the detailed expert information on the back of the postcard. Once complete, the postcards can be sent to members of the media along with a brief introduction letter asking that they file your expert postcard for future reference and when they need information pertaining to your field of expertise that you welcome any and all questions, interviews, and inquiries. Additionally, make sure to update your expert postcard annually and send the new version to all your media contacts.

WEB RESOURCE

🖉 www.postcardprinting.com: Custom postcard design and printing.

DON'T OVERREACT TO NEGATIVE PR
$ ⚒

A common reaction to any type of negative press or publicity that we might receive about us, our business, products, or services is to lash out at the source of the negative PR with a less than pleasant response, call it revenge at any cost. Don't feel bad if this describes a similar reaction that you have had to negative press because it is human nature to react in this manner, reactive anger is always the first line of defense. However, if you find yourself in the uncomfortable situation of receiving negative press in the future, resist the urge to react in an equally negative fashion. Instead allow yourself a cool down period of at least 24 hours so that you can truly assess the potential damage that the negative

press may cause to your business or reputation with a clear head. Often after the cool-down period what originally seemed horrible is really not that bad, and more times than not better left alone. Seldom is anything gained by reacting to negative press or an unfavorable review of your product or service. However, if you choose to react or respond in a negative fashion then you may well be opening an entirely new can of worms that you may have not been prepared for and therefore create an entirely new set of problems that you don't want or need. Professionals know that in business cooler heads must always prevail.

GET FAD SAVVY
$+ ⚒ ⚖

Public relations experts often tie their clients' PR campaigns into popular culture and fads that are hot at that particular moment. And because of this, many of their clients have profited handsomely. Now that you know the secret you too can put this clever PR trick to work for your small business. Look around you for ideas—what is currently hot at movie theaters, on television, in fashion, sports, music, politics, or even a local fad sweeping through your community. Once you have identified the latest and greatest craze then you can go about building a PR campaign around that popular fad. For instance, at the time of writing this book reality television shows such as the *Survivor* series are pulling in record audiences. This would make for a great foundation to base your event or PR stunt upon, a logical tie-in because most everyone at the time is familiar with it and has an opinion about it. Using the "survivor" example you could stage a contest that included contestants from your local community who had to outlast each other in a way that is relevant to your business. Securing media exposure for these types of "fad" events is generally quite easy as once again the subject, topic, or issue is hot at the present time and will appeal to the media's target audience in most cases.

NEVER STOP PROMOTING
$ ⚒

One of the greatest myths about success, be it business success or personal achievement, is that eventually your business, personal abilities, product, or service will get discovered and be embraced wholeheartedly by the masses. But how, if nobody knows about you, what you do, or where you are doing it? To quote from a famous movie business is not about "build it and they will come." Business is about build it and never stop promoting it and they will eventually come and keep coming providing you never stop promoting what you have built. Marketing success is best described as always being temporary. The world's most successful companies and people all share one common denominator business skill: They all learned the power of promotion and that when promotion stops or slows, so does success, revenues, profits, and public awareness of what you want the public to be aware. Consequently because of this, the world's most successful businesspeople have learned to become publicity hounds and never stop promoting what they do, what they sell, what benefits customers will receive by purchasing what they do and sell, and why they're the best at what you do.

WEB RESOURCE

☞ www.entrepreneur.com: Online business resource center.

BECOME AN EXPERT MEDIA SOURCE
$$ ✐

Let your business or career benefit from your specific expertise by becoming a national media contact source. For more than 15 years, Broadcast Interview Source has published a media directory that lists experts from every imaginable business, industry, and profession nationwide. The purpose of the directory is to give members of the media such as editors, producers, and journalists, quick and easy access to experts who can assist them in supplying information they need to complete a story or article for news. The media members using Broadcast Interview Source expands beyond print to include television, radio, and Internet interviews and feature articles as well. In 1996 Broadcast Interview Source expanded operations to include a Web site called ExpertClick, providing the same information as their print directory but electronically online. The big benefit of becoming a member of the ExpertClick site or paying a listing fee in the directory is that media will seek you out for your expertise, rather than you seeking them out to gain media exposure via press release, appointment, or telephone call.

WEB RESOURCE

☞ www.expertclick.com: Online directory listing expert services for media members to contact.

USE MEDIA DIRECTORIES
$$ ☎

Just about every type of media directory imaginable is available in print, online, or in CD-ROM format. And these directories can prove to be invaluable when it comes time to figure out what media you want to target for public relations purposes. The best media directories include important contact information such as key people, their titles, and the target audience. However, be forewarned, good media directories can be extremely expensive and must be updated annually to keep on top of changing circumstances and personnel within these media organizations. For that reason make sure that you have clearly defined and decided that public relations will be a key part of your marketing mix before you invest in media directories. Used properly, media directories will easily pay for themselves and more, but you have to be committed to using public relations as a marketing tool in order for these media directories to become a valuable business tool.

WEB RESOURCES

☞ www.mediafinder.com: Oxbridge Communications Inc. Publishers of print and electronic CD-ROM media directories covering magazines, newsletters, journals, and newspapers (subscriptions to online media directories also available).

☞ www.newslink.org Free online media directory service including print and broadcast media outlets and companies categorized by state.

HIRE A CLIPPING SERVICE
$$ 📞

You wouldn't send out a wedding invitation without some kind of response system in place. If you did how would you know who and how many people would be attending? Sending out press releases is very similar; you want to know who and how many media outlets are picking up the story and including it in their publication. This is important to know so that you can hone your skills in terms of developing effective press releases and so that you can learn what media outlets best reach your target audience. However, all of this is well and good if you have the time to purchase and read every publication that you send a press release to, but few businesspeople have that luxury. That's what makes hiring a clipping service to track what media picks up and runs your story such a good idea. Of course, clipping services charge for their service, but it's a fraction of what it would cost you to do the same when you factor in your time spent scouring various publications for your release. Clipping services work for many clients at one time, so economies of scale are at work and they are able to provide the service in a cost-effective manner based on volume. Most clipping services offer numerous packages based on a client's budget and needs, so before you start sending out press releases think about how you will track them and maybe you'll find that a clipping service will be your best bet.

WEB RESOURCE

🖰 www.factiva.com: Factiva provides media release and industry article monitoring services.

🖰 www.confirmedia.com: ConfirMedia provides broadcast monitoring services.

BUILD A MEDIA CONTACT DATABASE
$+ 🔨

Yes, you can purchase media directories, subscribe to online media services and databases, and even purchase media lists on CD-ROM format, but there are a few drawbacks to all these products and services. First, most do not allow you to personalize the information that is presented, which is very

important especially once you have made your own contacts and built relationships with key media personnel such as reporters, editors, journalists, and producers within the media industry. Second, these products and services can be very expensive to purchase and the free ones that are available mainly online often do not contain up-to-date information. Ultimately, you will want to combine different ways of collecting media contact information and build your own media contact database. This can be done the old-fashioned way with a pen and spiral pad for about $2, but that's not very efficient. Instead use your PC and a program such as Maximizer to record media contacts as you make them. This is a good way to do it because the software allows you to send press releases only to those you want to receive it. Basically you can set the field of parameters that best suits the task you want to complete. Building your own media database will take time, but in the end you'll have a very strong list of friendly media sources to get your news (promotional) message out and into the hands, eyes, and ears of the buying public.

WEB RESOURCE

🖰 www.maximizer.com: Prospect and client management software.

START A PUBLIC RELATIONS IDEA FOLDER
$ 🔨

One of the main reasons that small-business owners do not actively seek free publicity and media exposure for their businesses, products, and services is simply because of a lack of ideas. What makes news, well news, and not merely a promotional plug for your business that sounds like an advertisement? One of the easiest ways to get past the idea phase is to simply profit from other people's great publicity and news making ideas. You can do this by starting your own public relations idea folder or box. Every time you see, hear, or read a great publicity or news-making idea, write it down in detail or clip it out of the paper and put it in your public relations idea folder or box. Set aside a few moments each week to mine the box for publicity ideas or neat ways that you think would work in securing media exposure for your business, products, services, or a specific event that you have planned. Likewise, be sure to also encourage staff and friends to do the same; they collect great publicity and news-making ideas and you file them in your publicity idea folder for future review and with any luck, use.

THINK PHOTO OPPORTUNITY
$

You have banged our head against the wall and torn your hair out and you still can't come up with a newsworthy story or angle to use about your business, products, or services as a way to secure free media exposure. Don't focus so hard on trying to create a news story or angle that you overlook the obvious: Think about creating a photo opportunity instead. Print and television media love a good photo opportunity and often it is much easier to create one than it is to create a good news story. There are two ways to grab the media's attention about photo opportunities. You can contact them by way of a press release, telephone call, media advisory, or pitch letter and give details about the photo opportunity and why you believe it is a good one that should have their attention. Or, alternately, you can take the photograph yourself and send it to newspapers and magazines along with a paragraph or two explaining the details. Obviously, if you do it yourself, you will only be able to concentrate on print media unless you happen to get some pretty incredible video footage, which is rare. However, as good as photo opportunities can potentially be to secure exposure for your main message, you still have to keep in mind the target audience of the media outlet you want to be involved. The photo opportunity and accompanying story or news must be something that will appeal to a large segment of their readers or viewers; if not, you will get very little if any response. Here are a few ideas about what makes a great photo opportunity.

- Awarding contest prizes.
- Publicity events.
- Community and charity events.
- Company milestones, such as a store anniversary or 10,000th customer served.

- Grand opening or ribbon cutting to mark a special event or occasion.
- Winning industry, business, or community awards.
- Team sponsorships, especially sports teams that win a game or major tournament.
- Special holiday events such as Christmas decorations, Santa visits, and Easter egg hunts.

WHAT CAN YOU OFFER LOCAL MEDIA?
$

Every small-business owner has some sort of expertise that he can offer the media in exchange for free publicity and exposure, all that is required is to develop an angle and be creative in the process. Here are a few examples about various things that small-business owners have to offer.

- *Chef.* A chef and owner of a restaurant could offer to go to the local television station with a morning news and entertainment show one day a week and cook a new meal live on air.
- *Travel Agent.* A travel agent or broker could go on the local television station once a week or even daily and give a talk about travel information, tips, destinations, and the best travel deals of the week.
- *Fitness Instructor.* A fitness instructor could strike a deal to go live on the local television station every morning to show a fitness tip of the day to give viewers an energized start to the day.
- *Veterinarian.* A veterinarian could go on the local radio station weekly to answer call-in listeners questions about the health and training of pets.
- *Auto Mechanic.* An auto mechanic could offer to write a weekly auto maintenance column for the local newspaper.
- *Video Rental Store.* The owner of a video store could supply the local radio or television station or even the local newspaper with a weekly list of the hottest DVD rentals or a review of a specific new release of the week.

Once again, the key to successfully securing media exposure is to develop news or story angles that will appeal to the media's target audience, have broad or mass appeal, or ideally both. Once you have developed your story idea then contact your target media in any one of the ways featured in this chapter and pitch your idea. The ideas listed above are common; media outlets love this stuff for a few reasons. It's cheap to produce and feature and this type of information appeals to their target audience. Also, they need news, information, and activities to fill the airways or publications.

BENEFIT BY USING EDITORIAL CALENDARS
$+ ⚒

Media companies such as daily newspapers, magazines, and online news portals use editorial calendars mainly for two reasons. One, to plan key media features, usually a year in advance. For instance, on a newspaper's editorial calendar might be a ten-page feature section they will run in October covering pre-winter car maintenance information. And, perhaps on the same editorial calendar in April a feature section on camping and recreational pursuits for the approaching summer season. Two, media companies use editorial calendars for sales and marketing purposes. It becomes much easier to convince a business to advertise in the newspaper when they know that the paper will be doing a complete feature on the industry the potential advertiser operates in, giving them a higher chance of reaching the advertiser's target audience. Likewise, the benefit to you in securing media calendars is obvious. Media calendars give you the opportunity to fashion your news release and publicity events around forthcoming media events and features. For instance, if you operate an outdoor outfitters shop you could write a news release about outdoor activities including safety tips and the like, and submit it to media outlets that have forthcoming features on outdoor activities. Editorial calendars are a must for businesspeople who want to use public relations as a serious means of marketing.

WEB RESOURCE

⚲ www.edcals.com: Editorial Calendars, subscription-based online service providing annual editorial calendars for more than 4,000 media outlets.

TAKE OWNERSHIP OF AN EVENT
$$$+ ⚒ ⚖

One of the best ways that small-business owners can secure positive publicity for their business year after year after year is to create a special community event that is held on an annual basis. The event could be tied into charity, such as a 10K run held every August to support the American Cancer Society. Or, a just-for-fun event such as a restaurant that holds an annual hot dog eating contest. It should go without saying that the key idea behind this publicity trick is to name the event that you create and host annually after your business name or a main product or service that you provide, such as "Joe's Restaurant Annual Hot Dog Eating Contest." If financial budgets are too restrictive to develop and host your own event then look to other business owners in the community who could share the financial costs to host the event, but also share in the publicity and advertising rewards that can be derived from such community events. Also don't overlook media companies as potential sponsors or co-hosts of the event. Put together a proposal outlying the finer details, make appointments, and start pitching your ideas to local newspapers and radio and television stations. The potential rewards of annual events that are well received by the community can be well worth the financial and time investments.

BUSINESS AND MARKETING ACTIVITIES THAT SHOULD BE PUBLICIZED
$ ⚒

There are certain business and marketing activities that should automatically be publicized, but that is not to say that you will always secure media attention and exposure because you automatically contact the media for these featured business and marketing activities. However, you should get in the habit of publicizing the following business and marketing activities, it should come naturally like updating the books at the end of the week or taking inventory. Think of it as a necessary business activity and the payoff will eventually lead to increased attention from the media and increased exposure in the media.

Grand Openings and Expansions

Let the media know about the grand opening of your business or the opening of new expansion stores or branch offices. Likewise, create a press release around other types of "growing" related events such as merger or joint venture programs with competing and noncompeting business as well as when a business is being bought or sold and will be under new management. Additionally major renovations to an existing retail store or office are also a good reason to contact the media to let them know the details and why it is important information for their audience—"Growing to serve you better" kind of stuff.

New Product or Service Launch

Another business activity that should be automatically announced to the media is when you launch a new product or service or relaunch a vastly improved product or service. Once again take this opportunity to send the media a press release or hold a press conference if you feel the news is big enough and beneficial enough for the news-hungry public to know.

Special Employee Announcements

Take the time required to notify the media whenever you hire a new key employee or promote an employee from within to a new and senior position. Other employee announcements that could be released to the media would be things such as an employee who has won an internal or external award that is work or industry related. Or special employee milestones such as 30 years of service with no sick days or never missing a day of work or retirement after long periods of time with the organization.

Community and Charity Program and Event Sponsorships

News, information, and events that your business is involved in that directly affect the community is always a great reason to contact local members of the media and let them know the inside scoop. The news, information, or event could range from a sponsorship program that you would like to announce to a charity event that you will be hosting or participating in.

Winning Awards

Whenever your business wins an award for customer service, product design or development, a business or industry award, or just about any other type of award for that matter make sure to contact the media to fill them in on the details and why you think that it would make for good reading or listening for their audience. Small businesses that win awards are almost guaranteed to grab some free media exposure providing they take the time to contact the media to reveal the details of the award. The reason for this is that when a business wins an award it reflects positively on the entire community or city where the business is located and thus elevates the people who live in the area with sense of pride to be associated with a winner.

Public Safety and Health Information

Issues that relate to the public's health or safety are another reason to contact the media to get the story or news out. Health and safety issues could include product recalls from a manufacturer, safety issues related to crime in the area, or health information that would be beneficial to the general public. Or, announcements relating to health and safety information that has been revealed as a direct result of research that your business is conducting.

Contests and Special Promotions

Contests and special sales and promotions should always be announced to the media in hopes they will get picked up and featured. If the news is exciting, fun, and the average citizen has a chance to win or benefit from the event, then there is a better than average chance one or more media outlets will devote some ink or airtime to the event or promotion. These special events could range from a celebrity appearance to a "lookalike" contest to an announcement of a person who won a contest that you conducted to a special clearance sale that can potentially have an impact on the public, such as an under-the-tent sales event.

General Announcements

General announcements are another area that small-business owners should look at as potential news-making stories that can secure some free and valuable media exposure. General announcements could be any of the following:

- An announcement that you are lowering prices or alternately raising prices.
- A price freeze perhaps as a result of a slow economy, thus helping local citizens.
- Information about a poll or survey your business conducted.
- Impending government regulations or laws that will positively/negatively affect your business, employees, and customers.
- Extending business hours.

Company Milestones

Special company milestones should always be put to the media for announcement in print and on air, things such as a celebration commemorating 50 years in business, 10,000 customers served, or one million products sold. These types of announcements are especially important to people living in the communities that the business operates in. This is because small businesses become such a positive and important economic force, especially in small communities, and therefore when great milestones are achieved they are really a reflection of a collective effort between the business owner, staff, and the local community that supports the business and thus make great press features. And if you really want to increase the odds of securing exposure and the impact your PR message will have then try to tie the milestone in with a special promotion of sales event. This could be something as simple as "Helen's Bike Shop is celebrating 25 years in business with a special 25 percent discount to mark our anniversary."

Customer Success Stories

Like most people who read newspapers, watch television, and listen to the radio, I have always been a sucker for a good old success story, one that makes you say "hey, that's great to hear." And for that reason you should also get in the habit of automatically sending out a press release every time one of your customers has had a super positive or beneficial experience because of a product they purchased from you or a service you have provided. Of course you will want to get their permission first, but once you have it then craft a press release and get the story out to the media. Customer success stories could include just about anything that is interesting and newsworthy such as a physical therapist who helps a client to get better and regain use or have improved use of muscles that were previously damaged. Or, perhaps a tax accountant who took the IRS to task on behalf of a client and was successful. At the end of the day the media and the public love a great human interest story, especially one that has a happy ending.

PARDON OUR MESS
$ ✎

Build goodwill and a positive image for your business by asking clients and people in close proximity to work projects or jobs in progress to "kindly pardon your mess." This simple yet highly effective public relations trick is especially important for businesses such as remodeling companies, moving services, and landscape contractors to practice. Do this anytime your business activities disrupt a client's routine or the routine of other people who are in close proximity to your client because of noise or traffic congestion that is caused during the course of fulfilling your contract or servicing your client. Create a "Please excuse our mess and thanks for understanding" card and drop it off in person to offices next to your client's office, or to homes surrounding your customer's home where you are carrying out renovations or installations. A personalized card and a quick visit to explain what you are doing, how long it will take, and a verbal reassurance that if there are any problems they can contact you will go a long way to build goodwill. Not to mention the potential for securing new customers or referrals because you've taken the time to consider their interests. This is a champion public relations technique that will almost always secure you new business.

SAVVY TRICKS TO CREATE CHARITY GOODWILL
$$ ✎

Charity is a great way to promote goodwill for your business within your local community. However, it still has to be regarded as a business expense that comes directly off bottom-line profits. And as great as giving to charity is, you still want to make sure that you will get something in return for your kind gesture, especially if you are a regular contributor. Here are a few ideas that you can use to increase the impact of your charitable donations and in some cases save money while doing so.

Save Half

Safe half the cost of the donation but get twice the benefit by donating products or services as opposed to cash donations. A product that costs you $25 but retails for $50 is a $50 donation, wherein a $50 cash donation is $50 out of your pocket. Both have the same donation value but one costs you half as much. Likewise, donating a service that you charge $50 an hour for but only costs you $25 in hard costs is also a $50 donation.

Get Something in Return

Always try to get something in return for your donation. This something could be an advertisement for your business in the charity's newsletter or honorable mention at the charity's next dinner or social event. Most charities send out some sort of monthly printed information in the form of a newsletter, newspaper, or report, and knowing this is good information to have on your side. So that the next time your business is asked to make a donation you can in turn ask to be featured in the charity's publication in exchange for your gift.

Promote Your Good Deeds

Let your customers and clients know that you routinely donate to one or more charities within your community. Where and when appropriate include this information in promotional literature, on your Web site, in sales presentations, and in advertisements. Depending on the charities that you regularly donate to, some present business donators with a plaque or certificate that can be displayed in the store or office so make sure to ask if the charity has a recognition system in place.

Donate Resources

Give charities access to your resources as opposed to actual cash donations. The resources you donate could be storage space, transportation, meeting space, equipment, or services like bookkeeping or photocopying. Likewise when your budget is too tight to make a financial contribution consider inviting charities to use your business location for special events. The special events could be everything from collecting clothing for Christmas to bottle drives. These charitable events often attract media, and by getting involved this way you could end up with a ton of free media exposure right at your business location, especially if you tip off the media about the event prior to it taking place.

Encourage Your Customers to Donate

Establish a system that enables your customers to donate to charity and if you can afford to, match it with an equal donation. Perhaps one day you ask customers to give one dollar at the till and you match it with one dollar out of the till. Once again, this is also the type of good charitable work that media likes, and often they will feature businesses that go the extra mile to help out and do some good in the local community.

MAKE IT EXCLUSIVE
$ ✎

One way to up the odds of securing exposure in a specific media outlet is to offer that outlet an exclusive story agreement. What this means is that if they agree to run your story, interview you, or whatever the publicity vehicle might be, you in exchange offer the media outlet exclusive rights to your story, and to no other media company. This may seem like a complicated undertaking, but it is not. For instance, if you want to have your story, news, or photo opportunity featured in print then get started by making a list of the five most important publications that you would like the story to be featured in, in order of importance. Starting at number one, your first choice, contact each publication and pitch your story and offer them an exclusive to the story if they feature it in their publication. Alternately, send out a formal press release or pitch letter to your top five choices first. And, then follow up with telephone calls contacting each starting once again with your first choice. Ask if they received your proposal for an exclusive story and if they are prepared to act on the proposal. Exclusives work, especially after you secure a few good media personnel contacts who like to have exclusive access to your news because you have built a reputation for supplying great stories and news that talks directly to their target audience.

INCREASE THE VALUE OF YOUR KNOWLEDGE

$ ✎

If you keep what you know to yourself, then it benefits you and no one else—or does it? If no one but you knows this knowledge then it is of no value because you can only profit from what you share. If you share your knowledge and expertise with many then your knowledge increases in value with every person who comes in contact with it and benefits because of your knowledge. This is not rocket science, just a time-tested public relations strategy. Share what you know with as many people as possible and in turn you will become known as an expert in the topic, field, or within your business industry. Some of the best ways to share your knowledge are to write articles for print and electronic newspapers, features and columns for magazines and business journals, as well as by creating free reports and booklets that can be distributed to anyone who requests it, in print or electronically via the Internet. Likewise, share your knowledge by speaking at seminars and other events to an audience with an interest in what you have to say. Think of a well-known public speaker—the more knowledge they share, and the more people they share it with, then the higher their fee goes for speaking, even though more people already know about what the speaker will talk about and teach.

This holds true for writing, consulting, and teaching; the more you share what you know and the more people who benefit because of this knowledge of information, the more valuable that information becomes to you.

MAJOR PUBLICITY OPPORTUNITIES

$+ ✎

There are numerous publicity opportunities that every small business should consider developing stories or events around. However, the three best are charities, holidays, and contests. Orchestrated and executed properly, all three are about as fail-safe as it can possibly get in terms of securing media exposure in print, television, and radio. Below is a closer look at how you can benefit from all three publicity tie-in strategies.

Charity

Charity can be an extremely powerful building block for securing valuable publicity and exposure. Create, develop, or participate in a special event for a local or national charity such as a food drive for the needy prior to Thanksgiving, or a toy drive for less fortunate children before Christmas. Regardless if you are the creator or just a participating or sponsoring business in the charity event, make sure to contact the media by way of a press release or media advisory to inform them of the details, as well as the news surrounding the event and the photo opportunities. Ideally, you will want to create a charity event that can be held annually or semiannually with your business name attached to it, something along the lines of "Ralph's Family Shoe Fashions 10th Annual Running for a Cancer Cure Marathon," for example.

Holidays

Holidays are another hot time to create more fantastic public relations opportunities for the savvy small-business owners who are prepared to track these opportunities down and make them happen. For instance, a retailer who sold or rented costumes could develop a special reflective bag that could be used by children on Halloween to collect their candy. The retailer could give them away for free, "just come down to the shop and pick one up." The media loves this type of story because it includes children and a fun holiday event, but more important a great public safety announcement and even a freebie for the public as an added bonus. A great trade off for the exposure and win-win-win situation for the business owner, public, and media alike.

Contests

The third great opportunity to secure media exposure is to hold a contest that involves the community, something that everyone has an opportunity to get involved with and to win. Once you have created your unique contest, contact the local media and give them the details of the event. Or better, try to get one of the media outlets on board as a co-sponsor of the contest and in doing so really grab some great media exposure.

WRITE LETTERS TO THE EDITOR
$ 🔨

In addition to writing and sending out a press release, you might also want to consider writing letters to the editor as many newspapers, magazines, and trade journals print them on a regular basis. This can be a great way to get exposure for your small business, products, or services, but once again your letter must be far more than simply an advertisement promoting what you do or sell. Try to tie your letter into a local hot topic, or you might position yourself as someone with expert information or even inside information in regards to a particular subject or topic. The great thing about letters to the editor, besides the fact they can provide you with all sorts of free advertising, is that often the letter will be talked about for many days or weeks in the same publication via letters written by readers with supportive or opposing views of your original letter. Writing letters to the editor is a great way to secure some free publicity just make sure not to be too controversial and risk alienating potential or, worse, current customers. Additionally, your letter will also stand a better chance of being published if it is in direct response to a recent article the publication featured. For example, if controversy was brewing over a proposed new bridge being built over a waterway and you owned a water taxi service then perhaps the jist

of your letter would be why we don't need a new bridge, signed by you followed by the name of your business.

CONDUCT PUBLIC OPINION POLLS
$+ 🔨

Public relations specialists have long relied on public opinion polls and surveys as a method to secure their clients' exposure in print and broadcast media. Now that you know this closely held PR secret, so can you. Second only to a great photo opportunity of children and pets together, if there is one thing that media outlets of all sorts love to send out to their readers, listeners, and viewers, it's public opinion polls and surveys. The media and the news-hungry public have a love affair with statistics and numbers—mainstream, off base, or who would have thunk it, doesn't matter just as long as they are numbers that the media can sink their teeth into. Given this fact, it creates a fantastic opportunity for the savvy small-business owner to develop and conduct her own public opinion poll or survey. And once complete, release the results to the media so that they can pass this information along to their audience via print publications, over the radio, or on television, of course along with your business name as the source of the information. Below are a few simple examples of how everyday small-business owners can develop and conduct their own public opinion polls and surveys.

Example #1

A costume rental shop could survey kids to find out what the most popular and favorite costumes for Halloween trick-or-treating are, and send this random survey information to the media to feature a few days before Halloween. Or, even better, have the media outlet come to the shop and do a live on-air interview releasing the details of the survey with kids present trying on ghost and goblin costumes.

Example #2

A doughnut shop could survey 1,000 customers to find out what their favorite kind of doughnut is and how often they like to consume doughnuts. Use this information to put together some astonishing figures like "Based on our survey, Americans eat 300 tons of jelly doughnuts annually," or something similar. Once again, release this survey to the media in the form of news to be featured in print, radio, and television.

Example #3

An income tax accountant could poll 500 taxpayers to find out what their biggest pet tax peeve is, tabulate the results, and release this information to the media a few weeks before the beginning of income tax season.

CALL A PRESS CONFERENCE
$+ ✎

A press conference is simply asking reporters, journalists, editors, and broadcasters to come to a central location so that you can release your news or make a special or important announcement, answer questions, and hand out related print materials to a group of media personnel as opposed to contacting each individually. The downside to calling a press conference is the fact that you must have some pretty big "news shoes" to fill if you plan on dragging busy media personnel away from their work. In fact it must be groundbreaking and front-page stuff. This will obviously leave the majority of small-business people out in the cold in terms of calling a press conference simply because few will ever have or be able to create the type of news or hype about business-related issues that are required to draw out big media names to attend. Or is that really entirely the situation? Perhaps all that is required to call a press conference that can result in valuable media exposure is to think about drastically changing the guest list to include small media player names not big ones. Think about secondary methods by which people within your community get news and information and use these secondary formats to build your guest list. Invite key personnel from these organizations to your press conference. The secondary media can include school newspapers, business associations, local cable TV, small, radio broadcasters, special interest groups that regularly publish a magazine or journal in print or electronically, and local politicians.

Sometimes media coverage can go beyond being featured in traditional media and include word-of-mouth coverage from people who can influence others within your community.

More Great Press Conference Tricks

- Plan your conference for a time when the vast majority of media that you invite will be able to attend. Ten at night will draw few if any, but ten in the morning will definitely spike the interest of more than a few.
- Keep location in mind. If you can, hold the press conference at your business; if not, other suitable locations include small banquet rooms, the chamber of commerce, or a supplier or business alliance's location. Remember you will need chairs, a PA system, and basic refreshments like water, coffee, and a snack tray.
- Rather than long speeches about the information you want to get out to the media, if appropriate use live demonstrations instead of or in association with speeches. Also, try to have an expert on hand who can back up any claims that you may make about a product, service, or information. Your expert should be credible and be able to answer questions.
- Always think photo opportunity and, therefore, from the media's perspective when arranging the room where the conference will be conducted. Make sure that your products, logo, business name, and anything else that can identify your business or products will be included in photographs or film footage.
- Before the conference make sure that you create a complete media kit that can be handed out at the event. Additionally, consider handing out sample products, photographs, and promotional materials anything that you believe will help to explain your message and product or service in the best light possible.

BUILD A PR WEB PAGE IN YOUR SITE
$$ ✎

Don't forget to design a public relations page and include it in your Web site. Your PR Web page should be listed in your navigation bar and linked from the home page and include current and past press releases, and a downloadable full media kit in PDF format. Also include the latest breaking news about your business, key personnel, and detailed information about the products and services you provide to customers, especially information that details the unique benefits and competitive advantages associated with these products and services. Make sure to regularly update your PR Web page and include the fact that you have a PR page in your Web site when you send out press releases, pitch letters, and media kits to media outlets. As media personnel will often visit Web sites before contacting you for a better understanding of your business and "news" story or feature. It is also a good idea to have a dedicated PR e-mail link right on the page so that media personnel can contact the appropriate person directly if they wish to ask questions for possible media exposure or inclusion of your story. Another great idea to increase the effectiveness of your PR Web page is to submit additional keywords to search engines that are relevant to your press release, past and current. However, make sure that the keywords and phrases you submit are in the press release headline and repeated at least two or three times throughout the body of the press release. Also remember to submit new keywords to search engines every time you place new press releases or publicity materials on your PR Web page.

PRINT MEDIA INTERVIEW TRICKS
$ ⚒

Print media interviews can happen at any time and just about anywhere—your office, retail store, a restaurant, or at home. Consequently once you start sending out press releases, media advisories, and introduction letters, you have to be prepared for what can follow, namely media exposure and interviews. And with that said here are a few great tricks that you can employ to prepare for interviews as well as during the interview.

- When you prepare a press release, take a few moments to also jot down a few ideas, thoughts, and answers to questions that may come up in an interview should a reporter, editor, or journalist

call after they receive your press release. Think of this part of the planning process like a sales presentation; you know that your prospect, or in this case the reporter, will have questions, concerns, and objections so you have to anticipate what these may be and be ready to answer or overcome them during the interview.

- Keep track of what media you send your press release to and make a few notes on cue cards about each—their usual topics, their target audience, and the type of stories they generally feature. Write the name of the publication on the front along with the contact person and on the back write the rest of the relevant data, details, and information that you know about the publication. Knowing this information can help you prepare for a potential interview without having to spend a great deal of time researching beforehand and trying to remember the information after at the spur of the moment when a reporter calls. Cue cards such as these are a great reference tool that can give you basic details and information when you need it the most.

- When a reporter or editor calls, ask what their deadline is for the story and what types of questions they will be asking or information they would like to have. And if their deadline is not urgent then ask if you can prepare for the interview based on the information they want and return their call once you are ready. Providing they are not on a tight deadline, most media personnel are happy to give you some time to prepare for the interview so it is well worth inquiring right up front.

- Always be prepared for the potential that you will be interviewed and have a complete media kit ready to go. This way if you meet with a reporter or editor you will be able to give them the media kit which should help them to not only prepare their story for publication but also get a better understanding of the main message you are trying to relay.

- Before any interviews find out how much time the reporter has allowed so that you will be able to prioritize the information you would like to relay. This is very important because it is very easy to get sidetracked on secondary issues or explanations that take away from the true spirit of your story, news, or main message. Though the reporter will want to control the questions and pace of the interview, you must make sure that you can clearly explain the most important part(s) of your message and how this information benefits their readers.

- Try to review or summarize your main points, issues, or message at the beginning and at the end of the interview so that there is no miscommunication or misunderstanding between you and the reporter. If you want your message to be printed as you believe it should, then make every effort to ensure that it is understood the way you want it to be. Likewise if you do not want a comment to make it into print then simply don't make it. Contrary to what you may believe, there is no such thing as "off the record" or "strictly between you and me." Think of it this way: If you have to tell a person not to repeat what you say, then you shouldn't be telling him or her in the first place.

- Remain positive and upbeat during the entire interview even if things are not going as well as you had hoped. You do not want to come across as angry, upset, combative, or disappointed; if you do then expect that the published interview, feature, or article will have the same tone, voice, and message.

- Never answer a question that you are not 100 percent confident that you can answer correctly. If this situation arises then politely let the reporter know that this is not your area of specific expertise and that there are people better qualified than you to answer the question.

- If you do not fully understand a question that you are asked or are unsure where the questioning is leading, then give yourself time to mentally prepare for a response by restating the question back to the reporter for clarification. Or ask the interviewer to ask the question again, or even a reworded version that will help you to understand.

- Thank the reporter, editor, or journalist for his time and let him know that if there are any additional questions or information he needs to complete the story, then he should not hesitate to contact you. Additionally, a follow-up letter after the interview is also a good idea. Once again thank the interviewer for his time and let him know that you are available in the future as an "expert source" for information should he have the need.

WEB RESOURCE

⌁ www.newslink.org: Free online media directory service including print and broadcast media outlets and companies categorized by state.

BROADCAST MEDIA INTERVIEW TRICKS
$ ⚒

Radio and television interviews are much different than print media interviews. Broadcast interviews are almost never spontaneous and therefore you have time to prepare for them once you find out that you are fortunate enough to land some valuable airtime. But once again preparation is the key to coming off like a pro in any interview situation so listed below you will find some great tricks that you can use to prepare for broadcast interviews and a few for while you are being interviewed.

- When you send a press release or pitch letter to a radio or television station or program, let them know that you will make yourself available to meet their programming schedules. In other words make it more convenient for them than for yourself. This is a major point, especially if you want to turn a one-time appearance into a regular appearance or feature on the program. Producers like to work with people who are easy to work with frankly because their jobs are mass confusion at the best of times. The fewer road blocks and the easier you make it for them, the more likely you are to be called upon on a regular basis.

- Keep detailed records of the radio and television stations and programs that you send material to or that you pitch. Once again, cue cards with the name of the station, program, producer, and production assistant on the front and detailed information about the program on the back are very handy. Include information such as their target audience, the interviewer style, and the type of information they like to feature on the program. Also find out if the format of the show is taped or live.

- Ask the producer or production assistant if you should submit a sheet listing question-and-answer topics or a general tip or fact sheet of points that you think should be covered. Ask if there is specific information that they would like to discuss during the show so that you can best prepare yourself beforehand.

- If the radio interview will be conducted remotely—meaning that you will not be in the studio, which is usually the case—then make preparations for the location that you will be at during the interview. If at your office, then put a "do not disturb" sign on the door and lock it if possible. Make sure that no other telephone lines or intercoms are active during the interview. And if at home then take the same precautions and let family members know the importance of the interview, including the family dog. Don't laugh! I forgot the golden rule of at-home radio interviews and left my office door open, and during the interview my dog decided that I wasn't paying enough attention to her and starting barking and whining. Luckily the program host was a seasoned veteran and made a few humorous comments that quickly got us all off the hook.

- If the interview will be live in a radio or television studio then make sure you arrive early, introduce yourself to the production assistants, and get familiar with your surroundings. This is a great way to ease jittery nerves and ensure that you are not scrambling at the last moment. Also if the interview is for television broadcast make sure to inquire about appropriate attire beforehand and stick with conservative fashions that are always a safe bet and guarantee a professional appearance.

- Know the topic of the interview and information inside out and upside down, there is nothing worse than dead airtime while you try to think about a response or how to word a response. If

the interview is radio then you can take cue cards with topics that you want to cover during the interview and place your main points in priority of importance, or in logical sequence.

- Most speaking experts agree that for broadcast interviews you should try to limit responses to less than one minute in length, or break up the length or responses by allowing the interviewer to further elaborate questions or add secondary points. But don't worry, they will find a way to cut you off if they feel your response or explanation is getting long-winded.

- During the interview keep your main objectives in mind—the reasons that you first sought the publicity and coverage. Additionally, try not to push products or services on the air, instead give viewers or listeners options to contact you after the program. These options can include a mailing address, office or store location, as well as a toll-free telephone line, Web site, or an e-mail address. And always make sure that the program host or producer is aware of this information and can show it on screen or relay the information verbally on the air.

- Always remain upbeat and positive even if the interview is not going as expected and keep cool, calm, and relaxed. The only emotions that you should show is your excitement for the information or message that you want to get out, and how people will benefit from this information. In fact the main thrust of every response you give should be benefit oriented for listeners or viewers.

- I can tell you from experience that it doesn't hurt to have a ringer in your corner. What I mean by a ringer is that if the program you are being featured on is a call-in show, make sure to have a friend, family member, or business colleague call in and ask questions that you have rehearsed with them so that you will come off as a genuine pro and expert with the answers. This is not a deceptive practice, just a way to ensure that, number-one someone actually calls in to the show to ask a question, and number two, you can hold your head high and proud knowing that at least one call-in viewer or listener got all the right answers to all the questions they asked.

WEB RESOURCE

⚲ www.virtualtuner.com: Online directory of more than 10,000 Internet radio and television stations broadcasting from more than 100 countries in 75 languages directly to your computer.

TRICKS FOR GETTING ON TALK RADIO
$ ⚒

Talking to a captive radio audience about what you do or sell is like money in the bank, but before you go cashing that check you should make sure that you prepare to get on talk radio. Start by researching the show and its audience; nothing will scare off a producer faster than pitching a story or talk idea that is in no way even close to being relevant to their format, style, and target audience. Next develop a story idea, something that would be interesting to the producer and the audience and if you can tie it in with current or local events then do it. Once you have developed the idea, put it on paper in the form of a pitch letter. Basically a professional business letter that tells about your story and why it and you should be invited in to grace the airwaves. With your pitch letter, prepare and include a background sheet or bio to go along with your pitch letter. The bio sheet should be straightforward and clearly spell out your qualifications or expertise in the field. If possible try to back up your claim of expertise with facts or statistics, perhaps even a customer testimonial, or talk about special work you have done for a recognized person or business, the bigger and more recognized the names the better. Of course, if you have written books or articles, taught classes or courses, or anything else in terms of the topic, let the producer know about it in your bio sheet, anything to build and captialize on credibility. Send your pitch letter or set an appointment with the producer to meet in person. If you are an experienced public speaker and carry yourself well I strongly suggest a personal appointment approach to pitching. Producers like to know that they will be booking an exciting, knowledgeable, and engaging guest. Additionally,

try to develop an overall angle or concept that will secure a regular spot on one or more programs.

WEB RESOURCE

⚲ www.radio-locator.com: Online directory linked to more than 10,000 radio stations indexed by format and geographic location in the United States and Canada.

DON'T FORGET TO SAY THANK YOU
$ ⚒

In all the excitement of having your news, story, or article featured in the media, don't forget to take the time to say thank you to those who made it happen. Write a note, set a personal appointment, make a call, or send an e-mail that thanks the reporter, publisher, editor, producer, or journalist who gave you the media coverage. Keep your thank-you note brief, but appreciative and restate the date and subject matter of the coverage, as often media personnel have so many irons in the fire they might have forgotten who you are and not make the connection from the note unless you include a gentle reminder. Additionally if you have another story or news idea, don't be afraid to include it in with your thank-you note. But once again, keep your pitch short, to the point, and most important not too aggressive in terms of hard selling the idea. All media personnel share one thing in common, which is once they have found a reliable source for news that they like, they will return to that source for more news. Or in the very least be very receptive when you contact them to pitch another story idea. So it goes without saying that a quick "thanks for the coverage" will go a long way in securing your place in their good graces.

PLACES TO SEEK PUBLICITY AND PUBLICITY METHODS CHECKLIST
$+ ⚒ ☎ ⚖

The places that small-business owners can seek publicity go well beyond just the local newspaper, and the methods to gain free and valuable publicity go well beyond only writing a press release as the following checklists will illustrate.

Places to Seek Publicity Checklist

❏ National and metropolitan daily newspapers, print and online

❏ Weekly community newspapers, print and online

❏ College newspapers, print and online

❏ University newspapers, print and online

❏ High school newspapers

❏ Special interest newspapers, print and online

❏ Tourism newspapers and guides

❏ Trade school newspapers and newsletters

❏ Union newspapers and newsletters, print and online

❏ Corporate and employee newsletters, print and online

❏ Church newsletters

❏ Online news portals, e-zines, and e-newsletters

❏ Online discussion boards and forums

❏ Business associations newsletters and Web sites

❏ Social and sports clubs newsletters and Web sites

❏ National magazines, print and online

❏ Local magazines, print and online

❏ Business journals

❏ Trade journals

❏ Professional journals

❏ Special interest magazines and publications

❏ Local radio

❏ National radio

❏ College radio

❏ Public access radio

❏ Local television

❏ National television

❏ Public access television

❏ Mass market paperback-hardcover nonfiction books

❏ Ethnic foreign language newspapers and magazines

❏ Ethnic foreign language radio and television

❏ Seminars and public speaking engagements

Publicity Seeking Methods Checklist

❏ Write and distribute press releases, media advisories, and introduction letters

❏ Create and distribute a media or press kit

❏ Pitch producers for radio interviews

❏ Pitch producers for television interviews

❏ Pitch journalists and editors for print interviews

❏ Write and submit letters to the editor for print and online newspapers

❏ Call live talk radio programs

❏ Run for political office

❏ Hire a public relations firm

❏ Sponsor sports and community events

❏ Donate to and work with local and national charities

❏ Become known as an expert media source

❏ Write articles and features for print and online media

❏ Go to where the cameras are and where news is happening in your community

❏ Conduct public opinion polls and surveys and submit to media outlets

❏ Hold a contest

❏ Stage a wacky publicity event

❏ Attempt to set a local or world record

❏ Call a press conference

❏ Seek out public speaking engagements

❏ Write a book and get published

📖 SUGGESTED ADDITIONAL READING

Bly, Robert W. *Become a Recognized Authority in Your Field in 60 Days or Less.* Dulles, VA: Alpha Books, 2001.

Borden, Kay. *Bulletproof News Releases: Help at Last for the Publicity Deficient.* Marietta, GA: Franklin Sarrett Publishing, 1995.

Caywood, Clarke L. *The Handbook of Strategic Public Relations and Integrated Communications.* New York: McGraw-Hill, 1997.

Levine, Michael. *Guerrilla PR Wired: Waging a Successful Publicity Campaign, On-Line, Offline and Everywhere in Between.* New York: McGraw-Hill, 2001.

Levinson, Jay Conrad, Rick Frishman, and Jill Lublin. *Guerrilla Publicity: Hundreds of Sure-Fire Tactics to Maximum Sales for Minimum Dollars.* Avon, MA: Adams Media Corporation, 2002.

Mathis, Mark. *Feeding the Media Beast: An Easy Recipe for Great Publicity.* Ashland, OH: Purdue University Press, 2002.

Ries, Al and Laura Ries. *The Fall of Advertising and the Rise of PR.* New York: Harper Business, 2002.

Von Oech, Roger. *A Whack on The Side of The Head: How You Can Be More Creative.* New York: Warner Books, 1998.

Yale, David R. and Andrew J. Carothers. *The Publicity Handbook, New Edition: The Inside Scoop from More than 100 Journalists and PR Pros on How to Get Great Publicity Coverage.* New York: McGraw-Hill, 2001.

Yudkin, Marcia. *6 Steps to Free Publicity, Revised Edition.* Franklin Lakes, NJ: Career Press, 2003.

NETWORKING AND REFERRAL
Marketing Tips for Your Business

*Nothing is ever gained by winning an
argument and losing a customer.*

—C. F. Norton

WHY NETWORK?

$ ⚒

Without question personal contact networking is still one of the best and easiest ways to form long-term and profitable business relationships with like-minded businesspeople and prospects. It gives you the power of one-to-one relationship building that few other methods of marketing or advertising can match. Additionally, through proper networking activities, you are really building a super powerful sales force of alliances that work tirelessly at selling your business, products, and services to others, and best of all this sales force of eager sellers is not on the weekly payroll. Top businesspeople and sales professionals understand the power of networking and therefore make an effort to include networking activities in their weekly schedules. In fact, effort does not properly describe what top businesspeople do in terms of networking, it goes well beyond simply making an effort. They create networking plans so that they know who can have the biggest and most positive impact on their business. And because they take the time to identify these individuals, they know who they have to seek out and to build business alliance relationships. Networking works and will go a long way to help you reach your marketing and business objectives, but only if you make a conscious effort to master the art of networking, develop a networking plan, actively seek networking opportunities, and maintain and manage a networking schedule and base of contacts.

PROFESSIONAL BRAINSTORMING LUNCH

$$ ☎

Are you looking for fresh and effective ideas about how to market a new product or service, increase profits, ways to expand into new markets, or ideas to overcome a specific business challenge? If so, consider hosting a professional brainstorming lunch to get the answers that you seek to these and other questions and positive and productive ways to build your business. Mix up the guest list to include your banker, lawyer, accountant, local businesspeople, and a few of your suppliers. The more varied the guests' backgrounds the better the "idea generating team" you will have assembled. However, aim to invite people who you respect for their business and marketing savvy. Send out brainstorming lunch invitations to your guests with details such as location, date, and time, and more importantly the key objective of the meeting, "I'm considering expanding my business to include new products and your professional expertise and input is welcomed and much needed," as an example. Few people will turn down an "invited expert" opportunity, especially when you're picking up the tab for a fine meal at a nice restaurant. Who knows, you and your "brainstorming guests" might find the brainstorming lunches to be so productive that you collectively decide to hold them monthly or even weekly. Suggest a rotating schedule of who gets the floor to pose specific business challenges and the opportunity to benefit from the wisdom, expertise, and advice from the other invited guests.

HIGH-TECH CD-ROM BUSINESS CARDS
$$$ 🖐

Take your business card into the world of high-tech presentation by getting it put on disc. CD-ROM format business cards are the latest rage in high-tech business promotion and these mini CD-ROMs can be die cut into virtually any shape and have your picture, logo, or business name and telephone number silk-screened on the outside of the disk. Additionally, the disks can be played on any standard disk drive, hold the equivalent of 100 pages of typed information, and you can include graphics, sounds, and links directly to your Web site or e-mail from the disk. Imagine on one business card-sized CD-ROM you can give a virtual presentation highlighting the benefits of your business, products, or services. And get this powerful marketing presentation into the hands of prospects just by handing out these mini discs that prospects can play at their convenience. Wow, that is super powerful marketing and a great way to separate your business from competitors'. And best of all,

in bulk the end product costs about the same as it costs to produce a four-page color product brochure.

WEB RESOURCE

🖐 www.bizcard-cd.com: Manufacturers and distributors of CD-ROM business cards.

THE POWER OF YOUR BUSINESS CARD
$ 🖐

Business cards are an inexpensive and powerful networking tool when used correctly. Always introduce yourself when handing out your business card and give recipients a moment to review your card before initiating conversation. Also get in the habit of handing out at least ten cards a day—to the postman, store clerk, gas station attendant, and even to the police officer who just gave you a parking ticket. You never know where your next sale may come from, or who may refer it to you. Assume that everyone wants to do business with you and make it easy by giving out a business card. Be sure to take a moment to personalize every card you hand out, this could be writing a promotional offer on the back, a quote for the day, or a simple note that says "give me a call." And most importantly every time you hand out a business card let them know you are always seeking new clients and that you appreciate new business. Likewise when you receive business cards from people always take a moment after you disengage in conversation with that person to jot a few notes on the back of their card in relation to key points that came out of the conversation. Listed below are a few other clever ideas to use your business card as a cheap yet effective way to promote your business.

- When someone asks for your business card give them three, one for him or her and two extras so they can be shared with friends, family members, and co-workers.
- Include a business card with all outgoing mail and correspondences you send.
- Tack a few business cards onto every community bulletin board in your community, which are generally found in the laundry, library, schools, community center, grocery stores, public markets, and fitness clubs.

- Arrange with other businesses to leave a plastic cardholder and a supply of your business cards in their reception area, waiting room, or by the cash register.
- Leave a business card behind every time you pay a bill at restaurants, gas stations, dry cleaners, grocery markets, and movie theaters. Let people know that you are actively seeking new business and customers.

SET NETWORKING OBJECTIVES
$

Networking is no different than any other business or marketing activity you engage in, you will get the most out of what you are doing if you know why you are doing it and what you want to accomplish from it. Therefore make sure that you set networking goals and objectives so that you will know what you want to accomplish and so that you will have a yardstick to measure your performance. The objectives and goals you identify and set will vary as to each individual's situation, wants, and needs. However, common networking objectives and goals include generating new leads, making new personal and business contacts, introducing new products or services, forming new business alliances, finding new suppliers and vendors, reacquainting with past business associates, and conducting research. Simply stating that you want to increase business revenues and profits has little meaning or will generate few results unless you have a measurable plan in place that you can use as a map to reach your goals and objectives, be it increased revenues and profits or whatever. Networking is a terrific marketing instrument, but like any instrument you have to know how to play it and know when you have arrived at the sound you desire. Additionally make sure to identify the people that you would like to do business with. Keep your list short, say ten to begin with and then set about identifying ways that you can come into personal contact with these people and get the networking ball rolling. Find out what sports they play, what clubs or organizations they belong to, and the church they attend. Once you have identified this information you will be able to create a plan of action that can get you closer to the people you feel can have the greatest positive impact on your business.

MY NETWORKING OBJECTIVE(S) IS TO:
- make new and valuable business contacts.
- sell my product or service, or sell more to my existing customers.
- qualify prospects and collect leads.
- headhunt for employees, managers, and subcontractors.
- conduct market research.
- stay in contact with current customers and suppliers.
- maintain a high profile in my business community.
- find new suppliers and vendors.
- stay active and get involved in my community.
- seek new business and joint venture opportunities.
- secure valuable referrals.
- become known as an expert in my industry or field.
- keep in tune with trends and information that affect my business and industry.
- work hard to brand my business, products, or services through networking exposure.

THE HEADCOUNT RULE
$

Creating a simple headcount rule is a great motivational tool to ensure that you get out and network to make new business contacts and reinforce the business relationships that you currently have. A headcount rule means nothing more than you pledge that you will attend networking meetings, business functions, and community social events when the number of other people who will be attending exceeds the number you set as your "headcount" benchmark. For instance, if you set your headcount rule at 50, then you would endeavor to attend as many functions as possible when you know that there will be at least 50 people attending the function in question. Of course, you will want to prequalify the function to ensure that you get maximum networking possibilities out of each event, either by way of making contact with other people who can help your business grow or coming into direct contact with your target audience. As elementary as the headcount rule may appear to be on the surface, it is in fact a highly effective motivational tool that forces you to get out and network for new business and to make valuable new contacts. Much like the sound of a ringing alarm clock motivates you to get out of bed in the morning and on with your day.

TRICKS FOR BEING A BRILLIANT CONVERSATIONALIST
$ ⚒

Any person who ever met Dale Carnegie, noted author and motivational speaker, always commented about what a great conversationalist he was. The man himself described this as simply listening to what people had to say, asking them questions about what was important to them, and being interested in their responses. In short he kept the spotlight on the person he was speaking with and off himself. You control the conversation by asking the questions and carefully listening to what the person is saying. Talking is not controlling, listening is. A detective takes control by asking questions and taking notes. You should be taking mental notes and writing them on paper, the back of their business cards, or in your networking notepad after they leave. Here are some more great tricks for becoming a brilliant conversationalist.

- Take a greater interest in what the person you are speaking to has to say than what you have to say.
- Enter into a conversation knowing what you would like to say and learn, but don't have any preconceived ideas or judgments about the other person. In other words, keep an open mind.
- Don't interrupt, remain silent when the other person is talking.
- Never argue, even if you disagree with what someone is saying, or react emotionally to a statement and always keep your cool.
- Never offer an opinion unless you are asked to do so. And address the other person by first name frequently throughout the conversation.

As Mr. Carnegie noted, "There is no sweeter sound to a person's ears then the sound of their own name being spoken."

ENLARGE YOUR NETWORKING CIRCLE
$ ⚒

To truly master the art of networking and to leave no "opportunity for new business" stone unturned then you must go beyond your traditional networking model to include networking with people who are not like you and to places that you normally would not traditionally be networking. Build friendships and alliances with people who are from outside of your ethnic, social, economic, and cultural background. Develop a wide base of "people alliances" to broaden your networking circle, referral, and word-of-mouth marketing opportunities. At some point staying within your current networking circle will become counterproductive, not entirely but mostly as you reach critical mass. You could however make much better use of your networking time by including your current networking strategies and enlarging your networking circle to include new people and places. One of the best ways to enlarge your networking circle is to join a new club, a social or sports activity club, something that you have never tried before. Perhaps a skiing club, a book club, or even getting involved with a local charity. In a nutshell look for ways to make new contacts in new places so that you can broaden your marketing reach to include a new audience through networking activities. Here are a few ways to broaden your networking circle.

- Join or start a new networking club.
- Enroll in night classes or weekend workshops.
- Become involved in community politics and issues.
- Join social or sports teams and clubs.
- Get involved with community charities.

STAND OUT IN THE NETWORKING CROWD
$ ⚒

A decade ago I was at an evening social networking meeting at the local chamber of commerce. Most people in attendance were dressed in smart casual attire and some were wearing the business attire because they came straight from the office. The room was a mixture of business blue and brown. About halfway through this informal networking meeting a man showed up wearing a wetsuit and had goggles and a snorkel dangling around his neck. He was a new member who owned a scuba dive shop that gave lessons and sold equipment, and this was the first meeting he had attended. Needless to say he stood out in the crowd and for the next hour was bombarded with questions, humorous greetings, and the odd strange glance. A few months after this meeting, my wife and I were planning a vacation to Mexico. High on our agenda was to learn to scuba dive so we could take full advantage of the many scuba diving opportunities in the area where we would be vacationing. Guess who we called to take the required training to get PADI certified before the trip? You got it, the man in the wetsuit. In fact we didn't even bother to inquire at other dive shops in our area. He made such a positive impression on us that we felt totally comfortable with dropping into his shop and signing up for the required courses. Not all networking meetings are suitable places for these types of unforgettable promotional tactics, but at the social mixers there is no reason you cannot dress to leave a lasting and positive impression by standing out in the networking crowd.

DEVELOP A PERSONAL TRADEMARK
$ ✎

Good advertising causes us to remember something about the advertisement or the product that was being advertised and creating your own personal trademark can have the same effect on people that good advertising has. Sports broadcaster Don Cherry is known for his highly starched shirt collars, musician John Lennon for his round granny eyeglasses, and comedian George Burns for his constant companion, a cigar. All are personal trademarks that help to instantly identify these people as these items have become a part of their identity and will never be forgotten. A personal trademark can extend beyond an item to include a physical appearance like Don

King's wild hair, a pattern of speech or phrase like Ali's "Float like a butterfly and sting like a bee," or a physical movement like Rodney Dangerfield's continuous necktie straightening and eye rolling. The common denominator of personal trademarks is that they are remembered and instantly linked to the person who uses or owns them. Developing your own personal trademark can be very effective for networking purposes. Once again it can make you stand out, and be easily remembered. Of course you have to keep in mind your profession and the practical approach in terms of creating a personal trademark. Try to find a balance and not go to extremes. A lawyer with dyed red hair will likely be remembered for all the wrong reasons, while a lawyer who wears tennis sneakers with a suit will likely be viewed and remembered as a down to earth professional who is on the move. Both memorable trademarks, but one is likely to be viewed and remembered in a more positive way than the other. Try to create your own personal trademark as a way to stand out and get remembered in networking circles.

MAKE A MEMORABLE DONATION
$+ ✎

Help meet and exceed your networking goals and objectives by making a memorable donation to the networking club(s) that you belong to and participate in on a regular basis. The memorable donation that you make should be an item or number of items that will continually remind all the people at these networking meetings and functions about your business and about the products and services that you sell. Wise donations that fit the memorable bill include an oversized wall clock emblazoned with your business name and logo in the center, or a set of coffee mugs imprinted with your business name and promotional message that everyone in the group can use at meetings. The idea is to donate one or more items to your networking group that will get used during every meeting, thus continually reminding other people in attendance about your business, products, and services. Networking is like advertising; in order for it to be effective it must be memorable and repetitive, resulting in establishing brand

and image awareness over the long term. Get creative and think of ways that people in your networking group will remember you by donating an item imprinted with your business name and logo that will be used over and over by members. Of course if you can donate an item that you sell, then you can really ramp up the effectiveness of this easy low-cost marketing trick.

WEB RESOURCE

☞ www.promomart.com: Billed as the world's largest online source for promotional and advertising specialty products.

GET INVOLVED
$ ⚒

Build a strong network of potential salespeople and customers by getting involved in your community. It's a proven fact that people like to do business with people they know and like, and they also like to refer other people to businesses run by those people they know and like. Your church, a local charity, or even a run for a seat in municipal government, getting involved in your community can have an enormous beneficial long-term effect on your business. Get out and shake hands, smile, pitch in and help out for a good cause, and make the decision that you will get in the game instead of watching from the sidelines. In terms of building a positive business image and loyal customer base, no marketing effort can match getting involved with and giving back to the community that supports your business and success. However, be genuine in your efforts and get involved because you want to help out your community, not just because you want to promote your business. Don't worry about the upside because over time the business promotion aspect of getting involved will take root, flourish, and show positive and beneficial results. And best of all, it will be the people in the community who benefit from your involvement who will take up the cause and promote your business for you. Besides think of all the fun you can have and all the friends you'll make by getting involved and becoming an active member in your community.

FIRST IN, LAST OUT
$ ⚒

As a rule of thumb the best networking opportunities generally take place 20 minutes before a function or meeting starts, and in the first 20 minutes after these same meetings and functions end. Consequently, if your number-one objective is to make as many valuable contacts as possible then it is wise to always arrive early for meetings, seminars, and business functions and stay late to maximize the number of networking opportunities that may be available. Think of yourself as the host of the event even if you are just a guest and make sure that you try to greet and speak to as many people as possible before the event and see them off after the event. The majority of people in attendance will not know the difference or particularly care if you are the host or not. They will however, be very thankful and remember you as the person in the sea of people who was thoughtful enough to take the initiative and break the ice by greeting them warmly, thus making them feel more comfortable, relaxed, and a welcomed member of the group. Remember that old adages and clichéd sayings such as "the early bird always gets the worm" were never born out of bad advice.

GO OUT OF YOUR WAY TO WELCOME NEWCOMERS
$$ ⚒ ☎

Be the first to welcome new people to your community, either through supporting a newcomers program like Welcome Wagon or by developing your own newcomers program. If you decide to go it alone, one the best ways to find out who is moving into the area is to establish working relationships with real estate agents and brokers as well as property managers who specialize in renting residential accommodations. And of course local schools and business associations can also supply you with this type of information. These contacts can let you know who is moving into the area, how many people are in the family, and in what line of work or business they are involved. The goal is to provide the newcomers with something that will benefit them; a free product or service as a welcome-to-the-community gift. Just the fact that you have taken the time to greet them and say hello and make newcomers feel welcomed and part of the community will go a long way to ensuring that these people remember you and your business. Don't expect everyone you welcome to the area to become a customer, but take heart in the fact that many will. Besides, it's a great way to build your business image and promote goodwill within the community.

WEB RESOURCES

- www.welcomewagon.com: Untied States Welcome Wagon Association.
- www.welcomewagon.ca: Canadian Welcome Wagon Association

IT'S ALL IN THE NAMETAG
$ ✎

Here is an effective and virtually free networking trick that any businessperson or sales professional can benefit from using. Before you attend your next networking function, meeting or seminar, take the time to create an interesting nametag that will get noticed, be memorable, and work as a real icebreaker and open the lines of communication with guests in attendance. How you might ask? By stating a message on the nametag—in addition to your name, and something that will prompt people in attendance to ask you questions, not to mention get a few laughs. Your printed statement could be your favorite movie, where you were born, what breed your dog is, or just about anything else that is perhaps a little out of the ordinary. But remember to make it bold. This tactic works very well as an icebreaker in a room full of people you do not know, as instantly you'll get a few puzzled looks followed by questions about what your nametag says. A nametag that says, "Hi my name is Bob and I can show you how to make $100,000 next year," is sure to get notice and prompt more questions than an ordinary nametag that says "Bob, Financial Planner." Wouldn't you agree?

DEVELOP A FOLLOW-UP SYSTEM
$ ✎

Effective networking is not meeting someone today and then ten years later giving him a call to see how things are going. No, effective networking is a three-part strategy that begins with making the contact, following up with your new contact almost immediately, and staying in contact with your new alliance forever. The focus of this trick is part two, immediate follow-up. Get in the habit of following up with new contacts that you make while networking right away. Give them a call, send a letter, send an e-mail or fax, or better yet set an appointment with them even if it is a quick drop by just to let them know it was a pleasure to meet them and that you enjoyed the conversation. Use this time to reconfirm what they do and sell as well as restating your business and the benefits that people receive from buying your products or services. In the sales profession it is true that the real work begins after you close a deal, that work being to build and maintain a strong relationship with your new customer by way of follow-up contact. Effective networking is no different; it is easy to make new contacts, but the real work begins after you have made the contact. It is at this point where you must build the relationship so that it will generate mutually beneficial results for both parties and in order to do so you must follow up and stay in contact.

DEVELOP YOUR OWN MINI SALES PITCH
$ ✎

Drop the long-winded explanations about what your business does or sells and instead develop a high impact mini sales pitch to replace it. Keep the pitch short, simple, and directly to the point, which should be what you do or sell and the biggest benefit your customers receive because of it all clearly stated in plain English. For example, as a basic and mini sales pitch that is meant to get the conversation rolling a financial planner might say, "I help people retire young and very rich." Bingo. Who doesn't want to retire young and rich, and who wouldn't want to hear more about this? I would venture a guess that few would not want to find out more, especially when young and rich are used in the same sentence. Definitely more people would want to find out more this way than would want to hear jargon about financial markets relayed in technical terms and explanations that most people would not understand. The financial planner can get right to what will grab attention and possibly land new clients without boring them to tears in the process. We all meet new people every day, on the street, in restaurants, on the bus or in line at the grocery store. So why not get to work on creating your own mini sales pitch, use it religiously and watch your customer base and sales go through the roof as a direct result.

NETWORK THROUGH CURRENT PROJECTS
$ ⚒

Take full advantage of your current projects and work-in-progress projects to spread the word and promote your business, products, and services to new prospects. Companies that specialize in business-to-business sales or businesses that specialize in direct-to-consumer sales can employ this simple yet effective networking trick to ignite sales, especially companies that conduct in-home product installations or provide in-home consumer services. Here is how to get started. After an in-home or in-office meeting with a client, take the time required to visit surrounding homes or offices. Introduce yourself and let people know about the work you're doing for their neighbors. This is very powerful networking and marketing, simply because in all likelihood the people you talk to will know your clients, which in turn forms instant credibility for your business. Hand out promotional material about your business and let the people you're talking to know that you appreciate all new business and referrals. Additionally, use this networking opportunity to promote a little goodwill by asking people if they have any concerns about the work you're carrying out at the neighbor's that they can talk to you directly any time. And if you find that people are not at home or everyone in the office is busy then leave behind printed promotional materials. Once again, the promotional literature should inform people that you are working in the area and are available any time to meet and see

if your products or services would be of interest to them.

GO ONLINE TO NETWORK
$ ⚒

Take advantage of technology and the Internet to go online and network for new customers and business alliances alike. Do this by joining online discussion groups, posting messages in chat rooms, and joining online communities with people who share similar interests or fit into your target audience for the products or services that you sell. Additionally, in recent years many new online networking clubs are starting to spring up offering members traditional networking opportunities, but online without an actual bricks-and-mortar meeting location. Networking via the Internet can be a great way to find new prospects, customers, and to build business alliances; however, be aware that it will take time to establish a base of people who you network with and many will also be networking. Meaning that effective networking is when two separate but equally invested parties benefit by sharing information. Therefore expect to hand out referrals and advice to others when called upon to do so.

WEB RESOURCES

⚒ www.leadsclub.com: Ali Lassen's Lead Club, with 400 chapters representing in excess of 5,000 people.

⚒ www.bni.com: Business Network International, billed as the world's largest referral organization comprising more than 2,600 chapters worldwide and thousands of members.

CREATE A CONTACT LIST
$$ ⚒

Profit from the business cards and personal information you collect while networking by developing a contact list so that you can stay in touch with your new prospects by sending them your newsletter, a special offer, or your monthly e-zine if you publish one. Build your contact list using customer and prospect management software, such as

Maximizer. One of the most valuable mailing and contact lists that you can use for direct-marketing purposes is the one that you have personally created, a compilation of names of the people you have personally been in contact with, a putting a face to the message approach. This is called a house list and can be considered as one of your most valuable business assets. Additionally, the first time you mail to a new prospect make sure that you include where you met and the fact that it was a pleasure to meet and you enjoyed the conversation you shared.

WEB RESOURCE

✍ www.maximizer.com: Sales and contact management software.

MAKE IT A DOOR PRIZE
$$ ✎

Offering your product or service as a door prize is another great networking technique that can also be effectively used to generate a ton of prospecting leads. For instance rather than just attending a seminar, contact the promoter and offer your product or service as a door prize. And, if they accept, which often is the case, then simply collect business cards from people as they enter the room and explain that it is for a free door prize drawing. Or, trade the prize for the attendee mailing list, which can be provided by the seminar promoter or host. The seminar emcee can do the drawing and announce the winner for your free door prize. Of course your business, products, or services get the exposure while the emcee describes the prize and your business to the guests. Likewise if you belong to a networking club, business association, or a social club then also make sure that you regularly provide your product or service as a door prize at these club meetings and events. This simple networking and prospecting trick can be expanded beyond seminars to include just about any type of business function or meetings. And in some situations could even be expanded to include social functions and community events by having people complete a door prize entry form instead of supplying business cards.

CREATIVE INTRODUCTIONS
$ ✎

Make a memorable impact on people when you introduce yourself by developing a creative and memorable verbal introduction. Here are a few before and after examples, you decide which you think will have the greatest impact, create the most interest, and be the most memorable.

BEAUTY ADVISOR
Before: "I sell makeup."
After: "I help people look ten years younger and feel more confident."

MORTGAGE BROKER
Before: "I arrange mortgages."
After: "I turn dreams of home ownership into reality."

CLOTHING RETAILER
Before: "I sell clothing."
After: "I make sure that people do not get arrested for indecent public exposure."

MARKETING CONSULTANT
Before: "I help small-business owners market their products and services."
After: "I help small-business owners with limited marketing budgets grow their businesses and increase profits."

As the examples above clearly demonstrate, the way in which you introduce yourself can be serious or a little fun depending on the situation and the guests in attendance. But the key to a great introduction is to make it memorable and to instantly tell people what the biggest benefit of what you do or sell is. This message must be clear, easy to understand, and directly to the point. In short your creative introduction should be your unique selling proposition and become the cornerstone of all your marketing activities.

BECOME A PORTABLE ADVERTISEMENT FOR YOUR BUSINESS
$$ ✎

Being a portable advertisement for your business simply means that you are a walking and talking example of what your business does and sells. So finely tuned and refined is your ability at being a portable advertisement that in less than 30 seconds you can explain what you do and how people benefit because of it. And most important, the people you speak to instantly understand your advertisement and associate you with your business and the goods and services you provide. Additionally, as a portable advertisement for your business you are always ready and armed with information, promotional items, business cards, samples, and just about anything else that is related to your business and that promotes it in such a way as to invite new business. How many times have you been engaged in conversation and asked for a business card only to watch the other person flounder helplessly for one and come up red-faced and out of luck? Often I am sure, but don't let this happen to you. Instead become a walking, talking, and well-armed advertisement for your business and people will remember you and refer you to others because of the extra effort you put forth to promote your business, products, or services.

FOR PEOPLE WHO HATE TO NETWORK
$+ ✎

Let's face it, some businesspeople, for whatever their personal reasons might be, simply hate to network; in fact some refuse to network at all. So if you are one of those people who hate to network here are a few ways that you can market your business, products, and services without having to network.

Media

Share your knowledge and write articles, stories, and press releases to market your business. The more your name and what you do is out there in various form of media, the more chances of people contacting you to learn more about your products and services.

Advertise

Create advertisements or hire a professional agency to create advertisements for your business. Run your new advertisements in newspapers, magazines, business journals, Yellow Pages, television, radio, and on the Internet.

Hire Others

Perhaps the best approach is to hire people to network your business in your absence of networking. The people you hire could be general employees, contract professionals skilled in public relations, and hands-on management types who like to get involved and network. Or, commissioned sales staff who thrive in a personal contact, prospecting, and networking environments.

Teach

Teaching is another way to market your business without networking, though in effect teaching is a form of networking, just not as aggressive as some networking methods. You could teach or speak at learning institutions, community functions, churches, clubs, seminars, or by creating your own educational workshop and classes relevant to your business and products or services.

Bid on Projects

Strictly aim your marketing efforts at securing service and supply contracts by bidding for them. Bid on tenders and requests for proposals for both private and government contracts. Go online to find tender directories, such as www.securetenders.com, for tender opportunity listings. And visit the U.S. Small Business Administration Web site at www.pronet.sba.gov for up-to-date information on government service and supply contracts.

Internet

Build, maintain, and market a value packed Web site and put it to work for your business 24 hours a day, 365 days a year. The Internet provides business owners thousands of faceless and non-in-person marketing opportunities.

SORRY LETTERS WORK WONDERS
$ ✎

Thank prospects who did not buy from you. The "sorry letter" approach to follow-up and new business generation can increase your closing and referral rate by 5 percent or more! A sorry letter is simply a letter that you send to prospects who did not become clients or customers. The letter should be sent within two days of the proposal rejection and include the following points:

- Thank the prospects for the opportunity to fulfill their product or service needs.
- Restate the value and benefits of your product, service, and proposal.
- Close with "should you have a change in decision or direction, I would like the opportunity to earn your current and future business.

The benefits of the sorry letter rejection follow-up are many, including the following:

- The prospects will keep you in mind for future proposals.
- Should the winning bidder not live up to expectations, you may very well be called back to save the day.
- The prospect may very well refer your company, product or service to others even though they did not purchase from you. Especially if you ask for referrals in your letter and even go as far as offering an incentive for referrals.
- And most importantly, the door is left open with no burned bridges. Professionalism at the highest level.

In a nutshell, you would not invest time and money into the restoration of a house just to walk away from it if the roof leaked. Building a long-term and repeat customer base takes an ongoing effort. You invest time and money to attract business, so do not simply throw in the towel if you are first unsuccessful with an account or customer you want to land. Try the sorry letter approach and you will be very surprised with the favorable outcome.

SPEND 3 PERCENT TO GENERATE A 100 PERCENT REFERRAL RATE
$+ ✎

Here is a clever idea that will go a long way to ensure that just about every customer you do business with will refer your business to their friends, family, and business associates. What is this clever trick you might ask? Simply add 3 percent onto every job estimate or quote that you submit to prospects and customers. And when the job is complete, rebate the 3 percent back to them in the form of a check, nicely wrapped in a customer appreciation thank-you card. No one wants to pay more; we all want to pay less and are thrilled to pay less, and are especially thrilled to get a rebate in the form of cash money when we weren't expecting to receive one. At the end of the job pay a surprise visit to your customer and present them with the rebate check and an explanation that you managed to stay under budget while still providing the best quality products and the most qualified labor. But don't say you overestimated in the first place, as this could raise suspicions and make you appear dishonest in your business practices. This simple marketing trick can generate an enormous amount of new referrals. You may want to implement it even without building the 3 percent in the first place if you can afford to do so. As we all know, referred leads are ten times easier to close than cold leads and way less costly to generate, given that as much as 50 percent of the selling price of goods and services include the costs associated with marketing these goods and services. Therefore 3 percent just might be a bargain.

SET REFERRAL TARGETS
$ ✎

It's no mystery that warm prospects are much easier to close a sale with than cold prospects. Therefore it's a safe assumption that the more referrals you secure, the higher your closing rate, revenues, and, consequently, income. It's not rocket science, just a proven system for increasing sales and profits, while reducing the sales cycle time and cost associated with finding new prospects and developing profitable relationships. The first step toward securing more sales referrals is to simply set a target amount of referrals you want to secure. Don't be fooled by the simplicity of this strategy. Most businesspeople and salespeople do not set a referral target; thus there is no system in place to measure the success of how referrals are secured and how these referrals affect revenues and profits. If you set a referral targets then the act of securing sales referrals is an ongoing conscious effort or marketing technique, which it should be at all times. Once you have set a goal for the amount of referrals you want to secure then you can implement strategies to reach these goals and secure more referrals.

PROVIDE INCENTIVES FOR REFERRALS
$$ ✎

Offering incentives for referrals is truly a win-win situation. These incentives could range from a gift certificate to product or service discounts to cash payments, much depends on the circumstances and the value of the goods or services you sell. I used to send all customers a simple and quick-to-complete referral form along with a self-addressed, stamped return envelope asking that they kindly complete the form and return it. Enclosed with the referral form was a discount coupon related to what I sold that they could pass along to a friend, and a letter stating that if any referrals led to securing work that I would send them a gift certificate for dinner at a nice restaurant. The incentive was basic, but month after month the referral forms would pour in by mail and I would make new contacts and close new sales as a direct result of the referral forms I sent out. This worked because of the honesty—I wanted more sales, we offered an excellent product and service, and because of that customers were happy to refer other people

they knew who would benefit from what I sold. The small incentive I gave was just a way of saying thank you and the dinner was always welcomed and appreciated.

SIMPLY ASK FOR REFERRALS
$ ✎

Asking customers, business associates, and friends for referrals is still the best way to secure them, but many people find this difficult to do because they feel as though they are imposing, or, worse, begging for business. However, a simple fact is true: The more often you ask for referrals, the easier and more comfortable it becomes and the more referrals you will secure. A colleague I've known for years can't ask for a referral; he's tried but just can't bring himself to do it, simply feeling too uncomfortable. Not wanting to miss out on the obvious benefits referrals can provide he developed a clever system to secure them. His system is nothing more than a simple fill-in-the-blank form that he created on his company letterhead. He presents this referral form to customers and asks them to complete it. When they ask why, he tells them that it is company policy, something management has cooked up to help grow the business. No one ever refuses because they don't want to see him get in trouble; he's a very likable person and they want to help him out and this is an easy way for them to do so. In the end he has created a clever way to

Sample Referral Form

Name: _____

Occupation: _____

Address: _____

City: _____ State: _____ Zip code: _____

Telephone: _____ Fax: _____ E-mail address: _____

How do you know this person?   ❑ Friend   ❑ Family   ❑ Co-worker secure plenty of referrals by shifting who is asking for them to an intangible, in this case being a business identity and not a person, and this system has proven to be highly effective.

GO NETWORKING FOR REFERRALS
$ ⚒

Network for referrals by attending business and social functions in your community. Networking can be a great way to secure referrals; of course you'll want to brush up on your networking skills in advance to be the most effective that you can. But this is easy as there are lots of books and even trainers around that can teach you basic and advanced networking techniques. There are, however, two things to remember about networking for referrals: Rule number one, be prepared to give referrals, and rule number two, be prepared to invest a considerable amount of time before you will see results. By freely giving out referrals to others, it opens the lines of communication with that person, and more often than not they will want to return the favor by providing you a referral. However, don't be in a rush to

receive referrals, as mentioned this is rule number two. Building and maintaining a strong referral network requires patience as some time can pass before circumstances arise wherein a fellow networker can refer your business, products, or services to someone who needs what you sell.

TAP SUPPLIERS FOR REFERRALS
$ ⚒

Take advantage of the working relationship that you have established with your suppliers and ask them for referrals. Get started by making a list of all the suppliers that you purchase products or services from. Next, create a referral form that includes predetermined questions to help you qualify these referrals, as well as collect their required contact information. Below you will find a sample supplier referral from; use this form as an outline to create one for your business. Once the referral form is complete, send it to each of your suppliers along with a cover letter thanking them in advance for taking the time to complete and return the referral form to you by fax or in with the monthly invoice they send you. If you

Sample Supplier Referral Form

(Your company information here)

Kindly supply three referrals as outlined below.

Referral #1

Name: _____

Business: _____

Occupation/Title: _____

Address: _____

City: _____ State: _____ Zip code: _____

Telephone: _____ Fax: _____ E-mail address: _____

How do you know this person? ❑ Friend ❑ Family ❑ Co-worker

Can I/we mention your name? ❑ Yes ❑ No

Sample Supplier Referral Form, continued

Referral #2

Name: _____

Business: _____

Occupation/Title: _____

Address: _____

City: _____ State: _____ Zip code: _____

Telephone: _____ Fax: _____ E-mail address: _____

How do you know this person?   ❏ Friend   ❏ Family   ❏ Co-worker

Can I/we mention your name?   ❏ Yes   ❏ No

Referral #3

Name: _____

Business: _____

Occupation/Title: _____

Address: _____

City: _____ State: _____ Zip code: _____

Telephone: _____ Fax: _____ E-mail address: _____

How do you know this person?   ❏ Friend   ❏ Family   ❏ Co-worker

Can I/we mention your name?   ❏ Yes   ❏ No

Referred by: _____

(Important so we can send you your gift right away!)

Name: _____

Business: _____

Occupation/Title: _____

Address: _____

City: _____ State: _____ Zip code: _____

Telephone: _____ Fax: _____ E-mail address: _____

Thank you for your assistance.

Once complete please mail/fax to [your number/address]

want to see this simple referral strategy really pay off, then include a few referrals for your supplier's business when you send out your form. That's right, give them a few referrals and an opportunity to increase their own business and you will see the response rate skyrocket. Don't be shy when it comes to asking your suppliers for referrals and make sure to repeat the process every few months. Sending out one referral form monthly to 50 of your suppliers can generate a whopping 600 new referrals or sales leads a year. Now that is using great marketing savvy.

TAP COMPETITORS FOR REFERRALS
$ ⚒

Even business competitors can become an excellent source for securing well-qualified sales leads or prospect referrals. The key to success is to establish a reciprocal lead exchange program with competitors who service geographical areas outside of yours or who may specialize in niche products or services within the same industry that slightly vary from your specialty. For instance, a friend operates a very successful roofing sales and installation business, but specializes only in installations of new roofs, the service does not do roof repair work other than on roofs that they have installed. Instead they give all repair inquiries to another roofing company that also happens to be one of his main competitors. Why? Because they have found that working together has strengthened both of their positions in the marketplace and that each has their own specialties within the industry that the other does not concentrate on or rarely does. And because of this they are both able to benefit by freely exchanging referrals and sales leads back and forth, though once again both companies are in and compete for the same market and target audience. Get creative in the way that you exchange leads or referrals with competitors and all can benefit.

BUILD STRATEGIC ALLIANCES FOR REFERRALS
$$ ☎

A quick, effective, and inexpensive way to secure referrals and sales leads is to develop a referral exchange program with other business owners and professionals from within your community. Doing so can potentially boost your sales revenues and profits dramatically. In addition to establishing referral exchange programs with other businesses also be sure to develop strategic alliances with referral brokers in your community. Referral brokers are what I like to refer to as the people who other people will ask for advice and assistance because these people (referral brokers) are perceived as honest and leaders within the community, basically a great source of credible information and knowledge. Referral brokers most often include real estate agents, lawyers, doctors, accountants, and bank managers, just to mention a few. Create a complete package composed of print brochures, coupons, and fliers that explain your business, products, or services, and the big benefit for customers who purchase your goods and services. Send this package to all the referral brokers in your community, or, better, set appointments and give it to them in person. It shouldn't take long until your telephone starts ringing with new people who want to do business with you as a result of being referred to you.

MAXIMIZE YOUR ODDS OF GETTING REFERRED
$$ ⚒

Don't leave to chance that business alliances, which include suppliers, vendors, and subcontractors, will refer your business to their customers; instead opt to maximize your odds of getting referred and securing sales leads. One of the best ways to do this is to help your business alliances make more money, therefore maximizing the odds that they will be appreciative and want to return the favor by referring people to your business. For instance, sending a real estate agent tickets to a seminar about how to prospect for first-time homebuyers is sure to keep your business on their mind and high on their referral agenda. Likewise, if you had a business alliance in retail and you could find them a cheaper, better quality, and more reliable source for wholesale goods, then chances are you would also be on their mind and high on their referral agenda. Once again, don't settle for the chance that business alliances are referring your business and not the competition. Instead get creative and proactive and find ways that you can help these businesses succeed and profit, and in doing so you will be maximizing your odds of getting referred.

NETWORKING AND REFERRAL CHECKLIST
$+ ⚒

The following is a networking and referral checklist comprising numerous questions that will assist you in becoming a more effective networker, and help you to secure more referrals. The correct answer for all of the questions is yes. The questions that you answer no to would be considered areas that you need to improve upon to become 100 percent effective in networking and asking for and securing referrals.

Networking and Referral Checklist

Yes	No	
❏	❏	Do you set networking and referrals objectives and goals, and use these objectives and goals to measure your success?
❏	❏	Do you carry a file in your car stocked with a good supply of marketing brochures, business cards, and promotional items for handouts at meetings and functions?
❏	❏	Do you have created and maintain an up-to-date prospect and customer contact database?
❏	❏	Do you follow-up immediately with all new networking contacts you make? And do you follow-up immediately with all referrals that your receive?
❏	❏	Are you one of the first people to arrive and one of the last to leave networking meetings and functions?
❏	❏	Do you always exchange business cards when you meet someone and write notes on the back of the card you receive that better describe the person's business?
❏	❏	Do you provide special incentives and gifts in exchange for referrals?
❏	❏	Do you regularly ask clients for referrals?
❏	❏	Do you make a point of tapping suppliers and business alliances for referrals?
❏	❏	Do you freely offer business owners you meet referrals with no strings attached?
❏	❏	Do you keep the lines of communication open with past clients and try to develop strategies to lure them back as customers?

Yes	No	
❏	❏	Before attending an event or meeting do you get names of people and companies that will be participating and conduct basic research so that you know something about them?
❏	❏	Do you carefully track your referral sources and dedicate more networking time where it will have the greatest impact on your business?
❏	❏	Do you try to set up meetings right away with people you meet rather than telling them you will call, or they can call you?
❏	❏	Do you promptly follow up on all referrals you receive, at least within 48 hours?
❏	❏	Do you have the current membership lists for all of the clubs, groups, and associations that you belong to, business and social?
❏	❏	Do you strive to know other people's businesses better so that you can secure them better qualified leads?
❏	❏	Do you swap customer and lead lists with other businesspeople in your community?
❏	❏	Do you write columns and articles in your field of expertise and seek out opportunities to get them published in print and electronic media?
❏	❏	Do you mine newspapers and magazines for new selling and business opportunities?
❏	❏	Do you offer free reports, conduct training workshops, speak at seminars, and teach in your field of expertise, and share as much of your expert knowledge as possible?

Networking and Referral Checklist, continued

Yes	No	
❏	❏	Do you know your customers' and business contacts, special dates, such as birthdays and anniversaries, and, you always send a card or gift on these dates?
❏	❏	Do you keep in close personal contact with all current customers, at least once a month?
❏	❏	Do you commit to attending at least one function a week where there may be networking opportunities available?
❏	❏	Do you regularly attend trade shows and seminars to form new business alliances and make new contacts?
❏	❏	Do you sit beside people you have not met before and introduce yourself to new members at meetings you attend?
❏	❏	Do you often host brainstorming meetings and sessions with employees, suppliers, and business alliances to seek input and advice in terms of marketing activities and ways to generate new business?
❏	❏	Have you created a memorable personal trademark so that you stand out at meetings and events?
❏	❏	Have you developed a mini sales pitch that is short, powerful, memorable, and that clearly states the biggest benefit of what you do or sell?
❏	❏	Are you known as a credible and reliable source of information at the meetings you attend?
❏	❏	Can you clearly explain the products or services you sell in less than 30 seconds?
❏	❏	Do you know your competition inside out and upside down, but never slander them in any way, shape, or form?
❏	❏	Do you listen more than you talk when you meet new people?
❏	❏	Do you keep abreast of current events so that you can carry on meaningful conversations?

Yes	No	
❏	❏	Do you freely share great marketing ideas with people you meet?
❏	❏	Do you always take time out to make introductions and network in the vicinity of your current projects and jobs in progress?
❏	❏	Do you go out of you way to get involved in community groups, associations, clubs, and events?
❏	❏	Have you joined business groups such as the chamber of commerce and specific business networking groups in your area?
❏	❏	Do you go out of your way to welcome newcomers to the area and freely give them helpful advice about their new community?
❏	❏	Have you created and use a bold nametag and have you developed memorable introductions that clearly state the biggest customer benefit of what you do or what you sell?
❏	❏	Do you continually measure the effectiveness of your networking activities?
❏	❏	Do you have the attitude of a host at meetings and events as opposed to the attitude of a guest?
❏	❏	Do you always try to say yes when asked to speak publicly?
❏	❏	Have you made memorable donations such as imprinted coffee mugs or a wall clock to your networking group?
❏	❏	Do you go online to network for new business and participate in online discussion groups and forums?
❏	❏	Do you hold an annual contest or sweepstakes of some sort to collect leads for follow-up and qualifying?

📖 SUGGESTED ADDITIONAL READING

Baber, Anne and Lynne Waymon. *Make Your Contacts Count: Networking Know How for Cash, Clients and Career Success.* New York: AMACOM 2001.

Berg, Bob. *Endless Referrals: Network Your Everyday Contacts Into Sales.* New York: McGraw-Hill, 1998.

Bly, Robert W. *Become a Recognized Authority in Your Field in 60 Days or Less.* Dulles, VA: Alpha Books, 2001.

Burley-Allen, Madelyn. *Listening: The Forgotten Skill A Self-Teaching Guide.* New York: John Wiley & Sons, 1995.

Carnegie, Dale. *How to Win Friends and Influence People.* New York: Pocket Books, Reissue Edition, 1994.

Esposito, Janet E. *In the Spotlight: Overcome Your Fear of Public Speaking and Performing.* New York: Strong Books, 2000.

Grant, Lynella. *The Business Card Book: What Your Business Card Reveals About You and How to Fix It.* Scottsdale, AZ: Off The Page Press, 1998.

MacKay, Harvey. *Dig Your Well Before You're Thirsty: The Only Networking Book You'll Ever Need.* New York: Doubleday, 1999.

Silber, Lee T. *Self-Promotion for the Creative Person: Get the Word Out About Who You Are and What You Do.* New York: Crown Publishing, 2001.

Von Oech, Roger. *A Whack on The Side of The Head: How You Can Be More Creative.* New York: Warner Books, 1998.

KEY

COST TO IMPLEMENT $

DO-IT-YOURSELF

CALL IN THE
PROFESSIONALS

LEGAL ISSUES

BOOK RESOURCES

ONLINE

PROSPECTING
Marketing Tips for Your Business

Always think of your prospects as suppliers first. Work with them closely, so they can supply you with the information you need to supply them with the right products and services.

—SUSAN MARTHALLAER

WHY CONTINUE TO PROSPECT FOR NEW BUSINESS?
$$ ✎

There are a multitude of reasons you should always continue to prospect for new business, regardless of how busy your sales schedule might presently be, or how rosy your sales future looks. One of the most important reasons is that continual and systematic prospecting will ensure that your business pipeline remains full. Your pipeline consists of the prospects you are currently working with to turn their interest into sales. Take your core group of friends in high school or college and add up how many of those people you are still in contact with daily, weekly, or even yearly. If you're like most people, I'll bet you're in contact with less than 25 percent of them. The same thing happens to customers, they move, get lured to competitors, die, or their buying habits change. Where have my customers gone? This is one of the largest complaints of business owners

and salespeople. After years in business or in selling, sales and profits begin to slide and their once loyal customer base is slowly vanishing for the above-mentioned reasons. Just like the group of friends from your school days. This is why it is important to continually prospect so that you can continually refill your pipeline with new contacts, prospects, and customers with whom you can sell to and do business.

A LEAD VERSUS A PROSPECT
$ ✎

A common error made by people new to a selling career is to mistake a lead as a prospect. A lead is a name of an individual, organization, or business, whereas a prospect is a business or an individual that might have a need or that might benefit from taking ownership of your product or service. Leads are easy to secure—just open any telephone book and you'll have hundreds if not thousands of leads in front of you. Prospects are not as easy to come by because they require homework to identify. This homework is called prospecting. You sell photocopiers and decide to cold call on businesses in your area. At this point every business you see is a lead, but until you have identified if they use or need a photocopier they are not prospects. You walk in and see that they have a photocopier in the corner; the lead has just become a prospect, why? Because you now know they use a photocopier and you sell photocopiers. This does not necessarily qualify them as a *good* prospect, but a prospect just the same. It is the art of qualifying that truly determines a strong prospect from a weak prospect, nothing more. Understanding the difference between a lead and a prospect enables you to spend time where your chances of securing sales are the best.

SET DAILY GOALS
$ ⚒

Most sales professionals and business owners understand the importance of setting short- and long-term goals, but don't overlook the benefits of setting a daily goal as a way to increase your prospecting productivity. I have always set daily goals in business and when selling; even as I write this and other books I set daily goals to use as a yardstick to measure performance and increase my productivity accordingly as required. Setting daily goals is an easy strategy to develop, especially if there is a reward at the end of the day for meeting the set goal. The reward could be something as simple as a night out at the movies or perhaps a fitness workout session at the local gym. Additionally, daily goals can be a great way to solve challenges. For instance, if your weakness is prospecting then an obvious daily goal to set would be related to increase performance in terms of prospecting, perhaps setting a daily goal to make ten prospecting cold calls and five personal visits. The more you work at these problems and reward yourself for meeting goals and increasing performance daily, the easier these seemingly difficult tasks will become. Give it a try—start off by setting easily attainable daily goals and the better you become at reaching them, increase the difficulty. Before you know it you might find yourself increasing all aspects

of your business and sales performance by double-digit gains.

PROSPECTING BASICS
$ ⚒

Ninety-five percent of what you have to say, the actions you have taken to get to this point in the sales cycle, or information related to and about your company is for the most part irrelevant to your prospect. They only want and need to know the remaining 5 percent, which when boiled down are these three basic things.

The Basic Information

Your product or service and how you market it must be clear and easy to understand in moments, not hours or days. Consequently you must develop your sales message around clarity in order to appeal to the largest segment of your target audience. Make it plain English, easy to understand, and free of boring technical jargon that fits in great with scientific reports, but only works to confuse the vast majority of people. Never make what you do and why you do it hard for people to understand just for the benefit of your ego or to feel that it gives you a superior edge, because it doesn't. Sell more and profit, by making your sales message clear and keeping your overall approach to sales and marketing simple and straightforward.

Benefit

What you sell has to benefit the person to whom you are trying to sell it. Living in balmy Vancouver, I have little use for a snowmobile no matter how many features it has and how much horsepower is stashed under the hood—but a rain jacket? Yes, that would be beneficial. Appeal to your target audience by giving them what they need, helping them fix a problem, making them rich, saving them money, or making them feel better. Selling is all about matching what you have to sell to what people need. Once again, if I need an umbrella and you're selling umbrellas, then your job of persuading me to buy one becomes rather easy, wouldn't you agree?

Value

What you sell has to represent value to your prospect. This means regardless of what the price is, they see and can justify a direct correlation between your offering and the price that goes with it. And what your product or service will do for them—fill a need, solve a problem, or whatever it may be. Products and services are only worth what people will pay for them, but the more value (benefits) that a person can derive from a product or service then the more they are likely to be willing to pay for that product or service.

GREAT TELEPHONE COLD-CALLING TRICKS

$ 🔨

Cold calling prospects on the telephone can be a tough grind even for the most experienced and thick-skinned sales professionals. To make your cold-calling job easier and more productive, below you will find some great telephone cold-calling tricks that you can use to secure more sales appointments and meetings.

- Before you call, write down what the objectives of the particular call are. Is it to set an appointment; send promotional literature or samples; introduce your company; products, or services, or to find out who the decision-makers are within the organization? Additionally plan out what you are going to say; write it down in brief script format and anticipate objections and be ready to answer and overcome those objections during the conversation.
- Always identify who you are, your company, and why you are calling right at the beginning of the call. Additionally during the introduction state the main benefit of your product or service and how this relates to your prospect. Be very clear about this, the person you call must benefit directly; if not, you will soon lose their interest.
- Only give enough information to get the prospect interested and involved in the conversation. There is power in mystery so use the mystery you create to reach your objective.

- Ask for an appointment in a way that it is assumed the prospect will agree, such as "Which is best for you, Thursday at ten or Friday at eleven?" Doing so the prospect is led into choosing one; not meeting is no longer an option.
- Don't give up if they say no, ask for a personal appointment at least three times and if you get nowhere ask if you can place them on your newsletter and e-mail notice list.

GREAT TRICKS FOR LEAVING VOICE-MAIL MESSAGES

$ 🔨

Leaving a voice-mail messages with prospects or clients is the easy part, getting them to return your call is an entirely different story. Here are a few simple and effective tricks that you can use to increase the odds of getting your voice-mail messages returned.

- One of the most important tricks to leaving a voice-mail message that will get returned is to anticipate that you will have to leave a voice-mail message with the person you are trying to reach. Therefore knowing exactly what you will be saying, why you are calling, and why they should call you back is one of the keys to getting your calls returned. Being caught off guard and leaving behind a broken string of umms, ahhs, and irrelevant information is a surefire way of never hearing from your prospect.
- After the beep speak clearly and slowly so that the person will hear and know exactly what you are saying without having to guess when they play back the message. Use your voice effectively and with energy, come across sounding enthusiastic like you have some ground-moving information that they must be aware of instead of sounding monotone and boring. Excitement and mystery combined will almost always get your call returned.
- Always say your name and the name of your company clearly and slowly at the beginning of the message and spell out your last name if this

is a new prospect you are trying to reach. Likewise any words that are difficult to pronounce should also be spelled out. This might seem time consuming, but it screams professionalism that all people like. Would you return a call if you had to guess at the person's name or their company? Not likely, so don't expect others to.

- Leave your main contact telephone number at least twice, once near the beginning and repeated at the end. Additionally, leave a best time to call you back or blocked window of time such as "I will be in the office Tuesday between noon and four in the afternoon and would appreciate it if you would call me back then." This will reduce the potential for telephone tag.

- Finally state the main reason you are calling; this should be something that will benefit the person you are calling so that they will call you back right away. The benefit should be your biggest gun, something mind boggling that they could not possibly resist. Tell them you'll make them rich, save them money, make them more productive, make them feel and look 20 years younger, or that you have information that will be shared with no one else, providing they call you back right away. Tie the biggest benefit of what you do or sell into your prospect's biggest need, desire, want, or problem, and I guarantee that your call-back response rate will skyrocket.

QUALIFYING: NEEDS
$ 🔨

Qualify your prospect's needs is perhaps the most overused advice featured in a multitude of marketing books, but very sound and timeless advice just the same. The first rule of qualifying is to determine if the prospect needs what you are selling. If not, you are wasting your time and theirs by continuing with the conversation. If you have an in-depth knowledge of what you sell and how it will benefit buyers then qualifying a prospect in terms of needs should be easily accomplished with a few simple questions. What problems need solving? What are their requirements?

What needs to be improved? What is wrong with what they currently have, or alternately what would make their job or life easier? Of course, there is one exception to the "qualifying needs rule," which is appealing to emotions in such a way that it overrides and sometimes defies logic. Good examples of this is the fact that few people need a hot tub, but many want one, or few people actually need a Rolex wristwatch, but once again many want them. However, even with that said, unless you are selling a product or service that can be sold strictly on an emotional level wherein for the most part logic can be thrown out the window, stick with the time-tested and proven qualifying concept of only pursuing prospects who truly need what you are selling, regardless of how tempting the challenge might be to try to close them. Always ask yourself what the best use of your time is at that very moment, and I will guarantee it is not trying to sell something to someone who doesn't need or want it.

QUALIFYING: DECISION-MAKER
$ 🔨

Take the time to ask and make sure that you are dealing with the person who can ultimately make the decision in terms of buying your products or services. And if the person you are dealing with is not the decision-maker then find out who is and deal with that person or group of people. Nothing is more frustrating than having a hot prospect on the line only to discover after spending much time and energy with this person that he cannot make a decision about buying your product or service. Or, that there are other people who will be involved in the decision-making process besides the person you are dealing with. The best way to find out who the decision-maker is is to simply ask your prospect with questions such as: "Who will be making the purchasing decision?" "Will you be making the decision on your own, or will there be other people involved in the purchasing decision?" "If you find my [product] suitable are you authorized to make the purchase?" However, take your prospect's response with a grain of salt because even if someone tells you that they will be personally making decisions in terms of buying, that is not always entirely the case. Lower and middle managers sometimes want to feel important, but ultimately they have to secure approvals from people higher up on the management chain before they can give the go-ahead. You can get around this by asking your prospect a few times throughout the initial questions phase more qualifying questions to do with decision-making. Generally if they are not truly the decision-maker that will come out in the conversation through their responses to your qualifying questions.

QUALIFYING: TIME LINE
$ ⚒

What is the prospect's buying time line? Meaning when does she want to buy a particular product or service? And, the second aspect of qualifying time line is how committed is your prospect to her buying schedule? Very committed, somewhat committed, or just tentative based on other factors that could influence the final buying decision? Reveal this by asking questions. You can learn more about a prospect's needs in terms of timing by asking easy open-ended questions such as: "How soon do you need the [product]?" "When will you be ready to have the product installed?" "What is your time frame for completing this project?" "When would you like to take delivery?" These are very nonthreatening questions and the beauty of asking time line questions early on when you first meet a prospect is the fact that the answers she gives will also give you a good indication as to her openness to an early close in the sales cycle. Top sales professionals have discovered that if a prospect answers positively to a qualifying time line question then an early trial close is not out of the question even if you have not completed the entire qualifying process. So if a prospect tells you she needs it next week, then respond, "If I can arrange for delivery next week, are you prepared to make the purchase?"

QUALIFYING: OBSTACLES
$ ⚒

Effective qualifying means that you are carefully listening for or watching for obstacles that can stand between you and making the sale. Obstacles are usually the quiet deal killers, the stuff that was overlooked during the qualifying process because salespeople did not think to look for it, or the prospect was not forthcoming with information about potential obstacles. Here are a few examples of potential obstacles that can stand between you and the sale.

Health

Don't laugh, the condition of your prospect's overall health can be a major potential obstacle in terms of the sale. Is his health strong enough to complete the sales cycle? Because of any potential health problems will the prospect get value and benefit from what you are selling?

Geographical Location

Does the prospect reside in the geographical area, if this is relevant to your offer? Tourists, people out for a Sunday drive, visiting family and friends, there are various reasons that some people will not be living in the geographical area, but still go shopping to pass time. Therefore before you spend a lot of time and energy with these people, you have to know if they are from the area and serious buyers or just passing time.

Training or Education

Is the prospect qualified or trained to use what you are selling? Training is another potential obstacle that must be exposed. For instance if you are selling scuba diving holidays and your prospect is not PADI-certified to scuba dive, then that would be considered a major obstacle standing between you and the sale.

Priorities

A prospect's priorities are the biggest hidden obstacle. While a person might be genuinely interested about purchasing a new car, is the leaky roof at home that needs to be replaced the true priority instead of the new car? A prospect might really want to buy a new house, but is her priority to get a law degree first? Priorities can be a tough obstacle to identify and overcome simply because by nature they are hidden and few prospects will bring them into the conversation and qualifying process. Once again a salesperson's best bet in terms of identifying a priority obstacle is to listen carefully for any telltale signs in what prospects are saying .

These are only a few examples and there are many more. The trick is to listen carefully to what your prospect is telling you so that you will be able to identify potential obstacles. Sometimes it will be subtle, while other times the obstacles will be glaring. Of course if you think that there might be a hidden obstacle in the way of the sale, it is always best just to come out and ask your prospect.

QUALIFYING: FINANCIAL
$ ⚒

Qualifying prospects financially is where many salespeople become unglued because they feel uncomfortable asking people questions about their personal or business financial situation. Add to this, even if you do ask the right questions, the answers you receive might be somewhat embellished simply due to the fact that everyone wants to be perceived as being better off financially than they are in reality.

So where does that leave you? It leaves you knowing two things for sure. The first is that you must get comfortable and in the habit of asking prospects qualifying questions about their abilities to pay for the product or service, or their abilities to secure credit to pay for the product or service. Ask your prospects if they have the money put aside to pay for the purchase, if they will be using credit cards or arranging financing, or if you can take the liberty of arranging financing for them. You have to know that your prospect can financially afford to pay, by whatever means, before you invest time, energy, and money into the sales process. Second, you have to be realistic in regard to your prospect's purchasing power. This is not to say that you should assume your prospects cannot afford what they want or that they are blowing you a little smoke—not at all. But you should be prepared with an alternate and less expensive option or choice should financial matters become an obstacle to the sale. If you spend all your time focused on one product or service and suddenly

money becomes an issue, then you have little latitude to move. However, if you keep in mind the notion that money could become an issue or obstacle and have a plan in place should that happen then you will be armed to save the sale and still do business with your prospect.

QUALIFYING: ASSUMPTION
$ ⚒

One critical yet often overlooked aspect of qualifying prospects is the fact that you can make one generalized assumption, but only one. Seldom do people stray too far from what they already have, what they are comfortable with, or what they understand and therefore do not fear or doubt. Call it the nine-times-out-of-ten rule of qualifying. For instance, nine times out of ten people who currently drive a family type vehicle such as a mini van, station wagon, or four-door sedan will purchase the same or a similar type family vehicle when it comes time to do so. How many people do you know personally who have been to the same travel destination multiple times? This is because they know the area and therefore do not fear going or have doubts about going. People in general are creatures of habit and not the adventurous types we would like to be or think of ourselves as being. And much of our purchasing habits are also based on needs, making consumers extremely transparent to the well-seasoned sales professional. Knowing and believing this fact can help in the qualifying process because much of your work is already done for you, if you take the time to ask what people are currently using or have. Of course there are dangers with making any assumptions, especially in sales. However, wise salespeople have learned that the best use of their time, energy, and money is to make this one general assumption that will cover the vast majority of prospects.

QUALIFYING: COMPETITION
$ ⚒

Knowing who you are battling against for a sale in terms of the competition can be just as important as knowing what your prospects' needs are, especially in highly competitive industries where thin profit margins are the norm. Knowing who your competition is will be helpful in preparing your presentation, develop special benefits and advantages for individual prospects, and enables you to know where your product or service is positioned against the competition's products or services and how this relates to your prospects' needs and wants. The easiest way to find out who the competition will be is to simply ask your prospect; more times than not they will tell you providing you ask in a nonchalant or nonthreatening fashion. "Who else will be bidding on the job?" "How many other companies have you spoken to about this project?" "What other companies have you spoken to about this project?" "What companies have given you an estimate or quote for this?" Knowing who else you are bidding against for the sale is not important for trying to find out the competition's price, simply because if you are selling based on price you won't be in business long anyway. The importance of knowing who you are competing with is so you can design the best and most beneficial package for your prospect, stuff the competition does not do or sell, or perhaps special permits or training that you know they do not have. The more information you have about your prospect and about their wants and needs, and who the competition for their sale will be, the better you can position your own offering to meet and exceed your prospect's expectations.

QUALIFYING: OPEN-ENDED QUESTIONS
$ ✎

Key to the success of effective prospecting is asking qualifying questions. However, to truly be effective, the qualifying questions not only must be aimed at getting the proper response but also must be asked in a way that you do not close the conversation with the question you ask. A common example of asking a question that is not open-ended is the sales clerk who asks the shopper who just entered the store, "Is there anything I can help you find?" This is not an open-ended question and will result in a yes or no response—generally a "no" because people are pre-programmed to say no to an approaching salesperson

or clerk. Even a small change such as "What brought you into our store today?" is a vast improvement. At least the prospect or in this case the shopper must reveal information that the clerk can then use to determine if she can help the shopper fill a need or not. By asking open-ended questions you get the prospect involved in the conversation and sales process.

All salespeople should experiment with various open-ended questions that are related to what they do or sell and keep a log of the success or failure rates of these open-ended qualifying questions. Doing so will enable you to put together an arsenal of open-ended questions that you know will be effective more times than not. Here are a few examples of open-ended questions.

- How did you hear about our company?
- Ultimately what would you like to see happen?
- What challenges does your business face?
- When do you need to take delivery of this?
- Who are the other people who will be involved in this decision?
- What financial budget has been established for this?
- Who else will be supplying a bid on this project?

QUALIFYING: COMFORT AND COMPLIMENTS
$ ✎

Two final important aspects of the qualifying process are comfort and compliments. First, you must learn to become comfortable asking all types of people questions, in all types of situations, and under all types of circumstances. Many salespeople feel uncomfortable asking questions because they wrongly think they are invading their prospect's space or to some degree begging to be heard so they can sell. But realize that just about every person must ask questions in order to help others or to determine what the other person needs. Doctors ask questions about symptoms and your health so they can make informed diagnoses. Mechanics ask questions about what strange things your car is doing so they can narrow down what might be wrong with it. And fitness trainers ask about fitness goals so they can develop a fitness program that will help people reach specific goals. You have to get comfortable asking questions, even when your prospects are not so forthcoming with answers, simply because it is the only way you will be able to determine if you can help them. Second, get in the habit of complimenting your prospects, especially the ones who are not so thrilled with being asked questions. Doing so will help to establish mutual trust and make them feel important. Let them know that you appreciate them taking time from their busy schedule to meet with you. Tell them that they have nice homes, offices, or families. Basically, look for any opportunity that you can to compliment them on their looks, their intelligence, their material things, their families, and their wise decisions.

TRICKS FOR BECOMING AN EFFECTIVE LISTENER

$ ⚒

The importance of effective listening skills cannot be overstated in terms of prospecting and selling. It is in fact, one of the most important skills to learn and master as being able to listen to what prospects and customers are telling you is the cornerstone to all selling. It is the starting point where you learn the most, and therefore have the ability to close more sales because of what you listened for and learned from. You can ask the greatest qualifying questions in the world, but unless you carefully listen to what your prospect or customer is telling you, then your qualifying questions will be of no value. Below are a few great tricks that you can utilize to become more effective in the art of listening.

- This is the hardest one to master, but to be an effective listener and truly hear and understand what people are telling you, you must be prepared and willing to shut up and stop talking.
- Let the person you are talking to know that you hear what he is saying by nodding occasionally. And when you did not hear or understand his point, make sure to ask for clarification.
- Get rid of any distractions or try to create an environment with as few interruptions as possible. Give people your full and undivided attention and kindly ask that they do the same. Ask the question, "Can we speak uninterrupted?" when you book the meeting.

- Never finish someone else's thoughts or sentences during a conversation, be patient and allow the speaker to finish what she has to say.
- Even if you disagree, never get argumentative and never let your emotions get the best of you. If you have to get emotional make sure it is a positive emotion like excitement, appreciation, or happiness. As the old saying goes, "It is impossible to win an argument with a prospect or customer, even when you are right."
- Be empathetic to what the other person is telling you, look at the situation from his point of view and never assume that any concern he has is a small one. People don't mention concerns or objections unless they are important to them; otherwise, they would not bring them into the conversation.
- Listen closely to any obstacles that could be buried in what your prospect or customer is telling you. These quiet obstacles that come out could be financial, decision-making abilities, timing, or quantities.
- Ask lots of questions and keep digging to get to a prospect's true needs, motivations, objections, and wants. The more clear you can get your prospect or customer to paint the picture of what she wants, the better position you will be in to help her by giving her what she wants and needs. And the only way you will know for sure is to ask questions and closely listen to every single word of her response.

TIME MANAGEMENT FOR PROSPECTING SUCCESS

$$ ⚒

It stands to reason that the better you manage your time, the more time you will be able to devote to prospecting for new business. Here are a few tricks that you can employ to maximize and make the best use of your time so that you will be able to devote more time to prospecting and closing.

- Maximize your prospecting and selling time by using prospect and customer management automated software, such as Maximizer. Visit them at www.maximizer.com.

- Set aside a block of time each day strictly for the purposes of prospecting, creating new ways to promote your products or services, and unique ways to position what you sell in the marketplace.

- Prepare your daily to-do list the evening before and strive to check every item off before you call it quits the following day.

- Develop a scheduling system and stick to it. Prospect the same time each day when you are most likely to reach your target audience on the phone or in person. Group presentations together to save time and stay in the same focused mindset. And, do all administrative work at the same time, once again to save time and stay focused on an individual task. Basically, organize your time so that you group activities together such as prospecting, presentations, research, follow up, and administrative tasks.

- Never procrastinate—clear all inquiries, problems, and customer requests by the end of each day. Only carry over things that cannot be immediately accomplished or resolved because of situations that are beyond your immediate control or information, people, products, or services to which you do not have immediate access.

- Block off rest and relaxation time to pursue hobbies and family activities each week and strive not to forgo them or alter the time you assign for them.

- Carry a "hot prospects" folder with you so that you can benefit from any unexpected down time by calling them or working on solutions to fix their product or service problems or needs. Inspirational ideas are lost if they are not written down in an easily retrievable format.

- Keep your goals and objectives written down and in front of you as a daily motivator.

THOU SHALT NEVER PREJUDGE
$ ⚒

Prospecting rule number one: Thou shalt never prejudge prospects' abilities to buy and pay for purchases, or their motivation for their choices. We have all heard the tale of the person who goes into the car dealership dressed shabbily only to be treated poorly by the salesperson on the floor. The salesperson prejudged the prospect based on appearances and without asking a single question came to the conclusion that this person could not possibly afford to purchase a new car. The story goes on to reveal that the prospect later returned to the dealership asking to talk to the sales manager. He then produced a bag of cash and said that because of the way he was treated earlier by the salesperson he just thought the manager should know that his bag full of money would be spent at the competition, where he would be purchasing a new car. There are many versions of this story floating around and some may be based on fact and others fictional urban legends. But nevertheless the general premise is very accurate—never prejudge prospects' abilities or motivation until careful questions and answers have established what they need, when they need it, if they can make the buying decision, and if they have the financial ability to pay for it. Until these questions have been asked and answers given, everyone must be considered equally as a prospect regardless of looks, actions, dress, or speech.

THOU SHALT NEVER EXPRESS PERSONAL OPINIONS
$ ⚒

Prospecting rule number two: Thou shalt never initiate or be drawn into a political, religious, cultural, egotistical, or moral debate or discussion with any prospect or customer regardless of how strong you may feel about the topic or subject matter. The best way not to offend a prospect or customer consciously or subconsciously is to simply avoid any controversial topics and issues. More than a few times I have sat through lectures, ramblings, and long-winded speeches given by prospects about what is wrong with everything under the sun and then some. Once I was even lectured by a university professor for close to an hour about how I should aspire to higher things in life than selling home renovations. (I was

28 years old at the time and earning in excess of five figures monthly and, more important, loved what I did.) Needless to say I bit my tongue a few times during his rant, smiled politely and when I left I had a signed contract and a deposit check toward a $30,000 renovation project. The point is this; all people have a right to express their own opinions and take comfort in their own beliefs regardless of what their beliefs and opinions might be. But the job of a sales professional is not to debate issues or express opinions and thoughts on topics not related to the sale; it is to seek, qualify, close the sale, and ask for referrals, period.

THOU SHALT NEVER PUSH ONLY WHAT YOU LIKE
$

Prospecting rule number three: Thou shalt never sell what you like personally. Who cares what you like or what your preferences are in terms of the various products or services that you sell? You're not the one who will be using it and more importantly paying for it with your hard-earned money. There are two major problems when you are selling purely based on what you like. The first is that if you are telling prospects what you like about a particular product or service you sell, then you are not listening to what the prospect wants and needs, which in all likelihood is not even remotely similar to what you like. And by doing so you break the golden rule of selling: listen to what your prospects and customers are telling you at all times. Second, by constantly pushing what you like on to prospects you'll soon discover that patterns start to develop. And within no time you'll only be able to sell one product or service because that is all you know, understand, and believe in. Because of this habit of only pushing what you like, you will miss out on a lot of selling opportunities. Sell what the prospect likes, even if you don't happen to agree with his choice. Once again, if he's happy with his choice and is prepared to pay for it with his money then shut up get the contract signed, thank him, ask for referrals, and tell him that you look forward to doing more business with him in the near future.

PRACTICE IMMEDIATE FOLLOW-UP
$

All salespeople should get in the habit of immediately following up with new prospects after meetings to reconfirm what was discussed during the meeting and the course of action that will follow. You can do this in various ways: e-mail, fax, on the telephone, or by writing a letter and mailing it to them or having it delivered by courier. The benefits of immediate follow-up are many. Number one, it is an opportunity to compile all the information that was discussed at the meeting and to reconfirm the information, right down to the smallest detail. Number two, it illustrates to prospects that you are interested in their needs, you want to solve their problems, and that you conduct business in a very professional manner. And third, practicing immediate follow-up provides you with a great opportunity to reconfirm all of the details with your prospect so that there will be no miscommunications when you get back together for the sales presentation. Personally, I like to talk by telephone with the prospect and take notes; from that I write down everything from the first meeting and the follow-up telephone call, reconfirming all the details. Then I fax the notes to the prospect and often ask that she sign or initial the pages and fax them back.

CLONE YOUR BEST CUSTOMERS
$$

You know who your best customers are—they are the people who frequently buy products or services from you, always pay on time and in full, refer others to your business, and rarely complain. Now wouldn't it be nice if all of your customers were the same and you had thousands just like them? Well the thought might not be as big of a pipe dream as you think. Industry-leading businesspeople take the time to identify who their best customers are, and then set out to clone them. This means they identify common characteristics of their best customers and develop marketing and action plans aimed at people who are similar to their best customers. Granted, few small businesses can afford to conduct such in-depth research and have these analysis plans created.

However, every small-business owner can afford to create a simple questionnaire and ask your best customers to kindly complete it. Questions should include their interests and hobbies, the type of publications they like to read, and radio and television programs they like to listen to and watch, and basic questions pertaining to education, income, family, and career. You can use this information to identify patterns, things your best customers have in common with each other. Perhaps a high percentage of them subscribe to the same newspaper; then it would be wise to advertise your business in that newspaper to appeal to people who are like your best customers. Or, maybe a high percentage of them belong to one or more community associations; then logically you would want to join these associations and network with the members. There is much wisdom to the old adage "birds of a feather flock together." Identify as many feathers that your best customers have in common as you can and you won't be far from discovering where the entire flock is located.

GETTING TO KNOW THE GATEKEEPER
$ ⚒

If you plan on selling to senior management and corporate executives then you'd better get to know their gatekeepers if you want to succeed. These gatekeepers, sometimes known as executive assistants or secretaries, are good at their jobs, in fact some can be downright intimidating. They know that more often than not they hold the key that opens the decision-maker's office door. Therefore, not only do you have to get to know them, but you also have to get them to like you. This means not being aggressive or pushy with them and understanding that they have one of the most demanding jobs within the organization and as a general rule are overworked and underpaid. Going out of your way to be polite and not creating extra work for them will win over many gatekeepers, so much so that it might even get you preference in securing appointments in person and on the phone. Of course the other way to get past the gatekeeper is to position yourself as an expert in your industry, and in doing so, CEOs and senior management executives will seek out your expertise. Consequently

there will be little or no need to rely on tricks to get past the gatekeeper because the gatekeeper will be calling you to set appointments with the big boss.

WEB RESOURCE

⌀ www.smallbizbooks.com: Online retailer of business and marketing specific books, guides, and software.

DONATION PROSPECTING
$$ ⚒

Donating a product or service to a local charity or special event can be another great way to prospect for new business. And best of all, this prospecting technique often results in people contacting or seeking you out as a result of the donation as opposed to you trying to track them down. The key to a successful donation is exposure by means of media or by way of printed literature or signage stating that it was your business that donated the product or service to the cause. One of the best types of donation events is a charity auction wherein you make a donation of a product or service and the charity auctions it off to raise money for its cause. I have used this prospecting technique many times with great success, often recouping ten times the value of goods donated by securing new business as a direct result of the event. Other ways to benefit by donating include giving products and services to local charities; participating in hospital and library food, clothing, or toy drives; and donating to local schools. Regardless of what you donate, or who you donate it to, as long as many people know that it was your business that made the donation then you stand to gain new prospects because of your donation. People tend to support businesses that support the community at large.

TRY REVERSE PROSPECTING
$ ⚒

Think of all the ways you prospect for new customers, then simply reverse the way in which you contact them. If you use the telephone book or mailing lists then contact people with a last name starting with the letter Z working forward to A. If you cold call on businesses, then start on the top floor of an office tower and work down to the first floor. If you speak or demonstrate at events and seminars to prospect, then position yourself at the rear of the room or near the exit door after your speech or demonstration. This reverse prospecting technique will give you the ability to make contact with almost everyone in the room rather than just those who rush the stage while the bulk of people in attendance quietly exit behind. The theory behind reverse prospecting is sound. From a young age we are taught to start at the beginning of the alphabet or that the front of the line is the best place to be. This learned behavior carries into adulthood and for most it only comes naturally to prospect for new business in the same manner, alphabetically or geographical proximity. Therefore people with a last name starting with the letter Z or people the farthest away geographically are less likely to be solicited as much as people with a last name starting with the letter A or are in close geographical proximity and so on. Who gets picked on by the comedian during a stage routine? Always the people sitting closest to the stage in close proximity, rarely the people in the back. Give reverse prospecting a try and you just may be pleasantly surprised by the favorable outcome.

TROLL FOR PROSPECTS ONLINE
$ ⚒

The Internet is home to thousands of prospecting possibilities and growing daily if not hourly. In fact the number of prospecting possibilities is so large that it is quite likely that it cannot even be calculated. Go trolling for prospects online by joining usenet newsgroup forums or discussion groups, post messages in online classifieds, and get involved with various online communities wherein the people who belong to and participate in these communities meet your target audience. Even places like auction sites and classified advertisement sites can be used for prospecting purposes. For instance, if you're a commercial real estate agent specializing in selling businesses then there is a good chance that a person who is selling a business online via an auction or classified

advertising site would be a good prospect to purchase a new business, if not now then perhaps in the future. However, as a word of caution, make ads sound like stories and be careful not to offend, as many discussion groups, clubs, and community sites do not like selling taking place.

WEB RESOURCES

⚒ www.leadsclub.com: Ali Lassen's Lead Club, with 5,500 members in more than 400 chapters.

⚒ www.bni.com: Business Network International billed as the world's largest referral organization composed of more than 2,600 chapters worldwide and thousands of members.

EXPERIMENT WITH LIFECYCLE PROSPECTING
$$ ⚒

Hidden lifecycle prospecting opportunities are abundant if you take the time to conduct a little research. Every product has a definable lifespan, both in terms of usefulness and time. In the postwar era residential housing subdivisions became a popular way to develop large tracts of land to provide affordable housing for returning military personnel to start families. This was the start of what is now known as the baby boom generation and tract housing developments. From postwar times to current day, building houses in subdivisions has remained popular, in fact about 90 percent of all new homes built in the past 60 years have been constructed in subdivision developments. I mention this as an example of hidden lifecycle prospecting opportunities. A residential housing subdivision that is now 15 years old represents a wealth of lifecycle prospecting opportunities. Especially, when you consider the vast amounts of products used in the construction of these homes that have reached or are nearing the end of their useful lifespans. This would include roofing, kitchen and bathroom fixtures, appliances, windows, concrete and pavement driveways, decking and fencing, and the list goes on and on as most building products and fixtures have a definable lifespan of 15 to 20 years. Therefore, if your business is installing roofing, you would want to initiate a marketing and contact program in this subdivision. The greatest benefit of lifecycle prospecting is the fact that most contacts you make in this way are already qualified to a certain degree. They have no choice because the product you are trying to replace is nearing or has reached its useful lifespan. And in most cases it is the sum of the parts that makes the whole. Or as is the case with roofing, without a new roof the home-owner would be risking water damage to the rest of the home, or the whole because of a single part. Every product and even most services have a defin-able lifecycle and the key to successful lifecycle prospecting is to know exactly what the lifespan of your product or service is, then go about reaching and planning strategies to capitalize on this. Simply put, lifecycle prospecting means that you are seeking out prospects with products or services that are near-ing the end of their useful lifespan before these people contact you—and your competition—for bids.

DEMONSTRATION PROSPECTING WORKS
$$ 🔨 ⚖️

For centuries street performers have been using demonstration as a successful way to prospect for new business. A street performer who juggles sets up in a busy park and begins to juggle bowling balls (demonstration). Soon people start to take notice and crowd around to watch (prospects). Some people leave while others stay to watch (qualifying). The performer continues to demonstrate juggling skills to an amazed audience (presentation). The juggler com-pletes the presentation and takes a bow as people drop loose change into a box (closing). Doing no more than demonstrating a service (entertainment), the juggler has attracted prospects, qualified some, presented to a crowd, and closed a few sales. The complete sales cycle, all in a matter of minutes. This leads me to this point: Most products and services can be demonstrated in public for prospecting pur-poses beyond what we consider as acceptable demonstration forums of trade shows and seminars. For instance, if you sold fishing poles and went to a crowded beach on the weekend and cast a line it would not take long before people approached you and asked if the fish were biting. Or if you operated a martial arts training facility and took the class to a

local park for a training session, once again it would not be long until a crowd gathered and questions about your school ensued.

EXPERT PROSPECTING MAY BE THE BEST
$$ 🔨

What's easier, less time consuming, better quali-fied, less costly, and stands the best chance of taking buying action? The answer is easy—prospects who seek you out for your expertise, products, or services. Prospecting does not always mean that you will be searching for customers, it can also mean developing strategies to have people seek you out. This prospect-ing technique is known as expert prospecting. Society in general accepts the notion that published authors or speakers on specific topics and issues are mostly experts within their fields or industries. And when seeking assistance, guidance, or help do you start at the bottom or do you go straight to the top and seek out an expert to help solve a problem or fulfill a need? Obviously you go straight to the top and seek out the expert. Sales professionals searching for an effective prospecting technique should look no farther than their own expertise. You are an expert in one or more disciplines, if not you wouldn't be a sales professional. Use your expertise to persuade people to come to you. Get started by writing a book, newspaper column, or magazine feature, or seek out opportunities to speak. The medium is sec-ondary, getting published in print or electronically or securing speaking forums is the first objective; build and expand your expertise base from there. Becoming known as an expert not only distinguishes you from the competition, it also means that in all likelihood people will seek your advice when they are trying to solve a problem, need advice, or help in a decision, all of which can be turned into selling opportunities.

SWAP CUSTOMER LISTS AND LEADS
$ 🔨

A great way to prospect for new business and sales leads is to establish a customer list and lead swap program with other business owners and sales professionals from within your geographic area who represent noncompeting, but compatible products and services. For example, if you sell home renovation products and installation services of these products then swap your customer and prospect list with the owner of an appliance store. Both are noncompeting businesses, but share common characteristics that would benefit each party. In this example it's likely that customers and prospects for both businesses would own a home, and the lifecycle of many building products such as bathroom fixtures is about the same as major appliances at approximately 20 years. Therefore, it's a safe assumption that someone having a laundry room renovated would also need, or soon need new appliances. Customer list and lead exchange programs are a very efficient way to prospect for new business, as it can reduce the time you spend finding and qualifying new prospects. And in many cases you'll be dealing with warm prospects vs. cold because many of the leads you receive through the swap can be contacted under the umbrella of a referral.

RESPECT YOUR CLIENTS' TIME
$ ✎

Maximize the value of your client management database by listing all of your customers' preferred choices of contact times and the method in which they like to be contacted—fax, e-mail, ground mail, telephone, or a personal visit. Not only can this simple trick save you time and money in terms of not having to play telephone tag with a prospect or customer you would like to speak with, or by being turned away by the receptionist because of a spontaneous drop-by visit, it also perfectly illustrates to customers that you place value on and respect their working time. Ask clients and prospects when the best time to contact them is, and how they prefer to be contacted. Enter this information into their file in your customer management database and remember to update this information every six months or so because of changing circumstances in terms of your prospects' preferred contact times and method. Respect your customer's time and in return they will reward you with their undivided attention when you do meet in person or talk on the telephone.

MINE NEWSPAPERS AND MAGAZINES
$ ✎

Newspapers and magazines can be a great source in terms of prospecting for new business. Start by subscribing to publications that you think your target audience reads including newspapers, magazines, trade journals, and newsletters, both in print and electronic format and scan them for information about people or companies that you could contact in regard to your business offerings. For example, almost every community newspaper features a weekly announcement section listing births, engagements, weddings, graduations, company management appointments, and more, thus creating many great prospecting opportunities for the salespeople who are prepared to work and chase them down. A financial planner might contact the new parents featured in this section to discuss creating a scholarship fund for their newborn child. A wedding planner might contact the newly engaged couple to make a pitch about planning their forthcoming wedding, and so on. This prospecting method really is as easy as picking up the telephone and calling the people, business, or organization that was featured in the newspaper and setting an appointment with them to discuss how your product or service can benefit them.

GET IN THROUGH THE BACK DOOR
$$ 🐶

Are you having trouble getting your products placed in retail chain stores? Or, are you finding it near impossible to break into selling your products to a large corporation or organization? If so, perhaps you are taking the wrong approach by prospecting in the wrong places and targeting the wrong people. Selling into chain stores or large corporations is very difficult to do. Not to mention it can also be an extremely time-consuming process that involves many layers of management to claw your way through until you reach the person who can green light the purchase of your products, for consumption within the corporation or for resale purposes. However, often there is a much better approach available for getting your products into chain retailer's stores, and having large corporations purchasing them—go after their suppliers and brokers and get these established suppliers to include your products on their supply lists and in their catalogs. Yes, another hand stirring the pot will mean fewer profits for each unit, but increased volumes and revenues can easily make up the shortfall. And if all goes well you may at some point be able to break away from the supplier or broker and sell directly into the chain retailer or corporation once you have established a market for your product. Therefore get started by targeting the supplier that already has an established business relationship with the corporation that you want to do business with or to sell your products to.

PROSPECT BY PROMOTING A CONTEST

$$$+ ⚒ ⚖

Another great way to prospect for new business is to hold a contest that has been carefully planned to appeal mainly to your target audience to ensure the maximum prospecting benefit for you. An example of this is the classic "Ugliest Kitchen Contest," wherein a kitchen cabinet manufacturer or kitchen renovation company stages a contest that calls for people (entries) to send in photographs of their ugly and outdated kitchen. Along with their name, full contact information, and a brief essay about why they need and think that they deserve a new kitchen. The winner gets the new kitchen and the company that holds the contest is left with hundreds if not thousands of entries, which are in effect qualified prospects because the kitchen company has already established by virtue of the contest that these people (contestants) want and need a new kitchen. Contests such as these can be very productive in terms of collecting leads to turn into sales. In fact, when cross-promoted with a media outlet such as a newspaper or radio or television station it is not uncommon for these types of contests to draw thousands of contestants. Get creative and try to identify what type of contest that you can hold that would leave you with many new prospects that can be turned into new customers. The results can far outweigh the investment and work to organize and execute the event.

IDENTIFY THE BIG PROSPECTING OPPORTUNITIES

$$ ⚒

By targeting one key prospect can you gain access to many more prospects? This is a question that all sales representatives and small-business owners should be asking themselves, because the answer could potentially unlock a number of new and gigantic selling opportunities. This prospecting technique is very straightforward and has proven extremely effective for many who have learned to identify the big prospecting opportunities and turned them into big selling opportunities. These key prospects to identify and target include executives, business owners, company managers, presidents of clubs and organizations, and leaders of all sorts who have a team of people under them, be it employees, club members, or students. If you can persuade the leaders as to the merits of your proposal, products, or services by identifying how the people under them will benefit by your offering, then in all likelihood you have identified a new marketing and big selling opportunity. For example, if you operated a shoe store you could set appointments with business owners or human resource managers of local companies such as manufacturers whose employees are required to stand to perform their jobs. Pitch them on the benefits of orthopedic shoes for the staff—less injury and better performance may mean increased productivity and revenues for the company. Therefore making it in their best interest to grant you access to their employees to sell the shoes, or better to have the employer buy the shoes and sell them or give them to their employees. This is only one example of the big prospecting opportunities, there are many and almost any business can identify and develop these opportunities with a little bit of creative brainstorming.

PROSPECT THROUGH PRO-NET

$ ⚒

Many small-business owners and salespeople are discovering that securing government service and supply contracts is not as difficult as they may have thought, and that's largely due to Pro-Net, which is operated by the U.S. Small Business Administration. Pro-Net is an online database that gives all levels of government contracting officers and purchasing agents access to some 200,000 small businesses and contractors listed with the service. Government officials simply log on to the Pro-Net Web site and search for and find qualified businesses and contractors to fulfill government goods and services needs. Likewise, member small-business owners and contractors can search the database to find forthcoming government contracts and the requirements and bidding information that goes along with them. Additionally members of the Pro-Net database also can network with other small-business owners listed and even form business bidding coalitions to estimate and bid on larger contracts that may be too large for their businesses to handle alone, but can be tackled by the coalition they have formed.

Web Resource

*   www.pro-net.sba.gov: Small Business Administration, Pro-Net: Procurement, Marketing and Access Network.

PROSPECT BY SHARING YOUR KNOWLEDGE
$$ ✎

Sharing your expert knowledge is a great way to prospect for new business, especially when the knowledge you share is free and valuable to the recipient. This is not a new prospecting technique; many business owners and sales professionals have successfully used it for a long time, both service providers and product sellers. For instance, many software development companies give away basic working models of their software in hopes that prospects will find it beneficial enough that they will purchase an upgraded version of the same software or pay a monthly fee for technical support related to the software. But it doesn't end there; just about every business can benefit by sharing their expert knowledge with prospects to secure new business. A house painter could operate a free 24-hour tip line wherein people who wanted to paint their houses could call for painting tips. Many of the same people who call will soon discover that there is much more

to house painting than they anticipated and will ask the house painter for a quote to paint their houses. Giving away expert knowledge is a great way to secure new business, as prospects will learn about the product or service that interests them or fills a need, and understand the benefits. This will ensure the desire to have an expert carry out the service or supply the product to ensure that all the benefits associated with it will be professional.

LOOK FOR PROSPECTING GOLD IN YOUR JUNK MAIL
$ ✎

Carefully examine your junk mail before you toss it into the recycling box because you never know if your next big selling opportunity will be hiding in those printed pages just waiting for you to find it. Companies and marketers' who send out direct mail on a regular basis do so because they make money from it, or they would not be sending it. Therefore look for ways that you can sell to these businesses, or for ways that you can sell your goods or services through these businesses. For instance if you provide copy writing and editing services can you improve their mailer? If so contact them, set an appointment, and pitch them with your ideas how they can improve their mail outs and benefit because of it. If you're in the printing business, can you land their printing account? Who knows, but it's worth a telephone call or personal appointment to find out. And if you sell widgets, can you take advantage of this company's mail order distribution channels to sell your products to their existing customers and new prospects? Maybe, if your widget is relevant in some way to their business and target audience and of course if an equitable and mutually beneficial deal can be arranged for both sides. In a nutshell, examine all junk mail, because sometimes it contains opportunities that just have to be identified and developed.

FISHBOWL PROSPECTING
$ ✎

Fishbowl prospecting simply means that you strike a deal with a local restaurant or two to place a clear glass fishbowl by the front entrance or cash register so that diners can drop their business cards in for a chance of winning a free lunch draw, which is drawn weekly. The key to getting the maximum benefit from this simple prospecting trick is to make sure that you pick a restaurant frequented by business-people and that you switch restaurants every couple of months so that the business cards that you collect and turn into leads stay fresh and new. Generally you'll find that restaurant owners and managers are very receptive to this type of joint venture. It benefits them because it works as a drawing card to attract diners who want to win the free lunch contest back to the restaurant more often, and of course there is no cost to the restaurant to participate. However, remember to place a limit on the value of the prize, perhaps in the $20 range. And if you want to lower the overall monthly cost of this unique prospecting trick, just find likeminded businesspeople or sales reps who want to share the list compiled from the business cards you collect from the fishbowl and split the costs of the prize lunches with them.

FACT-FINDING MISSIONS
$ ✎

To increase your chances of closing more sales and building long-term selling relationships with prospects, treat every first or original contact with new prospects strictly as a fact-finding mission. Far too many salespeople spend far too much time trying to sell their products or services when they make new contacts. Instead of carefully listening to prospects and asking well-crafted questions to truly identify what the prospect's needs and wants are. Top sales producers generally will not even take promotional materials such as product samples or printed sales literature with them on first visits with new prospects. They have learned like I have from experience that the first contact meeting is the time to find out everything they can about their prospects' situations, wants, and needs. And use this information to determine if they can help the prospects and then go to the next stage if they identify a selling opportunity based on the facts they have learned during the first meeting. You can also benefit by implementing this same

strategy by simply treating every first contact with a new prospect as a fact-finding mission.

WEB RESOURCE

✍ www.entrepreneur.com: Online small business and sales resource and information center.

MULTIPLY YOUR PROSPECTING EFFORTS VIA E-MAIL
$ ✎

Here is a very simple prospecting trick that you can use to get the word out about your business and secure some prospects in the process. Get in the habit of creating "something" every day. This "something" should be relevant to your products or services and present value to those who will come in contact with it, read it, and share it with others. Such as a tip of the day, important article of the day, a law or regulation of the day, or an opportunity of the day. You decide what will be valuable in terms of information you share with your prospects and clients. Send it out to everyone on your database list and kindly ask them to share it with their friends, families, and co-workers. Your original e-mail should include a signature file at the end that identifies your business and that is linked back to your e-mail and Web site. Like the old saying goes "and they told two people, and they told two people, and so on." Except today word-of-mouth advertising is called word-of-mouse advertising and this particular technique is referred to as viral marketing. And it works great to get information out to the people who it can benefit and who in turn can help build and buy from your business.

IDENTIFY THOSE WHO CAN INFLUENCE OTHERS
$ ✎

To master the art of prospecting is to know exactly who needs your product or service and who will benefit by owning and using it, even if the prospect doesn't currently realize it. This part of prospecting is very straightforward. The difficulty lies within persuading even well-qualified prospects to spend time and hear why they need your product or service and how it will benefit them by solving a problem or enriching their lives in another way. This is when it becomes necessary to identify those who can influence others. The others in this case being the prospects to whom you want to target and sell your goods or services. For instance for a photographer, influential people would be wedding and event planners; simply because these people have the ear of people who would benefit by taking ownership of photography services to take pictures at their forthcoming weddings or special events. They have influence over these people because of their relationship with these people. Once you identify the people who could influence the people you wish to reach then you can develop a strategy to get to know them and develop a long-term and mutually beneficial business alliance.

LEAN MEAN DATABASE MACHINE
$$+ ✎

Creating a database for marketing, prospecting, follow-up, and customer service purposes is great and something that every small-business owner and salesperson should pursue and develop. However, your database is only as good as the information it stores and manages, so the following are a few ideas for maintaining a good working database.

- Create two uniform ranking systems, one to identify your best customers and the other to identify your hottest prospects. This will save time and money when it comes to sending out direct-mail marketing materials or telemarketing to present new offers.
- Develop a system wherein you update your database daily, focusing on new client and prospect information input, updating files and deleting outdated information.
- Include only information that is helpful in terms of meeting your database objectives. And information that assists in recognizing your clients and prospects as individuals, including birth dates, hobbies, family members, etc. This information is especially important when developing presentations and proposals that will

appeal to each individual based on needs and wants.
- Develop and maintain a system as to how information will be entered. This could be by company name, by personal name, alphabetically, or in order of importance.

Information You Should Capture

Though the type of information that you choose to capture and record about your customers will change depending on your business and your marketing needs, the following are a few suggestions.

- Name of individual, customer, or prospect (consumer)
- Name of company, including contact people and titles
- Type of company and related information such as product/service description, number of employees, etc.
- Address, including mailing address if different
- Telephone number, fax number, e-mail address, Web site URL
- Job description/job title
- Demographic information including age, sex, education, etc.
- Buying history including date of first purchase, date of all subsequent purchases, types of purchases, units sold, average units each sale, average value each sale, sale value to date
- How he became a customer, for instance networking, cold call, advertising, trade show, sales visit, etc.
- Customer ranking
- Special requests, complaints, payment history
- What specific benefits and features are needed and or wanted

WEB RESOURCES

- www.oracle.com: Oracle/Netledger Small Business Suite
- www.maximizer.com: Customer and contact management software.
- www.salesforce.com: Customer relationship management solutions.

B2B PROSPECT RESEARCH CHECKLIST

$$+ ✎

Knowledge is power, especially when the knowledge you acquire can be used to sell your goods and services to business owners and managers. The following is a checklist of research that should be conducted prior to meeting with new business prospects.

📖 SUGGESTED ADDITIONAL READING

Berg, Bob. *Endless Referrals: Network Your Everyday Contacts Into Sales.* New York: McGraw-Hill, 1998.

Burley-Allen, Madelyn. *Listening: The Forgotten Skill: A Self-Teaching Guide.* New York: John Wiley & Sons, 1995.

Sample Prospect Research Checklist

❑ Get to know your prospect's specific industry by reading industry publications, visiting industry-related Web sites, and by attending industry-related seminars, workshops, and trade shows. You must have a good understanding of your prospect's industry and the challenges she faces if you want to be able to effectively communicate with your prospect.

❑ Learn as much as you can about your prospect's competition and what their strengths and weaknesses are. Use this information to create a complete package showing prospects how they can compete effectively in the industry and beat their competition based largely on the benefits of taking ownership of your products or services.

❑ Collect as much statistical data as you can about your prospect's industry and use this information to add value to your goods and services that you sell.

❑ If the expense is justified by the potential payoff, then conduct your own in-depth and independent research into your prospect's industry. This can include commissioning a report or study, consumer focus groups, surveys, and questionnaires. The conclusions can be used to support your selling position and to motivate your prospect to buy.

❑ Collect and study your prospect's marketing materials including presentations, company reports, newsletters, product and service reports, brochures, warranties and guarantees, and Web site. Get to know your prospect's business better than your prospect does.

❑ Invite your client and the company's key people to your office so they can educate your staff about their particular business, needs, wants, and problems they need fixed. This will put you in a better position to understand their business and how your products or services can solve their problem.

❑ Talk to your prospect's employees, vendors, suppliers, and most important clients to find out as much as you can about your prospect, his business, products or services, employees, and management. All that you can learn from this can be very valuable and applied toward creating customer solutions to fulfill his needs.

❑ Identify that your product or service would fit the company's needs and make it more profitable, save money, make it more productive, solve or fix a problem, give it a competitive advantage, or best, all of the above.

❑ Make sure that you have clearly identified all the players— who they are, what they do, how you can get to them on a one-on-one basis, and who will benefit most by the company taking ownership of your goods or services. And, find out who the decision makers are and the extent of their ability to spend money and make decisions independently or as part of a group.

Carnegie, Dale. *How to Win Friends and Influence People*. New York: Pocket Books, Reissue Edition, 1994.

Dyche, Jill. *The CRM Handbook: A Business Guide to Customer Relationship Management*. Boston: Addison-Wesley Publishing, 2001.

Kahle, Dave. *10 Secrets of Time Management for Salespeople*. Franklin Lakes, NJ: Career Press, 2002.

Parinello, Anthony. *Secrets of Vito: Think and Sell Like a CEO*. Irvine, CA: Entrepreneur Media Inc., 2002.

Salant, Priscilla. *How To Conduct Your Own Surveys*. New York: John Wiley & Sons, 1994.

Schiffman, Stephen. *Cold Calling Techniques that Really Work*. Avon, MA: Adams Media Corporation, 1999.

Sewell, Carl, Paul B. Brown, and Tom Peters. *Customers for Life: How to Turn That One Time Buyer Into a Lifetime Customer*. New York: Pocket Books, 1998.

Smith, Douglas K. *Make Success Measurable: A Mindbook-Workbook for Setting Goals and Taking Action*. New York: John Wiley & Sons, 1999.

KEY

COST TO IMPLEMENT $

DO-IT-YOURSELF

CALL IN THE
PROFESSIONALS

LEGAL ISSUES

BOOK RESOURCES

ONLINE

PRESENTATION
Marketing Tips for Your Business

There won't be anything we won't say to people to try and convince them that our way is the way to go.

—BILL GATES

GREAT IMPRESSIONS: BE PUNCTUAL
$ 🔨

Seldom do we ever get the opportunity to reinvent ourselves to people we have previously met. The old saying that you only get one chance and a few brief moments to make a favorable first impression is very true. In fact, most presentation and public speaking gurus contend that you are indeed limited to less than three minutes to make a favorable first impression on new people that you come into contact with. While this may not be very relevant for a nighttime security guard to know, it should be considered very important information if you earn your living selling where personal contact with prospects is your number-one sales and marketing tool. Start making a great first impression by being punctual. Arrive to all meetings on time, or better yet five minutes early. If you are going to have to reschedule then notify your prospect at least 24 hours in advance of the meeting.

Additionally, if an emergency arises or you are running late then call your prospect to explain the situation and ask if it is okay to still meet or would she prefer to reschedule. Time is valuable and nothing frustrates busy businesspeople more than when their time is wasted by others arriving late or not at all for meetings. Make a pact to make a great first impression by always being punctual.

GREAT IMPRESSIONS: BE RESPECTFUL
$ 🔨

The golden rule of personal contact with people is to treat everyone with the same respect as you expect yourself. Treat every person you meet with respect. This includes the prospect's employees, receptionist, managers, and all others who may sit in on the meeting or be involved in the business, not just the decision maker. For in-home or showroom presentations this includes spouses and other family members—from kids to grandparents—who might be in on the decision-making process. Nothing projects professionalism more than treating all people you meet with the utmost respect. The added benefit of treating all with respect is the simple fact that most of these people around the decision maker have much more influence on the decision maker than you do, or likely ever will. These people work or live with the decision maker and have a bond of trust and mutual respect that has long been formed. The people around the decision maker often have a greater influence on the buying decision than most salespeople realize, thus it pays off to treat everyone with respect. Also, go out of your way to make sure to treat your surroundings with respect. This includes your prospect's property, office, or home furnishings, equipment, and personal belongings.

GREAT IMPRESSIONS: BE EDUCATED
$$ ⚒

Top sales professionals always take the time necessary to learn as much as they can about the entire "situation" prior to meetings or sales presentations. For business-to-business sales meetings and presentations, the "situation" means learning as much about the company as you can. Information such as what they do, who their key customers are, how long they've been in business, where their business has come from and where it is going, and who the key players are in the business. You want to impress your prospect with your knowledge of her business, and what makes her business special. Show your prospect that you have done your homework and know as much about her business as possible, but never more than the prospect herself. For meetings or presentations with consumers, researching beyond the prospect's needs and wants generally is not required unless it will have a positive impact on the meeting. However, with that said, try to see things from your prospect's perspective to truly understand what she wants. Additionally being educated means that you know a little about everything—not a lot, but enough to carry on informative conversations on a wide variety of general topics.

GREAT IMPRESSIONS: BE PREPARED
$ ⚒

Make a great impression by being prepared well in advance of the meeting and have all aspects of your meeting or presentation organized and ready to use. Nothing will sink a potentially good meeting faster than bumbling for information, samples, or other sales aids like an amateur in training. Likewise, make sure that all your sales and marketing tools are clean, work properly, and are in tip-top condition. Recently I was contacted by a salesperson I had purchased a photocopier from years earlier and asked if I would like to come to their showroom so he could show me the latest and greatest model. While I was not really in the market for a copier, I accepted the invitation anyway when he told me that they would give me 10 percent off trade-in value for the first copier I purchased some years earlier. This seemed attractive enough to find out more. I arrived on time for his presentation and waited 20 minutes while he finished talking with another client in the showroom. When he finally began to demonstrate the new copier it was out of ink; this took another ten minutes to rectify before I could actually see what great things the machine did, but not before the machine also had to be refilled with paper. Needless to say after wasting a half-hour, I was not in the mood to make deals. This is perhaps the worst prepared product demonstration I have ever had the displeasure to participate in. The moral of the story: Be 110 percent prepared for every presentation and leave nothing to chance. Your first opportunity to make a great first impression is your best so make the most out of it.

GREAT IMPRESSIONS: LISTEN
$ ⚒

Never try to sell or offer solutions until the prospect's needs have been determined. The reason that the topic of needs is worth talking about over and over is the fact that the more polished your meeting and presentation skills become the easier it is to forget how you got there, which in almost every case was by listening to what prospects want and need before you can flog benefits, features, and solutions.

This is a critical factor in making a great impression. We all have been in a first meeting with a salesperson who rambled on and on about his great products and services while we're thinking to ourselves, "Yeah, but what does this have to do with what I'm looking for?" So don't get caught in the rambling-on trap; instead listen closely and intently to what your prospect has to say. Think of it this way: If your prospect is prepared to talk and tell you exactly what he wants, then all you have to do is listen closely, take note of what he is telling you, and give him what he wants at the end. Price objections are born out of a prospect not getting what he wants, generally because the salesperson did not hear what the prospect was saying.

GREAT IMPRESSIONS: BE PROFESSIONAL
$ ⚒

To make a great and professional impression on new prospects and current customers alike, avoid small things like slang, bad posture, and trying to come across as clever. Remember, big words and technical jargon that might be commonplace and understood by people who work within your industry will more often than not leave your prospects scratching their heads wondering what in the Sam Hill you were talking about. Without question it is always best to stick to straightforward terms and language everyone will understand and feel comfortable with. Set professionalism standards and strive to exceed them with every contact you meet. This will include appropriate attire, good manners, and using your expertise within your business and industry to dazzle your prospects when you respond to their questions. Always project a professional image with every new contact and you will always make a lasting and favorable impression.

GREAT IMPRESSIONS: BE READY FOR ACTION
$ ⚒

People appreciate other people who don't try to skirt issues and hide behind bad policies, weak excuses, or seemingly clever but meaningless explanations that go nowhere or benefit no one. People do however like people who are ready for action and to do business. When you set up sales meetings and presentations go to them with an attitude that you know why you are there and what you want from the meeting. Action means a number of things including listening carefully, asking questions and clarifying the responses, and guiding your prospect to the desired resolution that you know is right and in their best interest. Be a salesperson who delivers and expects action to be taken at meetings and presentations and you will be making a good and lasting favorable impression with your prospects. If you cannot be decisive in terms of the results that you want to produce from a meeting or presentation, then how do you expect your prospects to act any differently? They won't nor will they even try to be decisive. Therefore be direct, ask questions, expect answers and keep asking until you get them, and always go to every sales presentation expectating action and you will create a favorable and lasting impression.

SIMPLE TRICKS TO IMPROVE YOUR B2B SALES PRESENTATION
$$ ⚒

The following are a few simple, yet highly effective tricks that you can use to improve your business presentations.

Create an Outline

Prepare a professional and visually appealing agenda prior to the presentation and give it to your prospects in place of any other type of printed sales materials. The outline will serve as a roadmap for the presentation and it will keep your prospects focused on the presentation and not handouts. Additionally, the outline will help to pace the presentation.

State Your Expectations

Make a statement of expectations to your prospects right up front before you get going, such as, "Once we are done I am sure you will see how our widgets will help you increase productivity while saving money." Let your prospects know how you would like them to respond at the end of the meeting. Do you want them to buy, book a second meeting, or use your product or service for a trial period? Stating your expectations right up front accomplishes two things: First, it sets the tone of the meeting in terms of the information that will be shared, and second, your prospects will concentrate more closely on those sections or segments of the presentation that will reinforce your statement of expectation.

Focus on Needs

Always revolve your presentation around your prospects' core needs or problems they need fixed. Your entire presentation should be needs based: how what you sell fills their needs, solves a problem, creates new opportunities that they need to compete, or increases productivity that they need to be profitable. Selling to business does not have to be complicated because, unlike all consumer purchases, businesses buy for a reason, something they need, such as

- the need to make more money.
- the need to save more money.
- the need to increase productivity.
- the need to expand market share.
- the need to expand into new markets.
- the need to increase cash flow.
- the need to decrease debt.
- the need to be more competitive in the market place.

Focus on Results

Never assume your prospects saw, heard, read, or understood what you wanted them to during your sales or product presentation. Instead restate the benefits of what your product or service will do for them in terms of results: Make more money, reduce workload, save money, or give a competitive advantage. Talk is cheap; results that can be clearly demonstrated are a tangible deal-closer.

Make It Memorable

Make your presentation unique and interesting by utilizing every available media and presentation aid. Demonstrations, charts, graphs, video, pictures, live customer testimonials, and online technologies. To keep your prospects' attention and make your presentation more memorable, make sure to get your prospects involved, interested, and invested in every aspect of the presentation.

Ask Them to Take Action

Your presentation must end with some sort of action taking place, preferably the action you want your prospect to take. Therefore, never just end a presentation. Instead end your presentation by asking once again that your prospect take action. The action might be to buy, buy more, buy more frequently, or set up a follow-up meeting. The desired action should be directly related to your initial objective of the presentation; people are not mind readers and unless you tell them what you want them to do next, then do not expect that they will arbitrarily take action.

CONSIDER A PREPRESENTATION SURVEY
$ ✎

Get prospects to help you clearly define their needs by creating a prepresentation survey and kindly ask that they complete the survey prior to meeting with you. Give the prepresentation survey to prospects during your initial contact with them in person, or it can be faxed, mailed, or e-mailed to them. Likewise, when the survey is complete, they can fax, mail, or e-mail back to you. You can also pick it up in person, giving an extra opportunity to build the relationship and find out even more about the prospect. Include questions on the survey that you would like answers to, such as the prospect's needs, current problems, financial budgets, and timelines or when the client might want to buy. The more detailed and plentiful your questions, the better the responses will be in helping you to identify problems and find solutions. Send prospects a prepresentation questionnaire prior to meeting with them and you will be amazed by how much information they are willing to give you. Tell them the company created the survey to best service customers. Don't forget to ask questions about competition for the sale. Additionally, make sure that you ask specific questions about who will be making the buying decision to ensure that you are dealing with the right person. Prepresentation questionnaires are not meant to replace qualifying prospects, they are just another tool that can give you a better perspective of the prospect's situation and, therefore, a competitive advantage.

LET PROSPECTS SET THE TONE
$ ✎

Always keep in mind that prospects and customers want to feel comfortable in the selling environment and each will have his own idea of what comfortable means. As a result, let your prospects set the tone of meetings, presentations, and all follow-up contact. Letting them have control over this very small aspect of the presentation will enable them to sit back, relax, and be more open to what you have to say without worrying about the pace, tone, or their physical surroundings or location. You might approach every presentation in the same style, tone, pace, language, and body language; and while repetition is a great learning tool, this particular systematic presentation approach could actually be hurting your closing ratio. Learn to hold back and let your prospect set the tone during meetings and then get in synch with your prospect's tone. If they are jovial, then you should be jovial. If she is serious, then you should also be serious. If she wants to be the center of attention, then make her the center of attention. If she wants to have the meeting at her office or home, then pack up your displays and go to her. If she is somewhat shy and introverted, then don't force her to come out of her shell. You have to be a chameleon and come across as nonthreatening to all prospects by showing that you are just like them. They have to feel that they have some control over the process in order to be comfortable and not defensive about the selling process; allowing them to set the tone gives them a small bit of control and will pay back many times over in turning resistance to the sales process into embracing the sales process.

USE PHYSICAL AND VISUAL DEVICES
$$ ✎

Great presentations should not be spectator sports for your prospects; they should be involved players in the presentation or better yet the MVPs. Always use props and physical devices during presentations, ones that will appeal to your prospect's emotions or logic. A financial planner can tell a prospect that he has devised a plan for the prospect to be able to retire at age 55, and using only black-and-white facts and figures on a page, show the prospect how this can be achieved. Or, in addition to the facts and figures the financial planner can also use colorful charts, graphs, and pictures of retired young-looking 55-year-olds frolicking on the beach and having a lot of fun. Which presentation do you think will have a greater impact on prospects? If you're a travel agent selling vacations then use themes in your office and presentations that are relevant to the vacation packages you specialize in. Devise ways to incorporate flowers, sand, and surf into your sales presentations for tropical destinations. Develop a strategy for incorporating art and other items of great cultural significance into your sales presentation for European destinations. Your presentation objective should always be to take advantage of every emotional and logical appeal that you can; include the five human senses of taste, sight, touch, hearing, and smell, and get your prospects physically and mentally involved in the sales process.

WEB RESOURCE

🖱 www.entrepreneur.com: Online business and marketing resource center for small-business owners and sales professionals.

LOW-COST DIGITAL VIDEO PITCH
$$$ ✎ ☎

With the advent of digital technology, every business owner can now afford to have a simple business presentation or sales pitch recorded digitally and placed on CD-ROM. Even if restrictive financial budgets do not allow you to hire a professional to film and produce your digital corporate video, you can still have one produced for a fraction of the cost by simply contacting a film school and inquiring about the possibility of having students write, direct, and produce a corporate video for you in digital format as a class or student project. Many film schools are open to these types of proposals and joint make-work projects with businesses, as they understand the importance of real-life training for students. Likewise many individual students are also open to these types of proposals so that they have samples of their work that they can use as references and sales tools to secure more film work once they complete school. In addition to video sales pitches and presentations, you may also find a series of digital videos that cover other topics such as employee training and customer service to be extremely helpful tools to assist in the growth of your business.

TRICKS FOR OVERCOMING THE FEAR OF REJECTION
$$

Face Rejection to Overcome the Fear

The first rule of not fearing rejection is to face it by getting busy making appointments and facing your biggest fear head-on. Procrastination fuels the fear of rejection; the longer you think about the possibility of being rejected the more you grow to fear rejection. The more you fear it, the more fear will consume you and the more people will pick up on this through your voice, mood, and body language. So by facing the possibility of rejection, you are in fact overcoming the fear of being rejected.

Control Rejection to Overcome the Fear

Take back control over your own life and destiny. When you fear that other people will reject you or reject what you do or sell, you are in effect letting these people control you, and therefore they are also making your decisions for you. Never let another person control you by fearing that they might reject you. Instead continually ask yourself, "Am I going to let someone else control my life?" No way.

Set Goals to Overcome the Fear of Rejection

One of the best ways to overcome the fear of rejection is to set goals—not sales or business goals but something that you really want on a personal level. This could be to retire young, afford to pay cash for a summer home, or perhaps just a week-long vacation in the sun every year with the family— basically whatever you truly desire. Print you goals on numerous pieces of paper and put the papers in places where you will come into contact with them on a regular basis throughout the day. Seeing and reading your goals constantly is a fantastic way to understand that to get to the big things in life you have to overcome the small obstacles, such as fear of rejection, that stand between you and what you want.

Team with Others to Overcome the Fear of Rejection

Work with someone you trust and admire and learn from his or her success. Ask another salesperson in your office or business to team up with you for presentations, but never sit idly and let him do the work. Instead learn how he handles both success and rejection firsthand and develop ways to build on his successes and make them your own.

Reverse the Situation to Overcome the Fear of Rejection

Reverse the situation and understand that the prospect sitting across from you likely also does not like to be rejected. Always remember that you are not alone, the fear of rejection is universal. Understanding this will help alleviate your own fear; think of it as a safety-in-numbers approach to eliminating the fear of rejection.

Use Proven Techniques to Overcome the Fear of Rejection

If you have done it once and survived, you can do it again. The easiest way to overcome the fear of rejection is not to get rejected. This may seem obvious, but it's true. Keep detailed records of your successes and failures; build on your success by using proven scripts, closing techniques, and more to minimize the odds of being rejected by prospects. In other words what did you do right when you were not rejected and closed the sale?

Focus on the Prospect to Overcome the Fear of Rejection

Forget about your fear of being rejected and instead focus on the prospect and the business at hand. If all you think about and fear is hearing your prospect say no, then you will never hear what the prospect is telling you and therefore you increase the chance of him saying no and rejecting your offer.

NEVER TAKE REJECTION PERSONALLY
$ ⚒

As outlined above there are numerous ways to overcome the fear of rejection, but how about taking rejection personally? What if your prospect jumps up and down screaming at the top of his lungs, telling you how much he hates your company, your products or service, and finally asking you to leave his office posthaste. As tough as this may seem to be, don't take rejection personally. Instead use rejection for two things. One, as a measure to know where your stand with your prospect. If he has rejected your offer, find out what he didn't like about it. If you have asked the right questions then you also likely have a good idea of what will be required to get them back on board. Two, learn from the rejection and what caused the rejection so that it never happens again. You cannot control people and they will say and do things just like you do when they are under stress, having a bad day, rushed for time, and just about anything else. Rejection is seldom aimed at or based on the salesperson but rather what the salesperson has to sell, or what the prospect needs to buy, or even something that is internal and well beyond your control. A prospect without the financial resources to buy a swimming pool might get nasty during the presentation and reject your offer, which has nothing to do with you and everything to do with him. He wants the pool but just cannot see his way clear to afford the pool; thus negativity and rejection surface as a defense mechanism. There is an old saying that has been around for decades that is still true today in the sales game, "don't feel bad or get mad because of rejection, just get marketing."

KEEP THEIR ATTENTION
$ ⚒

More often than not a piece of paper will not close the sale. That task is left up to you and the interaction you establish and maintain with your prospects. For that reason, it is important that you keep your prospects' attention at all times during presentations and the best way to accomplish this is not to distribute sales materials or a typed presentation at the beginning of the meeting. Instead hold printed sales materials back until the end of the presentation and then distribute them to prospects once you have presented your information and demonstrated your products. The focus of the sales presentation should be on persuading the prospect to buy through questions, answers, and demonstrations. None of this can be achieved if your prospects are busy flipping through and concentrating on printed sales material; your words and actions will be lost. And worse, prospects will form opinions and make decisions based on what is in print, and unfortunately all these printed words can do is tell; they cannot show the best and biggest benefits of your product or service.

BE ON THE LOOKOUT FOR COMMON INTERESTS
$ ⚒

One reason that I have been very successful in sales is because of my ability to instantly find a common interest with a prospect and use that common interest to break the ice and create a more comfortable and easygoing meeting or presentation environment. However, there are two important aspects to consider about finding common interests. The first is that you must make a conscious effort to educate yourself in a wide variety of issues, topics, and things such as sports, recreational pursuits, entertainment, the arts, and a whole lot more even if you have no real interest in these any of these. How important is this? Very. In fact I once carried on a conversation about the game of tennis with a new prospect for more than an hour. The odd thing about this was I had never, and still to this day have never played tennis. But I have a friend who does and often I would talk to this friend about the game even though I had no intention of taking it up as a hobby or sport. The second important point to consider about common interests is to continually be on the outlook for them. Getting back to my tennis story, when I arrived at the prospect's home I noticed a tennis trophy on a shelf and immediately asked who the tennis player in the family was to which he responded "me." Presto, an icebreaker right off, it doesn't get any better than that. I got the sale based largely on my ability to instantly find a common interest, use it as an icebreaker, and got the prospect to drop his defenses to being persuaded into my way of thinking.

TRICKS TO EARN A PROSPECT'S TRUST
$ ⚒

The easier you make it for prospects to trust you and to trust what they are buying, the simpler the process of persuasion becomes. Consequently, it makes sense to always strive to reduce your prospect's fear of buying by reducing doubt and by earning her trust in you, and in what you sell. Here are a few great tricks that you can use to earn your prospect's trust.

Focus on the Prospect to Earn Trust

Ask questions to find out what prospects want and need and listen very carefully to their answers. Match the prospects needs and wants to your products' or services' benefits and advantages, not the other way around. You can talk about features, price, and color until you are blue in the face and all this can add up to zip if it does not interest your prospect or meet his needs. People notice when you keep your attention and interests focused on what they are telling you, and they will reward you for this by buying what you are selling.

Be What You Sell to Earn Trust

Show prospects that you truly believe in what you sell by being a walking, talking example of the benefits of your product or service. If you sell Ford cars then you better drive a Ford if you expect your prospects to trust you when you tell them that Ford builds the best and most reliable cars in the world.

Obviously not every salesperson can be a walking, talking example of what they sell; few salespeople who sell $100,000 photocopiers need one at home; that's not realistic. However, if your product or service is something that you can use and benefit from, then always strive to clearly show your prospects that you use or own this product or service and let them know how you have personally benefited from ownership.

Be Helpful to Earn Trust

Help your prospects to really identify what they need. Dig deep for small things that they themselves might be overlooking or may not have realized about their situation. Go the extra mile to be extremely helpful in all areas of the sales cycle: prospecting, presenting, closing, and especially in continuous contact after the sale.

Be Honest to Earn Trust

Always be honest to a fault with your prospects; if your product or service is not right for them then let them know and explain why. Likewise, if they could get by with three widgets instead of four then also let them know, or if a basic model will fill their needs as well as an upgraded model then spill the beans. This is not to say that you want to brush off a sale or reduce the value of a potential sale, just that you should be honest with your prospects and let them know what their options are when appropriate.

Be an Expert to Earn Trust

Know what you sell inside out, and just as important, know who your customers are, why they buy from you, how often they buy, and what benefits they receive from buying from you. Once again, it is all about eliminating doubt, and if you can answer prospect objections before they are even raised then you crush their doubts and are subconsciously building a trust rapport with them that is rock solid. You take your car to a mechanic you trust. If you lose that trust in a mechanic you find a new one to repair your car. As consumers, we all really do think and act in these basic terms, and price become much less of an issue when trust in the relationship is elevated.

NEVER IGNORE EVEN THE SMALLEST CONCERNS

$$ 🔨

What might seem like a small point to you likely isn't to your prospects, especially if they took the time and effort to raise it during the presentation. People do not talk about concerns regardless if it seems minor unless there is some significant reason for doing so. Often in a presentation environment the salesperson will have already mapped out a strategy and agenda for how he would like the presentation to flow and keep pace, and this includes the potential objections the salesperson thinks that the prospect will bring up. This is good and every presentation should be planned in this fashion, especially anticipating potential or likely objections and concerns that the prospect will have. However, remember that you cannot anticipate all of your prospect's objections and concerns no matter how much qualifying, research, and planning you have done prior to the sales presentation. Which brings me to the point that small concerns raised by prospects during the presentation often get swept under the carpet or brushed off by the salesperson because they had not anticipated these concerns and/or feel they are too small to deal with. Or the salesperson is concentrating so hard on the flow of the presentation he is not listening to what the prospect is telling him or revealing about his situation. Once again even if it may seem to be something small like a color option, delivery schedule, or payment terms, this small concern is still an obstacle to you closing the sale. One of the golden rules of selling is resolving 100 percent of the prospect's objections and concerns, regardless of how significant or insignificant they may seem to be. Skip over three small concerns a prospect may have and those three will add up to one unanswered major concern that will kill the sale.

CAREFUL QUESTIONING

$ 🔨

Never ask questions that you know your prospects cannot answer; all this will accomplish is to make them feel stupid and extremely uncomfortable and awkward during the presentation. Instead ask direct questions that will reveal your prospects' knowledge about the topic, product, or service that is being discussed and sold, and that will unlock secret motivations and desires about why they need or want what you are selling. The problem is that many salespeople think that by asking questions only they or a limited few know the answers to, they will appear smart, well-educated, and an expert in their field. However, this cannot be farther from the truth. In fact, all top-producing salespeople have learned that it is best to treat and assume that every prospect is more intelligent than they themselves are. In doing so you heighten your prospects' feelings of self-worth and confidence, make them feel important, and make them feel as though they are educating you. The goal should be to make your prospects feel more important and more intelligent than yourself; sell on the same level or slightly below your prospects, but never try to sell above. Starting today make a pledge never to ask your prospects questions that you know they cannot answer or that you know will make them feel stupid. Check your ego at the door and keep an open mind to learning something new from every person you come in contact with.

FIND THE ACHILLES HEEL

$ 🔨

Dig deep and usually you will find that almost all prospects have an irritation, or something that is so important to them that it goes well beyond identifying their needs, wants, and solutions. I like to refer to this as finding your prospect's Achilles' heel, typically their weakness, though it could also be a strength, pride, or even a material object. For example, one time when I was estimating a complete exterior renovation for clients, it came up repeatedly in the conversation that they had just installed a new and very expensive custom stone driveway. I made note of this fact and when I returned to present the estimate a few days later my prospects were very surprised to discover that I was about 20 percent higher than the rest of the quotes they had received for virtually the same renovation job and using the same materials. Why? I decided that their Achilles heel was their new driveway and therefore they would appreciate if trucks and equipment where not on it, so I quoted high because of the additional labor it would take to remove the old materials by hand and wheelbarrow to the road and carrying the new materials by hand. Basically I made a promise that, in addition to protecting the driveway with plywood and tarps, no truck or piece of heavy equipment would travel on it. I got the job and if memory serves a few referrals down the road.

START WITH DOCUMENTS
$+ ⚒ ⚖

Build confidence with all of your prospects right from the get-go by laying your cards on the table at the beginning of all meetings and sales presentations. In this case your "cards" are the important documents that might be required to operate your business or sell specific goods and services. For instance, if workers' compensation is required as an employee safeguard in your business then show prospects your workers' compensation coverage form. If liability insurance is needed then show prospects a photocopy of your liability insurance coverage. And if special permits or licenses are required for your business or employees, then make copies of those as well and show them to all prospects at the beginning of the presentation. Insert copies of all of these documents in a special binder and show them to prospects right at the beginning of the presentation, even if they didn't ask to see them. Not only will you be building confidence in your prospects, but also it also clearly demonstrates your commitment to your business. Not to mention it is also a great icebreaker and a great way to separate your presentation from the competition's presentation.

WHAT POWERFUL DOCUMENTS SHOULD YOU HAVE READY TO USE?
- Insurance coverage
- Training certificates
- Workers' compensation coverage
- Client testimonials
- Professional accreditation
- Business licenses and permits
- Vendor permits
- Materials handling or transportation permits
- Industry or association memberships
- Better Business Bureau membership
- Industry, association, and government awards

GREENER GRASS SYNDROME
$ ⚒

All salespeople have suffered from the greener grass syndrome at some point in their careers, but the successful salespeople were quick to identify what it was and how it had a negative effect on their ability to sell and generate income. Greener grass syndrome simply means that you cannot get out of one sales presentation and to another sales presentation that you perceive as being better fast enough; in fact, you're probably on fire. Sound familiar? It should because we have all suffered from greener grass syndrome at one point or another. The difficulty is when a pattern starts to form and before you know it the "next" sales presentation, meeting, or opportunity is always looking better than the one you are currently or soon to be giving. Beat back the urge to get moving on by telling yourself that every presentation you do is the last, there simply are no more opportunities to sell, this is the one and only. Let's face it, it can be difficult to stay involved and motivated when things are not going as planned, or worse when the presentation seems to be spiraling out of control. However, remember if you have carefully planned the presentation prior to arriving then in theory all you have to do is ask for the sale. This is because if the selling cycle has been followed, everything else should fall into place and there should be no reason to move on to perceived greener pastures.

IDENTIFY ALL THE PLAYERS
$ ⚒

Long before it is time to present, make sure that you take the time necessary to identify who all the players in the organization are, what they do, how your product or service will benefit each, and why they are important to the business. Knowledge is power and if you can use names in a presentation and include those people in your sales pitch and how your product or service will increase a particular person's performance, productivity, or make her job easier then you have won half the battle. To find out who the key players are in a business try the following.

Web Site and Online Information

Visit your prospect's Web site; often you'll find a page that lists key players in the organization, their titles, what they do, and information about their significance to the business. Likewise, "Google" each of the key people by submitting their names to the search engine to see what other information you can learn about this person that might be buried in the four billion Web pages that call the Internet home.

Company Reports

Try to acquire annual and quarterly reports of publicly traded companies as they also list key personnel and their direct relationship to the business.

Organization Chart

Call the company and ask for an organization chart. These charts list key personnel, management, and executives and their duties within the organization. Most companies will gladly hand them out when asked.

Make Inquiries

Call and ask secretaries and middle managers for a complete list of names and titles for key personnel. This can take some time and a few kind words, but it is possibly the best way to learn as much as you can about the people you will be presenting to and who ultimately will be making a decision on your proposal.

NO ONE WANTS TO SAIL INTO UNCHARTED WATERS ALONE
$

It's a proven fact that few people want to be the first to try or buy something new, most people prefer the comfort in knowing that someone else has gone first. Who would believe an advertisement that stated you could lose 50 pounds without actually

backing up the claim. Not many. But add in before and after pictures of an actual person who has visibly lost 50 pounds and all of a sudden the waters are no longer uncharted, someone has gone before and survived, and, better, benefited because of the decision. Always share customer success stories with your prospects to clearly demonstrate to them that others have gone before them and benefited. Use customer testimonials, drop names of people your prospects might know, and rely heavily on any aids that demonstrate that your product or service is widely known and used by people just like your prospects. Remove as much anxiety, doubt, and fear about the buying process as you can by showing your prospects that people no different from them have purchased and benefited because of their decision to purchase.

TRAIN ALL THE PITCHERS
$$$

No one knows your product's features better than you do, or what specific benefits consumers will get by taking ownership of your products better than you do—and they shouldn't. That's why it is important for you to personally train any and every person who will be selling your products, be it in a retail store environment, marketing events such as trade shows, or through service providers. And of equal importance is the fact that you must also train this sales force to push your products instead of the competition's, or better yet train them to love and want to push only your products to their customers and prospects. If your products sell through vendor distribution channels then make sure to develop a training program wherein you visit all vendors who sell your products and train their staff about the benefits of your products. Additionally create incentives for these salespeople so that they will want to sell your products over competitors' products. These incentives could be money, but better is to make your products easier to sell than the competition because they are better to begin with and the people selling them have been trained to understand all the benefits and what the product will do for the customer. In the end if this is achieved then businesses and people selling your products will make more money and have an easier time doing it.

WEB RESOURCE

✍ www.trainingregistry.com: National online directory listing professional business, management, and employee training consultants, and training courses and products indexed geographically and by topic.

DEVELOP A WINNING ATTITUDE
$ ✍

It is certainly no mystery that people like to be around other people they like to perceive as winners, and who are self-confident—not egotistical or uncaring of others but confident in their actions, words, and professionalism. It is of great importance for every salesperson to develop a winning attitude, assume that people want to do business with you because you are knowledgeable, professional, and really do care about who they are and what they want and need. When you feel good and confident about yourself and what you do, it rubs off on those around you. We all know negative people, complainers, doomsayers, and these people are simply no fun to be around period. In fact, these people are downers; they never win because they do not think they can, therefore it becomes a self-fulfilling prophecy every time they lose. Project a winning image and you will make others feel good about you, about themselves, and about doing business with you. How much easier would your job be if you knew that every sales presentation was a formality, and that you were there to answer a few straightforward questions, collect a signature, and fill in the finer details on the paperwork? Obviously much easier, and that is my point—if you have a winning attitude then this enables you to focus on your prospects and not on your own fear, doubt, and insecurities about what they are thinking about you.

WELCOME OBJECTIONS
$ ✍

Selling would be much easier if prospects didn't object to what you say or what you sell, right?

Wrong, in fact the exact opposite is true. When prospects raise objections at any point during the sales cycle, but especially during the presentation and closing segments, what they are really telling you is that they are interested in what you have to say and what you are selling. If not, they would just say, "I am not interested," which is not an objection but a flat out refusal to even be involved in the process because they simply do not want what you are selling. When prospects raise objections, they are in fact asking you to do one of two things. First, they are giving you a signal to do your job. They think that buying is the right decision, but they need that decision reconfirmed; they need you to persuade them that buying is the right decision. Second, they have one or more points or things that they do not fully understand about your product or service or the buying process and they need these points explained by you in greater detail and cleared up before they can commit to buying. Therefore, the savvy salesperson knows full well that objections are really just a yes in disguise and a positive step closer to the confirming the sale.

THE FIVE-POINT OBJECTION PROCESS
$ ✍

There are five key points to consider in terms of prospect objections. These five points are:

1. be prepared for objections.
2. don't sidestep objections.
3. listen to objections.
4. confirm the objection.
5. answer the objection.

This logical sequence to overcoming objections will eventually clear the way to closing the sale. Here are some further thoughts on each of these key points in the objection process.

1. Be Prepared for Objections

It is not enough to welcome objections simply because if you are not prepared to answer and overcome an objection, you will lose sales. Consequently, prior to meetings and sales presentations, you must anticipate that there will be objections raised by your prospect and therefore develop a strategy or plan to overcome objections raised. Seasoned veterans have a good idea from experience what objections prospects will raise in meetings. This is a luxury that novice salespeople don't yet have, but they will eventually go in with practice and experience. So rule number one of the objection process is to anticipate that there will be objections raised and plan for these objections prior to the meeting or presentation.

2. Don't Sidestep Objections

When prospects do raise objections or concerns during a meeting or sales presentation, never sidestep the objection; if you do you will in fact sidestep closing the sale. Every single objection that prospects raise during presentations must be listened to, confirmed, and answered, all of which are discussed below. However, many salespeople have a tendency to sidestep objections during presentations and they do this by pretending the objection was not raised, by ignoring the objection and quickly changing the topic, or by rushing to the next point in the presentation to take the prospect's mind off of the objection. Generally this happens because the salesperson did not plan for objections and therefore cannot answer and overcome them when raised. Or, the salesperson does not give weight to the objection. Both are deadly, simply because prospects seldom forget about the objections they raise, they are always in the back of their minds like a beacon in the fog, flashing, as a constant reminder of why they should not buy.

3. Listen to the Objection

Never assume that you know exactly what objections your prospect will raise. While it is true that you must anticipate objections and plan for them, it is still very possible that a prospect will raise a new objection, one that you have never heard before or had to overcome. Likewise, you must give your prospect the opportunity to voice her objection and be prepared to listen to what she has to say with an open mind so that you can consider the merit of the objection, if it is a major or minor stumbling point or obstacle in the way of the sale, and how you will respond to and overcome the objection.

4. Confirm the Objection

Next, always confirm every objection that your prospect raises so that you fully understand what she is saying and how it relates to what you are selling. Do this by simply asking her to restate the objection and any other details she thinks relevant, or in other words why she feels as though it is a valid objection. Doing this will afford you three things: 1) you hear the objection again and why your prospect feels it is important thus giving you the opportunity to understand the objection from her perspective; 2) you will have extra time to consider how you will respond to and overcome the objection; and, 3) perhaps the most important, when prospects restate their objections many times they will see things in a new light and realize that they have misunderstood something along the line and end up answering their own objections or overcoming it before you even have to respond, clarify, or explain.

5. Answer the Objection

Finally the last point in the objection process is to answer and preferably overcome the objection by revealing additional information about your offering that will satisfy your prospect that the objection has been overcome. Once you have answered the objection, make sure that the prospect is happy with your response by asking if he understands and agrees with your explanation.

GREAT TRICKS FOR OVERCOMING THE PRICE OBJECTION
$ ✎

Listed below are a few great tricks for overcoming price objections.

- It is no mystery here that many people will automatically respond to an offer with the objection that the price is too high. Often they have not even considered if the price is too much, instead just state it because it comes naturally for many of us. Perhaps the best way to debunk this all too common response is to put it back in your prospect's court by simply asking, "The price is too much in comparison to what?" This simple question will throw the majority of people off balance, as once again they have not considered why the price is too high, they only believe that it is because they are automatically programmed to think it is, regardless if that is the case or not.

- Another strategy for overcoming the price objection is to simply agree with your prospect that indeed your price is more than competitors', but then explain why your price is higher. The quality, warranty, special training, or some other competitive advantage or specific reason you are justified in charging more for your goods and services. This is my favorite; the majority of people object to price only because they feel they have to, so by justifying your price through valid reasons and explanations you can actually increase your prospect's desire to buy because she can understand the value of your offering in relation to the price that you are charging.

- Explain to your prospect that he is not buying price, or for that fact, even a product or service. He is buying a solution, something that will benefit him immensely and help solve a problem, make money, save money, better his health, or whatever your product or service will do for him. When you can clearly demonstrate that the benefits or the results far outweigh price, then price will become less of an obstacle that stands in the way of the sale.

- Ask your prospect, "Is price the only objection you have, or are there also other objections that would stop you from proceeding with the sale?" Another great way to get beyond price, if indeed it is your prospect's only objection, is to use the good old "in hindsight" close. Perhaps something along the lines of "I know you really like our widgets and everything else besides price seems to be fine. I don't want you to look back down the road and say in hindsight 'I should have purchased those widgets.'" Many roads are paved with missed opportunities and if you can clearly show your prospect that he would be missing out on a great opportunity to buy over a silly little thing like price, then you

can greatly reduce the impact that "price" will have on the buying decision. Let's face it, in hindsight shares of Microsoft were the deal of the century at a buck apiece some years back. See my point?

- Maybe your prospect honestly feels the price is too steep for his budget or comfort zone. If so, then perhaps you could give him the option of cutting something out of the deal that would reduce the cost. Or, propose a second option that is less costly. Both are great ways to get beyond the price objection for the simple reason that when you give people a choice between 'A,' a more costly buying option, and 'B,' a less costly buying option, not buying is no longer an option. The option is now do I spend more for something better, or less for something almost as good?

GREAT TRICKS FOR OVERCOMING THE NO-MONEY OBJECTION

$ ⚒

Listed below are a few great tricks for overcoming no-money objections.

- In a business-to-business selling environment the first way to overcome a no-money objection from prospects is to make sure that you are calling on business prospects and making proposals when they are planning their budgets for the forthcoming year, and not in the process of spending their budgets for the current year. Of course, the danger is that you educate your prospects and open the door for them to secure competing bids. Hence, you have to be clever in how you approach this particular method of overcoming the no-money objection.

- When you receive a no-money objection suggest that you try to arrange a suitable financing option for the purchase. When you can show people that they can purchase by using financing means that they did not think of, often the no-money objection fades as they begin to warm up to the idea of buying because now they can.

- When a prospect tells you that she cannot afford to buy, ask why. Once again, when you know all the details and the reasons for the decision then you can develop mutually workable solutions that might otherwise go unnoticed.

- Clearly demonstrate to your prospect that the benefits of buying are so important to her particular situation that a no-money objection would not be wise. In other words, the cost of not buying far outweighs the cost of buying.

- This particular trick won't help you overcome the no-money objection today, but it could help to keep the lines of communication open for a future sale: When you are positive that your prospect does not have the financial resources to make the purchase and you have exhausted all other means of finding available money then try to get her to commit to the purchase in the future when money does become available. The key to successfully using this trick is to stay in regular contact with your prospect by putting her on your newsletter or e-zine mailing list, and by including her in holiday card mailings. Likewise, make sure to call her once in a while to see if her situation has changed to the point where a purchase can be made.

GREAT TRICKS FOR OVERCOMING THE "LET ME THINK ABOUT IT" OBJECTION
$ ✎

Listed below are a few great tricks for overcoming "let me think about it" objections.

- When a prospect says he wants to think about it, "it" being whether to buy your product or service, suggest that you go over things again while the details of the deal are fresh in everyone's minds. Often this will catch prospects off guard and they will agree that it makes sense to reconfirm or discuss the details, thus giving you another opportunity to open the lines of communication and to persuade them to buy.

- If you feel as though you are at the end of the line with your prospect, then now is the time to pull that ace from your sleeve and offer the prospect an incentive for completing the deal right now on the spot. Justify offering the incentive to your prospect as a way to save time for both parties by not having to meet at a later time. However, be firm and tell him in no uncertain terms that your incentive, whether it is a discount, a better model at the same price, extended warranty, or whatever it may be is only valid immediately; he must make a decision to buy right now if he wants to take advantage of your buying incentive.

- Try the Benjamin Franklin closing technique and list all the pros or advantages to buying in one column; list the cons or disadvantages associated with buying in a second column. When people can see in black and white that the advantages of buying far outweigh the disadvantages, often that is all the persuasion needed to make a buying decision. However, if you are going to use this closing technique to overcome the "let me think it over" objection just make sure that the advantages of ownership really do outweigh the disadvantages. If not, you will come off looking like a fool and lose any chance of closing the sale.

- Ask your prospect why she needs more time to think it over. Doing so makes her give you a concrete reason for not buying at that moment instead of the "let me think it over" excuse. The answer she gives to this question will greatly assist you in determining if your prospect is still truly interested in your product or service or not. Likewise, by forcing the prospect to give reasons she is not ready to buy, you are in effect opening the lines of communication once more and in doing so gain the opportunity to overcome these true objections which will likely surface in the absence of "let me think about it."

- Finally, simply ask your prospect what the chances are that he will go ahead and buy tomorrow, next week, or next month. If the response is positive then suggest that you save time by completing the paperwork now and should he decide not to go ahead with the sale that you will tear up the contract. This is a logical enough approach for many people, especially given the fact that if they say they will buy now you are placing them in a position of having to do so.

BE PREPARED TO NEGOTIATE
$ ✎

Perhaps one of the most important aspects of successful negotiation is to be prepared to negotiate. Since information is the cornerstone of preparation, the more information you have, the stronger your position becomes to get what you want and at your terms and conditions. Start by finding out as much as you can about your prospect's wants and needs and how these wants and needs are prioritized: by budget, by benefits, by the ability to solve a problem, or by schedule. I like to think of it as having all of your ducks in a row before you're ready to present or close the sale. Come armed with relevant documents and data; nothing will kill a negotiation faster than having to come back with one missing element at a later date, or telling a prospect that you will "find out" and let her know. The act of negotiation is useless and serves no purpose unless you can take advantage of the exact moment you have successfully negotiated to close, reconfirming the point to always be prepared before you negotiate. You cannot close and return later with the contract, there are far too many variables or things that can upset the apple cart for that. Being prepared also means that you are prepared mentally to negotiate: Your mood is good, your confidence is high, and your rapport with your prospect is excellent. And you have a good understanding of what your prospect is trying to achieve through negotiations, whether it is a better price, faster delivery, more features for free, or a longer guarantee.

SET YOUR NEGOTIATION OBJECTIVES
$ ✎

One of the most important aspects of successful negotiation is to know what exactly you want before you negotiate by setting negotiation objectives prior to the meeting. Your objective might be to get the sale at any price because of the potential spin-off, repeat, or referral business that can result from the sale. Or your objective might be to get your current customer to order more products or order products on a more frequent basis. There are numerous objectives in terms of what you want or need negotiations to do for your particular situation; the key is to write down what you want the outcome of the negotiations to be prior to every meeting with a prospect or customer. In doing so, once the negotiation process begins you will have a point that you want to reach and more importantly a formulated a plan to get to the point you want to reach in the negotiations. Negotiating without a clear idea of what you want or need by the end of negotiations is like leaving for a vacation with no destination—how will you know when and if you have arrived?

POSITION YOUR VALUE BEFORE NEGOTIATIONS
$ ✎

Long before negotiations begin you must position the value of your product or service with your prospect. This is a very important step in the negotiation process because if your product or service is properly positioned then it gives you increased leverage and power to get what you want out of the negotiations process. However, you do not want to value the wrong things in terms of your product or service, things such as the price or the specific features. You want to value the benefit to the prospects, what your product or service will do for them, how they will benefit by using and owning it, or what problem it will fix for them, these are a few of the things that you want to base the value on. You have to create a situation wherein your prospects have a real need and desire for your product or service; anything less and you will be in a weak negotiating position. This is important partly because some prospects will want to push to see how low you will go on price. This is deadly because if you have not clearly positioned the value of your product or service in terms of what it will do or solve for your prospect, you lose the ability to justify your price as compared to the relative value of what the product or service does for the prospect. For example, say I sell a car with a five-star safety rating and my prospect has a family. Then I would want to position the value of this five star safety rating and why it should be priority number one with my prospect (protect the family) prior to negotiating the sale. In doing so I would place myself in a strong negotiating position simply because you cannot put a price on safety, thus justifying a more expensive price. Remember that without a high perceived value, the price of a product or service will always be too much.

LEARN TO NEGOTIATE WITHOUT HOME COURT ADVANTAGE
$ ⚒

One of the key skills that every salesperson must learn is to be comfortable negotiating in all situations and all locations. This skill is an especially important one to learn and master because you want your prospect to be comfortable, relaxed, and not feel under pressure or on the defensive during the negotiating process. With that said, the most comfortable location for the prospect is to be in a familiar and friendly environment, the home court advantage, be it their office, home, favorite restaurant, or wherever they feel the most comfortable. The best way to find out where your prospects are most comfortable is to simply ask them where they would like to meet, what is most convenient for them? Generally if you ask the question in such a way as to let them choose they will almost always subconsciously pick a location that they are comfortable in and most don't realize this it is just a natural reflex. Once again, the reason you want your prospects to be in their comfort zone is so they will concentrate on the task at hand in a relaxed manner and not be distracted by an unfamiliar setting and strange surroundings, which can lead your prospect to take a defensive position rather than an open and freely communicating position.

GET THE NEGOTIATION BALL ROLLING WITH YES
$ ⚒

It is always best to get the negotiation ball rolling along in a positive and upbeat fashion by getting your prospect to agree to and say yes to a few issues up front, small things that are not threatening in any way, shape, or form. Perhaps you have learned that there is a time issue regarding delivery of the product and therefore can use this to your advantage early in the negotiations and say to your prospect, "I can assure early delivery if you still want it." Of course, the prospect will say yes because they have already indicated that they want early delivery. Thus you have asked a question that is guaranteed to get a yes—a small question, one that does not threaten the prospect but gets her in the mood for saying yes. Continue to ask small-issue questions that you know your prospect will say yes to, such as product colors, features, warranty information, and so forth, and in the end try to narrow the negotiations down to a single point. Doing this will make it much easier for you to make perhaps one small compromise if any at all, and for your prospect to accept it and feel like she has won.

DEVELOP STRONG NEGOTIATION QUESTIONS
$ ⚒

Stay upbeat and positive during negotiations and learn to ask question instead of making "no" statements or responses. Your questions should ultimately lead the prospect to the close and, just as important, a win-win negotiation situation. Never assume you know what your prospect is thinking or what she needs. There is only one way to be certain and that is by asking questions. What might seem like a small stumbling point to you, one hardly worth worrying about, could in fact be a major stumbling block to your prospect. Additionally use questions that begin with "what," such as "What would you suggest?" Or, "What are the alternatives?" Or, "What would you think about if...?" Remember that there is one golden rule that transcends all segments of the sales cycle including negotiations: The person who is asking the questions is the one who is in control of the process and, ultimately, the outcome of the negotiations. By asking questions, you force your prospect to reveal what she wants and therefore weaken her position in the process. And, you can only weaken your prospect's negotiation position if you ask questions, there is no other way of being 100 percent sure.

NEGOTIATE UNDER FIRE

$ ⚒

Never allow yourself to get pushed into a corner and react in a argumentative way with a prospect or client over a price objection or any other aspect of the negotiation or sales process. You must learn to keep emotions in check and rely strictly on logic to guide you past the rough spots that will invariably arise during some negotiations. Emotions can come in many forms—fear that you won't get the sale, excitement that you will, anger because of something your prospect said, or frustration because negotiations are not going as planned. Regardless of the emotion, any emotion can take over and greatly reduce your ability to think clearly, stick with your plan, or weaken your negotiating abilities. At the end of the day you must remove yourself from the process and view your involvement in the negotiations as that of an unbiased mediator. In doing so you can orchestrate a win-win compromise that keeps your prospect happy and ultimately yourself, too. Additionally, learn to keep your objectives to yourself as these can also weaken your negotiation power if your prospect finds out what it is you want out of the negotiations.

LEARN WHEN TO WALK AWAY FROM A DEAL

$ ⚒

Always be prepared to walk away from negotiations if you are positive that you have nothing to gain by continuing with the process. One certain time to walk away is when a prospect's only concern is price and nothing else matters. Ultimately a person who shops solely on price will never become a long-term loyal and repeat customer. She will always be searching for the lowest price, and if you take her business you will always be looking for ways to reduce your price to satisfy. This type of prospect is loyal only to a low price and grinding you out of a buck, and nothing else. This type of customer is a real waste of your time. Which is the perfect segue into the next type of negotiation situation that you should walk away from—time wasters. There will always be prospects who have already made a decision not to do business with you for any number of reasons, but do not come out and tell you so. Instead you qualify by asking all the right questions and believe that you have a valid chance at closing a sale. However, this type of prospect's true motivations will surface during the negotiations; she will continually refer to another company's offer, or insist on bringing up the same questions or objections repeatedly even if she tells you she is satisfied with your response. Politely thank her for her time, collect your samples and presentation, and bid adieu. When the outcome of the negotiations is no longer beneficial to you or your business, it is time to walk away. Never take or make the sale just because you let your ego and stubbornness get the best of you during negotiations.

WIN-WIN NEGOTIATION TRICKS

$ ⚒

Know that every negotiation has to have two winners, you and your prospect. Never go into negotiations expecting to get everything you want while your prospect doesn't get anything he wants. If you do, you should expect to close far fewer sales and do a lot more work to get the ones you do close. In every successful negotiation there has to be some compromise; without it one side will feel skinned and hoodwinked, which is no way to start a long-term customer relationship. Win-win negotiations means that both sides gain and benefit as a result, that long-term relationships are established, and that multiple issues on each side are appeased at the table through fair, honest, and straightforward negotiations. Never try to negotiate with someone who is unwilling to find a win-win settlement, or as some like to refer to it as "a common middle ground." If you do, in the end the negotiating effort will be for nothing because every time that customer wants something in the future he will expect to get it on his terms and conditions and at a price he sets regardless of what you want out of the business relationship.

CONFIRM THE NEGOTIATION DETAILS

$ ⚒

I cannot overstate the importance of confirming all the details once negotiations are complete and an agreement has been successfully reached. These details have to be recorded on paper and it is best if they are also mutually signed off on, or at least initialed beside each major point in the deal. A handshake is fine on a small job or order if you have established a long working relationship with a client; if not you must get all the details on paper, and when you're done, reconfirm these details with your new customer. Also, just as important as reconfirming the details of the contract and negotiations is to reconfirm to your client that he has made a wise decision in terms of the purchase and the fact that you appreciate his business. Remember that in all likelihood this is the start of a long-term business relationship. As I have mentioned in other chapters in this book, the work really begins after a prospect buys and not a minute before.

BE A PATIENT NEGOTIATOR
$ ⚒

Successful negotiations can take a great deal of time, often spanning more than one meeting or even more than a few weeks or months depending on what is being sold and at what value. Consequently, understand that the true value of the sale is not in the immediate value of what is on the table presently, but in the value the customer represents over a lifetime of loyalty to your business and brand. Selling a car for $25,000 today is great, but taking the time to build a strong relationship with your customers that can result in selling ten $25,000 cars over a lifetime is ten times more valuable. Likewise, do not rush prospects to make a decision if you see that they require time to do so. Not everyone is comfortable or used to making buying decisions on the spot; some need time away to collect their thoughts and rationalize or justify the purchase and you must give these people that space. In the end if you have done your job properly and stay in contact with "slow deciders," the majority will eventually go ahead with the deal.

LEARN TO STOP NEGOTIATING
$ ⚒

Stop negotiating once an agreement is reach. Strange as it seems, salespeople have a tendency to want to keep talking and negotiating after the prospect has said yes. Some will even start to concede points that have been agreed upon already or start to throw small incentives—"you're a nice person" discounts and more—into the deal without being asked to do so, and when it is totally unnecessary do to so. Sound familiar? If so, don't feel bad, at one point or another we all have gotten so caught up in the process of negotiating the deal and closing the sale that once it is done, we're not. We are too wound up, too excited, and too ready to keep talking and negotiating when we should be quiet and leave. So here are a few ways to make sure that when the negotiations are over you stop negotiating. As soon as an agreement is reached

- reconfirm the details of the sale.
- complete the paperwork, get it signed, and thank your customer for his time and business.
- ask your customer for referrals.
- switch the conversation to one of mutual interest as you complete the paperwork.
- complete the paperwork and say nothing, let your customer choose the conversation.
- (the one I like the best) say thank you, and as you complete the paperwork restate the main benefits and value of the product or service that the customer just purchased.

MORE GREAT NEGOTIATION TRICKS
$$ ⚒

Sales professionals and business owners can never have enough weapons in their negotiation toolboxes. Here are a few more great negotiating tricks that you can use to improve your negotiating skills and to create fair yet favorable results at the negotiating table.

The Decision Maker

Be absolutely positive beyond any reasonable doubt that you are negotiating with the final decision maker, the person who can sign the purchase order and check once you have reached a mutually beneficial agreement. Do this long before negotiations through a series of qualifying questions to determine your prospect's ability to make a buying decision.

Financial Ability

Next to being positive that you are negotiating with the decision maker, also make sure that the decision maker's signature can be backed up with the ability to pay for the purchase or the ability to secure the money required for the purchase upon successful negotiations. You would be amazed by how many people negotiate in what I would refer to as bad faith, knowing perfectly well that they cannot or do not have the financial means necessary to pay for the purchase. People do this for two reasons. The first reason is that some salespeople let them by not getting this qualification out of the way early in the sales cycle. And the second is because they often believe that the salesperson has a magic wand and can finance the purchase, or alternately secure financing for them even though they have a poor credit history.

Restating the Value

Never stop reconfirming the value your product or service represents to the prospects. This means continually reminding them of the benefits they will receive or the problem that will be solved when they buy. Likewise, reconfirm or restate the value of your product or service after the sale has been successfully negotiated and closed to reduce the probability of buyer's remorse that can ultimately kill the sale after the close. Do this immediately upon agreement, once more while you are completing the contract or paperwork, and a final time before you part company with your customer.

Listen

Be prepared to listen to and understand your prospect's position in the negotiations and learn to be comfortable with uncomfortable periods of silence. Often the first to crack when negotiating is the first to concede to a major point. More than once I have sat across from a prospect during negotiations with periods of silence that have lasted greater than five minutes while each of us ponders a offer or counteroffer. To get past the silence often you will know what your own response will be, but hang on to it a while and use this silent time to figure out what your prospects are thinking and where they are in the negotiating process.

Avoid First Offers

Never accept your prospect's first offer, if you do without doubt you will be leaving money on the table. Few people will walk away from the table when you tell them that you need more money in order to go ahead with the deal. Besides if you do automatically accept their first offer most people will begin to doubt their entire buying decision and "what ifs" and "maybe I should think about this some more" will begin to creep in to the conversation. This is because you have made it too easy for them to get a discount and they will think that there is something wrong with what you are selling or that the price was too high to begin with. Quickly accepting a prospect's first offer can ultimately kill the deal, therefore always counter even if you are satisfied with your prospect's first offer.

Leave the Door Open

And finally, there is great wisdom in the old saying, "never burn your bridges in case you want to cross back some day." So it should go without saying, if things do not work out in terms of completing or closing the sale during negotiations, always leave the door open for future business and more importantly let your prospect know that the door is open through regular follow-up and contact.

NEVER LEAVE EMPTY-HANDED $$ ✎

Calculate the amount of time it takes to prospect, qualify, prepare, and present, and you will quickly discover that you have a substantial "time money" investment into every prospect. I learned early in my sales and business career that to truly succeed, every single personal-contact sales presentation I conducted had to result in a sale, a second selling opportunity, a referral, a decision, or a learning experience. What I decided is that selling was like following a rope, it twisted and sometimes got knotted, but as long as I never left a sales presentation empty-handed the rope would not be severed. Consequently, developing a "never leave empty-handed" strategy is a way that you can protect and profit on the investment you have made and secure a high rate of return in exchange. Aim to leave every sales presentation with one or more of the following.

Leave with the Sale

The number-one thing you want to leave a presentation or sales meeting with is a sale, a signed contract, and a guarantee from your client that this is a done deal that won't collapse in the following hours, days, weeks, or months. Obvious yes, but still leaving with the sale is the first objective and if each and every presentation is approached in this manner then you'll find that you become a master in the assumption close. Also, assuming that every presentation will result in a sale is a great way to stop thinking about how you will close and concentrate on the presentation. Which if you have done all your homework prior to and have clearly identified a prospect's needs, wants, and situation, then a close is a natural progression to wrap up the presentation anyway.

Leave with a Second Meeting

Every salesperson, myself included, has walked away from a sales presentation saying to themselves and most likely others, "Wow that went great, these people are going to buy for sure they just need a little breathing room." True sometimes people do need breathing room prior to making a purchasing decision and you have to be able to identify that requirement and act accordingly by giving them space; it's all part of the sales cycle and perfecting the craft of persuasion. But, and this is a big but, you have just left empty-handed unless you have specifically asked for and confirmed with your prospect a second or following meeting so that you have the opportunity to close the sale. Preferably a face-to-face meeting with your prospect, not a telephone call, an e-mail, or a follow-up letter. Following this strategy alone has the potential to increase your closing rate by 10 percent or more, but you must be persistent in getting and confirming that second meeting. Like asking for the sale multiple times, ask for that second meeting until you get it. Why? Unless there is absolutely no hope in closing a sale, a warm prospect you have already developed a relationship and rapport with is

much easier to get to the close with than starting the prospecting, qualifying, presentation cycle over again with a new and cold prospect.

Leave with Referrals

Get in the habit of asking for a referral at every sales presentation, so that regardless the outcome you won't be leaving empty-handed. I remember many a sales presentation that went horribly for various reasons, but once I committed to the strategy of never leaving empty-handed, I always asked for a referral no matter how out of order it may have seemed at the time. And guess what? Seldom did I meet with resistance and more often than not people were more than happy to provide me with names of friends and family who might benefit from what I was selling, especially if the presentation went really bad and the prospect just wanted to get rid of me! If you find that you are really stuck when it comes to asking for a referral then create a quick and simple referral form. Before you leave every presentation give it to the prospect and kindly ask that they complete it because it's company policy. If you say it in a matter-of-fact fashion not emphasizing or making issue out of this, people will accept that this is your company's policy and simply complete it, usually without any hesitation.

Leave with a Decision

Obviously the decision you want to leave a sales presentation with is a yes, but when you cannot leave with a yes still aim for a decision. Sometimes a final no is just as good as a yes, it lets you know where you stand and we have already identified that time is money so at least a no decision allows you to move on to make the best use of your time. Beyond a yes or no decision there are others that you would like prospects to commit to. A second meeting as described above is a good one. That means a firm decision and date for a second meeting, not a "let me think about it and I'll give you a call." Another decision that you want is a commitment from your prospects that they won't make a final decision until they talk to you first. This can be a tricky one to get because in essence you are asking your prospect not to purchase from the competition until they speak to you. However, if you are open and honest with your prospects and let them know that their business is important to you, and that you have invested substantial time and energy into meeting their needs and wants, then most people will be happy to accommodate and at least give you a final kick at the can so to speak.

Leave with an Education

If you understand and believe that every single sales presentation you conduct is an educational experience then you will never leave empty-handed. No two presentations play out exactly the same thus there is always something to be learned in each. However, if you remain close-minded to this fact then you will leave without gaining valuable insights to what went right with the presentation or subsequently wrong. Superstar salespeople never stop learning; you can never know everything and those who believe they do are talkers and not listeners, and generally will soon find themselves to be failures in sales. You have the power never to leave empty-handed because you can choose to learn and educate yourself with every presentation you conduct, so adopt this winning strategy today and never stop benefiting from education.

📖 Suggested Additional Reading

Camp, Jim. *Start With No: The Negotiating Tools that the Pros Don't Want You to Know About.* New York: Crown Publishing, 2002.

Craven, Robin and Lynn Johnson Golobowski. *Complete Idiot's Guide to Meeting and Event Planning.* Dulles, VA: Alpha Books, 2001.

Dawson, Roger. *Secrets of Power Negotiation.* Franklin Lakes, NJ: Career Press, 2000.

Fisher, Roger and William Ury. *Getting to Yes: Negotiating Agreement Without Giving In.* New York: Penguin, 1991.

Heiman, Stephen E., Diane Sanchez, and Tad Tuleja. *The New Strategic Selling: The Unique Sales Systems Proven Successful by the World's Best Companies.* New York: Warner Books, 1998.

Jaffe, Aziela L. *Starting From No: 10 Strategies to Overcome Your Fear of Rejection and Succeed in Business.* Chicago: Upstart Publishing, 1999.

Maxwell, John C. *The Winning Attitude: Your Pathway to Personal Success.* Nashville, TN: Thomas Nelson Publishing, 1996.

Parinello, Anthony. *Secrets of Vito: Think and Sell Like a CEO.* Irvine, CA: Entrepreneur Press, 2002.

Rackham, Neil. *The S.P.I.N. Selling Fieldguide: Practical Tools, Methods, Exercises and Resources.* New York: McGraw-Hill, 1996.

Ury, William. *Getting Past No: Negotiating Your Way From Confrontation to Cooperation.* New York: Bantam Doubleday Dell Publishing, 1993.

CLOSING
Marketing Tips for Your Business

*If you are planning on doing business with someone again,
don't be too tough in the negotiations.*

—MARVIN S. LEVIN

WHAT IS YOUR PROSPECT'S MOTIVATION?
$

In order to consistently and successfully sell a product or service you must understand the reason(s) prospects will buy—what is their motivation to buy? In a perfect selling environment each party has something the other party wants. The salesperson has a product or service that the prospect wants to buy, and the prospect has money that the salesperson wants in exchange for the product or service. It's a basic premise, however, in almost all selling situations the major challenge that salespeople face is the fact that they want the prospect's money much more than the prospect wants what the salesperson is selling. From the prospect's perspective this is partly due to influences such as competition, a lack of trust in the salesperson or the company, and fear of not truly understanding the product or service that is being offered. Consequently, throughout the years many sales techniques and closing methods have been

developed to tip the scales in favor of the salesperson or at least level the playing field between the salesperson and prospect. However, these same sales and closing techniques can only be useful to a salesperson who has taken the time to identify and understand what the target audience's motivation is for buying, the true reason they need or want a product or service. Therefore, to be successful in sales, you must be able to identify your prospect's motivation for buying and make this the basis or cornerstone of the entire sales cycle, from prospecting right through to the presentation, negotiations, closing, and the ongoing relationship after the sale.

CONFIRM THE DETAILS
$

Unfortunately, once in a while a good sale that you work hard on to close can quickly turn bad because of a small written or oral miscommunication between the salesperson and the prospect. The product was delivered at ten o'clock instead of nine o'clock, the color was blue instead of red, the customer said she wanted 20 gadgets but received and was consequently billed for 50. Theses simple examples are why it is wise to get in the habit of reconfirming all the details of the contract including price, product or service details, and delivery information. Basically, review all aspects of the sale with every client before potential disaster strikes and turns a good sale into a bad one. Taking the time to confirm all the details will go a long way to ensure that a small miscommunication error does not lead to a full-fledged customer service complaint. Or, worse a lost client because of the ensuing fallout that might erupt from the error or miscommunication. You should try to design your contract, proposal form, or bill of sale so that your customers must sign off on important details such as delivery times, financing details, and other key elements of the sale. Explain to your customers that this is an important part of your job because you want them to get exactly what they believe they are buying without exception. Your customers will appreciate the extra attention you pay to the details by reconfirming everything, as they will see the level of customer service and professionalism you use, which of course will be rewarded by customer loyalty and referrals.

SURVEY LOST SALES
$$ ⚒

More times than not, when a salesperson quotes or estimates on a job and does not close the sale, that is it, game over, no further communications with the prospect in the future. If this describes what happens when you do not close a sale then do whatever it takes to break the habit and in doing so greatly increase your potential closing referral rate on future sales presentations. Get started by creating a survey form along with a self-addressed stamped envelope and kindly ask prospects who did not buy from you to complete the survey and send it back. Ask questions on the survey form that will help you better understand why your prospects did not buy based on their responses. The questions you ask on the survey form will be relevant to your business, industry, and

what you sell, so carefully consider the type of information that would be helpful to know and a suitable question that would get the desired response. Let's face it, you would rather have closed the sale than have to ask prospects why they did not buy from you. But with that said, at least by surveying prospects to find out why they did not buy, you can gain valuable insights and knowledge you need so that you can make corrections or changes in the way you sell and or the products and services you sell. I have used this type of survey in the past frequently and always found the response good, in the range of 25 percent, making the exercise well worthwhile. Not winning jobs or orders is not the end of the world. However, not knowing why is, so get smart and find out directly from your prospects why they didn't do business with you. What you learn can be invaluable.

TALKING OWNERSHIP IS A BUYING SIGNAL
$ ⚒

Let's face it, knowing when to ask your prospects for the sale is one of the most important skills needed to succeed in sales and small business. Given that, here is one of the easiest and most common buying signals that can help you identify when your prospect is ready to buy or at least getting closer to a purchasing decision—when a prospect talks about or refers to taking ownership of the product or service that you are selling. Talking about ownership is a very strong buying signal, as generally your prospect has already determined and is satisfied that the product or service has met her needs, represents value, and taking ownership would be beneficial to her and have advantages or deliver the desired results she wants. For instance, in the appliance store a prospect looking over a dishwasher might say, "This is great, I won't have to wash dinner dishes by hand any more." Or, in the sporting goods store, a shopper kicking the tires of a bicycle might say something along the lines of, "I'll be able to take this bicycle with me on my camping vacation this summer." Both are clear examples of buying signals, as the prospects are talking about the benefits of taking ownership prior to actually purchasing the goods. Consequently, the next time your prospects start talking about taking ownership and the benefits of taking ownership of the product or service you are selling, you know that they are in fact sending you a clear signal that they are ready to buy. And that is your wake-up call to ask for the sale in no uncertain terms "Do you want to take it with you or shall I have it delivered?"

COMPREHENSIVE QUESTIONS ARE BUYING SIGNALS
$ ✎

You can usually boil down a prospect's questions into two main categories: surface questions and comprehensive questions. Surface questions are questions that ask for general information without probing a particular point about what you are selling in greater detail. Prospects ask surface questions to gain a general knowledge of what is being discussed, enough to understand and then continue on with the conversation. Comprehensive questions on the other hand are questions that your prospect will ask that go into greater detail about a particular point or points about your product, service, or proposal. For instance, a prospect may ask about a product warranty, and follow your response with a further product warranty question that goes deeper trying to flush out more detail about the warranty, and follow your response to that question with a further product warranty question that goes even deeper and so on. Some sales professionals refer to comprehensive questioning as the prospect talking himself into purchasing, or justifying the purchase. This is because as the comprehensive questions go deeper and deeper, prospects will eventually start to answer their own questions before you even have the opportunity to respond. The deeper the questions go in terms of one particular point or number of points during the presentation, the stronger the buying signal becomes and it is time to trial close. However, keep in mind that comprehensive questions are not objections; your prospect is not objecting to anything that you are saying or anything about your product or service. The client simply is trying to justify the purchase in a way that makes sense. Objections as a buying signal is explained below.

OBJECTIONS ARE BUYING SIGNALS
$ ✎

When prospects raise objections, especially a minor point objection during the closing segment of the sales presentation, what they are really telling you is that they are interested in taking ownership of what you are selling. It is a clear buying signal, but they are also letting you know that they are no pushover and what they are really saying is, "OK, I am interested, now do your job and convince me." This is the precise moment that separates the successful sales professionals who drive new Corvettes from the not-so-successful salespeople who drive rusty Pintos. Why you might ask? Because the professional salesperson loves objections and views them as a clear buying signal from a prospect. While the not-so-successful salesperson hates objections and regards them as an obstacle that the client cannot overcome and therefore will not close the sale. When a prospect says to me, "Look Jim I am not interested in what you have to sell, now for the last time leave me alone," this is not an objection; the signal that is clearly being sent is that the customer does not want to do business with me, period. However, when a prospect says, "Jim I am not going to buy because the price is just way to high." Now that is a buying signal loud and clear because he just told me that he wants to buy, and that the only thing stopping him from buying is a small concern about the price of what I am selling. Great. I am off to the races, now all I have to do is help the prospect understand the true value of what I am selling to justify the price and the deal is done. The moral of the story; welcome your prospects' objections and take them as a buying signal because of what the objections are telling you. They are saying they are still in the game and just want you to do what your are being paid to do—to help them understand and see things your way.

OFFERING REFERRALS IS A BUYING SIGNAL
$ ✎

Personally the buying signal that I like the best is when prospects give you a referral before they have even purchased what you are selling. The reason that I like this buying signal best is that it clearly illustrates to me that I have done my job properly. My prospect is so impressed with the entire buying process, even though there is no commitment yet, that she is prepared to reward me by helping to find new sources of business. And, just as important to the client is to help out the person who they refer to me.

The "offering a referral" buying signal is quite common. Usually a prospect will say something along the lines of "Wow, I know that my friend George would really like to have this gizmo, boy would it save him time." Nine times out of ten the prospect is so impressed with the advantages and benefits of your product or service and dealing with the salesperson that they are thinking about others, be it family, friends, or co-workers who would also benefit by taking ownership of your product or service. When prospects start offering referrals during a sales presentation get out your pen for two reasons. The first reason is to ask for the sale and to get them to sign the contract. And, the second reason is to write down the name and contact information of the referral they're giving so you can follow up with the referred person right away. Of course, it should go without saying that once you close any sale you should be asking for a referral regardless if your new customer if offering one or not.

ARRANGE FOR PROSPECTS TO MEET YOUR CUSTOMERS

$ ⚒

Let your best and most satisfied customers close prospects for you by arranging for the two parties to meet. This closing technique works great on prospects who are not quite ready to sign on the dotted line. There are numerous benefits to using this powerful closing technique.

- Your prospect will see and hear firsthand how your product or service has benefited another person. This makes the benefits and features of your product or service tangible; they now have proof directly from the source, proof that your printed or spoken words cannot supply.
- Your prospects will feel more confident knowing that they're not the first to buy, that someone has tested the waters before them and was satisfied with the results. This is extremely important due to that fact that the vast majority of people in society are not risktakers by nature—they want to know that what they are doing or buying is proven to work, be safe, be beneficial, or better yet, all combined.

- Your customers' enthusiastic testimonial and praise for your product or service and you as well can help motivate your prospect to buy, thus speeding up the sales cycle substantially.
- Giving a prospect full access to customers clearly demonstrates that you operate in a professional and, more important, honest and open manner with nothing to hide. Many salespeople fear "world collisions" between their prospects and current customers simply because they do not tell a consistent story. Keep your story honest and consistent with all prospects and customers and you will be able to benefit from them meeting each other.
- Your prospects will feel at ease knowing they are talking with someone who truly understands their circumstances as they share common problems. In effect this takes the selling pressure off of the relationship and allows finding solutions and beneficial results to become the common goal.

These are only a few benefits to having prospects meet your best customers to help close a sale; there are many more. However, you may even want a prospect to meet with a customer who was not completely satisfied with your product or service at first, but was won over and brought back on board by your commitment to customer service that resulted in a happy ending. I have taken prospects to meet with customers who were not initially 100 percent satisfied. And I can tell you firsthand that this tactic works extremely well to convince the prospect that at the end of the day there can sometimes be an unforeseen problem, but what really matters is how these challenges are dealt with and corrected to everyone's satisfaction.

EXTEND CREDIT TO CLOSE

$+ ⚒

Many small-business owners have a difficult time in securing credit lines or accounts with suppliers and banks, especially if the business is new and without a proven track record of honoring debt and paying for inventory, supplies, and services. This fact could be your golden opportunity to benefit and close more sales by providing your business prospects with a basic line of credit. Of course, you'll want to keep the amount of credit you offer small at first and conduct a very basic credit check. However, you will find that the vast majority of small-business owners will pay their bills on time, especially small-business owners who have a difficult time securing credit because by you paying on time and in full they improve their chances of securing higher and new lines of credit in the future with you and others. By taking a small chance and extending credit to a business that cannot secure credit on its own you can close a sale, and in all likelihood secure a customer for life in the process. The vast majority of small-business owners are fiercely loyal and will not forget the people who helped them to get started and to ultimately succeed.

CLOSE BY CHANGING PROSPECT'S EXPECTATIONS

$ ⌟

Changing your prospect's expectations can be an extremely powerful closing tool, but one that does require much practice to perfect. For example, most people will enter a shoe store to check out what's new in footwear and at most expect to purchase one pair of shoes. But what if the shoe salesperson focused on changing the prospect's expectations? Instead of focusing on selling shoes, the focus would be to persuade the prospect that purchasing more than one pair of shoes would be a wise decision for whatever reason is valid at that point. This technique works because when we have determined our expectation prior to shopping or making a purchase, we have set the parameters of what we expect will happen and what we expect to purchase. When that expectation is suddenly changed or influenced by a professional persuader it throws our thought pattern out of whack and, more importantly, changes our built-in defense mechanisms to salespeople, clearing the path or opening our minds to new ideas. The

easiest way to shift expectations is to tie in an excellent reason for the prospects to forget about why they are buying and motivate them to buy more than or something other than what they expected to purchase. The reason that is created to change expectations has to benefit the buyer more than anything else does in the sales equation. This could be a discount for buying more or a relevant incentive, such as buy the two pairs of shoes and receive a free ticket to a local running clinic or seminar. Once you have established what the prospects' expectations are you can then devise a plan to throw them slightly off balance by introducing something that will greatly change their expectations and in doing so greatly increase your odds of closing and at a higher value.

THE QUIET CLOSE

$ ⌟

Always ask for the sale but be quiet after you do. Even if you feel you have more to say, resist the urge to speak. This can be very difficult especially if you think there is one last point, benefit, or story that might sway your prospect's decision in your favor. The goal of the quiet close is to place your prospect in the position of having to make a decision, or in the least respond to the close question with an objection, which we all know is a buying signal and just a desire for further information or persuading. If you choose to talk after you ask for the sale, you negate the closing question thus the prospect is no longer bound to answer or respond to the closing question. Often if you have done your homework and have an in-depth knowledge about what you sell then you already will have a feeling of what the prospect will say or what objection(s) will be raised. So use this quiet time to think about what your response will be; a yes then proceed to paperwork, a no or objection then overcome and ask for the sale a second time. The majority of people do not like to be placed on the hot seat especially if all around them is quiet, waiting for them to reply. This works in your favor simply because a "yes, let's go ahead" gets them off the hot seat and out from under the spotlight. The quiet close should be used early in the presentation. Not only can it save you time should the prospect be ready to buy, but it can also help identify your prospect's key objection(s) and in doing so you keep the sales momentum moving forward and understand the position you must overcome.

THE TRIAL CLOSE

$ ⚒

The trial close is always a good way to determine early in the sales presentation if your prospect is ready to buy what you are selling. And the trial-closing question can be put across to prospects with something that is as simple as "OK, any questions before we do the paperwork?" If your prospect says nothing, then start completing the paperwork, get the signature, and be on your way. OK, now that is an overly simplified explanation of the trial close—or is it? In reality the trial close is exactly that: You ask for the sale regardless if you know what the answer from the prospect will be. Though if you have spent any time with your prospect to that point, which is generally the case, you will already have some idea of what her response will be. There are two reasons for asking a trial close question early in the sales presentation. First, your prospect might be just as eager as you are to get the deal closed but you will never know unless you take a quick moment to ask him for the sale. You must do this because few prospects will readily offer you the sale unless they are asked to do so. Second, think of all the time you can save. Why try to sell something to someone who is already ready to buy? You could actually end up talking yourself out of the sale if the wrong information surfaces during the presentation. The trial close can be used at any point during the sales presentation, just by asking your prospects if they would like to go ahead with the sale. However, be sure not to overuse this basic closing method too often in one presentation. If you cannot secure the sale with the trial close then move on to a more advanced closing technique.

THE ECHO CLOSE

$ ⚒

This closing technique is referred to as the "echo close" because when a prospect asks a questions that clearly sends a buying signal on their behalf you return the prospect's question in the form of a confirming question that requires a decision. For instance, a prospect might ask a window salesperson "Can I have these new windows installed within two weeks?" To which the window salesperson better reply, or echo, by asking, "If I can arrange to have the new windows installed within two weeks are you prepared to go ahead with the job?" In doing so the prospect is placed in a position of having to make a decision or raise an objection. Obviously if the answer is yes, the salesperson would get started on writing the order without hesitation. If objections are raised then you know exactly where you stand and what hurdles are left to overcome to close the sale. Be aware that there is one problem with the echo close: many salespeople fail to recognize when their prospect is sending a buying signal and therefore miss the opportunity to use the echo close. Now I say this because a natural response from a salesperson to the question above would be something along the lines of "I am not sure I will have to check with the installation manager and let you know." Now you can see that there is a vast difference in these two responses from the salesperson. The first clearly picks up on the prospect's buying signal by responding with an echo close. While the second response misses the target completely and leaves the prospect and the salesperson no closer to a confirmed sale or the installation of new windows, which is what both parties want to happen.

THE SUMMARY CLOSE

$ ⚒

The summary close is perhaps the most common closing technique and one of the easiest to master and use in most selling situations. In a nutshell, you carefully take note of the advantages, features, and benefits that your prospect found to be the most interesting, valuable, and useful about your product or service during your initial contact and during the sales presentation. You then use these points or "hot buttons" to close by restating or summarizing these benefits to the prospect at the end of your sales presentation. In doing so you place the emphasis on all the things that your prospect finds beneficial about your offering, while conveniently leaving out any disadvantages. Almost like a Benjamin Franklin close (see page 273), but without actually writing it down on paper and leaving the cons or disadvantages out of the picture completely. The key to successfully using the summary close is to really work the most important points that your prospects believe to be the most beneficial in their particular situation. You must constantly remind your prospect of these hot-button benefits throughout the presentation and get your prospect to reconfirm that indeed these are the most important and beneficial aspects to them. However, make sure not to totally ignore any small concerns they may have; you still have to be able to reduce concerns, obstacles, and objections down into easily digestible parts not for your benefit, but for your prospect's benefit.

THE TAKE-AWAY CLOSE

$ 🔨

One of the best ways to motivate people to make decisions that you want them to make is to tell them that they cannot have something, or that they cannot do something. This is called the "take-away close." For decades top hotels have trained front desk clerks to master the take-away close. Does this sound familiar?

> *Guest:* Do you have any rooms available?
> *Desk clerk:* Sorry. No, I do not think so. (dramatic pause) Wait let me check, maybe there has been a cancellation. If there is a room available do you want it?
> *Guest:* Yes, please.

Miraculously the clerk will find a room after a few moments of fidgeting with the computer and a few "it doesn't look good" sighs. Of course, the room that is suddenly available will be a premium room like a honeymoon or executive suite and will cost an extra $50 over a standard room. Hotels do this because they know that travelers are tired and more agreeable if they think that every hotel and motel in town is full. The thought of having to sleep in a car does not appeal to many people, a motivating

factor to buy. Not deceptive, just using effective closing skills that are required in the extremely competitive accommodation industry. Another example of the take-away close is to give your prospect something, providing they buy; the best something is generally money. For instance, if you sell hot tubs, at the beginning of the presentation (not during or near the close) in the showroom, at the trade show, or wherever the sales presentation was being conducted you could give your prospect a "$200 Hot Tub" coupon. The coupon could be redeemable or applied against the purchase of any hot tub in stock on that day. Now the prospect has something of value, namely $200 and if she does not buy a hot tub today you will take that $200 away. This is a powerful closing simply because no one wants to have something taken away, especially money once she already has it in her possession.

THE FEAR CLOSE

$ 🔨

Fear is an extremely powerful closing tool. It is often underutilized by the majority of sales people for various reasons, but mainly because they do not know how to use fear properly to close a sale. For proof of how powerful fear selling is, look no farther than peer pressure among kids. One child will do something that they normally would not do just because of peer pressure and the fear that if they do not do it they will not be accepted by the rest of the kids. This is merely an example of how fear can change the way we behave, but fear can also come in many other forms such as the fear of missed opportunity, the fear of poor health, the fear of what other people think about us, the fear of not understanding and so forth; fear represents many different things to many different people, yet is an emotion that at some point we are all influenced by. The fear close is obviously more productive for some salespeople than others. It would be very difficult to make a prospect fear not buying pair of shoes. However, place this same closing technique in the hands of a seasoned stockbroker and watch the success rate soar. The fear of not having money or not making money is by far the most compelling reason or way to motivate people to do what you want them to do. But there are also other ways to introduce and use fear to close a sale such as the car salesperson who uses fear of an auto accident to persuade a young family to purchase a vehicle with a five-star safety rating or the property developer who uses the fear associated with a violent society to sell houses in gated and security patrolled community or, the roofing salesperson who uses the fear of what damage can be caused to the interior of a home because of water ingress to motivate the homeowner to replace her old roofing shingles. I suppose you can develop ways to use fear-based selling techniques for nearly any product or service if you thought about it long enough. However, with that comes a great responsibility to be honest and only use fear as a selling or motivation tool because there are underlying issues that are real and should be feared.

THE CHIP-AWAY CLOSE

$ ⚒

Another great closing technique is to lead your prospect to agree to a few small or minor points during the sales presentation prior to asking for the entire sale. This method is referred to as the "chip-away close." By getting the prospects to agree to small or minor points about your product or service during the course of the sales presentation you are actually gently leading them to a buying decision. What makes this such a powerful closing technique is the fact that you are greatly reducing the risk to the buyers—you are not placing them in a situation of having to say yes to the entire deal all at once, but only to small pieces of the deal along the way, the least risky elements of course. These small non-threatening pieces of the deal that you want them to agree to could include the color of the item, delivery schedules, product features, or warranty information. Try to get your prospect to agree to at least four or five minor points during the sales presentation and restate the benefits of these minor points prior to asking for the sale. Often you will find the prospect becomes used to saying yes and along the way a trust relationship begins to form as you eliminate risk and doubt and subliminally show the prospect that saying

yes does not have to be difficult or have dire consequences.

THE ALTERNATE-CHOICE CLOSE

$ ⚒

Many top-producing sales professionals have built their entire selling career on mastering and applying the "alternate-choice" closing technique. Like the name suggests this technique is nothing more than giving your prospect more than one option regarding the product or service you sell. By doing so and asking a question similar to "so which choice would you prefer?" you pull the prospects into making a buying decision and selecting one of the choices presented to them; not buying is no longer an available option, based on the alternate-choice closing question. Likewise, the alternate-choice close can also be used effectively to increase the quantity of a particular product that you want your prospect or customer to buy. For instance, a sales clerk in the sporting goods shop might ask "Will that be one dozen golf balls or two dozen?" Once again, pulling the customer into a buying decision of having to choose a quantity of golf balls. But not purchasing is still not an available option, based on the question and this closing technique. The alternate-choice close works best when you truly have the prospects' undivided attention and they have shown great interest in your product or service. However, keep in mind that you do not want to introduce so many choices that your prospect becomes confused or overwhelmed by having to make the decision. Introducing two or three alternatives is about the limit before the close starts to lose its effectiveness.

THE IN-HINDSIGHT CLOSE

$ ⚒

What would you have done differently in your life if you had access to a crystal ball? Perhaps you would have purchased shares of Microsoft stock way back when they were trading for a buck and before they split ten for one numerous times. In hindsight we all wish that at various times in our lives that we would have made different decisions or choices, taken a different path than we did, or taken advantage of an opportunity that we did not when we had a chance to do so. No one person is immune to these kinds of thoughts and this fact is the basis of a very powerful closing technique known as the "in-hindsight close." When prospects are indecisive about going ahead with a purchase or about upgrading to a better and more expensive model try the in-hindsight close as a way to persuade them to make the desired decision, which more times than not will be the right decision anyway. The true power of this closing technique is being able to make what you sell relevant to an in-hindsight decision. For instance, if you sell camping trailers and your prospect is having a difficult time deciding between the smaller cheaper model or the larger more expensive model, you might say something along the lines of "Mr. Jones, I know that this is a difficult decision for you. But I don't want you to look back two years from now and say, 'In hindsight I wish that I would have purchased the bigger camping trailer, but now it is too late.' Because I have a feeling that is what might happen." Or, for another example, I remember when my wife and I were in the market to purchase our first home. We had narrowed the field down to two choices. The only problem was that one of the houses we liked was considerably more money than we wanted to spend, but of course was also the home we both liked much better. Upon crunching the numbers our real estate agent figured out that the mortgage on the house we liked better would cost about $350 more each month. At the time this was a lot of money, so we made the decision that we would have to forget about the more expensive house that we liked better and instead consider the less expensive house as our only option. At this point our real estate agent made a suggestion that was the in-hindsight close. He said that while $350 a month was more than we wanted to spend at that moment, we must keep in mind that our incomes would be rising annually, while the mortgage on the more expensive home would remain the same and eventually drop. So in effect the extra $350 a month would be short-term pain, and that soon our income would increase enough to cover that extra amount monthly. He was right. In hindsight we are glad we decided to spend a

little extra and get what we wanted, instead of saving a little over the short term but being stuck with something we weren't as happy with for the long term.

THE YES CLOSE
$ ⬉

Much like the summary close, the yes close is designed to have the same impact and power of persuasion on the prospect. The key to using the yes close successfully is to make sure that you have fully flushed out the prospect's needs and explained the benefits of what you are selling in such as way that the prospect agrees and is excited about what the product or service will do for her. Once this is complete then you can develop a series of questions that you ask the prospect and her answers will restate the benefits of your product and service and how this meets, and if possible exceeds her needs. Here is an example of how a series of questions posed by the salesperson can be used to get the prospect to respond yes, eventually leading to the close.

Salesperson: Ms. Jones you did say that you liked the high safety rating our van has?

Ms. Jones: Yes. Safety is very important to me.

Salesperson: Me too. And you like the fact that it comes with a five-year warranty?

Ms. Jones: Yes. I am sick of my old car constantly breaking down.

Salesperson: You won't have to worry about that anymore, this van is guaranteed not to break down. You also said that you liked our low interest financing that we have available for our best customers like you?

Ms. Jones: Yes. I can't even get that low of a financing rate at my bank.

Salesperson: Great. I see we agree then, this van is perfect for your family needs.

In this example, you can see that by asking a series of questions that you know the prospect will say yes to (because these points have already been flushed out during the qualifying process) the prospect is left with no decision but to proceed with the purchase. Not to proceed would mean that she has lied to herself or the salesperson. Additionally, these are small nonthreatening points to say yes to. You're not asking for the sale yet and every time the prospect restates or responds yes to what she likes the best about what you are selling it takes you one step closer to the sale.

THE ASSUMPTION CLOSE
$ ⚒

The assumption close is the one that I learned to master early in my business career and the closing technique that I personally use the most often. Using the assumption close means that you simply assume that every prospect you present to will buy and you do this by making statements during the presentation like "I will have this shipped to you buy the end of the week." Or, "I just need a simple signature on this agreement so we can start processing your order." If your prospect says nothing or is agreeable then complete the paperwork, avoid further conversation about the job or order, thank him for his business, and move on to your next presentation. If your prospect raises any objections then you will know exactly where you stand and what you must do or say to overcome these objections or obstacles to close the sale. The assumption close is especially effective once you have established a working relationship with a repeat client who frequently orders from you. In these selling situations always use the assumption close and automatically write their order, don't even give the hint that there is a choice involved—the only decision is how many or how much to order and if you are bold you can also assume that decision for your client. You can also cleverly build to an assumption close by asking your prospect small and nonthreatening questions as you do such as, "What is today's date?" As you are filling out the paperwork or contract, continue to ask a few more questions such as "That's two L's in Fellows right?"

THE CHANCES-ARE CLOSE
$ ⚒

The next time you are in a sales presentation and facing the "Let me think about it" obstacle, counter by asking your prospect "Sure no problem, but tell me what are the chances that you will go ahead with this purchase?" Generally you will find that if for no other reason then to appease, your prospect will respond by saying, "It's looking pretty good" or something similar. Now, if the response is favorable as illustrated in this example then suggest to your prospect that you go ahead and write the order or complete the paperwork. And reinforce this suggestion quickly with a follow-up statement such as, "It will save us having to get back together to complete it later." Now you have placed your prospect in the position of having to state her true objection to the sale and not rely on the "let me think about it" excuse. Or, she will simply agree to what seems to be a very logical request if her intentions are indeed to go ahead with the purchase. Especially if you tell her that if for any reason she decides not to go ahead you will just tear up the contract no questions asked. The main objective of the chances-are closing technique is to get some kind of physiological commitment from your prospect, because once you have it few will go back on the commitment they made because they will feel as though they are bound to the deal. Think of it this way, if you tell a friend that you will help him move, then you have made a psychological commitment to that person that you are not likely to break even if you do not want to help him move. The chances-are close is built on the same premise.

THE 30-MINUTE FOLLOW-UP CLOSE
$ ⚒

Many prospects often will have committed to or made a decision about whether or not to buy within 30 minutes after a sales meeting or presentation, especially when it comes to purchasing consumer goods. Therefore, wise sales professionals have learned that following up with prospects within 30 minutes after a sales presentation is a highly effective way to close the sale. The difficulty often comes in justifying to your prospect the reason for the quick follow-up. However, there are a few easy ways to navigate these murky waters. The first is to leave something behind at the presentation such as your eyeglasses or a favorite writing pen, then use the item that you "accidentally" left behind as the reason for the follow-up call and a segue to asking for the close on the phone. Or, alternately go back to retrieve the forgotten item and ask for the sale in person. Another valid reason for the follow-up call is to state that it is company policy, set at the top to ensure 100 percent customer service and complete understanding of the products or services as they were presented. This is a great approach as not only does it open the lines of communication with the prospect once more, but also provides an opportunity to close the sale; and it illustrates your and your company's commitment to customers. Regardless of the approach you use to follow up and get back in front of prospects within 30 minutes after the presentation, the fact remains that many people will make buying decisions within that timeframe after a sales meeting or presentation, providing an incredible opportunity for you to take advantage of the situation and close.

THE COMPLIMENT CLOSE
$ ⚒

Everyone likes to be complimented, on their looks, their intelligence, their expertise, their homes, their offices, and more. In fact, some people are so ego driven that the conversation must be revolving around them all the time, and the moment that it is not they quickly find a way to get the spotlight back on themselves and nothing else. Which is actually great. Get to know this personality type for the simple reason that when your prospects are this kind of person you can often close the sale with little more than complimenting them by making them out to be an expert, important, and very special to be around. Likewise, the same can be said about people with low self-esteem; they also will respond favorably to a compliment or two from you. Now this is not to say that you must be constantly complimenting your prospects and customers in rapid succession; you will come off as phony and insincere. However, be on the lookout for nice things to say about people, their surroundings, or their families. Basically, be a nice and likable person and people will always

respond favorably to you and your compliments because they believe them to be honest and sincere. Let's face it, half of the battle in sales has little if anything to do with what you are selling, how much it costs, and in what color it is available. Much has to do with whether people like you, because people want to do business with people they like. Would you do business with someone you didn't like, or you thought didn't like you?

THE "CLOSE EVERYONE AROUND THE DECISION MAKER" CLOSE
$ ⚒

Take a strength-in-numbers approach as a way to close more sales by first closing everyone around the decision maker. While you may be very persuasive and an excellent closer, you will never be as good of a professional persuader as the person who is standing next to the decision maker on a regular basis. And more importantly the same person who has established a trust relationship with that decision maker, be it an employee, friend, or family member. When Mom says no to the kids, the kids instantly go to work on Dad because they realize they need an ally in their corner, someone who can champion their cause, make it his own, and help to close the true decision maker. Of course, once Dad has been successfully recruited, the kids then send him in to close the sale, often with success, but not before a lot of promises and compromises on other nonrelated issues such as painting the garage, mowing the lawn, and a few others. For that reason, it is important to get the entire family involved in the buying process, as they may have much more influence on the buying decision than you think they might have. Therefore, don't take any chances and be sure to close everyone around the decision maker so that you will have numerous allies in your corner and championing your cause.

THE BENJAMIN FRANKLIN CLOSE
$ ⚒

The Benjamin Franklin, commonly known as the T balance account close, is another time-tested successful closing technique that many salespeople still rely on today. This closing technique got its name from the manner in which Benjamin Franklin would reach decisions. He would draw a line down the middle of a piece of paper and in the left-hand column list the pros, or the positive benefits or advantages that would be derived by saying yes to a particular decision that he had to make. In the right-hand column he would list the cons, or how this decision would have a negative impact on his life, business, or family, and any disadvantages that would be a direct result of his decision. If the pros or beneficial advantages outnumbered the cons or disadvantages then he would make the decision to proceed. If the cons outnumbered the pros he would not proceed. Now here is where it gets a little tricky. You can fill in the pros and cons for the prospects or you can give them the paper, hand them a pen, and have them fill in the pros and cons. The danger in both cases is that you reveal the cons and highlight them for the prospect. Of course, the premises behind the success of the technique is that if you have done your homework identifying the prospect's wants and needs then the pros will far outnumber the cons and make the decision to proceed a logical one for the prospect. Personally, I have used this closing technique with success. However, when I fill in the pros in the left column I write larger and bolder and often place a star beside the benefit word or phrase. And in the cons column I tend to write smaller, almost faint and illegible as to distract from the impact of the negative word or phrase. Likewise, if you choose to use this closing technique make sure that you push every hot button and consistently hammer the benefits in the pros column while ignoring the disadvantages in the cons column.

WEB RESOURCE

↗ www.smallbizbooks.com: Online retailer of business specific books and guides.

THE FISH-OUT-OF-WATER CLOSE
$ ↖

Another highly effective closing strategy is to get your prospect out of her usual environment or out of a defensive environment that she controls. This is especially important for business-to-business sales as often your prospect—be it the CEO or senior or middle management—will associate her office or the boardroom with a defensive position in terms of meeting with salespeople. In her mind this particular location is a battlefield and there must be winners and losers. So if you can take her away from the battlefield, you have a better probability of getting her to drop her natural defenses to the sale, at least to a certain degree.

Even from a selling-to-consumers standpoint the fish-out-of-water close can also be an effective closing technique. Great automobile salespeople know that they have to get you in that new car and off the lot and away from the showroom right away on a test drive. The majority of people associate the car lot or dealership showroom as a battlefield; they want to pay less for the car and you want them to pay more. So once again the prospect is in a defensive position long before negotiations even start. Therefore, get your prospects out of their usual environment, or create a more pleasant environment to assist with closing the sale. I used to take prospects out for a sail on my boat; instantly they would drop their natural defenses to buying and enjoy the sail. Of course, along the way we would discuss the deal and before we tied up back at the marina I would always have a signed contact and a new customer. All my clients loved it and thought it was a great change of pace and scenery: often they would suggest that our next meeting should also be out on the water and they would bring along a co-worker, a spouse, or another family member. This is not to say that by simply getting your prospects away from an environment that they associate with having to be on the defensive will automatically close the sale for you. Obviously this closing technique, like all others, is only a cog in a much larger sales closing machine. It is completely useless if you don't take the time to identify what your prospect's motivations are for wanting to buy from you.

THE CONVENIENCE CLOSE
$ ↖

Often people will make buying decisions based on nothing more than the convenience of the buying process. How many times have you chosen to buy at one shop instead of another because there was lots of free and convenient parking? Or, the shop's operating hours conveniently fit in with your schedule, or they offered free delivery and set-up, which was perfect because you own a hatchback and have two left thumbs when it comes to product assembly? Most people base buying decisions on convenience, whether consciously or subconsciously. Consequently, from a professional salesperson's perspective it is a wise move to make it as easy as possible for all prospects to say yes by making it as convenient as possible for them to do so.

- If permits or licenses are required to buy what you are selling then secure these items for your prospect or help him through the entire process of securing any required documents.
- Meet with prospects at times and locations that are convenient for them, not you. The very first sales job I had was selling household appliances. I was 19 years old at the time and received a call from a couple asking how to get to our showroom on public transit because they didn't have a car. I asked a few qualifying questions and then suggested that I would pick them up personally the next day and take them to the showroom to talk about their appliance needs and show them the floor models. The following day I picked them up as arranged, we went to the showroom and within an hour they purchased. Our prices were not the lowest, nor was the quality of the appliances the best. But the buying process was so convenient that the prospects were left no option but to buy. The decision was made easy because I went out of my way to make the sales process convenient.
- Complete warranty cards and registration for customers.
- Arrange for any pre- and postinspections that might be required.
- Arrange financing for prospects if they need financing.

These ideas are only the tip of the iceberg; in effect, you want to create a convenient buying atmosphere that requires your prospects to do nothing but sign the contract and enjoy the benefits of what they have purchased. This extremely easy closing technique works wonders; go the extra mile to make it as easy as you can for people to buy and a certain percentage will buy based on nothing more than the convenience of the process.

THE COMPROMISE CLOSE
$ ⚒

You want one thing and your prospect will want another; this is called negotiations. Negotiation isn't always in direct response to money, but usually money is one of the negotiation factors. You want more of it and your prospect wants to hand over less of it. The compromise close is an effective closing technique providing it is not based on giving a discount that can become habitual and cost you bottom-line profits and commissions as a result. The best way to compromise a close is when both parties get something of perceived value. Obviously to you it will mean the sale, full payment, and a profit. To the prospect this could mean additional features, a lower financing rate, or a value-added product or service such as free delivery or an extended warranty. Always have the proverbial ace up your sleeve, a compromise that can be used to close the sale at the appropriate time. You state your case to your prospect in many ways such as "if I can find a way to extend the warranty period at no additional cost would you be happy with this arrangement?" Or, "I would like to suggest that we make a compromise. I know that a lower price is very important to you, but unfortunately my fair pricing structure leaves no room for a discount. But if I can arrange to break the total investment into three equal payments would you be willing to work with me on that?" Once again, in sales negotiations and closing there must be two winners, never one. Both sides have to be prepared to negotiate and compromise in good faith. Knowing this is what makes the compromise close an excellent backup strategy so that you do not leave the table empty-handed.

THE MAKE-A-SUGGESTION CLOSE
$ ⚒

Not all people are comfortable with making decisions. Often in a sales presentation or meeting situation this can cause your prospect to come across as uninterested and aloof, when in fact he just may be unsure of and uncomfortable with the process and with making buying decisions. There are many personality types and you must be able to effectively deal with each and not place all prospects into the same mold. Learn to identify this personality type and by doing so you can begin to use the "Can I make a suggestion?" closing technique. When you see that your prospect is uncomfortable in the selling/buying relationship, ask "Do you mind if I make a suggestion?" More times than not you will see instant relief wash over your prospect's face as he eagerly agrees to listen to your suggestion. At this point simply tell him what and why you think he should buy. Remember that making a suggestion that someone buy from you is not a bad thing, it is your job. We have all made bad decisions in the past and wished that someone at the time had helped us see the way to the right decision by making a suggestion. So as long as your intentions are honest and you believe that your suggestion is the right decision for your prospect and his situation, then by all means when a prospect is struggling to make the right decision then help him do it by making a suggestion. I know that from my own experiences in these situations, once I have made suggestions to my prospects about what I think they should buy and why, they are for the most part very grateful that I helped them understand better and interpreted what they were thinking.

THE CASTING-DOUBTS CLOSE
$ ⚒

The casting-doubts close is a super advanced closing technique that requires much practice in order to master properly. Think of the main reasons prospects will object to moving forward with the sale. One will be the fear of the unknown or the fear of doubt because we fear what we don't understand, it is human nature. Take this proven concept, but instead of allowing your prospect to have the exclusive right to use it, use it yourself by casting doubt on any bid, proposal, or estimate your prospect has from competitors (but not your own). Play the devil's advocate about the competition. Use gentle and subtle statements like "I

never knew they did that type of work," or, "they must be spreading their wings." The idea is to cast doubt on the competitor's bid while continually restating the benefits of your products and services. Once again, this is a very advanced closing technique that takes time in order to properly use and master it. Many times I have closed deals simply by casting doubts on my competitor's ability to successfully complete a project. I do it in such a way as not to bash the competition, but rather raise suspicions and with that fear. So the more doubt that you can cast on your competition's ability to perform, the more your prospect will fear a decision and leave the door open wider for acceptance of your bid or proposal.

THE LAST-ONE-IN CLOSE
$ ⚒

I have always believed that every selling opportunity deserves just one last kick at the can in terms of closing the deal. For that reason I have always practiced the "last-one-in close," a technique that you may also find helps you to close more sales and secure more referrals in the process. This is a very uncomplicated strategy; in fact the last-one-in close is nothing more than getting a commitment from your prospects that they will not make a buying decision until they have spoken to you last. Believe it or not this actually works and most won't buy from a competitor until they have spoken to you one last time for two reasons. One, they don't know what you have up your sleeve, why do you want to speak to them last, a special offer perhaps? Mystery and suspense are great for keeping prospects involved and invested in the sales process, or more importantly involved in your sales process. Secondly, if you have done all your homework properly and taken the steps necessary to establish a trusting relationship with your prospects, then to a certain degree they will feel obligated to meet with you and hear you out one last time. Being the last one in or last persuader to speak with a prospect enables you to play the devil's advocate in terms of competitors' bids, and also enables you one last opportunity to persuade your prospects to your way of thinking. Once I realized the power of this closing technique my closing ratio increased from 40 percent to in excess of 60 percent. Which for the construction and renovation industry where prospects commonly secure six quotes or more on a job, is an incredible closing ratio, even more so as I was always one of the highest quotes in terms of cost on the project.

THE EVENT CLOSE
$$ ✎

Use event marketing as an opportunity to close prospects who are indecisive about going ahead with the sale. Let's say that you are participating in or hosting a trade show, seminar series, workshop, or training class; invite your prospects to attend and use the heightened excitement surrounding the event to close the deal that you have on the go with these prospects. This closing technique is especially effective if you can mix current clients with the prospects you want to close. Often in these situations you will find that your current clients' satisfaction with the product or service they buy from you will rub off on your prospect. Meaning that your prospect will see and learn firsthand how your customers benefit from your product or service and from doing business with you. This is powerful marketing because no longer are you in the position of having to persuade prospects, your customers are doing it for you. And often this can have more impact on prospects because they share common problems and challenges with your customers that they do not share with you. However, as a cautionary note, never invite prospects to events where your competition will also be exhibiting or marketing. You do not want to inadvertently send your prospects to your competition and risk losing the sale and perhaps a long-term selling opportunity.

THE MAXIMUM BENEFIT CLOSE
$$+ ✎ ☎

In today's super competitive selling and business environment, more companies and professional salespeople are starting to use the maximum-benefit close more than ever because it works. For those not familiar with this closing technique, it simply means that you go to great lengths to ensure that your prospect will get the maximum benefits from owing and using your product or service. And you introduce these maximum benefits that you develop to your prospects as a method to close the sale. Think of the maximum benefit as the ace up your sleeve that you remove precisely at the right time to wow the prospect and close the deal. For instance, a recreational vehicle dealer might include a driver training program with every new or used motor home sold and use this maximum benefit to close more sales—not only can this type of specialized training potentially save their lives in hazardous driving conditions when driving a new, unfamiliar, and oversized vehicle, but also it will ensure that the buyer will get the maximum benefit from the RV by knowing how to operate and maintain it properly so that it will provide many years of safe travel enjoyment for the entire family. Creating your own maximum benefit can also be a great way to separate your business, products, and services from your competitors,' making the effort more than worthwhile.

THE PRODUCTIVITY CLOSE
$ ✎

Selling to business owners and managers must be done on a logical level as opposed to selling on an emotional level, as often is the case of selling to non-business consumers. This means that CEOs, small-business owners, and managers want to hear how much money they can save or how much money they can make by purchasing a product or service or ultimately both if you can orchestrate that. The easiest way for salespeople to turn this fact into a closing technique is to translate the key benefits of their product or service into productivity terms, because that is what businesspeople understand and want to hear. Use charts, graphs, case studies, and client testimonials to illustrate how your product or service will boost productivity, thus earning the business-people more profits or saving them hard cash. Here is an example that is perhaps the toughest sale that one could make to business in order to make my point. A fitness equipment retailer wanted to sell more fitness equipment, but the consumer market locally was very competitive and to a large degree saturated. Knowing this the retailer decides that perhaps selling the fitness equipment to local small businesses and corporations is the answer. A plan is developed and the retailer calls on a local business to pitch the fitness equipment not as what would normally be considered as a consumer purchase but as a very worthwhile business purchase that can potentially increase profits. How? Using scientific data the retailer proves to the business owner that increased employee fitness levels are proven to reduce on-the-job injuries, reduce stress, and result in fewer employee sick days—all of which increase employee productivity, and thus efficiency and profitability for the business. The business owner agrees that this may just work and orders $20,000 worth of fitness equipment to be installed at the workplace and hires a fitness consultant as suggested by the retailer to develop an exercise and fitness regimen for employees who want to participate. Anything can be sold to businesses when increased productivity and profitability is the carrot dangling at the end of the line. I can tell you firsthand that it works as a closing technique. This example is in fact real and the plan to sell the fitness equipment to corporations was hatched over lunch one day by me and a friend who owns the store. When selling to businesses always keep in mind that you must find ways for them to do things easier, faster, with less headache, with less competition, and above all that it will make the business more efficient, productive, and profitable.

THE TRY-BEFORE-YOU-BUY CLOSE
$+ ✎

There is no mystery to the fact that if you can get people to try what you are selling and they like it and benefit because of this trial period, there is a good chance that they will purchase the product or service so that they can continue to benefit after the trial period is over. That is the basis of this powerful closing technique known as the try-before-you-buy close. When I think of the try-before-you-buy close I am always reminded of one of my dad's businesses, which was the sales of canoes, kayaks, and related

accessories. He has never claimed to be a professional salesperson; in fact his motto has always been if you like it then buy it, and if you don't like it then don't buy it. Yet this motto is what made him a very effective salesperson for the simple fact that rather than trying to sell the benefits and features of his canoes, he would let prospects decide for themselves. He did this by letting potential customers take a canoe home or away for a few days to use it on a trial basis, and if they liked it they simply paid him and kept the canoe. And if they didn't like it they brought it back and were off the hook; that was pretty much his entire sales and closing strategy, but it worked. Almost all bought. How could they not after spending a peaceful few days gliding effortlessly across the water? Who wouldn't want to be able to do that every weekend? Now obviously the try-before-you-buy close is not suitable for all products and services, but for many it will work. This closing technique works because you get your prospects involved and invested in the product or service and the buying process. Once again, if someone benefits and likes what they are using, it becomes pretty tough to say no when the time comes to buy. Here are a few products and services where you might be able to take advantage of this closing technique.

- Recreational products: anything from boats, to campers, to bicycles
- Educational products: audiotapes, books, and software
- Entertainment products: music CD's, musical instruments, home electronics, satellite televisions, and opera tickets
- Health products: massagers, scooters, lifts, and spas
- Training services: everything from cooking classes, to karate classes, to fitness classes

Think of it this way: There is no greater way to reduce the doubt involved with a potential purchase than by letting a potential customer use a product or service on a trial basis.

THE WHAT-WILL-IT-TAKE CLOSE
$ ✎

When all else fails and you feel as though you have nothing to lose simply ask your prospect "What will it take to close this deal?" I have even asked prospects "I've done everything I can, turned over every rock, and bent over backward trying to figure out a way we can make this thing work for both of us. At this point I'm at a bit of a loss so I ask you from your perspective what do you think that we have to do to move forward?" The answer can sometimes be very surprising. And more often than not it will have nothing to do with price and everything to do with a lingering problem, doubt, or small need or concern that your prospect still has and that was overlooked during the lead-up to and during the sales presentation. By asking this type of "help me to help you" question you place the prospect on the spot of having to reveal what would be required to close the sale. Obviously, sometimes you'll find out that there is nothing that can be done to close the sale. That's fine, but at least you have reached the point where you can then focus on securing referrals and spending your time where it will have the biggest impact on sales with other prospects. Of course, once your prospect has revealed what it will take to close the deal and if you feel that you can meet this request, then make sure to maximize your odds of closing by asking your prospect one more simple question: "If I can make that happen are you prepared to complete this deal right now?"

GREAT FOLLOW-UP TRICKS
$$ ✎

Top salespeople know and have learned through years of practical experience that you cannot close every sale at the time of presentation and that it often requires one or more follow-up meetings, visits, or calls to get the job done. For that reason, the following are a few great follow-up tricks that you can utilize to maximize the use of your "follow-up time" and close more sales.

- Start by developing a complete follow-up system that includes an overall follow-up plan, follow-up schedule, and a tracking system so that you will know who, when, and how to follow up with your hottest prospects and best customers.
- Always set aside enough time to properly follow up with each new prospect and existing customer, regardless if it is by telephone or in person. Never rush the follow-up meeting, as every contact that you make with prospects and clients must be regarded as a new fact-finding mission, an opportunity to learn how to better understand your prospects' needs so you can create reasons for them to buy—and so you serve your customers better so that they will buy more and more frequently.
- Always let your prospects or customers set the pace of the follow-up meeting so it will give them the opportunity to cover the issues they want to clarify or touch on, and not just what you want to cover.
- Create a system for recording the details of follow-up meetings and calls; a prospect and customer management database is best but a spiral notepad will work to get you up and running. The information you record can be used to better understand prospect and customer needs as well as help choose proper methods for reaching your clients for direct-marketing purposes.
- Keep a list of your hottest prospects with you at all times, those with the greatest chance of closing. Use the majority of your follow-up time where it will have the biggest benefits in terms of sales. Use any down time to work on these files and ways to close your hot prospects.
- Listen closely to what prospects and customers are telling you so that you can create a follow-up and contact plan based on each individual's needs and conveniences and not just what suits you or that is convenient for you.
- Never procrastinate, follow-up is as important as any other part of the sales cycle. Remember following up with a prospect or customer after a meeting is very easy, so just do it. If you choose not to follow up, be assured that your competition will take every available opportunity to follow up.
- Never follow up with a prospect without a great reason. If you don't you will come off as pushy and a time waster. The best reason to contact prospects or customers is to give them information that will benefit them. So instead

of spending your time wondering and worrying if you should contact a prospect or customer, maximize the use of your time by thinking or creating ways that your contact will be beneficial. Know what you want and how you will lead them to what you want.

- Create a plan so that each follow-up contact with prospects will result in getting one step closer to closing the sale. Follow-up means that you are inching forward not backward. The same holds true with clients; every contact you make with them should result in strengthening the relationship, and persuading them to buy more and more often.

- When you make a promise to prospects or customers that you will do something for them, find out information for them, or whatever that promise might be, always follow through on these promises and commitments. The vast majority of sales that do not close during the sales presentation, but could easily be closed through follow-up contact and meetings do not close because the salesperson did not follow through with something as they promised they would. You cannot differentiate between 1 percent and 99.9999 percent closed, as both mean the same, which is no sale. A closed sale is 100 percent and more often than not that can only be achieved by following through on promises and commitments.

WEB RESOURCE

⟡ www.entrepreneur.com: Online business resource center.

MAKE THEM ALL TRUE BELIEVERS
$ ⚒

Let go of the concept of selling and embrace the concept of making them all true believers. No one wants to be sold. Being sold means you have lost control, your will is weak, and you have been taken for the proverbial ride. Regardless if you believe this to be true or not, perception prevails. One of life's greatest contradictions is selling. Society in general

goes to great lengths to distance itself from the salesperson, an arm's length relationship like the strange cousin to whom no one wants to admit being related. But if you step back and analyze this you'll quickly discover that we are all salespeople. We sell ourselves daily—to an employer: why we deserve a raise; to a potential spouse; why we would make a good life partner; to family: why we will miss that special occasion; to a product or service: supplier why we need and deserve special payment or delivery terms. Therein lies the contradiction, society distances itself from the salesperson yet we are all salespeople as living life is a constant state of persuading others to share our points of view or beliefs. It's often been said that nothing in the world would happen without salespeople, and this is true. However, the fact remains that selling to or being sold generally has negative attachments. Wherein not selling to, but making customers, friends, family, and business alliances true believers in you, your business, and your products or services is viewed positively. Think of it this way: When people truly believe in what you do and what you have to offer they in effect become your fan club. Attempting to make others true believers only works if you truly believe in yourself and your products or services. Once you have let go of the concept of selling and embraced the concept of making them all true believers the path to success will become apparent.

📖 SUGGESTED ADDITIONAL READING

Blachard, Kenneth H., Sheldon Bowles, and Harvey Mackay. *Raving Fans: A Revolutionary Approach to Customer Service*. New York: William Morrow & Company, 1993.

Gitomer, Jeffrey H. *The Sales Bible*. New York: William Morrow & Company, 1994.

Hopkins, Tom. *How to Master the Art of Selling*. New York: Warner Books, 1994.

———. *Sales Closing for Dummies*. New York: John Wiley & Sons, 1998.

Kennedy, Dan. *No B.S. Sales Success*. North Vancouver, BC: Self Council Press, 1999.

Parinello, Anthony. *Secrets of Vito: Think and Sell Like a CEO*. Irvine, CA: Entrepreneur Press, 2002.

Salant, Priscilla. *How To Conduct Your Own Surveys*. New York: John Wiley & Sons, 1994.

Schiffman, Stephen. *Closing Techniques: That Really Work*. Avon, MA: Adams Media Inc., 1999.

Singer, Blair. *Sales Dogs: You Do Not Have to Be an Attack Dog to Be Successful in Sales*. New York: Warner Books, 2001.

Tracy, Brian. *Advanced Selling Strategies: The Proven Systems of Sales Ideas, Methods and Techniques Used by Top Salespeople Everywhere*. New York: Fireside, 2001.

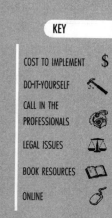

KEY

COST TO IMPLEMENT $

DO-IT-YOURSELF

CALL IN THE
PROFESSIONALS

LEGAL ISSUES

BOOK RESOURCES

ONLINE

CREATIVE SELLING
Marketing Tips for Your Business

I buy when other people are selling.

—John Paul Getty

THE ART OF DUPLICATION
$ 🔨

Much of what we do in life is simply duplication of an original action that we have learned. Like learning to walk and talk, once you have mastered it you pretty much have it down pat for life barring unforeseen catastrophic events. So it stands to reason if you can sell your product or service once, then selling it a second, third, fourth time, and so on should not be a problem, right? In theory yes but in practice no, simply because the vast majority of salespeople do not view the act of selling as being that simplistic. In fact it is that simplistic, hence the old adage "keep it simple, stupid." Many people have tried selling as a career only to give up a week, month, or year later because they were not selling and not generating an income. However, most failed to realize that if you can sell your product or service once, then the second time should be no more than duplicating your efforts you used during the first sale. Perhaps this is

oversimplifying the selling process, but for argument's sake the theory is sound; if you can do something once then repeating it only requires the duplication of the act itself. That said, you must be aware of this and be prepared to duplicate your efforts. This means you must carefully write down exactly what you did step by step, point by point in order to duplicate successes in sales. And from your notes you can begin to develop routines, systems, key qualifying information, closing techniques that work for what you sell, and you can begin to identify common objections and obstacles and therefore anticipate these and have solutions ready to overcome them.

CONSULTING? APPLY FOR A JOB
$ 🔨

Marketing, management, computers, software, and just about every other type of specialty consultant can benefit from this simple yet effective prospecting trick. Hundreds if not thousands of new employment advertisements appear in print newspapers and in online employment Web sites daily. So if you operate a consulting practice then why not tap into these help wanted ads to prospect for new business? The answer is you should. Get started by creating a specialized resume and introduction letter that explains the details and benefits of your service, as well as past client success stories and testimonials. Send your consulting service package to companies that are seeking employees and professionals in your area of consulting expertise. You may just find that recipients decide to contract with your consulting service rather than employ a person who may not be as qualified as you. Additionally, don't forget to attend job and career expos to make introductions and network with business owners and managers who could also benefit from hiring your service as opposed to an employee. Just because a corporation, organization, or small business thinks that they are looking for an employee, doesn't mean that in fact they are really seeking the services of a highly skilled consultant to help fuel their growth or solve specific challenges. The very fact that they run an employment advertisement means that they are to a certain degree qualified and definitely have a need to fill. Maybe all that is required is an in-depth explanation about how hiring your consulting service will be more beneficial and productive than hiring an employee. Certainly an option that consultants should carefully consider.

WEB RESOURCES

⌲ www.monster.com: Site listing thousands of employment opportunities in the United States.

⌲ www.monster.ca: Site listing thousands of employment opportunities in Canada.

PROFIT BY MAKING YOUR VENDORS SALES CHAMPIONS
$$$$ ✎ ✆

As a manufacturer or wholesaler of goods, your ability to succeed or fail is often beyond your immediate control and in the hands of those who resell your products—distributors, retailers, sales agents, and so forth. However, don't let others hamper your

ability to succeed. Instead take back control over your business's future and success by designing and implementing a training and information program that will help your vendors sell more of your products therefore ensuring the future success of your business. One of the best ways to train your vendors to be sales superstars is to develop an annual trade show or seminar series. Invite all your vendors to learn about the latest and greatest sales and marketing techniques taught by top-producing and industry-respected professional salespeople and marketers, as well as you as no one should know your products and how to sell them better than you. Not only will making training your vendors to be more productive sellers benefit your business, but also your vendor's businesses as well, as they will be able to apply what they have learned to increase revenues and profits in all areas of their businesses at your expense. If your budget is tight and you cannot afford to host a sales training seminar or workshop you can also develop a *Vendor's Sales Manual* in booklet format packed with outstanding sales tips and tricks that will turn vendors into sales superstars. And back up the training featured in the sales manual by personally meeting with each over time to answer questions and offer ongoing sales support and ideas. Remember, the easier you make it for people to sell and make money, the more motivated and harder they will work to sell your products or services.

WEB RESOURCE

⌲ www.smallbizbooks.com: Online retailer of business specific books and guides.

BREAK THE FEAST-OR-FAMINE SALES CYCLE
$$ ✎

Common to the sales profession is the feast-or-famine sales cycle. A good run during the feast usually means sixteen-hour days, a glut of presentations, and stacks of signed contracts ready for fulfillment. On the other end of the spectrum the period of famine generally leaves most sales professionals second-guessing their choice of profession as they desperately scramble to find new business and generate sales. The easiest way to break the feast-or-famine sales cycle is to develop a weekly marketing schedule that includes prospecting and networking for new businesses as well as contacting current and past clients. Yes this type of new business generation program can be difficult to commit to, especially during the feast periods. However the payoff can result in dramatically decreasing or eliminating the famine periods entirely, as you will always have a full and current pipeline of prospects to work with and sell to. Additionally, seasonal incentives can be used to help break the famine cycle or period and these marketing efforts should be conducted in opposite seasons. If you want winter sales and work, then promote seasonal incentives in the summer to defer clients to the winter and vica versa. Using seasonal incentives is a terrific method to ensure that your pipeline does not get depleted during the feast period. Often there is a cost to provide seasonal incentives, but these generally will be offset with higher volumes and the potential for increased referral business.

DEVELOP YOUR OWN MISSION STATEMENT
$ 🔨

Be bold and self-confident by developing your own personal mission statement that describes in perfect clarity exactly what your goals as a sales professional are, and what customers can expect from you as a result of your commitment to professionalism. "My purpose is to provide my customers with unsurpassed quality and service and always conduct my business in an ethical manner," as an example. Include your mission statement in sales letters, printed marketing materials, and promotional products like calendars, thank-you notes, and memo notepads that you distribute to your clients. Selling is very much a business like any other business, and to say, "I am a sales professional" simply is not enough. The world is full of salespeople; the ones that succeed have purpose and goals and they put these in writing in the form of a mission statement so that they have a written document that they can use as a reminder and as a yardstick to measure their progress and success. A mission statement is a fantastic sales tool. Not only does it state why and what, but it is also a great way to separate yourself from competitors and gives prospects an opportunity to form an instant favorable impression right from the start. For a better understanding of what a mission statement is and how you can develop one for your sales career, look in the Research, Planning, and Competition chapter of this book for a complete explanation.

B2B SHIFT SELLING
$+ 🔨

If you can provide prospects with a lower price than they are currently paying for a product or service is that enough to win their business? How about if you could give them better service or a better product than what they're currently getting from a competitor, would that be enough reason for them to come on board? Now what if you could combine a lower price and a better product or service, would that be enough incentive for a business to switch to your team and become a customer? Maybe not, in fact you could have a far superior product or service and a much lower price and still not win them over. Why? Newton's third law, "For every action, there is an equal and opposite reaction." When selling into businesses, especially large corporations, you have to carefully consider what reaction(s) there will be resulting from a change in the way business is conducted directly relating to your proposal. Perhaps you sell robotic equipment that can increase line production for a manufacturing company and cut end product costs by 10 percent. That's great and a good starting point, but what will be the true cost to the manufacturing business if they buy, install, and use the robotic equipment in their manufacturing process? Meaning, what will the opposite reaction be? Will there be down time during installation of the equipment, and how long if ever before this money is recouped? And could that down time send their customers to the competition? Will they have to lay off unionized employees because the robotic equipment will replace humans, and if so what is the buyout package of the employees going to cost? These are just a few questions that would have to be asked and there are many more, but I'm sure you see where this is going. In this scenario as good as increased production and decreased end product cost would be, there are equal and opposite reaction scenarios that must be considered. Therefore, trying to shift businesses from one product or service to another can be a tough sale; you cannot concentrate persuasion efforts on the obvious, which are generally surface things like price and great service. Instead you have to identify what new problems will be created by the shift and have solutions that are 100 percent solid and workable in theory and practice in advance of the sales pitch.

USE EXTENDED WARRANTIES TO MAKE IT EXCLUSIVE
$$ ✎ ⚖

What is your competitive advantage? Every salesperson needs to develop a competitive advantage that differentiates his products and services from his competition's products and services. Perhaps your competitive advantage could be the warranty you provide. If so carefully examine your warranty and your competitors' warranties. Is there an opportunity to provide an extended warranty that goes beyond what is currently covered or included? Extended warranties not only give you an advantage over competitors with standard warranties, but there is often even the opportunity to develop an extended warranty and turn it into a profit center by offering this as an upgrade to your standard warranty. For example, ABC Roofing has been in business for 15 years. The roofing industry is competitive and ABC needed a way to distinguish itself from the competition as all the roofing companies in the area sold and installed similar roofing products. ABC knows that they have a good installation and service track record with few warranty callbacks, so they decide the best method to separate themselves from the competition is to provide customers with an exclusive ten-year workmanship warranty in place of the industry standard five-year workmanship warranty. Presto, ABC Roofing has just made their roofing installations exclusive in the area and because of their good service track record this move costs them little to implement and maintain. "Roof your home with ABC and we'll provide you with our exclusive ten-year workmanship guarantee." This is a great way to separate them

from competitors and create a powerful sales tool at the same time.

REPORTS CAN BE A POWERFUL SALES TOOL
$ ✎

Creating your own exclusive report or manual that complements your business, products, or services is not only easy and inexpensive to do, but is also an extremely effective method of making your offering exclusive and separate from your competition's. If you sell real estate, then develop a free and exclusive "first-time homebuyer's report," packed with valuable information and tips that first-time homebuyers would find useful and beneficial. If you sell investment services, then create a free and exclusive "how to invest wisely for early retirement guide." If you sell vending machines then develop a free and exclusive "how to make $100,000 a year part time operating your own vending business." These are only a few examples of free and exclusive reports or books that can be easily developed for little cost. The fact remains that not only can providing potential prospects free reports separate you from the competition that do not take advantage of this powerful marketing technique, but it also will go a long way to establish you as an expert in the field and industry in which you operate. Reports, guides, information booklets, whatever you want to call them, they work, so develop one of your own to help make your offerings exclusive in the marketplace. But don't stop with one; once you have an exclusive report update it often and continue to use this as your competitive advantage and main sales and marketing tool for years to come.

FREE OFFERS TO GAIN EXCLUSIVITY
$$+ ✎

If you want to separate yourself from the competition and make your products and services exclusive then one way to do this is to give something of value away for free. For example, let's say that Joan sells vitamins and to stand out in this extremely competitive market she hosts free and exclusive monthly health seminars for consumers who would like to learn more about the health benefits that can be derived by adding vitamins to supplement their diets. Not only are Joan's seminars free to attend and exclusive to her business in her trading area, but she has also created a captive audience to sell to with no competition present. As this example illustrates, you have to get creative and seek out ways to make your offering different from your competition, and providing prospects something of value for free is a great way to do it. The objective of the free offer is to have and hold a captive audience long enough so that you can present the goods or services you want to sell in a noncompetitive environment. Creating this environment can be by way of free seminars, workshops, or group training and information sessions.

GETTING BEYOND LANGUAGE BARRIERS
$ ✎

The United States and Canada are two of the most culturally diverse nations in the world. This fact often makes it difficult for small-business owners and salespeople trying to expand their markets and customer base to include new immigrants as potential customers due to language barriers. However, online translation services have been popping up such as Babelfish and Free Translator that will enable you to translate English into as many as 12 different languages all with the easy click of your mouse. Simply go to one of these sites and type in the text that you want to translate, select the language you would like to translate your message into, and push "Translate." Within seconds you'll have translated your English language message into the language that you choose, which can be download, printed, or pasted into your sales and promotional materials. Best of all, you can use these language translation services to create sales letters, advertisements, and numerous other marketing materials in various languages to prospect for new business. There is no charge at the present time to use the services.

WEB RESOURCES

✆ www.freetranslation.com: Online translation service providing free and paid options.

✆ www.babelfish.altavista.com: Free basic online translation service.

PACKAGE YOURSELF
$$ ✎

You better believe that a book is judged by its cover and like it or not so are people. Packaging yourself is all about how you dress, the length and style of your hair, body language, and how you speak and handle yourself in conversation. Marketing is not selling, it is in fact persuasion and perceptions. We perceive that a doctor must be dressed in a white lab coat, a banker in suitable business attire, a mechanic in gray oil-stained coveralls, and that a boxer with a black eye must not be very good at the sport (though her opponent might have two black eyes). Hence, you have to package yourself appropriately for the situation and for what you sell. Without question I am talking stereotypes, but like them or not most stereotypes are so well ingrained into our minds and culture that no matter how hard you try to change them, you'll be fighting an uphill and ultimately a losing battle. Given this and the fact that much of sales is based on compromise, then isn't it better to fit into what people perceive and sell, rather then buck the trend and place an obstacle in the way of the sale before you even get a chance to sell? The answer is yes. I am not saying that perceived stereotypes are right, but from a practical standpoint if you want to sell then go with the flow. If people expect you to be wearing a suit then wear one; if they expect you to be in a specific uniform then wear one; if they expect that your hair will be a certain style, then try to meet their expectations. Corporations spend billions of dollars annually on product packaging research simply because they know that the packaging has a great impact on consumers and how they regard those products. So why not take advantage of this fact and package yourself to what people perceive to be "normal" for what you do and sell, and sell more because of it? Blue jeans might be more comfortable today, but appropriate business attire will likely put a lot more money in the bank and make for a more comfortable living and retirement tomorrow.

THE REAL WORK BEGINS AFTER THE SALE
$ 🔨

Never be under the illusion that once you have made a sale that "it's" over, because "it" isn't. In fact top sales professionals know that the real work begins after you make a sale, the real work being follow-up, great customer service, and establishing and maintaining a close working relationship with your customer for life. It is what you do once you make a sale that will determine the true value of the sale. If your goal was simply to close that particular sale then you're done, but if your goal is to continue to profit from the work and time that you have invested into establishing a trust relationship with your new, but still fragile, customer then get back to work. Assuming that customers will stay loyal to you because they have purchased from you once is false thinking. According to the U.S. Small Business Administration in excess of 60 percent of consumers stop doing business with a company because they feel they are being ignored and forgotten after the original sale. Couple that startling statistic with the fact that it costs ten times as much to find and sell to a new customer as it does to existing customers, and I am sure you see why the real work begins after the sale—building and maintaining a lifetime business relationship with all customers.

DITCH THE COMPETITION WITH FLEXIBLE PAYMENT OPTIONS
$$+ ☎

Make your offering different from your competitors' by developing a wide range of flexible payment options that can be provided to prospects on an exclusive basis. Flexible payment options can mean many things such as: If your competition does not accept credit card payments, then you should. Or, if your competition does not provide consumer or business financing and leasing options for purchases, then you should. When I was operating my renovation company I continually ran into the same obstacle when selling to strata corporations. A strata corporation is a housing cooperative, such as condominiums or townhouses, wherein each unit owner is a shareholder in the strata. The obstacle that continually surfaced was that some strata

unit owners had the financial resources to pay for their portion of the renovation work to the complex, while others did not. The result was that in many cases I lost the sale because each unit owner must be able to pay his portion of the bill and when some couldn't then the work would not be unanimously approved by the strata council. Determined to overcome this obstacle I visited a few local banks. Armed with a presentation promising substantial business I was able to convince one bank manager that the strata as a corporation should be able to apply for a loan in the amount of the renovation work and each unit owner would simply sign onto the loan as a guarantor. And, through increased monthly strata maintenance fees each owner could pay off his portion of the loan. It worked, and was the first time in British Columbia that such financing was granted by a chartered bank. Needless to say, you can guess who secured the bulk of strata renovation work in the area from that point forward. This examples clearly illustrates that by getting creative in terms of offering prospects payment options you can develop a competitive selling advantage and a very powerful marketing tool at the same time. Here are a few payment options you should consider providing customers as a way to separate your business from the competition and to create a tool that can be used to motivate prospects to buy.

Credit Cards

Accept credit cards such as Visa, MasterCard, and American Express, especially if competitors do not. Most credit card companies have a point system or credits in place that enable holders to redeem these point for trips and products. Therefore many consumers will pay for purchases with credit cards so they can collect these points, even if they have the cash on hand to pay for the purchase out of pocket. Therefore, if your competitors accept credit card payments and you do not, then you can be potentially missing out on people who want to collect the points via the cards.

Accept Checks

Allow customers to pay by way of personal checks, business checks, and electronic checks over the telephone or through your Web site.

Creative Installment Plans

Create in-house installment plans that allow customers to pay for purchases over a short period of time without interest being charged. One in-house installment plan that I used with great success was three months the same as cash, one-third due on completion, one-third 30 days later, and the one-third balance 60 days after completion. This worked especially well because I had arranged 60 days with suppliers, so in effect the installment plan did not cost anything to offer or manage and was a very powerful sales and closing tool.

Arrange Financing

Arrange consumer financing and leasing options for big-ticket items. Never make your prospects and customers go looking for money when they want to give it to you. Instead find the money for them to make sure they give it to you and not a competitor.

WEB RESOURCES

    🖉 www.visa.com: Visa credit cards

    🖉 www.mastercard.com: MasterCard credit cards

    🖉 www.discovercard.com: Discover credit cards

    🖉 www.amercianexpress.com: American Express credit cards

    🖉 www.internet-e-checks.com: Software enables you to accept electronic checks by mail, fax, telephone, and e-mail.

SEPARATE YOUR OFFER BY PROVIDING INCREDIBLE SERVICE
$+ ✎

Providing incredible service is an excellent way to make your offering exclusive and distinguish yourself from the competition. However, you can't just say we offer great service, you must be able to demonstrate this fact in a way the makes it tangible. For instance, if you sell roofing and install roofing products you could provide prospects with a written preinspection report detailing the current condition and deficiencies with their roofs. Should they go ahead with the roof installation, then you would follow up with a written postinspection report. In effect what you are telling a prospect is that you have their best interests in mind and that you provide these extra services at no charge to ensure that what they think they need and what they actually need are the same thing. And you're ensuring that after the installation what they thought they were buying and what they got was as good as or better. This is just one example of providing and being able to demonstrate incredible service to your prospects. Perhaps in terms of making your offering exclusive in a competitive marketplace providing various forms of incredible customer service is the best.

WEB RESOURCE

    🖉 www.entrepreneur.com: Online business resource center for small-business owners and sales professionals.

TRICKS FOR CRAFTING GREAT SALES LETTERS, PART ONE
$ ✎

It is a proven fact that great sales letters help to close more sales, motivate prospects to buy, and existing customers to buy more and more frequently. This is all music to the sales professional's ears. Here are a few great tricks for writing highly effective sales letters that demand the readers' attention and motivate them to take action.

Focus

Develop a central theme that is focused on wants, needs, desires, benefits, hopes, and dreams. Focus on emotional appeal when targeting consumers, and focus on logistical appeal when targeting business owners and managers. Basically, know the answer to the question that every prospect asks before making a purchase, which is "what is in it for me." Focus your key message on those points and the big benefit that they get, and not yourself or your company.

Make It Personal

Address the letter to the person it is intended for and continually refer to her by name and "you" throughout. Single out the reader as an individual, make her important, special, and your second highest priority, next to the main benefit. Of course, the two should go hand in hand, for instance "Jane, the P-3 widget will increase your productivity on the line by 59 percent! I guarantee it or I will personally return your money, Jane."

Grab Attention

Grab attention right away with a bold headline that solves a problem, creates a fantastic opportunity, passes a special limited offer, presents controversial or provocative ideas, or highlights an important and informative statistic about the prospect's business, industry, or target market. Additionally, ramp up the impact of your headline by including the reader's name into it whenever possible. Likewise use subheadlines throughout the letter to introduce other interesting information you know that will benefit the reader. Subheadlines keep the "skimmers" in the game and involved in your letter.

Relevant

Keep the content of the letter relevant to the topic or purpose and, more so, the action you want to reader to take. Keep it brief, to the point, and in perfect clarity. If what you have on the page is not 100 percent relevant to your objective, the reader, and your main message, then zap it by punching the delete key. Only relevant information needs to be included; anything else is likely only for the benefit of your ego.

Sell

Always write to sell. Even if the message or theme is not selling the subcontext should be leading the reader on a path, and each contact you make with them be it a letter, call, or personal appointment should take you and the reader one step closer to the sale. Simply handing out information is useless unless it helps you reach your ultimate marketing objective, which will always be sales. Think of it as connecting the dots, each line you connect to a dot takes you one step closer to the sale and great sales letters do that: get you one step closer to making the sale.

Would You Buy?

Ask yourself, "Would I buy?" If yes, list the reasons you would buy. What is the appeal, what is the advantage, and what is the motivation and urgency to buy? And if not, list the reasons why not, what's missing? Be honest if you or someone close to you who you entrust to read the letter are not excited by what you are offering or how you are offering it. Then get back to work until you are satisfied that you would buy.

TRICKS FOR CRAFTING GREAT SALES LETTERS, PART TWO
$ ⚒

Here are a few more clever tricks that you can use for crafting great sales letters that are guaranteed to get you the response that you want.

Action

Use action-oriented power words and phrases like free samples, call now, set an appointment, and delivery on time. In the advertising chapter of this book you will find a list of the 200 most powerful words to use in advertising and sales letter writing. Action words and phrases get the reader instantly involved in the message and theme of the letter and excited to learn more.

Page-Turner

Never end a page with a completed sentence if the letter is more than one page long. Instead force the reader to continue reading. Do this by stating an incentive or special offer at the bottom of the first page and completing it at the top of the second page. Or use an additional benefit that your product or service provides the readers as a way to keep them involved in the letter. Basically, be it an incentive, guarantee, or second big benefit, use something that is powerful and important to the readers to ensure that they turn the page and continue to read and stay involved.

Visually Appealing

Make your sales letters visually appealing with color, graphics, and bold paragraph headings on attractive professionally printed letterhead emblazoned with your business logo and catch phrase. Likewise make sure that your color selection, font, and logo are all consistent with the rest of your printed business materials. People visually link consistent styles with a business when they are repeatedly exposed to the business' unified corporate image—prospects and customers can begin to instantly identify your business just by the envelope, letterhead, or color scheme that you use in a consistent manner throughout all your marketing and promotional activities.

Plain English

Make the letter easy to read and understand. Always skip the technical jargon and just use plain English. Never go out of your way to make the reader feel stupid by using language and terms that they could not possibly understand. Nothing will turn a reader off faster then this. Likewise check spelling, grammar, and structure and if time allows try to let the letter sit for a few days then return to complete the editing. You will almost always find information that you want to include and some that you want to delete.

Tell the Reader What to Do

Tell the readers what you want them to do: call, stop by the showroom, order now, or log on to our Web site for more exciting information. Tell the readers what you want them to do next and make sure that you give them the tools required for them to take that desired action. The required tools can include full contact information, a coupon if used as an incentive, a customer testimonial if you want them to contact happy customers, or a self-addressed and stamped envelope if you want them to respond by mail, just to mention a few. Once again the easier you make if for people to do what you want them to do, the more people who will do it.

Postscript

Include a postscript that reinforces the benefits and values of your offer or the key elements and message of the letter. For example, "P.S. We have the best widgets in the industry and if you call now I'll prove it by sending you ten free samples by rush overnight courier and give you $100 credit toward your first order, but only if you call before the end of the month!"

TAKE "SALES" OUT OF YOUR JOB DESCRIPTION
$ ⚒

Always avoid using the term sales or salesperson in your job description, printed marketing materials, written proposals, or verbal presentations. The vast majority of consumers have a negative predisposition to the word "sales," especially when it is used to describe a person's career. The "sales" word can instantly place prospects on guard and worse on the defensive and digging for reasons to say no. Just mentioning the word sales instantly creates doubt and fear, which of course are already the salesperson's biggest obstacles standing in the way of a sale. Instead of salesperson change your job description to a title that portrays you as an industry expert and customer service specialist, a true knowledgeable leader in your chosen field. Great job titles that build instant credibility and confidence include Service Advisor, Product Advisor, Systems or Technical Estimator, and Consultant. Besides, selling is not selling anyway, it is persuading prospects to believe in you, your products, or your services. Once they do they do not need to be sold.

MINING YOUR DEAD FILE
$$ ⚒

Hang on to those old estimates and proposals for at least a few years because you just might be sitting on a boatload of new sales in your "dead file" and not even realize it. There are a number of reasons prospects don't go ahead with a purchase, or, perhaps they say that they have purchased somewhere else when in fact they haven't. These reasons for not going ahead can range from lack of financial resources, poor timing, changing circumstances, or just about anything else, but at the end of the day new sales can always be secured from mining your dead file even after a prospect has said no. Mining the true value of your dead file begins with creating a standard form letter, which thanks your prospects for their time during the original presentation. The letter should also restate the benefits of your product or service and a special incentive offer as a way to motivate them to take action and reopen the lines of communication with you. Personally, any proposal that I gave and that did not result in a sale I would follow up with in this manner for a two-year period, even if the prospects initially said no or said that they were going to do business with a competitor, which again is not always the true situation. As a result of this post- "no" follow-up system I would always secure at least a few new sales and at the bare minimum a few referrals.

NEVER BE A HIT-AND-RUN ARTIST
$ ⚒

Hit-and-run artists are salespeople who, after spending countless hours preparing a proposal or estimate for a prospect, they choose to simply fax, mail, or drop it off and leave right away, as if scared of what may happen if they have to meet with the prospect face to face to properly present their proposal. If you sell on a personal level, meaning face-to-face contact with prospects and clients, then never be a hit-and-run artist and drop off your proposal. Personally I refuse to give any prospect pricing, ideas, and solutions relevant to his needs, or explain product or service benefits and features unless he is prepared to meet with me face to face. This is not to say I am difficult to do business with; on the contrary I'm very accommodating and will travel to a prospect's location and meet with him at his convenience not mine. But I will never release details of my proposal unless I meet with the other party face to face. Why? Unless your prospect is an expert on the product, service, or industry, how can he possibly understand your offering in the proper context and how can he compare it to the competition's offering? It could be apples and oranges and who would know? Likewise how can you properly listen to a prospect's objections and concerns and overcome these to close the sale? Always get a commitment in advance to meet face to face when it comes time to

present your proposal, ideas, or pricing estimates. If you can't get the commitment, then the prospect may just be using you to keep a competitor honest. Never educate someone just so he can purchase from someone else.

MAKE CLIENTS LOOK FORWARD TO YOUR NEXT VISIT
$ ⚒

Wouldn't it be great if all your clients looked forward to your weekly sales visit? This just may be easier to accomplish than you think. First, it is no mystery that people look forward to spending time with people they like, so it makes sense that you should go out of your way to be a friendly and likable person. Second, people look forward to a surprise, so again it makes sense that you should go out of your way to surprise your prospects and customers with small gifts—perhaps candy one week, a book of humorous jokes the next, and a company embossed T-shirt the following week. Third, people look forward to talking with people they respect, so once again it makes sense that you should be honest and straightforward in all of your business dealings so that prospects and customers will respect you and look forward to your visits and calls. You will be amazed at how much you can grow your sales and referrals just by having clients look forward to your sales visits and calls. This is not rocket science, it is a proven formula that top sales professionals have utilized for decades. Make your clients look forward to your visits and you will build a very loyal customer base for life. It is really that simple.

AVOID THE WATER COOLER TALK
$ ⚒

Thousands of promising sales careers have been destroyed around the water cooler or coffee machine before they even had a chance to really get going, but you don't have to let this happen to you and your sales career. The old saying a "rotten apple will spoil the entire barrel" is true, especially in sales. Whatever you want to call it, water cooler talk, a smoke break out back, or an informal gathering in the corner of the showroom, be careful of customer-bashing conversations as they will quickly undermine your ability to be an effective persuader and producer. Customer bashing is common in selling because it is an easy way for poorly trained and performing salespeople to pass their inability on to customers in the form of faults, strange personalities, or general disrespect. We have all heard these comments and some of you reading this I'm sure have even joined in on one level or another. This is dangerous territory because once you begin to believe or think about customers in a negative way, it will spread like cancer and it won't be long until there is something wrong with every prospect who walks into the store or office. Break the cycle; if you hear customer bashing even if meant in fun, simply walk away; don't join in and don't allow yourself to believe it, because rarely is any of it true or based on fact.

GOOD ADVICE, BAD ADVICE
$ ✎

Much like water cooler talk mentioned above, many salespeople will take it upon themselves to dispense advice and guidance to other salespeople, even when they are not asked for their advice or opinions. In fact there are likely more experts per capita selling than in any other profession or industry; just take a random sampling and ask a few and you'll find experts oozing out of the woodwork. Seeking advice or learning from other people's successes and failures is something that every salesperson should commit to doing; without question it is the second best way to learn valuable selling skills short of actually getting out and selling and learning from your own experiences. However, before you take what is being said as the real McCoy make sure that you first consider the source of the advice. Is this person more successful than you? Is he a top producer in the field or industry? Do people respect his opinion and does he have a rock solid reputation? If the answers are not a resounding 100 percent yes to all of these questions, then in all likelihood his sales advice and guidance is about as valuable to you as catching the flu would be. The number-one rule of learning is never take advice from people who are not the top in their fields or who are worse off than yourself. This rule

of learning transcends just about every profession, task, and job. You wouldn't take fitness advice from someone who was not fit, or important medical life-or-death health advice from someone who was not a licensed medical doctor, so why take advice from a salesperson who is not a top producer? The answer is simple, don't. Seek advice, help, and guidance and never stop striving to learn more, but only from people who are at the top of the sales game. Finding top producers is easy; they are the sales professionals who don't randomly dispense advice until they are asked for their advice and opinions.

THE POWER OF A DOG BISCUIT
$ ✎

Never underestimate the power that a simple dog biscuit can have on your prospect's buying decision. Don't laugh—if you conduct presentations in your prospects' homes do yourself a favor and invest in a two-dollar box of dog biscuits. I'll guarantee you won't be sorry. It's a fact that dog lovers share a certain bond with other dog lovers, kind of like motorcyclists on the highway who wave to each other as they pass, but never to someone driving a car. The theory is that people who share similar interests feel more comfortable with people who share the same interests and this theory is sound; in sales it can be referred to as using similar interests to break the ice. That's why carrying a dog biscuit in your pocket is important, especially when you consider that approximately one in five homeowners in the United States and Canada have a dog. I've never kept a tally, but I'm sure if I went back over my client records I would discover that dog biscuits would likely be responsible for helping secure a million dollars or more in sales over the years. Like the famous credit card commercial says, "never leave home without it," except "it" should be a pocket full of dog biscuits and not a plastic card.

ASSISTANTS PAY OFF
$$$$ ✆

Are you at the point in your sales career were hiring an assistant would earn you more money? Only you can answer this question, but more professional salespeople are likely at this point than they might think. It may seem callous, but the number-one objective of salespeople is to live and breathe their ABCs, Always Be Closing. If you're not closing, you're not going to be in business or have a job for long, it's just that simple. Some aspects of selling cannot be placed in the hands of an assistant, but many can. Free up time to sell and close by delegating time-consuming tasks associated with selling by hiring an assistant, even if the assistant's wages come directly out of your pocket. The rich don't get richer because they are better than you or I, they get richer because they have learned to concentrate on what they're the best at and that makes them the most money, while delegating lesser tasks and responsibilities to assistants.

WORK THE TENDER PROCESS
$$+ ⚒ ⚖

Don't overlook product or services supply tenders as a way to find new prospects and secure new business. Tenders are something that most salespeople avoid simply due to the fact that successfully winning a tender can be a long, drawn-out process that often requires a lot of accompanying documents and reinforcement facts in the form of research studies and reports. However, the payoff can be good for those salespeople who are prepared to invest the time to work the tender process properly. Get started by conducting research into tenders and the tender process, educate yourself about how tenders work—time lines, financial commitments, liabilities, basically the who, what, where, when, and how of the entire tender process. A good place to get this information is from the Internet. Once you find and request information about a particular tender that interests you, you can ask to be included on the e-mail list for further tender consideration as the need arises. Give tender selling a try and you just may be pleasantly surprised by the outcome.

WEB RESOURCE

🔗 www.securetenders.com: Online service connecting buyers and sellers worldwide.

BE WHAT YOU SELL
$+ ⚒

Chances are you wouldn't hire a personal fitness trainer who was overweight or take flying lessons from a person who was not a certified pilot and instructor. Perhaps these examples are somewhat extreme, but they perfectly illustrate the point; if you want people to take you seriously and buy from you then you'd better truly believe in what you sell to the point that you can speak from personal experiences. If you sell high-end men's suits then you'd better wear one when you're talking to customers. Likewise if you sell sailboats then you'd better be a sailor. When I was operating my renovation company I sold a lot of heated bathroom floors, why? Because I installed one in my own home and could explain firsthand the benefits, which were actually a luxury. Never was my goal to sell only flooring; I ran a large renovation company and we would have starved if that were the case. However, I could always count on squeezing an extra thousand dollars out of each bathroom we renovated by using and having firsthand knowledge of what I was selling—some call it building buying excitement through personal experience. But whatever you want to call it, be what you sell, know what you sell, and love what you sell and it will rub off on your prospects.

WHAT TOP PRODUCERS HAVE IN COMMON
$ ⚒

Top Producers Focus on Results

One consistent trait that top-producing salespeople share is that while they are very organized and place a high priority on time management, they also know the limit in terms of when to be preparing to sell and when to be actually selling. At the end of the day the yardstick that all salespeople are measured by is results, not how nice their presentations looked or how neatly organized and displayed their product samples were at the meeting. Results means ironclad closed deals that not only generate revenues and profits in the short term but also have the ability if managed properly to continue to generate revenues and profits for many years to come. The desire to produce results must never diminish even when in negative situations or dealing with less-than-ideal prospects. Regardless of the selling environment, top producers stay focused on the results they want and expect to win every time they begin the sales cycle with a new prospect, or the continued sales cycle with an existing customer. Anything less would be letting another person control them and their livelihood.

Top Producers Develop Routines

Top-producing salespeople recognize that by developing and maintaining systems, they maximize the use of their time and in doing so free up more time to prospect, present, close, and become far more efficient and productive salespeople. However, like any business activity, it will require creating, implementing, and testing various ways of doing things and when results happen you duplicate them and systematically follow them through to ensure that favorable results continue to roll in. Systems will include the time that you prospect that will have the best results, when to do less important tasks such as administration, and computerizing your complete operation so that you can become more productive.

Top Producers Stay in Close Contact

Top-producing salespeople are always on their customers' and prospects' minds. And they do this by constantly staying in contact with them. They use all available means to do this—telephone, e-mail, fax, newsletter, mail, and personal visits. They do this before the sale, during the sale, and after the sale. It is a cycle that never stops even if the prospect did not buy; because top producers know that even the hardest-nosed prospects who scream no from the top of their lungs will eventually buy and become your best customer if you stay in contact.

Top Producers Create Competitive Advantages

Top-producing salespeople develop a competitive advantage that separates them from the competition and they use this competitive advantage as their main sales and marketing tool. They understand that without a competitive advantage they cannot give their prospects a valid reason to do business with them instead of the competition. The competitive advantage that they develop becomes the cornerstone of all their sales and marketing activities.

Top Producers Listen Carefully

Top-producing salespeople firmly believe that good selling means that you are a good listener. They talk only to ask questions, explain benefits, confirm details, ask for the sale, and ask for referrals after they have the sale. The rest of their time is spent listening to their prospects and customers so that they can better understand their situation and develop solutions that are second to none.

Top Producers Are Accountable

Top-producing salespeople hold themselves personally accountable for their actions and words, they never point fingers or lay blame. They simply accept negative situations even if they did not create the situation, apologize, and work with prospects and customers to find mutually beneficial solutions in a timely manner. They do this because they know that people will respect them for it and buy more from them because of it.

Top Producers Stay in Control

Top-producing salespeople stay in control of their careers by having goals and objectives and an action plan for how and when they are going to reach their goals and objectives. They also stay in control of their prospects, customers, and presentations by asking questions, being respectful, and always being professional. Top-producing salespeople are never in the backseat giving directions, they are always up front, behind the wheel, in control, and personally choosing their own path to success.

MAKE YOUR PRODUCT OR SERVICE AN EMPLOYEE BENEFIT
$$+ 🖊 ⚖️

Many mid- to large-sized corporations in today's competitive employment environment have had to increase the number and variety of benefits they offer to employees as a way to attract and retain top-producing personnel. These employee benefits can range from a clothing allowance, to dental plans, to free transit passes, and just about anything else that you can think of that is beneficial to employees. Get creative with the product or service you sell and seek ways to turn it into a viable and valuable employee benefit. Once you have created your "employee benefit" then contact business owners and managers in your area and set appointments to pitch your newly created employee benefit product or service to them. The key to success is that the employee benefit you create must also benefit the employers by assisting them to attract and/or retain great employees. An Internet service provider might offer an employer a 25 percent discount to hook up every employee's at-home computer to the Internet. The benefit to the employee is free at-home Internet connection. The benefit to the employer would be an increased ability to keep all employees communicating via e-mail, thus reducing miscommunications and increasing decision-making time and productivity. This is only one example, there are many ways to turn your product or service into an employee benefit. Though it will often mean having to reduce the per item or transaction sales value, this discount can easily be made up in higher sales volumes and the potential for referral business.

BE PRESENT AT DELIVERY
$ ✎

One of the best ways for salespeople to earn a customer's respect and continued trust is to be present at delivery, be it a product delivery, product installation, or major service call. It is not always practical for salespeople to be present at delivery due to time conflicts such as sales meetings and presentations. However, far too many salespeople try to make a habit of not being present at delivery simply because they feel that once the contract is signed their job is complete. This could not be farther from the truth. By being present at delivery you have the opportunity to collect new prospect referrals from clients, to ask for testimonials, to snap a few pictures of your happy

clients with their purchases, and even to sell new products or services—a strike-while-the-iron-is-hot approach if you will. Additionally, by being present you can also develop a checklist and have clients sign off on key points. By doing so this can nip potential problems or miscommunications in the bud before they become complaints. And above all, by being present at delivery you represent yourself to your customer as a true professional who has the customer's best interests in mind.

WAYS TO BEAT DESPERATION
$ ✎

Customers can smell desperation, not in the literal sense but by your actions—the way you conduct the sales presentation, your body language, and by the tone of your voice, just to mention a few. We all have bills to pay and we all must meet or exceed sales targets to stay in business or to remain gainfully employed in sales. Circumstance might be the internal cause, but unfortunately desperation is the external result that prospects and customers see. Here are a few ways to focus on persuading and closing, and forgetting about your desperate situation whatever the cause of it might be.

Beat Desperation by Dealing with the Business at Hand

When desperate to make a sale we have a tendency to look too far forward, sizing up what we believe to be our best selling opportunity, trying to get to greener pastures so that we can close an easy sale. Unfortunately, this is never the case and every prospect and sales presentation should be treated in the same professional manner, as they all can be closed.

Beat Desperation by Getting into Contact with Past Clients

The contact you make might not result in new sales or referrals, but speaking with past and current customers who are happy with their purchases and the level of service you provided them is a great self-confidence boost. Ask them why they purchased from you, try to get specifics, and build on those positive aspects of your skills with new prospects.

Beat Desperation by Turning to Your Business Team for a Hand Up, Not a Hand Out

If you're good at generating leads then do so and let someone else on your team close. Split commissions and use this success once again as a platform for rebuilding your confidence. Teaming special talents together is one of the best ways to build self-confidence and increase productivity and positive results.

DOWN-SELL FOR THE LONG TERM
$ ✎

Most salespeople are taught and believe in the up-sell approach to increasing sales values and therefore their commission on each sale. However an equally effective way to increase total sales values and commissions over the long term is to down-sell to customers in the short term. If you think a prospect or customer could get by with fewer widgets then tell him so and why you believe this and sell him less. Or, if a less expensive model with fewer features would work perfectly fine for his needs and more appropriately match his budget, then speak up, state your case, and don't let it go unnoticed. People appreciate the truth, especially when it can save them money or alternately make them money. This is not to say that you have to be telling customers to spend less money, just illustrate how they can spend less while still fulfilling their needs or finding suitable solutions to problems. In the end the customers will make the final decision about what will work best for their situation, but by introducing options you can separate yourself from competitors. And more importantly you keep the customers on your side by giving them one, two, or maybe a few options; think about it, with more than one option they are forced to select one, selecting none is no longer an option.

LET YOUR CUSTOMERS CONVINCE THEM
$ ✎

You can talk, demonstrate, and try to persuade prospects until you are blue in the face and falling down tired. Or, you can make things easy and adopt the strategy of letting your customers convince new prospects for you in regard to the value of your goods and services. What is this amazingly simple sales strategy you ask? Client testimonials, the more the better. Put together a binder of testimonials and take them with you to every presentation. Let your prospects flip through and read them and watch their expressions turn from skepticism to true believers with each testimonial they read. Even the King of rock and roll, Elvis himself, benefited from this simple yet powerful marketing premise when back in 1960 boldly printed on the front of his "Elvis's Gold Records" was "50,000,000 Elvis Fans Can't Be Wrong," referring to the number of records he had sold to that date. Given that even long after his demise Elvis is now closing in on one billion records sold, it would be a safe assumption that this statement is as true today as it was five decades ago. No one wants to be first, especially to spend money, try a new product or service, or buy from someone she has just met; all people want to know that others have gone first and it has worked out for them. This is what makes customer testimonials such a powerful marketing tool; they clearly demonstrate to prospects that others have gone first, purchased, and were happy with their decisions.

TESTIMONIALS WITH IMPACT
$ ✎

As mentioned above, one of the best sales and marketing tools available to business owners and salespeople is great testimonials supplied by happy customers. However, to increase the impact of customer testimonials, make sure that each includes as many of the following elements as possible, even if you have to walk your customers through the process of writing the testimonial letter or putting together a testimonial package step by step.

Contact Information

All customer testimonials should include the full name of the author printed as well as signed in their writing. This carries much more clout than just a first name, or an initial and a last name. Likewise whenever possible always try to include a photograph of the person(s) giving the testimonial, this will help appeal to an emotional level. People love to hear and read about good things that happen to people who don't look so different from themselves, or their family members and friends.

Pull Out the Big Guns

If you have a celebrity client or customer who is well known in your local trading area ask that person to write a shining testimonial about your business, product, or service. Celebrity testimonials can be used as a wonderful icebreaker, as most people feel at ease knowing that others have gone before them, especially if the "others" include a person or name they recognize. I once received a glowing testimonial from the captain of the local fire station because of a few renovations my business completed at his home. The renovations went well, on time, and on budget. I never missed an opportunity to use that testimonial when meeting with new prospects. And even though the fire captain was not a celebrity so to speak, he was so well known and trusted in the community that just having his recommendation in print was all the persuading that many people needed to go ahead and hire my firm to carry out renovations at their homes. A testimonial from a well-known and trusted person from the community cannot be duplicated through advertising and marketing activities, no matter how much money you throw at these activities.

Business Clients

If the testimonial is being given by a business client then it should include the author's business mailing address, title, and contact telephone number, and preferably be printed on her company letterhead. Once again, this will make the testimonial much more tangible and credible than just a testimonial with a few words jotted down followed by an illegible signature scribble. However, do be sure to ask the author if other prospects and customers can contact her from time to time for verbal confirmation.

Highlight the Benefits

And finally, ask the author to use a bulleted list or short quotes highlighting or featuring what they like about your product or service, the benefits. And

make sure that you ask them if it is okay for you to reprint the testimonial or use it in other forms of marketing and advertising. Get their permission in writing when possible.

ENLIST A LOBBYIST
$$ 🐖 ⚖️

Attempting to land lucrative corporate and government supply contracts is a time-consuming and very competitive process. You need to take the time to identify and build an alliance with someone within the organization or corporation who can lobby the decision makers on your behalf. Start by identifying who the lobbyist could be, keeping in mind that there has to be a benefit for this person to really get motivated and take up your cause. Money obviously is not the benefit, not only is it illegal, but it's also unethical. However, recognition, promotion, and making their jobs easier are all-powerful benefits that can be the source of motivation for many people, enough reason to happily get involved and lobby their superiors on your behalf—perhaps a city councilor who can push your company as the best choice to install new playground equipment or a line foreman who can convince management that your widget would save time and increase workers' productivity. Big business and special interest groups have used lobbyists since the beginning of modern industrial times to create prospecting and selling opportunities and so can you. All that is required is to identify who in the prospect's chain of command or team can have the biggest impact championing your cause and then get to work persuading that person to be your number-one supporter and spokesperson within the organization. Though seeking to identify and persuade a person to lobby can also be a time-consuming process, the potential rewards can be well worth the effort.

FIVE-POINT TIME MANAGEMENT
$$ ⚒️

Revenue

The first priority of managing your sales career is to identify the money hours. These are the hours during the day when you have the ability to generate the most revenues because of being able to actively reach or meet with prospects and customers. The money hours will not always be consistent every day and will largely be based on what you sell and to whom you sell it. For instance in the home renovation business I found my money hours to be evenings and Saturday afternoons. Mainly because that's when homeowners were not working and I could have their undivided attention during sales presentations. And because I knew when my money hours were I would purposely base my schedule around these hours because I knew that these were the hours that I had in any given week to generate the most revenues.

Prospecting

Dedicate a certain number of hours each day to prospecting. The productive prospecting hours are the hours when you stand the highest probability of reaching your target audience via various prospecting methods, cold calling on the telephone, personal visits, and attending networking events. But, as a rule of thumb skip Monday mornings and Friday afternoons, most people are too wrapped up in starting their week or finishing their week to give you their undivided attention.

Follow Up

The follow-up hours of your schedule are hours set aside to call your hottest prospects and to keep in constant contact with your current clients. Clients should be contacted at least once a month, but better if it is every two weeks. Additionally to maximize your follow-up time, develop and implement a system of form letters, gifts, and anything else that can be reused in template form.

Development

Set aside a specific block of time weekly and dedicate it to personal development building activities such as reading sales and marketing books, attending seminars, and enrolling in sales building workshops and training courses.

Administration

Set aside a block of time weekly to stay on top of administration aspects of your career. Keep accurate sales records and measure your progress to date against a sales forecast sheet and against your goals and objectives sheets.

WHAT IS EASY TO DO IS EASIER NOT TO DO $ ⚒

"What is easy to do is easier not to do, and most people will take the path of least resistance and simply choose not to do." These words spoken by Brian Tracy at a seminar have stayed with me for more than a decade. In fact, hardly a day goes by that I don't think about and try to apply them to a current situation or problem that I might be facing or a decision that must be made. Basic motivation yes, but very truthful just the same. Yes it's easy to meet with a client on a rainy night, but it's easier not to. It is easy to make just one more cold call every day, but it's easier not to. It is very easy to ask every customer for a referral, but once again it's easier not to. It's easy to provide great customer service, but it's easier not to. I am sure you see the pattern that is starting to develop. When you are facing a task, decision, or challenge and doubt begins to creep in think about these words and you'll quickly realize that this simple motivational message can be the catalyst for taking positive action that can make the difference between sales and business success or failure. Give it a try, you'll be amazed with by the results.

WEB RESOURCE

⚒ www.briantracy.com: Sales and motivational training, information, products, programs, and services.

INCENTIVES MUST HAVE VALUE $+ ⚒

At some point every business owner or salesperson will use an incentive as a way to help motivate a prospect to buy or entice existing customers to buy more and more frequently. As effective as providing an incentive to generate more business might seem on the surface, you must in fact make sure that the incentive you are offering is of real value. Meaning, that if you were not giving the incentive product or service away for free or including it in the deal at no additional cost, then it would be valuable enough that it could actually be sold on its own as an individual product or service. Ideally the incentive used to increase the value of your main offer should be a product or service that you are currently selling. A hat embossed with your business logo is a prime example of a product that is commonly used as an incentive to try to build value and as a tool to motivate prospects to buy. Without question a hat is very useful to keep the sun and rain off your prospects' heads, though I highly doubt that you would be able to find someone who would actually give you $20 for a cap embossed with your logo. For $20 they may as well buy a brand name cap with a recognized logo on it like Nike's swoosh. Instead your incentive must be something that is far more beneficial to your prospect if you expect it to motivate them to buy your main offering. A good example of this would be to include an extended warranty in the deal for free. This way you can actually indicate the value of the incentive in terms of dollars, and the benefit to your prospect, which is extra security and piece of mind that extended warranties provide. Other examples of prime and valuable incentives that could be sold individually include more product or service for the same price, free upgraded features, free delivery or installation, or a free $50 gift certificate that can be applied toward future purchases on other products and services you sell. In summary strong incentives that add real value to your main offering and that create motivation to buy should include the following characteristics:

- The incentive enhances your main offering.
- The incentive can be sold as a stand-alone product or service.
- The incentive is relevant to your main offering.
- In addition to your main offering your incentive will also benefit your prospect.
- You are able to attach a realistic and exciting dollar figure to your incentive.

THE SALES PROFESSIONAL'S CHECKLIST
$+ 🔨

The following is a checklist that you can use to help identify your selling weaknesses so you can formulate strategies to improve.

Sales Professional Checklist

❏ Set clear objectives for every segment of the sales cycle with each new prospect and current customer. Know what you want out of each contact with every prospect and customer.

❏ Create a personal mission statement, the purpose of what you do, why you do it, and who benefits because of what you do.

❏ Project a winning attitude and never let your emotions get carried away or cloud your judgment or decision-making abilities.

❏ Always strive to make a great first impression with every new prospect and learn to never take rejection personally. Instead treat it as an opportunity to provide your prospects with more information that will help them to understand your products or services better and how they will benefit by owning them.

❏ Listen closely to your prospects and ask in-depth questions, especially questions that can identify even the smallest obstacle that stands between you and the sale.

❏ Qualify all prospects by asking questions to determine their interest in your products or services, their individual and specific needs, and their abilities to make a buying decision and pay for products and services they wish to purchase. Qualify all prospects beyond a reasonable to doubt so that you can make the best use of time.

❏ Know what you sell inside out and be a walking, talking example of what you sell by using it, believing in it, and most of all knowing exactly how customers benefit by buying it and taking ownership.

Sales Professional Checklist, *continued*

❏ Be likable and the type of person with whom other people want to do business. Take a real and sincere interest in your prospects and clients, beyond what they represent to you financially.

❏ Always sell the benefits first, what it will do for them, the problem it will solve; anticipate objections and look forward to overcoming them because you are be prepared.

❏ Always be honest and never stop building a great reputation, credibility, and trust with all prospects and customers.

❏ Know your competition and develop your own competitive advantage and unique selling position. If you do not have a competitive advantage then develop one ASAP.

❏ Never overlook any prospect or customer concern no matter how small you may think it is. All prospect and customer concerns are big concerns; otherwise they would not reveal them.

❏ At all times practice your ABCs—Always Be Closing—and never stop asking prospects and customers for referrals, even if you didn't get the sale.

❏ Take advantage of all current and new technologies as they arise to develop and maintain a customer and prospect management database that will save you time and money. And that will enable you to customize individual files so that you can better understand and serve each prospect and client as an individual and based on their specific needs.

❏ Set aside time to prospect and network for new business and never stop researching and surveying your current best customers so that you can identify common characteristics they share and develop ways to clone them and sell to a broader audience.

❏ Verbally confirm the details with prospects and customers about every sale or discussion then reconfirm in writing a second time to make sure there are no miscommunications that can potentially come back to haunt you down the road.

❏ Learn to master and practice the art of fair negotiations at all times.

❏ Share your knowledge and expertise in your field by seeking out places to speak and by writing articles, newsletters, and features for publication. Likewise, never assume that your knowledge has no value, you might think that everyone knows what you know, but seldom is that reality.

❏ Develop a bulletproof follow-up plan and schedule so that every contact with prospects will take you one step closer to a confirmed sale, and every contact with customers will strengthen the relationship.

❏ Never stop thanking customers for their business and continued support.

📖 SUGGESTED ADDITIONAL READING

Blachard, Kenneth H., Sheldon Bowles, and Harvey Mackay. *Raving Fans: A Revolutionary Approach to Customer Service.* New York: William Morrow & Company, 1993.

Fox, Jeffrey J. *How to Become a Rainmaker: The Rules for Getting and Keeping Customers and Clients.* New York: Hyperion Books, 2000.

Johnson, Spencer. *The One-Minute Sales Person.* New York: Avon Books, 1991.

Jones, Laurie Beth. *The Path: Creating Your Mission Statement for Work and for Your Life.* New York: Hyperion, 1998.

Page, Rick. *Hope Is Not a Strategy: The 6 Keys to Winning the Complex Sale.* Alpharetta, GA: Nautilus Press, 2001.

Rackham, Neil. *The S.P.I.N. Selling Fieldguide: Practical Tools, Methods, Exercises and Resources.* New York: McGraw-Hill, 1996.

Schiffman, Stephen. *The 25 Sales Habits of Highly Successful Salespeople.* Avon, MA: Adams Media Inc., 1994.

Tracy, Brian. *Be a Sales Superstar: 21 Great Ways to Sell More, Faster, Easier in Tough Markets.* San Francisco, CA: Berrett-Koehler Publishers, Inc., 2002.

———. *Eat That Frog: 21 Great Ways to Stop Procrastinating and Get more Done in Less Time.* San Francisco, CA: Berrett-Koehler Publishers, Inc., 2002.

Underhill, Paco. *Why We Buy: The Science of Shopping.* New York: Simon & Schuster, 1999.

KEY

COST TO IMPLEMENT $

DO-IT-YOURSELF

CALL IN THE
PROFESSIONALS

LEGAL ISSUES

BOOK RESOURCES

ONLINE

RETAILING
Marketing Tips for Your Business

I am the world's worst salesman, therefore,
I must make it easy for people to buy.

—F. W. WOOLWORTH

ASK YOUR CUSTOMERS HOW THEY HEAR ABOUT YOUR STORE

$

The best way to track the effectiveness of your marketing activities is to simply ask your customers how they heard about your business. Create a simple form like the one shown on the next page, listing all the marketing methods you are currently using to promote and market your shop such as print ads, radio or television ads, direct marketing, coupons, referral, drive past, and any other types of marketing you use. Print numerous copies of the form and keep them beside telephones and the cash register so they can be completed quickly and conveniently. You will find that the vast majority of customers you ask will not mind telling you how they heard about your business, in fact most will likely be impressed that you care enough to ask. Also make sure that all staff get a quick rundown in the theory behind the new practice, that they fully understand the importance of asking customers how they heard about your business, and that the forms are completed accurately. Tabulate the results monthly, and use the results to increase the marketing activities that work and drop marketing activities that are not working and therefore not cost efficient. This is a really simple marketing trick that can pay off large so be sure to create "how'd you hear about us" forms and put them to work for your shop today.

Here is a sample form that you can use. Additionally, ask for specific information such as the name of the person who may have recommended your business (so you can thank him), and the newspaper they saw the ad in if you're running more than one display advertisement at any one time. Once you and your staff are in the habit of asking you'll be amazed at how quickly the form can be completed and even more amazed by the results this simple exercise can have on bottom-line profits.

How Did You Hear About Us Form

How Did Your Hear About Us?

Advertising
- ❏ Newspaper
- ❏ Magazine
- ❏ Yellow pages
- ❏ Trade publication
- ❏ Business directory
- ❏ Newsletter
- ❏ Internet/Web site
- ❏ Billboard

Direct Marketing
- ❏ Insert
- ❏ Mail drop
- ❏ Telemarketing
- ❏ Sales letter
- ❏ Response card
- ❏ Entry form
- ❏ Catalog
- ❏ Door hanger

Promotional Activity
- ❏ Sales visit
- ❏ Trade show
- ❏ Seminar
- ❏ Sponsorship
- ❏ Newcomer program
- ❏ Contest
- ❏ Cross promotion
- ❏ Gift certificate/coupon

Referral
- ❏ Business alliance
- ❏ Supplier/vendor
- ❏ Customer
- ❏ Networking
- ❏ Business club
- ❏ School/institution

Publicity
- ❏ Print article
- ❏ Radio
- ❏ Television
- ❏ Community event
- ❏ Charity event
- ❏ Internet article

Location
- ❏ Drive past/walk past
- ❏ Service vehicle
- ❏ Lawn sign
- ❏ Job in progress
- ❏ Store signs
- ❏ Window display

Additional Comments: _____

_____

_____

Completed by (staff): _____ Date: _____/_____/_____

LOCATION, LOCATION, LOCATION

$$$$

Location, location, location, it is the mantra of successful retailers worldwide. Let's face it, many types of retail businesses rely heavily on passing pedestrian and motorist traffic to survive; in fact some retailers rely entirely on passing traffic to survive. Now in fairness, the topic of selecting a location for a retail store really is worthy of an entire book on the subject. However, given that this is a general marketing book, I have boiled down what I believe to be a few of the most important questions that you should be asking and answering when selecting a location for a new retail business. I have turned these questions into a yes or no checklist. Use the checklist to analyze each location that you are considering for your retail business from the results of completing the checklist. Obviously the higher the "yes" count, the better that particular location will be for your new retail business venture. Some of the questions will not be relevant for every type of retail operation and those questions can simply be left blank.

Retail Location Checklist

Yes	No	Retail Location Checklist Questions
❏	❏	Is the location large enough for your current needs and is there the potential to expand within or outside of the location to accommodate potential growth?
❏	❏	Is the exterior and interior of the building in a good state of repair?
❏	❏	Does the location meet zoning, fire, and handicap accessibility regulations?
❏	❏	Is the rent within your budget range, and are the long-term lease terms favorable?
❏	❏	Is the location one where your customers would expect your business to be located? For instance, shoppers might not expect a jewelry store carrying a high-end merchandise line to be located in a strip plaza surrounded by doughnut shops and dry cleaners. Consequently, this could have a negative impact on sales.
❏	❏	Does the location require an unusually large amount of leasehold improvements?
❏	❏	Are the mechanical requirements such as electrical, heating, plumbing, air conditioning, and communications wiring suitable for your type of retail business?
❏	❏	Is the interior layout compatible with your design and merchandising display fixtures, equipment, and ideas?
❏	❏	Does the exterior have the "curb appeal" that is consistent with your image or the image you would like to project?
❏	❏	Is there suitable parking at the location, close by, or within reasonable distance? And is this parking free or paid if this affects your customers?
❏	❏	Is there good access to public transit?
❏	❏	Does the store have the type of visibility that you want or require?
❏	❏	Is there competition in the area that will enhance business or detract from business?
❏	❏	Is your potential business compatible with the other businesses on the street and in the general area?
❏	❏	Is the neighborhood safe and improving?
❏	❏	Is the neighborhood crime plagued and declining?
❏	❏	Is there suitable space for exterior and interior signage, and will local ordinance permit the type of signage you want to install?
❏	❏	Are the existing windows suitable for the type of displays that your want to create and if not can additional window display space be easily added?
❏	❏	Are there other businesses in the area that would be suitable matches for cross-promotional activities?
❏	❏	Does the pedestrian foot traffic count and the passing motorist traffic count meet your requirements?
❏	❏	Is there interior or exterior space available for special sales and events such as under the tent sales, celebrity appearances, and for the creation of large interior merchandise displays?
❏	❏	Is the location suitably set up to handle deliveries of merchandise from suppliers?
❏	❏	Is there availability to suitable labor force in the area?
❏	❏	Are there any restrictive covenants in place that would prevent you from marketing and promoting in the style that you want to, such as reduced hours of operation at shopping malls, or restrictions on the number of displays you can place outside of your business during operating hours and so forth?
❏	❏	Is the store located in an area that is composed mainly of your target audience?

RETAIL LOCATION PROS AND CONS

$$$$ ✎ ☏ ⚖

There are obvious pros and cons in terms of what type of retail location you choose for your store—a shopping mall, a strip plaza, or the downtown core. Considerations such as budget, visibility, and access all play a major role in determining where your store is located. While you may not want to pay an extra $1,000 a month in rent to have your store located in a shopping plaza, does this decision make good business and financial sense? Of course only you can answer that question, but you could end up spending a lot more than $1,000 in advertising trying to reach your target audience that may be at the shopping mall. Just food for thought. Listed below are a few of the pros and cons associated with three types of retail operating locations.

Location	Pros	Cons
Downtown core	Accessible transit	Limited parking
	Drawing power	Limited operating hours
	Street visibility	Higher rent
Strip plaza	Lower rent	Limited street visibility
	Longer operating hours	Limited geographic market
	Promotional freedom	Limited parking and transit
Shopping center	Broad market appeal	High rent
	Superior parking	No street visibility
	Upscale image	Often restrictive rules

RETAIL LOCATION, COMPETITION, AND BIG BOX STORES

$$$$ ✎ ☏ ⚖

When selecting a location for your new retail shop or for an expansion shop carefully consider what other businesses are in close proximity. Is there a big box retailer close by, and is there competition close by that sells the same or similar products as yours? If not, you might want to consider selecting a location that has both—a big box retailer and competition close to your new shop—for two reasons. First you can profit from a big box retailer's high volume of shoppers because it is a proven fact that small niche or specialty retailers in close proximity to a big box retailer fair better than similar types of shops that are not. Additionally, you can use the well-known big box retailer in your advertisements to create instant understanding of where your business is geographically located. And even more important, by using the big box retailer's name in your advertisements and marketing materials you benefit with added credibility because people will associate your business with theirs. In terms of the competition look no farther than automotive dealership malls, food courts, and public markets for proof that being beside or grouped in with one or more competitors is good for business. Each competitor is like a building block and the sum of the blocks creates the overall shopping experience. Why drive a half-hour to shop at one car dealership, when you can drive the same half-hour to an auto mall and have almost unlimited choices in what make you want to view, style of car, and price considerations? In a growing or stable marketplace, competition creates more business; it is a proven fact and one that top retailers understand and look for when selecting a location for their stores.

DESIGN YOUR STORE FOR YOUR TARGET AUDIENCE

$$$$ ✎ 🕐 ⚖

When selecting a location for your retail store or designing or redesigning the layout, always make sure to keep in mind who your customers will be. For instance, if your target audience is mature folks, then make aisles wider, lights brighter, sign lettering bigger and bolder, make sure convenient parking and good access to transit are close by, as well as easily accessible areas for sitting and resting. Alternately, if your target audience is young children then paint the shop in bright colors, lower displays, and make all fixtures more durable to avoid damage, and give extra attention to safety-related details and issues. The objective when designing a retail store is to appeal to the largest segment of your target audience in the broadest way so that they will feel comfortable in the store and therefore will want to return and shop often. This is one area where it pays to hire a professional designer and decorator with experience in commercial retail store applications. Listed below are general design tips that can be handy in any retailing situation regardless of the products you sell.

- When arranging displays and merchandise keep in mind that the most "profitable zones" are the areas around the sales checkout, immediately inside the front entrance, and on a direct path to the sales checkout counter. These are the areas that will account for the largest percentage of impulse buying; therefore it is wise to display your bestselling merchandise in these highly visible profit zones.

- Occasionally try new designs in terms of how you position your displays and merchandise. The majority of retailers find that a grid pattern, much like that used in a supermarket works best as it enable shoppers to have to pass most of store merchandise to get to certain product sections or displays within the store, increasing the chance of impulse buying. This is referred to as directing shoppers where you want them to go. Additionally, rotating merchandise will give shoppers the perception that the stock and displays are new and fresh.

- Always group products together that enhance or complement each other and that make for logical package sales. For instance, a pet shop should display bags and cans of dog food on the bottom and middle shelves while leaving the top open to display food dishes and bowls even if they have a bowl display elsewhere in the store. This sets off shopping triggers "Hey Fido hasn't had a new bowl in two years. I better get one while I am here." Likewise, men's shirts should be displayed by ties and socks, women's blouses by scarves and undergarments, batteries by toys that require them, light bulbs by lamps, cooking utensils by pots and pans, and so forth. Always think about how to increase the value of each sale and group products together that would accomplish this.

- Keep clearance bins and sales racks to the back of the store so customers who come in to browse have to walk past the other merchandise to get to the back of the store to go through the sales merchandise. However, do clearly promote clearance bins and sales racks with signage displays on the back wall or hanging from the ceiling over the racks. You want shoppers to take note of the sale not only to clear dated and out-of-season merchandise but also to pass your newest merchandise with the possibility to create impulse buying.

- Always think about key vertical profit zones when displaying products. The best zones are between 18 inches off the floor to a maximum of 66 inches off the floor. These are the zones that are the most visible and easily accessible to the vast majority of shoppers.

WEB RESOURCE

✐ www.visualstore.com: Online retail store design and visual merchandising resources.

BUY AND SELL LIQUIDATED INVENTORY ONLINE

$$+ ✎

Harness the power of the World Wide Web to buy and sell liquidated inventory and merchandise online; it's fast, easy, safe, secure, and the only technical skill required is to be able to click a mouse. In recent years many merchandise liquidation services have gone live on the Web to provide retailers with fantastic forums, which bring buyers and sellers of liquidated merchandise together to meet and conduct business transactions online. Regardless if you are looking to sell slow moving, excessive, or out-of-season merchandise to increase cash flow to purchase you're most saleable and profitable store items or if you are looking to buy merchandise at incredible savings that are often considerably less than wholesale, then Internet liquidation services are a great place to get started on your quest. Listed below are a few online liquidation services. Additionally, a simple query on any major search engine will reveal hundreds more.

WEB RESOURCES

- ✒ www.liquidation.com: Inventory liquidation service brings buyers and sellers together.

- ✒ www.merchandiseusa.com: Inventory liquidation service brings buyers and sellers together.

- ✒ www.quittingbusiness.com: Inventory liquidation service brings buyers and sellers together.

- ✒ www.sell2all.com: Inventory liquidation service brings buyers and sellers together.

PROMOTE ENVIRONMENTALLY FRIENDLY
$$+ ✎

Get in tune with going green and become an environmentally friendly retailer. Educate yourself about how you can utilize a wide range of recycled products such as paper, packaging materials, point of purchase displays, and more, so you can incorporate these environmentally friendly byproducts into the day-to-day operations of your business. Also carefully investigate your current product line to see if there are more environmentally friendly product options available that you can stock and sell in place of or alongside of less environmentally friendly products. Once you've made the switch to green partly or entirely, promote this fact by letting your customers know by way of "nonjudgmental" printed marketing

materials that can be handed out at the cash register. And you can also have signs made promoting your new go-green attitude that can be placed around the inside of your store on product displays. The go-green retailing premise is simple. You will never alienate consumers by being an environmentally friendly and conscious retailer, but you just may attract a few new customers simply because we all know that aiming for a healthier planet is not only good, but a must for this and future generations. Going green just makes good business sense.

WEB RESOURCE

- ✒ www.greensites.com: Information, articles, and links pertaining to environmentally friendly retailing.

WINDOW SPACE: THE 24-HOUR SILENT SALESPERSON
$+ ✎

Store windows are unquestionably one of the best and least expensive marketing tools that most retailers have at their immediate disposal. Windows can be used to display new products, demonstrate products, and to motivate people to impulse buy. They are in reality the 24-hour silent salesperson that never sleeps. Well-planned and -executed window displays can increase revenues and profits for every retailer who takes the time to create, maintain, and continually update her window displays for the benefit of her customers and ultimately also for her business and bottom-line revenues. Window displays are a form of advertising and like in any great advertising strategy there are main objectives that must be met, which in this case are attention, interest, desire, and action.

Attention

The first goal of the window display or window advertisement is to grab the attention of people passing by your shop. This can be accomplished by adding movement to your displays, creatively using lighting and bright color to grab attention, and by the use of bold signs that make a marketing statement such as "sale in progress."

Interest

The second step is to create interest once you have the attention of people stopping to look in your windows so that they do not simply take a quick glance and then continue on their way down the sidewalk. Creating interest will greatly depend on what you display and the products that you sell. However, the obvious way to create interest is by having great products that are always in high demand. Another way to create interest is to become known for changing your window display regularly. Or providing something that people get used to seeing in the window and go looking for every time they pass by such as the daily weather forecast or scrolling sports scores on an electronic message board or a clock.

Desire

The third element that your window display or advertisement must create is desire for the products that are being displayed in the window, meaning that people want to buy what is on display right away. You can create desire for a product the good old fashioned way by demonstrating how it will benefit the buyers, fill a need, or do something for them such as save time, save money, make them more healthy, and so forth. Or you can create desire by making what is displayed in your window an offer that is too good to pass up such as a product of the day that is on display and priced at cost or less—a legitimate "loss leader." Remember the name of the game is to get them inside. You can sell them on the sidewalk, but you can only close them in the store.

Action

And the final and obvious step is to have a call to action. Tell people what you want them to do, come in and buy. As attention grabbing and interesting as your window display may be, it will have missed the point entirely if it does not motivate people to come into your shop or return to your shop at a later time when you are open. So beyond telling them what you want them to do next you also must provide the motivation for them to take that action. So in the example of the loss leader pricing to create desire for a fabulous product that will benefit your potential

customers you now have to make them want it today and not tomorrow or the next day and you do this by using deadlines: "50 percent off today only" or "$50 off to the next ten people who buy." In doing so you tell people that this is a great deal, get in here and get it now or you will miss out on a great shopping opportunity. Many retailers frown on selling products at or below cost, but don't. You want people to come into the shop and you must offer legitimate deals for them to do so, then you can up-sell or sell more.

WINDOW SPACE: PROFESSIONAL LOOK ON A BUDGET
$$+ ✎ ☎

In terms of the budget you establish and maintain for your window display program you basically have three options: 1) dress the windows yourself; 2) locate and occasionally employ an intern; or 3) hire a professional window dressing and display service. Of course, there are advantages and disadvantages associated with each.

Do It Yourself

The first option available to you in terms of dressing your display windows is the least expensive option—dress the windows yourself or have an employee do it. I caution that while it is the least expensive option up front, it can also cost you sales if your window does not grab attention, create interest, and draw shoppers into your store. However, with budget in mind here are a few ideas that you can use to get your creative energies flowing prior to tackling your window displays.

- Buy books about window design and displays or if they are available at your local library then sign them out to study great displays and creative ideas.
- Armed with a camera, put on your most comfortable walking shoes and get out to see what other retailers are doing with their windows. Take pictures and make notes about window displays that look great and not so great. Also if you see people looking in the windows ask them what they think about the display; this is

grassroots learning and research that can really pay off when it is time to create great window displays for your shop.

- Make a few basic sketches of your ideas before you commit to building the displays. Storyboarding can also save time in the long run and help to identify weak areas of ideas that you didn't think of previously.
- Don't clutter your display, keep it lean and mean with one central focal point. The idea is to grab attention and pull people into your shop. You don't want your entire inventory on display in the window, this only serves to confuse and lessen the display impact.
- Be careful about the amount of time you devote to your displays. Creating ideas and building interesting window displays have a real way of chewing up valuable time and before you know it you would have been better off hiring a pro to do it. Try to set aside a fixed amount of time each week to create a new display; this probably should not exceed one hour.

Hire a Student

The second option is to locate and occasionally employ an intern or student to create great designs and build the window displays. Though there are only a few programs in North America that train people to become professional window trimmers, you can enlist the help of other types of design students such as interior designers, residential and commercial designers, product designers, and graphic designers. Most have an eye and a knack for what looks great and can grab attention. Post a notice at the local college or university stating your needs, or call the student union and let them know what you need.

Hire a Professional

Hiring a professional window trimmer should not be viewed as an expense as much as it should an investment in advertising. Once again, I cannot overstate the importance that window displays play in terms of grabbing the attention of people passing, building interest and desire from what they see in the

window displays, and pulling them into your shop. Not occasionally, but often. Great window displays do that and for that reason if you can afford to pay a professional to create exciting and attention-grabbing window displays then this option should be carefully considered. To find a great window trimming service, ask other retailers for advice and referrals and also look in the telephone directory. Generally window display services will be listed under window dressing or window display designers and builders. Another way to find a window dresser is to contact your local chamber of commerce, if one is not a member they will likely be able to direct you to a service. If budget restrictions are a real concern, yet you still want the beneficial results that a professionally designed and displayed window can have you might try to barter products in exchange for the service. Or perhaps join together with neighboring businesses. If the window dresser can save driving time and do two or three retailers on the same day of the week, it may enable them to pass this saving on to the participating businesses in the form of a substantial (in the range of 25 percent) discount.

WINDOW SPACE: CREATIVITY COUNTS $$ ✎

One of the best aspects of keeping up "window appearances" is that it allows you to be creative in the way you dress the window, what types of props you use, and how you grab people's attention as they are passing by. Think of your window displays as a creative outlet that enables you to separate your business from a competing business that sells the same products. In fact your window displays could even become your competitive advantage. However, you have to pull in the reins a bit and remember that your window displays and advertising should be used as a natural extension of what is going on in your shop at the time of creating the display. If you're holding a sale, then the focus of window displays should revolve around the sale. If you're introducing a new product line then the focus of the displays should revolve around the new product line. This is not to say that your window displays should not be creative because they should beyond expectations; just that there should always be a central theme that complements or enhances your main marketing objective at that period of time. In other words, your store's theme and marketing message should be consistent right from the window display to a reinforcing message on the entrance door to in-store displays and finally to the sales counter and the staff—one central theme and message designed to meet your marketing objective and maximize results. What will work for one retailer in terms of a creative window display will not work for the next; much has to do with the products you sell, the image that you project, and how you price products. However, with that said the following are a few creative ideas that can be incorporated into window displays or used as a catalyst to think a little more creatively when developing your own window displays.

A Few Creative Window Display Ideas

- Try before-and-after displays featuring products that your sell. For instance a low cost yet effective window display for a shoe store would be an old ratty pair of shoes beside a new one and a sign that ask "Is it time to treat your feet to a treat?" Before-and-after displays will work with just about any type of product, especially for retailers who not only sell goods but also repair them.

- Create window displays around popular entertainment, sports, or musical events that are hot at that moment. At the time of writing this book *Survivor* was the hot television reality show and therefore would make a wise choice as a theme for a window display and sale inside the store. Other examples would be window displays created around other events such as the Super Bowl, the top movie at the box office, a big community event such as a parade or political election, or even something as simple as the current season.

- If you have been in business a while then use products that you sold many moons ago in your displays along with photographs of how your store, staff, and community used to look. Tie this type of display in with a storewide anniversary sale to celebrate the milestone. If you do not

have access to old photographs and products then contact the local museum, city archives, or the library to see if they do and if these items can be borrowed to create your displays.

- Use props and movement to make your displays come alive and exciting. Remember the goal is to get people passing by to stop and take notice and create enough interest that they will wander into the shop and buy. So use things like LP players to create a low-cost way to rotate products on top and add movement, and other low-cost items like small water pumps and bowls that can be used to create water effects in the window. Additionally, flashing lights, music, a television or monitor running a promotional message or product display on a loop can also be highly effective in terms of grabbing attention. Of course the most effective props are those that reinforce the benefits of the product that you are displaying. For instance, if you sell bicycle helmets with a shatter proof guarantee then create a simple display with a hammer that automatically and repeatedly hits the helmet on the side to illustrate the fact that the product truly is shatterproof.

- Live demonstrations are another way to get super creative in terms of using your window space for maximum marketing efforts. Here are a few ideas for live demonstrations.

  - A fashion retailer could hold a Friday afternoon fashion show in the window space using real models (customers) accompanied by music and bright lights to create an exciting atmosphere.

  - An exercise equipment retailer could set up various pieces of exercise equipment right in the window space during the week and have people using it in front of consumers passing by. One day a person running on a treadmill, the next day a person working out with free weights, the following day someone working out on a stationary bike and so forth.

  - A pizza or sandwich shop could prepare foods and lunch specials right in the window space.

– A jewelry store could let people in the community use the window space to propose marriage to each other. Accompany the occasion with music, photographs, and more to make it special.

– A hardware store could set up a small woodworking shop in the window space and invites customers to use it free of charge to make small projects much to the interest of people who stop to watch.

The point is that live action draws a crowd, demonstrating products can show onlookers the benefits associated with owning or using that particular product, and create desire and motivation to enter the store and buy.

APPEAL TO THE FIVE SENSES
$+ ✎

To the vast majority of consumers shopping is not merely the process of buying, it is an entertainment experience, an event to be enjoyed much like going to the movies or out for a meal at a restaurant. With that in mind, you have to get every person who walks into your store involved by creating an entertaining atmosphere that makes them want to stay, shop, and return often. In short your store must appeal to the five senses.

Sight

Your store must be visually appealing. Most impulse buying is based on the sight sense: We see, we desire, we buy. In fact, studies have shown that 70 percent of retail purchases made by consumers are on an impulse basis, after they had already entered the store and without premeditation. Product merchandising in your store is one of the most important aspects of retailing. Placing merchandise at specific areas in the store can increase your profits significantly, and this is generally referred to as zone merchandizing. Key zones include at the entrance, changing rooms, windows, and at the cash register area or point of purchase. Commonly customers impulse buy at the cash register so place smaller, lower priced items near the cash desks and train your staff to suggestively sell while they are ringing up the

sale. Regardless of the size of your business it is very important that the customer can browse freely and comfortably. Presentation really is everything. Display your products in a way that would help the customers visualize your products in their home, or in a way that they can visualize the benefits of ownership, such as a life-sized cutout of a really physically fit person displayed beside a running treadmill. Likewise visually appealing product displays can also easily be achieved with some creative decorating, adding color and anything else you feel will punch up the overall presentation so your displays look great. Visual merchandising extends beyond product displays and also includes your shop inside and out, window displays, signage, sales and marketing materials, and staff. Keep a clean store that is in good repair and get your employees into sharp-looking uniforms emblazoned with your business name, logo, and promotional message. Go the extra mile during all holidays and create fantastic theme displays and merchandising packages that your customers will find visually exciting.

Touch

When people can reach out and touch a product it makes that product real, tangible, which is a very important aspect in retailing. Create displays that are interactive with your customers, give them the opportunity to pick up and look at your goods, touch them, test the quality and texture, thus adding to and increasing the value. Even better if possible, give customers the opportunity to use the products in a controlled area of your store so that they can see firsthand the benefits associated with the product. Toys "R" Us sells more toys than any other retailer because they leave many toys unpacked and let kids (and parents) try them out, play with them, get emotionally involved by having fun; all this creates motivation to buy. Cosmetic and fragrance companies have also long been aware of the touch and benefit marketing approach. A simple visit to your local drug store or department store will show you exactly what I am saying. Sample products are displayed right on the counter for the customers to touch and try, creating desire to want to own. Depending on what you sell, with a little bit of imagination you can create the same environment for your customers.

Taste

Taste is one of the best and easiest senses to appeal to. For instance, if you operate a bakery then always have free samples of your products sitting by the cash register and encourage people to try them. Likewise if you are a food manufacturer, wholesaler, or processor, then give away free samples of your products in grocery stores, mall kiosks, trade shows, and other special events. Create awareness and make it exciting for the taste buds. Once again the goal is to create impulse buying, get people hooked on your goods so that they will return and continue to buy. If you sell something that tastes great then let people taste it and they will buy it, it really is that simple.

Smell

Realtors have learned that the power of smell can increase their sales. That is why they encourage home sellers to bake a loaf of bread prior to an open house, or place fresh cut flowers in a vase and on the kitchen table before a showing. You can use the sense of smell to your benefit. For example, if you operate a bath and fragrance shop, arouse the interest of customers by simply using the products you sell: Burn a fragrant candle, create a bubble bath in a large bowl, the opportunities are endless. If you operate a bakery leave your front entrance door open; the smell will attract passersby and help increase sales. If you operate a restaurant then make sure your exhaust fan is strong enough to carry the aroma of your cooked food to the outdoors, especially during breakfast, lunch, and dinner times. And if you sell perfume then spray some outside your store, around the entrance, and just inside the door as a way to lure people passing by to stop, smell, and come on in.

Hearing

Create a comfortable atmosphere with background music or if relevant to your business and products then develop other clever ways to appeal to people's sense of hearing. Use this sound to increase sales. A clothing store that targets teenaged shoppers would best attract their customers by playing the top ten hot pop hits, at a slightly louder volume than most adult ears can bear. A music store allows free record sampling, an electronics shop turns up the volume of their best sounding stereo systems and stereo television sets. All these create a comfortable environment for their customers. Sounds can be used as a powerful tool to motivate people to buy around the holidays. Retail outlets generally start to play Christmas music near the middle to the end of November. Why? Simply to get the customers thinking about and in the mood for Christmas, thus motivating them to buy for friends and family members.

MAKE IT EASY FOR CUSTOMERS TO GIVE YOU MONEY
$$ ✎

Make it as easy as possible for your customers to give you their hard-earned money. As elementary as this marketing secret may be, many retailers still shy away from convenient payment options for customers usually because of the cost associated with providing these payment options. But in today's competitive retailing environment retailers must provide customers with as many payment options as possible, including cash, check, debit card, credit card, and often even consumer financing or leasing solutions. Eliminate just one and you are in effect reducing your potential market by a proportionate amount. One way to reduce the merchant rate for credit cards is to check with your local chamber of commerce or other small-business association in your area to inquire if they provide association members with reduced credit card merchant rates. Often business associations like the chamber of commerce negotiate lower merchant rates with banks and credit card companies based on the number of people who use the service. I have routinely heard members can reduce merchant rates by as much as three percent just by joining, and often these savings on credit card merchant rates alone can offset membership cost. Beyond increasing sales through providing customers with convenient payment options you can also benefit by reducing the amount of cash on hand, thus reducing security concerns for staff and the potential for theft. Below are a few payment options you should consider implementing in your store if you do not currently offer them to your customers; check off the ones that you think will help your business grow.

WEB RESOURCES

- www.visa.com: Visa credit card financial services.
- www.mastercard.com: MasterCard credit card financial services.

- www.discovercard.com: Discover credit cards financial services.
- www.amercianexpress.com: American Express credit card financial services.
- www.internet-e-checks.com: Software that enables you to accept electronic checks by mail, fax, telephone, and e-mail.

Payment Option Checklist

- ❏ Visa credit card
- ❏ MasterCard credit card
- ❏ American Express credit card
- ❏ Discover credit card
- ❏ Diners Club credit card
- ❏ In-house credit card
- ❏ Business checks
- ❏ Personal checks
- ❏ Electronic checks
- ❏ Debit cards
- ❏ On-site Automated Teller Machine (ATM)
- ❏ Money orders

- ❏ Foreign currency
- ❏ Gift certificates
- ❏ Travelers checks
- ❏ In-house revolving credit account
- ❏ In-house creative 90-day same-as-cash financing
- ❏ In-house 30-day bill-me-later programs
- ❏ Consumer and business financing options in association with lending institutions
- ❏ Consumer and business leasing options in association with leasing companies
- ❏ Barter and exchange programs and points

SEEK OUTSIDE OPPORTUNITIES

Are there selling opportunities for your business outside of your current retail store location? And if so, can these selling opportunities be efficient and profitable? The answers are as varied as the different types of retailing ventures out there. But in almost every retail situation there are ways to seek outside retailing opportunities beyond the store that can complement your business and generate additional income and profits. The best way to seek outside retail opportunities is to first analyze what you sell and to whom you sell it. For instance, if you retail women's fashions aimed at the mature market you already know who your target market is and the fact that your business relies on these people coming to your retail location to purchase products. So this information about your products and target audience can be used to consider outside selling opportunities. Perhaps given this example an outside selling opportunity may be to organize fashion shows at senior complexes and retirement homes. Basically, with this example you would be taking your business to your target audience rather than your target audience coming to you, and you'd also be providing an element of entertainment for your customers at the same time. Additional outside opportunities could be in the form of developing a Web site, or contract sales people to seek out and service new business outside of your geographic locations. Just because your business operates from a fixed location doesn't mean that you can't go looking for and developing new sales opportunities. Here are a few more ways to extend the reach of your business beyond your store to create and profit from new selling opportunities.

Show Homes

Let's say you sell products for the home such as furniture, appliances, electronics, art, or kitchen and bathroom accessories. Then make a list of new home developers and real estate agents in your area and get in contact with them to explore the potential to include your products into their show or model homes. Create small yet descriptive and elegant signs to go with the products you supply or lend to be featured in these homes with your products on display, along with a small plastic business card holder so that people can take your card home with them when they leave. To increase the effectiveness of this trick, also ask that the property developer gives each of their customers a gift certificate or coupons, giving the holder 10 percent off the products you sell. Open houses and model homes can draw hundreds if not thousands of new visitors each month giving you access to a broad audience.

Vacant Storefronts

Take a drive or walk through your local community and count how many vacant storefronts are available for sale or lease. If your community is like most, there will be quite a few, and best of all most will be in high-traffic areas that are highly visible to passing motorists and pedestrians alike. Write down contact numbers from the for sale or lease signs and get in contact with the owners or managers of these premises to inquire about the possibility of installing temporary window displays until the location is tenanted. The displays you create will reflect your business and products or services that you sell. Setting up temporary window displays in vacant stores is a wonderful low-cost way to display your products and services, and benefits the landlord by making the location more attractive thus viable from a potential tenant's prospective. In some situations you will have to pay a monthly rate to secure the storefront window, and only you can determine what amount is fair

based on what benefits you believe will be realized by this unique and effective promotional activity.

Trade Shows

Trade show and community events such as parades and fairs also present savvy retailers with product display and sales opportunities, as a stand-alone venture or in conjunction with other businesses that are participating in these community events. Give out sample products for free, set up a kiosk and sell your products, or host a free seminar under a tent to explain and demonstrate your products.

Cross Promotional Displays

Strike deals with other retailers throughout your community to cross-promote each other's products for marketing purposes. If you sell patio furniture and the local spa dealer does not then strike a deal to set up patio furniture displays in his showroom to enhance his spas and promote your products to his customers. Likewise, if you sell high-end furniture then strike a deal with local art galleries to furnish their interiors with display models of your products. Cross-promotional activities such as these are a great way to showcase your products to a broader audience and in doing so you create new selling opportunities.

Special Event Planners

Strike deals with special event planners, wedding consultants, and interior designers to supply your products for their events in exchange for the marketing, advertising, and promotional opportunities that go along with such an arrangement. Once again hundreds if not thousands can attend special events, a good portion of whom I am sure will have never heard of your business and the products you sell. Therefore, giving you ample opportunity to secure a few new customers and increase sales.

CLEAN FOR MORE CUSTOMERS
$+ ✎

One of the best impressions you can make on customers is the first. Top retailers understand the value of always putting their "cleanest foot" forward; customers appreciate this and return the favor by becoming repeat and loyal customers. A rusty car immediately makes you think that in addition to looking bad it must also be mechanically bad—regardless if this is true or not, that's the perception most people will have. What people see on the outside or inside of your store will greatly influence what they think about your products or services. Here are a few quick cleanup suggestions that will keep your store looking great for your customers and that can drastically increase the amount of drop-in and return visits.

Clean for More Green Tips

- Take five minutes before opening in the morning and closing at night to pick up trash outside your business—off the sidewalk, in the alley, and around the parking lot and sidewalk areas, even if you share them with other businesses.
- Wash interior and exterior windows and in-store displays at least every week (daily if you feel that it is required due to the amount of traffic your shop receives). However, the front door glass should be cleaned every day without exception as this is the most visible surface area to customers coming and going.
- Keep a can of paint handy that matches your wall colors to touch up nicks and scratches in the paint as they occur. Additionally, try to keep a few floor tiles handy that match your existing flooring to occasionally replace any that begin to show wear, especially in the high-traffic areas around the front door, changing rooms, washrooms, and cash register.
- Remove clutter around the cash register and boxes that seem to magically get stacked up in back corners. Follow one simple rule: If it cannot be sold or used to sell other things then you do not need it hanging around, regardless of what it may be.
- Pitch handwritten signs into the trash and replace them with computer-generated signs that you can make right on your computer or have made inexpensively at the local sign shop. If your budget is tight then try bartering your goods

with the sign maker in exchange for the signs you need to improve the look of your business. Great looking signs are proven to increase impulse buying from customers who are better informed about what you sell.

- Vacuum the carpets daily or polish floors daily if you have hard surfaces and place wear mats at entrances, exits, and other high foot traffic areas within the store. Likewise, keep on top of gum, pricing stickers, and tape that will become part of the surface unless they are removed from flooring and displays daily.
- Dust daily and don't forget to include around and inside light fixtures and display cases. Nothing will turn potential customers away quicker than having to blow dust off a product just so that they can read the label or pricing sticker.
- Public washrooms should be checked, cleaned, and restocked with paper products and soaps throughout the day as needed. In general strive to keep your place of business cleaner than the competition; your customers will love you for it and reward you by being loyal buyers.
- Keep on top of graffiti on the outside of your store. Most communities now have graffiti removal services that for a flat monthly fee will automatically check the outside of your shop weekly and remove any graffiti caused by spray paint, markers, or chalk. Though another expense, this type of service can return your investment many times over.
- Keep a supply of light bulbs on hand to replace burned out lights inside and outside your shop as required including signage and display case lights.

PUT A PROMOTIONAL FLIER IN EVERY SHOPPING BAG
$ ✎

Here is a simple and inexpensive marketing trick that can have real bottom-line impact in terms or revenues and profits. Design a promotional flier on your computer and have it photocopied at the local copy center for pennies apiece. Place a promotional flier in every shopping bag before customers leave your store with their purchases. Get in the habit of changing your shopping bag promotional inserts on a weekly basis and be sure to mix up the offering a bit. Perhaps a new product promotion one week, the printed history of your business the next, and staff spotlights the week after. Of course, the best promotional inserts are ones that motivate people to take action. In retailing that simply means your insert should motivate customers to come back to your store and purchase, refer others to your store to buy products, or ideally both. These types of little marketing promotions such as shopping bag inserts can have a really positive impact on your marketing efforts. Imagine your valued customer getting home and unpacking their purchases only to find a printed voucher inside their shopping bags that gives them a few dollars off their next purchase from your shop—what a pleasant surprise for them and a low-cost yet effective customer retention trick for you.

CONSIDER A RESALE PROGRAM
$$$+ ✎

Initiating a resale program may not be a viable option for all retailers, but for some it could prove to be a profitable business opportunity waiting to be identified and developed. Online bookseller Amazon has mastered this. Consumers purchase books from Amazon and when and if they're ready to resell that same book, Amazon is right there offering a highly effective forum to do so, for a commission fee of course. For decades auto dealers have provided customers with a resale program, under the guise of a trade-in or trade-up program. Though a bit different the general marketing principle at work here is the same. Sell a product and when the purchaser is ready to resell, trade up, or trade in that same product, offer them options to do so. And most importantly secure their new product purchase at the same time. Not unlike leasing companies some clever retailers have even gone to the extent of developing a system that guarantees consumers a fixed repurchase price or product value at a fixed future date. The bottom line is this;

all retailers should conduct a feasibility study to determine if a resale program is right for their businesses and product lines. The following are a few examples of creative resale options that you could provide your customers.

Consignment Space

Offer to resell their previous purchases on a consignment basis. The consignment arm of your business could operate right from your current location or you could establish a secondary location that sells the consigned goods and retain a percentage of the sales value.

Web Site

Develop a Web site that enables customers to resell products that they had previously purchased from your shop. You could charge a fee for the listing, a commission on the sales value, or simply provide the service for free as a way of securing their future business.

Newspaper

Much like a Web site, you could use your desktop computer to create a resale newsletter that enabled customers to list their products for sale and distribute the newsletter through your store. The newsletter would be in the form of classified listings and you could charge for the service or once again provide the resale option as a customer service.

ARE YOU PREPARED TO INCREASE SALES?
$$+ 🐾

In the majority of situations when revenues and profits are lagging or decreasing, what is the fastest way that retailers can increase sales by 50 percent or more with a relatively small investment, in a relatively short period of time, and continue to do so week after week, month after month, and year after year? There is only one answer. You must transform you and your staff from being order takers into sales professionals. Get started by enlisting the services of a retail sales trainer to come into your business and train you and your staff as a group or on a one-on-one basis to become professional up-sellers and closers, instead of order takers. There are three key ingredients to making a successful transformation from order taking to sales making in retail.

Getting the Right Coach

Obvious, but the professional retail sales trainer you enlist must be great, a true professional who helps train your staff to get the results you want. Talk to at least three and ask for and check their client references. Basically, do your homework to ensure you're getting the best your budget will afford. However, as a word of caution make sure that you seek out and secure a sales trainer who specializes in retail store sales and training.

Stay Focused on the Customer

Understand that your main motivation for making the leap from order taking to sales making should be done with the customer's best interest in mind. It is a proven fact that simply taking customers' orders without truly understanding their needs and wants is actually providing a disservice that can eventually lead your customers to competitors who take the time to truly understand their needs. A big part of the retailing mix is understanding customers and what they want. This can be revealed in sales training education and exercises.

Keep an Open Mind

Keep an open mind to the process, learn from the trainer, implement the selling strategies that are taught, and be prepared to take the time required to master the art of persuasion and track the beneficial changes and results. If you take the time to follow the program step by step in almost all situations the revenue and profit increases can be dramatic.

WEB RESOURCE

✍ www.trainingregistry.com: National online directory listing professional business, management, and employee training consultants, and training courses and products indexed geographically and by topic.

ASK CUSTOMERS FOR REFERRALS
$ ✎

Often the most productive and beneficial marketing techniques are the ones that are obvious, yet easily overlooked and therefore never practiced. And, asking your current customers for referrals may just top the list of overlooked and underpracticed great marketing tricks. Many sales professionals have built their entire sales careers strictly on referral business, but the vast majority of retailers never ask their customers for referrals. It's true. As a retailer, when was the last time you asked a customer for a referral? Or, as a consumer, when was the last time a retailer asked you for a referral? My guess is the answer in both cases is likely never, simply because the majority of retailers focus on advertising or special promotions to prospect for new business instead of mining their existing customer base for referrals as a method of gaining new customers and sales as a result. Asking customers for referrals will work for every retailer, regardless of the types of products that are being sold, and best of all for a fraction of the cost associated with attracting new customers using traditional advertising or special promotional methods. If you really want to maximize results, be sure to offer incentives to customers who refer new business to you. These incentives can be in the form of product discounts, free product upgrades, gift certificates, or even a nice dinner out at a local restaurant. You decide, but nothing says thank you better than a handwritten note with a special gift as a token of appreciation. Here are a few ways to ask your existing customers to refer their friends, family members, and co-workers to your store.

- Get in the habit of telling all customers at the till and before they leave, "Thank you for shopping and please tell your friends about our store and products. We appreciate all new business."
- Design and print a basic coupon that entitles the holder to a 10 percent discount on in-stock items. Give all your customers a few at the time of purchase and kindly ask that they share the coupons with friends.
- Hold an "out to win your business sale" and tell all your customers that if they bring a new

customer into the store for the event both of them will get a special discount of gift.

- Ask customers to kindly fill out a simple referral form (like the one shown below) at the cash register and give them a special gift for doing

so. Contact your new prospects by way of telephone or a direct-mail campaign and let them know that there is a special gift or discount waiting from them when they shop at your store.

Sample Referral Form

Your Business Name Here

Name: _____

Occupation: _____

Address: _____

City: _____ State: _____ Zip code: _____

Telephone: _____ Fax: _____ E-mail address: _____

How do you know this person?   ❏ Friend   ❏ Family   ❏ Co-worker

We appreciate your help.

PROFIT FROM GIFT CERTIFICATES
$$ ✎

Gift certificates are a great marketing tool and a terrific way to increase revenues and profits, but are often overlooked by many retailers. You can have gift certificates printed professionally or even make them yourself using your computer. However, if you decide to create and print your own gift certificates just make sure that you develop a numbering system that cannot be easily duplicated, and make sure to sign each one in ink when they are handed out or sold at the cash register. One trick to really promote your gift certificates is to offer them to customers at 90 percent of the redeemable value, meaning you sell a $10 gift certificate for $9. The theory behind this is that it creates a motivation for your customers to buy them to hand out to friends and family. Thus you create an opportunity to lure new customers to the store and a further opportunity to win their loyalty and keep them coming back. The discount you offer will easily be recouped when the person

redeems the gift certificate because as a general rule they will spend two to three times the amount of the gift certificate value on other items in the store. You may even want to give out free $5 gift certificates around holidays as a way to thank your best customers for supporting your business. Of course, it should go without saying that you should promote your gift certificates hard during the holiday season and special times of the year such as graduation, Valentine's Day, Easter, and Christmas.

SMALL PURCHASES PRESENT BIG SALES OPPORTUNITIES
$ ✎

Never overlook the true value of any sale, regardless of how small the initial value of it may be today. Each and every sale you make has the potential to payoff large if you develop strategies for building long-term relationships with customers, instead of considering only short-term or immediate sales value. This retailing concept is often referred to as the lifetime value that each customer represents to the retailer. For example, consider the pet food retailer who sells one pound of dog food to a customer for $2. On the surface a small sale, certainly not one to get overly excited about, right? Wrong. According to the American Kennel Club the average dog eats seven times its weight in food annually and on average will live to be 12 years old. So, upon closer examination this "small $2 sale" has the potential to mushroom into in excess of $8,500 over time, based on a puppy that will grow to be 50 pounds and live the average 12 years. Now $8,500 is a far cry from $2, and it doesn't end there when you factor in referrals that this customer may give, and the fact that this customer will likely have more than one dog over her own lifespan. The moral of the story is never underestimate your customer's purchasing power, no matter how small the initial purchase may be today, because it is the lifetime value of each customer compounded that will create the big sales opportunities.

IMPLEMENT A DIRECT MAIL PROMOTIONAL PROGRAM
$$$ ⚒

All retailers regardless of size or the type of product sold should take the time to build and maintain an in-house customer mailing list, which is nothing more than capturing customer contact information at the point of sale or by way of surveys. The information you want will vary depending on your marketing objectives, but at minimum will include full name, complete address, telephone number and a valid e-mail address. Doing so will enable you to take advantage of your customer list by developing a direct mail promotional campaign with the potential to boost sales while you drive down marketing and promotional costs by using direct mail to reach your best customers. Without question direct mail is the easiest and most straightforward way to target exactly who you want to market to, in a very measurable and cost-effective way to sell your products. Studies haven shown that retailers who create and maintain a current customer lists receive the best results from their promotional mailings. You can purchase mailing lists from brokers, however, your own in-house

list of 250 names of well-qualified repeat customers is far more valuable than a random list of 10,000 unqualified names and in the end will return far more and you'll spend far less to reach them.

WEB RESOURCE

⚲ www.the-dma.org: Direct Marketing Association.

BECOME KNOWN FOR OFFERING SOMETHING FOR FREE
$$ ⚒

Who doesn't remember when they receive something for free? It makes people feel like they won something. I'm sure we can all recall something a retailer or service provider has given us, a product or service at no charge and I'll bet you felt special and appreciated as a customer at the time. Do you think that the first pizza shop owner to offer free pizza delivery understood at the time that he was forever changing the way pizza was delivered to homes? Probably not, but that one decision is likely the main reason that pizza has become one of the most consumed fast foods in North America. Basically the businessperson responsible for free pizza delivery created an entire industry. Now I'm not suggesting that your free offering has to have the same impact, but it's a fact that people remember getting something for free and will return to buy in the future because of it and refer others to also buy. A restaurant may offer a bottomless cup of coffee. A car dealership may give away a free tank of gas with every new or used car purchased. A clothing retailer may give away a free dry cleaning coupon with every article of clothing sold. Carefully examine what you are currently doing, is there one or more things that you are giving to customers for free? If so make a big deal out of it, don't let it go unnoticed, advertise it, talk about it, and most of all get the most mileage you can from it. But make sure that your customers are aware of the true value of the freebie, especially if a competitor charges for this item or service that you are giving to your customers. Become known for giving something away for free, promote that fact in all marketing materials, and watch your sales and customer loyalty skyrocket. Here are a few good ways that retailers of commonly sold goods can become known for providing customers something free.

Auto Dealer

A free tank of gas with every new or used automobile purchased.

Restaurant

A bottomless cup of coffee or soda with every meal purchased.

Fashion Retailer

Free replacement buttons for as long as you own the garment that you purchased.

Toy Store

Free batteries on every item purchased that requires batteries to operate.

Electronics Retailer

A free universal remote control on every television, stereo, DVD, or CD player purchased.

Computer Retailer

Free in-home delivery and setup on all complete computer packages purchased.

Grocery Store

A free bottle of spring water with every purchase more than $25.

Hardware Store

A free screwdriver or new small hand tool of the week included with every purchase more than $25.

Lighting Retailer

Free light bulbs included with every light or lamp purchased.

START A CLUB
$$ ⚒

Creating your own club is a terrific way to provide great customer service and secure a few new customers in the process, not to mention build a loyal customer base and increase revenues. The club you create should appeal to your main customer base

or target audience and be relevant to your core business. For instance, if your store specializes in retailing cookware, then an after-hours cooking club held at a local community facility with cooking amenities would be a wise choice. Or, if you were in the business of retailing camera equipment then starting a photography club that was held at your business location one night a week would be a great choice. The principle behind initiating a club is to keep your customers active and involved in your business and to provide customers with an opportunity to participate with other like-minded people in one or more areas of interest related to your product line. In both of the examples above the extended selling opportunities beyond the original purchase are amazing. In the first example these selling opportunities would include additional cookware, cookbooks, and perhaps a gourmet food selection, all on a regular and continued basis. And in the second example the extended selling opportunities would include film, film processing, lenses, and additional camera and related photography equipment, especially as the skill level of the members improved. And these selling opportunities would also be on a regular basis. But also let's not forget the customer service aspect of this great marketing trick. Not only would the creation of the club give customers the opportunity to meet, mingle, and learn from like-minded members, but also the cost to participate would be nothing. One of the best aspects about starting a club relating to your business is that after the club and operating format have been established you quickly find that members will take roles as leaders within the club, reducing the amount of time that you have to commit to operating the club leaving you more time to market to the members.

LURE CUSTOMERS IN BY PROVIDING CONVENIENCES
$$ ⚒

What amenities or conveniences can you provide existing customers to keep them coming back and to entice new customers to shop at your business? Sometimes it's just the small conveniences that customers remember the most, consciously or subconsciously. For instance, I consistently go to the same market to shop for groceries because they are the only one in my area that provides a bicycle lock-up rack outside of the store and I like to leave the car at home when I can. A simple bicycle rack that might cost $500 to purchase and install is in this instance returning the store in excess of $5,000 a year just based on the purchases I make because of a convenience they provide. Simple conveniences that you could provide your customers could include shopping carts or baskets, a courtesy telephone for local calling, inside and outside bench seating, a carry-out

service, selling stamps and transit passes, free delivery and set up, 24-hour shopping via a company Web site, or even litter disposal cans in the parking lot for people who want to give their car a quick clean up. Perhaps the best way to find out what conveniences your customers would benefit from and appreciate the most would be to simply ask. Listed below is a customer convenience checklist. Not all ideas featured will be suitable for every retailer. Therefore go through the list and determine which are best for your situation.

Customer Convenience Checklist

❏ Free product delivery

❏ Free and paid product assembly and set-up options

❏ Free and paid product installation options

❏ A toll-free number

❏ Sales of handy items such as stamps, transit passes, and calling cards

❏ 24-hour emergency telephone service line

❏ Shopping carts or baskets

❏ Carry out to the car service

❏ Umbrellas for rainy days that can be returned later

❏ Ordering by telephone, fax, e-mail, or Web site services

❏ Free inside courtesy telephone for local calls

❏ 100 percent handicap accessible store

❏ Free coffee in the winter and water in the summer

❏ Free while-you-wait gift-wrapping service year round

❏ Good parking and close to public transit

❏ Extended business hours, especially during holidays, sales, and in-store promotional events

❏ Accepting various payment options such as credit cards, debit cards, financing, and checks

❏ A gift registry and management service

❏ Gift certificates and gift baskets available with free delivery

❏ Rain checks provided on out of stock items, along with a special discount

❏ No-hassle product return and refund policies

❏ Follow-up service on all large purchases

❏ Benches inside and outside the store

❏ Exterior bicycle lock-up rack

❏ Automatically fill out and submit all warranty cards for customers free of charge

❏ Offer an automatic product replenishment system so that high-volume buyers do not run out

❏ Prompt service and knowledgeable staff

❏ Free and helpful information booklets and tip sheets about the products you sell

❏ Stock a wide selection of products that customers want and need

❏ Free seminars to inform customers about new products or how to use specific products

❏ Valet parking

❏ Coat, bag, and hat check service

CREATE TIP SHEETS

$ ✎

Create tip sheets or handout fliers for your best-selling products and include information that your customers would find very useful in regard to the products they are purchasing. Information featured on the tip sheets or fliers could include things such as maintenance tips; how to use to get the best performance from the product they have purchased; or very detailed step-by-step instruction to make product use, installation, or setup easier. Even if the manufacturer has included such information in the packaging, your information could be much more detailed. Recently I switched my dog's diet to foods that had to be measured and mixed by hand to arrive at the correct portions. The pet food retailer that I purchase the ingredients from had a tip sheet that highlighted all the need-to-know information pertaining to this specific type of diet. The sheet was easy to read and in bulleted form, and now hangs on the back of the pantry door where we keep the dog food. I found this especially useful and have referred this business many times based on that tip sheet and what I believe to be outstanding customer service. That is the point: Make your customers' lives easier, show them how to get the most benefits out of their purchases, and they will in turn refer your business and products to their friends, family, and co-workers. You can use your desktop computer to design tip sheets and print them out right on your printer. Buy or build a small pamphlet rack, place the rack by the sales counter, and stock it with tip sheets and fliers that feature detailed information about your bestselling products. And of course encourage your customers to take one home with them—or better two, so they will have an extra to share with a friend.

IMPLEMENT YOUR OWN CUSTOMER LOYALTY PROGRAM

$$$ ✎ ☏ ⚖

Air miles, shopping points, and more, there are a wide range of customer loyalty programs in place right across the country, and wisely so because customer loyalty programs will not only increase repeat business but also often increase the average value of each sale. The objective is pretty straightforward: Create a program reward that is valuable and beneficial enough to keep customers coming back to further amass whatever is being collected. And from the customers' perspective this mean they will have to buy more of your products to get more points, miles, or whatever scoring or tracking system is used in the program. Boiled down, it is a great concept: Buy products and when you reach a certain point you will be rewarded for being a loyal customer. Customer loyalty programs work, but they have to be truly beneficial and present real value to earn and hold the attention of shoppers simply due to competition from customer loyalty or frequent buyer programs that are available. One of the most successful and longest running customer loyalty programs in Canada has been "Canadian Tire Money," which is issued to consumers who purchase products from the Canadian Tire Hardware chain. Basically you get 5 percent Canadian Tire money back on your total purchase and this money can be used to purchase anything in the store at any time without restriction. This program has been so successful that older Canadian Tire bills are now commanding huge sums as collectibles. Considerations prior to developing and implementing a customer loyalty program should include the following:

- The first consideration is budget. Though on the surface these programs appear to be straightforward, they can be very costly to establish and manage over the long run.

- Think about how you will motivate people to join your program. Obviously one motivation is to make it free to join, but beyond that what will you put in place to motivate people? Perhaps special incentives such as free products or bonus points for joining or maybe a discount on the purchases they are making at the point of joining; you will have to decide what will get the results you want.

- How will you track and record the transactions and points system? Will it be computerized, in a spiral notepad, or by using a card and punch out system?

- What products will be eligible for the loyalty program? All, a small selection, or will it vary on a monthly basis?
- How will the points, miles, or whatever system you have in place be redeemed? Will there be restrictions placed on this by way of time restrictions, product restrictions, or the price of products?

These are only a few considerations in terms of establishing a customer loyalty program. One of the best ways to really dig in and see if the program would be beneficial for your business is to talk to other retailers in your community that have these programs in place. Ask them about the success of the program, what it requires in terms of financial commitment and management, as well as other related questions that will help you to decide if a customer loyalty program is right for your business and more importantly your customers.

WEB RESOURCE

⊘ www.cardlinksystems.com: Cardsmart loyalty program integrated points-based reward system.

DON'T BE UNDERSOLD
$$+ ✎

Be bold by putting a price guarantee in place that states you will not be undersold model for model. Tell your customers in all of your advertisements and promotional materials that you will give them the lowest price and if they find one lower you will match it and give them an additional 5 percent off, even if you are selling for less than cost. Why? Two reasons. First, you get the last kick at the can and an amazing thing happens when you tell people that you sell for less; they will find a lower price then come to your store to see if you are indeed lower. If not, you would lower your price and have the opportunity to secure a lifetime customer. Second, people will automatically assume that you sell for less, regardless if you do or not. Thus, you will find that shoppers are attracted to your shop because of your low price guarantee and many will not check out competitors, but rather assume that you have the lowest price because you advertise the fact that

you will not be undersold. Remember that there is nothing wrong with stating that you sell for less or that you will not be undersold even if your products are more expensive than competitors'. This only becomes an issue if you do not live up to your claim and agree to match a lower price when a consumer clearly proves to you that they can get the exact model elsewhere for less than your store is charging. Now remember, I said that it is the consumer's responsibility to prove that your price is higher, not yours. That's not to say that you shouldn't make yourself aware of competitors' prices, because you should. Just that the onus is on the consumer to prove that you are not the lowest price, and if they do, they are rewarded for their effort by receiving a lower price from you.

BENEFIT BY BUILDING CLIENT FILES
$$ ✎

The best way to get to know what your customers want and need is to build individual client files on each of them and update the files regularly. Building client files can really pay off simply because they make such a wonderful marketing tool; you have access to the information you need at your fingertips to make or propose a special offer based on each individual client's needs or wants. Get started by asking every new customer to take a few minutes to complete a form. Ask questions on the form that can be used to determine what your customers really want, or problems they need addressed, along with their contact information, especially an e-mail address if you can get it. Offer a small incentive or free gift to customers who take the time to complete the form, and ask them if you may contact them by phone, fax, or e-mail when you have new or special offerings that you think will benefit them. Most people will be more than happy to take the time to complete the form and receive these offers, because you are taking a true interest in what they want. And isn't that what we all want?

WEB RESOURCE

⊘ www.maximizer.com: Sales and client management software.

PROFIT FROM BLACKBOARDS
$$ ✎

Don't laugh, the good old blackboard is one of the handiest and low-cost marketing tools that retailers of every sort can profit by using. Blackboards work extremely well to get your promotional message out to the masses who past by your store. Create a daily or even an hourly special and using your best handwriting and colorful chalk or markers write it down on a blackboard. Hang the blackboard over the cash register, by the front entrance in the window, or outside the front door to let people know that you are actively marketing and what your special or promotion of the day is. Include the action you want people to take, "Come on in!" Restaurants have successfully used blackboards for decades as an inexpensive and powerful way to advertise meal specials; just about any other type of retail business can benefit from this same principle. When we see a neat and legible handwritten message about a sale it immediately tells us it must be a real deal, hot off the press so to speak. The combination of a sidewalk sandwich board sign with a blackboard incorporated into it is also an extremely effective and handy sales tool to promote sales. The fixed portion of the sign can promote your business name and logo, while the blackboard insert can have a new marketing message added daily.

WEB RESOURCE

✐ www.usmarkerboards.com: Distributors of hundreds of various style blackboards, chalkboards, and markerboards.

EXPAND VIA MAIL ORDER
$$$ ✎

Do you sell products that ship well, have a long shelf life, good profitability, and are difficult to get everywhere? If so, you may be able to increase sales and revenues by adding mail order catalog selling to your business. This works especially well for retailers that are located in areas frequented by tourists and that do a large volume of business. Often the products that people purchase in one country or even state are not available when they get home.

This creates an opportunity for you to develop a mail order catalog listing your products, and making sure that every person who walks into your store leaves with one. The premise is simple; they get home and order more products for themselves, their friends, and their families. To really ramp up the effectiveness of this marketing activity also make sure to add a Web site and let your visiting customers know that you have safe and secure online shopping options for them in addition to your mail order catalog.

WEB RESOURCE

✐ www.smallbizbooks.com: Online retailer of business and marketing specific books, guides and software.

PROMOTE HARD WITH FLIERS
$$ ✎

Paper fliers are a fast and frugal way for retailers of all sorts to promote their businesses and products. Design the fliers right on your desktop computer and use them to promote a new product, a special event, or a change in a store policy. In bulk, fliers can be copied for pennies apiece at local printing centers and freely distributed to every customer who walks into the store. You can even use a few different fliers at any one time promoting any number of in-store special events or offers. Additionally, get creative and come up with reasons customers should hang on to the flier once home rather than tossing it in the trash. Reasons to hang on to the flier could include something as fun and simple as a quiz on the flier or a calendar of in-store specials or discounts for the week or month requiring your customers to keep the flier posted in a conscious place in the home so they will know what's coming up. The key to a great promotional flier is that it is filled with beneficial information that is aimed at your target market. Fliers are a cheap and a very effective marketing tool that every retailer should get in the habit of using regularly and with creativity. Here are a couple more great ideas for great fliers.

- Make your fliers visually appealing by using bold fonts, graphics, photos, and illustrations.

The objective is that anything you put in the flier should be a tool that helps prospects and customers better understand your product and the benefit they will get by using it.

- Great fliers have a bold attention-grabbing headline that screams out the biggest benefit that customers get by buying.

- Great fliers always ask for the sale and give readers the information they need to take action; telephone numbers, store address, Web site address, e-mail, and fax. And just as important, great fliers give readers a reason to take action, limited quantity, date deadline, or a special gift or discount if they take immediate action.

RUN FREE SEMINARS TO INCREASE SALES
$$ 🔨 📞

One of the most powerful words in retailing is the word free—free delivery, free gift with purchase, free refills, free extended warranty, and so forth, as long as "free" is a central theme. So why not combine the power of "free" with the power of an informational seminar and offer a free seminar to potentially increase revenues and secure new customers. For instance, if you sell cosmetics you could run free monthly beauty seminars at your location during nonbusiness hours or rent a suitable location to host the event. Promote the event through your store and by word of mouth. Invite local experts to the event to talk about the topic and give demonstrations. In the case of a beauty seminar this could include hair stylists, fitness consultants, massage therapists, just to mention a few. Securing the experts for free should not prove difficult, as they will be promoting their own businesses, products, or services at the same time as you promote yours. Free seminars are a terrific way to introduce your products and services to a wide range of people who can be turned into new and more important repeat paying customers.

PROMOTE PRODUCTS AFTER HOURS
$ 🔨

Here is a nifty trick that retailers can use to promote their businesses and products after hours once their shops are closed. Give customers 24-hour access to learn about your products even when your store is closed by installing a "please take one box" outside your shop, either by the main entrance or in another well-lit and signed area. Use your desktop computer to design basic promotional fliers describing products or services that you sell during business hours. And, make sure to change the after-hours promotional flier weekly to give people passing by after hours a reason to stop, pick one up, and read it at home. Ideally, what you say on the flier will prompt people to return during business hours to purchase products featured on the flier. Also try to date the material for the entire week giving them a reason to hang on to the flier. This may be a special offer on Monday, a discount on Tuesday, a new product launch on Wednesday, and so on. Fliers are very cheap to produce when copied in bulk, and are an effective way to make sure that after-hours window shoppers know what goods you carry and what specials or events may be forthcoming that will be of interest to them. "Please take one" boxes combined with great signage and window displays can go a long way to market your goods when your shop is closed.

GET CREATIVE WITH SPECIAL SHOPPING DAYS
$ 🔨

Senior discount days have always been a popular method for retailers to attract seniors to shop in their stores and pass along a small seniors discount as a sign of appreciation. This system works well and both parties benefit, the retailer can select what might be normally slow sales day as their seniors discount day be it once a week or once a month, and seniors living on a fixed income save a few dollars on items they want and need. However, special shopping days can be extended well beyond just seniors as a way to attract new customers, that with careful planning and a little luck will frequent your store and become loyal customers beyond just the special shopping day. Perhaps the 15th of every month is a hero's appreciation day and local police officers and firefighters receive a 5 percent discount on purchases they make. Or, a day every month that rewards office workers with a special reward as an incentive for coming in and making a purchase. Or, you can appeal to everyone and have a wacky Wednesday promotion that gives any customer wearing a pink hat a special discount. Promote your special shopping days by initiating a direct-mail campaign aimed at your target audience. For instance, if your target audience is office workers then send out a memo to all the offices in your area stating your special offer. Special shopping days aimed at a specific audience work, all that is required is a little bit of creativity to come up with something that is original and memorable for your business.

"TRY BEFORE YOU BUY" EVENTS

Increase revenues and profits easily by letting your products' special features and benefits sell themselves by hosting "try before your buy" events. Try before you buy demonstration events are not a new retailing technique, automobile dealers have been using "test drives" for decades as a method of creating excitement and motivating consumers to buy cars. However, many more retailers could be benefiting from these great hands-on promotional methods than currently are. For instance, a retailer selling canoes could hold a "try before you buy" event on a Sunday at the local river or lake. Invite prospects and customers alike to come down and go for a free paddle. Or, a retailer of home theater equipment could set aside a complete system that can be set up at prospect's homes for a few days to try it out. Few people could go back to watching their 19-inch mono television after experiencing the big game on a 50-inch screen with surround sound. Especially if the retailer had taken the liberty to arrange preapproved financing for the prospect illustrating that an incredible entertainment experience could be secured for a mere monthly investment of a few dollars. There's no secret formula at work here to make these product demonstration events successful. You can talk until you're blue in the face about features, but by getting the prospect involved in the buying experience and letting them discover and enjoy the benefits of ownership firsthand you create a motivation and urgency to buy. Get creative with a "try

before you buy" event for your business and I'm sure that you will be pleasantly surprised by the outcome.

GET CREATIVE WITH IN-STORE DISPLAYS

Retailers must constantly remind themselves that all consumers do not shop just to get what they need, many also go shopping for the entertainment value, and for some shopping is even a pastime or hobby. Consequently, you have to keep this in mind when creating in-store merchandise displays and go out of your way to make them exciting, attention grabbing, memorable, and above all entertaining and visually appealing. Here are a few great tricks to help accomplish just that.

Themes

Create storewide themes that tie all merchandising together with a central message that revolves around a sale or special event. The central theme could be tropical, outer space, or the old west just to mention a few; the choices and options are unlimited when creating storewide themes. Likewise, in-store decorating and display themes can also revolve around popular culture, such as the biggest movie at the box office, a hit television show, or music and art. The objective is to keep your displays fresh, interesting, unique, and appealing to customers while enticing them to impulse buy and buy more frequently.

The Good Old Days

If you have been in business for a longer period of time then create in-store product displays mixing how products used to look compared to how they look and are used today. A 50-year-old pair of skis beside a current pair of skis is sure to grab some attention and interest from shoppers. Especially if you can also add in old black-and-white skiing photographs and other accessories to liven the display up and give it real impact.

Interactive Displays

Interactive displays are another consumer favorite, simply because these displays make the products tangible; people can test or try them out without having to first lay down their hard-earned cash only to find out later that the product doesn't measure up to expectations. Likewise when customers can see firsthand the benefits and features of a product, it works to increase impulse buying. Interactive displays would include things such as a computer terminal so shoppers can test software and computer games before buying or a wall lined with audio and visual equipment that can be listened to, watched, and fiddled with to find out what it does best. Other types of interactive product displays can be constructed simply for your customer's entertainment, such as a hobby shop that displays a large ship model or jigsaw puzzle and encourages customers to pitch in and help complete the project.

Adding Movement

Adding movement or motion to in-store merchandising displays is another great way to grab the attention of shoppers and provide a little entertainment at the same time. Mechanical and motorized displays that rotate, flip, and turn can be purchased from fixture and equipment dealers that specialize in retail display products. However, for the budget-minded retailers for about $10 you can purchase secondhand record players and with a little creativity produce the same rotating product displays for a mere fraction of the cost.

Show Stoppers

Show stopper displays are the ones for which you pull out all the stops. They are truly spectacular and sure to grab the attention of shoppers. If you regularly create new show stopping merchandise displays they can even increase repeat business and lure new customers to your store. Examples of show stopper displays would include a complete camping display right down to the fire and roasting marshmallows in a recreational equipment store. Or, an incredible "dream workshop" display featuring all the latest and greatest tools and equipment for the handyman in a hardware store. Show stoppers take time, money, and energy to create, maintain, and regularly change, but the financial reward can easily justify the effort.

Demonstrations

Product demonstrations and even displays that are solely met for the entertainment of customers are another consideration for retailers. Demonstration displays could include things like a clothing retailer who hosts a weekly in-store fashion show for customers. Or, a sporting goods store that constructs an in-store rock climbing wall so that customers can try out rock climbing equipment and test their skills at the same time. Or, something even as simple as displaying a waterproof watch in a clear fishbowl appropriately signed "see, it still works—guaranteed to be waterproof."

WEB RESOURCES

- www.displays-store-fixtures.com: Supplier of retail store displays and fixtures.
- www.fixtures-displays.com: Suppliers of retail store displays and fixtures.

ASK ME ABOUT TODAY'S DEAL
$ ✎

Sometimes the simplest and least expensive promotional gimmicks have the biggest impact on increasing revenues and profits. And without question one idea that fits the bill is using simple promotional buttons worn by staff and emblazoned with "Ask me about today's deal" to spike impulse buying and reduce slow-moving or out-of-season inventory levels. This is an easy yet highly effective way to increase the average sales value of each transaction without being perceived by customers as pushy or aggressive at the point of purchase. The idea is to simply let your customers ask you what today's deal is. And don't worry they will, especially if you become known for providing a good deal that changes daily. Once again, this is another great way to get customers involved in the buying process without having to twist their arms in the process. And it works well as an alternative to simply discounting dated or slow-moving inventory or displaying it in a sales bin or rack. Try this simple yet effective promotional trick and you will soon discover that people will buy a discounted item on impulse regardless if they need it or not.

START AN INSERTION SWAP PROGRAM
$$ ⚒

In addition to stuffing promotional fliers and coupons into your own customers' shopping bags before they leave your store with their purchases, also consider starting an insertion swap program with other retailers and service providers from within your community. This easy trick will give you access to a whole new prospect base that will be warm to your promotion offering on the insertion flier. Warm, because the prospect has established loyalty with the business that promotes your business, meaning that by distributing the promotional materials your ally business is in effect referring your business to their customers. And the same holds true for their business when you distribute your ally's promotional materials through your business. Building and maintaining business alliances for cross-promotion and marketing efforts should no longer be viewed as a point to consider. Instead it has to be considered as an absolute must in order to survive in today's highly competitive retail selling environment. In fact, these cross-promotional marketing activities are often referred to as fusion marketing and can go well beyond simple flier insertions to include Web site links, interior and exterior sign cross-promotions, community building cross-promotions, and public relations and customer referrals exchange programs, just to mention a few. Yet at the core, starting a frugal flier insertion swap program with other community businesses is a great way to widen your marketing reach without breaking the bank in the process.

NONINTRUSIVE WAYS TO BUILD A CUSTOMER DATABASE
$$ ⚒

The benefit to a business that takes the time to build, maintain, and mine a customer database properly is invaluable. But some businesspeople find it difficult to ask customers for personal information that can be used to build a valuable customer database. Here are a few nonintrusive ways to secure customers' personal information that can be used to build your in-store database for marketing and promotional purposes.

Personal Checks

Get in the habit of recording customer information from their personal checks before you deposit them in your business bank account. Almost all personal and business checks include customer information such as name, address, and telephone number all of which can be used to build a customer file and database.

Contests

Create an in-store contest that requires participants to complete an entry form listing their complete name, address, telephone number, and e-mail address. Use the information collected from the entry forms to build a customer database. Change the contest weekly to ensure a continuous supply of new names for the database. Give away small items, but still valuable enough to generate enough interest that most customers that come in will take the time to enter.

Free Delivery

Offer free delivery on items that you sell and have customers complete a free delivery instruction sheet that requires their full name, address, telephone number, and e-mail address. Use the information from the delivery instruction invoice to build and add to your database.

Warranty Cards

Have customers fill in manufacturer's warranty cards on site and tell them that you will save them the cost of postage by mailing it for them. Transfer the customer's information from the warranty card into your database before mailing the warranty card back to the manufacturer.

Loyalty Programs

Create a customer loyalty program that requires people to complete a registration card to join. The loyalty program could be discounts on products, special services, or VIP treatment; you decide, as the value for you is using the registration information to build your database.

Subscription Forms

Create a print or electronic newsletter that is packed with information about the products you sell and special discounts and distribute your newsletter monthly. Ask customers at the cash register to take a moment to fill out a subscription form so that they can receive your free newsletter monthly. Ensure a near 100 percent positive reply by offering them a 5 percent discount on the purchase they are making at that moment as a way to say thank you for taking the time to fill out the subscription form. Once completed add the customer's information to your database.

Prized Data

The following is some of the types of customer information that you would like to capture, if possible. Though the type of information that you choose to capture and record about your customers will change depending on your marketing needs, the following are a few suggestions.

- Name of individual
- Address, including mailing address if different
- Telephone number, fax number, e-mail address(es)
- Job description/job title
- Demographic information including age, sex, education, etc.
- Buying history including, date of first purchase, date of all subsequent purchases, type of purchases, units sold, average units each sale, average value each sale, sale value to date
- How the person become a customer, for instance advertising, walk-in, etc.
- Customer ranking
- Special requests, complaints, payment history
- What specific benefits and features are needed and/or wanted

WEB RESOURCES

⌀ www.oracle.com: Oracle/Netledger Small Business Suite

⌀ www.maximizer.com: Customer and contact management software.

⌀ www.salesforce.com: Customer relationship management solutions.

SALES SPECTACULAR

To hold sales or not to hold sales? That is the question. Actually there are a few more questions that must be answered before this question, of which the responses will help to determine if holding a sale is the right decision for your particular business, situation, and marketing objectives. A few of these questions that you should ask prior to developing and holding a major sales event include the following:

- What do I want to achieve from a marketing perspective by holding the sale?
- Will the sales event increase repeat visits from current customers?
- Will the sales event attract new customers to the store, and will these new customers become loyal customers or are they strictly one-time bargain hunters?
- Does the type of sales event fit in with the image that the store has now, or with the image that I want to develop for the store?
- How will I advertise and promote the sales event? Given the cost associated with promotion, can I realistically expect to gain a return on investment?
- Is the purpose of the sale to move outdated or seasonal inventory, and if so at what price am I prepared to do so—above cost, at cost, or less than cost?
- By selling products at reduced prices will I alienate regular customers who have purchased these products at full price recently?
- Will the sales event start a price war with competitors, or am I holding the sale to combat a current competitor's sales event?
- Do I have the additional resources required to conduct a major sales event, things such as access to extra staff, floor space, and promotional aids and materials?

- Will the sales event enhance my business or detract from my business by taking time away from my main marketing objectives and focus.

These are only a few questions that have to be answered prior to holding a major sales event. Obviously if you're thinking about clearing out a few leftover seasonal items or some slow-moving stock then there is little planning required, just mark it down and move it out in any method that is fast, cheap, and effective. However, major sales events which are becoming the trend in today's competitive retailing environment need to be carefully planned prior to undertaking the event. Listed below are a few ideas for various types of in-store sales and clearance events that you could hold.

Axe-the-Tax Savings

Give customers a much-needed break from the taxman by selling your products free of state sales tax in the United States and Provincial sales tax and the Federal goods and services tax (GST) in Canada. Retail sales taxes charged at the register are a real sore spot for most consumers and often the perceived value of no tax is greater than any other type of discount you could provide.

Midnight Madness

As the name suggests, start your sale at the stoke of midnight and run it until 6:00 A.M. the following morning. These types of unique sales are customer favorites and stand an excellent chance of being featured by local media because of the distinctive time that the sales event is being conducted.

Red, White, and Blue

Get patriotic and celebrate Independence Day with a Red, White, and Blue sales event. Merchandise marked with a red sticker 10 percent off, a white sticker 20 percent off, and find something you like marked with a blue sticker and receive a whopping 30 percent discount. Neighbors to the north will have to settle for red and white stickers or can mark special sales merchandise with a Canadian flag for a Canada Day celebration sales event.

Christmas in August

Break out the Christmas decorations including bright lights, Santa's suit, the plastic tree, and the CD of Bing Crosby's Christmas favorites and hold a Christmas sale in August. Customers love theme sales that take place at the wrong time of the year, and the Christmas sale in August is perhaps the best. Offer free gift-wrapping, Christmas cards, photos with Santa, and cups of eggnog. Basically do everything you do in December before Christmas, but in August.

Tropical January

Much like Christmas in August, buck the "Snow Days" sales trend in January and instead hold a tropical theme sale. Bring in some artificial palm trees, hula dancers, and give anyone brave enough to shop in their bathing suit or shorts and a flower shirt an additional 10 percent off your already discounted prices. Once again, shopping is very much an entertainment experience for customers. So go out of your way to create an interesting and fun shopping and sales event entertainment atmosphere in your store and one that customers can participate in.

The $10 Shopping Bag

Create a $10 Shopping Bag sale or charge a different price for your shopping bag relevant to what your sell. The $10 Shopping Bag Sale means that customer cram as much as they can into a specific size shopping bag that you supply to them and they pay only $10 for the total contents of the bag. Though not suitable for all retailers to use, the $10 Shopping Bag Sale draws an enormous amount of interest from shoppers who cannot resist finding out how much they can actually cram into the bag. You can also limit the items that are available to be put in the bag to slow-moving inventory or out-of-season merchandise.

Continuous Knockdown

The Continuous Knockdown sale is one that every retailer should give careful consideration to using. For those not familiar with the concept, continuous knockdown simply means that you continue to reduce the price of a product by a certain percentage or dollar amount each day until it has sold. The benefit of this type of discount sale is the fact that often you will secure a higher price for the item using this method because shoppers who are interested in it don't want to risk waiting a day to return only to find the product has sold.

Storewide Liquidation

Much like an "everything must go" sale, few people can resist a Storewide Liquidation Sale-a-Thon; they simply cannot bare to think of the savings they will be missing out on if they don't go. That makes this a great theme for a sale for retailers who want to drastically reduce inventory levels, or who are moving to a new store location but don't want to move all the stock, especially dated or out-of-season stock.

Just in Time

Create a fun Just in Time sales theme to cover just about any reason for holding a sale: Just in Time for Spring Sales Event, Just in Time for the First Snowfall Sales Event, Just in Time for Christmas, and so on. As you can see, the choices are limitless. Additionally, Just in Time sales events are great to tie in with local community events, such as Just in Time for the Fireman's Picnic or Just in Time for the 10th Annual Bathtub Races.

48 Hours in February

Beat back the winter sales revenues blues by holding a 48 Hours in February Sales Extravaganza to get the cash register humming. February is traditionally one of the slowest sales periods of the year for the vast majority of retailers making it a great time to hold a sale and get customers out to your store and shopping. Cross-promote the event with other community retailers and offer shoppers incredible savings and specials for a 48-hour continuous period in February.

Welcome Back Snowbirds

If your store is located in the sunny south, especially Florida or Arizona, hold a sale in January that welcomes back the snowbirds who flock south when the temperature dips below freezing in the northern states and Canada. Create snowbird coupons, featuring your own unique snowbird logo and other snowbird discounts and special offers to keep them coming back year after year.

The Boss Is Away Sale

Let your customers think that they are getting great deals from the staff because you are away. The Boss Is Away Sale is a simple sale to develop and promote and should include more than just products that you want to clear out of the store. You have to give customers the idea that everything in the store is discounted to move out the door, and create a sense of real buying urgency by stating a specific date that the boss will be back, "The boss is back on Sunday, so get in to take advantage of all of the great deals while she's outta town."

Just One Day Only Sale

Just One Day Only sales are a incredible way to motivate customers to repeat shop and lure new customers to the event simply because they know from advertising and promotional activities surrounding the sale that the sale will be held for just one day—miss the sale and you will miss out on the opportunity to grab some great deals.

Two-for-One Extravaganza

Who can pass up an offer like two for one? Not many and that is what makes this such a fantastic sales event to hold for just about any reason. Two shirts for the price of one, two hats for the price of one, or two lunch pails for the price of one. The two-for-one sale covers just about any type of stock that you want to clear out or reduce levels on. However, make sure that you put in the small print in your advertising that the second item that customers receive for free has to be of an equal or lesser value than the first item that is being sold at full price.

Scratch n' Dent Days

It doesn't matter if the merchandise you want to liquidate is scratched or dented, just call your sales event a Scratch n' Dent Sales Event and watch increased business and revenues shoot through the roof. All consumers love Scratch n' Dent sales because of the perception that they will save huge amounts of cash just because of a small flaw in an otherwise perfectly good product. And you can capitalize on this perception by ridding yourself of out-dated, seasonal, or manufacturers' seconds merchandise under the Scratch n' Dent sales banner.

Ring in the New Years with Savings

Given that from mid-January to the end of March is traditionally one of the slowest sales periods for retailers, you could take advantage of this slow time to hold a Ring in the New Year with Savings sales event. The terrific thing about this sale is that you can hold it from early January right into February as a way to lure customers into the store and create buying motivation. After New Year's is perhaps one of the only times during the year when extending a sales event will not do harm, only good.

Factory Clearance

Just the mention of a Factory Clearance sales event can turn even casual shoppers into maniac bargain hunters. Strike a deal with your major suppliers so that they unload their leftover merchandise and sell it through your annual Factory Clearance sales event. Hold the sale-a-bration in-store, out in the parking lot, or even rent a location to host the event if you expect a large turnout. However, keep in mind that you do not want to pay manufacturers for the merchandise in advance, only after the sale. You also want to be able to return what doesn't sell at no restocking cost to you. So negotiate hard to make this sale work, because the financial reward can easily justify the effort.

Under the Tent Event

If you have the outdoor space required then rent a tent and hold an annual Under the Tent Event. Not only can this type of sale increase repeat business for your regular customers, but just the sight of a large tent set up in the parking lot with huge "tent sale in progress" banners strung across the side will dramatically pull people in off the street to shop, save, and return to buy another day.

Customer Appreciation Days

There is no better way to thank your best customers for their continued support of your business than by holding a special Customer Appreciation sale. The event can be open to the public and all customers and held during regular business hours. Or, alternately if you want to single out only your best and most loyal customers and say thank you, then hold the event by invitation only and at night after the store has closed. Make it a grand affair complete with music, snacks, and beverages.

Door Crashers

Door Crasher specials are without question one of the best ways to secure repeat business and increase new business to your store. They should be used in combination with a planned sales event and promoted by advertising a few outrageous door crasher specials to get the event cooking. Use outdated or slow-moving inventory as your door crasher special even if it means practically giving it away. The true value of the door crasher special is to get people into your store where they will impulse buy regularly priced items.

Bring a Friend and Save

Build your retail business for the long term by securing new customers by way of conducting a Bring in a Friend and Save sales event. When two people come into the shop together and if both people make a separate purchase then they receive a special discount. I love this type of sales event because you stand a greater than average chance that your regular customers will bring in a friend to shop so that they both will receive the special discount. Of course, the upside is that you then have the opportunity to retain the new customer (friend) and turn him into a loyal and repeat customer for life.

Truckload Sale

Truckload sales have always been a consistent consumer favorite because of the perceived notion that they will get amazing deals much like a factory clearance sale or warehouse sell off. And remember that just because the sale is called a Truckload Sale you don't actually have to have your own truck, just rent a truck signed with a "Truckload Sale in Progress" banner strung across the side and park the truck out in front of your shop. The curiosity and the fear of missing a deal of passing motorists and pedestrians will do the rest.

Graduation Sale

Mrs. Robinson never imagined a Graduation Sale could be so financially rewarding. For a little extra fun ask graduating customers to bring in their final report cards for kindergarten through to grade 12, and for the young adults their diplomas for college and university as proof of graduation. Graduation sales can mean a general storewide sale of all products or more specific products that would appeal to kids and young adults graduating from school or to the next grade level. All of the major car manufacturers have long offered graduates a special discount of between $500 and $1,000 off any new car purchase as a way to attract new business and reward them for their scholastic efforts. There is no reason that you cannot do the same.

Labor Day Clearance

Move out the last of the summer stock by holding an annual Labor Day sales event. In recent years Labor Day has become one of the most popular times of year to hold a sale that gets action and moves product out the door and money into the cash register. You can also capitalize on the end of summer and back to school savings at the same time and hold a Labor Day/Back to School sales event. Thus appealing to a broader audience.

Anniversary Sale

Another terrific reason to hold a sale is to celebrate a company milestone such as your anniversary. If you can swing it financially give customers a discount equivalent to the number of years that you have been in business on the anniversary date. Ten years equals 10 percent off, 20 years equals 20 percent off and so forth. Or, if you really want to be creative then reduce your prices for one day only and sell products at their selling prices when you opened

for business—of course providing that it wasn't in 1912 and you're not selling cars.

TARGET CLUBS TO INCREASE SALES
$$ ✎

Increase revenues and secure more customers by targeting clubs and associations in your community whose members can benefit from your products. Far too many retailers take a "let them come to me" approach in terms of marketing their goods. Well it's time to get creative and take control of your business future by seeking out new customers rather than starving to death while you wait for them to find you. Thankfully you already know who your primary and secondary target markets for your products are—seek those people out at local clubs and associations. For instance if you operate a clothing store specializing in sportswear then do a little homework to find out what athletic clubs and associations are in your community. Develop a marketing strategy to get in front of these people and present your goods. This can be accomplished by becoming a member of the club, or by arranging to speak to club members at their next meeting or group event. Great retailers never stop seeking ways to get their goods into the hands of people who need them, benefit from them, and can afford to pay for them, and neither should you.

GREAT CROSS-PROMOTIONAL IDEAS
$+ ✎ ☏ ⚖

Strategic alliances, relationship marketing, or joint ventures, the business world is abuzz with such terminology as we enter into a never before seen truly global marketplace with fierce competition around every corner. Given this new business environment perhaps one of the best ways to grow your small retail business is by joining forces with other small-business owners from within your community to create powerful cross-promotional activities. These cross-promotional activities should be developed so they increase brand awareness, have the ability to reach a wider audience, and drive new business into your store, all the time driving down the cost for each cross-promotional partner to market and promote her respective business. Call it a strength in numbers approach to cross-promotional marketing in the 21st century wherein entrepreneurs who share similar goals and objectives can band together to reduce financial risk and share in financial rewards. Listed below are a few great ways that you can build cross-promotional marketing activities with other small-business owners.

Cross-Promotional Coupons

A very easy and inexpensive way to get started with cross-promotional activities is to find a suitable "promotional partner" match for your business. Have discount or special offer coupons printed and each business hands outs the other's coupons to its customers. The coupon swap program could include more than two partners and extend beyond only retail businesses to also include service providers.

Cross-Promotional Product Displays

Another great cross-promotional idea is to have each business display the other's product in its store, or use the products to help enhance its own in-store displays. If you go this route I would suggest that signs and promotional literature be displayed with the products that indicate where they are for sale and other details relating to the products being displayed. Additionally, you could also co-purchase displays and fixtures that could be shared between the businesses that participate in the cross-promotional program. The fixtures could include mannequins, POP displays, and props for window display purposes. Not only will this trick give you access to a wider number of display fixtures that you can use in your store, but you will also save a pile of money by splitting the cost to purchase these displays among a few cross-promotional partners.

Cross-Promoting Contests

Finding partners to help offset the costs associated with developing and holding a contest is another very worthwhile cross-promotional activity to pursue for retailers of all sorts. The grand prize can be shuttled from participating business to participating business as a way to promote the event and increase customer visits in each store so they can fill out and submit entry forms. And speaking of which, all of the businesses involved could also be featured on the entry forms and supporting contest material. Also look to get the media involved in the contest so that you can potentially secure free and valuable publicity for the event.

Cross-Promotional Frequent Buyers Clubs

Extend your own frequent buying or customer loyalty program beyond your own store to include other businesses in your community. In doing so you will attract their customers as they will attract yours. Try to develop one central recording and tracking system for the frequent buyers club and create a promotional budget to market the club to all existing and new customers. Additionally, to build a membership base quickly consider offering an incentive such as 1,000 free bonus points to sign up, product discounts, a mystery gift, and so forth.

Cross-Promotional Lifestyle Packages

Creating cross-promotional lifestyle packages is one of my favorite cross-promo ideas because it enables you to get extremely creative and clearly separate your business from competitors'. For instance, if you sold billiard equipment and accessories then a logical match to create a lifestyle package would be a spa or hot tub retailer as well as a home theater or electronics retailer. Together you could create a "Family lifestyle entertainment package" that could include a billiard table, a home theater, and hot tub, but sold as one complete package and at a discount. The great thing about forming lifestyle packages is that these are generally larger ticket purchases so you can sell them on installment plans. Thus appealing to a broader audience that may not have $15,000 in cash to purchase the lifestyle entertainment package, but do have the good credit required to qualify for a $300 a month installment plan.

Cross-Promote with Shared Locations

Another way to cross promote with other businesses is to open satellite locations within another cross-promotional partner's store. For instance, if you operate a bakery then perhaps you would open a satellite location to complement your current location and your promotional partner's location within a grocery store. Or if you operate a electronics repair business specializing in televisions, VCRs, and DVD players then you could open up a secondary location within a video rental store. Satellite locations within other existing business locations are a great way to grow you business on a budget and gain access to a much broader marketplace.

Cross-Promote through Sponsorships

Band a business team together and share the expense of sponsorships. The sponsorships could be in the form of a little league team, an event that you create and host annually, or even an individual you sponsor for promotional purposes.

Cross-Promotional Advertising

An obvious but nonetheless effective cross-promotional activity is to form an advertising club of sorts with noncompeting businesses. In doing so you will generally find that you can negotiate lower costs for print and broadcast media as well as printed promotional literature such as brochures and product catalogs.

Hire Sales Agents to Cross-Promote

Here is a great cross-promotional idea that many retailers could benefit from. Expand your marketplace by hiring an outside sales agent or representative to prospect and find new buyers for the products you sell, but don't go it alone. Instead, find a few other noncompeting but compatible businesses in geographical trading and as a group hire or contract with the agent to sell all of the products these businesses represent.

Build a Community Web Site to Cross-Promote

Let's face it, great e-commerce Web sites can be expensive to build and very time consuming to maintain, especially for small-business owners who are short on both of the aforementioned resources. Consequently, banding together with other noncompeting but like-minded small-business owners to create and maintain a "community Web site" that features all of the participating businesses products and services is a great way to create an award winning and highly usable Web presence with out breaking the bank to get the job done. I would suggest that if you go this route that you hire an outside contractor to build and maintain the site for all of the businesses that participate in the program.

STOCK UP ON CONSIGNMENT GOODS
$$ ⚒

One way for cash-strapped retailers to increase inventory levels and potentially revenues and profits without having to invest thousands of dollars to do so is to accept goods from suppliers on a consignment basis. Not only can accepting consignments be used to increase salable inventory levels, but you can also accept consignments as a way to test market new products before committing to purchasing them in large quantities. Likewise you can also accept consignment products as a way to enhance your core product line. Handmade jewelry from a local craftsperson would complement the core product line of a fashion retailer. Or, custom designed and constructed wooden patio furniture taken in on consignment from a local carpenter would complement the core product line of a pool and spa dealer. As a general rule you will want to earn a minimum of 40 percent on the consigned items that you stock, market, and sell. And based on this if you sold $100 worth of consigned items, you therefore would retain $40 and pay the consignee the balance of $60 or 60 percent of the gross sale before taxes. The key to successfully accepting and selling consigned goods is that they must be high quality, represent outstanding value, complement or enhance your core product line, and help fill a niche in the local market. Additionally, make sure to strike an exclusive deal with the consignee wherein you will be the only retailer in your trading area to market their goods. Once you make the commitment to marketing their goods you don't want any unnecessary competition.

WEB RESOURCE

🖱 www.entrepreneur.com: Online business resource center for small-business owners and professionals.

GETTING CREATIVE WITH CONTESTS

Holding an in-store contest is another great way to increase repeat business from current customers as well as to lure new customers to the store. However, like any form of promotional activity you first must consider a few main points in terms of developing and conducting a contest.

Objectives

You have to start by knowing what the objective is for holding the contest. Or in other words what do you want to achieve or want the result to be? Common objectives for holding promotional contests can include

- increase repeat business from existing customers.
- lure new customers to the store.
- secure publicity and media exposure and coverage.
- build or update a valuable customer database.
- cross-promote with suppliers and business partners in the community.
- build awareness of a new, expanded, or improved product line.
- mark a company occasion or milestone such as an anniversary or specific number of customers served.
- brand the store, location, and product line, and become known for hosting the same contest annually.

Once you have determined what your objective of the contest are then you will be in a better position to decide which type of contest is best suited to meet your marketing goals.

Legal Issues

The next consideration will be legal issues. I strongly suggest that once you have a basic outline of the type of contest you will be holding and the prize that will be awarded that you seek legal advice to make sure that you will not be placing yourself or your business in a position of liability as a direct result of the contest, prizes, and entrants. Of course,

if the contest is just a small weekly draw or similar type of small promotional event, then legal advice is likely not warranted. Which brings up the next point—liability. Once again, you do not want to place yourself, your staff, or your business in a position of liability as a result of the contest. Therefore, once you have sought legal advice the nest stop should be to your insurance broker to find out about liability insurance to cover the event and matters relating to the contest.

Budget

Budget will also be a major consideration—the money to promote the contest and for the prize has to come from somewhere. Also, will you be able to secure a return on investment? Once again, in terms of budget considerations much will depend on your marketing objectives and how the contest is promoted in the community. Here are a few ways to reduce the overall cost to develop and hold a contest.

- Ask suppliers to furnish the prize(s) or at least give you the prize(s) at a reduced wholesale cost.
- Seek to build a cross-promotional partnership with one of more noncompeting businesses in the community and split the cost of the prize and the cost associated with promoting the contest.
- Try to build a contest partnership with a local media company such as a radio station, television station, or newspaper. Doing so will dramatically reduce the amount of money that you spend to advertise the contest, as the media outlet will have the vehicle for marketing exposure at their immediate disposal.

Prize

The next consideration will be a prize. What will you award as the grand prize and will there be other prizes also awarded? The prize you award should be relative to your business and complement what you sell. For instance, a good drawing prize for a video rental store would be a large screen television set or home theater components. Likewise, for a kitchen and bath retailer a bathroom and kitchen accessories prize package makes sense. And an additional consideration will be if you partner with other businesses. Will the prize consist of numerous prizes donated from each partner to create a prize package? These are a few considerations in terms of the prize(s) you award, but above all the prize(s) should enhance and complement your core product line.

Advertising and Promotion

How will you advertise and promote the event to ensure maximum benefit or return on investment? Once again how you advertise and promote the event will largely be based on your objectives, prize, and budget. Here are a few suggestions.

- Create simple promotional fliers revealing contest details and place one in every shopping bag as well as pinning the fliers to notice boards throughout the community.
- Have signs made promoting the contest and place them in your store windows, at the cash counter, and in other highly visible areas of the store.
- Give all customers entry forms when they make purchases. Or better, hand deliver the contest entry forms to as many households in the community as possible. This trick has the potential to lure more new customers to the store.
- If budget allows, create and run advertisements on the radio, television, and in print publications promoting the contest and details.
- Seek to gain free publicity and media exposure for the contest by contacting local media by way of a press release, media advisory, call, or personal visit. Let them know that it is a great photo opportunity for a human-interest story. Everyone loves to hear and read about people who win. Check out the Public Relations chapter for more ideas about securing media attention and coverage.
- If the contest is a cross-promotional event then use each partners individual advertising resources and contact to help promote the contest.

Type of Contest

The type or style of contest you hold will be in direct relationship to your marketing objectives and budget for the event. The following are a few different types of contests you may want to consider.

- *Entry ballot.* Requiring contestants to complete a ballot and deposit it in a box for drawing is perhaps my favorite type of contest because you have the most to gain from it. First, you can use the information you collect on the entry form to build a customer database, which can be exploited for direct-marketing purposes. And second, you can ask additional questions on the entry form that can assist in marketing research and planning purposes.
- *Counting games.* Simple "guess how many" counting games are another easy and inexpensive contest to hold. Yet they can be highly effective at greatly increasing traffic into you store, especially if you put what is to be counted in the front window along with the prize for the closets count match, and a big bold sign promoting the contest. What can be counted? Jelly beans, ping pong balls, golf balls, marbles, bolts, toothpicks, golf tees, and just about anything else that is compact and not easily counted when it is contained within a clear glass or plastic container on public display in the store or in your store window display.
- *Spin or scratch for a discount.* Another favorite contest for retailers to hold is spin or scratch for a discount. The spin part is very straightforward, simply rent or borrow a roulette or crown and anchor wheel from a local charity service club and replace the icons on the wheel with discount numbers. Ten percent discount, 15 percent discount, 20 percent discount, and so forth maybe right up to one space on the wheel wherein the customer wins a purchase entirely free. When customers bring their purchase to the checkout counter they or you spin the wheel and wherever the arrow stops then they win that corresponding discount off of their purchase. Scratch discounts are more involved and costly because you have to get the scratch cards professionally designed and printed for the contest. But the scratch contest is similar in nature to the spin the wheel discount contest. Except instead of spinning a wheel you give the customer a scratch ticket at the point of purchase and they scratch it and win the discount that is revealed off of their purchase.

- *Customer interactive.* Customer interactive contests can be anything from look-a-like contests to best costume wins to naming a new store or product contests. These are probably my least favorite type of contest simply because they can be very time consuming to manage and judge. The real point of a great contest is that it is self-explanatory, manages itself largely, and attracts new business. There are better contests to do that than customer interactive contests.

- *Hidden treasure.* And finally, though there are still many, many more types of contests that can be held, another one is a hidden treasure contest. And the hidden treasure could be a key that opens a box with a mystery prize inside or the actual prize hidden in a product's packaging.

Awarding the Prize

Awarding the prize is another important consideration simply because you want the maximum promotional bang possible. Once again contact local media and attempt to get them interested in covering an official prize awarding ceremony held in your store. Additionally, take pictures of the winner and the event and use these pictures in other promotional literature as well as hanging the prizewinner's picture in the store with a write-up about the contest. Ask the prizewinner to submit a testimonial about how happy she was to win, why she entered, and a few nice comments about your shop and use this in other areas of marketing. Basically seek out ways to make awarding the prize a grand event. The more people, media, and interest you can create the more exposure you will receive. Never just call up the winner, tell her she won, and award the prize quietly, behind closed doors. Always make a big deal and big fuss regardless of the size of the prize.

CONSIDER A RENTAL PROGRAM TO INCREASE REVENUES

$$$$ ✎ ⚖

Another clever way to increase retailing revenues and profits is to give potential customers access to goods that they could not otherwise afford by creating a rental program. For instance, a retailer of high-end woman's fashions could set aside a few exquisite evening gowns and start an evening gown rental business to complement sales, much like rentals of men's tuxedos. Many women need access to such formal wear for special occasions, but all cannot afford to purchase such fashions, especially considering the limited number of times the garment might actually be needed. This example would give these women access to what they need now and more importantly to the retailer, potentially these same people will become buying and repeat customers down the road as financial circumstances change. Likewise a retailer of camping equipment such as tents and the like could start a rental program for camping equipment, once again appealing to customers who do not have the financial means to purchase the equipment or for the person who camps occasionally but not enough to justify purchasing equipment. Added benefits of creating a rental program include access to a new and larger potential customer base, building customer loyalty for future purchases, increased customer referrals, and maximizing current resources.

NEGOTIATE EVERYTHING

$ ✎

Another clever way to increase profit is to save money by simply paying less for everything that is required to operate your business on a day to day basis and for the products you stock and sell. Do this by getting in the habit of negotiating with all your suppliers to lower prices and provide longer payment terms, even the suppliers that you have an established long-term buying relationship with. Likewise, get quotes from other suppliers and wholesalers once in a while on the same products to keep your current suppliers honest and to ensure you are receiving fair pricing and payment terms. The reason many small-business owners do not practice a policy of "negotiate for everything" is simply because many lack the self-confidence to do so, and have not learned to master the art of negotiation. Tackle the first obstacle with practice, practice, practice. The more times you ask and negotiate for a discount the easier it becomes. Tackle the second obstacle by educating yourself on how to become a master at negotiations.

Do this by reading books on the subject and attending seminars and workshops on negotiation skill topics. Don't be fooled by the simplicity of this trick. Even a small discount of say a mere 3 percent—which by the way is very easy to negotiate—can result in $6,000 more in your pocket every year based on total business expenditures of $200,000 per annum. Now imagine how much more revenues and profits you could turn that $6,000 into, if the new-found money were spent on additional marketing activities such as advertising, radio, direct marketing, and more to promote your business, products, or services?

TAP SUPPLIERS FOR THE WORKS
$ ⚒

As mentioned above you should learn to negotiate on all purchases you make for your business. Likewise you should also learn to tap your suppliers for everything you can, and then some. Ask for help to cover the cost of shipping, use their toll-free telephone lines when ordering, inquire about co-op advertising opportunities, nail them down for brochures and marketing literature, and make sure you get free in-store POP displays and lots of free samples. Basically, abuse their resources and generosity. As harsh as this may sound, if you don't, your competition will. This is not to say you do not respect your suppliers or that you should grind them to a point on price where it no longer becomes profitable to do business with you, because you shouldn't. However, you must remember the more of their products that you sell, ultimately the more money they will make so it is in their best interests to assist you in every reasonable marketing request. Of course, make sure that your approach is one that the savvy business owner would use and predesign a basic presentation outlining the details of your assistance request and ultimately how your supplier will benefit financially by agreeing to these requests. Here are just a few things that suppliers can assist your business with. Not all will be relevant to your particular business and situation, but many will and you can add and delete from this checklist as required.

Supplier Assistance Checklist

❑ Interior and special event signage

❑ Exterior signage

❑ Product packaging and design

❑ Product labels and price tags

❑ In-store product displays and point of purchase displays

❑ Specialized equipment as required such as freezers, counters, scales, and soft drink machines

❑ Product catalogs

❑ Promotional fliers

❑ Business cards

❑ Color brochures

❑ Sales receipts

❑ Advertising specialties such as pens, notepads, hats, and totes

❑ Printed gift certificates and coupons

❑ Co-op print display and classified ads

❑ Co-op radio spots

❑ Co-op television commercials

❑ Co-op Internet advertising

❑ Newsletter and e-zine ads

❑ In-store and event marketing posters, banners, table tents, and signage

❑ Product samples for presentations, demonstrations, and gift and prize giveaways

❑ Contest assistance and prize donations

❑ Expert personnel at no charge to assist in special sales and marketing events

❑ Training in specific marketing and merchandising disciplines such as sales, public relations, customer service, store design and layout, and small-business bookkeeping

SEEK EXCLUSIVE AGREEMENTS

$+ 🔨 🌐 ⚖️

There is no mystery to the fact that if you are the only store selling a popular product that people cannot get anywhere else in your local trading area then it stands to reason that in the least you will have one profitable product line. And for that reason you should be pressing your current suppliers to give you exclusive rights to sell their products within your geographical sales area, especially on your bestselling products and the ones that you put the majority of your marketing time and expense into promoting. If you find that your suppliers are not receptive, then start to seek out suppliers with similar products who will be receptive to this arrangement because in many retailing situations exclusive agreements can be that important. Of course, any agreement you strike with a supplier should be in writing. You are also best to have a lawyer check it over to ensure that your best interests are protected. The following are a few things that you want in an exclusive agreement as well as a few things that you do not want in an exclusive selling agreement.

What You Want in an Exclusive Product Distribution Agreement

- An exclusive agreement in writing to sell the product(s) in question and any new or expanded models based on that product line.
- The ability to transfer the agreement should you decide to sell your business, as these types of exclusive product line agreements can dramatically increase the value of your business.
- The right to cancel the agreement on short notice, without having to give reason and with no financial penalty for doing so.

What You Do Not Want in an Exclusive Distribution Agreement

- You do not want to have to purchase a certain amount of the product or meet a sales quota, though most suppliers will push hard for this. If you find that you must give in on this point then make sure the agreement stipulates that the more of the product you sell, the lower the unit cost will go.
- You do not want to have to commit to spending a certain amount of money each month, quarter, or year to promote and market the product line. Once again many suppliers or manufacturers will want this in the agreement; however, avoid this one if possible and try to turn it around so they have to spend a certain amount promoting the product in your exclusive sales area. Or in the very least match your promotional expenditures dollar for dollar.
- You do not want to pay a premium because it is an exclusive product line. You want the product at the same unit cost, or less, and you also should never pay an up front fee for the right to sell the product on an exclusive basis.

CONSIDER PRIVATE LABELING

$$+ 🔨

Myth

Only retailers with deep pockets can afford to develop, stock, and sell their own private label merchandise.

Fact

Never in the history of private labeling or private label merchandise have the costs been lower or the opportunities more abundant than right now.

The Rest of the Story

Free trade, global economy, marketplace, and emerging new world economies, chalk it up to what you want but one thing is true; regardless of size, number of outlets, or financial budgets just about all retailers can offer their customers merchandise under their own private label. For the vast majority of retailers private labeling is perhaps the only way they will ever be able to establish a brand name, awareness, and image for their business. Private labeling comes in many forms and, therefore, price entry points. Everything from the super elite practice of having a product line exclusively designed and developed for your retailing venture, right down to small manufacturing outfits that will simply add a name to a common product to make it private and exclusively you. The easiest way to find out about immediate private labeling opportunities is to first talk to your suppliers, especially if they are also the manufacturer of the goods that you stock and sell, to see what programs they may already have in place or what private labeling opportunities can be created. If that fails then simply turn to the Internet or the SBA to conduct research and contact manufacturers who manufacture goods specifically for private labeling purposes. To find out more about private label merchandise contact the SBA, or conduct your own research on the Internet. A simple "private labeling" search on Google will return thousands of matches representing numerous industries, products, and manufacturers.

SMALL, BUT MIGHTY, TRICKS FOR INCREASING PROFIT MARGINS

$$+ ✎

In today's competitive retailing environment all retailers need a few tricks up their sleeves that they can employ to increase profit margins and not have to spend a small fortune to do it. With that said here are a few simple ways that you can increase profit margins in a cost-efficient manner.

- Make sure that you computerize your business to streamline your entire operation, including a computerized inventory management, tracking, balancing, open to buy, and automated ordering system. Over the long run you will save, time, and money and eliminate impulse buying.
- Liquidate excessive amounts of inventory in slow-moving and unprofitable areas. Use the cash proceeds to buy more of your bestselling and most profitable stock. Do this even if it means selling off at cost or below.
- Make your business stand out by carrying merchandise your competitors don't. Find new supply sources and buy products that are not available in the area or at your competitors. In other words, find a niche in your marketplace, fill it, and sell products that no one else is selling locally.

- Understand that inventory, especially seasonal inventory is not like fine art, it never appreciates in value over time no matter how much you wished it would. Therefore create and implement a timely markdown strategy to dispose of out of season and outdated inventory.
- Concentrate a good portion of your marketing efforts at retaining your current customers. It costs ten times as much to secure one new customer as it does to retain an existing customer. Devise strategies that will motivate that customer to spend more and purchase more often.
- Buy close to the season to avoid carrying too much stock even if it means missing supplier discount deadlines. Often these discount deadlines are created by suppliers to motivate you to buy, which is commonly called creating buying urgency. Don't fall for it unless you think the supplier will run out of stock, if not hold tight and demand the discount even if it is after the season purchasing deadline.
- Make sure that you keep good financial records and pay particularly close attention to your overhead costs to gross sales ratios. Remember that you have fixed overhead costs such as rent and increasing sales a mere $50 a day can substantially boost this ratio and put more profits in your pocket.
- Never accept merchandise from suppliers that you cannot use, or that is late, damaged, or substituted. If they can't tell you up front so that you can work out mutually agreeable terms, then simply send it back at their expense and let them know that you're no pushover and that you do not tolerate subversive selling tactics.
- Create an annual financial budget and follow a detailed open-to-buy plan to ensure that you eliminate over buying, impulse (seemed like a great deal at the time) buying, and out of season buying.
- Seek out and attend trade shows relevant to your industry and products you sell to find new and lower priced suppliers. Likewise join business clubs and buyer groups to help find new

suppliers and better values. Buyers clubs are especially good because buying in quantity greatly reduces the per unit price you pay.

- Implement an automatic reordering system with your key suppliers so that you never find yourself out of your bestselling and most profitable products. Consumers don't like rain checks anymore; they don't have to, there is far too much competition in the marketplace for that. They want what they came in to purchase and they want it now, so make sure you don't run out because in doing so you'll be sending your customers directly to your competition and maybe forever.

- Always price your merchandise at what customers are prepared or willing to spend for it. Never base your retail-selling price on what the product cost, or on the suggested selling price set by the manufacturer or supplier. This is a balancing act and can take a while to establish, but well worth the effort.

- Look for products that you currently sell that can be packaged together and sold to customers at a slight discount as opposed to purchasing these products individually. The increased per transaction value resulting from selling products as a package will easily make up for the reduced profit margin as a result of the discount.

- Use year-over-year sales records to assist in and determine what and how much merchandise to buy. Your year-over-year records should indicate sales trends of all the products you sell, and you can therefore adjust your orders up or down based on these figures.

- Always be on the lookout for opportunities to increase prices on products that you stock, but your competitors do not. This is not monopoly prices, but rather receiving a fair return on the investment that you have made and for the service you provide. Profit is not, and should never be considered a dirty word.

WEB RESOURCE

✍ www.smallbizbooks.com: Online retailer of business and marketing specific books, guides, and software.

GREAT CURB APPEAL

Real estate agents will tell you that all things being equal a house with great curb appeal will sell faster and for more money than a house without great curb appeal. And this same premise carries over into retailing; with nothing more than a passing glance, consumers will form an opinion about your business based on the exterior presentation or the curb appeal that your shop projects. Many things go into great curb appeal for a retail store: signage, window displays, the front entrance, color selections, and lighting just to mention a few. However, while all of these above mentioned "curb appeal" elements are covered within this chapter, the focus of this marketing trick, or more correctly store presentation trick, is aimed at the space directly in front of your store—the sidewalk, street, and curb.

Take a survey of the general condition of all three (or whichever of the three is relevant to your store location) and decide what would make the store more appealing from a consumer's perspective. Perhaps the first would be replacing cracked and crumbling concrete work if it needs to be, or maybe installing planter boxes that can be filled with flowers, shrubs, or plants. The idea is to create an eye-catching presentation for your store, something that separates your business from every other storefront on the block. Of course, before you go tearing up the sidewalk and planting trees and so forth you will want to check with your local city and parks department to see what can be done to improve the look or the condition of the infrastructure and for what they are prepared to pay and for what you will have to pay.

Even if you find that you are in the position of having to pay for the work yourself this can still be a wise investment from a business point of view. Number one, the expenditure will likely be a legitimate business write off, and number two, by improving the front appearance of your store you will be increasing the curb appeal factor therefore increase the potential of drawing more people into your shop, with an objective of turning them into lifetime customers. Once again with local government approval here are a few things that you can do to increase the curb appeal of your store.

- Install decorative planters and fill them with flowers, trees, and shrubs.
- Install decorative street and building light fixtures.
- Replace broken and cracked concrete and cement work with new concrete or alternately interlocking brick or stone work.
- Install seating benches and decorative garbage receptacles.
- If space permits install a raised deck area with an outside patio if you operate a restaurant or an outside area for product displays if you sell merchandise.
- Have the local newspaper company and telephone companies install a pay phone and newspaper coin boxes, but you agree to maintain them so they remain looking clean and in good repair. Having these out front can force people to stop and use them and potentially through window displays draw them into your store.

CLEVER CALENDARS
$$ ✎

Give your customers calendars at Christmas time as a gift and a way to say thanks for your support. But not any old typical calendar, instead get creative and have your own calendar designed and printed that includes promotional specials printed right into the calendar boxes for each month. For instance, if you provide a 10 percent seniors discount on Tuesday then have 10 Percent Senior Discount printed on every Tuesday in your calendar for each month of the year. It doesn't matter if every customer is not a senior because it will remind those who are every time they look at the calendar and those who aren't likely know people who are and will refer them to your business to take advantage of the special discount. Likewise, print other special sales dates in the calendar and in the appropriate month. These special sales and promotion dates could include your anniversary, customer appreciation sales in March,

back to school sales in September, out of school sales in June, and so forth. The options really are unlimited. Additionally, use the larger space at the top of each month that would usually be reserved for a generic landscape photo for tear off or cut out promotional coupons, or to spotlight a new product each month of the year.

WEB RESOURCE

✑ www.thediscountprinter.com: Custom calendar printing service.

CONSIDER THE EBAY ADVANTAGE
$$ ✎

There are three basic ways to sell your goods through eBay, which by the way is one of the most visited Web sites on the net and at the time of writing this book is generating sales in excess of $2 billion a month. The first is single or multiple items via their auction service. The price can be a reserved amount you set, meaning that if you set the reserve at $25 then someone would have to bid higher than $25 in order to buy your product. Or, you can sell your products on the auction unreserved; meaning the highest bidder in the allotted time buys it. The second is single or multiple items can be sold through their fixed price sellers system, kind of like a catalog of thousands of products listed in various sections. And the third is to open your own eBay store, where in effect you could list your entire inventory, if you wished. There are numerous categories, so don't worry you'll find one no matter what you sell. Additionally, eBay has created various ways to promote your store or the items that you are selling, including picture listings, feature listings, and more. You can use your existing payment systems to accept payments from customers or you can sign up for the various payment services offered through eBay such as electronic checks and PayPal and have the money automatically forwarded to your business bank account. The fees vary greatly in direct response to the number of services you want and need, but in large part are more than reasonable, especially when you consider that overheads are low, you will have no sales staff or few distribution costs, and you will not have the expense and maintenance associated with operating your own e-commerce Web site. Many top retailers and manufacturers have found eBay to be a convenient and profitable way to sell and distribute their goods, definitely worth consideration, especially if you want access to a global audience via a Web site that is billed as the World's Largest Online Marketplace.

WEB RESOURCES

⌀ www.ebay.com: eBay United States.

⌀ www.ebay.ca: eBay Canada.

TRY GIFT WITH PURCHASE
$$+ ⚒

Give customers a gift when they make a purchase and watch repeat business and customer loyalty skyrocket because of this crafty trick. The cosmetics industry has been successfully using "gift with purchase" promotions for decades as an extremely powerful marketing tool. Purchase a lipstick set and receive a free makeup bag, buy a face cleanser and receive a free eyeliner, and the list goes on and on. Look for ways that you could use this same promotional tool as a way to build customer loyalty and attract new customers. Check with your suppliers to see if they have a new product launch coming. If so, perhaps you can strike a deal to get some of this new product for free or at a discount to give to customers as a gift when they make a purchase. Or, check with suppliers to inquire if they have discontinued products that you can purchase inexpensively to once again give away to customers as a gift with purchase. And if you're really creative then try partnering with another local business and distribute each other's products as your gift with purchase. There are many ways to use this promotional technique effectively; all it takes is a little bit of homework and some creativity, but the bottom line is that it works great as a customer loyalty building tool and well worth the effort to develop and implement a gift with purchase promotion.

BOOST SALES WITH VIC CARDS
$ ⚒

Contact your local printer and have VIC (Very Important Customer) cards printed that entitle the cardholder to terrific discounts on products and services that your business sells as well as access to special any VIC promotions that you create through out the year, such as free product or service training workshops, special manufacturers discounts, and VIC appreciation parties and events. Create and distribute VIC cards as a way to thank your best customers and secure new customers, as well as bolster sales and profits. Distribute the VIC cards to customers and employees and let them in turn give them to friends and family members as a special gift. Also make sure to include a line on the card where the giver can sign their name so you can gift that person with something for helping to promote your business by distributing your VIC cards. A special incentive to show that you appreciate their hard work and effort, VIC cards are a powerful marketing tool that just about every business can benefit from, not to mention they are very inexpensive to have printed professionally or you can even design them on your PC and print them yourself if your budget is tight.

BRING IN THE ENTERTAINERS
$+ ⚒ ☎ ⚖

I have mentioned numerous times in this retailing chapter that for many consumers shopping is not merely buying to fill a need, it is also a form of entertainment. And judging by the number of retail stores and shopping malls across the nation, it is safe to say that shopping is a very popular entertainment pastime. So with that said you should not overlook the value of bringing in entertainers to the delight of your customers. Of course, not all of the suggestions made below will be suitable for every retailer but some will be, or a variation will be suitable. Along with the various entertainers listed, I have also included a few tricks on how you can get the biggest promotional bang out of each.

Music Performers

Now in terms of music performers, they could range from a complete band—rock, jazz, blues, or country—right to a soloist with a cello on a Sunday afternoon. But regardless of the type of music or number of musicians, live musical entertainment is one of the most popular ways to keep customers entertained and in your store longer and coming back more often providing that live music is a regular feature. And guess what? Both add up to the potential of your customers buying more and more often. You shouldn't have to pay for the musicians providing that there is a benefit for them to be there entertaining, which is namely the money they can receive by selling their CDs, and other related materials such as T-shirts, hats, or whatever they use to generate revenues. However, make sure that customers are not dropping coins into a guitar case, this is tacky and uncalled for. You can get the most marketing mileage from live music performances by having the musicians build your products into their songs, or by wearing the products (fashions), sitting on the products (furniture), playing the products (musical instruments), and a whole host of clever ideas.

Theatrical Performers

Another form of entertainment to feature in-store on a regular basis is theatrical performers from a local theater troupe, high school, or performing arts institution. Once again, the vast majority of performers will perform for free or in exchange for product or for cross-promoting an event they have forthcoming by hanging fliers in your windows or selling performance tickets at the sales counter. And to really increase the effectiveness of having live theatrical performances in your store, try to convince the performer to create a play to perform about your products. This could be a spoof of a popular Shakespeare play with your products mixed in, or a completely new play that is specifically developed around what you sell.

Magicians

Like live music, magicians are also a favorite form of entertainment especially if your shop caters to children and families. Have the magician use your products in her routine to make them disappear, reappear, or solve a problem right before your customers' eyes. In exchange for the magician coming in and entertaining your customers offer to set up a service wherein customers can book the magician's services for parties and events right at your store; provide this service for the magician in exchange for the service she provides you.

Psychics

Psychics are always a crowd favorite, who doesn't want to know their future or their lucky numbers for playing the lottery? However, while most forms of entertainment discussed in this chapter can be secured for free, you will likely have to pay for psychic services or perhaps negotiate to barter with products instead of hard cash. Try to feature the psychic appearances on a specific day of the week and maintain that schedule so that customers will begin to associate that day as the day the psychic is in, thus potentially increasing repeat visits to the store and the potential for more frequent purchases. Likewise, if you do you will also be increasing the chances of word of mouth advertising between customers who have had a psychic experience at your shop talking to people who have yet to have the experience.

Artists

Painters, sculptors, and craft artists who make just about anything useful from a doily also can be a great form of entertainment for customers. Perhaps one of the best to have is a caricaturist who can come in one afternoon a week and make funny, yet lifelike drawings of your customers as they shop. These drawings can be given away to the customers as an appreciation gift before they leave the store. What may seem to be just small forms of entertainment, such as bringing in artists, can actually go a long way to increase word-of-mouth advertising. This is due to the fact that if you regularly have the artist or entertainer present, your store will become somewhat of a local landmark and known for the entertainment you bring, which can dramatically increase word-of-mouth advertising.

Sports

Sports demonstrations are yet another fantastic form of entertainment to bring into the store for the benefit of your customers. The sports demonstrations could range from karate or other martial arts demonstrations, to table tennis, to a batting cage if you have the space required. Additionally, if you sponsor little league or other community sports teams make sure to bring them in for autograph signings and picture taking with your customers, especially if they have won major championships.

SHOOT FOR A RECORD
$$+ ⚖

Attempting to set a world record is an interesting and fun way to promote your business and potentially get a ton of media exposure because of the event. Get started by going through the *Guinness Book of Records* to determine if there is a record that is suitable for you or a staff member to attempt breaking. If not, start making inquires locally to find out if any residents in the community are attempting to set a world record in the near future and offer to sponsor that person or group of people in exchange for the record attempt taking place at your business location. World record attempts generally attract a lot of media attention and exposure, which is why this is a very worthwhile promotional activity to pursue. Even if the attempt fails, the media exposure, lingering goodwill, and word-of-mouth advertising can have a very beneficial impact on business. Find out before you sponsor any type of record-breaking attempt, be it you, a member of your staff, a customer, or a member of the community, if your business and personal liability insurance will cover such a promotional activity in the event of unfortunate circumstances as a result of the attempted record.

WEB RESOURCE

✍ www.guinnessrecords.com: Official online *Guinness Book of Records*.

FREE GIFT WRAPPING
$ 🔨

How many times a year do you purchase a gift for a friend, family member, or business associate? If you're like most consumers you are probably purchasing gifts for others more than twice a month. And I'll bet that other than at Christmas or special holidays the store clerk has never asked you if you would like your purchased gift wrapped. Get a leg up on the competition by providing free gift wrapping for customer purchases on a year round basis. Install a professional looking sign right at the cash register that says, "Is your purchase a gift for a special someone? If so we'll gift wrap it for *free* while you wait." Or better yet don't wait for customers to ask you, instead get in the habit of asking customers if they would like their purchases gift wrapped. The small investment you make into fancy wrapping paper and ribbon can pay off huge. Consumers remember when they have been treated like royalty and have received a valuable service at no extra cost. Start now and you'll be amazed by how this simple low-cost service will build customer loyalty and increase new business through word-of-mouth advertising and referrals.

TRY TRADE-IN PROMOTIONS
$$+ ✐

As a way to bolster retail sales and profits consider holding an annual or semiannual trade-in event wherein customers can bring in their old products and trade them in for new ones, and receive a special discount in the process. For years clever automobile dealers have been using "push, pull, or drag" trade-in events with great success. There is no reason you cannot also profit from this excellent promotional activity. For instance, if you sell shoes then give customers $10 trade-in value for their old shoes when they buy new shoes, or if you sell mattresses then give a $50 trade-in value when customers buy new mattresses. And to really ramp up the effectiveness of trade-in promotional events, make sure that the traded-in items that are in the best condition go to local community charities. Even if you have to do a little clean-up or repair work on the items prior to sending them to the charity. Additionally, if you do donate the traded-in items to charities make sure that you contact local media outlets via the telephone or a press release to let them know what you are up to. These types of events that support local charities often get media coverage and all retailers can use a little extra media exposure now and then.

OVERUSE DEADLINES
$ ✎

Far too many retailers fail to understand that to create buying urgency there must be a deadline in place or some other type of cutoff that will motivate customers to buy right away, to buy more, or to buy more frequently. Constant sales with the same product stuck in a bin or on a rack for an eternity are useless, in fact they do more harm than good because shoppers will begin to associate your shop with the same old, same old in terms of ongoing sales. Consumers get used to this and therefore will go searching for other retailers who offer new and fresh specials and deals on a regular basis. Therefore, it is important that you use deadlines in association with sales, special offers, and clearance events. In fact, you should overuse deadlines, not underuse them, as a tool to motivate buying. Be firm with your cutoff dates even if you have not cleared out the inventory you wanted to, or not met all of your sale objectives. If you bend the rules, once again your customers will pick up on this and get numbed by it, because it will become commonplace. We have all seen the television commercials wherein a retailer announces they are going out of business and to rush in for great savings. However, many of these same commercials seem to drag on and on, never ending and sooner or later you catch yourself thinking you wish they would just go out of business so that you won't have to watch this stupid commercial anymore. Of course, such marketing activities do little if anything to create a sense of buying urgency or to motivate people to take action and buy before it is too late. So get smart and use deadlines with every sale or promotional event you conduct as a way to create buying urgency.

RANK YOUR CUSTOMERS
$$ ✎

Develop a simple customer ranking system so that you can identify who your best customers are and any similarities they might share. Assign each customer a rank, base the ranking system on A, B, C, or D, or 1, 2, 3, 4. Rank each customer on factors such as buying frequency, types of products they buy and the profitability associated with these products, special requests, complaints, and if they pay on time or are slow payers. By ranking your customers you will be able to pinpoint who your best customers are, thus enabling you to develop a strategy to find more like them. Or, by directing more of your marketing efforts at your core target group to increase sales values, introduce new products, and ask for referrals. By ranking all of your customers generally you will discover that 20 percent are responsible for 80 percent of sales and profits; this is called the 80/20 rule and is a widely accepted measure of customer loyalty principles. It is this 20 percent that you should focus the majority of your marketing efforts and activities on, these are your customers that you want to go the extra mile for; shower them with appreciation and continually seek out ways to ensure they remain loyal customers to your business for life.

DON'T FORGET THE GOOD OLD SUGGESTION BOX
$ ✎

You never know where that next great marketing, promotional, or customer service idea will come from and with that in mind all retailers should install a suggestion box and encourage customers to make suggestions. In fact, insert a "please help us by making a suggestion" card right in with their purchases. Customers can drop the suggestion card in the box the next time they are in or you can be really creative and print remittance options right on the back of the suggestion card. These options could include going online to your Web site to post comments in your "electronic suggestion box," leaving a voice mail, or sending in a suggestion by fax or e-mail. But remember it is not enough just to encourage customers to make helpful suggestions in terms of marketing and customer service ideas, you must also reward the ones who go out of their way to do so. Give them a special gift or discount as a way of saying thank you. If you give customers a way to make suggestions and encourage them to do so, many will. And you just might end up with a great marketing, customer service, or product idea that will help to increase revenues and profits as a result. Suggestion boxes are cheap, easy, and have the potential to really pay off, making them a wise addition to any retail business.

CREATIVE GIFT PROGRAM
$$ ✎

Here is a fantastic and simple marketing trick that all retailers can implement right away and start enjoying the benefits immediately. Develop a creative gift program for your store. What this means is that people can come into your store and select a product they would like for their birthday, Christmas, or any special occasion as a gift, and supply you with a list of people or even a single person who might purchase the gift for them—very much like a wedding gift registry, but in reverse. Instead of the potential buyers contacting you to find out what gifts are on the list, you contact them and let them know that a certain person submitted their names and the gifts they would like to receive on their special occasions. You can contact these potential gift buyers by way of mail, fax, e-mail, or telephone because you got detailed contact information from the person who completed the registry card. This is a win–win–win situation. The person gets exactly the gift he wanted, the buyer does not have to guess and risk gifting the wrong gift, and you profit by selling the gift and providing a valuable service.

CLEVER WAYS TO BUILD REPEAT BUSINESS
$+ ✎

While sales and special promotions may bring customers into your store, the real trick is to turn these one-time shoppers into lifetime loyal customers. To do that you need to offer customers more than just great service, selection, and fair pricing, you have to develop clever marketing strategies that will encourage repeat business. Earlier in this chapter we covered loyalty programs, air miles, points, frequency discounts, and a few other promotions. All of which are aimed at encouraging and capturing

repeat business. So given the importance of turning all customers into lifetime customers, here are a few more clever ways to encourage and build repeat business.

Product of the Month Club

Book and music retailers are not the only ones who should be benefiting from creating a product of the month club; in fact with a little ingenuity just about every retailer could develop their own product of the month club regardless of the products they sell. Sign your customers up for the club right at the point of purchase, and as an incentive to join let them know that all the products of the month are discounted by 10 to 15 percent. The club could operate on a basic model. Every month you send out the product of the month to members, and if they want to keep it they simply remit payment for the product. If not they send it back to you at your expense—easy, basic, and simple to implement.

Gift Basket Service

An effortless way to increase repeat business is to develop a gift basket service and offer this service to all customers. Promote your gift basket service in the store at the point of purchase and with signage and also include the details of the service in all advertising and promotional material you use in marketing. To streamline the service try to create perhaps six standard gift baskets from an economy model or option right up to a full luxury option. The baskets can be sold to customers who want to give them as personal and business gifts. Likewise, make sure to also create holiday gift baskets to match the various holidays such as Christmas, Valentine's, and Mother's Day.

Automatic Replenishment Service

If you sell consumable merchandise such as food products, office supplies, pet foods, bottled water, or cleaning supplies then be sure to sign your customers up for an automatic replenishment service and deliver their goods right to their homes or offices free of charge. This is one of the best ways to secure repeat business, because as long as you are automatically refilling your customers' supplies on a regular basis then they won't be out shopping at your competitors.

Reminder Service

Reminding customers to shop is perhaps the easiest way to increase repeat business. It doesn't really matter what you sell, just as long as you remind people to buy it. For instance, the pizza shop could send out a letter along with a $2 off pizza coupon to customers who hadn't ordered pizza in a couple of months. "Hey you must be starving. Just to show you that we care about your stomach, here's $2 off your next pizza to help fill it up. See you soon."

Gift Registry Service

Start a gift register service for weddings, anniversaries, birthdays, graduations, and just about every other type of special occasion. Promote your gift registry service in your monthly newsletters by inserting promotional pamphlets in your customers' shopping bags and by telling customers at the checkout counter.

TRICKS FOR SUCCESSFULLY MARKETING A MOVE
$$+ ✎

Moving to new retail location can be very costly both in terms of the costs associated with the move and more important lost revenues resulting from down selling time and lost customers. Here are a few tricks that you can use to successfully market a store relocation.

Create a Moving Plan

The first trick to successfully marketing a move is to create a moving plan as soon as you know or have decided to move your shop to a new location. Two items should top your moving plan list. First, how can you eliminate or reduce the amount of non-selling time that can be lost during the move? Do this by trying to move during a time that you would not normally be open such as overnight or on a holiday. Or, spread the move out over a longer period of time so that you will be able to continue to sell

products during most of the move. Also, if you can afford to, be sure to allow at least a one month overlap between the time that you take possession of the new store location and the time that you have to vacate the old store location. Trying to accomplish the move all in one day is a recipe for disaster, no matter how well the move is planned. The second item on your moving plan list should be this question: What steps can you take to ensure that your current customers continue to shop at your new store once you have relocated? The number-one way you can ensure that current customers will continue to be loyal is to let them know that you will continue to provide excellent customer service and a wide selection or products they want and need at fair prices. You can also do the following.

TELEPHONE

Use a recorded voice message for customers on hold and during nonbusiness hours to advertise the fact that you are moving and give details such as date, new location, telephone numbers, and a reason for the move, such as to a larger location to serve you better. Record this message as soon as you know that you will be relocating, and after the move also continue to use a message. But reword your recorded message to say that you have already moved and once again give new location and contact details. Additionally, if you're moving far enough away to require a new telephone number make sure to retain the old number and have it forwarded to your new shop for at least 12 months after the move.

FAX

Advertise all the details of your move on all outgoing faxes. Do this a few months prior to the move and a few months after the move. Place the notice near the top of the fax you send or preferably on the cover page if you use one. Also send a separate fax to all your suppliers stating the details of the move and asking them to update their files.

MAIL

Create a simple one-page flier listing all the move details and include this with outgoing mail. Once again send the moving notice to suppliers asking them to take note and update files.

WEB SITE

Place a headline on your home page linked to a separate page that gives moving details. Leave the page posted for as long as possible before the move and at least 12 months after the move. Additionally, send out a moving notice e-mail correspondence to everyone on your store opt-in mailing list or database. Do this once a week starting six weeks prior to the moving date and follow up with at least a few more electronic correspondences after the move.

SIGNAGE

Have signs made announcing the move and details, and place the signs inside and outside of your existing store and the new store location. Additionally, if possible try to have the new tenant at your current location leave a sign in the window or in a noticeable place for a few months after you have moved. Also arm the new tenant with brochures showing where you have moved. Most will be happy to help out because it will be easier for them to hand a person a brochure or point to a sign as opposed to having to explain to people where and why you moved.

PRINTED HANDOUTS

Create a brochure listing all the details of the move including keys dates, location, telephone numbers, a map to the new location, and why you are moving to a new location. Of key importance is to create a positive spin for the move, one that demonstrates benefits for your customers. The benefits could be "moving to a larger location to better serve you." Regardless of the reason for moving, it must be for your customers. So make sure to create a reason that illustrates that you have your customer's best interests in mind and that is why the store is moving.

LOCAL MEDIA

Identify ways to make the move newsworthy and develop and distribute a press release to local media stating that news. Do this at least a few months in advance and likewise after you move look for ways to create another newsworthy story about the move and your new location. The media can play a key role in helping to market a move, all it takes is a little bit of creativity on your behalf to create a news angle and secure free media coverage.

TELL EVERYONE

Tell all your customers about the move, not once or twice, but at least three times. Also make sure that employees do the same, in person or on the telephone with customers. Print a note about the move and stick it by the telephone and cash register; this will help to remind you to keep telling customers. And of course make sure to ask customers to tell as many people about the move as they can. Tell anyone and everyone until you're blue in the face.

ADVERTISE

Take out as big and as many advertisements as you can in the medium that you usually advertise in, whether it be print, radio, or television. Yes it's costly, but so is lost business and customers. If you can't afford big print ads, try classified advertisements. Also hang moving notices on every community bulletin board you can find and enlist students to deliver your moving brochures door to door as well as placing them on windshields of parked cars in the area you are moving to.

GRAND REOPENING CELEBRATION

Hold a grand reopening celebration once you're settled into your new location and place the emphasis of the event on customers. Give them food, beverages, entertainment, and fabulous discounts. Try to make the grand reopening a community event by enlisting the help of noted community leaders to be present. Cut the ribbon and make sure the picture hits the local paper, basically make your grand reopening as grand as you can and as your budget will allow.

WHAT SIGNS DO

Interior and exterior signs are the lowest cost highest impact form of advertising that retailers can invest in, hands down. They tell your customers, and people who you want to become customers about your business in a passing glance, 24 hours a day, 365 days a year. A study conducted by the International Sign Association and in partnership with the University of San Diego concluded that on average, the addition of one exterior sign increased sales by 4.75 percent annually for retailers. And that through the use of professional interior signage it was possible to increase revenues by an additional 3.93 percent annually. Combined you have the potential to increase sales in excess of 8 percent per annum by paying close attention to your interior and exterior signage. Consequently, the value and power of store signs should be a very high priority for all retailers regardless of the types of products they sell. Below you will find a more detailed view of what exterior and interior signs can do for your business as well as ten great tricks that can help you maximize the value and impact of your signage.

Exterior Signs

Above all, exterior signs brand your business or store location within your community. At a glance they tell people who you are and what you sell or do. People see a "Pet Store" sign and they know instantly they can buy food for their pets; they see a "pizza" sign and instantly they know they can buy pizza at that location. In short they drive traffic into your store and therefore help to increase impulse buying and repeat business. The types of exterior signage is near limitless and ranges from building-mounted canopies and awnings to pole-mounted freestanding signs, to complete walls or the entire building wrapped in billboard style signs. The style or type of sign you choose will depend on budget, local regulation, and what message or image you want to send. It is always best to seek the advice of a professional sign design and installation company to help you with signage decisions.

Interior Signs

Much like exterior signs, interior signs also brand your store but on the inside. Interior signs let people know where products are located, where the cash counter is, where products that are on sale can be found, and more importantly information on signs and stickers that tell people why they should buy—the big benefit. Also like exterior signs the options for types, style, usage, and design are nearly unlimited, but above all the signs should be professional, easy to read, and direct in the message they send. Once again, a professional sign designer can help you to create signs that will meet your marketing objectives and increase sales.

Ten Great Signage Tricks

1. Exterior signage should be bold, brief, easy to read, and tell people at a glance exactly who you are; your business name should be the largest lettering on the sign. Trying to fit too much text or multiple messages on a sign will only confuse people.

2. Exterior signage should also tell people at a glance what you do and how well you do it such as "We Dry Clean All Clothes in One Hour Guaranteed." What you do and how well you do it should be the second largest lettering on the sign. Outside of perhaps a telephone number or Web site URL if relevant, you do not need your sign to say anything else.

3. Always include your business logo on your exterior sign to help build awareness of your image. Additionally include a subliminal message that speaks volumes that words cannot, such as a picture or graphic of a camera if you sell cameras or a pizza if you sell pizzas. Remember you sell inside the store not out on your sign, but your sign should grab attention, build interest, and drive people inside your store so you can sell them.

4. Keep your sign in tip-top condition as things such as peeling letters, burnt out bulbs, and faded paint can also send a subliminal negative message. We all make assumptions based on first impressions. So if the first impression you are sending out is a sign that is in need of maintainence and repair then expect that people will feel and think the same about the products you sell. Think of your sign as your handshake and that first impressions are often lasting impressions.

5. Keep your sign consistent with your corporate image by using a unified color scheme, the same font and style, and a consistent logo and marketing message. Additionally make sure that your sign lettering contrasts with your sign background color for maximum visibility. Use a color contrast chart if necessary, but colors such as blue on white, white on black, and red on white are highly visible, easy to read, and stand out. Likewise to ensure maximum visibility watch for obstructions such as tree branches, competitors signs, and power lines. Try to install your sign at the maximum height allowed in the zoning as well as the farthest allowed outward toward public spaces.

6. Studies have also shown that certain colors represent certain things to the majority of people. For instance, red is associated with stop or halt making it one of the best choices for exterior signage. Yellow is associated with cheery but must be used on a dark background; blue represents calm and therefore is best suited for a service provider such as a plumber. And purple is seen as luxury and suitable for professionals and retailers of high-end merchandise.

7. Always incorporate some sort of attention-grabbing devise or element into your exterior signage, which could include things such as a scrolling message board; time and weather readouts; rotating, flashing lights, elegant bright neon; or a reflective background such as mirror or silver Mylar coating. Additionally, adding flags to your sign or above the sign is also a proven attention-grabbing devices. Beyond grabbing the attention of people passing by all these devises will work in making your sign sing and therefore your business a landmark within the community.

8. Lighting also plays an important role in exterior signage. Obviously the first thing it does is make your business visible after dark but it also adds an element of safety by illuminating the surrounding area both for staff and customers. By using various styles and colors of lighting you can grab attention and use lighting for decorative or design purposes to enhance your store's image.

9. Invest in a wide variety of interior signs that can be switched regularly to promote an in-store event or special and at the point of purchase and window displays. These signs should include electronic message boards that can be programmed with new marketing messages as required. Large banners that can be draped or hung from the ceiling with bold marketing messages such as "Sale in Progress" or "Clearance" emblazoned across them. And simple signs that can be used to describe your products in perfect clarity. However, keep in mind that all interior signs, pricing labels, and stickers should be professionally printed, in good repair, and used regularly.

10. And perhaps the most important sign that you can invest in is a simple "Open for Business" sign. But don't make it too simple as it is well worth the extra cost to purchase an attention-grabbing neon or flashing light open for business sign.

WEB RESOURCE

www.signweb.com: Helpful information and links regarding the sign industry.

SIGN REGULATIONS

Long before you invest hundreds if not thousands of dollars into new store or office signs or renovate existing signs make sure to check local ordinances about signs. Just about every community across the United States and Canada has regulations in terms of commercial signage, including size, style, and usage. Don't forget about Uncle Sam either because in addition to local or regional sign regulations there are also federal sign codes that are written to protect public health, safety, and welfare. The federal sign codes include such things as materials and structural issues such as wind load for exterior signage, electrical regulations, and Americans with Disabilities Act

(ADA) regulations such as Braille and wheelchair accessible sign requirements. Given the importance that signage plays in terms of marketing your business it is always a good idea to hire a professional sign design and installation firm for large or major overhauls of signage. In addition to creating signs that will attract the desired response these companies can also give advice and guidance on federal and local sign regulations. And as a general rule they will also obtain permits and variances as required as part of the contract, but make sure to inquire first before you sign on the dotted line for your new sign.

BECOME AN OFFICIAL SUPPLIER
$ 🔨

An often overlooked yet fantastic promotional tool that the vast majority of retailers could take advantage of is to become known as an official supplier and promote this fact in-store and in printed marketing materials. Take a careful look at your current customer list; does it include local celebrities, government offices, a sports team, well-known local corporations or businesspeople, or institutions and charities? All of the above are generally known as sources of influence in every community, and by being known as a official supplier to any or all, you build instant credibility and create a fantastic promotional tool at the same time for your business. For instance, let's say that you operate a sporting goods store and supply all the local softball teams and clubs with balls, bats, and other related equipment. Then you could make up a certificate to hang in your shop that proudly states "We are the official supplier to the hometown softball league. 2003 State Champions" or something similar. And once you have determined your "official supplier" status, extend this promotional message into other areas of marketing such as print and broadcast advertising, printed promotional materials, and on your Web site. However, before you make the official supplier statement, first ask the person, organization, or business that you supply if it is okay that you make the statement that your store is the official supplier.

GET NEWSLETTER SAVVY
$ 🔨

Every retailer should create and maintain a monthly newsletter that can be distributed to customers right at the point of purchase. Pack your newsletter with detailed information about the products you sell, upcoming special events and sales, and tips about how to use and maintain products so they will provide maximum benefits and enjoyment. Also try to create a reason that people will want to hang on to your newsletter once home and not trash it after a quick read. To do this you could include a calendar or games such as crosswords and find-a-word puzzles that require time to complete. The newsletter can be designed right on your computer using basic software and copied at the local print shop for pennies each. Here are a few additional ideas about content for your newsletter.

- Interview your customers and include their stories in your newsletter, especially customers who have benefited from buying products that you sell. Try to include a photograph of them actually using the product. This can motivate others to also buy the same product.

- Company milestones such as years in business, number or customers served, complaint-free or employee injury-free days on the job and so forth.

- Include some fun stuff—trivia, crosswords, word puzzles, and quizzes—and reward readers with small prizes for the first person to correctly answer skill-testing questions and submit the result to you.

- If you have been in business a number of years then include little tidbits of information about the history of your business such as the founder, what your products cost 25 years ago, and first store locations.

- Have a new product or service spotlight each month and perhaps a special discount to entice customers to try them. You can extend this to include new products and services that you will soon be introducing as well.

- Print question and answer interviews with experts in the industry, real and valuable information that will benefit your readers and your business. For instance if you sell bicycles then feature information about the best riding trails in the area, or race statistics and so forth.

- Include tips of the month, how-to articles, and case studies on competitors' services that do not stack up against yours. And don't forget information about your own products.
- Put in community and charity news, events, and volunteer opportunities.

WEB RESOURCE

- www.howtowriteanewsletter.com: Newsletter tool-kit software.

BECOME KNOWN AS A LOCAL ATTRACTION

Another way to increase free word-of-mouth advertising for your retail business within the community, in fact drive it through the roof, is to become known as a local attraction of sorts. What attraction that you become known for will greatly depend on what you sell. But as a creative catalyst, here are a few examples of various businesses that could become known as a local attraction for different reasons.

FAMILY RESTAURANT

The largest and widest selections on the Sunday buffet in the area.

PET SHOP

Install a huge aquarium packed with rare tropical fish.

ICE CREAM SHOP

The biggest scoop of ice cream in town.

HOBBY SHOP

Assemble and display the largest jigsaw puzzle in the state.

BICYCLE SHOP

Build a gigantic bicycle and install it on the roof of your shop.

The premise behind this marketing trick is that people will begin to associate your shop or business

with the attraction or thing that you build, install, or whatever the attraction you develop might be. And, because of what you become known for your business or shop will become memorable. Or in the case of the bicycle retailer with the huge bike on the roof when people discuss bicycles that particular shop is sure to come up in the conversation. "Where did you buy your new bicycle?" "You know that place with the 20-foot tall bike on the roof?" People may not always remember your business name, but they are sure to remember your business if you go out of your way to become know as a local attraction.

SHOPLIFTING PREVENTION TRICKS

Okay, so what does shoplifting prevention tricks have to do with marketing your retail shop? Actually quite a bit, in fact a lot when you take the time to consider that the potential to be victimized by shoplifters can greatly affect your marketing and business decisions. The decisions that can be affected include things such as how you design your store's interior, market and display your merchandise, price your goods, and compete for market share. Especially, when you consider that studies have revealed that in certain sectors of the retail industry as much as 5 percent of potential annual revenues are lost through shoplifting crimes. So back to the opening question, what do theft prevention tricks have to do with marketing your retail shop? For one, imagine what could be accomplished if you had an extra 5 percent a year to spend on marketing activities that would build your business, instead of being lost to criminals. Or, for that matter how much would your own personal lifestyle improve if you could turn shoplifting losses into personal income? Dramatically, I am sure. The difficulty with this type of crime is that you cannot take one brush and paint a portrait of a shoplifter; theft crosses all boundaries of humanity regardless of age, race, sex, religion, or education. Likewise, there are also countless reasons people shoplift: peer pressure, to support addictions, thrill seekers, career criminals, and mental illness just to mention a few. Given that there is no one profile of a shoplifter or one reason people shoplift, the best that you can ever hope to achieve is to increase your knowledge about how you can best prevent shoplifting. Or, in the least greatly reduce the impact that it has on your business and bottom-line profits. With that said listed below are 35 great tricks that you can employ starting today to prevent your store from becoming a victim of shoplifting crimes.

1. Start by hiring a shoplifting prevention consultant to train employees and set up a shoplifting prevention program. The shoplifting prevention program should also include the development of an employee handbook that features shoplifting prevention, deterrent, and detection examples and explanations. Likewise, make sure that all new employees receive this training before being pushed on the sales floor and that existing staff receives an annual refresher course.

2. Ensure that staff greet every shopper who comes into the store and let him know that you are aware of his presence while he is in the store by occasionally making eye contact, asking if he needs assistance, introducing specials or promotions, and generally providing great customer service. When people know that they are being watched they won't steal, and by making the thrust of your efforts customer service as opposed to sizing everyone up as a potential thief only the true thieves will feel uncomfortable and leave. The rest of your shoppers will feel right at home and be highly impressed by your heightened level of great customer service.

3. Install security and surveillance cameras in key areas of the store that are highly visible to shoppers. If your budget won't allow for the purchase of security cameras make inquiries to local alarm companies about the possibility of renting surveillance equipment. Or, if all else fails you can purchase "mock" security cameras that are designed and built to look like the real thing, especially when they are hovering ten feet in the air overhead. Cameras are a great deterrent to shoplifting.

4. In addition to security cameras also install security convex mirror in corners, at the ends of aisles, in inventory receiving areas, and in stockrooms. Make sure to position the mirrors so that blindspots can be easily monitored by staff from any location within the store. Security mirrors are very inexpensive and readily available at most glass and mirror suppliers, and can be installed even by a novice in minutes with only basic hand tools. Additionally, consider installing two-way mirrors from management and administrative offices that look out over the sales floor.

5. For shops with few employees on the sales floor or behind the sales counter on a regular basis then install a motion buzzer or bell at the entrance door so you will know when people are entering or exiting the store. This $10 device can potentially save you hundreds if not thousands of dollars annually.

6. Let people who enter your store know that you mean business by posting "shoplifters will be prosecuted" signs in highly visible areas such as around the cash register, fitting rooms, and above pricey merchandise displays. Also add "this store protected by surveillance cameras" stickers on the front entrance door. The name of the game is to deter shoplifting before it happens, not to react after the theft or attempted theft.

7. Hire plainclothes or uniformed security personnel for peak shopping periods like Christmas and special sales events that you conduct during the year. Rates for trained security personnel start at less than $20 an hour making this a very recoverable sales promotion expenditure.

8. Always limit the number of items that can be taken into fitting rooms and keep fitting room doors locked and install a "ring for service bell" on the outside. Make sure employees count the number of items before opening the fitting room, but in a nice way so that customers don't feel uncomfortable.

9. Keep merchandise away from entrance, exit, and fire escape doors to prevent grab-and-run theft. Likewise, if you retail clothing then turning hangers backward on the rack can also prevent people from being able to

quickly pull garments free during grab-and-run attempts.

10. Ensure that sales staff and all employees for that matter get in the habit of checking all merchandise at the register to make sure that other merchandise has not been hidden inside. The prime culprits are tool boxes, products that are packaged in canisters and decorative boxes, and larger items of clothing with small items hidden inside. Shoplifters will try to conceal small items in just about anything or anywhere.

11. Keep unused checkout aisles or lanes closed and gated during slow periods and hand out keys for washrooms as opposed to leaving washrooms open and unattended. Unattended washrooms are prime places for thieves to hide merchandise under clothing and then leave the store.

12. Lower merchandise displays around cash and customer service desks, as well as promotional stand-ups, POP displays, and signs and banners hanging from the ceiling so employees have a clear view of the selling floor. Likewise, keep the cash counters clear of any items that obstruct the view of the store. You may also want to elevate the floor behind the sales counter so that staff have a better view of the entire store.

13. Design your store display counters and racks in such as way that you create central exit paths so that every person leaving the store regardless if they have made a purchase or not must pass cashiers or reception personnel. In doing so you will be able to monitor what people are leaving with and how they are acting as they exit.

14. Always make sure to tear up unclaimed sales receipts at the cash register. Shoplifters often find them on the floor or in garbage receptacles, and using them as proof of purchase they will then remove merchandise from displays on the sales floor that match the items on the receipt and return these items asking for a refund without ever leaving the store.

15. Check all interior garbage cans and exterior garbage dumpsters prior to regular collection and dumping. A favorite tactic of seasoned shoplifters is to dump merchandise into garbage cans while in the store and return after the store is closed and riffle through exterior garbage dumpsters in search of the merchandise they hid earlier. Unfortunately, this is also a tactic favored by less-than-honest employees, which makes it doubly necessary to check garbage cans and dumpsters prior to collection.

16. Perhaps not shoplifting by definition, but make sure to purchase and use counterfeit money detection equipment. Additionally, ask for two pieces of identification from people who want to write personal checks to pay for purchases, one piece should be photo identification. Counterfeit bills and bum checks cost retailers millions annually, yet both are relatively easy to prevent if you make a conscious effort to do so.

17. Make an effort to control backpacks and other tote bags that enter the store and leave the store. One way to do this without upsetting customers is to offer a free security locker service, similar to those found in bus stations and airports so that they can safely and securely store their bags while they shop.

18. Assign staff sales floor monitoring zones during their shifts and never leave sections or departments unattended. Especially, when new merchandise is being unpacked and priced for display. Unpriced merchandise is a price switcher's dream come true.

19. Prior to hiring any candidates to fill jobs within your store carefully check their backgrounds and references to make sure they do not have past theft convictions. And, insist that employees' friends do not visit during working hours and discourage staff from socializing on the sales floor in groups so that they are not distracted when they should be selling and keeping their eyes and ears open.

20. Install extra interior and exterior lighting and make sure that the lighting is bright enough that people outside looking in through the windows as they pass by can see inside the store. This is also a wonderful deterrent to shoplifting; once again thieves do not like to be watched while they work.

21. Try to keep small and expensive merchandise such as jewelry, cameras, watches, expensive batteries, cell phones, and so forth in locking display cases and in highly visible areas of the store. Shoplifters prefer to steal small and expensive items such as these items that are easy to conceal and resell on the street once they are out of your shop with the goods.

22. Train sales staff and cashiers to be aware of price switching tactics used by thieves. You can deter the potential for price switching by using machine-printed price tags and never handwritten price tags. And also use plastic, nylon, or other tough-to-tear string or wire to affix price tags onto merchandise. Of course, the best way to deter price switching is to use electronic tags that are removed or swiped to desensitize them by staff at the checkout counter. And if budget is tight and you cannot afford any of these methods you can always include a second price tag that is hidden inside or on the merchandise for price verification at the register if required. Thieves hate getting caught by this simple method.

23. Remind all staff and cashiers to check the lower racks of push-out shopping carts before people leave the store with them. Likewise, also ask them to check under larger boxed packages that customer's carry out themselves for concealed merchandise. Most clerks have a tendency to only use a handheld scanner or ring in large items without actually coming out from behind the sales counter to inspect the package for other merchandise that may be concealed inside or underneath. Shoplifters know this and will use this method to get out of your store with merchandise that they have not paid for.

24. If possible instruct cashiers to staple all shopping bags shut upon purchase with the receipt also stapled on the outside of the bag. Doing so will make it easy for other staff or security personnel to verify what is in the bag if they feel it is warranted prior to the customer leaving. Additionally, it makes it harder for people to slip items into their shopping bag on the way out after they have passed through the checkout aisle.

25. Keep your stockroom doors and receiving area doors locked at all times, unless they are required to be unlocked during business hours to meet fire regulations. Likewise, consider installing locking steel cabinets for smaller and expensive merchandise that remains in the stockroom area until it is cataloged for inventory, priced, and displayed on the sales floor.

26. Develop clear policies for employees regarding when they can shop, how merchandise is checked out and cleared, and how they store personal belongings such as bags, jackets, and totes they bring into the store. Unfortunately employee pilferage is on the rise and accounts for millions of dollars in lost merchandise sales annually.

27. Post a sign that restricts freight and delivery drivers from entering receiving areas and stockrooms beyond the check in point. Likewise, when service personnel are hired to carry out repairs or routine maintenance in the store make sure to carefully examine their toolboxes, push carts, and other equipment for your merchandise before they leave. Don't feel bad about doing this, professional service providers expect it and most prefer you do so that there is no potential for disagreements relating to accusations of theft.

Be Aware of Commonly Used Tactics by Shoplifters

28. Watch out for people asking you or staff to check on merchandise in the stockroom, especially when there is limited staff on the sales floor. While you're out back, they're robbing you blind and flee before you even notice.

29. Train employees to be on the lookout for people who are carrying concealment devices such as newspapers, large books, umbrellas, tote bags, jackets, baby carriers, briefcases, camera cases, bulky packages, and shopping bags. These are all favorite concealment devices for shoplifters to hide the goods so they can make a clean getaway.

30. Be on the lookout for large groups of people shopping together, especially younger people.

Also watch for large groups of people who come charging into your store on a looting spree. Once again, generally younger people perform this increasingly common practice called swarming.

31. Take notice of people who regularly browse the store, but rarely make purchases and when they do the items are small and low cost. It is a proven fact that when successful, shoplifters will keep returning to the same store time after time often until they are caught, which could come thousands of dollars too late.

32. Be on the lookout for people who seem nervous and avoid direct eye contact with staff, but appear to be watching or scanning everything but the merchandise. When honest people want to shop and buy they pay attention to the merchandise and not so much to what is around them. On the other hand when shoplifters steal, merchandise takes a backseat to their surroundings in terms of where their attention is focused.

33. Watch out for people who are wearing unusually baggy clothing or clothing such as heavy winter coats that do not suit the current season. Still the favorite of shoplifters is to stash merchandise under clothing and slowly make their way out of the store. The bigger, bulkier, or baggier the clothing, the more they can conceal.

34. Sadly, also be on the lookout for parents pushing baby carriages; as alarming as this may sound some have recently been caught stashing merchandise under their babies in the strollers or carriages while no one is watching then calmly exiting the store.

35. Be on the lookout for people who unnecessarily distract sales staff and clerks, with extensive or prolonged questioning, "accidentally" knocking over displays, fainting, choking, complaining, or causing a general disturbance. Shoplifters love to work in pairs or worse teams and while one is keeping sales staff busy the other is looting your shop for whatever they want.

📖 SUGGESTED ADDITIONAL READING

Blachard, Kenneth H., Sheldon Bowles, and Harvey Mackay. *Raving Fans: A Revolutionary Approach to Customer Service.* New York: William Morrow & Company, 1993.

Butcher, Stephan A. *Customer Loyalty Programs and Clubs.* Brookfield, VT: Gower Ashgate Publishing, 2002.

Kingarrd, Jan. *Successful Retail Business.* Irvine, CA: Entrepreneur Press, 2002.

Krause, Jim. *Layout Index: Brochure, Web Design, Poster, Flyer, Advertising, Page Layout, Newsletter, Stationery, Index.* Cincinnati, OH: North Light Books, 2001

New York Institute of Store Planners and Visual Merchandisers and Store Designers, The. *Stores and Retail Spaces 2.* Watson Guptill Publications, 2000.

Portas, Mary. *Windows: The Art of Retail Display.* London, UK: Thames and Hudson Publishing, 1999.

Salraneschi, Luigi. *Location, Location, Location: How to Select the Best Site for Your Business.* Central Point, OR: Entrepreneur Press, 1996.

Segal, Rick. *Retail Business Kit for Dummies.* New York: John Wiley & Sons, 2001.

Sewell, Carl, Paul B. Brown, and Tom Peters. *Customers For Life: How to Turn That One Time Buyer Into a Lifetime Customer.* New York: Pocket Books, 1998.

Walton, Sally. *It's a Wrap: 50 Inspirational Ideas For Your Gift-Wrapping.* London, UK: Southwater Publishing, 2001.

KEY

COST TO IMPLEMENT $

DO-IT-YOURSELF

CALL IN THE PROFESSIONALS

LEGAL ISSUES

BOOK RESOURCES

ONLINE

SERVICE PROVIDER
Marketing Tips for Your Business

Most of us never recognize opportunity until it goes to work in our competitor's business.

—P. L. ANDARR

TRANSFORM YOUR WAITING ROOM INTO A SELLING ROOM
$$+

We have all sat in reception areas and waiting rooms at doctors, lawyers, car dealerships, and many more. As a general rule what you'll find to keep you occupied while you wait for your appointment is a stack of outdated magazines and newspapers. If your business uses a waiting room as a holding area for customers and clients, then it's time to break the rule and toss the magazines and newspapers into the recycling bin. Instead, use your waiting room as a marketing center for the products you sell and the services you provide. Take advantage of the fact that you have people's undivided attention while they wait and use this opportunity to display marketing materials such as a monthly newsletter, product and service brochures, and maybe even a promotional video that plays on a continuous loop—anything that highlights all the products and services you sell and how people benefit from taking ownership of them. Waiting rooms can provide incredible marketing opportunities, so get creative and put your waiting room to work promoting your business.

LEVERAGE YOUR CURRENT BUSINESS ASSETS TO GROW
$$

All operating businesses have assets that can be leveraged and used as a tool for fueling the growth of the business. These assets can generally be leveraged very inexpensively.

Referrals

Embrace and practice the three R's of referrals: request, reward, and reciprocate. This means that you must get in the habit of requesting or asking for referrals—ask your customers, suppliers, and business alliances and not just once but often. Reward those individuals who give you referrals. This could be by way of a simple but sincere thank-you card or a gift such as tickets to a concert or a certificate to a restaurant. And finally, reciprocate; if business alliances or suppliers give you referrals then work hard to find some that you can give them and return the favor.

Direct Marketing

You know who your best current customers are so why not create a profile of them and seek to clone them based on the information from the profiling exercise? Once you have identified the common characteristics of your best customers—and this could be what they read, their hobbies, or associations and clubs they belong to—then create a direct-mail package promoting the benefits of your service and send it to the "clones."

Diversify

You already have a core customer base so why not survey them to find out what additional services they need and that they would be willing to use if you supplied them? Diversification is one of the easiest and quickest ways to grow an existing business. For instance if you operate a house painting service, ask current and past customers about window and rain gutter cleaning. Find out how often they get these things done, who does it, how much they pay for it, and most importantly if they would like your business to do it. Trust and credibility are the two biggest assets any business has; if your business is credible and your customers trust you then the job of persuasion (selling) becomes a nonissue.

Discount

Once again build a profile of your best customers, seek the clones, and offer your service for half price for a fixed period of time, like 30 or 60 days. Yes this can be a tough pill to swallow in the short term, but long term you can build a larger repeat client base, gain additional referrals, and even use this tactic to expand into new geographic markets. To ease the pain of a 50 percent short-term discount, calculate the lifetime value of each customer you service. Seeing on paper that shaving $100 now to secure thousands in future business makes this pill much easier to swallow.

SELLING SOLUTIONS
$$ ✎

By the very nature of being a service provider you are in fact selling solutions that fix a problem; you are a problem solver and this should be the cornerstone of your marketing campaign and underscore all of your marketing activities. Carefully analyze what you sell to figure out what problem(s) you are solving. An exterminator rids a house of cockroaches, a financial planner makes sense out of hard-to-understand financial and investment matters, and an appliance repairperson fixes broken washing machines. All problems that from a prospect's perspective are creating difficulties or inconveniences of varying degrees need to be fixed or solved. Once you have clearly identified the problem your service solves then boldly use this in all your marketing to remind prospects that these are the problems that you fix. However, keep in mind that you want to make the problems you solve appear as bad as they possibly can be, in fact down right horrible and nasty. Of course, you will depict your solution or how you fix the problem as easy and as convenient as possible. Service providers should always boil down what they do into the most basic of terms so that it is easily understood and digested by prospects who have problems that need to be fixed.

WEB RESOURCE

⚲ www.briantracy.com: Sales and motivational training, information, products, programs, and services.

PROACTIVE WARRANTY INSPECTIONS
$$ ✎

You may have no control over the manufacturer's warranty of products that you sell and install but you can make sure that all your customers get peace-of-mind security by examining products that your business has installed a few months prior to the manufacturer's warranty expiring. Call customers and let them know that the manufacturer's warranty is about to expire on the product(s) that you have previously sold and installed for them. Tell customers that you would like to come out or send a service-person by to inspect the product and make sure that it is still performing the way it was designed to do and that there are no problems with the product. And if you find that the product is not working properly then you can make adjustments, repairs, or replacements before the warranty expires, thus potentially saving your valued customers money down the line, for which of course they will love you. There is a cost to providing a free "prewarranty expiration" service, but in the end customers will be blown away that you have their best interests in mind. And ultimately this relatively small expenditure will go a long way to ensure that your customer becomes a customer for life and refers many more people to your business. Call it a proactive way to secure repeat business before your customer needs to buy again and the competition gets a kick at the can.

EXPAND BY PHONE NUMBERS
$$ ⚒

Project your company's image as wide and as an industry leader by expanding geographically using only telephone numbers in the absence of an actual office location. There are a few methods to do this. The first is to set up a telephone number and answering service with a call center, and the second is to establish a new business number in the area you want to expand in to and have that line forwarded to your existing location. Both methods work well and each generally costs less than $150 a month, a mere fraction of what it would cost to actually establish a bricks-and-mortar office in new geographical areas. This simple idea really gives the illusion that your business is big. Imagine having your stationery printed with New York, Los Angeles, Miami, Seattle, and Dallas across the top as office locations, each with its own distinct telephone number. Now that is impressive and gives prospects a feeling of reassurance that they're dealing with a large firm capable of handling their business needs. Additionally, vehicle signs showing multiple service areas and telephone

numbers also project the same image. And lastly, don't forget to project your image in cyberspace as larger and wider also by creating different e-mail addresses for various departments in your business, such as customerservice@yourbusiness.com, public relations@yourbusiness.com, or marketingdirector @yourbusiness.com.

STEP-BY-STEP DETAILS SELL
$ ⚒

An amazing thing happens when you clearly demonstrate to prospects exactly how something will happen in precise step-by-step detail; sales and profits skyrocket because the precise explanation elevates doubt and fear of buying because the prospect better understands the product, service, or process. For that reason it is wise to use the step-by-step approach in your marketing materials and during presentations with prospects. Lay out what you want your prospect to understand about your service starting at the beginning, then in careful step-by-step detail build through to the end to what the exact results will be when you are done. Of course the results should be what the prospect will get as a result of using your service: save money, make money, solve a problem, or fill a need. This strategy also works in reverse if you lay out what steps you want your prospect to take in terms of responding to your offer and acting right away. Think of this kind of detail as a road map, when you want to get somewhere you rely on one. The same premise holds true for getting your prospect from point A to B. Additionally build your step-by-step instructions around what you anticipate the prospect's key objections are going to be; once again this can eliminate the need to raise objections, build trust, and eliminate doubt.

TAKE A PACKAGED APPROACH
$$ ⚒

Take a unique approach to the various services you offer by packaging one or more together and offering these packages to new prospects and existing clients. The upside to this type of marketing is that while it can reduce your profit on a individual transaction basis, it can increase the value of your per sale and per customer transactions. In turn this can lead to overall increased profitability because of the economies of scale—meaning in most cases your fixed costs of doing business such as office rent, utilities, and transportation—remain constant regardless if your gross sales are $20,000 a month or $30,000 a month. A good example of packaged services is the simple oil change that typically costs in the range of $25, but you'll find that few service garages sell the basic oil change. Instead they will offer various packages that usually top out at around $99 and include an oil change, lube, filter, filling of the fluids, and 30 point mechanical check of items like the tires, exhaust, belts, and lights. Why? Because it only takes about an extra ten minutes to service each vehicle, making it extremely profitable for the service provider. And even more important is the perceived value from the customer's perspective simply due to the fact that if all of these services were provided and billed for separately it would run the cost from $99 to a few hundred. Service garages aren't the only businesses that are benefiting from taking a packaged approach to selling services; the cable company bundles specialty stations, the telephone company bundles specific services, and even the local car wash offers numerous packages to get your car clean to various degrees. Carefully examine the services that you are currently providing customers and look for ways to package a few together and increase your sales value for each transaction and possibly your profitability at the same time.

CREATE A NEW CUSTOMER KIT
$$ ⚒

Thank new customers for their support by creating a new customer kit and give the customer kit to them at the point of purchase. The new customer kit should include printed promotional materials that give details about the benefits of all the services and products that you sell. The kit should also include client testimonials, discount coupons, and special incentive programs to motivate more frequent buying along with a few advertising specialties such as pens, notepads, fridge magnets, and more that can be emblazoned with your business name, logo, and

promotional message as a special thank you and as a way to stay fresh in your customer's minds as they use these items daily. Also make sure to include a half dozen referral cards that your new customers can pass along to their friends and family, and that entitle the holder to a special referral discount or other promotional incentive. New customer kits are an extremely effective marketing tool and can be customized to suit each business that distributes them to their valuable customers.

SIZZLING WORKMANSHIP WARRANTIES
$$ ⚒ ⚖

Separate your business from the competition by implementing a workmanship warranty program that will live up to your claim that your business is an industry leader and the best at what it does. If the competition's workmanship warranty is one year, then make yours two. If the competition's workmanship warranty is loaded with small print that does not have customers' best interests in mind, then zap the small print from your warranty. And, if your competition's workmanship warranty is nontransferable or charges a transfer fee, then make your workmanship warranty easily transferable and free to do so. People want to know that should problems arise after the sale and after the work has been performed and paid for, that they have a guarantee from your business that you will stand behind your work and word and will be there to correct workmanship-related deficiencies if they arise. In short, a powerful workmanship warranty is one of the best marketing tools that service providers have to secure new business and build lifelong selling relationships with all customers. Not too mention that a great workmanship warranty is also a fantastic credibility booster, as who can doubt the company that is so confident of their work that they are willing to make it the strongest warranty in the business.

BE MORE MEMORABLE
$ ⚒

Go the extra mile and make your service more memorable than the competition's and reap the benefits, which generally include more referrals and repeat business. Being remembered means that you do something that your customers do not expect and this impresses them enough that they tell others and continue to be loyal to your business. Or, it can mean something as simple as appealing to their emotions, which once again can make your business more memorable and therefore increase the likelihood of word-of-mouth advertising. The things you do to become more memorable can be small and very inexpensive, such as the hand car wash service that leaves an air freshener hanging from the mirror. Or the carpet cleaning service that leaves a vase full of fresh cut flowers on the kitchen table when they leave. Or the TV repair service that gives every customer a package of microwave popcorn when they repair television sets. Or, even the house painting service that cleans the rain gutters for free and without being asked to while they have the ladders on site painting. It is these very small, inexpensive, and non-time-consuming extras that your customers will remember, and as the story goes, they tell two people who tell two people who tell two more people and so on.

WEB RESOURCE

ʃ www.entrepreneur.com: Online business and marketing resource center for small-business owners, managers, and professionals.

INVOICE GREETINGS
$ 🔨

Unfortunately all too often complacency sets in and the only contact that service providers have with their customers is via the monthly account statements they send out. This is actually an opportunity in disguise to strengthen the working relationship that you have with your customers. Take the time to personalize each monthly statement to appeal to each individual customer who will receive it. Boldly print across the top of it that you appreciate their business and even stamp a "our best customer since" date on top of your invoice. Include other greetings that are related to the season or a special holiday that falls within the billing month. Include brochures that introduce new services or upgraded service options, or include a

"please fax back" survey form loaded with questions that can help you to learn more about your customers and additional products or services that they might require from the answers they provide. In short, use your monthly invoice to further build a bond with your customers by giving them information that will benefit them and by telling them that they're a very important and appreciated member of your business team. You're already paying for the stamp, envelope, paper, and ink so get the most out of it both in terms of promotional efforts and building strong relationships with your customers.

OFFER FREE SECOND OPINIONS
$$ 🔨

No one wants to be taken for a ride and pay too much, or pay for a service and have a poor job done. You can play on these customer fears by offering even the most doubting prospects a free no-obligation second opinion to alleviate doubt and win them over. Many service providers advertise and promote free estimates as a way to get people calling and get their foot in the door. However, you can turn this around and advertise free second opinions and come off looking like the good guy with the customer's best interests in mind by not estimating a job, but by scrutinizing a competitor's estimate and then undercutting their price. Or, alternately by offering superior products or services at a higher price. I have personally used this marketing tactic many times in my home renovation business with great success, and more times than not prospects were more than happy to show me competitors' estimates and bids on their job. In turn this was my opportunity to be the last bidder in, and more importantly knew all the other prices and the job details they proposed. Offering free second opinions removes your business as a threat; you become the mediator and lead prospects to wise and honest decisions that can save them time, money, and increase the value of what they receive in exchange for their money. Give it a try—banish free estimates or quotes and strictly offer free no obligation second opinions; you will be amazed at the positive impact this can have on your business and bottom line.

NEWSLETTER MARKETING

$$ ✎

Publishing a monthly newsletter is a great way to keep your name and the services you provide in front of prospects and clients alike in a consistent manner. Not only are newsletters highly effective in terms of their marketing power but they are also extremely cost effective, especially if you take the time to learn how to put together and publish the newsletter yourself. Newsletters should provide valuable information that is aimed directly at your target audience. They should be brief, yet be long enough that the reader forms a favorable opinion about what they have learned from reading it. For the service provider, newsletters can create a fantastic forum for up-selling in a very nonaggressive fashion. For instance if you operate a property maintenance service you could include a section in your newsletter every month that describes a new type of property maintenance service and the benefits of the service. Existing customers reading this will feel compelled to give you a call if they find the service would be beneficial to them, powerful because it enables you to build on the existing credibility and trust that you have established with customers. However, with all that said newsletters still require time and energy to put together and to make professional, not to mention the fact you must consistently come up with new ideas to base your newsletter content on. So here are a few ideas around which you can build your newsletter content.

- Interview your own customers and include their stories in your newsletter, especially customers who have benefited from doing business with you. Include their photos and if they are in business thank them by giving them a plug that describes their products and services and how they can be contacted.
- Have a section with news concerning your industry, joint ventures, mergers, impending government legislation, statistics and special events. Include stories on local, national, and international news concerning your industry.
- Post company milestones such as years in business, number of customers served, complaint-free or employee injury-free days on the job.

- Include some fun stuff—trivia, crosswords, word puzzles, and quizzes—and reward readers with small prizes for the first person to correctly answer skill-testing questions.
- Print product and service spotlights, a new one each month and perhaps a special discount to entice customers to try them. You can extend this to include new products and services that you will soon be introducing as well.
- Question-and-answer interviews with experts in the industry will have real and valuable information that will benefit your readers and your business.
- Show tips of the month, how-to articles, and case studies on competitor services that do not stack up against yours.
- Community and charity news, events, and volunteer opportunities will be of interest to your customers.

WEB RESOURCE

✍ www.howtowriteanewsletter.com: Newsletter toolkit software.

TURN SERVICE VEHICLES INTO MOBILE SHOWROOMS

$$+ ✎

Take advantage of every customer contact opportunity to increase revenues and profits by converting your service vehicles into mobile showrooms and by also converting your service personnel into professional service and sales specialists. Turning service vehicles into mini mobile showrooms is very easy to do and need not be expensive just professional looking such as shelving stocked with a few samples of the bestselling products that you sell and install. Or, a binder full of extended warranties that service personnel can show and explain the benefits of to customers on site after they complete a service call or install a product. Basically, any additional product or service that you normally sell can be pitched on site as an upgrade, add-on, or something entirely new to your existing customer. It is a fact that 70 percent of purchases made in a retail store environment are done on an impulse basis—meaning the people who make these purchases had no intention of doing so until they entered the store and were motivated to do so by way of salespeople, displays, and in-store signage. There is no reason that you cannot create the same impulse buying atmosphere, but right from your service vehicles and on a mobile basis. Train your service personnel in the art of one-minute sales pitches and reward them above their normal salary with a commission on all new sales they generate on site. This simple and effective marketing trick can generate thousands of dollars in new sales annually and dramatically raise your average per customer sales value, which in return will decrease your average unit marketing costs.

COVER THE COSTS OF CUSTOMER CALLS
$$ ⚒

At one time not too long ago providing customers with toll-free calling options was expensive and out of the financial reach of many small-business owners. Fortunately that has now changed with the deregulation of the telecommunications industry right across North America; toll-free calling services are now very affordable and a must-have marketing and customer service tool for every business regardless of size and revenues. Promote your toll-free calling line on all printed marketing materials and business communications to get the most benefit from it. Given two identical advertisement offers, but one with a toll-free number and the other without, just about every interested consumer would opt to call the business with the toll-free line. On the surface this marketing trick may seem elementary, but it is highly effective—your toll-free telephone line works year round as a silent salesperson that cleverly persuades prospects to call your business. Additionally, extend the toll-free line to your fax machine for customers, suppliers, and sales reps to use. It can be a worthwhile expenditure simply to keep people happy by providing a valuable service. These same happy people might just buy more and refer more people to you because of your toll-free calling and fax service.

WEB RESOURCE

⚒ www.ultimatevoicemail.com: Toll-free calling programs and services for small businesses.

CATCH AFTER-HOURS CALLS
$$ ⚒

Most business owners rely heavily on the telephone to generate new business, especially service providers. This makes it a good idea to develop a rotating after-hours call schedule for all employees to participate in. Buy a cell phone and after regular business hours have your business telephone line call forwarded to the cell phone so that you do not miss a single customer call. Many people work nine to five and therefore cannot call a business or make inquiries until after five, after many businesses have already closed for the day and the employees have gone home. Ask that each employee take the phone home one night a week and pay a small "on-call" fee for doing so. This fee will easily be recouped by the amount of new business you secure as a result of talking to customers on the telephone after hours. Most people have become so numbed by answering machines and answering services that they no longer bother to leave a message and instead keep calling competing businesses until they finally reach one that is open or that has wisely chosen to take after-hours calls.

CHOOSE WORK CAREFULLY
$ ⚒

Is that proposed contract or new job one that you really want? One problem that has always plagued service providers more than any other type of business or industry is not getting paid for work completed or having to wait long periods of time to get paid, especially for service providers subcontracting for other businesses. Before saying yes to a job, always question your customer's motives for wanting to contract with your service. For instance if you run a house painting service and a general contractor or homebuilder has asked you to paint five houses for them, a red flag should go up. Assuming the contractor is established then why is their usual house painter not painting these houses? Is the contractor a slow payer, or non-payer, or is it a legitimate case of the contractor seeking new subcontractors? Secondary service providers are often the last in line to get paid and the first not to get paid when money runs short for whatever reason. Before jumping at what on the surface may seem to be a great opportunity to expand your business make sure that you protect yourself. Know who your dealing with and how and when you will be paid.

"WHY I NEED AND DESERVE ____" CONTEST
$$$ ✎ ⚖

Create your own "Why I need and deserve ____" contest as a way to collect a ton of valuable leads that can be followed up and turned into sales and, more important, loyal lifetime customers. For instance if you operate a residential house cleaning service create a contest that asks people to describe in brief essay form "Why I need and deserve free maid service for a year." You can advertise the contest by running display advertisements with cut-out entry forms tied into the ad in your local newspaper. Or use a direct-mail and entry card response system by renting mailing lists compiled from names of people who reside in the geographical area you want to target. The benefit to your business from creating this type of contest and awarding the prize is the hundreds if not thousands of entry forms (leads) that you receive and that can be followed up by way of direct mail and telemarketing and sold on the value and benefit of your cleaning service. Additionally, prior to staging the contest, seek to build alliances with other businesses or media companies that can cosponsor the event, as this can be a great way to reduce your marketing expenses in promoting the contest. However, as a word of caution make sure to carefully plan and layout the details of the contest. You may even want to consult with a lawyer to ensure that you do not bend any local contest or sweepstakes rules and regulations. The contest can be adapted to all sorts of businesses that provide services; here are a few ideas.

- Why I need and deserve to have my windows professionally cleaned.
- Why I need and deserve to have my house professionally painted.
- Why I need and deserve to have my car professionally cleaned and detailed.
- Why I need and deserve a day at the spa.
- Why I need and deserve a professional makeover.
- Why I need and deserve to have my carpet professionally cleaned.
- Why I need and deserve free dry cleaning for a year.
- Why I need and deserve to have my backyard professionally landscaped.
- Why I need and deserve to have my dog professionally trained.

Once again, these are only a few ideas. Get creative and develop your own "why I need and deserve" contest and put it to work promoting your business.

RATE OUR SERVICE
$$ ✎

Learn more about your business, customers' expectations, employees, and subcontractors by asking customers to kindly complete a postjob "Rate Our Service" survey form. Create the survey form using questions that ask specific questions about how customers rank each segment of your business, from initial contact right through to completion and overall satisfaction with the services you provide. Include a self-addressed stamped envelope with the survey form to ensure a high response rate. Use the results of the ongoing customer survey to identify ongoing problems or weak areas of your service, poor performing employees, and strengths that you can build upon and expand into other areas of your operation. Make sure that every customer rates your service, even if they are repeat customers because in business, especially a service-related business, there is no place for complicity. Keep in mind that this is also the perfect opportunity to ask customers to supply a testimonial as well as a few referrals. Below is a basic survey form that you can use as a general outline from which you can create a custom one to meet the needs of your business.

"Rate Our Service" Sample Form

Help us help serve you better by rating our service.

(Your company information here)

Great	Good	Poor	Customer Service Survey
❏	❏	❏	How was your initial inquiry handled?
❏	❏	❏	Did you find our employees helpful in answering your questions?
❏	❏	❏	Did you find our employees knowledgeable about our products and services?
❏	❏	❏	How would you rate the price of our service?
❏	❏	❏	How would you rate the value of our service?
❏	❏	❏	How would you rate your overall experience of our service?
❏	❏	❏	How would you rate the quality of our service?
❏	❏	❏	How would you rate the performance and reliability of our service?

Would you like to receive free and valuable information from us?   ❏ Yes   ❏ No

Would you refer other people to our business?   ❏ Yes   ❏ No

Would you be prepared to provide a written testimonial outlining your experiences with our business?   ❏ Yes   ❏ No

We welcome additional comments, questions, or concerns you may have:

_____

_____

_____

Name: _____

Address: _____

City: _____   State: _____   Zip code: _____

Telephone: _____   Fax: _____   E-mail address: _____

Thank you! We appreciate your support.

CALL TO CONFIRM
$ ✎

Never assume that an installation or service appointment with a customer, a sales presentation with a prospect, or an appointment with a patient or client is a sure thing unless you or a member of your staff has called to confirm the appointment at least 24 hours in advance. Often appointments are set days, weeks, or even months ahead of time, especially for service providers who install products or professionals such as medical and legal specialists with long waiting lists. When appointments are set far in advance it is easy for people to simply forget about them; when this does happen it unfortunately results in down time that you will likely never be able to make up financially. And worse a strained relationship with the customer can result because of the missed appointment that in the worst case scenario can result in lost future business and profits from that customer. Always get in the habit of calling customers to reconfirm appointments, installations, presentations, or routine service visits. This simple trick can save you time, money, and make your customers happy knowing that they're on your mind and valued.

OFFER FREE CHECKUPS
$$ ✎

Get creative in the way that you promote your service-related business by offering free and no-obligation diagnostic checkups as a way to cleverly get your foot in the door and selling. For instance an insulation contractor could offer prospects free "Heating Loss Evaluations," wherein they test homes to find out how much heat is being lost as a result of the home being poorly insulated and weatherproofed. Of course the "Free Evaluation" would also come with a list of recommended improvements that should be done to reduce heat loss, thus lowering energy costs. Likewise a retailer of bottled water could offer prospects free in-home "Tap Drinking Water" tests to find out how clean and safe their drinking water was for consumption. Once again this would provide more than ample opportunity to sell the bottled water should the water tests prove of poor quality. Free checkups work extremely well as a marketing tactic for two reasons: First, they offer consumers terrific value because they are receiving a very valuable service at no cost; second, your business will be perceived by prospects as reputable because you offer the free checkups with no strings attached. It's kind of like going to see the family doctor for a checkup; you trust her and believe the advice she gives you, even if it means having to spend money on a medical procedure or prescription drugs.

Who Can Offer Free Checkups as a Way to Potentially Secure More Business?

Here are just a few who can benefit, there are many more.

PLUMBER

Offer free checkups on pipes and fixtures.

ROOFER

Offer free checkups on roofs and chimneys.

ELECTRICIAN

Offer free checkups on electrical circuits and panels.

EYE DOCTOR

Offer free eye checkups and examines.

DENTISTS

Offer free dental examines.

SIGN COMPANY

Offer free checkups of outdoor signage.

HOME ALARM CONSULTANT

Offer free check ups on home security systems.

COMPUTER CONSULTANT

Offer free checkups of computer equipment.

GOLF PRO

Offer free golf swing checkups.

TRICKS FOR SURVIVING TOUGH TIMES
$$+ ✎

The economy runs in cycles and even long established and successful companies can find it difficult to survive in tough economic conditions. Here are a few tricks that you can employ to not only survive in tough times, but to actually increase your sales and profits.

Survive Tough Times by Staying Focused

Zero in on and get downright focused on your best customers for two reasons. First, you don't want them jumping ship when times are tough economically. And second, your existing customers are the fastest and least expensive way to increase sales. The fact of the matter is that it will always cost ten times as much to find new customers as it will to hang on to the ones you have.

Survive Tough Times by Prospecting

Don't let your pipeline dwindle or worse become empty. Instead pick up the pace with quality prospecting. Spend more time networking, on the telephone, and asking for referrals. Tough times tend to get businesspeople down emotionally and mentally: break the cycle and stay on track by always seeking new customers and business opportunities.

Survive Tough Times with Direct Marketing

Develop an incredible offer and launch a relentless direct-marketing campaign. Mail, e-mail, telemarketing, infomercials, or a combination of all, whichever works best for your business. In tough times businesspeople have a tendency to reduce the amount of time, money, and energy on direct-marketing activities, when in fact it should be the time that you increase these activities to remain strongly positioned in the marketplace and in your target audience's minds.

Survive Tough Times by Sharing

Use your expertise as a powerful marketing tool in tough economic times to increase sales and revenues by sharing your knowledge with the world. Send out press releases; write articles for print and online publications; seek out public speaking opportunities; and conduct free seminars, workshops, and training classes to prospect for new business and to motivate existing prospects to buy. Branding yourself as an expert in your field or industry is still one of the best and least expensive ways to secure new business. And the best way to become known as an expert is to share what you know with others.

Survive Tough Times by Increasing

Develop strategies to increase the value of every sale and to increase buyer frequency. Imagine if you have 20 people using your service once a month and spending $100 each; if you could increase the average transaction by only a mere $20 and the frequency to every three weeks you would then generate an additional $16,800 per annum.

CRANK UP THE PRICE OF YOUR SERVICE $$ ✎

Chances are your service is worth far more than you are currently charging clients for it; the trick of course is to get prospects to see this and be willing to pay a fair price for it. But before you can think in terms of how to get people to pay more for what you provide you first have to clearly identify and list what it is your service does for someone in order to be able to place a higher value on it. Does it save someone money? If so, how much and can you clearly demonstrate that to your prospect? If you can, then a percentage of the savings could be the value that you place on your service, saving a prospect $10,000 and asking for only 50 percent of that as a fee would be realistic and fair, especially if you could prove it beyond doubt with the assistance of client testimonials and even went as far as to provide a guarantee. Does your service make someone money? If so, can you clearly demonstrate that to your prospect? Once again what value can you place on earning someone money and what is that worth—10 percent, 20 percent, or more? Does your service positively benefit your prospects' health or prolong their lives? The list goes on, but at the core is that you have to know what your prospects get from buying and using your service if you ever hope to get past price objections and being able to justify the price you charge in exchange for the value you provide. In a nutshell, stop thinking of the value of your service in terms of an hourly or daily fee. Instead value your service based on what it will do for people.

INDEX YOUR CONTRACTS
$ ✎

Before you sign any long-term contract to provide a service or services to a client make sure that you have included a provision for indexing the contract. Inflationary and deflationary pressures on the economy can affect labor, materials, transportation, and all other costs associated with providing a service. These costs can rise dramatically or subsequently drop dramatically and have an effect on your business and ability to generate a profit. To protect yourself you should consider having an indexing clause written into all of your contracts. Depending on the value of the contract the clause does not have to be a legal document, just one that serves to protect your and your client's best interests. For instance you could tie the indexing clause to a specific indicator such as the cost of living inflation index and the contract would then be automatically adjusted annually to this selected indicator. Alternately you could mutually create your own indexing system with your client, basing the index on key components of the contract such as labor, materials, and transportation. And select a median number such as 100 based on today's prices, and should the index increase or decrease beyond a certain point such as ten points in either direction then the indexing clause would automatically change the contract pricing to reflect economic conditions. Be smart, be wise, and protect your business from outside pressures that you have no control over.

ENTER COMPETITIONS
$$ ✎

Winning business awards and competitions, as well as customer service awards is a fantastic way to build credibility and attract new business, especially for service providers who often must build their entire sales pitch and marketing campaign around trust, reliability, credibility, and the good reputation of their firms. Just about every community, city, and state has some sort of annual business competition classified by type, sector, or industry. Often these business excellence awards and competitions are sponsored and administrated by local business groups like the chamber of commerce, the economic committee of government, or even by local newspapers and radio and television stations. Likewise, many industry business associations also hold annual "best of" business award ceremonies as well, all of which are more than worthwhile to take the time to enter. Get started in your quest to locate a suitable competition for your business to enter by checking with community business groups, your local newspaper, and industry associations to find out which type of competition and awards are available for your type of service business. Learn the details of each and then apply or get nominated for the ones that interest you and the ones that you feel winning would have the most benefit for your business from a sales and marketing standpoint. The publicity and free advertising that winning can generate is priceless, not to mention the limitless marketing opportunities associated with being the best.

VOICE-MAIL MARKETING
$$+ ✎

Utilize your existing voice-mail system to maximize promotional efforts by having every employee with a voice mailbox leave a promotional message along with their normal message. This is a very powerful marketing technique that very few companies use, therefore they are not fully realizing all the promotional benefits that can be derived from something that you are already using, in this case voice mail. A sales rep can promote the newest product. A service rep can promote a monthly service special. A customer service rep can promote extended warranties, and so on. All this can be accomplished just by each employee adding a ten-second sales pitch onto their existing voice-mail message. This can also be extended and each employee's promotional message can be played when they have to place customers on hold. Every employee should understand that sales drive every single business and that each is responsible to some degree to generate new sales. Work with each employee to script and record the best pitches and make sure to change the promotional message every month. "Hi, you've reached Don at ABC Company. I apologize for not being available to take your call. Please leave your name and number and I will return your call as soon as possible. Be sure to ask me about this month's service special when we speak, it will save you $100."

WEB RESOURCE

⚲ www.americanvoicemail.com: Voice-mail marketing solutions.

CREATE A REPUTATION
$$$ ⚒

You can dramatically shorten or even in some cases eliminate the sales cycle entirely when prospects have either heard favorable things about your business, or they have taken steps to seek you out to do business. And the easiest way to achieve both of these favorable scenarios is to work hard at creating a rock solid business reputation, which in terms of providing a service is one of the most powerful marketing tools you can have in your arsenal. There are ways to go about building a solid reputation and the first is obvious; always go out of your way to ensure that you do what you say you are going to do, on time, on budget, and as promised. The second way to gain a solid reputation is to get your current customers to refer your business to other people. Once again this will require you to go that extra mile for all clients and ensure you deliver on promises and do it in true professional style. The third way to gain a solid reputation is to become known as an expert in your industry or professional field. This can be accomplished by writing articles, columns, and books about the subject or by actively seeking opportunities and being called upon to speak publicly about your area of expertise. Ideally both if you can. The fourth way is through consistent and ongoing marketing and promotional activities that are designed to be repetitious and everlasting.

SEEK OUT PIGGYBACKING OPPORTUNITIES
$$ ⚒

Small-business owners should always be on the lookout for innovative ways to piggyback their service with an existing business. For instance, if you operate a mobile automobile detailing service then contact local car dealerships and offer to operate your service through their dealership and for the benefit of their customers. Meaning that the dealership could sell your service at a profit to their customers, or alternately give your service away as a gift or incentive to persuade people to buy a new or used car. Likewise if you operate a mobile computer cleaning service then contact commercial office cleaners and strike a deal in that they market your computer cleaning services to their commercial office clients. There are many cooperative and joint venture opportunities available to the service provider, or at least ones that can be easily developed. Often all that is required is a little bit of creative thinking and clever planning to get the ball rolling and make these mutually beneficial joint ventures happen.

BENEFIT BY GIVING YOUR SERVICE AWAY FOR FREE
$$ ⚒

Try giving your service away for free to make more money. For instance a friend who operates a carpet cleaning service routinely gives away his carpet cleaning services for free. However, there is a catch. He carefully selects an apartment building, generally a large one and takes a name off of the front door registry. Using the white pages he tracks that person down and calls to offer the carpet cleaning services for free. Seldom does he get turned down, especially when he honestly tells them that he needs access to the building a few days prior to cleaning the carpets so that he can place a simple door hanger on each door in the building. The doorhanger states "We are going to be cleaning the carpets in apartment #_____ on _____. We can offer you a special discount of 20 percent to clean your carpets, too? However to take advantage of this special offer you must call within the next 24 hours and reserve your appointment." Without fail he always secures at least another six jobs to do at the same time and gets back the free and discounted work through volume and not having to lose time traveling between jobs. This system works well because you gain access to a market for peanuts and it works or acts like referrals.

BUILD A RECOGNIZABLE CORPORATE IMAGE
$$$ ✎ ☏

Every business must strive to build and maintain a strong corporate image and identity. But this is especially important for service providers as image, reputation, and reliability are the main selling tools that you have in your marketing toolbox. The following are ideas that you can employ that will go a long way to establishing and maintaining your corporate image.

- Select and consistently use the same color scheme and look in your corporate identity.
- Splurge on having a professional logo designed for your business and always make sure to include it beside your name in all business and marketing materials.
- Make it easy for customers to contact you by phone, fax, and e-mail. Additionally consider 24-hour-a-day calling options and toll-free calling options. If customers can't contact you they'll keep calling around until they find a business they can reach.
- Stick to a specific style and theme in all of your printed materials. This includes a central message, mission statement, tone, and font.
- Develop a mini sales pitch and use this pitch in all your marketing activities and printed promotional materials.

Additionally you should also strive to build a recognizable corporate image with a consistent look, tone, and message through the following:

- Company brochures and sales and promotional literature
- All company signage including vehicles, site signs, advertising, and displays signs
- Business identity package including business cards, letterhead, sales invoices, sales estimate sheets, and any and all materials that customers come in contact with
- All advertisements regardless of the advertising medium
- Employee and management uniforms, as well as advertising and promotional specialties such as imprinted T-shirts, caps, tote bags, pens, notepads, calendars, and jackets

- The company Web site, all pages, e-zine, e-newsletter, and response e-mails

SPECIALIZE FOR SUCCESS
$$ ✎

A general family doctor can earn a good living, but a doctor who specializes in neurology can earn substantially more. Likewise a mechanic can earn a good living, but a mechanic who specializes in repairing BMW cars can charge substantially more for her service. Specialization does not mean that you have to narrow the field of the services you provide down to one or two things. What it means is that you can still continue to provide a wide range of services and even expand the services you provide, but you become known in the industry and marketplace for providing one particular service, call it the backbone of your business, your anchor and main competitive advantage. For instance a roofing service may sell and install many various types of roofing products and services, but still specialize in installing copper roofing. Copper is a roofing product that has a narrow target market due to the high cost, but still appeals to that narrow target market that can afford it because of the durability and the beautiful aesthetic appearance of the roof. Of course the better known you become in terms of your specialty then the more likely you are to begin to drop other services to concentrate on your particular area of specialization. Many service providers find that they begin offering numerous services and over time and through trial and error they are able to identify those services that are the most profitable to provide, eventually those services or even one service will become their specialty.

INVEST IN YOUR MARKETING SKILLS
$$ ✎ ☏

The world's most successful businesspeople never stop investing in ways to improve their marketing skills. This is simply because they know and have learned firsthand that every dollar you invest into educational activities and tools aimed at increasing your marketing knowledge and skills will pay back many times the investment. Below is what top businesspeople invest in to improve their marketing skills, and so can you.

Invest in Tools

Top marketers invest in the tools they need to become a better and more efficient marketer. These tools include automated multifunction telephone systems, Web sites, portable computers, digital cameras, great marketing brochures and catalogs, employee uniforms, incredible signage, and just about anything else that will save time, be more efficient, and help reach their target audience.

Invest in Training

Top marketers invest in specialized training and educational pursuits because they know you can never have enough knowledge. They attend seminars, workshops, and invest in personal one-on-one coaching with professionals such as sales trainers, publicists, time management specialists, and public speaking coaches.

Invest in Publications

Top marketers invest in and read at least one new marketing book monthly and subscribe to numerous business and marketing publications, inside and outside of their own industry. They do this so they can learn from other businesspeople's great marketing success stories and crash-and-burn marketing failures.

Invest in Participation

Top marketers invest in getting out and involved with their communities. They are not wallflowers; instead they make a conscious effort to mingle with like-minded businesspeople and never stop promoting their businesses. They go to networking meetings, get involved in the local community, and join business and social clubs in their area.

WEB RESOURCE

🔨 www.trainingregistry.com: National online directory listing professional business, management

and employee training consultants, and training courses and products indexed geographically and by topic.

🔨 www.smallbizbooks.com: Online retailer of business and marketing specific books, guides, and software.

🔨 www.marketingsource.com/associations: Online directory listing more than 35,000 business associations.

CREATE AN ELECTRONIC RESUME
$$ 🔨

Benefit by creating an electronic resume that gives detailed information about the services you provide, and that can be quickly sent to prospects as a professional marketing tool. Electronic resumes are great for professionals, consultants, and service providers to use. You can include contact information, a detailed explanation of your services, price lists or fees, loads of client testimonials, your specialized training certificates, and other important documents such as insurance coverage, licenses, and permits. Create your e-resume in Microsoft Word, HTML, or as a portable document file (PDF), which enables recipients to open and read it providing they have Adobe Acrobat installed. Acrobat can be downloaded from Adobe's central Web site for free so it is a good idea to include the link in your e-mail if you use this format. The benefit of an e-resume is that it enables you to market your service very inexpensively; you can update the information regularly and without cost and you can send it to prospects within minutes and not have to rely on couriers or snail mail.

WEB RESOURCE

🔨 www.adobe.com: Adobe software.

MANAGING YOUR MARKETING CAPITAL
$$ 🔨

Marketing capital comes in three forms—time, money, and energy—and it is the smart service providers who must learn to manage, balance, and often juggle all three at once.

Manage Your Time

Implement systems so that you can manage your time efficiently and productively. Invest in software that will help to track and manage prospects, customers, and projects. Invest in books on subjects including time management, selling, marketing, and leadership. Organize your office, business, and work schedules to maximize the best use of your time and understand that time is just as valuable as money in terms of marketing capital.

Manage Your Money

Spend money on marketing activities that will have the greatest impact on your business. This may seem like obvious advice, but far too many small-business owners waste money on marketing activities rather than have a plan for how they can spend their precious marketing capital and maximize the value of it. This includes buying stuff that will transcend all your marketing activities, such as having one professional piece of artwork produced that can be used in brochures, advertisements, presentations, and packaging, rather than having artwork produced for each. Additionally, seek out and take advantage of low-cost and free marketing activities to stretch your marketing budget, such as cooperative advertising programs, low-cost and free classified advertisements, and cross-promotional activities with other businesses. And most of all try to stick to your marketing budget as closely as possible to avoid making impulse purchases that might seem like a good idea at the time, but rarely turn out to be.

Manage Your Energy

Marketing is time-consuming hard work and unfortunately because of this many small-business owners burn out, which sadly is one of the most common reasons businesses fail. It is hard to stay excited about marketing and keep your energy level high if you do not feel good physically or mentally. Prospects and clients will pick up on this instantly and think that you do not care about your business or helping them; ultimately lack of marketing energy will cause you to lose focus and customers. To keep your marketing energy level high, get in the habit of scheduling personal time for yourself, time away from your business and office. Make it a personal goal to stay fit and healthy, and never stop investing in your most powerful, effective, and best business and marketing tool—you!

SERVICE PROVIDERS WIN WHEN THEY ARE PREPARED TO OVERCOME OBSTACLES $ ✎

No longer view sales as how you can get people to buy your service. Instead identify what the most common obstacles are that stand in the way of people buying your service. Once you know what these obstacles are, then you can find ways to overcome them and sell more. Seems like obvious advice right? Wrong. Few business owners stop to think about why people do not buy. They instead focus their marketing efforts on trying to sell by way of broad but ineffective advertising, lackluster direct-mail campaigns, and lots of other well meaning but poorly planned marketing activities because they think that this is the way to sell their service. Anyone can try to sell, but few ever become truly great marketers, as the number of annual business failures in North America clearly illustrates. Marketers take the time to learn and understand why people buy or alternately do not buy and focus their time and efforts on creating sales strategies based on the information they discover through this process. Three common obstacles that stand between service providers and consumers are price, money, and need. Consumers will not buy if they feel your price is too expensive. So you must then be prepared to overcome that obstacle by clearly demonstrating the high value of your service. Consumers will not buy if they do not have the money to pay for your service. So you must then be prepared to overcome that obstacle by making it easier and more convenient for people to buy. Accept checks, credit cards, and offer consumer financing plans so that the availability of money is no longer an obstacle. And, consumers will not buy if they feel they do not need your service. So you must be able to overcome that obstacle by clearly demonstrating to prospects why they need your service and how it will benefit them, a point they did not consider, a safety issue, ways they will save money or alternately make money. There are many ways to create need, but first you must identify that lack of need might be an obstacle that stands between you and your prospect.

📖 SUGGESTED ADDITIONAL READING

Blanchard, Kenneth H., Sheldon Bowles, and Harvey Mackay. *Raving Fans: A Revolutionary Approach to Customer Service*. New York: William Morrow & Company, 1993.

Carter, David. *American Corporate Identity*. New York: Hearst Books International, 2003.

Collins, Jim. *Good to Great: Why Some Companies Make the Leap...And Others Don't*. New York: Harper Collins, 2001.

Dawson, Ross. *Developing Knowledge-Based Client Relationships: The Future of Professional Services*. Burlington, MA: Butterworth Heinmann, 2000.

Fox, Jeffrey J. *How to Become a Rainmaker: The Rules for Getting and Keeping Customers and Clients*. New York: Hyperion Books, 2000.

Gerber, Michael E. *The E-Myth Contractor: Why Most Contractors' Businesses Don't Work and What to Do About It*. New York: Harper Business, 2002.

Kotler, Philip, Thomas Hayez, and Paul N. Bloom. *Marketing Professional Services: Forward-Thinking Strategies for Boosting Your Business, Your Image and Your Profits*. Upper Saddle River, NJ: Prentice Hall Press, 2002.

Rackham, Neil. *The S.P.I.N. Selling Fieldguide: Practical Tools, Methods, Exercises and Resources*. New York: McGraw-Hill, 1996.

Salant, Priscilla. *How To Conduct Your Own Surveys*. New York: John Wiley & Sons, 1994.

Weiss, Alan. *Million Dollar Consulting: The Professional's Guide to Growing a Practice*. New York: McGraw-Hill, 2002

KEY

COST TO IMPLEMENT $

DO-IT-YOURSELF

CALL IN THE PROFESSIONALS

LEGAL ISSUES

BOOK RESOURCES

ONLINE

WEB SITE AND ONLINE
Marketing Tips for Your Business

*What's my return on investment on e-commerce?
Are you crazy? This is Columbus in the new
world. What was his return on investment?*

—Andrew Grove

WHY DO YOU NEED A WEB SITE?

 $+

The Internet gives small-business owners and marketers from all walks of life, geographic regions, and financial budgets the ability to level the playing field with larger and often much better-financed competitors. The reason for this is straightforward. You can reach a wider and broader audience, sell more to more people, share more information, keep your current customers better informed and serviced, and have the ability to test new products, services, and markets inexpensively, quickly and effectively, all with the click of a mouse. Not to mention the fact that the rent on the Internet is extremely cheap when compared to a bricks-and-mortar store or office lease. Though there have been recent glitches in online expansion and e-commerce sales, one thing is for sure—the Internet has forever changed the way the world does business and shares information. The

Internet will only continue to expand and prosper with each new online technology that is developed, introduced, and embraced by business and consumers alike.

The advantages of Internet marketing are many. Your store is open 24 hours a day, you can send information to customers and business alliances in moments, not hours, days, or weeks. And, you can update or alter your marketing message and strategy quickly, conveniently, and very inexpensively, just to mention a few of the benefits of online marketing. The question should not be why do you need a Web site? But rather why do you not already have one? However, with that said, to truly benefit from operating a Web site you have to first determine what you want your Web site to do for your business, what is the objective(s)? The following are only a few common objectives for starting and maintaining a Web site, as a stand-alone business venture or as a natural extension to complement your existing business venture.

- Sell products and services
- Advertise products and services
- Conduct customer and market research
- Conduct customer and market surveys
- Information sharing with business partners, employees, and customers
- Provide online customer service
- Provide online product support
- Train representatives, customers, and employees
- Find new representatives, customers, employees, and suppliers
- Test new products, services, and markets
- Expand into new geographic markets inexpensively
- Reinforce additional sales, advertising, and marketing activities
- Introduce new or updated products, services, and information
- Create or support corporate identity and brand image and awareness
- Share corporate and public relations information
- Support other marketing activities

BUILD YOUR SITE TO APPEAL TO YOUR TARGET AUDIENCE

$$+ ✎ 🐶

A common error in Web site design and development is not keeping the target audience in mind when constructing or updating a commercial Web site. Often, this is simply due to the fact that there are so many cool features and tools currently available that are quick and easy to incorporate into a Web site even for the novice webmaster or designer. This makes it easy to get carried away and lose sight of who the Web site is actually being designed for—your target audience—and what the objectives of your Web site are. For instance, cool graphics with sounds are likely lost on site visitors who are interested in financial investment information. But the same features would appeal to teens and young adults if they were your target audience. It's important to always keep your target market in mind when developing or expanding your Web site. Forget about Web tools and features that you might like and instead ask your customers what they like and want in terms of content, features, and useful tools that they would find beneficial. Additionally, keep in mind that human-compiled directories like Yahoo! will check out your site. And much having to do with the design and how you relay your central theme and information to your target audience will influence on their decision to accept your site and rank it for relevancy. Here are a few ideas that you can use to build a better Web site and stay focused on your customers and visitors.

- Spend your advertising money wisely. This means spend your money on ads and marketing activities that are aimed at your target audience. Likewise test online ads before committing to long-term contracts.
- Prospects will have objections to what you want them to do. Therefore you must anticipate objections and answer these within your site before prospects can turn them into reasons not to take the desired action you want.
- Always speak directly to your target audience. For instance if your target audience is campers, then use bold attention-grabbing headlines like Campers Wanted!
- Don't be afraid to "overbuild" your site, as triple-digit growth in terms of hits is not entirely uncommon, especially for new Web sites that are heavily promoted and linked.
- Always inspect your site, policies, and what you offer from your prospects' point of view. Keep an open mind and be honest and answer "what is really in it for them?"

CHOOSING THE BEST DOMAIN NAME

$+ ✎

Ideally you want your business name and domain name or URL (Uniform Resource Locator) address to be the same. For instance, if your business trading name was "Shoes For All" then you would aim to acquire the right to use the URL "shoesforall.com" or another designation such as .biz, .tv, .ca, .net, although the "dotcom" designation is still considered the best for online commercial enterprises. If you cannot match your online and offline trading names then try to make your online name as short as possible or use hyphens and numbers such as "shoe4all.com" or "shoes-for-all.com." Additionally, your domain name should be easy to remember and spell, and it should be something that best describes your business and what you do or sell in perfect clarity. Also make sure to take ownership of your domain name and not use one of the numerous extension services offered on the Web. They might go out of business and take your domain name with them after you spent years and thousands of dollars promoting it. And, if you are still having a difficult time picking a new and suitable domain name you might also want to search through recently dropped domain names. Dropped domains mean that the owners did not renew the registration contract or did not pay to re-register the domain name when it was time to do so. As a result these previously registered domain names become available into the public domain once more. You can check out new and unclaimed domain names at www.unclaimeddomains.com. This Web site boasts thousands of recently dropped domain name additions weekly. Here are a few more basic domain name tricks.

Easy to Spell

Try to avoid using words that are commonly misspelled as your domain name. If you have to use these types of words because of an existing business, product, or service name then also register the domain name with common misspellings and link that URL to your main Web site.

Rankings

When selecting a domain name or URL address keep in mind that some search engines such as Google and Inktomi have started to prioritize rankings based partly on selected keywords in a Web site's URL.

Register Early

Once you have decided to create a Web site as an extension of your existing business or as a stand-alone enterprise start the process of choosing a domain name right away and register a few variations as soon as you have a short list of names picked out. Good names are hard to come by and ones that do come available or that have not already been picked up go fast. Don't worry if your site is not ready as all domain registration services will allow you to park the domain and leave it there until your site is ready to go, of course providing that you have paid the registration fee.

WEB RESOURCES

⚲ www.register.com: Domain registration services.

⚲ www.unclaimeddomains.com: Directory listing once registered but dropped and now available domain names.

ANALYZE YOUR ONLINE COMPETITION
$ ⚒

One of the best ways to design and develop a Web site that will meet your customers' needs and wants is to use your competitors' Web sites as a yardstick when creating or revamping your own site. Chances are you already know who your competition is and who the competition is that leads the industry. If not try a few of the following tricks for finding out who your online competition is and what they are providing visitors.

- Conduct product and service searches related to own your business, industry, products, and services via search engines and directories such as Google and Yahoo! as well as online business directories.
- Visit your suppliers Web sites to find out who else they are selling to and visit those Web sites, your competition.
- Track down your competition by reading magazines, business telephone directories, and trade and industry publications to search for competitors' URLs featured or advertised in these publications.

Once you have identified your online competition, visit their Web sites and make extensive notes about what content they include, how it is designed, and what features and interactive tools they use to make their site a leader in the industry. Due to budget restrictions you may not be able to provide the same features as the competition, but you may be able to provide your visitors with a slightly watered-down version that can still come close. Additionally, if the competition has an e-zine, newsletter, or membership section be sure to join or subscribe. Doing so will enable you to track and monitor their marketing activities and judge the success of each. Online or off, you have to keep informed about what your competition is up to at all times. But don't stop there. Instead use the Internet to quietly stalk your competition by bookmarking their site so you can continually keep on top of new developments, and by visiting chat rooms and newsgroup discussion boards they post in so you can listen to what they are saying and what they might be planning.

KEEP YOUR WEB SITE CONSISTENT AND USER-FRIENDLY

$+ ✎ ☎

When designing or updating your Web site always aim to keep it simple and straightforward. Ensure your Web site is as user-friendly as possible and keep your target audience in mind when adding new features, content, and interactive or community building tools. Skip information that doesn't meet your marketing and Web site objectives and instead include tools that your visitors will use, find beneficial to their needs, and appreciate. The easier you make your site to navigate, and for visitors and customers to find exactly what they're looking for without having to search endlessly for it, the more likely you are to secure repeat traffic and sales. Also keep your online and offline image as consistent as possible including the way Web pages look and function, the tone and voice of your message, consistent navigation bars cloned from page to page, and corporate identity including logos and colors. Building an image or branding your business is a long process, therefore it makes sense to develop and stick with a consistent image so that people will begin to recognize it and remember it. Use white backgrounds with black lettering so that pages are easy to read, and add small features like "printer friendly" buttons. Basically, make your Web site as easy to use and navigate and your visitors will thank you by helping you to reach and exceed your online marketing objectives. Listed below are a few more ideas that you can use to make your site easy to navigate.

- Create a site map page and include the link in your navigation bar on each page.
- Create a frequently asked questions (FAQ) page so that your visitors can quickly find answers to the most commonly asked questions about your business products and services.
- Use standard icons and language terms that the majority of other mainstream Web sites use. People get used to them and if you buck the trend it can cause unnecessary confusion for some visitors.
- Consider using an internal search engine if your Web site is more than 250 pages or if you offer visitors a wide variety of products, information features, or archived news.
- Include a navigation bar on every page, ideally one that is consistent throughout your entire site. This is especially important due to the fact that visitors who found your site through keyword searches and links will not always land on the same page. And if you make it difficult for them to navigate your site, they will leave after the first page and not stick around to surf other pages.

SEARCH ENGINE BASICS

$+ ✎

The number-one way that people find the information, products, and services that they want on the Internet is by way of search engine and directory search submissions. In fact, some studies suggest as many as 90 percent of Internet users search for the information and products they want using search engine submissions. Consequently, you need to have your Web site and pages listed or registered with as many search engines and directories as possible simply because you never know which one people will use to find the information they are searching for on the Net.

But before you start registering with search engines and directories you should know the basics. First, the difference between search engines such as Google and directories such as Yahoo! is that search engines send out spiders that crawl through Web sites to index sites and pages on the Internet. In the case of directories, people called directory editors compile the information by hand generally indexed and grouped based on relevancy to the submitted search. However, with that said the line between search engine and search directory is becoming increasingly blurred as most major search engines and directories use mechanical and human power to build and index information or supplement each other's services. At the end of the day, search engine or search directory is irrelevant and you will want to submit your Web site and pages to be listed in both for search rankings purposes. Now this is where it begins to get a little frustrating for novice webmasters who want to get their sites registered so that people can start to find them. I say that because the rules and regulations of search engine submissions change regularly what is and more frustrating for the Web marketer is the fact that there is no one set of submission rules that covers every search engine or directory, most have their own individual search engine submission policies. You can opt not to register with the major search engines. And the ones that send out bots and spiders will eventually find you in time; sometimes a lot of time can pass before they do. But once again with an estimated 90 percent of Web surfers using search engines and directories to find the information, products, and services they want you would be well advised to take the time to learn how to submit to each engine and directory for registration purposes.

A Few Words about Search Engine Registration Budget

Another consideration prior to submitting your Web site to major search engines and directories will be your financial budget. While it is true that you can submit to many of the major and minor search engines and directories for free, this is not recom-mended for anyone who wants to operate a business Web site and wants to rely on search engines as a major marketing method of driving traffic to your site. Paying for search engine submissions will dramatically decrease the time it takes to get listed. In some cases this means you can pay extra to be listed overnight or wait a month or more if you plan to go the free submissions route. Likewise, paying for submission will almost always increase your chances of higher rankings in terms of search queries and results. Paid submission fees range from a low of $25 to more than $300 on Yahoo!, but in general you will want to budget at least $1,000 in total to get listed quickly and start driving traffic to your site. Listed below are the major search engines and directories. Log on to each to find out more about their specific requirements for submitting your site for registration and how to optimize your Web site, Web pages, and keywords for each.

MAJOR SEARCH ENGINES AND DIRECTORIES

- www.google.com: Google
- www.excite.com: Excite
- www.aol.com: AOL Netfind
- www.looksmart.com: LookSmart
- www.altavista.com: AltaVista
- www.dmoz.org: The Open Directory Project (dmoz)
- www.netscape.com: Netscape
- www.msn.com: Microsoft Network (MSN)
- www.yahoo.com: Yahoo!
- www.infoseek.go.com: InfoSeek/Go Network
- www.lycos.com: Lycos
- www.teoma.com: Ask Jeeves/Teoma

SEARCH ENGINE SUBMISSION SERVICES
$+ 🔧 🕷️

For anyone who does not want to take the time to individually submit a Web site and pages to each of the major search engines and directories manually there are a raft of search engine and directory submission services that will do it for you. These submission services automatically submit or register your Web site with all the major search engines and directories, often by only having to complete one relativity basic form. While some of these services are free to use, the majority charge a fee if you want quick listings, regular maintenance, and other premium listing services. For small-business owners with limited time to optimize their Web sites and keywords for the best search rank results, these online multiple search engine submission services offer great value for a relatively small fee. However, like any type of marketing activity, if you plan on using the Internet and your Web site to do business, make sales, and generate revenue then take the time required to select the right submission and maintenance service, regardless of the fee they charge for their services. Listed below are a few search engine submission services. To find more, simply visit any search engine and submit "search engine submission service" and you will have hundreds if not thousands of matches to select from.

WEB RESOURCES

⚲ www.addme.com: Add Me

⚲ www.submit-it.com: Submit It

⚲ www.ineedhits.com: I Need Hits

THE IMPORTANCE OF KEYWORDS
$ ⚒

How important are keywords in terms of search engine submissions and rankings? Well, let's just say that it is estimated that 90 percent of Internet users search for information, products, and services through search engines and directories using keywords and phrases that they think will help them find what they are looking for. So in other words if you plan on operating a Web site as a stand-alone business venture or as an extension of an existing business and want to generate revenues and profits from your site by selling products and services then keywords are of great importance. Below are a few great keyword tricks that you can use to select better keywords and secure higher search rankings.

Great Keyword Tricks

- The first rule is to make sure that you include keywords in your page titles, headers, keyword meta tags, and description meta tags, alt tags and hyperlinks. Below you will find a few online meta tag generation services that you can use to build your meta tags.

- The target keywords you use should be two or more words together. Selecting only one greatly increases competition for that keyword with other sites and reduces your chances of securing a top ten search ranking. Likewise, most sites are built from the top down and out from the entry or home page, so be sure to concentrate your keywords near the top of each page.

- Each page within your site is unique so be sure to select different keywords for each subsequent page in your site. Ones that are relevant to the information or content that is featured on that particular page. If you rely on just a few keywords and phrases to describe your entire site you will be greatly limiting your search results.

- Never try to fool search engines with keyword spamming; eventually they will catch on and you will run the risk of not being able to register—meaning if they catch you it's so long you're outta here. Common spamming tricks include repeating keywords numerous times throughout a page by making them undetectable to the eye by changing the font color to match the background color. Or, repeating keywords numerous times at the bottom of the document after the line break. And, excessive repetition of keywords on pages and in the title and meta tags.

- Use both plural and singular versions of your keywords and common variations of misspellings of your keywords. You may sell ink jet printers, but some people might search for inkjet printer. However, you do not have to repeat the singular and plural versions together on every page and make your copy read oddly, just remember to include what you believe to be the less popular misspelling keyword or phrase in your site.

- It is recommended that you aim for a keyword density of about 5 percent. What this means is that for every 100 words of content your keywords will comprise five of those words. Likewise, if you can keep your keyword frequency at least half of this rate you will increase your odds of higher search rankings.

- Always be very descriptive when selecting your keywords and phrases. Think about how people will search for information, products, and services that you sell. A good starting point is to list what you sell and begin to conduct your own search engine searches using variations you make up of the descriptive words you use to describe your goods or services. Narrow the field, until you have found suitable matches and repeat this exercise for each page in your site.

- Always include the maximum number or keywords that search engines will allow. If that is 50 then include 50 keywords, if it is 75, then include 75 keywords and so forth. However, keep in mind that directories base ranking much on the quality of the content and not keywords, so with directories concentrate on quality content.

- Try to link to as many relevant Web sites and with as many relevant keywords as possible. The majority of search engines base search ranking partially on links; but once again not on the number of links but rather the relevancy to your Web site and keywords. To do this conduct a simple search with your chosen keywords prior to submitting to see what Web sites are listed in the results and from these start to create your linking strategy.

- Take time and carefully determine what your keywords will be to ensure the highest search ranking possible. Once you push "submit" to register with search engines, it is very difficult to reverse the process, therefore keyword research and planning are critical.

WEB RESOURCES

🕹 www.wordtracker.com: Free and paid online services aimed at generating optimum keywords and phrases to describe your site, business, products, or services.

🕹 www.siteup.com/meta.html: Site Up Networks, free online meta tag generator.

🕹 www.addme.com/meta.htm: Add Me, free online meta tag generator.

🕹 www.vancouver-webpages.com/meta/mk-metas. html: Meta-Builder, free online meta tag generator.

PAY-PER-CLICK KEYWORDS
$+ 🔨

Another way to rank high on search engines is to purchase targeted keyword advertising. Most of the major search engines have various types of targeted keyword advertising programs in place. However, the two major players in this form of advertising are Google with their "AdWords" program and their affiliations with other search engines and directories such as America Online (AOL) and Earthlink. And, Overture with their "Pay-For-Performance" program and with their affiliations with Yahoo!, and AltaVista. Needless to say both have a broad range in terms of their reach to Internet search engine users. In a nutshell, pay-per-click programs are nothing more than bidding on choice keywords that you believe your target audience will use when they search for the products or services you sell or provide. For instance, if you sold basketballs then you would want to bid on keywords that are related to basketballs, such as "basketballs" or "buy basketballs." In the case of Google the results show up on the right-hand side of the screen separate from the regular search results and highlighted in a different color. In the case of Overture the results show up along with the regular search results on the page, and they will send the top three search results to their partner sites. Both programs have different requirements and rules for how you select your words and how they make sure your site is relevant to the keywords you select or bid on. However, both programs are similar in the way you bid for the keywords you want. For instance, you may bid $1 for a keyword; if that was the highest bid for that particular keyword then you win and would get top ranking. On the other hand if you bid $.20 and other Web marketers bid more for the same keywords then your ranking will be greatly diminished. But with both programs you only pay the amount you bid when someone actually clicks on your listing. This is referred to as a "click through." In summary targeted keyword advertising or pay-per-click keywords can greatly increase your search engine result rankings and dramatically increase your click-through rate. But with that said you will want to visit a few of these programs and carefully read through the information they provide to make sure that participating in any of these premium keyword advertising programs will help meet your online marketing objectives and your budget.

WEB RESOURCES

🖙 www.adwords.google.com/select/overview.html: Google AdWords programs.

🖙 www.overture.com: Overture Pay-For-Performance program.

MULTICULTURAL WEB SITE
$$+ 🔨

While your Web site may reach a global audience that certainly doesn't mean that a global audience will understand your Web site or what it says. Unless of course you take the steps necessary to give visitors from foreign lands language options for viewing your site so they will understand your message in their native tongue. Less than 25 percent of the world's population speaks fluent English, therefore expecting to appeal to foreign non-English speaking prospects in terms of marketing your Web site, products, or services will only work if you take steps to speak their languages so they will understand. Fortunately there is software available that can translate your English language Web site into as many as 30 different languages in mere seconds and in a relatively easy procedure. One of the more popular language translation software programs is called Systran. Systran has many language translation options available to meet a wide range of user needs and applications. The software can copy your existing Web site into various selected languages or you can display different languages right alongside of English on each Web page in your site. An added benefit is the fact that their software will also translate incoming and outgoing e-mail messages and personal documents into the language of choice and includes a spelling dictionary function to ensure minimal typos.

WEB RESOURCE

🖙 www.systransoft.com: Distributors of language translation software.

KEEP YOUR WEB SITE QUICK
$+ 🔨 📞

Skip large slow-loading graphics, scrolling messages, and other feature and functions that can slow down the speed of your Web site and delivery of your Web pages to visitors. Instead opt for thumbnail pictures and graphics and well-written, bold, attention-grabbing headlines to get noticed and to drive traffic to the desired areas within your Web site. Keep in mind that the vast majority of people are connected to the Internet with a 56K or slower modem—hence the importance of trying to keep every Web page in your site under 25KB so that most visitors will be able to download a complete page in less than ten seconds. In today's fast-paced world we have all come to expect, perhaps even demand what we want to be available to us quickly, right away, and without hesitation. You wouldn't wait a half-hour in a drive-through to get your lunch, so don't expect your visitors to wait through slow-loading pages or graphics to get to the information they came to your Web site to retrieve. Keep your Web site quick, provide useful tools, and give your target audience exactly what they want and you will secure lots of repeat traffic and meet your Web site objectives because of this focus. Additionally, make sure to test your Web site's compatibility with various browsers to ensure that visitors are seeing what you intended them to see and how you wanted them to see your site.

WEB RESOURCE

🖙 www.anybrowser.com: Check your Web site for compatibility by viewing it in various browsers via this online service.

WHICH SHOPPING CART?

$$+ ⚒

What is one of the greatest challenges facing online e-tailers today? Would you believe shopping cart abandonment? That's right a recent survey suggested that as many as 50 percent of online purchases are abandoned before the purchased has been completed. The number-one reason for this is simple frustration with the shopping cart—difficult to use, slow, and unreliable and because of this shoppers give up on the process and abandon their carts before checking out and paying up. So it stands to reason that which shopping cart program you purchase or rent is of great importance to your online business, perhaps one of the most important decisions you will have to make. Submit a shopping cart software search to any of the major search engines and you will likely be overwhelmed by the response. Thousands of choices and which shopping cart program is the best? The best shopping cart will largely be based on your needs and more so your budget. There are free shopping cart programs and services available, but most are highly unreliable and will ultimately cost you sales (remember cart abandonment because of poor reliability) and therefore not a very good value, even though they are free. Then there are shopping carts that you can rent and that operate from a remote server location. Some of these are of very good quality, reputation, and have a terrific performance track record and can be subscribed to for less than $100 a month. However, the downside is that many require your customers to link over to the shopping cart provider's Web site to complete the purchase and therefore you lose the opportunity to upsell and sell more because you lose control of your customers if they are not still within your site. Additionally, some of the remote server shopping cart programs are very limited in terms space for the amount of product description you can include for promotional purposes. Another option is to purchase your own shopping cart program and server, and operate the program yourself. Once again, this route can be very costly for quality software and hardware, thus eliminating e-tailers with restrictive financial budget. Ultimately the best way to find out which shopping cart program or service will be best suited for your particular needs and budget is to ask other online e-tailers. Also check with your Internet Service Provider as many have expanded operations and include reliable shopping cart programs and services or can refer you to a reliable source. Whichever route you choose make sure that your shopping cart is safe, secure, fast, easy-to-use, reliable, and cost effective for your needs. If it does not meet every one of these criteria then keep shopping for another, and keep asking other online marketers for advice and guidance until you find a cart that won't be abandoned before checkout.

GIVE INFORMATION THAT BUILDS CONFIDENCE

$ ⚒

Drop the shroud of mystery about who you are and where you are located and instead go the extra mile to instill a sense of confidence in your visitors by being an open online book. Include contact information within your Web site that enables visitors and customers alike to reach you offline. Let your visitors know who key employees and managers are within your organization, what they do, and how they can be contacted directly by e-mail and by conventional means including snail mail, fax, and telephone. Demonstrate to visitors that your Web site is secure for online financial transactions, and clearly state your company policies in terms of visitor security and privacy. If you are not confident enough to let people know who they are doing business with, how they can contact you, and what steps you take to ensure their security and privacy then you may as well pack up your cyberventure and hit the road. No one wants to do business with a computer, people do business with people. And, they want to know who is connected to the other end of the cord, especially small businesses that are not well known to a global audience of buying consumers.

FOCUS ON THE CUSTOMER

$ ⚒

Forget the boring facts and figures about how great your company is, and what a fantastic job you do of marketing simply because few people who visit your Web site will particularly care. Get rid of company puffery and keep your Web site and the content focused on and for the customer by making your customers the center of your online marketing strategy and not your company. Identify your primary and secondary target audiences and figure out exactly what their wants and needs are, and more importantly how you will meet and exceed these wants and needs. Steer visitors through your site and know what action you want them to take by anticipating obstacles and objections and overcoming these with answers and information in your site that will meet and exceed their expectations. The only time you should be tooting your company horn on your Web site is when customers do it for you with glowing testimonials or if you have received an online customer service or Web site design award. Back patting and ego stroking are best left where they belong, which is behind closed boardroom doors. Customers are people, and people want to hear about how great they are and what you will do to help them, not the other way around.

PROVIDE GREAT ONLINE CUSTOMER SERVICE, PART ONE
$$ ✎

Much like conducting business in the bricks-and-mortar world, customer service should also be priority number one in the cyberworld, because we all know that without paying customers you simply do not have a business. The following are a few fantastic customer service ideas that you can employ to ensure that your online customers remain loyal to your online business venture.

- Always strive to build long-term relationships with customers and visitors alike by staying in contact with them on a regular basis and in a consistent manner. Create and send out by e-mail a monthly e-zine or e-newsletter, send online greeting cards during holidays, and offline cards to your best customers also during holidays and special occasions.
- Respond to and resolve all customer complaints as quickly as possible, even if it means a refund, product replacement, or other forms of

discounts or incentives to cool irate customers. This is an extremely important online customer service tip as negative word-of-"mouse" marketing moves much more swiftly on the Internet than in the real bricks-and-mortar business world. An unhappy cybercustomer can tell thousands of other people about a negative experience with your business in a matter of moments.

- Make sure that you develop and implement a customer service plan with policies that have been created with your customer in mind and not just what is easy or convenient for you. Additionally make sure that all employees understand and treat customers in accordance with the plan and policies to promote a consistent message throughout the organization.
- Give customers and visitors options beyond e-mail to get in contact with you for whatever their reasons may be, including telephone, fax, a live online operator option, and standard ground mail. And add an online FAQ page to help them to get answers in a hurry without having to jump through hoops.
- Get in the habit of telling customers and visitors to your site how much you appreciate their business and their continued support. And show your appreciation by giving them gifts, great service, and above all access to a fantastic Web site that meets their needs and wants in terms or products, information, and great service.

PROVIDE GREAT ONLINE CUSTOMER SERVICE, PART TWO
$$ ✎

Remember that for every one customer who speaks up and complains that there are many more who simply stop doing business with you and start doing business with your competition. Given this harsh fact of business here are even more great ideas that can help you provide the best online customer service possible to ensure your customers don't take off and do business with the competition.

- E-mail customers a satisfaction questionnaire a few days after they have purchased, just make sure it is after the product has been delivered. Ask questions that are relevant to your business, Web site, industry, and products. Use the information they give you to identify weaknesses within your operation and ways to improve your business and boost sales. Ask customers what they would like and what they think should be improved, and implement the truly great ideas they give you. And always let customers know that you want them to be completely honest in their survey responses, good or bad.

- Interact with your customers and visitors through your online discussion boards and chat rooms on your Web site. This will show them that you take a real interest in what they think.

- Follow up after customer complaints have been resolved. Even if people say they are happy that is not always the case so follow up with them after the resolution just to be sure that they are truly satisfied with the outcome and your business. This should come from one of the highest if not the highest level in your organization.

- Give customers as many choices as they would like to have. This means payment options, product choices, service choices, and special user utilities and information on your Web site. Do this by constantly surveying customers to find out what they would like your site to offer them. Always strive to build lifetime relationships with customers by giving them exactly what they want; if you do then there will be no need for them to look and go elsewhere for it.

- Make all customers and visitors feel as though they are part of your online community and family. Freely hand out compliments and encourage them to share information about themselves and their families through chat rooms and discussion boards.

PRESENT A CRYSTAL CLEAR MESSAGE
$ ✎

Once you get visitors to your Web site you have but a mere moment to grab their attention and spark enough interest to keep them involved and in your

site. Given this fact be sure to present a crystal clear message of what you offer, what the benefit is, and what you want them to do right on your home page. Keep you main messages short, to the point, and linked to other pages that will provide more detail or direct the visitor to make a decision or to take action. Web sites have become the granddaddy of all advertising media and information-sharing forums and just like any advertisement in any medium your first goals are to get noticed and create interest. Therefore think of your home page as an advertisement and include information that will get noticed, grab attention, create interest, draw visitors in deeper, and persuade them to take the action that you desire them to take. All of this is best achieved by presenting a crystal clear message. But remember the opening, you only have a passing moment to draw visitors deeper into your site once they arrive, so put your best story right up front. Your best story is the one that makes people perk up and say "I want that" or, "I need that." It's what they get from buying into what you are selling, saying, or doing. Your best story is the answer to the question that every single person asks, which is "what's in it for me?" When visitors arrive, the purpose of your site and the message should be clear and at a glance people should be able to instantly tell what you do and why you do it. People want accurate online descriptions of your products and services without having to read between the lines or decipher what you might think are cute and clever messages.

TRICKS TO PUNCH UP YOUR CONTENT, PART ONE
$ ✎

Not all people doing business on the Internet need to continually update their Web site content as a strategy to keep people returning to learn and discover new and valuable information. For instance, if you sell furnace replacements chances are your content or online information will not need to be changed or updated as often as a business that sells financial services and investment advice. And for those businesses that must focus on information as a cornerstone of their online marketing strategy it is important to remember that content is king. Here are a few clever tricks that you can use to punch up the effectiveness of your Web site content and marketing message.

- Make a point of updating your content on a regular basis, always keep it fresh, new, and informative with your target market and customers in mind. Your visitors and customers will thank you for it and reward you by returning often to find out what's new and even stick around to buy.
- Let visitors know right up front what's in it for them, the big benefit, the reward for spending their precious time on your Web site. Place this information within the first line under your bold headline on your home page and make it exciting, something that will solve a problem or fill a need. Write to appeal to emotions or logic, meaning that you want to tug at the heartstrings. Give them a reason that makes sense or make them feel as though they are not alone and that you are talking directly to them as individuals.
- Always keep your content and writing focused on your customers and visitors and not yourself or your business. Likewise use bold headlines and subheadlines to catch the "skimmers'" attention so that they will stay interested and involved in your message and active in your site.
- Keep articles and explanations brief, powerful, and to the point by using bulleted lists and short paragraphs. And back up claims with facts, statistics, and photographs as proof. You can never have enough proof when it comes to backing up your marketing claims; it lends credibility to your message and helps to remove buyer doubt and fear.
- Avoid using all capital letters, elegant fonts, or too many words in boldface or accented with an exclamation point or in italics, all of which can make it *difficult to read* or seem like you are **SHOUTING AT YOUR VISITORS!**

TRICKS TO PUNCH UP YOUR CONTENT, PART TWO

$ ✎

Once again given that content is king, listed below you'll find a few more great ideas that you can use to punch up the effectiveness of your online content.

- Write to excite by using power words that are designed to grab attention and get readers hooked and motivated to take the desired action. In the advertising chapter of this book you will find the 200 most powerful words to use in sales, marketing, and advertising.
- Always ask your visitors to share your content information and articles with their friends, families, and co-workers by adding a "share me with a friend" tag at the end of your online articles, columns, tips, and product or service information and pictures.
- Let readers know right in your content that their safety and security is your number-one concern. Use a <u>linked word</u> in the body of your message that will take them directly to your security page or privacy protection Web page.
- Edit, edit, edit, and always make sure there are no grammar or spelling errors. Professionalism is number one. Also try to provide readers information that they cannot get anywhere else; this is very important if you can do it as it is a surefire way to keep visitors loyal to your site and content. If people can get the same information in 100 places that they can from your site, then it greatly reduces the chances of them returning.
- Remind readers what your product or service will do for them now and in the future, and even more important what will happen if they do not act and buy what you are selling. As effective as excitement building is as a motivator, fear is an equally powerful motivator. Use the fear of missing an opportunity to save money, make money, feel better, or win to motivate visitors to buy. Let them know that if they do not take advantage of your offer right away it will be over, gone, and too late if they wait until tomorrow. And finally use text links (<u>linked words</u>) to take readers to other pages or places in your Web site. Statistically it has been proven that text links are more credible than banners or icons while surfing within the same site.

PROVIDE A RETURN ON INVESTMENT
$+ ✎

If you expect people to spend their valuable time navigating your Web site and if you want them to return often then you have to be prepared to provide benefits that go well beyond trying to flog a product or service, especially if it is a product or service that they can get just about anywhere from anyone. What this means is that you have to anticipate what your customers' needs are going to be in advance and deliver benefits as a reward for time they invest navigating your Web site. The rewards or benefits will be consistent with what your target audience wants and needs, but should extend to include additional information, products, and services that will interest and benefit them, thus providing a return for time they have invested into your Web site. Providing this is accomplished, your visitors will continue to return so they can be further rewarded with benefits. The time you spend jogging is rewarded with an increased level of fitness; the time you spend working is rewarded financially, and so on. Time is precious and no one wants to squander it, so you must be able to provide your visitors with a solid and beneficial reward in exchange for the time they invest in navigating your Web site. For example, if you sell music CDs online then provide visitors with additional information such as nationwide concert listings, interviews with musical bands, music reviews, and discussion forums so that your visitors and customers can share information about music freely. Music CDs are available anywhere, but highly specific information that benefits your music loving visitors is a strong motivation to get them to return to your site and buy often.

PROMOTE THROUGH NEWSGROUPS
$ ✎

For those not familiar with Usenet newsgroups, they are simply discussion groups or forums on the Internet that focus on specific subjects or topics such as political issues, business, sports, or the arts. And each group is composed of members who interact with each other electronically through these discussion forums and who share a common interest in the subject or topic. At present it is estimated that there are more than 100,000 newsgroups on the Web and while some are extremely active and have many members posting daily, other newsgroups are not very active and rarely have new postings. So research is key to the success of using newsgroups as a promotional tool for your business. Likewise, some newsgroups are monitored or mediated while others are not. Monitored newsgroups generally mean that before your message will get posted it will be reviewed to make sure that it fits the theme of the group, and if not, it will be rejected. And unmonitored newsgroups generally mean that just about any message will be posted in the forum unchecked for content. Likewise there are also newsgroups that allow and encourage commercial or marketing postings while others do not. Much of this can only be learned by tracking groups that meet your target audience or that are relevant to your products and services.

Common Newsgroup Categories

alt	Any conceivable topic
humanities	Fine art, literature, and philosophy
biz	Business products, services, and opportunities
news	Information about Usenet newsgroups and administration
rec	Games, hobbies, and sports
talk	Current news issues, general conversation, and debates
comp	Computer hardware and software

Here are a few newsgroup marketing tricks to get you started; however be aware that all these tricks are not allowed in every forum. So once again you will have to spend time researching the specific rules of each of the newsgroups you want to use as a promotional vehicle for your business.

- Create various reports, brief articles, and messages ahead of time then choose relevant newsgroups and post your information. This will enable you to save time and cover more territory.
- Answer responses or questions to your post quickly and invite people to visit your Web site to learn more about the topic.
- When you sign off of each message you post, use your signature that includes a link to your site.

- Become known within the newsgroup for being a source of valuable information.
- Read other posts carefully so that you can better understand what kinds of information, products, and services people in the group are truly seeking.

WEB RESOURCES

⚓ www.groups.google.com: Directory listing more than 50,000 discussion forums and Usenet newsgroups indexed by subject.

⚓ www.messageboardblaster.com: Software that automatically submits your message to more than 1,300 online message boards and Usenet newsgroups.

GET BOOKMARKED
$ ⚒

Ask your site visitors to bookmark your Web site by incorporating a boldly displayed "Bookmark Us" icon on all of your Web pages. Adding a "bookmark us" button is one of the easiest ways to increase the number of repeat visits your Web site gets. Ask yourself how many times have you visited a Web site and a few days later wanted to return, but couldn't remember the URL or how you found it in the first place? This situation is played out thousands of times daily on the Web, and while having a bookmark icon included and prominently featured on all of your Web pages is no guarantee that visitors take the time to bookmark your site, it's no guarantee they won't either. The best aspect about bookmarks is that they're free and work as a gentle yet effective reminder, kind of like the yellow Post-It® note on the refrigerator door that reminds you to pick up milk on the way home after work.

GREAT TRICKS FOR BUILDING ONLINE CREDIBILITY, PART ONE
$$ ⚒

One of the greatest challenges faced by online businesspeople and marketers is credibility. How do you gain the trust of consumers in the faceless world of cyberspace? Fortunately, there are many ways to build credibility so that your visitors will know their security is protected when giving out personal information and releasing financial details. Here are a few great tricks that you can use to help build online credibility for your business and Web site.

Build Online Credibility by Providing a History Lesson

Create a page within your Web site that chronicles the history of your business and the key people who are involved with the business. Your online presence may be relatively new but your offline business activities may be well established and highly regarded. This information should be brought to a visitor's attention as it can go a long way in helping to build trust. Remember you're appealing to a global audience and while your business might be well known in Los Angeles, chances are someone from Toronto or Glasgow won't know it from Sam.

Build Online Credibility by Ensuring Privacy

Create a privacy policy that tells visitors in plain English about the steps your company takes to ensure privacy and protect security for all visitors and customers alike. Every page in your Web site should be linked to your privacy and security policy page.

Establish Key Alliances to Help Build Online Credibility

Establish alliances with larger more well-known companies and organizations by offering them free advertising, conducting research for them via your Web site, and by joining their affiliate vendor program. When your visitors see that your business is aligned with these well-known and trusted companies and organizations they will link your business with theirs, lending instant credibility and professionalism.

Join Associations to Help Build Online Credibility

Join professional business associations that are relevant to your business and industry as well as consumer protection organizations such as the Better Business Bureau. Not only will this assist in building trust with visitors but many of these organizations

WEB SITE AND ONLINE MARKETING TIPS

and associations have well-known logos and graphics that can be displayed on your site as a trust-builder once you're a member.

GREAT TRICKS FOR BUILDING ONLINE CREDIBILITY, PART TWO
$$ 🔨

Building and maintaining a credible online reputation is so important to the overall success of online marketing that it only seemed right to include some more great ways that you can build credibility and profit.

Overuse Testimonials to Help Build Online Credibility

Create a client testimonial Web page within your site that includes at least four testimonials from your happy customers. To get the maximum benefit from the testimonial make sure that the person who wrote the testimonial includes her full name, business, and title if applicable, contact information such as an e-mail address, and a photograph. Additionally, try to update the testimonial page twice a year with your newest and greatest customer testimonials. Client testimonials are without question one of the best ways that an online marketer can establish credibility for his business and products and services.

Become Known as an Expert to Help Build Online Credibility

Make your Web page a one-stop shop for expert information that is relevant to your business, products, services, and industry. Additionally, write articles and columns in your area(s) of expertise for other online news and general information Web sites, and link your articles that are featured on those other sites back to your Web site so that your visitors and customers become aware of your expertise.

Give Visitors the Good Stuff to Help Build Online Credibility

Include a page in your Web site that lists and describes in detail any and all the charities that your business supports. Also include fundraising activities you have participated in and any ongoing charity causes that your business is partnered with so that visitors can also become involved. And if possible show a dollar amount to add real impact. If your business has raised $100,000 through fundraising and donation activities for various causes then let your visitors know the amount.

Winning Awards Can Help to Build Online Credibility

Enter your business and Web site in competitions that focus on providing great online customer service, having a user-friendly Web site, or for being known as a leader in your industry. Proudly display your awards. This will go a long way to boost your credibility and help build visitor trust.

YOU WANT TO CREATE AN ONLINE COMMUNITY
$ 🔨

The most successful Web sites and most profitable e-commerce sites are the ones that have created a sense of community for customers and visitors alike. New and repeat customers and visitors feel as though they are part of the Web site through interaction with other visitors and by getting benefits be it information, products, or services that they really need or really want. Top online retailers and information portals have gone to great lengths in developing and testing various ways to create communities that people will want to participate in and return to often. Knowing this is beneficial to all small-business owners and online marketers operating Web sites because you do not have to spend thousands or in some cases millions of dollars to research and come to this same conclusion. The research has been done proving that Web sites that provide visitors with a sense of community fair far better at reaching their objectives than Web sites that lack a sense of community. Once again, top online marketers of products, services, or information like Amazon, eBay, and CNN have already done the bulk of the work for you. Imitation is often said to be the sincerest form of flattery. Therefore the only thing that you must research and decide upon is what type of features, content, services, and interactive tools will you incorporate into your Web site, ones that your specific target audience will find the most beneficial and want to become part of your online community?

GET THE BUGS OUT
$$ 🔨

Before taking your new or renovated Web site live on the net make sure that you have worked all the bugs out of the system so that your visitors and, worse, paying customers aren't the guinea pigs. Enlist the help of friends, workers, and family members to test every aspect of your Web site. Ask them to proofread content, order products, test links, submit keyword searches to search engines and directories to determine result rankings, and aggressively test all the other functions and features of your Web site prior to publishing it to the World Wide Web. Testing goes beyond just new Web sites and should also include sites that are undergoing minor or major renovations. Post the reworked or clone site with a variation to your URL and once again ask friends, workers, and family members to rigorously put it through the testing paces to get the bugs out before going live. Not only will this help to identify problems with your Web site, but it will also go a long way to ensure that when you do go live you have as close as possible to a Web site that is 100 percent perfect and efficient for visitors and customers alike. If you are going to ask people for money then you must make it easy for them to give it to you, and not make them work or test your site, it's that simple.

DON'T FORGET THE GRAND OPENING
$$+ 🔨

Just like a business launch in the bricks-and-mortar world, don't forget to hold a grand opening celebration for the launch of your new or substantially renovated Web site. Your grand opening marketing strategy should include both online and offline promotional techniques aimed at driving your target audience online and to your Web site. In addition to the promotional methods listed below that you can employ to market your online grand opening also make sure to use special offers and incentives to lure visitors to your Web site and include these special offers and incentives in your promotional mix.

E-mail

Rent opt-in electronic mailing lists and send out a grand opening message and special offer to promote the opening of your new or revamped Web site. To maximize the effectiveness of this grand opening promotional trick, repeat the e-mail blast two to three times prior to launching, one week prior, one day prior, and on the day of the launch.

Media

Send out electronic and print press releases, media advisories, and bulletins to announce the opening of your new or improved Web site. Keep in mind that you will want to follow standard press release format rules and guidelines and make your release read like news and not merely like a promotional message or advertisement.

Newsgroups

Post messages in Usenet newsgroups, discussion, and message boards related to your business, products, services, and industry to announce the launch of your new Web site.

Advertising

Purchase advertising space on Web sites that you believe are frequented by your target audience and in electronic publications that are read by your target audience. However, make sure that your ads are linked back to your Web site to ensure maximum impact. Also consider purchasing advertising space in print publications such as newspapers, magazines, and trade journals to promote your new or revamped Web site that are also read by your target audience.

Communications

If you are already in business and launching a new Web site to complement your existing marketing activities then take advantage of all business communications to promote your new Web site. These existing communications methods could include newsletters, voice-mail messages, outgoing invoices and mailings, and printed promotional materials such as brochures, catalogs, fliers, sales letters, and presentations.

Direct Mail

Launch a direct-mail campaign aimed at your target audience and send out information pertaining to your new Web site along with an exciting offer or incentive to drive traffic to your new site. Use your in-house mailing list or rent high-quality mailing lists comprising people who meet your target market and marketing objectives.

Cross-Promotion

Get suppliers, vendors, and business alliances on board to help promote your new or revamped Web site launch by having them include your URL on their Web sites.

HIGH-TECH WEB SITE POSITIONING TOOLS
$$ ⚒

When someone queries a search engine with keywords related to your business, Web site, products or services does one of your Web pages appear as a result of the search, or does a competitor's? Listing in the top 20 search engines is still one of the best ways to drive new visitors to your Web site. However, unless you are prepared to commit a lot of time to create a search engine submission plan, submit, resubmit frequently, and follow up with analyzing your rankings, then it just won't work. Fortunately for online marketers there are software programs available that will automatically submit your Web site to hundreds of search engines, online directories, and link exchange Web sites all with the simple click of a mouse. Additionally this same software will also analyze your keywords for optimum selection, and enable you to edit your Web site quickly and efficiently based on the analysts to ensure that you have selected the best keywords to get the best search engine rankings. In short for the do-it-yourself webmaster, Web positioning software might be one of the wisest investments you make for your Web site and business.

WEB RESOURCES

⚓ www.webposition.com: Distributors of Web Position Gold.

⚓ www.cyberspacehq.com: Distributors of Add Web Web site promoter.

CREATE AN E-MAIL COMMUNICATION MARKETING PLAN
$+ ⚒

With more than one billion e-mail messages being sent and received daily in the United States it's no wonder that top marketers understand the benefits of creating an e-mail communications marketing plan. Especially, if you ever hope to stand out in the increasingly jammed e-mail cybermessaging airways. Below is a basic outline for an e-mail communications marketing plan that you can customize to suit your needs.

Start by Defining the Objective of the Plan

What do you want to achieve? Drive traffic to your Web site; sell products or services; introduce new products or services; share specialized information; or train customers, vendors, or employees? You might even have more than one objective that will be reached in multiple contacts with prospects and customers via e-mail. Regardless, the first issue is to decide what you want to accomplish and how you will measure progress, success, or alternately failure of the program.

Identify the Target Audience

Who is your target audience for the information? Have you already identified them or is this an entirely new audience to your business? And if so what are their specific needs and wants? If you are trying to reach multiple audiences then you will have to take the time to carefully identify specific characteristics and how you will reach each target audience.

Pinpoint How Your Target Audience Will Benefit

How will your target audience benefit from contact with your business or the information you send?

This is an important step to identify simply due to the fact that you will have few takers even if your information is free if there is no benefit for the recipient. Ask yourself what is in it for the audience? If the answer is not "extremely valuable information that will be of great benefit to the audience" then you must create a new and more powerful benefit for the people you are trying to target. A reason they will want to participate and receive information from you is so that they can take action and benefit as a result of the information you send.

Decide on the Message You Want to Send to Your Target Audience

What type of information do you want to share with your target audience or audiences? In the highly competitive electronic information-sharing age content is king; your content must be fresh, original, and highly specialized to meet your target audience's needs and wants.

Choose How Your Message Will be Sent

In what form will your message and content be delivered? Will it be an e-zine, e-newsletter, e-tip of the day, short commercial advertisement or special offer, or e-catalog? And how often will this information be delivered to your audience?

Pick Who Will Be Creating and Managing the Program

Who will be responsible for creating the content, writing copy, managing your mailing list, and using the software and technology required for the entire program? Will you hire some or all of this out to a contractor and if so what segments of the program and to whom?

Forecast a Start-Up and Maintenance Budget

How much will it cost initially to create the program, to maintain the program, and to expand the program? Remember to include computer software and hardware technologies, as required, and training costs if needed. And where will the money come from to do so? What is the expected return on money invested in the short, mid, and longer term?

Decide How You Will Promote the Program

How will you promote your e-mail communications program, gain subscribers, and build your subscription list? Will it be through your own Web site or offline customer base or by renting opt-in mailing lists? Once again promotion is one of the most difficult aspects to get right as there are thousands of electronic publications being distributed each day, week, and month; in fact as many as 100,000 in any given month. Therefore you really must have a well-defined audience who needs and will benefit from your information; this may be the cornerstone to a successful promotional campaign.

Identify a Schedule and Implementation Timeframe

When will each phase of the program be implemented and how often will you send out new information? Will your e-publication be sent daily, weekly, monthly, or quarterly?

This is a basic outline of what is involved in setting up an e-mail communications marketing plan. Each step should be carefully researched and carried out to ensure the success of the program.

RESPOND AUTOMATICALLY
$+ ✎

Respond to hundreds even thousands of e-mail inquiries automatically and painlessly by installing or using a remote e-mail autorespond system that is integrated with your Web site communications system or with your electronic publication. The following represents a few of the timesaving and powerful marketing features available in today's automated e-mail response systems.

- The system can automatically detect what mail format the recipient can receive and send your message in HTML or plain text only.
- There are tools available so that you can integrate voice messages and digital video clips into your HTML e-mail responses.
- You can include an automatic "unsubscribe" link at the bottom of any message that you automatically send or use a response.

- Send follow-up e-mail offers to customers automatically after they have made purchases or product inquiries.
- Personalize your messages with mail-merge features so that you can single out and talk directly to individuals by using their first names in all electronic correspondence you send.
- Many autorespond systems have built-in tracking mechanisms so you will know who and how many recipients are opening your message and clicking on the links featured within.
- Change or update your autorespond marketing messages in minutes and as often as you wish.
- Choose to delete or save messages in the message library, or use opt-in features to help build a server or hard-drive based subscription list.
- Send order confirmations to customers automatically after they have purchased.

Autoresponders can help you stay in touch with thousands of customers, prospects, and visitors all in a matter of moments instead of the days that it would take to respond personally to each individual message. Autoresponders are a must for any entrepreneur who is serious about building a strong online presence. One word of caution, however—beware of some of the free autorespond systems as you will not have to pay for the service but other companies advertisements will appear on your responses to visitors and customers.

WEB RESOURCES

⌚ www.autoresponders.com: Online directory listing various autoresponder programs and services.

⌚ www.mailloop.com: E-mail and e-business automation software.

TELL A FRIEND
$ ✍

In the bricks-and-mortar world many business owners rely heavily on word-of-mouth advertising and customer referrals as one of their main sales and marketing tools and sources of new business. In the cyberworld this marketing technique is often referred to as "word-of-mouse" marketing. Make it as easy

as possible for your customers and visitors to spread the word about your Web site by tacking a "tell a friend" button to the end of feature articles and special interest content that appears on your Web site. When visitors find something that benefits them or fills a need regardless if it is a product, service, or just interesting information, they are likely to share that information with like-minded people they know. Don't be shy to freely use "tell a friend" tags—contests, columns, newsletters, games, special offers, coupons, workshops, and tips of the day are all valid reasons your visitors should be telling a friend about your Web site. And when they click on your "Tell A Friend" button they'll be prompted to fill in the e-mail address of the person they want to send it to and submit, just that easy. A second benefit is that there is software available that enables you to customize the e-mail that your visitor sends to his friend. In addition to the article or information that is sent you can also include a message in the e-mail body before the article. Use this feature to announce new products, special discounts, or to ask that they subscribe to your newsletter or e-zine. The options are endless, but one thing is for sure—top online marketers use this marketing technique with great success and so can you.

WEB RESOURCE

⌚ www.bravenet.com: A gigantic source for interactive Web site tools.

AIM TO GET THEIR PERMISSION
$ ✍

Permission-based marketing is the best way to build a solid and loyal online visitor and customer base for your Web site. What permission-based marketing means is that you ask customers and visitors for their permission to allow you to send them something via e-mail. The something you send can be a weekly or monthly newsletter, an e-zine that you publish, a special offer or discount that relates to your products or services, or just about any information that appeals to your target audience and that they would find beneficial. The benefit of securing a person's permission for this type of electronic marketing is twofold. First, if people ask for the information, then in all likelihood they have an interest in what you provide or sell, regardless if it is information, a service, or a tangible product; they fall into your primary or secondary target audience for your products and services. Second, by securing permission you won't be violating antispamming laws, which are laws against sending commercial e-mail messages to an individual without the recipient giving the sender permission to do so. The best way to get visitors' permission to send information or to subscribe to your electronic publication is to simply ask. Create an icon and include it on every Web page in your site. The icon could read "sign up for our free e-newsletter," or "enroll in our monthly e-recipe club." What you say will be directly related to your business and what you plan to use as the basis for extended marketing, be it a newsletter, discount offer, or what have you. One of your main online goals should always be to get as many visitors as possible to sign up to or agree to receive information via e-mail from your business. Of course once you have that information you have to manage the names and contact information. Fortunately there are numerous contact management software programs available that will enable you to build an opt-in list. Or, alternately you can have your contact list managed by an online contact list management service from a remote server location. The cost for this type of service generally starts at about $10 a month and increases based on usage. The benefits of a list management service is that they supply the subscription form link, automatically sign up visitors who want to join, and also remove people from your list (opt out) who no longer want to receive your messages.

WEB RESOURCE

✍ www.tridentlist.com: Online opt-in e-mail list maintenance company.

UNDERSTANDING COMMON BANNER ADVERTISING TERMS
$$ ✍

The following are a few key banner advertising terms, styles, and programs that you should take the time to familiarize yourself with prior to jumping into the banner advertising waters with an open checkbook.

CPM—Cost per Thousand Impressions

CPM is a standard term used to describe the fixed cost charged for a fixed number of banner advertising impressions, meaning the number of times the banner was displayed on a Web site or multiple Web sites. The 'M' in the acronym represents 1,000 impressions; therefore if the CPM of banner advertising on a particular Web site was $30 and the number of impressions the advertisement had was 5,000, then the cost to the advertiser would be $150 (5 x $30). Banner impression costs vary greatly from a few dollars per thousand to a few hundred dollars per thousand and is largely based on the audience that will be exposed to the message.

CT—Click Through

CT is an acronym used to describe the action of a visitor click on a banner advertisement or text advertisement link that takes visitors from the Web site they are in to another Web site, which is generally the advertiser's Web site.

CTR—Click-Through Rate

Click-through rates are typically shown as a percentage. For instance if 100 people click on a banner advertisement that has been displayed 10,000 times then the click-through rate of the banner would be 1 percent. Knowing the click-through rate is important so that you can judge the effectiveness of your ad during testing and after it has been implemented. Clicks-through rates greatly vary, from almost nil on untargeted or mistargeted sites to as much as 10 percent when displayed on highly targeted sites. Additionally, the cost per lead can be determined by your click-through rate by dividing the number of clicks the ad received by the number of impressions that were purchased multiplied times the CPM rate. For instance, if the CPM rate was $25 and you purchased 10,000 impressions then your total cost would be $250 ($25 per 1,000 x 10,000 impressions = $250). And, if you received 100 click throughs in total then the cost of each lead (click through) would be $2.50 (100 click throughs divided by the total cost of the impressions, $250 = $2.50 per lead).

CPC—Cost Per Click

Another term used to describe advertising rates is "cost per click." As an alternative to CPM you might agree upon a click-through rate prior to advertising and pay each time someone clicks through to your site via your banner advertisement or text link advertisement that is displayed on another Web site or search engine.

ROS/RON—Run of Site/Run of Network

Run of site/network means that your banner advertisement will be displayed on some or all of the pages within a particular Web site or network of Web sites with no guaranteed placement on any one certain page. The only way around this is to specifically negotiate for guaranteed placement on a particular Web page or section within a Web site. If not, expect that your banner ads will be ROS/RON. Guaranteed banner placements (targeted) are generally much more costly, in fact as much as ten time the average CPM rate, but highly effective in terms of reaching a very specific and narrow target audience.

Static Advertising Banners

Static banners remain on one particular Web page within a site without moving to another page within the same site until the advertising contract is over or the agreed advertising period or number of impressions has been reached. Therefore, unless you have more than one static banner within a Web site then visitors will only be exposed to your ad while they are on the page where your banner advertisement is displayed. As soon as they move to a different page within the site or exit the site, your banner is no longer visible. Keep in mind that every time your banner is exposed to a visitor through a page view it counts as a new impression. The term "static" also refers to the banner design and type, meaning that there is no movement in the banner and the message and graphics remain static in one place.

Animated Advertising Banners

Animated banners have movement, a changing message, graphic, or picture and have become extremely popular as a way to grab the attention of visitors. Animated banners generally run on a timed continuous loop and display your entire message and then start the process over. Animated banners can also be static and while your message on the banner changes, the position on the Web page or within the site does not.

Rotating Advertising Banners

Rotating banners means that the banner moves throughout the Web site or network of Web sites that you are advertising within. The rotation of the banner can operate on a time loop anywhere from a few seconds to a minute or more. Or, alternately the banner can rotate each time there is a new visitor to the page.

Advertising Banner Exchange Programs

Banner exchange programs have become extremely popular in the past few years, as they can be a very cost efficient and effective advertising method especially for small-business owners with a limited advertising budget. Most banner exchange programs work on a simple premise: in exchange for providing banner advertising space within your site you receive banner advertising space in other Web sites to promote your business, products, and services. Some exchange programs work on points, meaning that you get credits or points every time the banners within your site get clicked. You can use the points or credits to place your advertising banners on other Web sites free of charge by using your points as payment. Other banner exchange programs use a ratio system ranging from 2:1 to 4:1. For instance, if you belonged to a two-for-one program you would receive one banner impression for every two banner impressions that were displayed on your Web site. There are other systems in place in terms of how the banner program works. But at the end of the day you will find few programs that swap one for one as the service has to earn revenues and they do this by selling the excess advertising space to advertising marketers, brokers, corporations and small-business owners. However, before you sign up or commit to a banner exchange program check with the operator to make sure that there are restrictions in place that limit the banners that will be displayed in your site to reputable advertisers. You don't want adult theme banner advertisements displayed on your Web site if your target audience is children and families. Likewise, make sure that there are also size restrictions in place so that you do not end up with gigantic banners being placed on your site that take forever to download.

WEB RESOURCES

✆ www.e-bannerx.com: Banner exchange program.

✆ www.bannerswap.com: Banner exchange program.

GREAT BANNER ADVERTISING TRICKS, PART ONE
$$ ⚒

Banner advertising is the most common form of online advertising. In fact, one that is embraced by just about every online marketer, big and small. The purpose of the banner ad is very straightforward; use tempting copy, gimmicks, and just about anything else you can think of on the banner as a way to motivate people to click through to your Web site. The true power of the banner advertisement is its ability to create mystery, kind of like the old *Let's Make a Deal* game show; most people have a real curiosity about what they will find on the other side of the door, or in this case the banner. The following are some great banner advertising tricks you can use to create mystery, excitement, and motivate people to click through to your Web site.

- Keep your target audience in mind when purchasing banner advertising space. While the lure of cheap run of site or run of network deals might be alluring from a financial budget perspective, your results can suffer dramatically by not exposing your advertising message to your target audience. Taking the time to find suitable sites and networks to advertise on can greatly increase your click through rate, ultimately leading to a higher return on investment by way of direct sales and lead collection for follow-up marketing and opt-in list building.

- Keep the size of your banner small, ideally under 12KB for a 468-by-60 banner to ensure that it loads fast regardless of the speed of the site that it is featured on. You want your banner to be completely visible before the entire page loads, that way visitors will have something to read and look at while they wait for the rest of the page to load. Likewise test your banners in a few different browsers to make sure they look the way you want them to, regardless of the browser.

- Test every banner ad and the placement of the banner before committing to a large number of impressions. Try a four-week test campaign with 5,000 impressions a week in the same location. Track your results weekly and if after the fourth week the banner is not receiving the desired response then alter the message and try a new advertising venue. If the banner is working then commit to a longer run with a higher amount of impressions in the same forum, and similar forums aimed at your target audience. Additionally, negotiate for the test impressions by offering a longer commitment to a substantially higher number of impressions should the test generate the desired results.

- Studies have shown that banners that resemble Web forms and surveys pull a higher click though rate than banners that do not. However, keep your main marketing objective in mind and remember that if you only want to drive traffic to your site then this trick will work, but if you want to drive qualified traffic to your site then there are better ways to accomplish it.

- Studies have also shown that you can dramatically increase your click-through rate by telling people what to do next in your banner message by using words and phrases such as, Click Here, Start Here, Enter Here, and Win Here in your ad.

- When designing your banners use bright colors that are in stark contrast to the background colors of most Web pages (while) and the text color (black). Best colors are bright blues, yellow, greens, and orange. Bright colors grab attention and draw the eye to the ad; hence they can dramatically increase the response to your ad.

- Including a good incentive offer in your banner message can go a long way to increasing the click through rate and subsequently increasing sales. The stronger and bolder you can make your incentive the more pull power it will have, especially if the incentive is based on a well-known product or service. For example, a music retailer might use an incentive in a banner that states "Purchase one CD, get one free!" Or, an online retailer of books might use an incentive such as "Free shipping this month!" There is no question that incentives in advertising work; the key is to create one that works for your particular offer.

- A ton of click throughs are great if your goal is to drive traffic to your site, but what if you want the people visiting to buy? If you do, then carefully consider the message that your banner advertisement is sending out. Ten qualified click throughs that result in ten sales is much more valuable then 1,000 click throughs that result in no sales if your objective is to sell. Therefore, staying clear of clever wording or gimmicks in your banner message is well advised; instead use the space in your banner to prequalify prospects who are exposed to it. Do this by making statements or asking questions that would interest your target audience and not merely the online masses.

WEB RESOURCE

⌀ www.animationonline.com: Online banner generation service with free and paid service options for creating advertising banners.

GREAT BANNER ADVERTISING TRICKS, PART TWO
$$ ⚒

Given the importance of banner advertisement to the average small online marketer; one can never have enough tricks up their sleeves for creating great banner advertising strategies. With that said the following are more great banner advertising tricks that use can use to drive traffic to your Web site.

- Like any other form of effective advertising often the best way to design a banner ad is around a powerful headline that asks a questions, reveals the big benefits, solves a problem, or that appeals to a basic human need such as security. Powerful headlines in banners will motivate your target audience to click through to your site mainly because they feel the message in the headline directly speaks to them as an individual. Often you do not even have to create a headline for your banner you can just use a headline from your print ads, sales letters, or presentations that work and secure the desired results. If none of these are at your disposal then make a list of the main ways that people benefit by taking ownership of your product or service. Once you have the big benefit then start to design bold headlines that incorporate this message until you have the perfect headline for what you are selling.

- Depending on your marketing objectives, most advertising experts agree that your banner advertising campaign should be composed of two elements: banner ads optimized for direct response and click through and banner ads optimized for building brand awareness.

- To measure the effectiveness of your banners make sure that you put some system in place that can track the banner's performance and record the key data. There are software and shareware programs that will do this, as well as online advertising tracking and analysis firms that provide these services. To find one that is right for you submit "Advertising Tracking and Monitoring" to any major search engine.

- Beware of banner burnout, as it will dramatically reduce the effectiveness of your online marketing campaign. Most advertising experts agree that your banner ad begins to lose its effectiveness after your target audience has been exposed to the same banner and message more than six times; they become numb to the banner and message. Therefore, plan on making changes to your banners that you continually run on the same Web site or network. Keep them fresh so that your target audience will continue to click through to your site.

- Test your link to make sure that once your banner advertisement is clicked the visitor is taken to your Web site. Likewise give some careful consideration to the page that you want them to land on within your site. Ideally the landing page will be relevant to the message in your banner. Meaning that you do not want to make a promise in your banner and then force people to click through your entire site looking for it, because they won't but will simply exit your site. Also make sure that your landing page includes options for visitors to subscribe to your opt-in list to receive daily, weekly, or monthly electronic information and special offers that you send out.

- Bigger is not always better. While brand name Web sites and search engine sites attract untold numbers of visitors, that does not necessarily make them fantastic places to run your banner ads. Once again, it's all about reaching your target audience and meeting your marketing objectives.

- Your banner advertisements should be a natural extension of your marketing objectives and goals and consistent with your other marketing activities. Use your corporate identity logo in your banner and a consistent tone in the way the message is delivered. Think of your banner as an extension of your main sales and marketing message. Consistency is always the best policy when trying to build brand awareness and corporate image.

Web Resources

⚓ www.bannerdudes.com: Online banner generation service with free and paid service options for creating advertising banners.

⚓ www.webmasterbids.com: Online auction service where webmasters and small-business owners can bid on banner impressions and newsletter advertising.

CREATE YOUR OWN E-ZINE
$$ ⚒

It is a great idea to publish your own electronic magazine or newsletter, as not only can your e-zine be a useful tool to market yourself and what you do or sell, but it can also be a highly effective way to build an opt-in mailing list database and even

earn extra income by selling advertising space in your e-zine to other small-business owners and marketers who want access to market their goods and services to your e-zine subscribers. Or, alternately advertising space in your e-zine with other e-zine publishers for cross-promotional purposes. However, like any business or marketing activity that you undertake there are pros and cons to publishing and maintaining your own e-zine that have to be carefully considered.

Pros for Creating an E-Zine

- Automatically stay in touch with prospects and customers on a regular basis.
- Build trust and credibility, which can be turned into selling opportunities.
- Become known as an expert source of valuable and useful information.
- Build an incredibly valuable opt-in mailing list database.
- Inexpensive to publish and maintain, excluding time.
- Increase traffic to your Web site.
- Opportunity to sell, trade, or barter the advertising space within your e-publication once it has been established and proven successful.
- Opportunity to build lifetime customer relationships creating ample selling opportunities that can span years or even decades.

Cons Against Creating an E-Zine

- Continually finding fresh and original content to publish or having to maintain a writing schedule if you intend on writing your own content.
- Time consuming to put together and maintain a regular and strict publishing schedule.
- Managing your e-mail opt-in list to ensure 100 percent efficiency.
- Continually trying to increase your subscriber base.
- Selling advertising space if the e-zine will be used to generate income. (There are more than 100,000 e-zines published monthly and this creates a very competitive marketplace in terms of securing paying advertisers.)

WHERE YOU CAN GET CONTENT FOR YOUR E-ZINE

$$ ⬉ 🌐

Still one of the best ways to find content for your e-zine or other electronic publications is to write the material yourself, mainly because you will be assured that what you are publishing is fresh and original and not featured in 50 other e-publications. The downside is finding the time and making sure that you stay focused on your target audience with information that they will find beneficial.

Direct from the Source

Direct from the source means right from the author's computer to your e-zine. There are a few ways to find a direct source of content. The first is to surf the Web in search of good content by visiting numerous relevant Web sites. And when you come across information or an article that is suitable for your needs you simply contact the author or operator of the site and ask if you can borrow the information to feature it in your e-publication. Few authors will say no simply because they will receive lots of exposure and the potential to further their own cause via links back to their Web sites or e-mail. Additionally you can also post messages in writers' discussion broads asking for articles or submissions; believe me if you go this route you can get as many as 100 submissions in one day. The Internet is responsible for launching more writing careers (paid and unpaid) than all educational facilities combined.

Buy Content

Another way to secure content is to buy it by joining a content supply service. There are numerous content suppliers on the Internet and a simple "content supply" search on Yahoo! or Google will confirm that. The downside to buying content is that it can be expensive, as much as $1,000 for a feature article. But of course like the old saying goes "you get what you pay for." I would only suggest paying for content if your e-zine is generating enough revenue to cover the cost; if not, spend the extra time required to find good free content.

Free Content

And finally, the most common way that publishers get content for their electronic publications is for free. This could be by way of a free content supply service such as www.ezinearticles.com, or by visitor submissions and from hungry writers looking to build an audience and a name for themselves by getting exposure for their work.

In the end, regardless of how you secure content for your electronic publication a few things will always remain the same. The information must be relevant to your target audience, it must be fresh and original to hold your reader's attention, and it must be delivered on time and on a regular basis in order to build credibility.

WEB RESOURCE

⬆ www.freesticky.com: Providers of content and other useful online tools.

GREAT E-ZINE ADVERTISING TRICKS

$$ ⬉

The popularity of e-zines has exploded in the past few years with some 100,000 being published and electronically distributed every month reaching millions of people around the globe. Many small-business owners and professional marketers have found e-zine advertising to be an extremely inexpensive and effective way to reach their target audience. But before you create an advertisement and test the e-zine advertising waters, consider the following five essential tricks that are sure to help you get the most bang for your e-zine advertising buck.

1. Target Your E-Zine Advertisements

Though e-zines are broken into specific publishing categories like business, travel, profession, hobbies, or sports, before committing to advertising you still want to be sure that your ads will be reaching your target market. Get e-zine publishers to send you all the relevant statistics in terms of audience size, demographics, and geographical location if relevant. Also subscribe to e-zines that you feel meet your target audience and track the advertisements featured in each. If you notice advertisements that run continually, this generally means they are getting the desired response for the advertisers making the cost to advertise worthwhile. Also don't be afraid to contact a few of the advertisers via their Web site or published e-mail address in their ads, and ask them questions about the audience, success of their ads and for other information that will help you decide if the e-zine's audience is your target audience.

2. Track Your E-Zine Advertisements

Get in the habit of tracking the e-zine ads you place so you can analyze the response and performance. If you're advertising in more than one e-zine at one time there are a couple of ways you can track the effectiveness of each ad. Instead of a URL link, you can use an e-mail link with a different address for each advertisement, an easy way to track. Or you can duplicate your home page and use different URL extensions for each advertisement you run. Regardless of the tracking method you use just make sure to track your ads so you'll know where the greatest response is coming from so you can continue to advertise in e-zines that are generating the desired response and drop the ones that are not contributing.

3. Check Out the Competition

Before committing to a single ad or bulk ad purchase in any e-zine first check with the publisher regarding their competing ads guidelines. You want to be the only person advertising shoes for sale or selling consulting services. Also bigger is not always better, as e-zines with large subscriber bases often contain large numbers of advertisements, which sometimes can cause readers to grow "ad numb" and jump past ads and read only content that interests them. Be sure to careful select the e-zines you advertise in based on ability to reach your target market and not just on the number of subscribers.

4. Repetition Is the Key to Success

Like any successful advertising campaign, once you've discovered an advertisement that works and that's getting the desired response and action, then make sure to repeat it on an ongoing and regular basis. Most e-zine publishers have a discount insertion rate and sometimes you can even negotiate a free trial ad

or two if you are prepared to purchase bulk insertions based on favorable performance from the trial advertisements. As a rule of thumb always negotiate single and bulk insertion rates, because like you, e-zine publishers want to build long-term repeat customers and are prepared to offer incentives to secure them.

5. Your E-Zine Advertisements Must Have Impact

Create e-zine ads that are short and to the point. Instead of describing all the features your product has, tell readers what it will do for them in bold headlines and well-crafted phrases, and why they should contact you right away. "Do YOU want to be a millionaire? The next 10 people to contact me will receive FREE valuable information about how to make millions with our powerful real estate investing program!" The two most important objectives are to get the readers' attention and get them to take the desired action.

WEB RESOURCES

↗ www.ezine-universe.com: Online e-zine directory.

↗ www.ezine-dir.com: Online e-zine directory.

GREAT TRICKS TO TURN THEM ALL INTO SUBSCRIBERS, PART ONE
$$ ✎

Electronic newsletters, tips, and magazines are all very powerful marketing tools but without people to send them to they are of absolutely no value. For that reason here are a few ideas that you can employ to motivate your Web site visitors to join up and become subscribers to your electronic publication and in doing so, build your opt-in subscribers mailing list.

- Offer visitors free and valuable information if they subscribe. The information could be in the form of an e-book or e-report but should be relative to your business, what you sell, and your target market. For instance if you operate an online antiques auction then create a valuable antiques pricing guide and give it away as a free gift to everyone who subscribes to your weekly or monthly antiques auction newsletter, e-zine, or electronic forthcoming calendar of antiques auction events.

- Provide a free sample of your e-publication on your Web site. You will generally find by doing so visitors will read it and benefit from the information that is included within and therefore motivate them to subscribe so that they will be able to further benefit from the information you provide via your e-publication.

- Offer visitors two choices—an e-zine with advertisements and an e-zine without any product or service advertisements. Some people simply won't subscribe because they fear receiving an e-publication that is loaded with advertisements. So by offering them a choice you cover all the bases and potential objections up front. Of course you will still want to include advertisements for your own products and services, but just make them look and read like news rather than a traditional ad.

- Offer a discount on all the products and services you sell to people who subscribe to your e-zine. Be bold and tell your visitors that if they subscribe to your e-publication they will receive 5, 10, or 15 percent off all the products and services you sell. You can make up the lost revenues and profits as a result of the discount by increasing your overall sales volumes. Remember that 9 times out of 10 your fixed operating overheads will remain the same if you are doing $1,000 a week in sales or $2,000 a week in sales. Increased sales and cash flow equal increased profits, even if your per unit profit drops because of a discount.

- Create a members only section in your Web site and offer free and exclusive access to this members only section to people who subscribe to your e-zine. Increase the perceived value of your members only sections by including information, discounts, and other special offers that only members can gain access to via the members only section.

GREAT TRICKS TO TURN THEM ALL INTO SUBSCRIBERS, PART TWO
$$ ✎

Here are even more great ideas that you can employ to motivate your visitors to subscribe to your electronic publication.

- Host a subscription contest wherein everyone who subscribes to your e-publication is automatically entered in a drawing or contest to win fabulous prizes. Use deadlines to motivate people to subscribe or hold a new drawing every month so that you can continually add new names to your subscription list.

- Give away something for free that you would normally charge for. This is a great way to motivate people to subscribe. Your freebie could be free delivery, more products for the same price, or an extended warranty free of charge providing they sign up to receive your e-publication.

- Motivate people to join by telling them how many other people receive your e-zine now and how and why they benefit because of it. No one wants to sail into uncharted waters alone. If you let them know that hundreds or thousands of other people just like them are receiving and benefiting from your e-publication this will motivate a lot of people to subscribe.

- Place a dollar figure on the value of your e-zine or e-publication and then motivate people to join by offering it for free for a limited time, or to a limited number of people. "The next ten people to sign up will receive our monthly e-incredible tip sheet, a $200 value, absolutely free!"

- Ask current subscribers to enlist their friends and families to join and offer them an incentive for doing so. And finally, publish positive reviews and testimonials about your e-zine or other electronic publications on your Web site to motivate visitors to subscribe.

MAKE IT DIFFICULT TO OPT OUT
$ ✎

Make it very easy and accessible for your Web site visitors to opt in to your permission based e-mail marketing program, but make it difficult for them to opt out of the same program. This may seem like obvious advice, but there is a very sound marketing principle at work here. By making it difficult for people to opt out of your e-mail marketing program, be it an e-newsletter, e-zine, or e-alerts, you're in effect creating work for them. Most people will choose the path of least resistance and in this case that means simply not bothering to opt out. Thus increasing or at least sustaining the number of people on your opt-in list. Mail order record and book clubs have successfully used this marketing strategy for years. Lure people into the club with gifts and great deals, then send a monthly selection and give members the option to keep the selection and pay later or send it back and pay nothing. You got it, the majority of people will keep the selection even if it's something they do not particularly like simply because sending it back involves work. Remember the path of least resistance? Make it hard for them to opt out by redirecting them to a separate page on your Web site that requires a long code to be typed in, or a cut-and-paste code out of your last e-mailing. The more steps you put in place for people who want to opt out, the fewer people who will opt out. The benefit of doing so is that if you sell advertising space in your e-mailing you'll keep up the circulation, and if you sell products eventually the person who wanted to opt out just might step up to the plate and purchase the right offer.

MARKET BY WRITING E-ZINE AND ONLINE ARTICLES
$ ⚒

If you do not want to invest the time or money that is required to operate your own electronic publication or pay to advertise your business in electronic publications, you can still get involved in the electronic publication craze and benefit by reaching the estimate 50,000,000 people who read monthly e-publications. You can do this by sharing your expertise and writing articles and columns for any number of these electronic publications. There are a host of benefits to writing articles and submitting them for publication in e-zines and online news providers.

- You can position yourself and your business as an expert in the industry or field that you write about.
- You can brand your name and your business name through increased and continual publishing exposure to a broad online audience.

- You can gain access to hundreds if not thousands of new and well-qualified prospects by including your URL or e-mail link at the end of your articles or in the body of your articles using <u>text links</u>.
- You can secure free advertising for your products and services under the guise of "news" in the articles you write.
- You can build credibility and a reputation that would cost thousands to reproduce using traditional advertising and marketing methods.
- You can expand your market size, reach, and depth geographically without even leaving your keyboard to do so and continue to do so with each new article that you write that gets published.
- You can form new business alliances and partnerships focused on seizing or creating new business and selling opportunities as a result of the contacts you make through writing online articles.

MARKETING WITH PUBLICLY ACCESSIBLE LISTS
$ ⚒

Much like Usenet newsgroups, discussion mailing lists are publicly accessible and electronically sent to people who have subscribed to the discussion group to be kept informed and included in specific discussion topics that are of interest to them. There are primarily two types of publicly accessible electronic mailing lists: moderated and unmoderated.

Publicly Accessible Moderated Mailing Lists
Messages sent to subscribers in moderated publicly accessible mailing lists will be checked for suitable content by an editor or moderator to ensure the theme of the message is in keeping with the general theme of the discussion group. For the most part getting a commercial message or advertisement past the editor of moderated lists is tough; in fact, it's not worth your time or effort to try to create such a message. However, if your message is based more on news or in-depth knowledge and in keeping with the theme of the discussion group then moderated lists can be a good way to distribute your message.

Publicly Accessible Unmoderated Mailing Lists

Messages sent to subscribers in unmoderated publicly accessible mailing lists are automatically sent to all subscribers to the list without being checked first in terms of the content or theme of the message. The downside to unmoderated public lists is the fact that many subscribers soon leave the group or unsubscribe as a result of receiving too many commercial messages that are too far removed from the theme of the discussion group that they initially signed up to receive information about.

A Few Tips

Here are a few tips in terms of using publicly assembled mailing lists for marketing purposes.

- Keep you messages or responses to messages and postings brief, to the point, and in keeping with the central theme of the discussion group.
- Use a signature at the end of your message that includes a link to your Web site or e-mail. Some moderated lists will not allow the use of a signature at the end of postings, messages, and responses, but it is always worth a try.
- Subscribe first and get to know the rules and regulations of the group before posting messages that promote your business. Likewise watch for other businesses that use the list as a promotional vehicle and consider what they are doing right or wrong before posting.

WEB RESOURCE

🔗 www.paml.net: List of Publicly Accessible Mailing Lists, information about 6,900 public mailing lists.

MARKETING WITH OPT-IN LISTS
$+ 🔨

For anyone not familiar with opt-in e-mail lists they are simply name lists compiled from people who have requested to receive specific information or offers about one or more subjects or topics that interest them. The opt-in list could be specific to people with interests in antiques, business, education, and just about any topic, subject, product, service, or activity imaginable. Key to note is the fact that "opt in," means that people have requested to be sent information, which is different from spam. Spam is a term used to describe an e-mail promotional message that was sent to a person or people who did not request to receive the message; spamming on the Internet is illegal. Be aware not all opt-in lists are spam-free; there are still scammers out there who rent lists under the guise of opt-in lists, when in fact they are not. Some of these list renters send out robots to literally suck e-mail addresses, out of public and private online message and discussion boards. So be sure to deal with a reputable list owner or broker before you rent. At some point almost all online marketers will rent an opt-in mailing list to test an offer, send out an electronic publication, or to simply advertise to a specific audience. Outside of building your own opt-in list there are three sources from which you can secure these lists.

1. List Owners

Many online marketers and business owners who have spent considerable time, money, and energy to build optimal opt-in lists often rent these lists out as a method to recoup some of the expenditures and generate profits.

2. List Managers

Often list owners do not have the time to manage their own mailing list and therefore hire a list management service. The list owner and the management service divide the rental proceeds. List managers generally provide services for numerous list owners.

3. List Brokers

As the title suggests these are businesspeople who represent many opt-in lists. They may manage them as well but more often than not they simply find people to rent the list to and collect a commission from the list owner.

Knowing who to rent the list from is a challenge that all new online marketers face. If you can, try to get referrals from other online marketers, find out who they rent lists from and if they are happy with the results and service. And of course it goes without saying that you should always tests a smaller percentage of the list first to make sure that you are receiving the desired response and action to your message before you commit to the entire list or multiple mailings. The second challenge online marketers face is trying to decipher a good opt-in list from a bad one; the difference means reaching your target audience successfully or not, so it is important to have the right list to match the right offer or message. The first item you will want to review is the data card associated with the list that you are considering renting. On the data card you will find information such as list size or number of people on the list and cost per thousand to reach these people, which can range from one cent to a dollar a name for highly specialized lists. Additional information will include the list description, which is a brief background about the type people on the list; selection, meaning that you can separate out certain names that you want to reach; frequency that the list is updated or cleaned; and sometimes the list use report, which tells who else used the list. Ultimately renting a opt-in list is very much a *caveat emptor* (let the buyer beware) situation; therefore do your research homework prior to making a commitment. Listed below are a few additional questions you should ask the list owner or broker before you pay your hard-earned marketing money to rent the list.

Questions You Should Ask

- *Who is delivering the list?* This is an important question to ask especially if you are renting more than one list at a time. Many list owners subcontract the service of e-mailing the list and you do not want to have the same company sending out two of your messages at the same time to the same people on the list. A follow-up message is a great idea, but a few days after the original message or offer, not hours after.
- *Does the rental cost include layout of your message and delivering the message?* To entice online marketers some lists advertised cheaply do not include everything that needs to get your message from point A to B so be sure to clarify that the cost to rent the list includes all services.

- *Where are the opt-out replies sent?* Opt outs should be directed to the deployment service and updated regularly to avoid complaints from people who no longer wish to receive mail from you.
- *What is the URL for the opt-in site where the names where collected?* Get the address from the list owner or broker and go directly to the source yourself to make sure that the names are being collected in the manner the owner tells you they are. You don't want to be sending out spam. You want assurances that the people receiving your information have asked to be included.
- *Do you pay for e-mails sent or e-mails received?* Make sure that you are only paying for people who actually received your message and not for hard or soft bounce backs, which are messages that have been returned unopened.
- *Will your message be sent as a stand-alone or incorporated into an electronic publication?* Once again advertising can be deceptive, you may only be paying one cent a name, but that might be because your message is buried in an electronic publication with numerous other advertisements or offers. If you want your message to be on its own, then make sure to ask, never assume.

WEB RESOURCE

⚓ www.google.com: Search for opt-in list owners and brokers by submitting an "opt-in" keyword search, hundreds of matches to get you started.

ADD A "WHAT'S NEW" PAGE
$$ ⚒

One of the main objectives of any successful Web site is to turn new visitors into repeat visitors, which ultimately generates revenue for the Web site through sales of products, services, advertising opportunities, and more. Webmasters commonly refer to this activity as building the Web site's sticky ingredient and creating a "what's new" page is a great way to add sticky content. It can draw visitors to return to the site so that they can get updated on the latest news and information related to your business, products, services, or the industry in which you generally operate your business. Ideally, an icon should be placed on your homepage so that visitors can quickly navigate to the "what's new" Web page and to really get the most benefit out of this simple yet effective "keep them coming back" trick. Make sure to ask visitors if they would like to sign up for e-mail reminders that alert them electronically every time your what's new page has been updated with fresh and valuable information and features. However, avoid company "puffery" on your what's new page. Stick to information that will interest and benefit your customers by filling a need, a want, or solving a problem that they may have.

BENEFIT FROM A GUEST BOOK
$+ ✎

Adding a guest book feature to your Web site is another great way to learn more about your visitors and use the information you collect to market to them and to add products and services to your lineup that would appeal to them. You can customize many guest book programs so that you can add in your corporate identity, logo, and message, select colors that match your existing identity, add in music or video clips, ask questions in numerous languages, and receive automatic e-mail notification when a visitor signs in to the guest book. Some programs even have automatic profanity delete options so that you don't have to monitor your guest book 24/7 to ensure that no unwanted profanity is present. Once the guest book is installed, ask friends and family members to visit your site and sign in to the guest book to give you a jump start, sort of a catalyst to get other site visitors using the book. Remember to ask in the book if you can include those who sign in if you can include them in your daily, weekly, or monthly e-mails that you send out. Get them to agree by letting them know you don't share your opt-in list with anyone else.

WEB RESOURCE
♂ www.freeguestbooks.com: Online customizable guestbooks.

CYBERMALLS, STOREFRONTS, AND AUCTIONS
$+ ✎

The Internet is home to thousands of cybermalls—large, small, arranged geographically or by type of product or industry, and just about everything imaginable in between. And for anyone not familiar with the cybermall-retailing concept they are much like a bricks-and-mortar shopping mall wherein many retailers are grouped together to sell products and services from one central location taking advantage of an increased promotional effort to a wider and larger audience, all online of course. Even online giants eBay and Amazon have opened their Web sites to smaller retailers who wish to have access to their large audience and marketing machine. A few of the advantages of joining a cybermall include

- the ability to drive more traffic to your Web site or access to a larger online shopping audience.
- reducing the costs associated with purchasing the hardware and software that is required for operating your own online secure shopping cart.
- not having to continually update or maintain an independent Web site if you choose to market solely through one or more cybermall storefronts.
- low initial investment to get online and selling your products to a global audience.
- the ability to join the cybermall's credit card merchant account if you do not currently have your own merchant account established, or are having difficulty establishing your own account.
- group promotional and marketing activities.

Fees to join or participate in cybermall retailing are charged based on your needs and level of participation. Some malls charge a commission fee on all items sold, while others will charge only a monthly fee ranging from $25 to $1,000 depending on the services you subscribe to. Still others will charge both a monthly fee and a commission on every sale processed through the mall. What is best for you will largely be based on expected sales, your initial and ongoing budget, and the services that you require.

But, before you jump in and join any cybermall make sure that you confirm that the mall draws a large number of visitors each month and that this number is steadily increasing not decreasing. Also, be sure that the Web site is maintained and updated on a regular basis, the webmaster has a powerful promotional campaign in place to market the mall, and the mall has a safe and secure server for online credit card processing.

WEB RESOURCES

🖉 www.amazon.com: Amazon.com Inc. set up your own personal storefront within their site.

🖉 www.ebay.com: eBay, set up your own personal storefront within their site.

🖉 www.internet-mall.com: Online shopping mall providing retailers with vairous tenant packages and programs.

ASK AN EXPERT TO GET THEM BACK
$+ ✎ ☎

"Ask an expert" is unquestionably one of the best online services that you can provide for visitors and one of the best ways to keep them coming back on a regular basis to get more free and valuable expert advice. Even visitors to your Web site who do not use this service will be compelled to find out the answers to questions posted in this section of your Web site by other visitors. "Ask an expert" is a very powerful community building tool that every Web site can benefit from. Securing "experts" to answer questions and provide advice on topics that relate to your target audience, business, products, and service is generally easy, providing there is a benefit for the expert. The benefit can be money, but that is not necessary. Usually all that is required is to provide a link back to the expert's Web site, or feature her products or services on your Web site in exchange for her expert services. If you sell antique car parts, then enlist an expert in the classic car restoration field to answer visitors' questions. If it's gourmet foods you sell, then secure a highly respected chef to answer cooking and recipe questions. At the end of the day you want to create a sense of community on your Web site, a place where a person can go and interact with likeminded people; adding expert advice is a terrific way to accomplish this and more.

LINKS AND MORE LINKS
$ ✎

You may not have thought that encouraging visitors to leave your Web site for another would be an efficient way to secure repeat visits but it is. Once again it's all about creating useful and beneficial tools to meet your visitors' needs. Providing access to additional sources of information, products, and services via links is a way of telling visitors that you care and identify with their needs and are striving to provide the best place for them to fulfill those needs. However, don't be too quick to shoo visitors to another Web site and be sure to keep links off your homepage and a couple of levels down. You may even want to have visitors link to another site through an exit page where you can ask one last time that they bookmark your Web site or sign in to a guest book or subscribe to your electronic publication before leaving. The second benefit of providing links is that many search engines such as Google, AltaVista, and MSN use links found within your site as part of the formula to establish search result rankings.

Additionally you might also want to add a free-for-all links service in your site. What this means is that any business or organization that wants to can automatically sign up to be featured on your links page within your site. Of course, there are pros and cons to doing this. One pro is the fact that you can keep the linked site within yours, therefore keeping your own visitors within your site longer. One con is that unless you check your free-for-all links page daily or use a customizable program that enables you to approve the link prior to going live, you risk having a site linked to yours that is not suitable. Another way to link your Web site with similar-interest sites is to join a linking service. For a fee, a linking service will automatically link your site to other sites that are also members of the service. For online marketers short on time joining such a service should be considered. On the next page is a simple worksheet that you can use to keep track of the Web sites you would like to link your site to and why.

Web Site Tracking Worksheet

Yes	No	URL	Comments
❏	❏	_____	_____
❏	❏	_____	_____
❏	❏	_____	_____
❏	❏	_____	_____
❏	❏	_____	_____
❏	❏	_____	_____
❏	❏	_____	_____
❏	❏	_____	_____
❏	❏	_____	_____
❏	❏	_____	_____

WEB RESOURCES

✍ www.linkleads.com: Online Web site linking, link management, and advertising service.

✍ www.linkpopularity.com: Use this online service to find out how many sites are linked to your site and vice versa, as well as how many links and to whom your competitors' sites are linked.

CONTEST YOUR WAY TO INCREASED HITS

$$+ ✎ ☎ ⚖

Daily, weekly, monthly, or quarterly prizes, online contests are hot and a great way to attract new visitors to your Web site and keep the ones you already have coming back often. The type of contest you hold and the type of prize you give away will greatly depend on what your online marketing objectives are and of course your budget. Do you want to attract a lot of new visitors to your Web site, regardless of target market? Or, do you want the contest to appeal to your core target audience only? If it's big numbers you want then the contest must be broad with a large payoff. Even small businesses with limited promotional budgets can get involved—how? One way is to subscribe to a contest pooling service such as ePrize, which provides clients complete contest and sweepstakes services; they even manage the entire event, legal issues, entry form registration, and more. Of interest is a very popular service they provide called pooled eDrawings, which is a quarterly contest with huge grand prizes like luxury sports cars and dream vacations. What is so interesting is that Web sites pool together to offer prizes and share the expense of doing so, meaning that your small business can easily afford to offer a sports car as a contest prize. If you plan to host and manage your own contest, big or small, be sure to get the details listed in as many contest directories like Contest Hound as possible due to the simple fact that these online services can drive a lot of traffic to your site. Of course before holding any type of contest or sweepstakes be sure to research and conform to all legal issues and regulations.

WEB RESOURCES

- www.contesthound.com: Online directory featuring contest listings.

- www.eprize.net: ePrize provides clients complete contest and sweepstakes services.

PROFIT FROM AFFILIATE PROGRAMS
$$ ⚒

Associate or affiliate programs are simply establishing alliances with other online businesspeople to sell their products or services via your Web site and receiving a commission for doing so, which is generally in the 5 to 25 percent range, depending on the program and profitability of what is being sold. Or alternately having your new business alliances sell your products or services via their Web sites and paying them a commission based on total sales for doing this, once again in the 5 to 25 percent range. Online bookseller Amazon.com was one of the first major players to embrace the affiliate system and the program has proven to be so successful that they have grown their number of "affiliate sellers" from 30,000 in 1998 to more than 700,000 by the end of 2002. There are two ways to profit from affiliate programs. The first is to sell your products (services are not as popular in an affiliate program). The second is to join other retailers' affiliate programs and earn a commission on every sale that is made as a direct result of your efforts. This generally means that a visitor to your site has clicked through on a banner or button featured on your site to the affiliate's site and purchased the product or service that was featured. Once again, mammoth online retailer Amazon.com has successfully used affiliate programs to spread its wings throughout the Web. In fact, it is becoming more and more difficult to find a commerce Web site that does not participate in Amazon's program and why not—earning up to 15 percent of total sales that are generated through your site can be very profitable. Likewise offering your own affiliate program to other online retailers is also a very smart way to increase your market penetration and sales and revenues. However, if you are going to sell affiliate products on your site make sure that you do not include too many or your site will start to look like a garage sale. Likewise be choosy about the sites that you include in your own affiliate program so that you do not stray too far from your online objectives and that your "morals and values" stay intact.

WEB RESOURCE

- www.associateprograms.com: Online directory listing numerous associate and affiliate reseller programs and how you can get involved.

MEMBERS ONLY PLEASE
$$+ ⚒ ☎

Create a members-only or exclusive club section in your Web site packed with valuable bonus information, service, and tools for your best customers to use, and so they can interact with other customers, your employees, and your management team. Everybody wants to feel special and giving valued customers access to an exclusive club is one of the best ways to single out customers as individuals and make them feel special and important. Issue a simple password to grant entry and allow your customers to interact with each other through discussion boards, workshops, and instant messaging programs. Additionally, offer club members discounts on products and services you supply and allow them to do the same with their own products and services they sell if your site and private members club is business-to-business oriented. If the club revolves around hobbies or special interests make sure that you provide members with great features like expert online seminars and other events that revolve around the hobby or special interest that would appeal to your club members. Once again, establishing a community should be one of your main online marketing objectives and creating a membership or club section on your site is a fantastic way to promote and create community.

POP UP AT THE RIGHT TIME
$$ ⚒

Online marketers have mixed feelings about using "pop-up" windows for various marketing activities;

some like using them while others think they are an intrusive pest. However, when used correctly pop-up windows can be an extremely powerful and profitable marketing tool. Here are a few ways that you can put pop-up windows to work for your online business in a nonintrusive fashion. Use a pop-up window

- that contains a useful tip of the day on every Web page.
- that contains a subscription form for your e-zine or e-newsletter and ask visitors to subscribe or send it to a friend.
- to promote special discounts or printable coupons.
- as an entry form to promote a contest and add the names to your opt-in list.
- advertisement to promote one of your own specials or an affiliate product.
- that contains a reminder asking visitors to bookmark your site or sign a guest book.
- that contains a survey, poll, or suggestion box to find out valuable information about your company, products, and services. Ask visitors to complete the form and give them an incentive as a reward.
- to promote employment opportunities or business partnership opportunities that are available within your organization.
- at the point of purchase to offer customers free gift wrapping or delivery as an appreciation gift.
- at the point of purchase to up-sell or offer additional products or services at reduced prices.
- at the point of purchase to market extended warranties related to purchases made.
- at the point of purchase to sell co-branded merchandize such as an embroidered hat to go with the set of skis purchased.

As you can see, used correctly pop-up windows can serve for a wide variety of marketing, information, and customer service uses.

CREATE YOUR OWN ONLINE E-CATALOG
$$ ✎

Not that long ago only small-business owners with the deepest of pockets could afford to have their own promotional products catalog professionally designed, printed, and distributed to customers and prospects by way of direct mail. But fortunately thanks to the advent of the Internet and e-mail technologies now just about every small-business owner, marketer, and salesperson alike can afford to design and distribute his own online catalog packed with information about his products and business. That's right, armed with nothing more than a digital camera and a basic software program you can take pictures of your products and arrange them into a great-looking electronic catalog. Once your e-catalog is complete simply click "send" and out it goes to all your current customers on your electronic opt-in list and to new prospects by renting high quality targeted opt-in mailing lists. Once you have your e-catalog developed, be sure to update it regularly and use it as one of your main sales and marketing tools.

REMINDERS AND ALERTS WORK
$$ ✎

Leading online retailers like Barnes & Noble, Amazon.com, and Wal-Mart have perfected the art of "Alerts" as a way to ensure that visitors return to their respective Web sites, and often. In the case of Barnes & Noble they simply ask visitors to sign up for a writer or book alert service, and contact customers via an e-mail writer alert when their selected writer has a new book published and for sale. Simple, yet highly effective because in the case of Barnes & Noble they are trying to ensure that customers shop with them and do not stray over to the competition and by alerting customers they stand a good chance of securing their business before they go shopping for what they want elsewhere online or off. Once again, one of the main objectives of online marketing is to keep visitors active in your Web site and online community. Another benefit of a reminder service is that once you have the person's permission to e-mail her with the related reminder or alert this also gives you permission to send her other relevant news and offers about your business, products, services, or industry. In a nutshell asking visitors to sign up for a reminder or alert service is a great way to keep customers involved with your business and build your own opt-in e-mail list, a highly valuable online marketing tool.

DISCUSSION BOARDS CREATE COMMUNITY
$$ ✎ ☏

Installing a discussion board, online chat forum, or bulletin or message board in your Web site is an excellent way to secure repeat visits by providing like-minded visitors ways to interact with each other and become part of your online community. Additionally, you can use any of these forums to post a topic of the day relating to your business and even host online seminars and workshops in them. However, be prepared to play mediator once in a while as discussion and message boards can get a little wild and wooly when strong-willed visitors state opposing points of views. Discussion forums can also be used to conduct research to better understand your customers. For instance if you wanted to raise the price of a specific product or service that you are currently selling, you could "float a balloon" in your discussion board under an assumed user name and ID number about what you wanted to research or accomplish. To "float a balloon" means that you leak a few comments about what you'd like to do in order to gauge customer reaction in advance of taking action and implementing the proposed change. Or in the case of a price hike, you would release a message into the discussion board about a rumor of a price hike and see what visitors and customers think about it via their posts or responses to posts on the boards. Likewise if time allows you can also sign up for any one of the thousands of discussion groups on the net and use these boards to learn about your target audience and conduct quiet research. You can even do a little advertising, providing you can make your posts appear as newsworthy or helpful information and not just an advertisement.

Web Resource

✍ www.bravenet.com: A gigantic source for interactive Web site tools.

USE ONLINE POLLS AND SURVEYS TO GENERATE TRAFFIC OR LEARN
$+ ✎ ☏

Polls and surveys that are related to your business or industry, or generalized for fun and entertainment purposes are another terrific way to lure visitors back to your Web site on a regular basis and build a sense of community among visitors. Not to mention that conducting your own polls and surveys for research purposes to find out what your customers and visitors truly want and need is a great marketing and planning tool. You can even increase your opt-in database by using polls and surveys simply by asking visitors to sign up for an e-mail reminder service that alerts them when new polls or surveys are posted on your site, as well as creating a reason to e-mail them with the results of previous surveys, along with a new marketing offer. There are many content providers that supply poll and survey plug-ins at little or not cost to the user, and most can even be customized to meet your and your target audience's needs. Two such providers of polls and surveys are One Minute Poll and Web Surveyor; both of their respective Web site URLs are listed below. In terms of using polls and surveys for marketing research and planning purposes, surveys can be a very powerful tool. Through responses you can learn how customers feel about your business, products, and services, and learn from the responses to improve your marketing efforts and increase sales. Here are a few things to consider before and while you are designing your poll or survey.

What Are the Objectives of Your Poll or Survey?

Set the objective of the survey and be very specific about what type of information you want to discover. If you want information about your customers, visitors, products, services, Web site, customer service, or your competition? Ask yourself, "if I knew more about _____, it would really benefit my business." Whatever the "blank" is should be the objective of your survey.

Who Is the Target Audience You Want to Reach?

Once you have set the objective of your survey and you know what you want to accomplish, the next step is to identify the audience that can help you to reach your objective. Who are you going to ask to participate? Will you ask all your Web site visitors, your electronic publication subscribers, all customers, or perhaps only customers who purchase certain products or use specific services? Pick your survey audience based on your objectives and what you want to learn.

Create the Survey Plan

Now that you know the objective of the survey and who the audience will be, the next step is to plan your survey including design, time frame and implementation, survey questions, budget, and analysis methods of results.

Pretest Your Survey Prior to Launching

Once you have your survey designed pretest it before you launch the entire program. To pretest your survey you can give it to friends and family members to complete or to a small group of loyal customers, either online or off. The purpose of the pretest is to make sure that you have not left anything off your survey that should have been included and so that you can gauge the responses to find out if the answers you are receiving are meeting your objectives. Pretesting is an important step in the survey process as almost always you will be able to identify a weakness in your survey and improve it before you go wide with the final version.

Decide on Your Survey Topic and Questions

Once you have pretested your survey and fine-tuned your questions then you are ready to release the survey to your larger target audience and kindly ask that they complete it. If you want to increase the response rate then offer an incentive to people who take the time to complete the survey, something small such as a discount coupon or certificate. However, make sure that your incentive will not bias the survey results, you want honest and legitimate answers.

Analyze the Results of the Survey

Based on the questions you ask in your online survey and the objective you want to reach, the next step is to analyze the results you received. If you are using quantifiable information such as a question that requires a yes or no response then you can analyze the results statistically—70 percent said yes they would like more relevant content on the Web site, while 30 percent said no. Thus the results are easy to relate to statistical numbers.

Put the Survey Results to Work in the Form of Action

Oddly enough the action part of the surveying process is where most small-business owners become unglued and more often than not what the results of the survey revealed are never put into action. The results of a survey do little good if they sit in a drawer collecting dust; if so the entire exercise was for nothing. Hence only take the time, effort, and money to create and implement a survey if you are sure that you will use the responses to the benefit of your business.

In addition to online surveys and pools you might also want to consider adding a online suggestion box so that customers can provide feedback about your company, site, products, and services 24-7-365.

WEB RESOURCES

- www.oneminutepoll.com: One Minute Poll, customizable survey and poll software.
- www.websurveyor.com: Web Surveyor, customizable survey and poll software.

GIVE THEM USEFUL TOOLS
$+ 🔨

Attract new visitors and keep the visitors and customers you have coming back by providing useful interactive tools on your Web site. Is there a calculator that you can provide that your visitors would find useful and beneficial? Or, perhaps you can provide customizable templates that they could use to fill a need, solve a problem, enhance their businesses, or make their jobs easier? The best way to find out what tools and useful features you can add to your site to enhance visitor services is to simply ask your visitors what tools and features would be the most helpful and beneficial to them. Do this by conducting your own online survey and ask your visitors what they want in terms of interactive or specialized Web tools. From there you can set about developing these features or adding a link that would send visitors to non-competitive sites that already provide the same or similar tools. The objective is to pull visitors back to your site and developing and offering interactive tools and features is a great way to get started in the hunt for repeat hits. Not to mention the fact that the more times people return to your site, the higher the chances go of them buying and buying more often. A word of caution however: if you are going to provide useful and valuable tools on your site for visitors then the tools must be that: useful and valuable. The tools must be easy to use, always "up," and more beneficial to visitors than what the competition offers.

✍ www.bravenet.com: A gigantic source for interactive Web site tools.

TIE IN OFFLINE PROMOTIONS
$$ ✎

To help build your online presence try to route your offline bricks-and-mortar customers to your Web site by creating promotions that send offline customers online to learn details, or to take advantage of the offer. Additionally develop other methods to drive customer traffic to your Web site and encourage repeat visits. Methods include routing all customer service inquiries through your Web site so customers can speak to representatives via live operator software, or they can be directed to a frequently asked questions Web page within your site. The objective with offline promotions is to take advantage of all opportunities to promote your URL and drive traffic to your Web site. One of the best ways to promote your URL offline is to print it on all business materials including outgoing invoices

Offline URL Promotions Checklist

Your Web site URL should be included in or printed on the following items:

❑ Business cards

❑ Company letterhead and envelopes

❑ Invoices and sales receipts

❑ Sales letters and presentations

❑ Outbound faxes and e-mails

❑ Promotional fliers and brochures

❑ Product catalogs

❑ Estimate and tender forms

❑ Exterior signage

❑ Interior signage

❑ Window displays and signage

❑ Vehicle signs and bumper stickers

❑ Point-of-purchase displays and special event exhibits

❑ Product packaging and labeling

❑ Press release and media kit

❑ Yellow and white pages telephone directories

❑ Newspaper display and classified advertisements

❑ Exterior and interior billboard and poster advertisements

❑ Transits ads and other types of outdoor advertisements

❑ Radio spots and television commercials

❑ Voice-mail messages and on-hold messages

❑ Newsletters and company reports

❑ Advertising specialties such as imprinted T-shirts, pens, memo pads, and coffee mugs

❑ Warranty and customer comment cards and survey forms

and envelopes. Get creative with gimmick promotional and advertising specialty items such as key chains, bumper stickers, and T-shirts all of which can be attractively emblazoned with your logo and URL and distributed to customers and suppliers to promote your Web site and help build an online image. Use the basic checklist of additional ideas on page 416 to promote your Web site and URL offline.

LET THEM ALL SUBMIT
$$ ⚒ 🕮

Inviting people to submit to your Web site can be a great way to attract new visitors and keep them coming back to read, view, or listen to the latest submissions, whatever the submission might be. The topic or subject of these submissions will vary greatly depending on the purpose and objective of your Web site, so some creativity is required to identify what kind of visitor submissions will have the greatest impact for your particular business. For instance director/producer Francis Ford Coppola's online virtual studio Web site call Zoetrope allows members to submit screenplays, photographs, short stories, and more for the rest of the site members to review and critique. This site boasts more than 20,000 members, so in practical terms as you can see visitor submissions work. There is no charge to join so you might ask what the benefit for providing such a valuable service for free is to Mr. Coppola. I suppose one might be, how many of those 20,000 members go out and see his new films or rent his existing films, and how many refer others to do the same? More than a few I am sure. Once again the goal is to create a community that visitors will want to become part of and interact with other visitors within the community, and developing a system that enables visitors to submit something for the benefit of everyone is a great way to create that community. In turn increased traffic can provide increased revenue potential via product and service sales, or advertising sales opportunities. It is a proven fact that the longer people are in your Web site and the more often they return to your site, then the higher the odds go of them buying something.

GIVE THEM THE LATEST NEWS
$ ⚒

Another good way to increase your Web site's sticky content is to provide up-to-date headline news, sports scores, international and local weather forecasts, and stock market financial information. Many content providers of these types of information will customize content packages to suit your needs, and best of all much of this content can be featured on your Web site for little if any cost to you. If your Web site target audience is restricted to one geographic area such as your city or town, then you may want to enlist a local person or people to supply "content" that would be more suited to your target audience and geographic business area. This content could include local news, amateur sports scores and information, free local classifieds sections, and other types of local community-building features. Once again by providing visitors with free and valuable information and services, you entice them to return to your Web site often, and in doing so you increase the number of selling opportunities you have with each individual visitor. Studies have conclusively shown that the more a person visits one particular Web site the higher the odds go that he will make a purchase from that same Web site.

WEB RESOURCES

⚲ www.uspntech.com: USPN Tech, providers of current and continually updated free and low cost news, weather, sports, and business content.

⚲ www.newsclicker.com: News Clicker, providers of current and continually updated free and low cost news, weather, sports, and business content.

BUILD YOUR ARCHIVES
$$ ⚒

Think twice before you push the delete button on that old content, articles, and tips column you publish on your Web site or in your e-zine, because everything old can become new and very valuable once again, especially highly specific and valuable information that you publish on your Web site or in your e-zine. So instead of simply deleting this information put it to good marketing use by creating an achieves section in your Web site and make this information available by topic or subject or chronologically indexed for easy navigation for visitors. Not only can a value-packed information archive draw new visitors to your site, but it can also increase the number of return visits to your site, therefore increasing the number of opportunities you have to sell to each person. Additionally, you can also create a valuable e-book from your archived information and give it to prospects free of charge as a powerful incentive to motivate them to buy a product or service, or as an incentive to motivate them to subscribe to your monthly electronic publication.

MARKET WITH ONLINE COUPONS
$$+ ✎

Market your products and services to a global audience by designing a coupon that can be distributed online via any one of the many online coupon distributors or even right from your own Web site. In terms of the specialized coupon sites, shoppers simply log on and search through various categories that interest them, such as consumer products, business products and services, travel, sports, entertainment, and more. When they find a discount or rebate coupon related to a product or service they wish to purchase, then they simply link over to the featured business's Web site and buy. Or, alternately print the coupon and redeem it at a bricks-and-mortar store. Additionally you can also have your own coupon Web page right on your Web site. But make sure to make your offer a good one and change it often as a method to keep visitors coming back to your site to check out your new and incredible coupon offers.

Web Resources

- ☞ www.coupons.com: Online products and services coupons.
- ☞ www.rebateplace.com: Online service listing manufactures' rebates.
- ☞ www.giftcertificates.com: Online gift certificate service, redeemable at numerous e-commerce sites.

E-MAIL SIGNATURE
$ ✎

Business e-mail you send should have an e-mail signature or e-business card tacked on the end of your message. An e-mail signature is a text message that is automatically attached to the end of your outgoing e-mails that you send, or a template than enables you to create your message and send. Using an e-mail signature can provide many benefits.

Contact Information

Include business name, title, and contact information such as telephone and fax numbers, e-mail and Web site URL, and mailing address.

Links

Recipients of your e-mail can automatically link to and send you an e-mail or log on to your Web site from information you include your signature. Additionally you can also include in a site of the week or some other interesting information in your signature that people can link to and visit on the Web.

Marketing Message

Include a brief marketing message, less than ten words but powerful like your biggest benefit such as "Lose ten pounds in one week guaranteed! Click here to find out how." And to stay fresh you can change your marketing message weekly.

Some savvy entrepreneurs even use their e-mail signature to ask people to sign up or subscribe to their free newsletters or e-zines, so if you publish one you might want to try the same. However, on a cautionary note try to limit your e-mail signature to eight lines or fewer in total; any more and people can become annoyed because it starts to look and read like a pushy advertisement. Also make sure that all employees also create their own e-mail signature as well.

Signature Set Up

The majority of e-mail programs such as AOL and Outlook give you the option of setting up your own e-mail signature. On both under "Tools" or "Toolbar" will be a create new signature or set up new mail signature option. Simply click on these, complete, and use as your default outgoing mail option. If you have problems setting up an e-mail signature file consult the tutorial section of your e-mail program for a detailed explanation.

WEB RESOURCE

⚲ www.workz.com: Submit "signature files" into the Workz search engine to find numerous articles and information about establishing and using e-mail signature files as a promotional tool.

ADVERTISE ONLINE WHERE IT WILL DO GOOD
$+ ⚒

The Internet is home to many charitable causes, Web sites, and other ways that people can help support their favorite charities right from the comfort of their homes or offices with the simple click of their mouse. Many of these charitable organizations and Web sites also offer businesspeople and marketers ways to get involved and help their favorite charities through great advertising and sponsorship opportunities. By getting involved you can help wipe out world hunger, save the Amazon rainforest, find cures for breast cancer, or anything imaginable in terms of great and worthwhile charitable causes that do good. You will find various operating formats as to how your business, products, or services will gain exposure on these charity Web sites by way of an advertisement or sponsorship. However many have a standard operating format which goes something like this: A person gives to a charity via a Web site and they receive a response e-mail confirming their donation and some facts and figures about the charity or cause they have donated to. Included in the e-mail confirmation is an advertisement of the sponsoring business letting the giver know that this business also gives to this particular cause by way of donation or paid advertising sponsorship. The business' advertisement includes a link that the person can click on to get to that business's Web site or additional contact information. This is a great system because it enables you to spend advertising dollars in a way

that they will do good to wipe out any number of world threats, and it helps to build goodwill for your business in the eyes and minds of consumers.

WEB RESOURCES

⚲ www.thehungersite.com: The Hunger Site, fighting worldwide hunger.

⚲ www.thebreastcancersite.com: The Breast Cancer Site, helping to provide medical care for women who otherwise could not afford it.

⚲ www.thechildhealthsite.com: The Child Health Site, helping to cover costs associated with medical attention for children from around the globe.

⚲ www.therainforestsite.com: The Rainforest Site, money used to purchase and protect rainforest lands.

⚲ www.theanimalrescuesite.com: The Animal Rescue Site, rescuing and caring for animals worldwide.

⚲ www.igive.com: iGive helps to support numerous charitable causes.

PROVIDE SOME FUN STUFF
$+ ⚒

Even Web sites with serious themes, messages, and content can benefit by providing visitors light entertainment in the form of interactive games, trivia, cartoons, and humor. Of course, if you can relate these entertainment activities and tools to customers' or visitors' interests in the form of a quiz or challenge then these tools become even more powerful for luring visitors back to your Web site on a regular basis. Perhaps a joke of the day or cartoon of the day can be e-mailed to customers who sign up for the service. Once again, this would be another way to secure their permission for receiving e-mails from your business; thus you would be building a valuable and powerful marketing opt-in list just by providing some light entertainment. Whatever form it takes, jokes, cartoons, or games, fun stuff can be a great way to build a loyal visitor base for your Web site.

WEB RESOURCE

⚲ www.freesticky.com: Free Sticky is an online directory of free or low cost content based on data or graphic feeds including games, entertainment, trivia, cartoons, jokes, and more.

DON'T FORGET THE FREEBIES
$$ ✎

No one can resist getting something for free and that's what makes free giveaways such an effective marketing tool for attracting new visitors to your Web site and keeping them coming back. There are hundreds of "Free Stuff Directories" on the Web, which list and are linked to Web sites that routinely give things away for free. Being listed in these indices is a great way to increase your site traffic and potential customer base. To get listed in free stuff and giveaway indices, simply do a search on Google or Yahoo! using the keywords "Free Stuff Index," and hundreds of matches will appear. What you choose to give away should be related to your business, such as a mouse pad or T-shirt emblazoned with your URL and company logo. It is not always necessary to give something to everyone who visits your site; a daily or weekly drawing will suffice. But do make sure to ask everyone that enters the giveaway for permission to contact her to let her know who won. Not only will this enable you to stay in contact with visitors but you can also include some information or an offer with the response you send and you'll be building a very valuable e-mail opt-in list at the same time. Here are a few more ideas about things that you can give away that have a high perceived value that can boost your credibility and attract new customers.

- Give customers free shipping for anything they purchase, or alternately set a dollar amount that they must spend in order to qualify for fee shipping. This is a great way to increase the sales value transaction of each one that Amazon.com has been using with great success.
- Offer visitors free reports or correspondence courses. This trick works best when you break the report into chapters or sections and give each section or lesson to prospects over a period of time enabling you to build rapport, trust, and numerous point of contact selling opportunities. This simple trick can also be used to increase the amount of times a visitor returns to

your Web site if you opt to publish your training course or report right on your site featuring a new lesson or chapter weekly.

- Share your professional expertise in your industry or field and give visitors free e-mail or telephone consultations. Once again this is a great way to build credibility and trust with prospects and is a highly effective method to break down resistance to buying.
- Offer free samples of your product or service on a trial basis. This enables prospects to benefit firsthand from using your product or service making it much easier to convert to a sale. Think AOL—who can say no to an Internet connection after they have realized the benefits of being connected for a month?

MAKE YOUR "FREE" ONLINE OFFERS MORE VALUABLE
$ ✎

Everyone loves to get something for free and most businesspeople give stuff away for free all the time—a free estimate, a free gift with purchase, free delivery, and many more freebies. But anything you give away for free has to benefit the receiver in order for it to benefit your business and the best way to do this is to increase the value of your free offer. Below are a few ways that you can increase the value of your free giveaways.

- Start by listing all of the features of your freebie and more important all of the benefits prospects will get from owning and using what you are giving to them for absolutely nothing. For instance if you give away a free "how to play guitar" book with every guitar you sell as an incentive to motivate people to buy, or simply as a thank-you gift, then make sure to tell people how they will benefit from the freebie. In this example, they will get more enjoyment out of playing their new guitars because they know how, thanks to the instructional book you gave them for free.
- State the dollar amount that your free offer is worth. You might not charge a subscription fee for your monthly newsletter, but if you did,

what would it be? Translate it into a dollar figure, "Join now and receive our exclusive newsletter every month for absolutely free, a $240 value!" Or, "Companies pay me a $250 an hour consulting fee to have access to this information, but you can have it for free if you subscribe today!" Or, as mentioned above if the instruction book is worth $49 then boldly state it right beside the product you want to sell in the form of a headline.

- Use facts to increase the value of your free offer, "5,000 people just like you have already taken advantage of and profited from our free reports so join now so you can profit, too!" How can 5,000 people be wrong? Now that is a beneficial incentive.
- Package multiple free offers to increase the perceived value of your overall free offering. "Sign up today for our free e-mail tip of the day and receive our special e-book report that will make you rich!"
- You can also increase the perceived value of your free offering by limiting the offer. "The next 50 people to subscribe to our free outdoor living e-zine will receive our exclusive imprinted backpack, a $50 value, absolutely free!"

NEVER FORCE PEOPLE TO BUY ONLINE
$$$ ✎ 🐶

Even if you incorporate the latest and greatest encryption technology into your Web site to ensure safe and secure online shopping options for your customers, you'll find that many people are still reluctant to give out credit card information over the Internet. Especially to lesser-known businesses that lack brand name or instant recognition. For that reason don't limit your potential market share or take a chance on reducing revenues and profits. Instead make it easy for all of your Web site visitors to give you money by providing them with offline product ordering and payment options. These offline options should include a 24-hour toll-free telephone order hotline and mail-in payments; post the details on your Web site. In both cases you can enlist fulfillment services to answer the telephones, check post

boxes, and warehouse and ship products to your customers for a fee, based on a per customer order transaction basis, often for much less than it would cost an individual business to set up and operate these types of services because fulfillment operators work on volume for many customers at one time. In today's super competitive online marketplace often all that separates the winners from the losers is who empowers consumers to make choices that fill their individual needs. This can only be accomplished by providing people with options so they can decide which is best for them. You should still ask people to buy directly from your Web site; in fact you should encourage it with special incentives that are only available to online shoppers. But, at the end of the day if a person would prefer to shop offline for whatever reason then you also want that business, so make sure to give buyers options. Besides you will be in good company—even online marketing giant Amazon.com has recently included a feature that enables visitors to buy books through their partnership with Borders Books in the bricks-and-mortar world.

MOTIVATE VISITORS TO BUY BY PROVIDING INCENTIVES
$$ ✎

Providing special incentives is also a highly effective way to motivate your online visitors to buy products and services that are featured for sale on your Web site. Your special incentive could include free shipping on purchases over a certain dollar amount, two products for the price of one, extended warranties at no additional cost, or upgraded features for free to the first ten people who respond to a special offer and buy. The key to using incentives successfully as a motivational buying tool is that the incentive must be an individual product or service that could be sold on its own merits to truly represent value to the prospect. Additionally the incentive must be relevant to your main offer for it to have great impact. For example, if you sold computers online offering a free extended warranty that protected the customer's purchase for two years instead of one would be a valuable incentive that could be used to motivate people to buy the computer. Because this incentive is relevant to the main offer and it could be sold as a stand-alone item the perceived value of the incentives dramatically increase.

MOTIVATE VISITORS TO BUY BY REMOVING FEAR

$$+ ↖

One of the best ways to motivate your online visitors to buy and become customers is to remove the fear or doubt associated with making a purchase. This is especially important for online sellers, as unlike the bricks-and-mortar world where consumers can pick up and examine goods, they cannot do the same in cyberspace. Even if the product you are selling is relatively well known and accepted there will always be a degree of intangibility to your offering. Doubt and fear that it might not work, it might not fit, it might not be delivered, it might not be exactly what they wanted, and maybe they are paying too much. Doubt and fear are the two biggest obstacles that all online sellers face, period. Removing doubt and fear to secure more sales can be accomplished in numerous ways.

- Offer customers a 100 percent satisfaction and risk-free money back guarantee.
- Offer free product trial periods, a two-week no obligation trial period.
- Let customers buy now and pay later by offering "bill me later" payment option.
- Divide the total cost into installments over a fixed period of time, $20 a month for 12 months reads as less risky than $240.
- Offer financing options or convenient payment options such as e-checks and credit cards.

The easier you make it for people to buy, the more people who will buy. Likewise the more you can reduce or eliminate the fear and doubt of buying and the more people will buy.

FOLLOW-UP OFFERS INCREASE PROFITS

$$ ↖

It's no mystery that selling to a customer who has previously purchased from your business is much easier than selling to someone who hasn't. In fact it's about ten times easier and much less expensive the second, third, fourth, or tenth time around, simply due to the fact that you have already spent time, energy, and marketing dollars to find this customer. The "investment" to keep them as customers is much lower then the initial expenditure was to capture them. That is one of the many benefits of online marketing and e-commerce; it is much less costly to maintain electronic customer relationships than it is in the bricks-and-mortar world when you factor in the costs of personal visits, specialized printed promotional materials, and the like. Therefore wise online marketers have learned that once a customer buys you should immediately follow up after the sale via e-mail with another powerful offer, something that screams "buy me." You could offer something that is relative to the first purchase they made such as a book of recipes if the first purchase was a set of cooking pans. Or, a custom frame if the first purchase was unframed artwork. Your offer could even be more of the same product that they purchased, but at a discounted special offer price. While it is important to create and deliver a special follow-up offer to all people who have purchased, the real key to increased profits is that you must take the steps necessary to make the offer. One of the best ways to create and maintain a strong and powerful follow-up offer system is to use automatic e-mail responders, such as mailloop. In doing so you can predetermine great follow-up offers based on the various products and services you sell prior to people actually making a purchase. And once they have selected and purchased products or services, your follow-up system will automatically contact them with your special offer based on their purchases without you even having to remember to do it. The autoresponder will do it for you, thus greatly reducing the amount of time you spend responding to each customer purchase yet still increasing your selling opportunities and potential for added profits.

WEB RESOURCES

ℰ www.autoresponders.com: Online directory listing various autoresponder programs and services.

www.mailloop.com: E-mail and e-business auto-mation software.

MORE GREAT ONLINE MARKETING IDEAS
$$ ⟍

Online marketers can never have enough great marketing ideas, so listed below are a few more great online marketing ideas that you can employ to boost your sales and profits through the roof.

- Get clever in the way you use your banner advertisements mainly because to a certain degree Web surfers have become numb to them. So it makes a lot of sense to experiment with things like a banner advertisement in the form of a trivia question. Or animating pictures or characters on it to grab attention. Or even using your banner ads to advertise a contest that you are hosting as a way to drive traffic to your site.

- Add a classified advertising page to your Web site and let visitors use this very valuable service free of charge. This is a great way to secure new visitors and repeat hits. Advertise your free classifieds in classified advertising directories found on the major search engines such as Google and directories like Yahoo!.

- To separate your Web site from the millions of other Web sites on the Internet, consider coming up with a central theme that carries throughout your site and all of your marketing and promotional activities. Perhaps your site could resemble a mechanics garage, or an office tower, or a book. The theme you develop and use should be relevant to your business and what products or services you sell.

- Don't be afraid to use a loss leader to get visitors to your site and buying. Meaning that you will advertise and sell a particular product or service at or below cost to attract more visitors in the hopes that they will buy other products of services, become loyal and repeat customers, and ultimately both. Loss leaders have long been successfully used on and offline to build traffic and secure future business. The costs associated with selling below cost should be considered a marketing expense.

- Team up with smaller online competitors and use your newly formed coalition to do battle against your larger and better-financed competitors. The businesses you form an alliance with do not have to be direct competition; they could be nondirect in the sense that they operate in the same industry or sell similar products or services but are different in a specialty, or the way they build, deliver, or maintain the products they sell or the services they provide. Forming alliances on the Internet is a great way to broaden your marketing reach, appeal to a wider target audience, and share common expenses so that you can lower operating expenses and therefore deliver goods and services to the end user at reduced costs while maintaining or increasing quality and value.

- Consider selling your products at wholesale cost for much cheaper than your competitors do, but make up lost revenues by charging a membership fee to join your wholesale Web club. One thousand members paying $50 a month to have access to products at cost is the equivalent to selling one thousand products a month with a $50 gross profit margin.

- Offer to write free testimonials and product and service reviews for other online companies in exchange for a link to your site not only from the review you write for them but that is also prominently posted on their Web site. And clobber the competition by offering something for free that they charge for such as delivery, extended warranty, or specialized software. And be sure to use this as your unique selling position and your competitive advantage in all of your marketing activities.

- Offer visitors free product or service trial periods, and payment installments or bill me later options to reduce the risk or fear of buying. And also package products or services together for real impact. For instance, if you are selling a weight loss program, offer a free e-mail consultation to go with it for support.

DRIVING TRAFFIC TO YOUR WEB SITE CHECKLIST

$+ ✎

Below is a checklist of ideas that you can use to drive traffic to your Web site and secure more repeat visits and more selling opportunities. Create your own checklist from this one, ideas that would work to help increase traffic to your specific site.

📖 SUGGESTED ADDITIONAL READING

Bailey, Keith and Karen Leland. *Online Customer Service for Dummies*. New York: John Wiley & Sons, 2001.

Joyner, Mark. *Mind Control Marketing.com: How Everyday People are Using Forbidden Mind Control Psychology and Ruthless Military Tactics to Make Millions Online*. New York: Steel Icarus, 2002.

Driving Traffic to Your Web Site Checklist

- ❏ Register with online search engines such as Google.

- ❏ Register with online search directories such as Yahoo!.

- ❏ Build a powerful linking program with other Web sites, especially the ones that you feel would be most beneficial for driving traffic to your site.

- ❏ Drive traffic to your site by launching an affiliate sellers program.

- ❏ Send your offline customers online for customer service solutions and product support information.

- ❏ Write articles for online and offline publications and include your URL in all.

- ❏ Refer your offline customers to your Web site.

- ❏ Ask all customers to refer your Web site to friends, families, and co-workers.

- ❏ Publish a monthly e-zine or e-newsletter with links back to your Web site.

- ❏ Join and participate in Usenet newsgroups and online forums; readily display your URL in messages you post.

- ❏ Ask visitors to bookmark your Web site when they arrive and before they exit with a "bookmark reminder" pop-up window.

- ❏ Join professional, business, and industry associations and have your URL listed in online and offline association directories.

- ❏ Enter and strive to win online and offline customer service, business, and Web site excellence awards.

- ❏ Never stop seeking free publicity for your Web site by creating news and spreading the word with press releases and media kits.

- ❏ Use an e-mail signature that includes your URL in all outgoing messages and ask employees to do the same.

- ❏ Add a "tell a friend" tag onto content and information in your Web site and encourage visitors to share the information.

- ❏ Use offline direct-marketing techniques including mail, telemarketing, and personal visits to promote your Web site.

- ❏ Use online and offline classified advertisements to promote your URL.

- ❏ Include your URL in all offline business communications and printed promotional materials such as business cards, sales presentations, receipts, and product brochures.

- ❏ Host online contests and get listed on contest directories with links back to your site.

- ❏ Use free and paid banner advertisements to increase click-through traffic.

- ❏ Purchase keyword targeted advertising at the major search engines.

- ❏ Get your products and services listed in cybermalls, storefronts, and auction sites with links back to your site.

- ❏ Use pop-up windows to ask visitors to sign up for alerts and reminder services related to your site and the products and services you sell.

- ❏ Create coupons and girt certificates and get listed in online coupon sites.

- ❏ Build your own in-house opt-in list and send out valuable offers. Ask recipients to share with others.

- ❏ Rent opt-in lists and send out valuable offers on a regular basis.

- ❏ Give away free stuff and get listed in online "free stuff directories."

- ❏ Promote your URL in all online and offline marketing activities.

Kim, Amy Jo. *Community Building on the Web: Secret Strategies for Successful Online Communities*. Berkeley, CA: Peachpit Press, 2000.

Krug, Steve and Roger Black. *Don't Make Me Think: A Common Sense Approach to Web Usability*. Indianapolis, IN: Que Publishing, 2000.

Macpherson, Kim. *Permission-Based E-Mail Marketing that Works*. Chicago, IL: Dearborn Trade Publishing, 2001.

McGovern, Gerry and Rob Norton. *Content Critical: Gaining Competitive Advantage Through High-Quality Web Content*. Upper Saddle River, NJ: Prentice Hall Press, 2001.

Nielsen, Jakob and Marie Tahir. *Homepage Usability: 50 Websites Deconstructed*. New York: New Riders Publishing, 2001.

Usborne, Nick. *Net Words: Creating High-Impact Online Copy*. New York: McGraw-Hill, 2001.

Wilson, Ralph. *Planning Your Internet Marketing Strategy: A Doctor Ebiz Guide*. New York: John Wiley & Sons, 2001.

Zeff, Robin Lee and Brad Aronson. *Advertising on the Internet*. New York: John Wiley & Sons, 1999.

TRADE SHOW AND SEMINAR
Marketing Tips for Your Business

If opportunity doesn't knock, build a door.

—Milton Berle

WHY TRADE SHOWS?

$

Trade shows are a great way to showcase your specific expertise as well as the main benefits of your products or services to a large and captive audience at one time and in one place. Few other marketing activities afford this type of opportunity to make personal contact with numerous qualified prospects and existing customers over such a short period of time and in a relatively cost effective manner. Not convinced with the merits of trade show marketing? Perhaps these additional reasons you should include trade show exhibiting in your marketing activities will help you see the light.

Sell Products or Services

Over the course of a single day event, to a few weeks depending on the show, you can come into contact with hundreds if not thousands of qualified prospects, thus having hundreds if not thousands of opportunities to persuade and sell your products or services to them. Imagine how long it would take to see that same number of prospects by way of traditional one-to-one personal sales visits?

Collect Sales Leads

Trade shows are one of the best marketing methods to generate well-qualified sales leads. In fact, depending on how you generate and qualify leads at the show it is possible to collect thousands of leads at one single event, easily enough to last a small business a year's worth of follow-up and marketing.

Introduce Products or Services

Trade shows are a great forum to introduce new or improved products and services to a wide and qualified audience in one shot, especially at the more specialized industry shows and exhibits. Trade shows allow you to substantially drive down marketing costs by reaching a large target audience in one place and at one time as opposed to setting multiple individual presentations with each prospect to introduce your new products and services.

Build a Database

You can take advantage of the many opportunities to make new and valuable business and consumer prospect contacts to quickly build a database that is specialized and unique to your business, or update your current database with new names. I know of a travel agency that specializes in business travel exclusively and that exhibited at one trade show and managed to collect in excess of 5,000 names for their database, which they use for direct-marketing purposes. At the time of writing this book that single list had already generate more than $400,000 worth of new business for the agency.

Conduct Research

Use trade shows to conduct and collect valuable data and information about the competition, the industry, customers, and your business, products, and services. Trade shows are a great forum for conducting research, as once again you have the potential to come into contact with so many people in one location, making this a very cost effective research technique. And even more important the results of your research can often be far superior and more valuable than traditional research results. The reason for this is people who attend specific trade shows have an enhanced interest in the theme, products, and services featured at the show, making their responses to research questions extremely relevant and therefore valuable from a marketing perspective.

Reach the Media

Trade shows are almost always covered by one or more media outlets, giving you the opportunity to develop a plan to gain free media exposure for your business, products, and services. Free publicity can be worth hundreds if not thousands in terms of advertising dollars spent on similar exposure in other media such as print publications, radio, and TV.

Showcase Your Expertise

Showcase your expertise in the industry to hundreds if not thousands of people in a very short period of time. Do this via your booth exhibit and displays, and by way of live demonstrations, workshops, and seminars all taking place at the show and to what can best be described as a warm and interested audience.

Build Brand Awareness

Through trade shows you can come into contact with many current customers and new prospects and use this opportunity to help build a brand name image and awareness for your business. Additionally, you can use your promotional activities at trade shows to position your business, products, and services with your industry and in your customers' and prospects' minds.

Support Your Business Team

Use trade shows to support your field reps, agents, and vendors by generating leads for them, holding training and education workshops, or introducing and demonstrating new or improved products and services you plan on making available to them in the near future.

Recruit New Business Team Members

Trade shows are a wonderful way to find new suppliers, vendors, and employees. And many corporations use exhibition opportunities to recruit new people and headhunt for true professionals who, once brought on board, can help their businesses grow tremendously.

WEB RESOURCE

⚲ www.tsea.org: Trade Show Exhibitors Association, online news and information about marketing products and services at trade shows and special events.

FINDING TRADE SHOWS
$ ⚒

Once you have made the decision that exhibiting at trade shows and other types of special marketing events will become part of your overall marketing strategy, the next step is to locate shows that may be suitable candidates and meet your marketing and exhibiting objectives. And when you consider that there are more then 10,000 trade shows hosted annually in North America alone, this task could best be described as overwhelming if it weren't for the Internet. Fortunately thanks to the advent of the Internet, finding trade shows is a relatively easy and painless task, especially when compared to ten years ago when a great amount of time would have to be spent pouring through print trade show directories or calling various associations and agencies to find out about trade show listings in greater detail. However, now you can click through hundreds of online trade show listings in no time and gain valuable insights into each show and the target audience. For those who are technically challenged or lack access to the Internet the old methods of finding trade show listings include your local chamber of commerce, business and industry specific associations, and government agencies like the U.S. Small Business Administration.

WEB RESOURCE

⚲ www.tradeshows.com: Online directory listing trade show events indexed by location.

NEVER PROTECT YOUR BOOTH
$ ⚒

Make your exhibit and booth as open and inviting as possible to trade show attendees. Don't block the entrance or stand out front with your arms crossed like a security guard intimidating everyone who passes by. Instead move displays and tables back and to the sides of your booth space and greet prospects passing by in the aisle by using the circle approach and engage prospects from the side or from slightly behind. Far too many exhibitors, especially businesspeople who are new to trade show marketing, try to arrange their booths and product displays like a retail store or office and restrict the flow of people through like a funnel effect. This in turn makes people very uncomfortable. The idea is to draw prospects into your booth by displaying something that interests them, is beneficial to them,

or that will solve a problem for them. This can be done with creative and engaging displays, pictures, graphics, or live product and service demonstrations. The more inviting you make your booth the more truly qualified prospects will want to enter and learn more about your products and service.

WILL CREDIT PRE-APPROVAL HELP?
$$ ☏

Few people who attend consumer trade shows featuring high-end merchandise on exhibit can actually afford to pay in cash for what is being sold. However, many can easily qualify for credit or financing to make these same purchases. This begs the question, will having on-site financing and pre-approval credit applications help you to attract more prospects and close more sales? Chances are the answer will be yes for businesses that sell products with a retail value of more than $5,000. By providing financing options or pre-approved credit checks you can sell on more of an emotional impulse level as opposed to a logical level. Not many people need an expensive hot tub, but almost everyone would like to have one set up on the back patio deck. Therefore by having on-site credit and financing options you can appeal to those people who do not have the money to purchase the hot tub but do have the good credit that will enable them to purchase the hot tub. Yes large ticket items can be an emotional or impulse purchase; if they were not, the automobile industry would likely have crumbled decades ago. Consult with your banker to find out if they would be willing to have a loan officer in your booth accepting credit applications and offering immediate or fast approvals where applicable. If not the bank there are also many smaller financing and leasing companies that would take up the cause, but be careful because these businesses generally charge two or three times the interest that banks do and this can scare off a few would be customers.

AVOID TIME-CONSUMING GIMMICKS
$ ⚒

Contests and special promotions such as the time-tested old favorite "Trade Show Special Discount" are great ways to lure people into your booth and promote your business at trade shows and other special marketing events. But these same gimmicks are only productive when they are self explanatory; if you or staff have to take time out to explain contest details or how your special promotion works, then simply don't bother with the promotion or create a new and less involved special promotion or contest. The time, energy, and money you spend on exhibiting is not to promote a contest, it is the result of the contest that will meet your marketing objective; generally in the case of contests this means collecting leads via entry forms to follow up with after the show. The main objective of trade show marketing should always be to sell and if you are taking time to explain contest details or other promotions to prospects then you are in effect reducing the amount of time you have to sell, to make contact with, and qualify other prospects. Keep your promotions clear, simple, and easy to understand.

GET INVITATIONS OUT TO THE PRESS
$$ ✎

Sing your praises by creating a dynamic invitation outlining the special features and benefits about your products or services along with exhibition details and send the invitation out to media outlets two to three weeks prior to the next trade show where you exhibit. Let media know in advance the why, when, where, who, and how. Be sure to include that you are available for interviews and product or service demonstrations. Newspapers, radio, and television need news to relay to their audience, that's their business. So get media savvy and make it easy for them to get news by stamping your booth number across the top of the invitation and inviting them to the trade show or event where you will be exhibiting. Who knows, a little free publicity just might give you the competitive advantage and audience awareness that you've been looking for, turning your next trade show into an unequaled success. A few good reasons to invite the media to your booth would include

- new product or service launches.
- new technologies and their applications.

- improved products or services.
- specialized demonstrations or information seminars.
- celebrity or expert guest appearances in your booth.
- milestones such as number of years in business or number of products sold or accounts services.
- publicity stunts at the show such as record setting, highly specialized contests, or activities.
- trade-in events such as bring your old camping tent to the show and we'll give you $50 for it toward the purchase or a new one, refurbish your old one for free, and donate it to the Girl Scouts.

WEB RESOURCE

✐ www.newslink.org: Free online media directory service including print and broadcast media outlets and companies categorized by state.

USE A PRESS RELEASE AS A MARKETING TOOL
$ ✎

A few weeks prior to your next trade show, create a press release and send it to media outlets that are in the geographic area of the exhibition and to media outlets that have an interest in the type of trade show where you are exhibiting. Remember this is still a press release and the fact that it relates to a trade show does not change the critical makeup and format of the release. So you will still want to follow accepted press release format and structure guidelines and strive to make your release newsworthy and not just a promotional advertisement for your business. Also be sure to print extra copies of your release to hand out to media members who might visit your booth during the event, and also so you can drop off one each day of the show to the on-site media center if one is available. As a general rule members of the local media always cover trade shows in their geographic region. So it's best to be prepared and have a press release ready to go at all times so you can take advantage of free publicity opportunities as they might arise on the spur of the moment during the show.

WEB RESOURCE

⚲ www.newslink.org: Free online media directory service including print and broadcast media outlets and companies categorized by state.

BRING A PRESS KIT TO THE SHOW
$$ ⚒

In addition to sending out media invitations and a press release to media outlets and key media personnel also make sure to create a complete press kit about your business, products, and services. Include all the relevant details such as a company overview, product or service highlight sheets, bios for the key players, and client testimonials and success stories. Keep a supply of the press kits handy at your booth for visiting members of the media who drop by and make sure to leave a press kit at the on-site media center every day of the show. It's important to drop off a press release or press kit to the media center every day because media members change throughout the course of the show. And while your press kit and business might not be news to one journalist or outlet, it could very well be headline-making news to another.

What to Include in Your Press Kit

Here are the basic elements that most media kits include. Of course you can add or delete items as required to meet your specific needs and marketing and public relations objectives.

SUMMARY SHEET

A summary sheet is much like a table of contents, it allows the readers at a glance to quickly decipher what is in your press kit and what may be of interest to them. The summary sheet should also include your complete contact information at the bottom including your booth number and location, and it's best to print your summary sheet on company letterhead.

PRESS RELEASE

A current and up-to-date press release written with the current trade show you are exhibiting at in mind. Your release could include news about your product and service and how it solves a problem for the guests in attendance at the show or other worthwhile and beneficial type news. But remember "news" is the key word, keep your press release reading like news and not an advertisement.

REVIEW SHEET(S)

Generally a one-page sheet that lists the compelling reasons that a reader should give you media coverage. One paragraph can be devoted to describing the product or service. A second paragraph can be devoted to the benefits that result for the product or service. And a third paragraph can be used to describe how the product or service can be used to solve a problem and its competitive advantages. As with all the sheets contained within the media kit, the review sheet should be printed on company letterhead, which includes key contact information and once again your booth number.

FACT SHEET

A fact sheet, which briefly describes the history of your company and the vision for the future, can be included. You can use this sheet to also describe any awards your company has won and to point readers to a company Web site if you have one. If you are going to include a fact sheet in your media kit then make sure you print your company mission statement on this sheet as it will instantly provide readers with a clear understanding of what you do, how you do it, and what people get because of it.

BIO SHEET

A bio sheet is a list of the key people within your organization—their titles, their education, their specialties, their awards, what they do, and how they can be contacted. Often it is also best to list personal information about these people and their families as this can appeal to readers on an emotional level.

TESTIMONIALS

You can include testimonials that you have received from clients. However, make sure that if you include testimonials that they are complete in terms of the person who wrote it, their company and title, how they can be contacted, and what solutions your products and services provided them and how they benefited as a result. Know that if you include testimonials that there is a better than average chance that the reader will contact this person to back up or support your and their claims.

VISUALS

Visuals can include relevant photographs, condensed charts, maps, graphs, or illustrations. Remember a picture really is worth a thousand words, so if you can include a picture that leaves no doubt as to what your product or service is and how people benefit by using it, then make sure to include one.

KEEP YOUR EXHIBIT SIMPLE
$$$+ ✎ ☎

The job of a trade show exhibit and displays is to attract the attention of passersby and to project the appropriate image of your company. At a glance a person should be able to instantly know what your company does or sells. As a rule of thumb, the exhibit does not do the selling; you do through interaction with the prospect. Think of your exhibit booth as the backdrop for personal contact you make with prospects. Much like a movie scene wherein character interaction is the story, and not the background props or action. Your exhibit should not display all the products and services your company sells, or the benefits associated with these products and services. This is the information you use during personal contact with prospects or information you put into brochures and promotional handouts. Use the exhibit background to get noticed, impress people, and provide a quick glimpse of what you offer. The rest of the details they can get directly from you. And when in doubt follow the proven AIDA advertising formula.

A Grab the *attention* of passing prospects
I Pique their *interest* in your products or services
D Instantly create *desire* for what you sell
A Make them take *action* and inquire for more information or buy

SHOW GUIDE SUCCESS
$$+ ✎

Just about every consumer or business-to-business trade show distributes a printed show guide to the guests as they enter the event. In the show guides are floor maps indicating what companies are exhibiting, where their booths are located on the floor, and additional information such as seminar and workshop schedules and special demonstration events. The show guides are sometimes printed by the show manager, but more often by a separate publisher and done so for a profit by selling advertising space within the guide to companies that will be exhibiting at the event. These advertisements can be expensive but are extremely valuable in terms of grabbing the attention of people who attend the show and people who read the guide after the show has taken place. If you purchase an advertisement in the show guide make sure that you really get extra bang for your buck by striking a deal with the publisher of the guide. Ask that a specific product or service that you sell be featured in the guide in news article format and even offer to write the article. The article should sound and read not so much like an advertisement, but more like a feature news article with a gentle promo message about your business, booth number, and special trade show offers buried within. Bargain for this by telling the publisher that you will purchase a display advertisement space in the guide in exchange for also having your news article featured in the show guide, in effect giving you double the advertising exposure for one price. You will find that many publishers are open to this tactic simply because it serves two purposes; they sell advertising, which is their main objective, and they secure interesting and informative content related to the event that can be included in the show guide for free and without having to do the leg work associated with researching and writing the article.

CALCULATE YOUR AUDIENCE SIZE
$ ✎

What is the size of your potential audience? According to Exhibit Surveys, Inc., a leading trade show surveying firm, there is an industry standard formula for calculating your potential audience size at expositions and events.

Step 1

Determine the total number of attendees. Show management can provide you with attendance figures, which are usually based on an average of past attendance figures. However, be sure to ask if the attendance figures are based on gross or net numbers. Net attendance figures means the total number of people who attended the show less exhibitors, press, and service providers.

Step 2

Calculate the show's AIF (Audience Interest Factor). Once again, show management may be able to provide this number; if not, the all-industries average is 44 percent. AIF all-industry percentage average is based on interested attendees who visit two out of every ten exhibits.

Step. 3

Calculate the size of your potential audience by multiplying the AIF number by the percentage of attendees who indicate a high interest in your product or service. If you do not have these figures you can use the all-industries average, which is 16 percent.

Step 4.

By using the calculations illustrated above, you can now determine your potential audience size. For example, say there is a net audience attendance of 10,000. Multiply that by the AIF figure; in this case we'll use the all-industry average of 44 percent. 10,000 times .44 percent equals 4,400. Lastly multiply this number by the high interest figure. Once again we'll use the all-industries average of 16 percent. 4,400 times .16 percent equals 704 people, your potential show audience size. Or if you only use all-industries averages to calculate your potential audience size the fast formula is to multiply the show's net audience by 7 percent.

Web Resource

🖱 www.exhibitsurveys.com: A full service exposition research and marketing intelligence firm.

RANK YOUR LEADS

$ ✎

Hardly anyone has the ability to instantly recall critical information about people that they have come into contact with and had a conversation with. The broad topics and subjects yes, but never the small and most important details. Therefore never take chances trying to remember which prospects were great leads and which were fair at best. Instead create a lead ranking system prior to the event so that when the smoke clears and you are left with a pile of sales leads to follow up on you'll be able to instantly identify the hottest prospects. Contact them immediately after the show, while working your way down to the not-so-hot leads in due time. Leads can be ranked in various ways, from using the alphabet system such as A, B, C to numbering the leads on a sliding scale with "1" being the hottest and "4" being the poorest. The criteria you use to rank your leads will be a direct result of the qualifying questions you ask, and the responses your prospects give. The more qualified the prospect is, then the higher ranked the lead becomes. Additionally if you do not want your prospect to see you ranking their lead, then develop a ranking system based on how the leads are gathered and stored at the show. Red-hot leads might get placed in a red file folder, while cold leads might get placed in a blue file folder, and so on. In addition to ranking your leads also make sure that you include comments as to why they are ranked as they are, and what the prospect's biggest interests are. You can never really put enough information on a lead sheet, especially for the red-hot leads. Keep in mind when you create your lead form to cover key qualifying information.

Needs

Does the prospect need what you are selling?

Decision Maker

Is the prospect the person or one of the people who makes the final buying decisions? And if not who is?

Time Frame

When is the prospect seeking to buy and take delivery?

Obstacles

Identify obstacles that could stand in the way of completing a sale such as does the prospect live or work in the geographical area that your business services?

FINANCIAL

Can the prospect afford what you are selling, and if so has the budget been determined? If the prospect does not have the money to pay, can she qualify for credit, pay with a credit card, or have access to other money sources?

COMPETITION

Ask who else the prospect has spoken to in terms of your competition that might be exhibiting at the event, and competition that is not exhibiting at the event. This is not so much qualifying importance as it is good information to know so that you can better position your future offer in terms of a competitor's offer.

SAMPLE LEAD FORM

Below is an example of a simple lead form that you can use to collect names, qualify, and rank prospects. For example purposes the lead form chosen would be suitable for a window replacement company. You can use this example to create your own lead form that would be relevant to your business, products, and services.

Sample Lead Form

Prospect Information

Name: _____

Occupation: _____

Address: _____

City: _____ State: _____ Zip code: _____

Telephone: _____ Fax: _____ E-mail address: _____

What is wrong with your current windows?	❏ Steaming	❏ Poor condition	❏ Not energy efficient
How old are your current windows?	❏ Less than 10 years	❏ 10–20 years	❏ 20+ years
Do your windows need replacement?	❏ Yes	❏ No	
What type of windows do you currently have?	❏ Wood	❏ Aluminum	❏ Vinyl ❏ Other
Do you own the home where the windows are to be replaced?	❏ Yes	❏ No	
When do you want to have the windows replaced?	❏ 1–3 months	❏ 3–6 months	❏ 6–12 months ❏ 12+ months
Have you established a budget for your window replacement project?	❏ Yes	❏ No	

Do you want one of our qualified window replacement experts to give you a no-obligation free quote to replace your window? ❏ Yes   ❏ No

Have you received or will you be getting other quotes to replace your windows?   ❏ Yes   ❏ No

…and if so from which window replacement company or contractor: _____

Can we include you on our mailing list and send you valuable information periodically?   ❏ Yes   ❏ No

By   ❏ Mail   ❏ Fax   ❏ E-mail

Rank   ❏ Hot   ❏ Warm   ❏ Cold

Additional Comments: _____

Lead taken by: _____ Date: ____/____/____

ANSWER THE OBVIOUS QUESTIONS
$ ✎

The trade show pace can be fast and furious. Don't waste your valuable selling time answering obvious questions about your business, products, or services. Instead, in the limited time that you have with prospects, you want to listen, question, and qualify, generate a lead or close, and build mutual confidence and trust. For instance if you were in the classic car restoration business a display model of a 1957 Chevy that was in original but poor condition on one side and completely restored and beautiful condition on the opposite side would speak volumes in terms of exactly what it is that your business does. Now combine that display with some colorful signs and graphics and this would go even further to tell people exactly what your business does, and better it clearly demonstrates how customers benefit from doing business with your company: in this example having their classic car professionally restored to look and perform like new again. The objective is to generate new business, not spend hours explaining what you do. By carefully designing your in-booth displays and signage to illustrate this you can save time by not having to answer obvious questions and have more time to aggressively promote and sell your goods and services.

PREPROMOTE WITH DIRECT MAIL
$$+ ✎

Don't just sit back and hope that your current customers, hot prospects, and target audience will visit the trade show and find your booth in a sea of other exhibitor booths. Instead be proactive in your approach to marketing and promote your participation in all trade shows and other special events your business participates in. One way to pre-promote your exhibit at a trade show is to develop a direct-mail package and send it to existing clients and to hot prospects giving them all the details about the forthcoming show and your involvement. Get creative and provide an incentive to lure these people to the show, such as "present this letter at the booth for your mystery gift," or for a discount. To reach people through direct mail you can use your own in-house mailing list, buy from list brokers, or ask show management to provide the previous year's attendee list. Studies have shown that the vast majority of people who attend trade shows will return to the same show the following year and many do so with the purpose of buying in mind. So the attendee list can be very valuable in terms of direct-mail marketing. The direct-mail objective is simple; provide as much incentive as you can to get your new prospects out of their offices or homes and to the show and to your booth at the show and make existing customers feel obligated to visit your booth at the show. Addition-ally make sure to address your mailings to a person, preferably a decision maker and always include your booth number in your mailings, preferably on a few pages in bold print.

PREPROMOTE WITH PRINT ADVERTISING
$$+ ✎

Print advertisements are another great way to pre-promote your exhibit, products, or services at trade shows. If you're exhibiting at business-to-business events stick with trade publications, magazines, and journals that are related to the industry or theme of the show simply because in all likelihood your target audience who will be attending the show reads those publications. Often publishers of these magazines and journals are aware of the shows that are industry related and will pass along advertising specials and discounts to companies that will be exhibiting and wish to advertise in their publication. For consumer shows display ads in newspapers promoting your booth at the show are your best bet, providing the newspaper is distributed in the same geographic area where the show will be hosted. Remember to also ask show management and your suppliers about any cooperative advertisement programs they might have in place, as a method to reduce ad costs by sharing the expense. Also check with the ad sales reps for publications that you are considering advertising in, as many will have special sections and features about forthcoming trade shows, especially those publications that co-sponsor the event. Once again, keep your print advertisements consistent with your overall marketing message and directly related to your objective at the show—sales, display, seminars, demonstrations, new product introductions, or whatever your objective might be.

PREPROMOTE WITH TELEMARKETING
$$ ✎ ☎

Telemarketing still remains one of the best ways to reach prospects and clients to personally invite them to forthcoming trade shows that you will be exhibiting at simply because you can reach a large number of people in a very short period of time for a relatively low cost. However, before undertaking any telemarketing program make sure to first define what your message will be and how you will deliver that message. The best way to accomplish that is to create a script to follow before you start dialing. Start by listing a few keys reasons you will be exhibiting and why prospects and clients should visit your booth. Key to success is creating excitement; don't expect that clients and prospects will be excited about attending unless you give them a reason to feel excited about attending the show and visiting your booth. These reasons could be a discount; special promotion; introduction of a new product or service, or a live demonstration, workshop, or seminar that will benefit them personally or their business. Appeal to consumer prospects on an emotional basis, meaning that there will be a benefit for them to come to your booth that is tied in with one or more emotions. Appeal to logic for business prospects; make it clear that by attending the show and visiting your booth they will benefit by making money, saving money, or increasing productivity in their businesses. Use your own staff or employ a telemarketing service to call existing clients and new prospects to inform them about your exhibition schedule. Once again, create an incentive that will seduce clients and prospects to visit your booth.

PREPROMOTE WITH PERSONAL APPOINTMENTS
$$ ✎

Go one step further than telemarketing by setting appointments and meetings with hot prospects in the pipeline and let them know about your exhibit at forthcoming trade shows. Personally invite them to the show and create an incentive to motivate them to attend. The incentive could be free admission tickets or a special promotional item relevant to your business or theirs. Ideally the incentive will be one that will help close indecisive prospects, and motivate current customers to take advantage and buy more or more frequently. Trade shows are a great closing environment because the lively environment builds excitement and if you use the right incentive you can also create a sense of buying urgency at the same time right at the booth—your prospect will have to take advantage of the special offer at the show or miss the opportunity to do so entirely. Therefore getting a few prospects who you want to close out to the show is important, especially if the competition that you're batting against is not going to be exhibiting. However, if the competition is going to be present be careful about which prospects you invite because you do not want inadvertently to send your hot prospects to competitors.

PREPROMOTE ONLINE
$$ ✎

Use your Web site to let existing customers, new prospects, and all visitors to your site know about the exhibitions that you will be participating in annually by creating an exhibition calendar Web page. Include all the relevant details about each show or event and more important, create a valid reason for people to attend each show and stop by your booth. The reason could be a powerful show discount special; a free gift related to your products, services, or industry; product demonstrations; or information that is specific to the client and that will benefit the client or business and help fulfill a need or solve a problem. Additionally, if show management has Web sites promoting each of the events, make sure that you get listed on each one. Always include a link from your listing on the show manager's site or your trade show advertisement back to your Web site so that you can expand on your message and take inquiries from new prospects. Also don't be afraid to rent opt-in lists that are compiled from people who meet your target audience and marketing objectives. Though of critical importance is the fact that the electronic list you rent must be "opt in"—the people on the list have subscribed or asked to receive information, offers, and special announcements relative to your industry and products or services you sell. If it is not opt in then the message you send will be considered spam, which is illegal. High quality and targeted lists can be rented for about two to ten cents a name. However, there are two important things to consider. First, test the list by sending out your message to only a small number of people on the list. This can be accomplished by renting only part of the total list as a tester. Brokers and managers are use to this type of request. Testing the list will enable you to gauge the effectiveness of it prior to committing to renting the entire list. Secondly, only lists composed of people who live close to where the trade show will be held are of any value to you; businesspeople may travel far and wide to visit trade and industry shows, but few consumers will.

PREPROMOTE THROUGH PREREGISTRATION PACKS
$$ ✎

Often trade show managers will mail preregistration forms to companies and individuals who they believe will be attending the show. This is done for two reasons. First, it ensures the highest attendance rate possible. And second, it saves these individuals time by not having to line up at the ticket booth on show day. The preregistration forms are generally sent out as a complete package highlighting new exhibitors, special in-show events, and new product features. And more important to you there are also advertising opportunities within these preregistration packs that are available to businesses that are confirmed exhibitors. These advertising opportunities come in many forms including loose leaf promotional inserts in the package, event sponsorship recognition, and coupons and other special offers to attract attendees. What makes this an effective preshow advertising opportunity is the fact that a high percentage of the individuals and companies that receive the preregistration package attend the show because they have attended in years previous—which in turns gives you exposure to people who are for the most part sure to attend and generally do so because

they are in the market to buy, find new suppliers, or make new business contacts.

PROFIT FROM NONPARTICIPATION
$ ✎

Even cash-strapped small-business owners who can't afford to rent booth space can still market to trade show and special event audiences, all it takes is a little bit of creativity. Here are a few ways to promote your business, products, and services directly to trade show and special event audiences without actually participating or exhibiting at the events.

Utilize Fliers

Print low-cost promotional fliers detailing your business, products, or services and a special offer and tuck the fliers under windshield wipers of parked cars in close proximity to the event location. In all likelihood people attending the event will own the majority of cars that are parked in the general area where the event is taking place. Likewise, pay the price of admission to get into the event and then distribute fliers promoting your business to people in the food court, lounges, and even on the exhibition floor where the event is taking place. However, watch out for security because they'll throw you out if you get caught. Show managers don't like this, but lots of people do it and profit because of it and so can you.

Get In and Network

If it's a business-to-business trade show or industry event once again pay the price of admission to get in and network with the attendees for new business and to make new and valuable contacts. Be sure to laminate your business card and clip it to your jacket or hang it around your neck. This is a good strategy to blend in with the crowd and most will think that you are an exhibitor.

Buy Sales Leads

And my favorite one that I have personally practiced many times is to buy leads. Contact noncompeting businesses that you know exhibited at the event and that collected leads and offer to pay them for copies of their leads. Or better, see if you can barter with your own goods or services in exchange for the leads. Seldom did I find any resistance to this technique; in fact rarely did I pay for the leads or the cost to copy them as most businesses were happy to help out and I never forgot them when a sale resulted from one of the leads they supplied.

IN-SHOW EVENT SPONSORSHIP
$$+ ↖

Another good way to get your business name boldly out in front of the trade show audience and exhibitors alike is to sponsor a special event that takes place within the trade show. These in-show events range from seminars to grand opening and closing ceremonies and dinners, to preshow media receptions, and many more. Depending on the size of the trade show and number of expected guests and media coverage, event sponsorship can be costly but it can also go a long way to help build your image at the show and give you increased exposure to a broader audience. Check with show management at least six months prior to the show to see what event sponsorship opportunities may be available. Or, get creative and develop your own event that you can sponsor and pitch the idea to show management. Either way in-show event sponsorship can be an extremely effective marketing tool to promote your participation in the show and your exhibit booth on the floor.

CAPITALIZE ON NEW PRODUCT DISPLAYS
$$ ↖

Many trade show managers construct what are known as new products displays, and as the name suggests these unstaffed displays and exhibits are used to promote new products that are being featured or introduced at the show. There are many benefits to having your product featured and included in the new product display, even though there is a cost to do so. These benefits include increased exposure, as the new product displays are always located in highly visible and high-traffic areas such as by the front entrance, beside the food court, or around the main seminar or demonstration stage. Another benefit is that new product displays are also a favorite stop for members of the media, as this enables them to check out the latest and greatest products easily in one location without having to go hunting through the show floor in search of what is new and exciting. Of course this increased media attention can lead to the potential for increased media exposure should your new product be featured. Contact show management to inquire about new product displays at least six months in advance as these displays are usually limited in size and space often rents quickly because of the many marketing benefits associated with the displays.

IN-SHOW SEMINARS CREATE A CAPTIVE AUDIENCE
$$+ ↖

In a group format or in a one-on-one individual basis, conducting seminars at the show is also an excellent marketing tool that you can capitalize on to promote your products and services. You can rent and curtain off a second booth next to your main display and selling booth to hold the seminars. Or alternately you can conduct the seminars off site but close to the venue, give out personal invitations to the hottest prospects who drop by your booth, and usher them away to your VIP seminar location. Seminars are best used to shorten the sales cycle by building excitement and creating urgency that motivates prospects to buy on the spot before they leave the show. Likewise you can host and conduct open seminar series wherein any person at the trade show can attend for free. In using this method once again the objective is to build excitement about the topic (your product or service) then direct prospects to your booth to close the sale or collect information and generate leads directly after the seminar.

CREATE CLEVER WAYS TO PROMOTE YOUR BOOTH
$$ ↖

In addition to the time-tested and proven trade show promotional ideas also make sure to get a little creative and develop unique ways to promote your booth so that you can attract and appeal to a broader audience. A few of the more creative promotional ideas that I have heard about or have come across include sending mimes or actors dressed up in a costume related to a business out onto the show floor to mill among the audience and hand out promotional giveaways emblazoned with business names, logos, and a sales message. One company sent prospects a single high-quality running shoe along with a note that stated they would get the matching shoe if they came to the booth and participated in simple questionnaire. And yet another company hired a team of acrobats to wander the aisles performing and handing out fliers that promoted the company and their exhibit booth. By their very nature trade shows are a form of show business so don't be afraid to create a unique way to promote your booth. But a word to the wise: Before you decide upon any type of promotion make sure that you first run the idea past the show managers to secure their approval before you invest too much time and money into the promotion. You don't want to find out after the fact that there is a rule or regulation that prohibits you from that particular or certain types of promotion during the show.

PROMOTE WITH AD SPECIALTIES AT THE BOOTH
$$ ✎

Advertising specialties such as imprinted key chains, T-shirts, hats and tote bags emblazoned with your company name, logo, and promotional message have always been a popular giveaway at trade shows. However, many of these items have little if any impact on prospects unless they have been carefully planned and selected to be memorable, unique, and to specifically meet your marketing objectives at the show. First, the promotional giveaway should be related to your business and what you sell, be it a product or service. One of the better advertising specialties that I have come across recently at a trade show was a ballpoint pen given out by a canoe manufacturing firm. However, this was no ordinary ballpoint pen, it looked exactly like a miniature wooden

canoe paddle; the paddle portion removed like a cap to reveal the pen. Imprinted on the pen was the canoe manufacturer's business name, Web site address, and a toll-free telephone number. Second, never randomly give out these promotional items, instead save them for your best prospects and personally give them to them so that they will have the best impact.

WEB RESOURCE

✐ www.promomart.com: Billed as the world's largest online source for promotional and advertising specialty products.

PROFIT FROM PAPER
$ ✎

Instead of handing out high-gloss color brochures and product catalogs to every person who enters your booth, hang on to them and use them as a way to generate and collect qualified leads. Tell people that you will mail them a complete information package or even better set an appointment right in the booth to deliver the marketing materials to their office, business, or home in person after the show. The sad fact about brochures and trade shows is that most fliers and brochures that get freely distributed at trade shows end up in the garbage. This is because they initially made their way into the hands of people who had no interest in the information in the first place, or who had no intention of ever buying what was being sold. It's easy to spot these people; they are the ones tromping through the show carrying numerous plastic bags full of printed literature courtesy of every booth they have passed along the way. By mailing, faxing, e-mailing, or personally delivering brochures and promotional information, you will be able to collect full names and addresses to enter into your database and generate leads. Chances are if a person is prepared to hand out their address and wait for the material or meet in person after the show they are a pretty good prospect. Likewise avoid handing out complete product and service price lists as well. Not only can your price list end up in competitors' hands who might decide to use them to undercut you, but visitors can also take them to competitors' booths and use them to negotiate a lower price on what they think may be the same item even though it could be a case of apples and oranges. Either way freely handing out price lists can result in the loss of sales and profits.

HOLD A CONTEST TO GENERATE LEADS
$$+ ⚒ ⚖

Staging a contest at your booth is another way to promote your business and generate sales leads to follow up on after the show. However, the leads generated will not be qualified unless you put some measures in place to do so. These measures should include asking qualifying questions on the entry form that the contestant must answer in order to be eligible to win the prize. Likewise the prize can also be more specific—one that would only interest certain people, consequently qualifying them to a certain degree before they enter the contest. For instance, a window sales and installation contractor might run a contest wherein the winner receives $1,000 off the installation of new windows. Or a security company might give away a free alarm to winners hoping to secure monthly monitoring contracts. In both examples the prize is not complete; $1,000 off window installations still requires a balance payment and winning a free alarm still requires signing a monthly alarm-monitoring contract. And only people in the market for these types of products or service are likely to take the time to enter the contest. Of course it goes without saying that prior to committing to holding a contest make sure that you have checked with legal sources to ensure that the contest meets any and all regulations that might govern such promotional activities in the area where the show is being held.

PROFIT FROM CROSS-PROMOTION
$$ ⚒

Another great way to reach more people at trade shows is to create and engage in cross-promotional activities with other exhibitors. The key to successfully cross-promoting is to identify and peruse good noncompetitive exhibitor matches wherein the cross-promotional activities will enhance and benefit each other's booths and create more selling opportunities. For instance, a company marketing hot tubs could cross-promote with a company that sells patio and deck furniture. Each business could use the other's products for display enhancement purposes in their exhibit booths. On the displays could be a small printed sign stating the business name and booth number of the business that supplied the display item along with some printed handout materials describing the product and how and why to buy. In this basic example the benefit to both exhibitors is clearly obvious. The patio and deck furniture surrounding the hot tub paints a complete and inviting picture for prospects, or enhances the other product and vice versa. Get creative and seek out ways to develop and implement cross-promotional opportunities with other exhibitors as a way to appeal to a broader audience and enhance your exhibit. Do so a few months prior to the show; find out who will be exhibiting by contacting the show manager and asking for an exhibitors' list. Once you have the list spend some time researching the other companies that will be marketing at the show to find a few suitable cross-promotional matches. Once you have identified these matches call the companies and set up appointments to pitch your ideas. Generally you will find other exhibitors very open to creative promotional ideas that ultimately can benefit their businesses and increase selling opportunities.

DEMONSTRATE YOUR WAY TO SUCCESS
$$ ⚒

Exhibit booths alive with activity and product demonstrations draw considerably more prospect interest than static DOA booths do at trade shows. Therefore, carefully consider how you can invent or create a demonstration at your booth to draw large crowds. We have all seen and witnessed the dicer slicer pitchers at trade shows—they draw the largest crowds hands down. Why? Because their product demonstrations clearly show visitors what the result will be, the big benefit to the consumer who buys. In the case of the super slicing machine, the big benefit is perfectly sliced fruits and vegetables in seconds and safely completed with no worries about getting cut by the knife blade. These master exhibitors live by the proven sales method of "why tell it, when you can show it and sell a lot more because of the fact that you show it." As great as in-booth demonstrations are, be picky about who you choose to conduct the demonstrations; he must be a people person who loves to perform in a fast-paced speaking and selling environment.

TIMELY INTRODUCTIONS
$ ⚒

Get to the show and set up early; in fact try to be one of the first exhibits ready to sell so that you can free up introduction time before the show officially opens to the general public. An amazingly high amount of referrals are given out during trade shows, often the atmosphere among exhibitors becomes like a large friendly family or team. And when one member of the team cannot help prospects with what they need or solve their problems they are quick to refer them to someone else at the show who can help them out. Thus the importance of introducing yourself, business, products, or services to as many of the other exhibitors and their staff as possible and as early into the show as you can. Make the rounds armed with business cards and fliers describing your business, what you do, and what you sell. Hand out the cards when introducing yourself and ask for business cards in return. Also don't be shy and let exhibitors know that you are seeking referrals and that you are giving referrals in exchange. Of course also remember that exhibitors are also potential customers, so make sure to develop a special exhibitor discount or incentive and let them know about how they can benefit and save right up front.

PRESHOW STAFF TRAINING
$$+ ⚒ 🐞

You can design and construct the biggest and best exhibit, give away the coolest promotional gifts and

ad specialties, and employ the latest interactive tech demo gadgets. But all of this won't add up to a hill of beans unless your staff is happy to be in the booth and motivated to generate leads, close sales, and meet and exceed show objectives and goals. For these reasons make sure to develop a preshow training program to motivate staff and ensure maximum productivity in the booth. Your staff should know why they and your business are exhibiting at the show and what is expected of each individual. Use role-playing and other interactive exercises to teach staff how to greet prospects, ask qualifying questions, generate leads, and close sales in the booth. Also include staff in setting the objectives and goals of each event; this will help motivate them and get them excited about the process. Likewise each staff member should set a personal goal for the show, one that is separate from business or team objectives and goals. Additionally, carefully read your exhibitor's kit as most show managers offer a pre-show staff training seminar, which is generally focused on lead generation, presentations, and selling. And best of all these training seminars are often included in your booth rental costs and conducted by training experts specially brought in for the event. Remember it is the interaction between staff and prospects that will determine the financial success of the event—your exhibit, contest, displays, and promotional materials are all just props and support mechanisms.

MOTIVATING STAFF IN THE BOOTH
$$ ⚒

Here are a few tricks you can employ to keep staff energized, motivated, and productive in the booth during trade shows.

Unified Message

Prior to the show develop a unified sales pitch and set of qualifying questions for all staff to use so that you promote a consistent and powerful central theme and message that is designed to maximize results. Have staff practice the pitch before the show and master the delivery of the message to guarantee results in the booth.

Incentives

Provide incentives to staff based on group and individual performance. The incentive should not be easily reached, but once reached in terms of desired productivity or set goals related to your show objectives these same incentives should be very generous. Additionally, set daily lead and/or sales goals and provide an incentive in the form of cash, a product, or a gift for staff who reach their daily goals.

Work in Teams

Group staff together in terms of their expertise for scheduled shifts, technical personnel with sales personnel. Each will be far more productive when they are comfortable sharing information that they know and understand. Additionally, have staff work in maximum three- to four-hour shifts with a half-hour off in between. This will help to keep them fresh, focused, and reduce overall stress and fatigue in the booth.

WEB RESOURCE

✍ www.motivationusa.com: Employee motivation products, programs, and awards.

MASTER THE QUICK QUALIFY
$ ✍

Qualifying in the fast-paced trade-show atmosphere is very different than a non-trade show sales atmosphere simply because there are generally many potential prospects to engage and speak with in a very short period of time. Therefore, there is no time for social chitchat, detailed explanations, and a raft of ongoing and probing questions like would be the norm in a non-trade show qualifying and selling environment. When qualifying prospects at trade shows you must take control of the conversation immediately and within moments be able determine if they are potential customers. If so then conduct business according to your objectives at the show; if not you must immediately and politely dismiss them and move on to the next prospect. The best way to get this system down to a science is to develop a series of qualifying questions that are relevant to what you sell and your show objectives. Once you have developed this series of qualifying questions stick to them like

glue. If not you'll soon find yourself giving detailed explanations to people who have no interest in what you do or what you sell, but listen intently because they do not want to appear or simply have nothing else to do. And, while you're talking up a storm a raft of what might be well-qualified prospects will creep on past your booth without a word.

KEY QUALIFYING INFORMATION
$ ✍

As mentioned above in the Master the Quick Qualify tip, time is of the essence in terms of qualifying prospects in the booth. You have to be able to get enough basic information as quickly as possible so that you can determine on the spot if you should present or demonstrate your products or services right away in the booth; complete a lead sheet and contact the prospect after the show; or politely disengage them and move on to the next prospect.

Qualifying in the booth is tougher job then most think, but the following four key qualifying elements will assist you with this process.

1. Qualify Decision Maker

Determine right away if the person you are talking to has the ability to make the buying decision; if not ask who does and if that person is at the show or how she can be contacted after the show. Trade shows are not the place to waste your time talking with people who can't make the buying decision.

2. Qualify Time Line

What is the prospect's buying time line? When does he want to buy this particular product or service? If right away, good; if way down the road you will be better off taking basic information to include him in your mailing list and instead spend your time with someone else who is ready to buy now or in the very near future.

3. Qualify Obstacles

What obstacles come up in the conversation? A common obstacle at trade shows is the fact that many of the people you will speak with will reside outside of the geographic trading area your business services.

Trade shows draw visitors from far and wide so if location matters you must ask where they're from to qualify them as potential prospects. This is only one example, there are other potential obstacles so you must listen closely to what the prospects say, as obstacles may arise in their answers—if you're doing all the talking you will not hear these deal killer obstacles until it's too late and you have spent far too much valuable time with someone who for whatever reason (obstacle) cannot buy what you are selling.

4. Qualify Needs

Finally, is what the prospect is describing in terms of her needs really the same as what you are selling? If not you are wasting both of your time continuing with the conversation. You must be able to let the prospect know that you cannot help her, point her to someone who can if possible, politely disengage her, and move on. The only time that you should try to sell if there is not a need is when the decision to buy could be based on a want and on an emotional level such as is often the case with consumer goods like a hot tub or new furniture.

WAYS TO BEAT BOOTH FATIGUE
$$ ✎

Even the most experienced exhibitors can fall victim to booth fatigue. We have all seen the telltale signs—yawning, leaning against in-booth displays, deep knee bends and back stretching with a grimaced look, and sitting on anything that even remotely resembles a chair including the floor. The main downside to booth fatigue is that it sends the wrong message to potential prospects. You look tired, uninterested, and therefore they will not approach for fear that they may interrupt your nap. Here are a few surefire ways to avoid booth fatigue.

Fuel

A diet of French fries and burgers over a ten-day show will kill you—or at least make you sluggish and nonproductive. Avoid fast food and instead pack nutritional meals from home or from a local market. Likewise skip soda and coffee and drink lots of juices and water. Standing for long periods is incredibly hard work, much harder than most people think it is at first glance and the body requires lots of good fuel to make this possible.

Rest

The most important way to keep from being fatigued in the booth is to make sure you get lots of rest. Skip the "industry parties" and keep in mind that trade shows are not a social function, they are business and you have objectives to meet. Therefore, stay focused and reward yourself on the last night by unwinding at the postshow party.

Comfort

Never wear new shoes, make sure that the ones you wear are comfortable and worn in. Additionally comfort insoles are also a good idea, as well as comfortable two-ply runner's socks, which work wonders and are guaranteed to keep your feet blister free and feeling great all day long.

Schedule

Develop a booth schedule; ideally it will mean a maximum of three hours in the booth with thirty minutes off in between each shift. It is very important to create the schedule and stick to it for the benefit of all staff. This is one of the best ways to beat fatigue and remain fresh, interested, and involved for an entire show.

GREAT SHOWS START WITH GREAT ATTITUDES
$ ✎

If you're scowling, appear to be preoccupied, uninterested, or just don't appear to be enjoying yourself in the booth then expect that prospects will pick up on this immediately and pass your booth without stopping. Or, if they are already in it they'll get out of it like it is on fire. The key to success at every trade show is a great attitude; you must be personally invested and involved in the entire experience from the word go to get the most benefit from it. Know your products and services, as well as the booth and be prepared to help prospects out with stuff beyond things that will personally benefit you. Tell them about other great exhibits, workshops, and displays;

be helpful, friendly, and always professional. Likewise staff must also have a great attitude toward exhibiting and if they don't, banish them from the booth as they will do more harm than good. Great shows truly begin with great attitudes; you must want to be there, and you must want to be meeting and talking with potential customers. And most of all you must truly believe that all the hard work that goes into trade show exhibiting is worthwhile.

AVOID BORING JARGON

$ ⚒

Skip the technical jargon when explaining your products and services to prospects in the booth, mainly because they might not understand the terminology and feel threatened or stupid because of this lack of understanding. Instead stick with plain old English and make everything sound as simple and easy as possible; in fact most speaking experts agree that speaking at about a grade seven or eight level is perhaps the best way to converse with an audience to ensure your message is understood by all. Additionally, using scientific terminology will often lead into long-winded and boring detailed explanations about your products or services and generally serve no purpose other than waste time and limit the number of prospects you can come in to contact with—many of whom may be well-qualified buyers with pockets full of cash to spend. The only exception to the "no boring jargon while in the booth rule" is when a prospect engages you with detailed and technical terms and expects you to talk the same language—then go for it. Otherwise keep it simple and straightforward and remained focused on your objectives and maximizing your trade show results. Time is very limited at the show so make the most out of it.

CREATE EFFECTIVE OPENERS BEFORE THE SHOW

$ ⚒

There are three types of exhibitors: those who stand back in the booth and wait for prospects to approach them, those who approach prospects with irrelevant questions or opening statements, and those who are proactive and approach prospects with opening questions that are prepared before the show to get the desired response of engaging in meaningful conversation and qualifying the prospect's level of interest. Avoid the first type like the plague, you are there to meet the objective you have set and hanging back and hoping qualified prospects are going to engage you first is rarely going to happen. As for the second type, engaging everyone who comes into your booth with ineffective openers and irrelevant questions will only work to rob you of time that you could be spending on and with qualified prospects. Effective openers waste no time getting to the heart of the matter and meeting your objective for being at the show. For instance, if you are selling replacement windows, an effective opening question to engage prospects with would be something along the lines of "How often do your windows steam up in the winter?" This is an open-ended question that is designed to engage the prospect in meaningful conversation as an opener and quickly find out what their true interest in your products might be. The key to creating great openers is to do it before the show and narrow it down to a maximum of four that focus on the benefits of your product or service and that you continually use. In our example the benefit would be quickly revealed after the prospect is qualified as to their interest in new replacement windows.

PREPLAN YOUR PRESENTATION

$ ⚒

Avoid winging off-the-cuff in-booth sales and product and services presentations at all costs; all this will accomplish is to use up valuable time and leave to chance if you are really giving prospects too much or too little information for their ability to make decisions. As a substitute create one or two solid presentations prior to the show and make sure that all booth staff have input into this process as well as using the chosen presentation method. The goal of the presentation should be in direct relevancy to your objective. If you want to sell in the booth then create a presentation that will lead the prospect into making a buying decision; if you want to collect leads, then create a presentation that will secure leads from qualified prospects; and if your objective is demonstration, then combine a great presentation with your demonstration. Key to the presentation will be to focus on what important benefits buyers will receive from purchasing your products or using your service. The people selling chamois at shows have mastered the art of presenting benefits and selling tons of chamois because of it. This works because their presentations are well scripted and rehearsed long before the show and through testing and trial and error they know the repetitious presentations may be boring for the presenter, but they push all the right "hot buttons" in terms of the crowd.

NEVER STOP ASKING FOR THE SALE IN THE BOOTH
$ 🔨

In the fast-paced trade show environment, time is a commodity that you will never have enough of. Therefore it is important to start and never stop asking each prospect for the sale providing that "sales" is your main exhibiting objective. The trial close is a good way to determine early on if your prospect is ready to buy. This closing technique is also often referred to as the echo close because when a prospect asks a question that clearly sends a buying signal on their behalf you return the prospect's question in the form of a confirming question that requires a decision. For instance a prospect might ask "If I buy a hot tub could I have it delivered and installed within two weeks?" To which the salesperson in the booth should reply or echo by asking, "If I can arrange to have the hot tub delivered and installed within two weeks are you prepared to go ahead and buy it?" In doing so the prospect is placed in a position of having to make a decision or raise an objection. Obviously if the answer is yes the salesperson would get started on writing the order without hesitation. If objections are raised then you know exactly where you stand and what hurdles are left to overcome. The problem with the echo or trial close is that many salespeople fail to recognize when the prospect is sending a buying signal and therefore miss the opportunity to test the trial close. But by getting in

the habit of asking every prospect for the sale, then you needn't worry about identifying the buying signals. You will secure many more sales by asking for them than if you don't, it's just that simple.

WEB RESOURCE

🔗 www.briantracy.com: Sales training, information, products, and services.

CLOSE IN THE BOOTH WITH A SUMMARY
$ 🔨

The summary close is perhaps the most common closing technique and one of the easiest to master and use in most selling situations including trade show and special marketing events. For anyone not familiar with this closing technique, in basic terms it is nothing more than carefully taking note of the advantages, features, and benefits your prospect found to be the most interesting, valuable, and useful about your product or service during the in-booth sales presentation or live demonstration. You would then use your prospect's points of interests, likes, or as some salespeople like to refer to them as your prospect's "hot buttons" to close the sale by restating or summarizing these benefits to the prospect at the end of the presentation. In doing so you place the emphasis on all the positive aspects that your prospect finds beneficial about your offering, while conveniently leaving out any disadvantages. Almost like a Benjamin Franklin close, but without actually writing it down in column format and leaving the cons or disadvantages out of the picture. The summary close is a fast and efficient way to get prospects to buy in the booth simply because it reconfirms to them in their own thoughts, words, and actions what they like about your product or service and therefore why they should buy it and start benefiting.

CLOSE IN THE BOOTH WITH AN ASSUMPTION
$ 🔨

The assumption close is the one that I personally learned to master early in my business and sales career and use the most often, simply because it is the easiest and perhaps the most effective closing strategy in sales. Successfully using this closing requires nothing more than boldly assuming that every prospect you present to in the booth will buy and you do this by making statements during the presentation like "I will have this shipped to you buy the end of the week." Or, "I just need a few signatures on this agreement so we can start processing your order." If the prospect says nothing or is agreeable then get started on the paperwork. If the prospect raises any objections then you will know exactly where you stand and what obstacles you must overcome to close. Or, what fears or doubts that your prospect has that must be eliminated in order to close the sale. The beauty of the assumption close is the fact that many people who attend trade shows do so with the goal of making a purchase. So if you do not assume they will buy from you and ask for the sale, then you have to assume they will buy from your competition at the show, thus leaving you without the sale. Perhaps this is an overly simplified explanation of the assumption close, and in many selling situations much more work is required in terms of getting to the point in the sales cycle wherein a safe assumption can be made that your prospect is ready to buy. However, I cannot stress enough that selling in the trade show environment is not even remotely similar as selling in a non-trade show environment. You simply do not have the time available that would normally be required to qualify your prospects beyond reasonable doubt in terms of their interests, need, and abilities to purchase from you. Therefore certain assumptions must be made in order to maximize the use of your time and productivity at the show and one of the best ways to accomplish this is to assume that everyone you come in contact with wants to do business with you and buy. This is not to say that you should not take the time to qualify each prospect, because you should. But you must qualify quickly and concisely, disengage if the prospect shows no interest, and assume that they will buy if they do show interest.

CLOSE IN THE BOOTH WITH URGENCY

$ ✎

Creating a sense of urgency is still one of the best and most proven successful closing techniques to use to motivate prospects to buy in the trade show or exhibition environment. This is partly due to the fact that people attending trade shows often associate exhibition events with getting a deal or discount on products or services they wish to purchase. Smart exhibitors realize this and go out of their way to create exciting promotions aimed at creating urgency as a way to motivate and accommodate these deal seekers so they will buy and not leave the show empty-handed. Here are a few ways to create buying urgency in the booth.

Discount Urgency

One way to create buying urgency is to offer prospects a trade show special discount, one that is only available at the show. As a rule of thumb, trade show discounts are generally 10 percent, but go 15 percent if you can afford to to separate your offer from competitors who will once again generally offer a 10 percent trade show special discount.

Value Adding Urgency

Increasing the value of your product or service while still charging the same price for it is another surefire way to create excitement and build buying urgency in the booth. Trade show special, buy three and get the fourth free. Or, buy at the show today and receive an extended warranty absolutely free of charge, a $250 value! These are only two examples of ways to increase the value of what you sell to create a sense of buying urgency in the booth. The key to success is to increase the value as relevant to what you are selling. The larger the perceived value, then the more urgency and motivation it will create to buy. Hence adding a computer printer into a computer package yet still charging the same price for the package is relative value adding. But giving away a T-shirt or ball cap with every computer package sold is not relevant to your main offer, which is the computer package and therefore a poor way to add value to the offering.

Deadline Urgency

Of course to truly create a sense or buying urgency you must mix in a little fear, the feeling that prospects have when they fear they will not be able to benefit because they have waited to buy. This means that regardless of the method you use to create urgency there must also be a deadline attached to your offer in order for it to create urgency. Giving people 15 percent off is great way to motivate them to buy, but why should they act today if they can get the same deal tomorrow. However, 15 percent off today means buy now and save or miss out forever, thus urgency has been put into the marketing equation. Trade show deadlines should be extended beyond the show only in situations where the initial contact with the prospect was made during the show and a sale cannot be completed at the show, such as in the case of selling home renovation products and services. But even then a deadline must be put in place to create urgency after the show.

THE PROFESSIONAL DISENGAGE
$ ⚒

Once you have determined that a prospect is not qualified, your next goal should be to disengage from conversation as quickly, politely, and professionally as possible. This is important simply due to the fact that time is everything at the show; you must be able to get to the next prospect quickly, and there is little time available for idle chitchat. Unfortunately disengaging from conversation can be easier said than done, especially when you have a person who likes to chat in your booth. One way to disengage is to simply be honest and tell the prospect that you're sorry that you can be of no assistance, but you are at the show to help those you can, thank him, shake his hand, and say goodbye. A second method is to gently push him toward your show premium, be it a contest, drawing, or whatever and tell him to complete the entry card. While he is doing this you engage another prospect as quickly as possible. A third method is to tell him about another exhibitor who may be able to help him out and send him in the right direction. Whichever you choose you must get comfortable with disengaging from people while in conversation once you have determined that they are not potential customers for your goods and services. At trade shows this skill is a must to master and more important, to practice.

PROFIT FROM IMMEDIATE FOLLOW-UP
$$+ ⚒

Generating leads at trades shows and other exhibit marketing events is the easy part, but what do you do with them once you've got them? Obviously you follow up and attempt to turn as many leads into sales as quickly as possible to maximize the value of the leads and to get the highest rate of return on the money you invested into exhibiting at the show to collect the leads in the first place. Here are a few tricks that you can use to immediately follow up on leads allowing you to maximize the value of all your collected leads.

Lead Collection

Start by decentralizing lead collection in the booth so that interested prospects will not stray off waiting to give their contact information. Ensure that all staff in the booth are up to speed in terms of collecting and ranking the leads for follow-up. However, do have a centralized system for storing leads at the show, a special folder, lock box, or computer hard drive, whichever you find appropriate for your specific needs.

Lead Manager

Designate one person within your organization to manage all the leads that are collected at the show. Ideally the lead manager should not be actively participating in the event so that she can begin to contact and requalify prospects immediately, before the event is even over.

Follow-Up Package

Develop a lead follow-up package prior to the show so that when it ends you're ready to start following up on the hottest leads with no down time while you rush to create a follow-up package. The follow-up package should include sales letters, presentation templates, employee work and presentation schedules, extra staff to telemarket the leads, and just about any other item or service that will be required to maximize the value of the leads by contacting and requalifying prospects right away.

Requalify

Develop a system to requalify and rank leads immediately after the show or, in the case of a show that extends beyond three days. Then start the process of requalification and ranking almost immediately during the show, especially with leads that are ranked the hottest.

Competition

Remember that competitors who were also exhibiting at the show are likely chasing the same leads as you, so you'll want to carefully gauge the progress you make with each prospect, too fast or slow and the competition could scoop them out from under you. The key is to position your follow-up with the prospect so that you can maximize your chances of selling.

BOOTH PROPS

$$+ 🔨 📞

Unfortunately when it comes to trade show booth design and layout there is no one set of rules that works for every application and situation. But with that said here are a few tricks that you can use to help grab attention and maximize the interest of potential prospects in attendance.

- Create at least one freestanding and durable product display, preferably one that is a working model of what you sell and that can be used for interactive demonstration purposes with visitors.
- Use a prop or aid in the booth to grab the attention of passing guests. The prop or aid could be a flashing emergency style light or strobe lamp, a loud speaker playing a prerecorded promotional message or live message, a computer monitor or television set running a corporate advertisement or product or service video, or a lively ongoing hands-on in-booth product or service demonstration.
- Place interactive computer terminals, product models, and displays on swivel bases to avoid staff having to squeeze visitors out of the way during demonstrations or questions and explanation presentations.

- Keep a blackboard or whiteboard handy behind the curtain or under a table, somewhere that is easily accessible for staff who may have to construct diagrams to respond to unique visitor questions and situations.
- When unavailable due to size restrictions use scale models to showcase your products and make sure that they are durable enough to last an entire show's worth of poking, prodding, and general handling from prospects and booth staffers alike.
- Display products, scale models, and key photographs and graphics at eye level—as a general rule 60 inches from the floor to the key focal point or feature(s) of the product or display that you want to spotlight.
- And of course it should go without saying that you need to keep a spray cleaner and polish cloth close by so that you can keep all booth props and displays clean and looking in tip-top condition.

WEB RESOURCE

⌖ www.configurations.net: Trade show exhibits, displays, props, and specialty marketing programs.

GREAT TRICKS FOR CUTTING TRADE SHOW COSTS

$+ 🔨

Trade shows and exhibitions can provide incredible marketing opportunities for businesses that choose to participate. However, a recent survey conducted by the Small Business Administration indicated that more than 50 percent of small-business owners cited "cost" as the major factor in determining their decision not to exhibit at trade shows and special industry events. Here are a few tricks that you can use to reduce trade show costs, which in turn may enable your business to participate in and profit from exhibition opportunities.

Cut Costs by Booking Early

Exhibition space is the single largest direct expense for most exhibitors, accounting for as much as 30 percent of the total budget. Therefore, once you have identified the events you will be exhibiting at be sure to book early because most trade show management companies provide an early booking discount in the range of 10 percent off the total space rental rate. Of course, an added benefit of booking early is that you will be able to secure the best booth locations. Furthermore, for business owners who require minimal space, consider a partnership with an existing noncompeting exhibitor wherein you rent or sublet the space you require from them. Partnership strategies work well due to the fact that you only pay for the amount of space you really need and use. However, as a note of caution it is the business that rents the booth space that gets listed in exhibition marketing literature that goes out to attendees and the press.

Cut Costs by Negotiating

Adopt a 10 percent discount and 90-day payment policy for all your trade show product and service needs. This means that you want to negotiate with suppliers for a 10 percent discount and 90-day payment terms. The benefits of this strategy are apparent. First, you'll save 10 percent on purchases of products and services needed to participate in the event. Second, 90-day payment terms will often allow you to generate revenues from trade show sales before you have to pay for the goods and services yourself. For years I have used this cost-saving strategy with great success, often with little or no resistance from suppliers, especially when you explain that the discount will be more than offset with higher volume ordering due to new sales as a result of the trade show. In business, everything is negotiable and available with terms; all you have to do is ask.

Tap Suppliers to Cut Costs

Tap suppliers you regularly do business with for products and services that can reduce your trade show expenditures. These products and services can include displays, sample giveaway products, prize contributions, marketing materials, and much more. Your suppliers have a vested interest in the success of your business and with that said, a little gentle coaxing from you and they should be more than happy to assist in any way possible to ensure that your exhibition roster is a successful one.

Cut Costs on Exhibits

Renting or borrowing booths and displays is also a great way to reduce capital expenditures, especially for businesses that are new to trade show marketing and want to test the waters before committing large amount of money for booths, displays, and props. Most companies that sell trade show displays also rent them, usually the fee is about 10 percent of the purchase value. Alternately if you're a member of the chamber of commerce or another business association check to see if they have exhibit booths and displays for members to rent, many do. And lastly just ask around to alliance businesses and your suppliers to see who has a suitable booth that you can borrow. However, keep in mind you'll still have to pony up to have signs and graphics made for the booth and your displays.

Cut Staffing Costs

There are various ways to reduce staffing costs for trade shows and other event marketing with the first being to tap suppliers and have them provide technical staff. These would be people who could conduct demonstrations or assist behind the scenes. However, never place new people on the floor collecting leads or selling, especially if they are not associated directly with your business because the results are generally catastrophic. The only staff who should be selling and collecting leads are individuals who will directly benefit, meaning their job or income depends on it and preferably both. Another method to reduce staffing costs is to ask your employees to work the trade show on an incentive basis with no wages. This would mean a commission for leads they generate, or sales they make. This system works well especially when you demonstrate to staff that their potential earnings can be much higher based on individual performance.

Cut Marketing Costs

First rule in terms of reducing marketing costs: Carefully read your exhibitor's package because hidden in there somewhere will be marketing assistance programs provided by exhibition management. Why I say carefully read is because most trade shows are large and management simply does not have enough time to contact each exhibitor and explain all benefits. And because these marketing assistance programs also usually have a date deadline associated with them. Some of the programs that show managers will provide are free admission tickets, brochures and fliers, mailing list of attendees for B2B shows, and samples and marketing pre-show training seminars. Management wants you to have a good show and sell, and they want you to get the word out about the show to increase attendance. So work with exhibition management to help reduce your marketing costs and increase your productivity. But to do so you have to be proactive and take the initiative because it's your business and no one will do it for you.

Cut Travel Costs

Exhibiting at trade shows outside your local area or internationally can be very expensive when you factor in flights, display shipping, accommodations, and meals. One way to reduce these costs are to check with show management as often they strike deals with hotels, restaurants, and airlines for exhibitor discounts. Of course organizations such as automobile and travel clubs can also be a good source of reducing travel expenses. Usually the cost of membership can be saved by the discounts you receive from member businesses with just one trip. Additionally if all else fails form a group with other exhibitors and negotiate group rate discounts with hotels, freight companies, and airlines.

Being Prepared Is the Best Way to Cut Costs

The best way to ensure that trade show costs do not spiral out of control is to be prepared. Create a checklist and a complete trade show marketing plan at least six months prior to the exhibition and stick to it like glue. Also it is best to appoint one person—yourself or an employee—to manage the event and record and track all expenses, a centralized management system regardless if your business and the show is small or large. Like any aspect of business budgeting, it is always the unplanned events or last minute changes and purchases that blow the budget and leave you in a financial crisis.

GREAT PRE-TRADE SHOW PLANNING TRICKS $+ ✎

The following is a general outline that you can use to help plan for the next trade show where your business will be exhibiting.

One Year Before

- Visit trade shows that you are considering exhibiting at to make sure that the people in attendance meet your primary target audience and that the overall tone of the show and exhibitors are aligned with your marketing goals.
- Contact show management and request an exhibitor information package or exhibitor's kit so that you can create a short list of shows that you would like to participate in.
- Research demographics supplied by show management as well as other sources of information that you have secured about the show, industry, attendees, and competition that exhibit at the show.
- Depending on the show you might want to return the contract with a deposit one year in advance as some shows fill up fast, but only if you are 100 percent certain that this is a show that you want to participate in.

Six Months Before

- Develop a preliminary budget and assign a show captain, booth manager, and lead manager. Each person you assign these roles to should be trained for the tasks if he is new to trade show exhibiting.
- Confirm participation with show management and return contract and deposit if not already completed. Book booth space and from this point forward contact show management monthly or even weekly and try to secure a better booth location if you are not 100 percent satisfied with the one you have been assigned. Often

companies drop out of shows for various reasons so this is a very worthwhile exercise if you are at all concerned about securing a better booth location.

- Book show services, which are often contracted by show management so all exhibitors use the same. It is very important to contact show services early if your exhibit is elaborate and includes major utilities or staging platforms. Additionally reserve hotel rooms and transportation service if applicable.
- Set trade show objectives and goals with show captain, booth managers, and lead managers. Once again each must have clearly defined roles and understand them completely.
- Develop a complete show marketing and promotion plan including a budget for each marketing activity and a time line for when each will be set into action.
- Select the rest of the people who will be staffing the booth.
- Check your existing exhibit and displays and make repairs and updates as needed or secure a new exhibit and displays if required. If you require an entirely new display that is not a standard portable or knockdown exhibit make sure to start working with an exhibit designer and builder on this at least six months before the show. The more planning time the better your display will be at meeting your objective.

Three Months Before

- Confirm participation in any workshops or seminars that show management is making available to exhibitors.
- Plan exhibit layout and design and select signs, graphics, photographs, and props to be used in the booth and for displays. This is best accomplished by setting up the entire booth and displays for a trial run to ensure that all marketing and display pieces are constant and work together.
- Create a complete media kit and begin to draft a few versions of your press release.
- If applicable reconfirm schedule with outside contractors and show services.

- Order promotional and advertising specialties.

Two Months Before

- Finalize press release and send to target media outlets.
- Finalize any in-booth contest and giveaway details.
- Change current advertising and marketing activities such as newsletters and Web sites to include information and promote participation in the forthcoming event.

Four Weeks Before

- Confirm staff participation and make arrangements for any temporary help that may be required for the show.
- Confirm hotel and travel arrangements for staff, as well as confirming exhibit transportation details.
- Create in-booth scripts such as qualifying, presentation, and closing scripts and distribute to booth staff. Additionally conduct test runs of demonstrations, workshops, and seminars that you will be providing at the show.
- Create lead forms and lead generation and management system. Test this out if it is computerized to ensure the bugs are out of the system.
- Create all postshow follow-up packages including direct mailers, advertisements, and telephone scripts.
- Test all booth props, especially media and electronic props and gadgets.

Three Weeks Before

- Mail preshow direct-marketing promotional materials, as well as guest and press invitations.
- Re-release press release to selected targeted media outlets.

Two Weeks Before

- Reconfirm staff arrangements, travel and accommodation reservations, and show services.
- Hold a training session for any temporary booth staff.

One Week Before

- Conduct all last minute staff training and release any incentive details to energize and charge up the staff.
- Reconfirm all show details.
- Get ready, go, and have a great and profitable show.

POST-TRADE SHOW PLANNING TRICKS
$+ ⚒

Here are a few things to consider after the show.

- Hold a postshow meeting with staff to discuss how the show went overall. If possible this meeting should be held as soon after the show has wrapped as possible so things are still fresh in everyone's minds. Topics discussed should include preplanning accuracy, budget, staff training, the success of preshow promotion and in-booth promotion, the audience, the quality and quantity of prospects and leads, and reconfirm the goals and objectives of the show. This is also the time to give all booth staff a great big pat on the back and thank them for all their hard work and commitment.

- In addition to the above also be sure to discuss and analyze the competition present at the show, the effectiveness of your exhibit, displays, giveaways, lead collection system, demonstrations, and overall impressions of the show in general.
- And finally complete all budgets to see if your preshow budget stayed on track and over time conduct a complete analysis to decide if the show was a success and if goals and objectives were met and/or exceeded. If so make appropriate changes for the following year and book your space in advance.
- The vast majority of these should be completed by staff who will not be selling or following up on the leads or sales generated at the show. Postshow activities must be 100 percent focused on follow-up of leads to maximize the value of those leads and turn them into sales.

TRADE SHOW CHECKLIST
$+ ⚒

The following is a basic trade show checklist that you can copy and customize to suit your business and to make sure your next trade show is a successful one.

Trade Show Checklist Form

Your Business Name Here

Show name: _____

Street address: _____

City: _____

Show management company: _____

Contact person: _____

Street address: _____

City: _____ State: _____ Zip code: _____

Telephone: _____ Fax: _____ E-mail address: _____

Show start date: _____ / _____ / _____   Finish date: _____ / _____ / _____

Trade Show Checklist Form, continued

Show captain: _____

Lead manager: _____

Exhibit manager: _____

Booth staff
1. _____   4. _____
2. _____   5. _____
3. _____   6. _____

Section 1. Application

Item/Task	Budget	Date Completed/Details	Show Captain
Complete application	$ _____	_____	❑
Application mailed/faxed	$ _____	_____	❑
Confirm application rec.	$ _____	_____	❑
Booth location requested	$ _____	_____	❑
Booth location confirmed	$ _____	_____	❑
Booth rental deposit sent	$ _____	_____	❑
Booth rental balance paid	$ _____	_____	❑

Section 2. Booth

Item/Task	Budget	Date Completed/Details	Show Captain
Security	$ _____	_____	❑
Setup labor	$ _____	_____	❑
Tear down labor	$ _____	_____	❑
Temp booth staff	$ _____	_____	❑
Electrical	$ _____	_____	❑
Plumbing	$ _____	_____	❑
Telephone lines	$ _____	_____	❑

Section 3. Exhibit

Item/Task	Budget	Date Completed/Details	Show Captain
Exhibit cleaned/repaired	$ _____	_____	❑
Displays cleaned/repaired	$ _____	_____	❑
Carpet cleaned/repaired	$ _____	_____	❑
Lighting cleaned/repaired	$ _____	_____	❑
Props cleaned/repaired	$ _____	_____	❑
Signs cleaned/repaired	$ _____	_____	❑
Graphics/photos	$ _____	_____	❑

Trade Show Checklist Form, continued

Item/Task	Budget	Date Completed/Details	Show Captain
TVs/monitors tested	$ _____	_____	❑
PA equipment tested	$ _____	_____	❑
Rental equipment booked	$ _____	_____	❑
Rental equipment received	$ _____	_____	❑
Rental equipment returned	$ _____	_____	❑

Section 4. Promotion/Literature

Item/Task	Budget	Date Completed/Details	Show Captain
Preshow advertising	$ _____	_____	❑
Show advertising	$ _____	_____	❑
Client/prospect passes	$ _____	_____	❑
Preshow press release	$ _____	_____	❑
Press kits	$ _____	_____	❑
Staff uniforms	$ _____	_____	❑
Staff preshow training	$ _____	_____	❑
Lead collection system	$ _____	_____	❑
Lead forms	$ _____	_____	❑
Product samples	$ _____	_____	❑
Demonstrations schedule	$ _____	_____	❑
Workshop schedule	$ _____	_____	❑
Seminar schedule	$ _____	_____	❑
Preshow direct mail	$ _____	_____	❑
Preshow telemarketing	$ _____	_____	❑
Preshow invitations	$ _____	_____	❑
Giveaways/ad specialties	$ _____	_____	❑
Prospect/client hospitality	$ _____	_____	❑
Cross-promotions	$ _____	_____	❑
Cooperative advertising	$ _____	_____	❑
Promotional handouts	$ _____	_____	❑
Show program advertising	$ _____	_____	❑
Contest	$ _____	_____	❑
Contest prize(s)	$ _____	_____	❑
Contest entry forms	$ _____	_____	❑
Prize presented/delivered	$ _____	_____	❑
Celebrity appearances	$ _____	_____	❑

Trade Show Checklist Form, continued

Section 5. Shipping/Accommodations/Travel

Item/Task	Budget	Date Completed/Details	Show Captain
Hotel reservations	$ _____	_____	❑
Parking passes	$ _____	_____	❑
Airfare	$ _____	_____	❑
To: Shipping labels	$ _____	_____	❑
Return: Shipping labels	$ _____	_____	❑
Freight shipper	$ _____	_____	❑
Shipping containers checked	$ _____	_____	❑

Section 6. Post Show

Item/Task	Budget	Date Completed/Details	Show Captain
Information request kits	$ _____	_____	❑
Info request kits sent	$ _____	_____	❑
Sales/follow-up letters	$ _____	_____	❑
Sales kits	$ _____	_____	❑
Sales samples	$ _____	_____	❑
Leads requalified	$ _____	_____	❑
Leads assigned	$ _____	_____	❑
Phone scripts completed	$ _____	_____	❑
Show sales confirmed	$ _____	_____	❑
Show sales shipped	$ _____	_____	❑

Section 7. Tool Kit Checklist

Item/Task	Budget	Date Completed/Details	Show Captain
❑ Imprinted pens	$ _____	_____	❑
❑ Portable tool kit	$ _____	_____	❑
❑ Screwdriver/screws	$ _____	_____	❑
❑ Hammer/nails	$ _____	_____	❑
❑ Cordless drill/drill bits	$ _____	_____	❑
❑ Socket set	$ _____	_____	❑
❑ Adjustable wrench	$ _____	_____	❑
❑ Measuring tape	$ _____	_____	❑
❑ Ruler	$ _____	_____	❑
❑ Level (signs/displays)	$ _____	_____	❑
❑ Extra business cards	$ _____	_____	❑

Trade Show Checklist Form, *continued*

Item/Task	Budget	Date Completed/Details	Show Captain
❏ Staff 1—business cards	$ _____	_____	❏
❏ Staff 2—business cards	$ _____	_____	❏
❏ Staff 3—business cards	$ _____	_____	❏
❏ Staff 4—business cards	$ _____	_____	❏
❏ Staff 5—business cards	$ _____	_____	❏
❏ Staff 6—business cards	$ _____	_____	❏
❏ Plastic bags	$ _____	_____	❏
❏ Note pads	$ _____	_____	❏
❏ Tape/glue	$ _____	_____	❏
❏ Stapler/staples	$ _____	_____	❏
❏ Paper clips	$ _____	_____	❏
❏ Extension cords	$ _____	_____	❏
❏ Flashlight	$ _____	_____	❏
❏ Scissors	$ _____	_____	❏
❏ Spray cleaner	$ _____	_____	❏
❏ Broom/dustpan	$ _____	_____	❏
❏ Paper towels/tissues	$ _____	_____	❏
❏ Garbage bags/container	$ _____	_____	❏
❏ Camera/film	$ _____	_____	❏
❏ Extra display light bulbs	$ _____	_____	❏
❏ String/rope	$ _____	_____	❏
❏ Aspirin	$ _____	_____	❏
❏ Breath mints	$ _____	_____	❏
❏ Comfortable shoes	$ _____	_____	❏
❏ Power bars/fruit/water	$ _____	_____	❏

WHY SEMINARS?

$+ ✎

Much like trade shows, seminars are another great way to showcase your specific expertise as well as the main benefits of your products or services to a select and captive audience. Here are a few more reasons how seminars present entrepreneurs with many valuable marketing and business building opportunities.

Sell Products or Services

Use the seminar format to sell products or services. This is especially viable for the sales of software programs, training programs, books and audio visual tapes, vitamins, and other health related products. Seminars are a great way to reduce the length of the sales cycle and motivate prospects to purchase through building excitement, sharing vital information, and creating a sense of urgency at the event.

Collect Sales Leads

Seminars can be a great way to generate a ton of well-qualified leads, either by using the attendee list or by setting follow-up and sales presentations with as many people as possible on the day of the event. Ideally you will want to do both. However keep in mind that the more qualified the guests are in terms of matching your primary target audience for what you sell or do then the better qualified the leads you collect will be.

Introduce New Products or Services

You can use a seminar as a forum to introduce new products or services or products and services that have been revamped or greatly improved. The seminar format works extremely well for introducing new products and services into an existing client base, as it gives you the ability to reach many of your customers in one place and at one time in a cost efficient and effective manner. Perhaps saving you as much as 75 percent over the cost of a one-to-one personal sales visits.

Build a Direct-Marketing Database

Seminars give you the ability to help build your database even if all in attendance are not currently qualified prospects simply due to the fact that over time and through continual direct-mail or electronic mail contact many can become qualified or refer others who are qualified.

Conduct Research

By using audience interaction techniques and questions you can conduct research during the seminar and gain valuable insights into your business, products, or services. Once again, this can be done in a very cost effective and efficient manner when compared to other contact methods for research purposes.

Secure Media Exposure

Seminars present a fantastic opportunity to get the media involved and potentially secure a ton of free and valuable publicity. Send out a press release outlining your seminar details and your "news" to media outlets about three weeks prior to the event, and follow up the first mailing with a telephone call or a second mailing a week prior to the event as a gentle reminder. In addition to the press release your first mailing should also include an invitation to the event.

Showcase Your Expertise

Use seminars to position yourself as an expert in the industry or to reconfirm your expertise in the industry or your field. Becoming an expert is relatively easy. It is maintaining your expert status that can be difficult. That's what makes seminars a great forum for doing so; you can reach a large audience in a very efficient manner and give huge amounts of information that is not viable through other marketing formats such as print advertisements.

Build Brand Awareness

Use seminars to help position your business, products, and services in the marketplace. This is a great way to build and maintain a brand name image and awareness, especially in highly specialized and professional fields.

Support Your Business Team

Host a seminar annually or even more frequently to ensure that your vendors, employees, and contractors stay up to date and knowledgeable about your latest products and services. The more they know and understand about your business, products, and services then the more they will be able to help your and their customers understand it.

Recruit New Business Team Members

Use seminars to recruit managers, employees, sales agents, suppliers, vendors, and even customers. It is a highly effective and cost efficient way to recruit every type of person for every type of role you need filled in your business.

Educate Your Customers or Business Team

Training or educating a room full of people is a cost-effective way to ensure your employees or customers are trained to their maximum potential. This type of training would be far too costly to do individually for many small businesses, but in a seminar situation the cost of training or educating each person in a group format drops dramatically.

WHAT CAN BE SOLD THROUGH SEMINARS?
$+ ✎

The short answer is just about any product or service imaginable. The long answer is of course what people want, need, and are prepared to buy in a seminar-selling environment. Below are examples of selling products or services at seminars. In addition to selling at seminars, prospect qualifying and lead generation are other common objectives, which when handled properly through effective follow-up can result in extremely positive sales results and in building long-term customer relationships.

Selling Products

This is often referred to as back of the room selling because products are displayed at the back of the room behind the audience and sold to guests once the event is over and excitement during the speech or demonstration has been established. Some of the best products to sell at seminars include books, audio and videotapes, and computer software. Most commonly these products are written or produced by the speaker of the event and are often associated with solving a problem, personal motivation, and how-to information relevant to the topic and theme of the seminar. For instance a sales trainer or coach may host seminars that are free to attend, but sell books or audio or video tapes that they have written or produced that give further in-depth information that was only scratched on the surface during the seminar, but enough that buying motivation and excitement were created.

Selling Services

When selling services at seminars you have to be a little more creative about how you go about it. For instance a retailer who sells computer hardware and software could host a monthly free seminar night and invite all customers who had purchased a computer

the pervious month to attend. The purpose of the seminar could be to provide basic and free computer training, a beginners guide to working with specific hardware and software. During the event the presenter could let people in attendance know that an advanced course is also offered to people who have participated in the free beginner's course. The advanced course is taught for a fee and therefore built on the participation of the free beginner's course. Likewise a fitness trainer could host a free seminar about how to stay fit and live a healthier life through exercise. Though the seminar would be free to attend the goal of the fitness trainer would be to build enough excitement with the audience that a certain percentage of people in attendance would purchase or sign up for paid fitness training classes with the trainer.

PROFIT FROM CREATIVE SEMINAR LOCATIONS
$+ ✎

Seminars need not be conducted in a formal setting or even in an inside location to be successful at drawing the right crowd and meeting the desired objectives. For instance there are literally dozens of "seminar selling opportunities" held annually in every community right across the nation. These can range from community picnics and special events, to charity sporting events, to music festivals. I recently entered a 10K charity run and prior to the event I participated in a "healthy runner" workshop that was conducted by a local company that sold vitamins and nourishment supplements. The turn out for the workshop was great, about 150 people. It was not a hard sell type of seminar, yet many people still made a purchase at the end of the workshop and many more returned at the end of the run to make a purchase from the portable tent the business was operating from. . Likewise a music shop could give free instrument lectures and instrument tunings at a music festival, or a mechanic could lecture about car maintenance during the summer car "show and shine" events. There are literally limitless possibilities to create and take advantage of creative seminar locations and opportunities for entrepreneurs who are prepared to invest the time and hard work to profit.

OPTIONS FOR PROMOTING A SEMINAR INEXPENSIVELY
$ ✎

There are basically two ways to market a seminar. One, you can spend a small fortune on creating and implementing a direct-mail promotional program accompanied by a lavish ad campaign that includes print displays advertisements and radio spots. Or, alternately for the thousands perhaps millions of small-business owners and managers on a tight budget who would like to test seminar marketing without the financial risk, you can implement a few of the following ways to promote your seminar frugally, yet effectively. However, keep in mind the ideas listed below are best suited to be used to promote a free seminar, one that you do not charge people to attend but instead create revenues and profits by way of sales at the seminar or through follow-up on sales leads collected at the seminar.

Basic Fliers

Design a basic flier on your computer listing the details of your seminar event and have the flier photocopied inexpensively at a copy center. Once armed with a few hundred fliers, pin them to bulletin boards throughout the community and tuck them under windshield wipers on parked cars.

You Do It Telemarketing

Devote a few hours a day prior to the seminar event to call past and current clients to inform them about your seminar and invite them to attend. Maximize the impact of this low-cost marketing method by kindly asking them to also bring a friend or two out to the event.

Word of Mouth

Tell everyone you come in contact with about the event and ask that they spread the word. Employees and suppliers should be asked to do the same. This is an especially effective technique for informal seminars much like a retailer or community service provider might hold, wherein people are not asked to preregister, only to show up on the day of the seminar with a friend, co-worker, or family member.

Media Coverage

Create a newsworthy press release about your seminar event and send it off to local media outlets such as newspapers, specialty publications, radio stations, and television stations. Additionally, take the time to invite key members of the media to the seminar, as the coverage they might provide after can be just as valuable as the exposure before the event.

Outbound Communications

Include details about the seminar in all of your current outbound business communications and correspondences including telephone voice messages, company newsletters, invoices and sales receipts, outgoing faxes and e-mails, and by promoting the seminar on your Web site.

MARKET WITH NEWSLETTERS AT SEMINARS
$ ✎

Here is an easy and very economical way to promote your business at seminars, regardless if you're a guest speaker or just an invited member of the audience. Print extra copies of your latest company newsletter and hand them out to everyone in attendance at the seminar. Additionally make sure to have a special sticker printed and affixed to the newsletters that gives people instructions about how they can get on your newsletter mailing list and online electronic newsletter mailing list. Newsletters are great handouts at professional seminars as they are not pushy attempts to sell goods and services. Also, they are generally more than a quick read, which means that many people will likely take them home or to the office and read them at a later date. Making newsletter handouts is far more effective than a one-page promotional flier that often ends up being left behind at the event or in the garbage can right outside the front door.

WEB RESOURCE

⌕ www.howtowriteanewsletter.com: Newsletter toolkit software.

MAKE IT MEMORABLE WITH HUMOR

$ ✎

Not long ago I attended a commercial investment real estate seminar with a business colleague. The seminar was mid-sized with about 100 people in attendance and was the type of seminar that for most part was serious due to the nature of the topic. The speaker kicked off the speech with the usual introductions and a brief overview about the information that was to be presented and the order in which the seminar would proceed. After about five minutes into his talk, which was accompanied by a PowerPoint video presentation, a picture of a baby in a bathtub appeared on the screen much to the surprise and delight of the entire audience. The speaker apologized for the accident and stated that he couldn't understand how that picture got mixed up in the works as the audience continued to chuckle. An obvious setup yes, but one that worked well and made the seminar and speaker extremely memorable to those in attendance. Not only did he make his speech memorable but he also made the audience feel at ease and comfortable knowing that we are all people with families and friends regardless of how serious the subject matter of the event may be. Later I received a courtesy follow-up call from this speaker and he immediately introduced himself as the guy with the bathing baby picture, I laughed and said "How could I forget?"

ALWAYS GET SOMETHING IN RETURN FOR SPEAKING

$ ✎

Often businesspeople and professionals are asked to speak at numerous events and functions for just as many reasons, sometimes business and sometimes social. However, before committing time and resources to speaking at these seminars and functions make sure that you will recieve something in return for your effort, as more often than not unless you're a professional speaker these speaking requests are nonpaying gigs. Here are a few ideas about how you can get something valuable in return for speaking.

- Ask for a list of names and contact information of all the guests who have signed up, or have been invited to the seminar. Use this list as a lead source for direct mail, e-mail, and telemarketing promotional opportunities.
- Ask for a display advertisement promoting your business, product, or service in the seminar or function schedule and other printed literature that is handed out to guests at the seminar and mailed to people before and after the event.
- Request that your promotional literature be handed out or placed on all seats, and that the event manager or host picks up the cost of printing or duplicating these printed materials.
- Inquire about the possibility of selling or demonstrating your products or services in a post seminar wrap-up.
- Ask to be included in any and all postevent mailings to guests and pre-event press releases promoting the event and topic.

GREAT PUBLIC SPEAKING TRICKS, PART ONE

$ ✎

The fear of speaking in public is real; in fact it is the number-one fear shared by more American adults than any other. Not the fear of heights, claustrophobia, or even the fear of dying! Nope, the number-one fear is speaking in public. To help get past your fear of public speaking, below you will find a few great tricks that you can use to become more confident and convincing at the podium or at your next meeting or sales presentation.

- Arrive to the seminar or speaking location early and familiarize yourself with the room you will be speaking in. Walk around the floor and stage or dais area to get comfortable in your surroundings and test all audio and visual equipment before the seminar guests arrive. Practice speaking into the microphone to check suitable volume levels. Introduce yourself to the organizers and all of their staff, get to know everyone by name and what their responsibilities are so that if you have any problems you'll be able to go directly to the person who can fix it without wasting time.

- Get to know the audience before you speak by greeting people and making quick introductions as they arrive at the main entrance or refreshment area. You'll find it easier and much more relaxing to speak if you can look at the audience and see a few familiar and friendly faces smiling back.
- Use breathing and light physical exercises before your speech or presentation as a way to relax and ease nervous jitters. Additionally mentally envisioning your favorite television show or listening to your favorite music is another way to stay relaxed.
- Know the central message and theme of your speech inside out and upside down. Don't try to memorize your speech word for word; if you do you will come off as manufactured, rigid, and boring sounding. And make sure that the practice readings have taken place the day before the event and not ten minutes before you speak, as this last minute rush to remember and practice will only increase your nervousness.
- Understand that almost everyone in the audience will be sympathetic to your task. Public speaking can be difficult and nerve-racking even for professional speakers, so remember that the audience is behind you, they support you and want you to be informative and entertaining, and most of all they want to see and hear you succeed.

WEB RESOURCE

✍ www.public-speaking.org: Advanced Public Speaking Institute, public speaking information, articles, resources, and links.

GREAT PUBLIC SPEAKING TRICKS, PART TWO

$ ✍

The following are more great public speaking tricks that you can use to become more confident and convincing at the podium.

- The audience is there to hear your message. Therefore try to relax by focusing on the message and the audience. Think of yourself as the mediator between two sides, one being the audience, the other being your message. Your goal is to bring the two sides together so that they understand each other and by doing so you take the emphasis off your actions as you speak and place them where they should be, on the audience and message.
- Avoid rocking back and forth as you stand at the podium and speak; try to use normal hand gestures and voice fluctuations in your tone and pacing. Be slightly animated and move naturally so that you do not appear rigid.
- Keep your speech short, simple, and to the point. The length will depend on the situation and the information you want or need to share; however, as a rule of thumb after 30 continuous minutes of listening, the majority of the audience will start to lose interest unless there are preplanned breaks and intermissions. Talk at the educational level of the room or slightly below, never above, and skip technical jargon that might be lost on the audience and instead use easy-to-understand words.
- Make eye contact with various members of the audience, try to get them to acknowledge you and nod in agreement to what you are saying. Master speakers get the audience involved and invested in the speech within the first minute and keep the audience involved right until the end. And the best way to learn how to master this is through practice and repetition, therefore continually seek out places to speak.
- Always welcome questions and comments at the end of your speech or presentation. But never get into a debate with anyone in the audience; politely disengage them by telling them you'll speak to them at the end and then go directly to the next question or create a new discussion as a diversion.

WEB RESOURCE

✍ www.public-speaking.org: Advanced Public Speaking Institute, public speaking information, articles, resources, and links.

PUBLIC SPEAKING MISTAKES TO AVOID

$ ✎

Now that you know the best tricks for speaking in public to an audience, be it one person or one hundred, below you'll find the biggest public speaking mistakes that you can make; choose to ignore them at your own peril.

- Using big words, technical jargon, and generally talking down to the audience in such a way that you make them feel stupid because they do not understand what you are saying or the terminology. Amazingly, most public speaking experts agree that speakers should talk to guests at about a grade eight comprehension level. Of course, much of this will depend on the theme and topic of your seminar and the guests in attendance.

- Talking too fast, rambling on beyond the point made and speaking in a high pitch or monotone. A comfortable pace for yourself and the audience is about 160 words a minute, which gives you a reference point for writing and practicing your speech prior to the event.

- Failing to smile or make eye contact with anyone in the audience. Or, never getting excited or using body language and speaking without a trace of emotion or interest, and not getting the audience involved physically, mentally and emotionally in the topic, speech, and the way you deliver it.

- Talking so quietly that people cannot hear, or talking so loudly the audience feels as though they are being screamed at or scolded. Using slang, profanity, poor grammar, and politically incorrect humor is the kiss of death.

- Failing to use visual aids such as charts, props, printed handouts, and audio/video aids and media. And finally, not being prepared, presenting a crystal clear message, summarizing at the end by restating the main points and biggest benefits, and worst not asking the audience to take action.

TROLLING FOR SPONSORS

$ ✎

Planning and hosting seminars can be very costly and time consuming especially for small-business owners who most often lack both of these key resources, which are required to pull together a successful seminar that will meet marketing and other key objectives. Consequently many business owners forego testing seminars as a viable means of marketing their goods or services. However, before you eliminate seminars from your potential marketing tools consider seeking out and securing a sponsor for the event to share in the time, energy, and money investment that is required to plan and host the event—and of course also the potential rewards. I like to break down seminar sponsorship opportunities for small business into three main categories.

1. Hands-On Sponsors

Hands-on sponsors are ones who take an active role in planning and presenting at the seminar. An example of the hands-on sponsorship match would be a real estate broker who hosts a first time home buyers seminar. Co-sponsors such as a home inspector and a mortgage broker would be good potential matches as both have similar target audiences and can benefit from the seminar. Thus a three-way split in terms of financial and time resources required to pull the seminar together and host the event could be arranged with each partner making an equal contribution and sharing the leads collected at the event.

2. Hands-Off Sponsors

Hands off refers more to sponsors who can benefit from the exposure but don't necessarily want to play an active role beyond financial sponsorship. These types of sponsors typically include large financial institutions, manufacturers, and insurance brokers who want to be associated with the event and recognized through signage, ads, or article features in the printed seminar guide and all other marketing materials used to promote the event before, during, and after. To secure these types of key sponsors will require time, planning, and a formal presentation. You must be able to successfully demonstrate to the sponsor that the investment will generate a return on investment based on the exposure received at the event. Target audience plays a major role in securing hands-off sponsors. Insurance companies would have a keen interest in seminars focused on families and homebuyers and owners, but not likely in a seminar focused on growing organic vegetables.

3. Media Sponsors

Media outlets often co-sponsor seminar events, though generally not financially for small events but rather with marketing exposure through their particular medium. Once again the sponsor must benefit from participation, be it by reaching their target audience or by being seen as an active supporter of the community if the seminar is not for profit, charitable, or aimed at improving the community in general. However, with that said, regardless of the type of seminar that you plan to host, always try to get the local media involved in the event at some level or participation.

BRINGING IN THE SPEAKERS
$ ✎

One thing that every seminar requires is a presenter, someone or a number of people who will speak at the event and whose expertise or qualifications for doing so will be directly related to the topic or theme of the event. There are basically two types of presenters that speak at seminars.

Paid Speakers

Professional speakers are available to speak at any occasion right across the country and their fees to do so greatly vary from a low of about $250 a day to as much as six figures a day. And usually expenses such as transportation and accommodations are on top of these fees and paid by the seminar organizer or a sponsor of the event. Obviously for the majority of small-business owners paying professional speakers to present information at their seminars will be out of the financial reach of most business owners and therefore they will have to rely on the second type of presenter, unpaid speakers.

Unpaid Speakers

Unpaid speakers make up the bulk of presenters who speak at seminars which are hosted by small-business owners. And usually include the host or the organizer of the event. It is very easy to secure unpaid speakers for an event. However there must be a benefit for them in order for them to be motivated to want to participate and in order to secure high quality speakers. The benefit more times than not will be an opportunity to sell products or services, either directly at the event or by generating leads that can be followed up and turned into sales after the event.

ADDITIONAL CONSIDERATIONS FOR SEMINAR SUCCESS
$+ ✎

In addition to the topic of your seminar, how you will promote the event and meet your key objectives and secure a return on investment here are a few other critical considerations to keep in mind and plan for while creating your seminar action plan.

Competition for the Audience

I don't mean competition for the audience in the literal sense, meaning other seminars with the same topic are being held at the same time.. but more so by way of distractions such as live or televised sporting events, political elections, community parades or fairs, and other major entertainment events. Competition plays a major role in terms of drawing your target audience to the seminar and therefore must be carefully considered.

Timing of the Event

Timing of your event is another consideration and most seminar consultants agree that the best time to host a seminar is in the spring between late March to very early June. And in the fall from early September to early November. Of course much to do with timing will be greatly dependent on your seminar topic and marketing objective. However, one must still carefully select and plan for the timing of the event. Additional timing considerations include holidays, and things such as your target audience's availability. If you want to reach businesspeople, then a daytime seminar will work best. If you want to reach consumers then plan your event for when the vast majority of your target audience is not at work, which are generally weeknights and weekends.

Accessibility to the Event

The third consideration is accessibility of the event location and this can range from where the event is being held to weather conditions and road traffic. Is there good parking or public transit available to the location and is the seminar being held in general proximity to the largest segment of your target audience? Likewise weather conditions and road traffic also play a major factor and once again this gets back to the timing of your event.

SEMINAR CHECKLIST
$+ ✎

The following is a basic checklist that you can copy, customize, and use to plan your next seminar or group presentation.

Seminar Checklist Form

Your Business Name Here

Seminar Information

Seminar planner: _____

Seminar date: _____ / _____ / _____

Start time: _____   Break 1: _____   Break 2: _____   Finish time: _____

Number of participants invited: _____   Number of participants confirmed: _____

Seminar topic: _____

Seminar location: _____

Seminar address: _____   Room/unit number: _____

City: _____   State: _____   Zip code: _____

Location contact: _____

Telephone: _____   Fax: _____   E-mail address: _____

Seminar Objective(s)

❏ Sales

❏ Generate, qualify leads

❏ Introduce a new or improved product or service

❏ Public relations

❏ Support vendors

❏ Recruit vendors or employees

❏ Train vendors or employees

❏ Brand company products or services

❏ Information sharing with investors, suppliers, employees, and key business alliances

❏ Conduct research

❏ Community or charity involvement

Seminar Checklist Form, continued

Guest Speaker(s)

	Name	Topic	Fee
1.	_____	_____	$_____
2.	_____	_____	$_____
3.	_____	_____	$_____

Accommodations required: ❏ Yes   ❏ No

If yes, accommodation details: _____

Hotel: _____

Address: _____

Transportation: _____

Other: _____

Co-Sponsor Information

Company name: _____

Contact person: _____

Address: _____

Telephone: _____ Fax: _____ E-mail address: _____

Additional comments: _____

_____

General Seminar Checklist

Seminar location/room: _____

❏ Room booked   ❏ Room in good state of repair

❏ Parking   ❏ Preseminar room clean

❏ Transit accessibility   ❏ Postseminar room clean

❏ Suitable size

❏ Good lighting

❏ Telephone/fax on site

❏ Internet connection on site

❏ Washroom accessibility

❏ Handicap accessible

Seminar Checklist Form, continued

Seminar Promotion	Quantity	Budget
Direct mail/marketing		
❏ Mailing list rental	_____	$ _____
❏ Labels/envelopes	_____	$ _____
❏ Invitations	_____	$ _____
❏ Response forms	_____	$ _____
❏ Follow-up package	_____	$ _____
❏ Telemarketing	_____	$ _____
❏ Postage/courier	_____	$ _____
❏ Fax blast	_____	$ _____
❏ E-mail blast	_____	$ _____
❏ Personal visits	_____	$ _____
❏ Contest/prize	_____	$ _____
Advertising		
❏ Print	_____	$ _____
❏ Radio spots	_____	$ _____
❏ Television commercial	_____	$ _____
❏ Internet ad	_____	$ _____
❏ Cooperative program	_____	$ _____
Public Relations		
❏ Media invitations	_____	$ _____
❏ Press kit	_____	$ _____
❏ Press release	_____	$ _____
❏ Follow-up letter	_____	$ _____
Signage		
❏ Printed direction maps	_____	$ _____
❏ In-seminar promotional banners	_____	$ _____
❏ Outside direction signs	_____	$ _____
❏ Registration signs	_____	$ _____
❏ Sponsor signs	_____	$ _____
❏ Table tents	_____	$ _____
❏ Backroom product/sale signs	_____	$ _____
❏ Posters	_____	$ _____
❏ Photographs	_____	$ _____
❏ POP signs	_____	$ _____
❏ Level (signs)	_____	$ _____

Seminar Checklist Form, *continued*

Seminar Promotion	Quantity	Budget
Handouts		
❏ Name badges		$
❏ Promotional items/specialties		$
❏ Presentation folders/booklets		$
❏ Brochures		$
❏ Fliers		$
❏ Comment/questionnaire cards		$
❏ Business cards		$
❏ Pens		$
❏ Notepad		$
❏ Workbooks		$
❏ Photocopied handouts		$

Seminar Equipment	Quantity	Budget
❏ Lead forms		$
❏ Tables		$
❏ Chairs		$
❏ Flip chart/paper/markers		$
❏ Overhead projector		$
❏ Complete computer terminals		$
❏ Notebook computer(s)		$
❏ PowerPoint projector/screen		$
❏ Specialty software		$
❏ Television/VCR/DVD		$
❏ Audio/microphone equipment		$
❏ Still camera/film		$
❏ Video camera		$
❏ Room decorations/theme		$
❏ Product displays/sales table		$
❏ Debit/credit card processing		$
❏ Whiteboard/blackboard/markers		$
❏ Small tool kit/step ladder		$
❏ Power cords		$
❏ First aid kit		$
❏ Stapler/staples		$

Seminar Checklist Form, *continued*

Seminar Equipment	Quantity	Budget
❑ Paper clips	_____	$ _____
❑ Tape/glue	_____	$ _____
❑ Scissors	_____	$ _____
❑ Cleaning supplies	_____	$ _____
❑ Garbage bags/containers	_____	$ _____
❑ Complete catering	_____	$ _____
❑ Break refreshments	_____	$ _____
❑ Product samples	_____	$ _____
❑ Product giveaways	_____	$ _____
❑ Specialty displays	_____	$ _____
❑ Coat rack/check	_____	$ _____

Merchandise/Sales	Quantity	Budget
❑ Books	_____	$ _____
❑ Audiotapes	_____	$ _____
❑ Videotapes	_____	$ _____
❑ Workbooks	_____	$ _____
❑ Product	_____	$ _____
❑ Sponsor products	_____	$ _____

📖 SUGGESTED ADDITIONAL READING

Carnegie, Dale. *The Quick and Easy Way to Effective Speaking*. New York: Pocket Books, 1990.

Craven, Robin and Lynn Johnson Golobowski. *Complete Idiot's Guide to Meeting and Event Planning*. Dulles, VA: Alpha Books, 2001.

Esposito, Janet E. *In the Spotlight: Overcome Your Fear of Public Speaking and Performing*. New York: Strong Books, 2000.

Gleek, Fred. *Marketing and Promoting Your Own Seminars and Workshops*. New York: Fast Forward Press, 2001.

Jolles, Robert. *How to Run Seminars and Workshops: Presentation Skills for Consultants, Trainers and Teachers*. New York: John Wiley & Sons, 2000.

Levinson, Jay and Conrad Mark Smith. *Guerrilla Trade Show Selling: New Unconventional Weapons and Tactics to Meet More People, Get More Leads, and Close More Sales*. New York: John Wiley & Sons, 1997.

Miller, Steve and Robert Sjoquist. *How to Design a WOW Trade Show Booth without Spending a Fortune*. Federal Way, WA: Hikelly Productions, 2002.

Nelson, Bob. *1001 Ways To Energize Employees*. New York: Workman Publishing Company, 1997.

Weisgal, Margit B. *Show and Sell: 133 Business Building Ways to Promote Your Trade Show Exhibit*. New York: AMACOM, 1996.

Ziglar, Zig. *Zig Ziglar's Secrets of Closing the Sale*. Berkeley, CA: Berkeley Publishing Group, 1985.

INDEX